TO END WAR

TO END WAR

A New Approach to International Conflict

by
Robert S. Woito

The Pilgrim Press
New York

Copyright © 1982 by The Pilgrim Press
All rights reserved.

Library of Congress Cataloging in Publication Data
Main entry under title:

To end war.

    Rev. ed. of: To end war / by Robert Pickus.
3rd ed. 1970.
    Bibliography
    Includes index.
    1. Peace—Bibliography.   2. International
relations—Bibliography. I. Woito, Robert.
II. Pickus, Robert. To end war.
Z6464.Z9T63 1982 [JX1952] 016.3271 '72 81-15889
      AACR2
ISBN 0-8298-0464-1
ISBN 0-8298-0476-5 (pbk.)

The Pilgrim Press, 132 West 31 Street, New York, N.Y. 10001

In memory of John Lang and
Robert Maynard, two colleagues
at the World Without War Council—
Midwest, who encouraged the
re-publication of *To End War*.

Contents

Preface

This is the sixth edition of a work first published in 1967 as an annotated bibliography. That bibliography was revised and expanded in 1968. Critics pointed out that there was an argument implicit in the bibliography and that the argument, combined with introductions to the ideas, books, and work that could help end war, would make a useful book. Robert Pickus and I developed *To End War* into such a book for the third edition in 1969. A modestly revised fourth edition was published by Harper and Row in 1970. The fifth edition was prepared by Robert Pickus, Timothy Zimmer and others for release in 1975 but was never completed. The introduction to the fifth edition argued that the institutional and attitudinal requirements of modern war are the central realities in world politics today. War should be defined as a problem; thought should be directed toward its elimination. That introduction has been revised and updated and appears here.

While this sixth edition retains much of the original structure, it is, to a significant extent, a new book. World politics has changed significantly, and chapters on the shifting world economic order and on the environment have been added to reflect this. New regional powers require a chapter. The Soviet military build-up, the increased military spending of the last Carter and first Reagan budgets, the emergence of powerful conventional armies and the new military technology also add new dynamics to world politics. A chapter introduces the current debate about military strategy and explains why understanding strategies of war is important for someone wanting to develop a strategy of achieving a world without war.

America has changed. The Johnson, Nixon, Ford, and Carter Administrations have come and gone. Each President had his distinctive approach to world politics and defined peace as a valuable objective; each pursued that goal in different ways. None has succeeded in bringing nuclear or conventional armaments under control, much less advancing the goal of disarmament. Public attitudes have shifted from the preference for disengaging from world politics expressed in the post-Vietnam era to a cautiously internationalist attitude in the 1980s. The Reagan Administration is asserting America's presence in world politics to an apparently approving public, but the new assertiveness is largely military.

Peace studies have become an accepted part of American life and over 300 institutions in other countries define peace research as their central purpose. Many international relations courses now place war and conflict resolution at the center of their subject matter. Although written primarily for an American audience, this book ought to be useful in academic centers in other countries as well.

Citizen activity in the world affairs field has increased in the last 10 years. There are over 5,000 organizations in the United States which seek to influence this country's role in world politics. The ideas, books, and contexts described herein should be of use to them. The action section has been changed and enlarged to address the needs of such organizations. In addition, the conceptualization of the field, and the extensive, annotated bibliography should interest experts.

This book reflects the conviction that the conditions essential to a world without war are known *but* that little in the United States today which is self-defined as peace activity is helpful in bringing them into being. The section on the causes of war has been expanded to provide a test of any strategy of peace. By identifying the ideas, work, and organizations that could help end war, *To End War* challenges the prevailing State-centered approach to world politics. In realistically assessing conflicts in world politics, and the role of military power in deciding their outcome, *To End War* also challenges those who believe that the categories of the State-centered approach can be easily transcended or ignored.

This book, more than most, is the work of many people. Robert Pickus, who co-authored the third and fourth editions, was a critic. Much of the conceptualization of the field, the development of the peace initiatives strategy, and the approach to work with organizations is derived from his ideas and activities. My other colleagues in the World Without War Council have criticized drafts of this manuscript. Lowell Livezey and George Weigel have made extensive comments on every chapter. Sam and Nancy Starr provided encouragement. Steve Boyd, Deborah Zimmer, Sr. Helen Garvey, Fred Stevens, Will Reid, and other staff members provided various kinds of support. Karen Minnice aided in the work prior to her leaving the Council.

Much of the manuscript is a presentation of the ideas of others. The works of these authors are acknowledged in the text or, when that becomes awkward, in the bibliography.

I am grateful to the following for criticisms of draft chapters: Cathy Good Abbott, David Albert, Norman Alcock, Dennis Allred, Alan Anderson, Lee Anderson, Mary Appelman, Sister M. Applonia, Charles Bergerson, Doug Bond, Joan Bondurant, Kenneth Boulding, J.R. Burkholder, Richard Dean Burns, Dale Butland, Stephen Cimbala, Lloyd Cohen, Arthur Cyr, Don Durnbaugh, Peter Eng, Hahmond Fahmy, Ken Farmer, Bruce Fetter, Lawrence Finkelstein, David Finke, Michael Fleet, Duane Friesen, Ray Gastil, Larry Gould, D. Graf, Harold Guetzkow, Roger Hamburg, Larry Holmes, George Hudson, Ray Johnston, Chris Joyner, Bill Keeney, Ray Kim, Warren Kuehl, Anne Larson, Jerome Laulicht, Lawrence LeBlanc, Paul Lembesis, Woodrow Linn, Robin Lovin, Pat Lynch, Stephen Marks, Steven Marshall, Robert Messer, Don Miller, Sherry Minert, Jiri Nehnevajsa, Herb Neil, Burton Nelson, Jack Nelson, Alan Newcombe, Hannah Newcombe, Charles Okolie, Fr. John Pawlikowski, Rich Peacock, George Pickering, Cynthia Roberts, Rev. C. Theodore Roos, James Rosenau, J.D. Rummel, Terry Rynne, Phil Schrodt, Mulford Sibley, Derek Singer, J. David Singer, Louis Sohn, Herman Spector, Barbara Dodds Stanford, Joseph Wall, James Will, and Kale Williams.

Drafts of this book were the basis of intern training seminars of the World Without War Council—Midwest. Helpful comments were made by Misty Gerner, Doug Bond, Jamie Morrisey, Walter West, Bennett Caplan, Bruce Peterson, Vicky Singer, Barbara Page, Rebecca Levin, George Wagner, Kurt Carlson, Janet Mackey and Martha Tobak. Misty Gerner circulated the draft of the fifth edition for comments and updated the information in it. Bennett Caplan reworked many paragraphs. Janet Mackey and Kurt Carlson spent weeks checking every bibliographic entry and other information. Marnie Clark edited several chapters. Hilda Hoehl helped in ways too numerous to mention. Elda Maynard helped with the final editing, and provided a constant prod: "Isn't it done yet?"

Four editors went over earlier drafts: Susanna Davison, Bruce Smith, Jacqueline Phillips, and Charles Bloomstein. The prose and substance have greatly benefited from their volunteer labors. A Pilgrim Press editor, Esther Cohen, completed the editing. If the language remains cumbersome, the fault lies with the author.

Financial contributions in support of this project were received from Mary Appelman, Louise Barry, Bob Drake, Dr. George and Jean Fischer, Hilda

Hoehl, Binnie Lang, Mary Liebman, Elda Maynard, Gene Podulka, Fred Replogle, Bruce Smith and Kale Williams.

Five young adults have shared in the work. Katrina and Andrea Woito worked on the bibliographical and organizational information. Brian Woito, Jengis Alpar, and Aaron Alpar alphabetized, filed, and labored in other ways. Each of them joined Jacqueline Phillips and my mother Lois Woito to provide family support.

Although I am indebted to all those named above and many others, responsibility for the final form of this manuscript remains mine.

Robert Woito
June 1981
Chicago, Illinois

Introduction*

This sixth edition of *To End War* was prepared at the World Without War Council—Midwest. It presents the harsh realities of contemporary world politics and seeks, without romanticism or over-simplification, to explore a non-military, security strategy. It appears at a time when many in America will condescendingly refer to any systematic challenge to the institutions of war as "visionary." Indeed, in the present climate, even such visionaries are undergoing a crisis of confidence.

Despite nearly twenty years of work, the institutions of modern war are rarely consistently challenged today. Worse, they are affirmed nearly everywhere. Nuclear arsenals have grown; proliferation has taken place. Conventional wars are nearly constant. The Reagan Administration apparently has no strategy of peace other than a massive military spending program. In international organizations, ideologically loaded exchanges and the legitimation of war against America, Israel, and South Africa are as likely as searching out new areas of agreement, the promotion of constructive change, and non-military conflict resolution. In peace circles in the United States, where one could hope to find a strategy of peace, one finds

*Portions of this essay were originally prepared by Robert Pickus for inclusion in the unpublished fifth (1975) edition of *To End War*. He has graciously given me permission to rewrite that essay for this edition.

little more than a challenge to American military spending increases that is frequently combined with a denial or underestimation of others' use of violence and few ideas on how to conduct conflict without war.

Defining the conditions essential to a world without war and considering how to get world leaders to pursue them, remains a "visionary," not a political, task. That strikes at our confidence, for those working in the Council have always judged our work by its impact on national and world politics as well as its expression of religious and democratic values.

Despite the bleak present, we are not disillusioned with the ideas that have guided us, although these, like most ideas, need refinement. Two basic judgments continue to undergird our work: 1) the conditions essential to a world without war are known; 2) war is a problem that can and must be treated independently from much else that troubles contemporary world affairs.

CONDITIONS ESSENTIAL TO ENDING WAR ARE KNOWN

In the final analysis there is only one alternative to war as the legitimate means for conducting and resolving conflict between States and that alternative is *law*. Enforceable law, however, cannot be achieved in a world society divided by armed ideological, religious, ethnic, and economic adversaries unless a sense of community unites the antagonists. Such a sense of community could be expressed in agreeing to political processes through which differences are contested. A sense of community in world politics today is atrophied by the threat or fact of war, by gross human rights violations, and by economic deprivation. A sense of community grows as change is achieved and conflict resolved without violence. A sense of community is advanced as arms control agreements actually limit armaments and lead toward disarmament, as world economic development occurs, and human rights are observed. These six concepts—law, community, development, disarmament, human rights, and non-violence—constitute the conditions essential to a world without war.

These ideas, along with the ideas that currently prevail in discussions of world politics—power, military strategy, the national interest, and nationalism, are introduced in Section A, *Ideas.* Throughout Section A the state of the discussion in seventeen world affairs subjects is summarized and the ideas considered most helpful or relevant to ending war are identified. In Section B, *Context,* a strategy through which one country, such as the United States, could lead in their achievement is presented. That strategy is called a peace initiatives strategy. The resources gathered in Section C, *Action,* are designed to help American citizens and non-governmental organization leaders, turn this country toward developing and implementing such a strategy.

WAR IS A SEPARATE PROBLEM

It is the problem of war that takes us to the heart of the difficulty. "Inter-dependent" is the best one-word description of the situation of all States in the contemporary world. It also describes the calamities and the resources needed to remedy them. It is the fact of war between and within countries that reveals starkly our present inability to organize to address common problems. It is war—its structures and dynamics (and the beliefs that underlie them)—which occupies the ground that must be cleared if we are to build a sense of world community. That sense of community is needed if we are to gather the resources and sustain the institutions capable of addressing those calamities which, along with war, portend our demise.

War most clearly reveals the obstacles which block the way to a more humane global order. War requires that we cling exclusively to the State; that we treat our enemies, neither as people to love, nor as human beings with rights to respect, but as things. War speaks in absolutes, while the proposed solutions to the problems we face are at best approximate. War requires that our material resources be directed toward the destruction of other societies which threaten us, just as we threaten them.

There is nothing new in famine, in injustice, or in economic breakdown. What is new is the level of interconnectedness in the world today that spreads their effects, and the power of modern communications which forces the problems into our lives.

The upheavals that follow from leaving such massive problems unattended, or attended without widespread agreement, bring with them violence. Proof of this dismal result fills the pages of our daily newspapers and of history. Our present disorders, if unresolved, will lead to such mass violence—and this time in a world with nuclear weapons.

For many, it is world poverty, or population, or economic injustice, or ecological disaster that should be the focus of attention. For others it is refugees, or torture, or other human rights violations. For specialists in international relations, it is the problem of power in a world composed of sovereign States that must master their rivals to be freed from external threat. All these matters are explored in this book, for work on them is essential and could help promote an end to war.

This book, however, reverses the priorities which characterize most contemporary approaches to world politics—even those based on world order objectives. It places the problem of war above the problems of change or security. It does not ignore the need for change or the necessity for achieving security, but argues that the means must be appropriate to the ends sought and the knowledge available. It makes a difference whether solutions to problems are approached through an agreed upon political process, or are contested by adversarial States between whom political discourse is clouded in ideology with thinly veiled, or even explicit, threats of violence. We must find a way to agree on the terms of world politics, else we who are seeking to solve problems will ourselves make their resolution more difficult. At a minimum, we must agree not to destroy our political opponents. We must agree that constructive change will not be sought through mass violence. Our intention in this book is to introduce the ideas, the context, and the resources which make these goals credible in world politics.

OBSTACLES TO ENDING WAR

Many people who share the values and analysis which lead to work against war, nonetheless support military deterrence, or military threat in other forms, as the best alternative to war, appeasement, or acceptance of the status quo. For them, it is beside the point to define the conditions essential to a world without war in which democratic societies can survive. They have not been presented with a credible alternative strategy to achieve security and change. Those close to the prevailing ideas are, in many cases, stopped even from considering such a strategy by one or more of these obstacles:

1. The belief that war is rooted in human nature and cannot be eradicated.

2. The belief that nuclear deterrence can be maintained indefinitely.

3. The belief that the Soviet Union cannot be challenged or turned from an expansionist course by anything other than military power.

4. The belief that nationalism, or cultural or religious differences, pose insurmountable barriers. Nationalism is held to be the only politically effective belief providing cohesion in old States and the myth that holds new States together.

Those challenging the prevailing ideas, rarely develop a realistic, non-military strategy of peace. They are often stopped from considering such a strategy by these ideas:

1. The belief that strategic and conventional weapons *can* be significantly, unilaterally, reduced or abandoned without the loss of diplomatic or political influence.

2. The belief that significant change requires violence.

3. The belief that the United States is incapable of leadership toward alternative means of resolving international conflict and of promoting change.

4. The belief that the individual is powerless to effect change on the scale required.

We will in the course of this book develop responses to these ideas. We do not believe that war is fated by human nature. It has been unknown in some cultures, and it is illegitimate within some 170 places on earth today, called States. Some of these States are very large, with diverse people and problems. Many of these States have processed significant change without war—with violence, with riots, with intense conflict, but without the organized mass violence of war. Yet, many of their inhabitants live without any sense of impediments resulting from the renunciation of war in domestic politics. Our claim is that although conflict between people and groups *is* in the nature of things organized mass violence (war) is not. Although we cannot rid the world of hatred or individual and small group violence, we can rid the world of war because war is not spontaneous, but is socially organized, planned, and decided upon.

Nuclear deterrence remains the dominant concept in this country's strategy for peace. Many now managing the instruments of threat, knowing that the response-time is lessening, that the technology is constantly changing, that the nuclear club is enlarging, are joining those already worried. In the long run, many inside and outside the institutions managing military threat know it is a "dead-man's" game. If shown a credible alternative, they would surely try it.

The alternative presented in Chapter 19 does not assume that the current military force levels are redundant—that they represent meaningless overkill. It is *not* based on the futility, horrors, or costs of war, though it is, in part, motivated by a desire to avoid them. It accepts that there is significant political bargaining leverage provided by the possession of nuclear or conventional forces. As Paul Seabury has put it:

> Arms, even nuclear ones, are in the first instance political resources. They can be used to obtain political goals. They are a medium of exchange in the marketplace of world politics.[1]

Thus, a strategy for ending war must take into consideration, and provide a response to, the political uses of military force. The failure to recognize this blights many peace efforts that focus on the horrors, costs, or futility of war, but fail to address the world's armies in the field, or to develop non-military ways through which to conduct or resolve international conflict.

Significant change can be achieved with or without violence. But what kind? This book suggests how constructive change can be accomplished without the organized mass violence of war; this book identifies the institutions of war and the terror of violence as obstacles to the sense of community essential for achieving economic development that consistently meets human needs and promotes human rights.

---

[1]Paul Seabury, "Clausewitz: Visions of a Nuclear War," *The American Spectator*, August/September 1978.

CAN CITIZENS CHANGE THE U.S.? CAN THE SOVIET UNION CHANGE?

To achieve the conditions essential to a world without war, change is required in the policies of the United States and the Soviet Union, as well as others. The emphasis here is on changing U.S. policy. The critique offered (see Chapter 8) maintains that, despite the statements of constructive goals by Truman, Eisenhower, and Kennedy, the requirements of nuclear deterrence and military alliances shaped the day-by-day policy decisions during their Administrations. Few positive goals have since been articulated. Those defending those Administrations, maintain that the Soviet Union would not agree to the next steps toward the conditions essential to a world without war.

To End War describes how the United States could, through a non-military strategy, maximize the chances of achieving the needed agreements. This approach is the peace initiatives strategy mentioned earlier. Such a strategy does not commit itself to deterrence theory, but develops a non-military strategy within the existing system of deterrence. Such a strategy asks what non-military acts by one power could alter the cost-benefit calculations of others in such a way as to make negotiated agreements more likely than at present. A peace initiatives strategy offers a way through which governmental leaders could, without unacceptable risk to their own society, initiate progress toward a world without war.

At present, American governmental leaders are most unlikely to do so.

To End War, therefore, is addressed primarily to American citizens, not governmental leaders. We find them in world affairs organizations, in peace and international relations courses, and in a wide range of non-governmental organizations, such as religious institutions, labor unions, and business organizations. Why do we look to the American citizen for the sense of direction and strategy of change required? Can our citizens act effectively to gain a serious and sustained effort by this country? Could America lead in creating a sense of world community adequate to sustain law which, rather than violence, should be the preferred means to resolve international conflict?

We look to American citizens for three reasons: 1) present governmental leaders won't undertake these tasks; 2) citizens can; 3) the fulfillment of the best in our tradition requires that they do.

We live in a world dominated by preparation for war. Any American administration taking office gives a spoken or unspoken commitment to the people of the United States to depend on national military power for the security of this country. The Reagan Administration is no different from other recent Administrations in this. One can take some pride in efforts by our government to help resolve immediate crises, to press in specific situations for peaceful settlement; but we cannot count on present governmental leaders to initiate the changes in world politics needed to achieve a world without war. Their primary

commitment is dictated by military contingencies. Their choices are limited by
the degree of threat posed by other States' military programs. To enter a war or
an arms race prepared to come in second, or to lead a peace race when no one
else is following, is as likely to lead to war on the adversary's terms as to peace.
Contemporary governments talk peace, but essentially do as they always have
done: prepare for and wage war.

Only the American people can authorize a fundamental change of direction. Without the burden of immediate governmental responsibility, they can
initiate currents of thought and policy that break with traditional conceptions
of security and deal more adequately with a world of nuclear weapons. They
can call for a realistic engagement of this country in world politics; they can indicate a willingness to sacrifice to achieve the conditions essential to a world
without war, just as they sacrifice now for military programs; they can indicate
whether they prefer the risks of peace sought through nuclear deterrence or
peace sought through the attempt to build a sense of world community. Their
clear mandate would open the way for the needed changes in governmental
policies.

The means for citizen action are at hand. Contrary to the continuing attacks on the democratic process in this country, entry into public policy arenas
is wide open. American government does reflect public belief and concern. It is
hard to find an issue around which a majority has been built and sustained that
has not resulted in significant change in governmental policies. But, there is not
yet in this country agreement on policies that can seek the replacement of the
institutions of war, that can move us and others toward world order. Even
where such proposals are understood, there is little will to accept the risks involved in pursuing them. When the risks are analyzed and prepared for,
government will reflect public understandings and America will be able to lead
in work for a world without war.

Much that is important in our religious and political traditions requires
action to end war. The concept of conscience holds that individuals are morally
responsible for their actions and those of their governments. Only as the moral
values that defend the individual in domestic politics are embodied in the international policies of our government can we expect to resolve the dilemma (so
troubling to so many) presented by a democratic and religious country waging
war.

WHY THEN SO LITTLE SUSTAINED WORK?

Given the crucial role of the American citizen in work for a world without
war, the promptings of our major intellectual traditions, and the openness of
our political process, why has so little actually been done?

Too few have encountered a believeable perspective on how to pursue the goal of ending war. This book is an attempt to define such a perspective—one which offers an alternative to oscillation between militarily asserting American values in world politics and futile attempts to withdraw from efforts to shape international politics.

The crisis of confidence of the "visionaries," who take seriously the goal of ending war, can be overcome. A realistic visionary recovers confidence when others undertake this work without initial hope of significant financial, status, or political reward. In the final analysis, it is for such people that the resources in this book have been compiled. It is they who, in the next twenty years, will know the effort it takes to lay the foundations that make possible a world without war. While one cannot be sure that enough people will take up these tools and improve them, one can be confident that those who do will be rewarded. When the vision is clear, when the dangers of the moment are evident, then the work has a meaning that makes one ask: "How can you do anything else?"

Robert Woito
February, 1982
Chicago, Illinois

TO END WAR

SECTION A

IDEAS

To END WAR is divided into three sections. Section A introduces the basic ideas in the world affairs field, summarizes the arguments concerning them, and assesses their significance for resolving the problem of war. Extensive, annotated bibliographies are provided to facilitate further study. Section B presents a number of coherent views on world politics, each providing a "context." The questions which divide contexts in American politics are introduced, contending answers sketched out, and a context presented to guide efforts at ending war. Section C discusses actions which could help turn what are now only ideas into public policy. It offers a number of helpful resources. Taken together, the ideas, the bibliographies, the contexts, and the resources provide an introduction to the world affairs field.

Section A is divided into five parts, each presenting an approach to world politics with a distinctive emphasis. In Part I the focus is on States[1] and the management of State power. The basic standard for deciding policies is the

[1] States is used throughout this book, rather than "nations" or "nation-states," because of the close association of "nation" and "ethnic group," and because of the fact that over 90% of the States in the world today are composed of more than one ethnic group. "States" is capitalized to indicate a country as opposed to a region or province within a country.

3

national interest, and the critical problem is national security. Causes of war and military strategies for achieving security are considered. Part I makes clear why many knowledgeable observers of world affairs do not think ending war is a meaningful or realistic goal. For those of us who continue to pursue such a goal, the ideas in Part I provide a test of whether a strategy to eliminate war is feasible and adequate.

Conditions essential to a world without war are introduced in Part II. The emphasis is on building a sense of world community to sustain law, not violence, as the means of resolving conflicts. Among the ideas considered in Part II are arms control, disarmament, international organizations, world law, a sense of world community, human rights, world economic change, and political development.

Part III moves from an emphasis on concepts and goals to decision-makers, identifying the major actors in world politics. There is a separate chapter on each superpower and one on regional powers. The role of non-State actors is presented, including intergovernmental organizations, like the United Nations, and private voluntary associations.

Part IV focuses on several current crises and immediate issues in world affairs. Whatever theoretical concepts are adopted, whatever the judgment about the actors, these specific matters must be dealt with.

Part V completes the presentation of ideas. It considers how moral concepts can be applied in world politics, introduces non-violent strategies of resolving conflict and promoting change, and presents current trends in peace research. In each of these chapters, the focus is on whether a significant change in our ability to apply moral concepts in world politics, to promote change without violence, and to apply new knowledge will make likely what is now only possible: a world without war.

PART I

WORLD POLITICS
AND WAR

CHAPTER 1

THE STATE-CENTERED APPROACH

MANY engaged with world politics find themselves in a chaotic setting. The personalities, events, and issues change with bewildering rapidity, and the standards for conduct differ from the more familiar practices of a democracy. In world politics, there is seldom any public examination of facts or intentions of leaders, and lies and dishonesty prevail as often as truth and integrity; in democratic politics, doubts about facts and intentions can be reduced through public and private investigations. In world politics, the most powerful actors are States; in domestic politics, the contest for power and influence is shaped by political parties, interest groups, or other associations. In world politics, the threat or use of organized mass violence (war) is widely accepted; in domestic politics, the use of violence by citizens or associations is illegal. These differences between world and domestic politics suggest the following questions:

1. Can high standards of truth and honesty become the norm in world politics?
2. Can the sovereignty of States be limited?
3. Can war be ended as a legitimate means to resolve international conflict?

Many experienced students doubt that world politics will ever resemble domestic politics in a democracy. Such students may be committed to democratic values, such as the search for truth, accountability of the powerful, and non-violent conflict resolution, but find that these values do not easily apply to world politics. World politics, they argue, is dominated by States for which honesty, accountability, and a rejection of violence lead to powerlessness in deadly quarrels with other States. Those who argue that world politics will be dominated by States in the foreseeable future take a "State-centered" or "traditional" approach, which is the prevailing view today. From it, one can learn much about the history of international relations, the causes of war, and why a sense of world community is a condition of peace. The categories of the State-centered approach to world politics are introduced below. Only when the dynamics of the State-centered approach are clear can the possibilities and risks of an alternative approach be persuasively stated.

The State-centered approach to world politics (Bull, *The Anarchical Society,* 1-61)[2] is based largely on the judgments that States will remain the most powerful actors in world politics and that violence, though regrettable, cannot be eliminated. In the State-centered approach, the role of a country in world politics is motivated by the need to secure its territory, and by the desire to promote or defend its national interest in economic and political conflict with other States. Bull asserts that State domination of world politics cannot be changed, given the power of States to influence each other, the nature of their conflicts, and the absence of effective constraints in international law or morality. The key concept is power, and the primary conceptual problem is how to define and measure it. Permanent peace, an end to war, is not considered a reasonable objective; what peace is possible is usually sought through a balance of power.

The State-centered approach builds on the fact that a State is "the most durable and most efficient unit to which individuals and groups give their effective allegiance" (Duchacek, *Nations and Men,* 1-31, p. 5). Patriotic feelings are felt deeply and shared widely in most States today. Contending claims on allegiance are not as emotionally powerful or as politically effective. When contending allegiances do develop, they often lead to the establishment of a new State, for example, Bangladesh. A feeling of membership in a global society is perhaps growing, but it is not politically effective. Given political allegiance to the State, a world politics based on the pursuit of the national self-interest, as defined by national leaders, is to be expected. Governmental leaders gain power only if they appear able to advance the national interest. Thus, the transcendence of the State system is not considered imminent.

The State-centered approach is worthy of careful study because it is based on several obvious truths. The power of States, when compared with other

---

[2]The author's last name and the book title are included in the text when the work develops the idea being introduced. The number refers the reader to the number of the title in the bibliography at the end of the chapter. If the book is quoted, the page on which the quote may be found is indicated.

forces and measured by military and economic resources, is overwhelming. Leaders of States set and pursue foreign policy objectives that shape the course of world politics; they levy taxes and raise armies to pursue their objectives. And there is a long tradition of distinguished theorists and practitioners supporting it: Machiavelli, Frederick II, Metternich, Bismarck, and Henry Kissinger, to name only a few.

Some students of U.S. foreign policy, recognizing the failure of the United Nations to evolve into an effective instrument of world peace, feel that the wise management of State power is perhaps the only hope for maintenance of peace. They would limit U.S. commitments in world politics, and thus avoid the over-extension of American resources which could, they argue, in the pursuit of illusory objectives, jeopardize our vital interests.

Recent changes in world politics also suggest the continued importance of the State-centered approach. The ''sovereign equality of States'' is a principle asserted by developing States in their advocacy of a ''New International Economic Order'' (see Chapter 12). Raymond Aron *(The Imperial Republic,* 8-29) maintains that the U.S.'s lowered profile in Asia and Africa since the Vietnam war has not led to the achievement of self-determination or liberation, as many opponents of U.S. power expected; it has led, instead, to an increase in Soviet influence. This suggests a maxim of the State-centered approach: there are no power vacuums. China has dropped the attempt to organize the ''rural'' areas of the world against Soviet and American domination in favor of an aim derived from the State-centered approach — building a bloc of States against Soviet ''hegemonism.'' The emergence of newly industrialized States, and the use of energy as a weapon in world politics, plus the assertion of regional influence by Brazil, Nigeria, Saudi Arabia, and others, suggests a new and more complex distribution of power, and new problems in power management.

AT STAKE IN WORLD POLITICS

The State-centered approach becomes more credible when the stakes (what is at issue) in world politics are considered. The stakes include most of what is at issue in domestic politics and much more; for example, the defense or acquisition of territory, the maintenance of a political system, economic advantage, or fair treatment. Through the mechanisms of world politics, States are created, achieve independence, are destroyed. A comparison of political boundaries in 1900 and 1980 is startling. Europe has been drastically altered. The Ottoman Empire is no more. Germany and Korea are divided. Elsewhere, Israel has been created, and new States have emerged from old empires throughout Asia and Africa. Only in the Western Hemisphere have the boundaries been relatively stable.

Political systems have also changed. In 1900, old monarchies were declining; they are now nearly extinct as effective political institutions. Democracy, once the heir apparent to monarchy, now is in contention everywhere with 20th-century totalitarian and authoritarian forms of political organization. To be sure, political systems change because of domestic as well as international forces. But external assistance to a faction contending for State power is highly influential, even when domestic forces remain primary.

There are many tangible and intangible values at issue in world politics. Among the tangible objectives are trade policies, the rules of monetary exchange, the prices of raw materials and commodities, and, in the future, the utilization of ocean-bed resources. Intangible objectives include the moral and political credibility of each State's economic and political system.

Given these high stakes, those taking the State-centered approach conclude that a defense of the national interest is the best guide to what constitutes good policy. It can provide a standard which can restrain State power; moral ends like freedom or anti-communism or liberation too frequently turn into crusades in which the means used cannot lead to the ends sought. But critics point out that the national interest is difficult to define, and often gets confused with the interest of the strongest or most influential group within a State. The pursuit of the national interest in world politics can lead to war, support for dictatorial allies, acquiescence in starvation, and in massive human rights violations. "Can't we aim higher than that?" critics ask.

REALISTS AND IDEALISTS

Those who doubt we can aim higher than a world politics dominated by States and violence are frequently seen as the realists. Their survey of European and world history leads them to conclude that States and war will prevail. Those who challenge this view maintain that international institutions or morality can restrain States and help eliminate war. They are frequently called the idealists.

Since 1500 the diplomatic history of Europe has been, in large part, the history of the alteration of power relationships between States (Hinsley, *Power and the Pursuit of Peace,* 1-17). One State after another has sought and occasionally gained European hegemony only to be checked by a coalition of opponents. A sub-theme has been the persistent effort to establish peace through international institutions, law, or moral restraints. Around the turn of the century, idealists were arguing that the political conditions underlying world politics had changed. They asserted that monarchical or other autocratic forms of government needed to go to war occasionally,while republican and democratic governments did not. It was particular elite groups, not the public, who wanted war. Since democratic government was the superior political form, 20th-century diplomats could build international and supranational institutions to keep peace. The carnage of World War I, and the initially successful effort to blame autocratic governments for the war, did much to place the idealists' agenda at the center of world politics. Woodrow Wilson became the foremost idealist diplomat, fighting a ''war to end all war,'' and then seeking a League of Nations to help keep the ''world safe for democracy.''

E.H. Carr (*The Twenty Year Crisis, 1919 – 1939*) is frequently cited as exposing the shortcomings of the idealists' approach. Wilson in particular, and idealists in general, Carr argues, mistakenly believed that States naturally seek peace. The constraints on power which the idealists sought — open diplomacy, freedom of the seas, acceptance of the right of self-determination, arms control and disarmament agreements, peaceful arbitration of disputes — could abolish war only if all societies shared the same values, and accepted others as equals. Wilson thought that democratic values would become universal, that as industrialization through private enterprise occurred, a league of democratic, capitalist States would unite against any autocratic aggressors. Carr maintains that these were simply the values and the political ends of the dominant classes among the victors in World War I.

While Western European States and the United States might remain committed to democratic government and capitalism for a time, the belief that the institutions of liberal democracy would become universal received a rude jolt. The Bolsheviks overthrew the democratically-inclined government of Kerensky in Russia, and set about to demonstrate that a non-democratic government could industrialize a country through State-socialist forms of economic organization. A new model emerged in world politics, Carr asserts, one based on different values and institutions. The new model proved attractive to colonies who were denied the right of self-determination, smarting under European racism, and whose economic interests were subordinated to those of the colonial powers. A fundamentally different perception of what is morally appropriate in economics and politics gained ground when the Bolsheviks seized State power in Russia. With control of States in the hands of advocates of irreconcilable ideas — democracy vs. totalitarianism, capitalism vs. State socialism — world politics remained what it had always been: a deadly quarrel.

For idealists, however, the central question was one of values. Could the values underlying democracy and capitalism recover the momentum they once had and become universal enough to support international institutions? Or could some new set of values gain such credibility? The Bolsheviks, of course, had one answer. Others sought a synthesis in democratic socialism; and still others reconciled themselves to cultural relativism and a pluralistic view of economic and political systems within states, while seeking supranational authority to resolve conflicts between States. Today, Peccei (*The Human Quality*, 6-37) and Gerald and Patricia Mische (*Toward a Human World Order*, 1-58) continue the idealist tradition of attempting to define common values on which to build world political institutions. A view distinct from any of these, the view presented in Chapter 19 calls for agreement about the conditions essential to resolve conflicts without the organized use of mass violence.

The idealist vision faltered in the 1920s and 1930s. Many different reasons can be cited. The Treaty of Versailles assigned guilt for World War I to Germany and required that it pay large war reparations. This hardship on Germany provided a focus for German hatred of the League of Nations. The Soviet Union formed its own international movement, seeking not the resolution of conflict between capitalist States but a world of socialist States under Soviet leadership. The United States withdrew into its traditional isolationism, taking the world's largest industrial power out of the forum. The League did not implement its principle of self-determination, and the European States and the United States remained colonial powers. The collapse of the capitalist world economy in the Great Depression further undermined the hopes for a world order based on democratic and capitalistic values. For these and other reasons, the League of Nations was incapable of checking the expansionist aims of Japan, Germany, and Italy, which were expressed in military offensives against Poland, Western Europe, and China. World War II began.

The realists had been far more accurate than the idealists in describing what to expect in the pre-World War II era. The history of the period was dominated by States, not international organizations; power, war, and violence, not law, were the arbiters of disputes. Carr thinks this was so because class and ideological differences determine the foreign policies of States. His view is held by Marxists and others, who argue that foreign policies are decisively influenced by the internal social and economic structures of States. In this version of the realists' argument, we can expect peace (if at all) only when a classless society emerges, or when an egalitarian social basis is established.

Neo-Marxism shares the realist assumption that self-interest is the only real motivation in world politics. However, Neo-Marxists like Wallerstein (*The Modern World System*, 1 – 65) narrow the issue to economic self-interest in a "capitalist world system." In this conceptualization, the capitalist "core" States (Western Europe and the U.S.), are pitted in conflict against the "periphery" or dependent States of the non-Western world. Many in this school of thought also refer to themselves as "neo-mercantilists," because they believe as did the classical mercantilists, that the possession of wealth is only possible by taking it away from someone else.

Hans Morgenthau offers a different basis for the realist argument: human nature. Whatever the social structure, Morgenthau argues, conflicting national interests will be expressed in war. Morgenthau's widely influential *Politics Among Nations* (1-59) succinctly presents the major principles of political realism:

1. Political realism believes that politics, like society in general, is governed by objective laws that have their roots in human nature. . . . Human nature . . . has not changed. . . . the fact that a theory of politics was developed hundreds or even thousands of years ago — as was the theory of the balance of power — does not create a presumption that it must be outmoded and obsolete.

2. The main signpost that helps political realism to find its way through the landscape of international politics is the concept of interest defined in terms of power. . . . A realist theory of international politics, then, will guard against two popular fallacies: the concern with motives and the concern with ideological preferences. . . .

3. Political realism refuses to identify the moral aspirations of a particular nation with the moral laws that govern the universe . . . and is aware of the ineluctable tension between moral command and the requirements of successful political action. . . .[3]

Morgenthau does not deny the importance of either legal or moral concepts in world politics, but warns against the danger of ignoring the influence of self-interest and the mistaken identification of a country's or an elite's self-interest with morality.

The realists argue that Woodrow Wilson was, of course, right to prefer law to violence, but that he was wrong in believing that a sense of world community would grow out of the establishment of global institutions. A sense of community, the realists argue, must precede the creation of political institutions. Only when a socially, economically, culturally integrated world society exists, can we expect global institutions to be created. In the meantime, we must expect world politics to be dominated by States. While the allied powers in World War II developed a sense of community adequate for the creation of the United Nations, that sense was too weak to give the U.N. binding authority. The community was based on a common enemy, not on shared values. Recognizing this, the five major allies gave each other the veto power in the Security

[3]Hans J. Morgenthau, *Politics Among Nations: The Struggle for Power and Peace*, fifth edition (New York: Alfred A. Knopf, Inc., 1977), pp. 4–11. Copyrighted material, reprinted with the permission of Alfred A. Knopf, Inc.

Council. Given the absence of a consensus of values underlying the United Nations, the U.N. has proven ineffective in resolving disputes between the superpowers.

For most professionals in international relations, the idealist-realist debate is over. The realists have won. The idealists have failed to show how their conception of unifying values or of power centralized in global institutions can gain the agreement of State leaders and restrain the power of States. Professional interest in the international relations field has turned to a discussion of systems or models based on the complexities of world politics, or has turned to a focus on changing social structures. Advocates of different ideological approaches, as well as those with different assumptions about human nature, have united in seeking to enlarge the knowledge base upon which international policy decisions can be made. Systems theory provides another approach to international politics, permitting consideration of alternative distributions of power and of how a State-system might change into a world government.

SYSTEMS THEORY

There are today a number of systems theories. The systems approach developed by Morton Kaplan (*Macropolitics*, 1-71) analyzes international relations during historical periods. The power centers in each period are identified and their patterns of interaction determined. Different distributions of power are then described and the rules required to maintain the system, and to change it, delineated. Kaplan constructs six possible models of international political systems, briefly described as follows:

1. *Balance of power*. The classic form of a balance of power system was 19th-century European politics, when five major powers (England, France, Prussia, Austria and Russia) each prevented the other from gaining hegemony. In this model, each State seeks primacy but is checked by the others. The rules which must be followed to maintain this system include the following:

Each major power must:

    a. increase its capabilities, but negotiate rather than fight;
    b. fight rather than be prevented from increasing capabilities;
    c. stop fighting rather than eliminate another major power;
    d. oppose any coalition of States or any single major power that attempts to dominate the international system;
    e. discourage States from favoring a transition to a global collective-security system or to world government;

f. after a war, permit the defeated or constrained major powers to reenter the system as full-fledged major powers, or act to raise some previously weaker power to the status of a major power;

g. treat all major powers as equals.

Changes from this system to another occur when circumstances change. Thus, the significant loss of power by the European States in two wars ended the five-power balance of power system.

2. *Loose bi-polar model.* This system has two major actors, and others less significant though important, such as independent power and international organizations. This model closely resembles the post-World War II international system with the U.S. and U.S.S.R. holding the political initiative. India, Yugoslavia and Egypt, for example, acted independently, and the United Nations raised a distinctive voice or acted as an intermediary from time to time.

3. *Tight bi-polar model.* In this model, the two major actors prevail over other States and over international organizations. This model has not existed, but could if two countries were able to dominate all the others, dividing the world between themselves, as Portugal and Spain came close to doing in the 15th and 16th centuries.

4. *Universal-international system.* In this model, which also has never existed, international organizations acquire the authority to resolve conflicts through political processes, thus transcending the States. The international system has resources and powers that enable it to override the power drives of any particular State within it. As originally conceived, the League of Nations had similar features. Advocates of world federalism today seek to create such a system.

5. *Hierarchical international system.* In this model, a single State or interest gains control of the universal-international system or eliminates its rival in the tight bi-polar model. The *"Pax Romana"* (Peace of Rome) is a past example of this system: Rome imposed an order in the Mediterranean region of the world through conquest and imperial administration.

6. *Unit-veto model.* In this system, every actor can prevent the others from significantly coercing each other. A world in which every State possesses the capacity to destroy any other would be such a system, as would a situation in which every State could prevent any other from occupying its territory through non-military systems (See *Civilian Defense,* Chapter 16).

Other models can be described. For example, Couloumbis and Wolfe describe "multibloc models," "the national-fragmentation model," and "the post-nuclear war" model and go on to discuss the "conflict quotient" of each. (*Introduction to International Relations,* 1-37) Each model forces a student of world affairs to look at all the actors in world politics, to assess their powers and to consider how the actors interact. These are all necessary preliminary steps to decide what goals, what means, and what actions are appropriate in world politics. In addition, systems theory offers a theoretical framework within which to bridge the gap between the idealist-realist debate; it points out that the idealist model is, at least, a hypothetically achievable model. Consequently, a student must confront the pivotal questions with which this chapter begins: Can a truthful statement of intentions be usefully made in world politics? Can the sovereignty of States be limited? Can mass violence be ended? Whatever answer one now gives to these questions, one must recognize that the circumstances, within which world political choices are made, are now undergoing rapid transformation.

ELEMENTS IN WORLD POLITICS

Prior to his government service, Henry Kissinger described 20th-century world politics as follows:

> Since the turn of the century, international crises have been increasing in both frequency and severity. The contemporary unrest, although less apocalyptic than the two world wars which spanned it, is even more profoundly revolutionary in nature. . . . The current international environment is in turmoil because its elements are in flux simultaneously.[4]

Kissinger then went on to list some thirty distinct elements important to a diplomat's consideration of foreign policy. He would surely add to the list today. The debate is not so much about what goes on the list, but what are the most significant items, now and in the future:

I. *The General Character of World Politics*

1. Foreign policy has become global — all States must be considered, not just Europe.

2. Many States now have significant, independent power to initiate new policies in world politics — to the United States and the Soviet Union must be added Japan, Western European States (separately or through the Council of Europe), China, Israel, Iran, Brazil, Nigeria; and groups of countries like the Organization of Petroleum Exporting Countries (OPEC) and the Group of 77 (a bloc of some 121 developing countries) when acting in concert with each other in the U.N. General Assembly and other international forums.

[4]Henry Kissinger, *American Foreign Policy* (New York: Norton, 1977), p. 52.

3. Two States, however, retain significant military and economic power to influence issues throughout the world. The Soviet Union and the United States are the only States which have huge nuclear arsenals and the ability to deliver many nuclear weapons to distant targets, as well as conventional forces and the airlift capacity to move them or allied forces any place on earth.

4. Regional powers are a new reality: West Germany, Japan, Israel, Iran, Nigeria, Brazil, Taiwan, South Korea, South Africa and others are significant economic and military forces in world politics.

5. Ideas are transmitted world-wide almost instantaneously; although many States try to restrict the flow of ideas, they rarely are successful in doing so.

6. The boundary line between domestic and international affairs has broken down. Civil wars often involve aid by external forces.

7. Survival often seems in jeopardy with every new technological breakthrough — the same capability which can abolish hunger and economic deprivation, and can increase life expectancy beyond all previous imagination, can also destroy human life.

8. Nationalism has increased the resources which the State can marshall in competition with other States.

9. There is a lack of agreement even about key terms, such as democracy or ''the people.''

II. *The Division of Power in the World*

1. The world is divided militarily into a ''loose bi-polar'' system.

2. The world is divided politically into many different centers of power.

3. Small powers want both protection and independence; both aid and non-interference.

4. Separatist currents (i.e. groups within a State, seeking either autonomy for their region or the creation of a separate State) threaten many States.

5. Ethnic minorities sometimes seek to create new States encompassing all of their members. An example of this are the Kurds who live in Iran, Iraq, and Turkey.

6. Both regional and global international institutions exercise influence, but only occasionally effectively restrain the war-making capabilities of States.

III. *World Economic Issues*

1. The economic gap between the rich States and the poor is increasing.

2. A new group of countries — the newly industrialized States, has emerged with significant economic resources.

3. The economic gap between developed and developing countries is frequently paralleled by economic disparities within developed and developing countries. Many different claims are made about whether this gap is closing, within the United States, China, Taiwan, South Korea, and Tanzania.

4. While there are limits to the fossil fuel energy resources, those limits are not now known.

5. The use of fossil fuels to achieve a high level of affluence creates pollution and other environmental hazards which may be unacceptable or have damaging side-effects.

6. There is a significant amount of economic dependence of countries on each other. The United States imports about 50% of its energy resources. Other countries import cereal grains from the United States. The Soviet Union currently imports significant technological resources from other States.

IV. *Social/Cultural Issues*

1. World population has passed the four billion level and is climbing. Current projections vary from six to sixteen billion or more as a leveling-off point. Population growth is occurring more rapidly in the developing countries than in the developed ones where, in some cases, zero population growth has been achieved.

2. While the majority of the world's population lives in rural areas, the cities continue to attract significant numbers of new inhabitants. Urbanization is continuing.

3. Migration between countries remains large, with Indochinese and Cuban refugees part of a much larger pattern of migration.

4. Rapid technological innovations have thrust new social groups into prominence with a corresponding decline of others. This upward and downward mobility, and the social dislocation involved, presents an explosive situation.

5. A world communication network has informed nearly everyone on earth that poverty is not in the nature of things; it is susceptible to being ended through political and social processes. Whether the goal is stated as overcoming poverty, more equitable distribution of wealth or some form of equality, there are powerful pressures for rapid, significant changes.

6. Political loyalties no longer always coincide with national boundaries — there are people in nearly every society who prefer the political or economic system of a different society.

There are, of course, many forces transforming world politics, and the above-mentioned need not, of necessity, grow in intensity. New ideas, new concepts of what is right and wrong (or old conceptions applied in new ways in different areas) may offset such forces. But in today's world politics technological innovations and military power struggles between States are important determinants of the political result. The build-up of both nuclear and conventional arms at a time of rapid technological innovation creates a high degree of instability in the balance of power between States. The facts of war, weapons systems, and current military strategies are introduced in the next chapter.

This introduction to conflict in world politics recommends that the State-centered approach be studied carefully. From such a study, one can learn much about how the current system of world politics operates and how it can be changed. In the following chapter the search for an American military strategy of participation in world politics is introduced. In Part II the conditions essential to a world without war are presented. By placing both systems of thought alongside each other, a better understanding can be gained of what is and what might be.

Such a brief summary of major currents of thought concerning world politics is necessarily incomplete. The following bibliographical resources will be helpful in answering questions such as these: 1) What kinds of conflicts between States frequently end in war? 2) What is the relationship between power struggles within States and power struggles between States? 3) What new technological innovations could radically alter the power of the various States? 4) What existing or new systems of thought are influencing loyalties in world politics? 5) Does interdependence create a greater likelihood of cooperation or conflict? 6) On what specific issues and problems do the categories of the

State-centered approach focus attention? Which are ignored? 7) Can a decentralized or centralized system of world order provide greater stability, less war, and more responsive government than the current system dominated by large States? 8) What new elements and forces influence world politics today? 9) What definition of national-self-interest is consistent with the self-interest of every State? 10) What are the forces maintaining the current system of world politics? What are the forces changing it?

BIBLIOGRAPHY[5]

A. Reference Works

1 – 1 *Europa Year Book* 1980, 3,350pp, 2 volumes., 1980, (21st ed.), Gale, $150.00 (per set). Detailed information on every country and some 1,500 international organizations.

Intro.[6]

1 – 2 *World Almanac and Book of Facts,* 976pp, 1980, Newspaper Enterprise Association, $3.95. One of a number of inexpensive almanacs providing annual information on countries, the head of State, activities of international organizations and other information.

1 – 3 *Philips' Concise World Atlas,* Harold Fullard (ed.), 1977, International Publication Service, $8.50. Inexpensive, useful, reference.

1 – 4 *Current Affairs Atlas,* Donald Paneth, 192pp, 1979, Facts on File, $19.95. Introduces fifty major international issues, devotes two to six pages to each, offers

[5]The books annotated in this and subsequent chapters are listed in *Books in Print,* 1980 – 81 (New York: R.R. Bowker 1981). With rare exceptions, articles, out of print books and books published in other countries, are not listed. Bibliographies of such works are provided in nearly every chapter.

As long as these titles remain in print, they will be available through the World Affairs Bookstore, 421 S. Wabash, Chicago, IL 60605. Please check current price if possible, and add $.95 postage and handling fee.

[6]*Intro* means best introductory work; *classic* = seminal study defining a school of thought; INF = influential in shaping the present discussion; TEW = To End War — considered of aid in ending war.

Great care has been taken to record accurately the information for each entry. In some cases, however, the page numbers are from a hardcover edition, when the price listed is for a paperback edition. We have listed the lowest price of the publication known to us. The publisher's name has been shortened to save space in many cases; for example, the University of Chicago Press is referred to as Chicago. Other university presses are similarly shortened.

photos, graphs, and statistics on such subjects as "Rich World/Poor World," "Crossing National Boundaries," and "Spaceship Earth."

1 – 5 *Countries of the World and Their Leaders Yearbook: 1980,* Gale Research, 1,265pp, 1980, Gale, $44.00. Reprints 168 of the Dept. of State's "Background Notes on Countries of the World," plus lists the Chiefs of State and Cabinet ministers. Leaders in international organizations are also listed.

1 – 6 *Atlas of World Population History,* Colin McEvedy & Richard Jones, 368pp, 1978, Penguin, $4.95. Permits comparisons of populations of countries from 400 B.C. to the year 2000 through 130 graphs and interpretative essays. Rich bibliography.

1 – 7 *Political Handbook of the World: Nineteen Eighty,* Arthur Banks (ed.), 657pp, 1980, McGraw Hill, $29.95. An annual publication including political, economic, and geographic information on each country, maps indicating territorial disputes, summaries of activities of intergovernmental organizations and a list of major events from 1945 to the present.

1 – 7A *The State of the World Atlas,* Michael Hidron & Ronald Segal, 210pp, 1981, Pluto, $9.95. A graphic portrayal of national attributes, each labeled with a catchy title.

1 – 8 *International Yearbook and Statesman's Who's Who, 1980,* Marvyn Pragnell & Jean-Pierre Keillor (eds.), 1,454pp, 1980, International Publications Service, $105.00. Provides information on States of the world, international organieations, and prominent individuals of international significance.

1 – 9 *Handbook of the Nations,* CIA, 232pp, 1979, $24.00. Reprints the CIA's National Basic Intelligence Factbook providing information on 189 "political units," emphasizing economic and governmental data.

1 – 10 *World Economic Survey, 1979-1980, Current Trends in the #orld Economy,* United Nations, 116pp, 1980, U.N., $10.00. Compares the "developing countries, the developed market economies, and the centrally planned economies" growth, rate of inflation, trade and outlooks.

1 – 11 *1978 Report on the World Social Situation,* United Nations, 54pp, 1979, United Nations, $5.00. An analysis of population trends, growth and distribution of income, and availability of social services.

1 – 12 *UNESCO Statistical Yearbook, 1977,* UNESCO, 1,064pp, 1979, United Nations, $74.25. Provides statistical data from "200 countries" on population trends, educational enrollments, technological developments, publishing, and libraries.

1 – 13 *Annual of Power and Conflict, 1978 – 79,* Brian Cozier (ed.), 502pp, 197', Gale, $40.00. Summarizes each year's political violence, subversion, and wars for each geographical region and country.

B. Documents

1 – 14 *Documents on International Affairs,* 1962, D.C. Watt, *et al.* (ed.), 534pp, 1971, Oxford, $37.50. An annual collection of documents covering that year's activity.

1 – 15 *The Major International Treaties, 1914 – 1973, A History and Guide with Complete Texts,* J.A.S. Grenville, 575pp, 1975, Stein & Day, $8.95. A selection from the more than 20,000 treaties and agreements concluded during the period with introductory remarks providing the setting.

1 – 16 *Survey of International Arbitrations, 1794-1970,* Alexander Stuyt, 590pp, 1972, Oceana, $32.50. Provides an overview of negotiated and arbitrated conflicts and how they have been resolved.

C. Histories

1 – 17 *Power and the Pursuit of Peace; Theory and Practice in the History of Relations Between States,* F.H. Hinsley, 416pp, 1963, Cambridge, $11.95. Provides a broad overview of diplomatic history casting doubt on whether the weak and the strong should ever be united under one authority.

1 – 18 *The Philosophy of International Relations: A Study in the History of Thought,* F. Parkinson, 245pp, 1977, Sage, $8.95. A history of different approaches to international relations from ancient Greece to the present. The concluding chapter attempts a synthesis.

1 – 19 *World Politics Since 1945,* Peter Calvocoressi, 458pp, 1979 (3rd. ed.), $11.95. Focuses on diplomats, specific events, with a few generalizations.

1 – 20 *International Disputes: Case Histories 1945-1970,* M. Donelan & M. Grieve, 280pp, 1973, St. Martin's, $19.95. Offers case histories of major events.

D. Anthologies

TEW
1 – 21 *Readings in World Politics,* Robert Goldwin & Tony Pearce (eds.), 644pp, 1970, Oxford, $5.95. The best single introduction to concepts central to any discussion of world politics: goals, citizenship, nationalism, communism, other ideologies, peace, and morality. The editors present four or more selections from classic and modern sources on each concept. The ten selections on the causes of war provide an invaluable overview of the problem.

1 – 22 *World in Crisis, Readings in International Relations,* Frederick Hartmann, 519pp, 1973, Macmillan, $9.25. Readings in a State-centered approach introduce the

role of the super-powers and the place of crisis problems in balance of power politics.

1 – 23 *World Politics, An Introduction,* James Rosenau, Kenneth Thompson & Gavin Boyd (eds.), 754pp, 1976, Macmillan, $16.50. Three editors with different theoretical perspectives offer thirty authors defining their approaches to international relations. The nation-state is considered the primary actor. Selections focus on diplomacy, regional, and global systems.

1 – 24 *Great Issues of International Politics, The International System and National Policy,* Morton Kaplan (ed.), 598pp, 1974, 2nd ed., Aldine, $8.95. Thirty-seven essays disputing such issues as the role of world law, the strength of contemporary internationalism, as well as regional political and military controversies.

1 – 25 *International Politics, Anarchy, Force, Imperialism,* Robert Art & Robert Jervis (eds.), 567pp, 1973, Little, Brown, $9.95. The title describes international politics; it is a game now in which little law can be imposed, hence it is a state of anarchy. States must thus use force to defend themselves and thus end up taking territory or exerting control over other States. Selections from over thirty authors develop these concepts.

1 – 26 *At Issue, Politics in the World Arena,* Steven Spiegel (ed.), 500pp, 1981 (3rd. ed.), St. Martin's, $8.95. Thirty-six selections (thirty new with this edition) reflecting the new toughness of mind. Articles by Walter Laqueur, Edward Luttwak, Paul Nitze, and Carl Gershman contend with articles by Richard Barnet and Richard Falk.

E. Texts

Intro
1 – 27 *International Relations: Theories and Evidence,* Michael Sullivan, 400pp, 1976, Prentice-Hall, $16.95. Attempts to present the empirical evidence substantiating and calling into question contending theories.

1 – 28 *The Politics of International Economic Relations,* Joan Spero, 350pp, 1981 (2nd ed.), St. Martin's, $8.95. Describes the setting within which Western, North-South, and East-West economic issues are resolved and concludes with a call for *a* (not *the*) "New Economic Order."

1 – 29 *7304: International Relations on the Planet Earth,* David Finlay & Thomas Hovet, Jr., 374pp, 1975, Harper, $19.50. Asks "What might be the state of international relations twenty years (7304 days) from now?" This text is distinguished by its emphasis on "interrelated transactions" across national boundaries, particularly environmental, technological, economic, and military transactions. The focus is thus futuristic and emphasizes cooperation beyond the State system to solve basic problems.

1 – 30 *Comparative Politics: System, Process, and Policy,* Gabriel Almond & G. Bingham Powell, 435pp, 1978 (2nd ed.), Little, Brown, $9.95. Introduces the structural-functional approach to comparing political systems.

1 – 31 *Nations and Men: An Introduction to International Politics,* Ivo Duchacek, 596pp, 1973 (3rd. ed.), Holt, Rinehart & Winston, $12.95. Broadens the range of concepts considered central to the discipline, to include disarmament, world law, world community, nonviolence and moral concerns; in short, emphasizes the transnational in the current State system.

1 – 32 *Contending Approaches to International Politics,* Klaus Knorr & James Rosenau, 297pp, 1969, Princeton, $5.95. An anthology focused on the debate between "scientific" and "traditional" approaches with Morton Kaplan, David Singer, and Robert North defending the scientific approach, and Hedley Bull and Robert Jervis, the traditional. The problems of defining abstract ideas as concrete things, the use of models, quantification, prediction vs. retrodiction, fallacies of inference, complexity, goal-directed behavior, are all discussed.

1 – 33 *Introduction to International Politics,* Robert Cantor, 323pp, 1976, Peacock, $12.50. In ordinary language, the author presents the main concepts, theories, actors, stakes, and goals in world politics.

1 – 34 *Global Politics,* James Ray, 416pp, 1979, Houghton Mifflin, $15.50. Introduces world politics through a search for patterns in 20th-century history, and through an analysis of contemporary crises. Explores possible new roles for international organizations in a changing world society.

1 – 35 *International Relations, A Transnational Policy Approach,* Werner Feld, 433pp, 1979, Alfred, $13.95. A text including chapters on conflict and collaboration and emphasizing non-state actors.

1 – 36 *Games Nations Play, Analyzing International Politics,* John Spanier, 457pp, 1978 (3rd ed.), Holt, Rinehart & Winston, $11.95. A State-centered approach introducing different levels of analysis, the structure of the State system, the role of force, alliances and the major actors. Rejects political integration, functionalism and global approaches as inapplicable to the real world.

1 – 37 *Introduction to International Relations: Power and Justice,* Theodore Couloumbis & James Wolf, 399pp, 1978, Prentice-Hall, $12.95. Emphasizes international organizations, war, and "challenges to mankind."

1 – 38 *Theory and Reality in World Politics,* Carey Joynt & Percy Corbett, 147pp, 1978, Pittsburgh, $10.50. Includes the theories of Morton Kaplan, David Singer, Hans Morgenthau, Hedley Bull, and others, and offers a critical analysis of them.

1 – 39 *How Nations Behave,* Louis Henkin, 416pp, 1979 (2d ed.), Columbia, $7.00. An introduction to the role of law in international politics.

1 – 40 *International Relations, A Policymaker Focus,* Robert Wendzel. 288pp, 1980, 2d ed., Wiley, $7.00. Built around the information, concepts, and considerations policy-makers usually bear in mind.

1 – 41 *World Change and World Security,* Norman Dahl & Jerome Wiesner (eds.), 174pp, 1978, MIT, $14.95. Assessments of international relations issues such as

nuclear proliferation (Frank Church), population (Robert McNamara), security (Willy Brandt), human aggressiveness and conflict resolution (Hamburg).

1 – 42 *Principles of World Politics,* George Modelski, 370pp, 1972, Macmillan, $14.95. Seeks to identify "responsibilities that are willingly assumed by all" the actors in world politics — States, international organizations, world universities, global corporations, and world society. Argues that the value of survival has become an overriding preoccupation of the State system in the nuclear era and that different forms of order would permit the pursuit of justice.

F. Concepts and Theory

1 – 43 *Power: Its Nature, Its Limits,* Donald Harward (ed.), 1979, G.K. Hall, $18.00. Fourteen authors debate the meanings of power.

1 – 44 *Handbook on Social Philosophy,* Robert Beck (ed.), 220pp, 1979, Macmillan, $7.95. Offers a brief descriptive guide to the major schools of thought: classical realism, positivism, philosophical liberalism, utilitarianism, idealism, communism, pragmatism, existentialism, and analytic philosophy as they differ around six central topics: human nature, social political values, law, human rights, and justice.

1 – 45 *Concepts of International Politics, A Global Perspective,* Abdul Said & Charles Lerche, 385pp, 1979, Prentice-Hall, $15.95. Introduces the basic concepts: actors, power, change, conflict, war, ideology and circumstance.

1 – 46 *Diplomacy,* Harold Nicolson, 151pp, 1977 (1939),[7] Oxford, $4.95. Defines diplomacy as "the art of negotiating agreements between Sovereign States." Sets forth the "principles and ideals of correct diplomacy . . . which are considered necessary and immutable." A history of diplomacy, distinction between different types, the uses of various forums, and diplomatic procedures are all covered.

1 – 47 *In Search of Theory: A New Paradigm for Global Politics,* Richard Mansbach & John Vasquez, 544pp, 1981, Columbia, $22.50. Focuses on issues, psychological profiles, and characteristics of the actors.

1 – 48 *The Handbook of Political Science,* Vol. 8, *International Politics,* Fred Greenstein & Nelson Polsby, 450pp, 1975, Addison-Wesley, $19.75. An introduction to the key concepts and theories.

1 – 49 *International Politics, Foundations of the System,* Werner Levi, 320pp, 1974, U. of Minnesota, $12.50. A theoretical approach almost devoid of names, places or dates, which affirms the possibility of a unified theory adequate to understand and interpret international relations.

[7]The year in parenthesis indicates the year the book was originally published.

1 – 50 *Foreign Policy Motivation, A General Theory and a Case Study*, Richard Cottam, 374pp, 1977, Pittsburgh, $16.95. Argues that differences in world view lie at the heart of interstate conflict and domestic debate on foreign policy. Offers a study of the British in Egypt (1876-1956).

1 – 51 *Theories and Approaches to International Politics, What Are We To Think?*, Patrick Morgan, 293pp, 1981, Transaction, $9.95. Seeks to develop or contribute to the development of a theory of international politics which integrates influences on policy and simplifies their assessment.

1 – 52 *Contending Theories of International Relations*, James Dougherty & Robert Pfaltzgraff, Jr., 416pp, 1971, Harper & Row, $9.50. The authors present summaries of the major approaches: balance of power theory, ''man-milieu'' relationships, realism, systems theory, conflict theory, economic imperialism, microcosmic theories (anthropological and psychological explanations of conflict), macrocosmic theories (deterrence), integration of political communities, decision-making, and games theory.

1 – 53 *The Theory and Practice of International Relationships*, David McLellan, Fred Sondermann, & William Olson, 410pp, 1979 (5th ed.), Prentice-Hall, $10.95. Introduces the principal elements and processes of international relations and applies them to current issues such as the economic questions raised by the third world spokespersons, detente, and the nuclear arms race.

1 – 54 *Political Identity*, W.J.M. Mackenzie, 185pp, 1978, St. Martin's, $14.95. A study of political language and the literature about such powerful abstractions as race, religion, class and nation.

1 – 55 *In Search of Peace*, Waris Shere (ed.), 226pp, 1980, Exposition, $12.50. A policy maker's perspective on the best approach, with essays by Trudeau, Begin, Fulbright, and Alexander Haig.

G. Idealists vs. Realists Debate

1 – 56 *Wilson and the League of Nations: Why America's Rejection?*, Ralph Stone (ed.), 128pp, 1978 (1967), Krieger, $5.50. Brief selections from contending perspectives about the conflicts between Woodrow Wilson and Henry Cabot Lodge, and between the vision and the reality of the League of Nations.

1 – 57 *Henry Cabot Lodge and the Search for an American Foreign Policy*, William Widenor, 400pp, 1980, California, $18.50. An intellectual biography portraying Lodge as neither a bitter foe of the League of Nations nor an ardent supporter of Theodore Roosevelt but as a staunch defender of the national interest.

1 – 58 *Toward a Human World Order: Beyond the National Security Straitjacket,* Gerald and Patricia Mische, 399 pp, 1977, Paulist Press, $2.95. A contemporary idealist statement identifying a set of core values believed to be universally shared and suggesting that new political institutions can be built on those values.

INF
1 – 59 *Politics Among Nations: The Struggle for Power and Peace,* Hans J. Morgenthau, 640pp, 1978 (5th ed.), Knopf, $18.95. An introductory text by one of the leading political scientists of the U.S., which makes the case for realism, and maintains that the balance of power and the pursuit of national interest provide what basis the current international system offers for peace. Maintains that a world community must be created before a world State, and concludes that the "creation of an international community presupposes at least the mitigation and minimization of international conflicts so that the interests uniting members of different nations may outweigh the interests separating them." (p. 525)

1 – 60 *The Decline of Bismarck's European Order: Franco-Russian Relations, 1875 – 1890,* George F. Kennan, 466pp, 1979, Princeton, $6.95. A history based on balance of power, realist assumptions of the time when a complex structure of European political order was beginning to crumble.

1 – 61 *The Anarchical Society: A Study of Order in World Politics,* Hedley Bull, 335pp, 1979, Columbia, $6.50. Addresses these questions: "What is order in world politics? How is order maintained within the present system of sovereign States? Does the system of sovereign States still provide a viable path to world order?" Bull concludes that the "arguments to the effect that the state system was in decline, or was unable to serve goals of world order, were unconvincing" (p. 319).

1 – 62 *Defending the National Interest, Raw Material Investments and U.S. Foreign Policy,* Stephen Krasner, 404pp, 1978, Princeton, $5.95. A self-conscious defense of the State-centered approach: a State has interests above those of the dominant group within it or of its economic system; those interests should be defended by diplomacy if possible, by force if necessary.

1 – 63 *International Politics: A Framework for Analysis,* Kalevi Holsti, 548pp, 1977 (3rd. ed.), Prentice-Hall, $16.95. Seeks to "present a framework that will help the reader understand what States seek through their governments and political leaders; how they operate in relation to others in periods of stability and war; what techniques they use to achieve or defend their objectives; how they are restrained — or unrestrained — by moral, ethical or legal considerations; and how they resolve their conflicts." Unusual in the attention it gives to ethical and legal concepts as frail but real restraints on national power.

1 – 64 *The Nation-State and the Crisis of World Politics, Essays on International Politics in the Twentieth Century,* John Herz, 307pp, 1976, Longman, $9.95. A

collection of essays written over 20 years by a realist, examining the limits of the territorial State and the implications of nuclear weapons for contemporary politics.

H. Neo-Marxism

1 – 65 *The Modern World System II: Mercantilism and the Consolidation of the European World Economy,* 1600-1750, Immanuel Wallerstein, 220pp, 1980, Academic Press, $9.50. The second volume presenting the conceptualization and historical interpretation of the "world capitalist system," the "core" vs. the "periphery" and the economic determinist principles underlying their interaction.

1 – 66 *Processes of the World System,* Terence Hopkins & Immanuel Wallerstein (eds.), 320pp, 1980, Sage, $9.95. An anthology applying the "world systems" concepts to specific situations.

1 – 67 *Class and Nation, Historically and in the Current Crisis,* Samir Amin, 292pp, 1980, Monthly Review, $6.50. Argues that the "class struggle is taking place not only within separate national frameworks, but in the context of the world system."

1 – 68 *Critical Perspectives on Imperialism and Social Class in the Third World,* James Petras, 314pp, 1980, Monthly Review, $5.95. A specialist in Latin America offers a synthesis of class analysis with dependency theory using Puerto Rico, Chile and other Latin American examples.

I. Systems

1 – 69 *Theory of International Relations,* Kenneth Waltz, 1979, Addison-Wesley, $8.50. An approach to systems theory which includes both internal dynamics of States and world politics as part of the systems leading to predictions of foreign policy outcomes.

1 – 70 *Superpowers and International Conflict,* Carsten Holbroad, 178pp, 1979, St. Martin's, $25.00. A study of U.S. – Soviet relations since 1945.

1 – 71 *Macropolitics: Selected Essays on the Philosophy and Science of Politics,* Morton Kaplan, 234pp, 1968, Irvington, $18.50. Introduces systems theory and argues for its utility in studying politics; also treats ethical and methodological implications of contending values.

1 – 72 *Modernization and the Transformation of International Relations,* Edward Morse, 203pp, 1976, Macmillan, $14.95. A broad overview of the State system, which emerged after the Peace of Westphalia (1648), to the present, that concludes moderniza-

tion has caused the breakdown of that system and that no new world order is likely to replace it.

1 – 73 *The International System, Theoretical Essays,* Klaus Knorr & Sidney Verba (eds.) 237pp, 1961, Princeton, $2.95. A collection of essays in the systems approach to international relations defining conceptual, theoretical, and empirical problems in developing a coherent systems theory. Essays by Morton Kaplan, Thomas Schelling, J. David Singer, George Modelski, Stanley Hoffmann, and others.

1 – 74 *State Systems: International Pluralism, Politics, and Culture,* Robert Wesson, 296pp, 1978, Free Press, $16.95. Maintains that the treatment of world politics as a game played by States is ending, and doubts that the new system will be less violent — probably more. The State after all, was invented in part to control the violence of non-governmental associations.

1 – 75 *Dominance and Diversity: The International Hierarchy,* Steven Spiegel, 317pp, 1980, Univ. Press of America, $10.50. Describes a systems approach to international relations, how to get and keep influence, and the prospects for the re-emergence of Europe as a superpower.

1 – 76 *System Theory in International Relations: A Study in Metaphoric Hypertrophy,* John Weltman, 144pp, 1973, Lexington, $13.95. A critique of the enterprise.

J. World Order

1 – 77 *International Order and Foreign Policy, A Theoretical Sketch of Post-War International Politics,* Friedrich Kratochwil, 298pp, 1978, Westview, $26.00. Seeks to define how the rules of the game developed and their connection with conflict resolution and the problem of world order.

TEW
1 – 78 *The Logic of International Relations,* Stephen Rosen & Walter Jones, 504pp, 1980 (3rd ed.), Winthrop, $10.95. Introduces the contending perspectives in world politics and thus the reality of conflict, suggests the ways in which conflict has been conducted through balance of power diplomacy, deterrence and war, and the role of international organizations and law, to achieve world order.

1 – 79 *War, Peace, and International Politics,* David Ziegler, 444pp, 1977, Little, Brown, $9.95. This introduction is built around the theme of "the problem of war and what we can do about it." The book includes a realistic appraisal of contemporary conflict, a historical introduction to the causes of war and approaches to peace from world government to the balance of power. Ziegler concludes "there is no simple approach to peace that will end all wars."

1 – 80 *From National Development to Global Community, Essays in Honor of Karl*

Deutsch, Richard Merritt & Bruce Russett (eds.), 1981, Allen & Unwin, $14.95. Essays analyzing the communications networks forming the basis of global community.

1 – 81 *The Dialectic of World Politics,* Silviu Brucan, 163pp, 1978, Macmillan, $15.95. An unorthodox Marxist view of world politics which foresees the "disintegration of the present world system" by the year 2000 and the establishment of a "world institution" (p. 152).

1 – 82 *Principles of Foreign Policy: The Civil State in Its World Setting,* Roy Jones, 300pp, 1979, St. Martin's, $25.00. Argues on behalf of constitutional government and from that premise, suggests ways to work for peace, or at least to avoid a nuclear holocaust, with very different kinds of States.

1 – 83 *A Global Approach to National Policy,* Richard Falk, 384pp, 1975, Harvard, $17.50. Maintains that the State system is under siege, and argues that geopolitical concerns, not idealism, should lead one to think about the world in global terms and to search for a new world order. Concludes that a compromise between the State system and world government is "the most desirable conception of world order that is also both attainable within a reasonable length of time and does not rely on transitional trauma."

1 – 84 *World Politics, Trend and Transformation,* Charles Kegley & Eugene Wittkopf, 500pp, 1981, St. Martin's, $11.95. Maintains that politics is undergoing transformation; emphasizes the limits of the State without suggesting how the process will end.

K. The Setting

1 – 85 *New Forces in World Politics,* Seyom Brown, 224pp, 1974, Brookings, $11.95. Discusses transnational organizations, multinational corporations, ideas, and background conditions within the State-centered framework.

1 – 86 *Climatic Change and World Affairs,* Crispin Tickell, 78pp, 1977, Harvard Center for International Affairs, $3.95. Demonstrates if nothing else, that you probably had not considered everything in deciding your policies.

1 – 87 *World Handbook of Political and Social Indicators,* Charles Taylor & Michael Hudson, 464pp, 1972 (2nd ed.), Yale, $8.95. A valuable indication of many conditions underlying world politics.

L. Bibliographies, Dictionaries and Sources

1 – 88 *Foreign Affairs Fifty-Year Bibliography: New Evaluations of Significant Books on International Relations, 1920-1970,* Byron Dexter, 936pp, 1972, Bowker, $43.95. Provides insight into the changing focus of the discussion.

1 – 89 *International Relations Theory, A Bibliography,* A.J.R. Groom & C.R. Mitch-

ell, 222pp, 1980, Nichols, $12.50. Prepared by the Center for the Analysis of Conflict (London). It is a valuable overview of the literature.

1 – 90 *A Guide to Bibliographic Tools for Research in Foreign Affairs,* Helen Conover, 2 Vols, 1980, Gordon Press, $250.00. An extensive resource for the professional.

1 – 91 *International Bibliography of Political Science,* International Committee for Social Sciences Information & Documentation, Vol. 25, 1976, International Publications Service, $57.50. Both a periodical index and book list.

1 – 92 *The Information Sources of Political Science,* Frederick Holler, 5 volumes, 1981 (1975), ABC-Clio, $21.75. Over 1,700 annotated entries, including one volume on international relations.

1 – 93 *The Study of International Politics: A Guide to the Sources for the Student, Teacher, and Researcher,* Dorothy LaBarr & J. David Singer, 211pp, 1976, ABC-Clio, $19.75. Provides brief descriptions of the sources.

1 – 94 *The Political Science Concept Inventory,* Ralph Goldman, Philip Schoner, & DeVere Pentony, 500pp, 1980, ABC-Clio, $21.50. Analyzes and lists 21,000 terms and concepts used in political science.

1 – 95 *International Relations Dictionary,* Jack Plano & Roy Olton, 337pp, 1979 (2nd ed.), New Issues Press, $6.50. Provides one paragraph definitions of key words and explains their significance.

CHAPTER 2

WAR, WEAPONS, AND MILITARY STRATEGY

TODAY almost all States prepare for war. Almost all rely on military power — their own or their allies — for national security and as an essential instrument for their participation in world politics. War has long been an accepted means for fulfilling such functions. The organizational requirements of war, although always onerous and costly, have been accepted as necessary *(A History of Warfare, 2 – 1 to 2 – 13)*. For those seeking to end war, a central educational task of our times is changing people's minds about the utility, necessity, and legitimacy of war.

Most people maintain that war is legitimate until it is supplanted by some other process. The institutions of modern war (weapons development centers, military installations, strategic think tanks, military production facilities, and mobilized public opinion) are, it is claimed, maintained for necessary, indeed vital, purposes. The essential tasks, strategists argue, are to define a State's political objectives, and to develop the instruments and the strategy needed to achieve them. In the past these have been the instruments and strategy of war.

DETERRENCE

The prevention of war is the stated purpose of the prevailing military strategy: deterrence. Advocates of military deterrence (George & Smoke, *Deterrence in American Foreign Policy*, 2– 78, Kahn; *On Thermonuclear War*, 2– 52; and Kahan, *Security in the Nuclear Age*, 2– 55) argue that peace will be maintained as long as adversaries believe the price of war is prohibitively high. Deterrence requires that a society be prepared to use weapons of mass destruction, for as Robert Tucker has indicated:

> To convince the adversary that we would act in the manner threatened, it is indispensable to convince ourselves that we would so respond. As long as we believe, others will believe. As long as others believe, they will not act. The key to a successful strategy of nuclear deterrence lies wholly within ourselves.

Thus, the essential element in deterrence is *our own willingness* to use weapons of mass destruction. As long as that will is clear and adequate forces are maintained to execute it, deterrence theorists argue there will be no war. They cite the absence of nuclear war between the super-powers as evidence. They argue that military weakness can itself cause war, recalling in support of this view the events leading to the Munich Agreement (1939) and the subsequent German invasion of first Czechoslovakia, then Poland, and Western Europe.

For a time there was a significant debate in this country about the morality of nuclear deterrence. Those defending deterrence argued that theirs was a morality of intention. Opponents of deterrence argued that no society should even consider completely destroying another society. They argued further that the strategy of deterrence engenders suspicion and fear which are obstacles to the peaceful settlement of international disputes; it exacerbates tensions, thus blocking the path to possible cooperation in resolving common problems or in building the institutions and understandings essential to a world without war.

Despite the high financial costs, the risks of nuclear war, and the fear and distrust bred by modern weaponry, the deterrence strategists have clearly won the argument, at least for the moment. Even at the peak of the anti-Vietnam war feeling, few people challenged reliance on nuclear deterrence. Today, some advocates of disarmament recommend that the disarming power retain a few nuclear weapons (Myrdal, *The Game of Disarmament*, 4– 5). Thus, the focus of the debate about military strategies has turned to the question which deterrence strategists have asked all along: "How much is enough?" Those who continue to challenge deterrence theory are unlikely to succeed unless they develop an adequate alternative strategy of peace (see Chapters 4– 7 and Chapter 19).

THE STRATEGIC DEBATE

Today there is significant debate about nuclear strategy. Deterrence based on mutual assured destruction (MAD) has been called into question by the changed balance of forces between the Soviet Union and the United States, by increases in both superpowers' delivery vehicles and warheads, by the improved accuracy of weapon guidance systems, by possible technological break-throughs making anti-ballistic missile defenses conceivable, and by psychological factors. Nuclear strategists debate questions such as these:

1. Is nuclear war a "war or a holocaust"? If a war, what forces are needed to be prepared to fight it if deterrence fails?

2. Is the possession of an overkill capacity (the capacity to destroy an enemy's population many times over) a decisive factor, or must strategists consider what forces will be lost in a first strike, what forces in a war will not reach their targets, and what level of losses the adversary is willing to risk to achieve its objectives?

3. Is deterrence effective so long as you can destroy an adversary's population centers, or must forces be maintained for a number of contingencies?

4. If Western Europe were attacked by the Soviet Union's superior conventional forces, would the U.S. initiate a "limited nuclear war"? What forces are needed to convey to the Soviet Union (and to Western European allies) the credibility of that intention?

5. Could a war involving nuclear weapons be limited?

6. Is the rapid Soviet build-up of its strategic forces translatable by it into political bargaining leverage?

7. If the Soviet Union can destroy all of the land-based missiles of the U.S. with one-third of its land-based missiles, would the U.S.'s deterrent be held in check by the remaining two-thirds of the Soviet land-based missiles targeted on U.S. population centers?

8. Can a democracy maintain a willingness to accept millions of deaths to gain political leverage in world politics? the security of its allies? its own security? Can it maintain itself and others in any other way?

HOW MUCH IS ENOUGH?

For much of the cold war period (1947 – 1960s), the U.S. had a significant superiority in nuclear weapons and in strategic delivery systems. U.S. strategists felt that, if war were to come, the Soviets might launch their nuclear weapons and destroy a portion of our nuclear arsenal; however, with U.S. superiority the United States could make a devastating retaliatory attack. The second strike capability of the U.S. would thus prevent war between the super-powers.

Since the Cuban missile crisis (1962), however, the circumstances of the arms race have changed. The Soviet Union began to build up its strategic arsenal and to enlarge its conventional land forces. The Soviet Navy had been expanded from one capable of defending its coastal waters to one capable of global operations. At first it was thought the Soviet Union would build up to force levels equivalent to the United States. Most experts believe that the two super-powers entered the 1980s with a rough equivalence of strategic nuclear forces, with each having the advantage in some weapons systems — either quantitative or qualitative. The Soviets clearly have greater throw-weight or destructive capacity; the U.S. can deliver its weapons with greater accuracy. The Soviet Union did not stop building at equivalent force levels. Thus, current forces plus the momentum of Soviet expenditures can give them significant leads in the 1980s, particularly in land-based, strategic missiles (The International Institute for Strategic Studies, London, 2 – 16 and Stockholm International Peace Research Institute, 4 – 2).

Two additional changes in the 1970s haunt the strategic debate in the 1980s. One is the enormous increase in the size, destructive capacity, and precision of guidance systems. The other is the new technologies that may make possible what has not been possible since 1960: a defense that might limit losses to twenty million people. Both changes increase the danger of nuclear war. They do, because as the arsenals of the two super-powers increase, each may believe that it (or the adversary) has a first-strike capacity — the ability to destroy enough of the other's arsenal so that retaliation would result only in what political leaders or nuclear strategists consider "acceptable" damage.[1] Defensive weapons, if acquired by one power, would have the same consequence: providing that power with a first-strike capacity. But if sufficient retaliatory power remained to assure the destruction of the attacker, no State would risk a first strike. Thus, the objective of SALT (Strategic Arms Limita-

---

[1]There is no agreed definition of "acceptable" losses in the strategic literature. Between 1964 and 1967 Robert McNamara defined the ability to destroy 20 to 33% of an adversary's population and 50 to 67% of its industry as "an unacceptable degree of damage" in an effort to define precisely what U.S. strategic forces must do to effectively deter war.

tion Talks) was to limit nuclear forces of each side so that mutual assured destruction (MAD) remained. The growth of strategic arsenals which paralleled the SALT process, however, raised questions about whether either or both super-powers were seeking a first strike capability.

The fear among many American strategic thinkers is that the Soviet Union may be able to neutralize the land-based missiles of the U.S. U.S. strategic airplanes are also vulnerable to attack. If the U.S. submarine fleet remains immune to anti-submarine warfare, an effective deterrent would be maintained. But some U.S. strategists, doubtful that one leg of the "Triad" (submarines, planes, and land-based, intercontinental ballistic missiles) is sufficient, now advocate building the MX missile. The MX need not increase the number of delivery vehicles available, but would complicate targeting since it would be mobile. In addition, the cruise missile would permit aircraft to launch nuclear weapons out of range of many anti-aircraft defense. For some, in short, a significant new series of weapons must be built by the U.S. to restore an assured ability to destroy the Soviet Union should it launch an attack. For them, the ability of the U.S. to deter such an attack is in question at current force levels.

ASSURED DESTRUCTION OR FLEXIBLE RESPONSE?

The dispute about whether to build the MX or other new strategic delivery systems is, in part, about what forces are needed to hit what kinds of targets to maintain an effective deterrent. Robert Jervis describes this division as follows:

> . . . the basic question . . . can be referred to as the dispute between those who advocate a policy of Assured Destruction (AD) and those who call for Flexible Response (FR). Proponents of AD believe that any nuclear war will be all-out war and therefore that the United States need only have an assured capacity to destroy an enemy's cities even if forced to absorb a first strike. Proponents of FR hold that there is a range of military contingencies for which the United States must be prepared and that nuclear weapons can be used in a variety of such contingencies in a more flexible, limited way.[2]

Advocates of AD are accused of treating war like a holocaust, opening a credibility gap between the U.S. and its allies which the Soviet Union is exploiting, and of courting disaster by not continuously manifesting the will to retaliate through maintenance of, at least, equivalent force levels. Advocates of FR are accused of making limited nuclear war thinkable, of wasting funds, of

[2]Robert Jervis, "Why Nuclear Superiority Doesn't Matter," *Political Science Quarterly*, Winter 1979–80, p. 617.

building a first strike capability, and of exaggerating the risks the Soviet Union would take for valued political objectives.

SUFFICIENT AND MINIMUM DETERRENCE

"What does it matter if the Soviet Union does acquire superiority?" say those committed to sufficient and minimum deterrence. We still have an enormous overkill capacity and all we really need is the ability to destroy Soviet cities. We can decide on the force levels needed for that task without considering what forces the Soviet Union may build. If we tailor our strategic forces to that objective we can significantly reduce our military expenditures. The Carter Administration studied the feasibility of a sufficient deterrent force of 200 to 250 strategic delivery vehicles as opposed to the 2,400 limit agreed in the Vladivostok Accords (1974). Others have argued that a minimum deterrent of ten Trident submarines, each with twelve ballistic missiles, all with multiple-targeted re-entry vehicles (MIRVs) could launch 400 nuclear warheads which is surely enough. Some advocates of minimum deterrence cite domestic political or economic interests as responsible for excessive force levels.

STRATEGIC EQUIVALENCE

Those who want to keep pace with the Soviets and maintain a "strategic equivalence of forces" respond in several ways. What counts, they say, is not your capacity before the war begins, but what survives the first strike, what then reaches the target, and what the other side considers unacceptable losses. Some strategists, both Soviet and American, talk today about twenty million deaths as acceptable. The best way to avoid such losses, American strategists argue, is to maintain forces equivalent to those of the Soviet Union and to make a significant portion of them very difficult to attack.

Advocates of strategic equivalence believe there are other objectives besides the territorial defense of the United States and its allies for which strategic forces should be built. A large arsenal provides a reserve for many contingencies, they argue. We do not want a situation where our only response to Soviet provocation in Berlin, Western Europe, the Middle East, or elsewhere, is massive retaliation. We want the possibility of flexible response. Should an unauthorized attack occur against the United States, we would not want to respond with nuclear war. Should an ally be threatened, we want to be able to demonstrate that the U.S. could respond to that threat and still maintain sufficient forces to deter threats to the United States itself. Finally, in a time of rapid technological innovation, who can be sure that some new weapon system will not be developed capable of eliminating our forces? Even anti-submarine warfare, once thought technologically impossible, may become feasible in the 1980's. Given all these considerations, some even argue that the U.S. should seek to regain military superiority in order to deter the Soviet Union.[3]

But that is just the problem, many respond. Our technological developments and weapons system developments provoke theirs, and theirs ours; the arms race goes on toward Armageddon. Our government's new statement of the counterforce doctrine — that it is feasible and a matter of policy to target military installations instead of cities and the endorsement of the concept of limited nuclear war, may suggest to the Soviets that the U.S. is seeking a first strike capability. It makes no sense, after all, to initiate limited nuclear war, unless you can win it at other levels.

Being prepared to wage war is what deterrence requires, those advocating strategic equivalence respond — whether we target cities or military installations. Military targets are preferable in some cases, for they permit a flexible response or controlled escalation rather than just massive retaliation. The neutron bomb, they argue, is an effective deterrent precisely because the Soviets must believe we would use it if they attack Western Europe with their conventional forces or seek political concessions because they possess conventional military superiority in Europe. The neutron bomb does lower the nuclear threshold. That is why it is an effective deterrent to war.

Behind the debate about ''How much is enough?'' lie other issues. What are the Soviets' overall intentions? (See Chapters 9 and 18) Does military superiority (or military equivalence when only one power has the demonstrable will to use what it possesses) provide significant bargaining leverage in political arenas? Those who answer yes (Luttwak, *Strategic Power: Military Capabilities and Political Utility,* 2 – 57) agree that no one wants to fight a nuclear war. They argue that an aggressor State wants to get its way without going to war. The threat to go to war is an effective instrument of influence. Some seeking reduced U.S. military expenditures concede this point, arguing that negotiating a withdrawal of U.S. influence or abandoning current objec-

---

[3]See, for example, Colin Gray & Keith Payne, ''Victory is Possible,'' *Foreign Policy,* Summer 1980.

tives (*The Price of Defense*, 4 – 49) is the preferred course,[4] while others argue that military means are futile and do not yield political benefits (Hobbs, *The Myth of Victory*, 2 – 47).

ARMS CONTROL: STABILIZING THE DETERRENT

Closely allied to the deterrence theory is an influential school of thought which supports arms control. It argues that limited arms control agreements can stabilize nuclear or conventional arms build-up at current or lower levels; arms can be banned from certain areas, and particular types of weapons eliminated. Arms control can stabilize the deterrent posture, reduce cost, and assure that should war occur, it would be initiated with fewer and less deadly weapons (*Arms Control and Disarmament Agreements*, 4 – 7). Some arms controllers also seek to break the momentum of the arms race and open the possibility of disarmament (see Chapter 4).

IS A NON-DETERRENCE STRATEGY OF PEACE POSSIBLE?

Those working for peace sometimes ignore such discussions of military strategies and developing weapons systems. The debate among the advocates of deterrence is important, however. In any non-deterrence strategy of peace, the transition from an arms race to a world without armaments will reduce nuclear and conventional arsenals and eventually eliminate them. Can this best be done if some form of equivalence is sought at each stage of disarmament, or could one side reduce its forces dramatically without any adverse consequences? Which position — equivalence or a conceded superiority — is most likely to make successful negotiations for reductions by the other powers?

The answers to these questions must be convincing to those on both sides of the current debate, if we are to gain a consensus on a non-deterrence strategy of peace. Other issues involved in this debate include whether a freeze at current levels is a wise first step, and whether it makes sense to single out one weapon system, such as the MX missile, as the target for efforts in arms control or

---

[4]See for example, Earl Ravenal, "Under the Nuclear Gun: Doing Nothing," *Foreign Policy*, Summer 1980: "With respect to American allies and clients, the prescription would be disengagement for the United States, self-reliance for them. . . . A policy of strict non-intervention recognizes that the United States might have to let some countries be dominated by its adversaries or their supposed proxies"(pp. 34 – 35).

disarmament. "How does it help to limit one of many areas in which armament expansion is taking place?" those committed to disarmament ask.

CONVENTIONAL WAR

While it is possible that deterrence may have had a role in preventing war between the super-powers, it has not prevented over 115 conventional wars since 1945. The majority of these have not involved the super-powers directly, although they have frequently armed one or both sides. Military spending among third- and fourth-world countries exceeded $85 billion in 1978, and is rising. Many spend a higher proportion of their gross national product (GNP) for military purposes than do either the Soviet Union or the United States.

Conventional war is thus an urgent concern of those seeking a world without war. Post-World War II violent conflicts include Korea, Vietnam, the Sudan, Nigeria, Angola, the Middle East, Peru, Bolivia, Cuba, Cambodia, China, and Southern Africa, among others. Not only are the weapons available for conventional warfare increasingly destructive, but nuclear capacity is pending in many of the above countries. It may already exist in Israel and South Africa. Pakistan has announced its intention to rival India in detonating a nuclear device, thus providing an "Islamic Bomb."

The sale and transfer of weapons from one country to another is part of the problem posed by conventional war. The United States has, for most of the post World War II period, been the leading supplier of conventional armaments. During the 1970s the Soviet Union became a major supplier as did France, West Germany and England. In addition, many developing countries became manufacturers of their own armaments.

The Carter Administration initially tried to set a ceiling and then reduce American arms transfers. For the 1977–80 period, however, the U.S. total rose to a total of $24,893 billion dollars. The Soviet figure is given as $15,755 although estimates of Soviet exports to Syria, for example, vary, some putting them much higher. Indeed, SIPRI concludes that "Soviet deliveries of major arms to Third World Countries actually surpassed those of the United States. . . . "[5] In 1981 conventional arms transfers exceeded $50 billion and were growing.

The above forms of war are carried on by States. Guerrilla warfare and terrorism are executed by non-governmental organizations as well as by States.

[5]World Armaments and Disarmament, SIPRI Yearbook 1981, Stockholm International Peace Research Institute (Boston: Oelgeschlager, Gunn & Hain, 1981).

The strategies through which they are conducted, the public and private support given such forms of warfare, as well as the problems which give rise to them, pose another challenge to those seeking to build a sense of world community.

The prevailing strategy for preventing war is a military strategy: deterrence. Although a costly strategy, whether measured in lives or resources lost, an effective alternative must fulfill its legitimate functions. Those now committed to deterrence and those wishing to challenge it need to study carefully the debate. Whether one seeks peace through the maintenance of military threat or through a non-military strategy, the management of power entails assessing the role played in world politics today, by war, weapons, and military strategies.

BIBLIOGRAPHY

The bibliography for this chapter presents books on the history and nature of warfare, on military strategy, and on those forms of control related to eterrence. These books are helpful in answering the following questions: 1) What central concepts are helpful in understanding military organization, purposes, requirements, and limits? 2) Has the nature and character of warfare changed significantly? 3) Is Clausewitz's definition of war, as "the conduct of politics by other means," still an accurate assessment of the direct relationship between military capacities and political bargaining? 4) How does warfare affect a society that prepares for or engages in war? 5) What are the assumptions of deterrence theory? 6) Can escalation of modern war be controlled to achieve political objectives? 7) Does the possession of strategic nuclear superiority give bargaining leverage? 8) Do the size, number, and accuracy of current nuclear weapons delivery systems give either side an effective counterforce capability and thus add an incentive for a first strike? 9) Why have there been so many conventional wars since 1945? 10) Are defensive weapons now possible again? 11) How are current military strategies related to the development of a non-military security strategy?

A. A History of Warfare

2 – 1 *The Encyclopedia of Military History from 3500 B.C. to the Present,* R. Ernest Dupuy and Trevor Dupuy, 1,488 pp, 1977, Harper, $29.95. A detailed overview of the

history of warfare indicating the major technological innovations, shifts in strategic doctrine, and requirements of military organization.

2 – 2. *A History of Militarism, Civilian and Military,* Alfred Vagts, 542pp, 1937, 1973, rev. ed., Macmillan, $8.95. Distinguishes militarism, which the author deplores, from the requirements of military organization. He demonstrates that armies have traditionally begun each war with the weapons and strategies of the last.

2 – 3. *Men in Arms: A History of Warfare and Its Interrelationships with Western Society,* Richard Preston, Sydney Wise, 424pp, 1956, 1979 4th. ed., Holt, Rinehart & Winston, $9.95. Traces the changing relationship between military strategy, weapons developments and societal goals. Concludes that, even in the nuclear era, "the means adopted to avert (war) consist in building up the means to wage it." (p. 376)

2 – 4 *The Conquest of Gaul,* Julius Caesar, 283pp, 51 B.C., 1978, Penguin, $1.95. Caesar argues that Rome has a right to expand to civilize the barbarians and, in the bargain, preserve its frontier.

2 – 5 *The Military in America: From the Colonial Era to the Present,* Peter Karsten (ed.), 512pp, 1980, Free Press, $9.95. An historical anthology assessing the social and political, as well as military, role of American armed forces.

2 – 6 *The American Way of War: A History of United States Military Strategy and Policy,* Russell Weigley, 226pp, 1977, Indiana U. Press, $7.99. The military and political history of U.S. armed forces from 1775 to the Vietnam war.

2 – 7 *War in European History,* Michael Howard, 165pp, 1976, Oxford, $4.50. Traces the development of the instruments of war and the strategies for fighting them from the Knights to the Nations to the Nuclear age. Howard concludes that "nothing has occurred since 1945 to indicate that war or threat of it, could not still be an effective instrument of State policy. Against peoples who were not prepared to defend themselves, it might be very effective indeed."

2 – 8 *No Man's Land, Combat and Identity in World War I,* Eric Leed, 257pp, 1979, Cambridge, $17.95. Describes the immediate impact of the trauma of combat and the long-term political consequences of war experience.

2 – 9 *World War II, An Account of Its Documents,* James O'Neill & Robert Krauskopf, 269pp, 1976, Howard, $15.00. An interpretation of WW II identifying the political consequences of military strategies.

2 – 10 *Life Goes to War, A Picture History of World War* II, Life Editors, 304pp, 1981, Simon & Schuster, $12.95. Glimpses of the war as seen from American photographers' perspectives — full of patriotic heroism, self-sacrifice and courage.

2 – 11 *Preparing for the Next War, American Plans for Postwar Defense, 1941 – 1945,* Michael Sherry, 288pp, 1977, Yale, $17.50. Argues that defense preparedness advocates envisioned a powerful military force after World War II, contributing to the origins of the cold war.

2– 12 *The Secret Wars, A Guide to Sources in English,* Myron Smith, Jr., 3 Volumes, Vol. I, *Intelligence, Propaganda and Psychological Warfare, Resistance Movements, and Secret Operations, 1939 – 1945,* 256pp, 1980, ABC-Clio, $34.50; Vol. II, *Intelligence, Propaganda and Psychological Warfare, Covert Operations, 1945 – 1980,* 400pp, 1981, ABC-Clio, $42.00; Vol. III, *International Terrorism, 1968 – 1980,* 237pp, 1981, ABC-Clio, $33.75. Each volume has an introductory essay followed by roughly 3,000 citations of English language sources. Books, articles, government documents and dissertations are included.

2– 13 *The Atlas of Modern Warfare,* Chris Cook & John Stevenson, 254pp, 1978, Longman, $22.50. Detailed history with maps and diagrams of post-World War II wars.

B. Weapons & Budgets

2– 14 *Defense & Foreign Affairs Handbook,* Copley & Associations, 800pp, 1981 (4th ed.), Copley & Assoc., $97.00. Offers up-to-date information on 191 countries, including governmental leaders, defense manufacturers, military leaders, arms transfer patterns, military equipment, as well as economic data.

2– 15 *Defense & Foreign Affairs Handbook 1980, Political, Economic and Defense Data on Every Country in the World,* Defense and Foreign Affairs, 800pp, 1980, Franklin Watts, $70.00. Provides detailed information on countries, colonies, territories and atolls, including their present weapons, their manufacturing capability, and their military strategies.

2– 16 *The Military Balance 1981 – 1982,* The International Institute for Strategic Studies, 133pp, 1981, Westview, $16.00. A country by country listing of military weapons and armed forces and an assessment of the U.S.-USSR strategic balance and European theatre forces.

2– 17 *The Almanac of World Military Power,* Trevor Dupuy, et al, 418pp, 1980 (4th ed.), Presidio Press, $40.00. Offers data on the arms forces and military potential of every State in the world today. Includes forces, weapons, resources available and the political uses to which such weapons might be put.

2– 18 *World Armies, 1980,* John Keegan, 843pp, 1980, Facts on File, $40.00. Includes information on weapons, strategies, personnel, command structure, and military deployments of all countries from Albania to Zambia.

2– 19 *International Weapon Developments: A Survey of Current Developments in Weapon Systems,* Royal United Services, Institute for Defence Studies, 203pp, 1980 (4th ed.), Pergamon, $13.25. A survey of naval, land, and air weapons developments with speculation about future trends focused on NATO and Warsaw Pact weapons.

2– 20 *A Short Research Guide to Arms and Armed Forces,* Ulrich Albrecht, 112pp, 1980, Facts on File, $17.50. Compiled under the auspices of the International Peace

Research Association, this book details which powers have what weapons and provides an extensive bibliography of sources of information.

2–21 *Arms, Men, and Military Budgets: Issues for Fiscal Year 1981,* Francis Hoeber, William Schneider, Jr., Norman Polmar, & Roy Bessette, 186pp, 1980, Transaction, $6.95. Fourth annual analysis of U.S. military capabilities: this year it assumes alarm at the situation and outlines "quick fixes."

2–22 *False Science: Underestimating the Soviet Military Threat,* Steven Rosefielde, 200pp, 1981, Transaction, $7.95. Casts doubt on the CIA's estimates of Soviet military expenditures, given the agency's recent revising upward by 50% of its estimate for 1970. Argues Soviet expenditures have been underestimated throughout the 1960–1980 period.

2–23 *The New Generation of Nuclear Weapons,* Stephen Daggett, 20pp, 1980, Institute for Policy Studies, $2.00. A summary of Soviet and American nuclear forces and the new technologies lending credibility to limited nuclear war and preemptive first strike scenarios.

2–23A *Cruise Missiles: Technology, Strategy, Politics,* Richard Betts (ed.), 220pp, 1981, Brookings, $15.95. A comprehensive review of the implications of this weapon system.

2–23B *Yellow Rain: A Journey through the Terror of Chemical Warfare,* Sterling Seagrave, 324pp, 1981, Evans, $11.95. Surveys the constraints on chemical warfare (1899 Hague Convention and the Geneva Protocol of 1925) and chemical weapon use by the Soviet Union in Afghanistan and Cambodia and U.S. chemical warfare capability.

C. The Nature of Modern War

2–24 *The Encyclopedia of Modern War,* Roger Parkinson, 226pp, 1979, Stein & Day, $8.95. Everything you want to know and have been afraid to ask.

2–25 *Humanity in Warfare,* Geoffrey Best, 400pp, 1980, Columbia, $25.00. A study of the role of conventions and constraints in the conduct of warfare.

2–26 *Restraints on War: Studies in the Limitation of Armed Conflict,* Michael Howard (ed.), 173pp, 1979, Oxford, $16.95. Considers the difficult attempt to fashion the instrument of war to political objectives and the ways in which nuclear war and wars of national liberation make the problem more difficult.

2–27 *War, A Historical, Political and Social Study,* L.L Farrar, Jr. (ed.), 285pp, 1978, ABC-Clio, $26.50. Thirty-two essays by twenty-six authors range over subjects as diverse as films about war to whether Marx glorified war. Some are silly (Is there a close connection between sex and violence in war?), some broad in scope (warfare in pre-industrial societies), others narrow (the army in Argentine politics) — all seek "to understand war".

2 – 28 *The History of the German Resistance, 1933 – 1945,* Peter Hoffmann, 847pp, 1979, MIT, $9.50. Traces the forms, development, and size of the resistance.

2 – 29 *Hitler's War and the Germans: Public Mood and Attitude During the Second World War,* Marlis Steinert, 387pp, 1977, Ohio, $10.00. A totalitarian power first destroys public opinion and then wants to know what is the public mood. This study is based on Nazi intelligence agency reports.

2 – 30 *The War Without a Name: France in Algeria, 1954 – 1962,* John Talbott, 320pp, 1980, Knopf, $12.95. A judicious history of a war in which terror on one side led to torture on the other, and which divided French society as Vietnam was to divide America.

2 – 31 *The Lessons of Vietnam,* W. Scott Thompson & Donaldson Frizzell (eds.), 288pp, 1977, Crane, Russak, $19.50. A wide-ranging reassessment discusses both the military and political failures of American policy, but emphasizes the failed military strategy.

2 – 32 *The Limits of Military Intervention,* Ellen Stern (ed.), 400pp, 1977, Sage, $12.50. Studies the political circumstances, military requirements, and policy objectives that influence one State to intervene militarily in another.

2 – 33 *The Changing World of the American Military,* Franklin Margiotta, 488pp, 1979, Westview, $10.75. A wide-ranging discussion of the issues which face the American military in a time of changing domestic values and a more complex world political arena.

2 – 34 *War in the Next Decade,* Roger Beaumont and Martin Edmonds (eds.), 217pp, 1974, University Press of Kentucky, $11.00. Essays on weapons, technology and strategy in a setting set by this realistic note: "War is waged by men . . . to call it a crime against mankind is to miss at least half of its significance; it is also the punishment of a crime."

2 – 35 "Effects of a Nuclear Blast on Chicago," Ted Postel, 8pp, 1979, *The Progressive* (reprint), $1.00. A chilling block by block description of the effects of dropping a nuclear bomb on the loop in Chicago.

2 – 36 *The Effects of Nuclear War,* Office of Technology Assessment, 151pp, 1980, Allanheld, $9.95. Finds enormous consequences even in a limited nuclear war, some predictable, many not.

2 – 37 *Long-Term Worldwide Effects of Multiple Nuclear-Weapons Detonations,* National Research Council, 213pp, 1975, National Academy of Sciences, $8.50. A detailed study of the effects of an equivalent of ten billion tons of TNT being exploded in the Northern Hemisphere including the effects on the ozone, climate, radiation poisoning, somatic and genetic effects on human beings and ecological damage. "Despite 30 years of development and study," the report concludes, "there is still much that we do not know." And a lot we do.

2 – 38 *Nuclear Nightmares: An Investigation into Possible Wars,* Nigel Calder, 168pp, 1980, Viking, $10.95. An alarmist view of a coming nuclear war.

2 – 39 *Apocalypse: Nuclear Catastrophe in World Politics,* Louis Beres, 1980, Chicago, $20.00. Assesses the risks and consequences of nuclear war and terrorism.

D. Conventional War Strategy

Classic

2 – 40 *On War,* Karl Von Clausewitz, Anatol Rapoport (ed.), 461pp, 1968 (1832), Penguin, $2.95. The classic study of the nature, theory, and political uses of war.

2 – 41 *On War,* Karl Von Clausewitz, Michael Howard & Peter Paret (eds.), 717pp, 1976 (1832), Princeton, $19.50. Includes an introduction and interpretative essays by the editors and Bernard Brodie.

2 – 42 *Makers of Modern Strategy, Military Thought from Machiavelli to Hitler,* Edward Earle (ed.), 553pp, 1971 (1943), Signet, $2.50. A survey of military strategies from 500 B.C. to the present, with a focus on World War II strategies.

2 – 43 *Liddell Hart, A Study of His Military Thought,* Brian Bond, 289pp, 1977, Lander: Cassell, $18.00. An intellectual biography of an influential conventional war strategist.

2 – 44 *On War,* Raymond Aron, 143pp, 1957, 1968, Norton, $1.45. Written ten years after Hiroshima. Aron concludes that nuclear weapons have not yet altered the nature of war. War remains an instrument of diplomacy and of national influence in world politics.

2 – 45 *War: Controlling Escalation,* Richard Smoke, 419pp, 1978, Harvard, $20.00. On the assumption that North-South conflicts will add new wars to the traditional East-West competition, Smoke concludes that "wars in the final decades of the twentieth century are likely to be at least equally frequent (average three per year, 1945 – 1975) and more destructive. If wars must begin, their escalation should be limited. Smoke then studies what escalation means, presents historical case studies, and offers advice on how to control escalation.

2 – 46 *American Defense Policy,* John Endicott and Roy Stafford, Jr. (eds), 626pp, 1977, 4th ed., Johns Hopkins, $8.95. Developed as a text for the U.S. Air Force Academy, these articles cover international relations, changes in U.S. military strategy, limited war and counter-insurgency warfare, as well as arms control, policy-making and the role of the military in a democratic society.

2 – 47 *The Myth of Victory: What is Victory in War?* Richard Hobbs, 450pp, 1979, Westview, $30.00. Questions the results of war in the 20th century, while seeking to reconcile democratic societies' dislike of war and the appropriate use of military violence in world politics.

E. Nuclear Strategy

2 – 48 *Arms and Foreign Policy in the Nuclear Age,* Milton Rakove (ed.), 485pp, 1972, Oxford, $6.95. An anthology of theoretical arguments which clarifies conflicting views of international politics, the causes of war, pacifism, arms control, thermonuclear war, and disarmament. A thought-provoking introduction maintains that "the central political problem of our times" is "the revolution in military technology" (p.143).

2 – 49 *American Defense Policy from Eisenhower to Kennedy: The Politics of Changing Military Requirements.* 1957 – 1961, Richard Aliano, 325pp, 1975, Ohio U., $13.50. Calls for re-examining the Eisenhower era defense policy; he credits Eisenhower with the wisdom of maintaining a low profile so that the public would endure in a protracted conflict rather than burn out in a dramatic, crisis atmosphere like the 1960s.

INF

2 – 50 *National Security in the 1980s: From Weakness to Strength,* Elmo Zumwalt & W. Scott Thompson (eds.), 524pp, 1980, Transaction, $6.95. Eighteen essays by strategists close to the Reagan Administration outline a variety of quick fixes to offset perceived weakness.

2 – 51 "U.S. Defense Policy in the 1980's," Stephan Graubard, 209pp, 1980, Daedalus, $4.00. A special issue complements earlier editions published each decade: the 1960 edition focused on disarmament, the 1970 edition on arms control, and the theme here is what new forces are needed to strengthen regional and global deterrence.

2 – 52 *On Thermonuclear War,* Herman Kahn, 668pp, 1978 (1961), Greenwood, $42.25. A pioneering work establishing nuclear strategy as a province of rational thought. Sets forth the available military alternatives, and the forty steps in escalating war.

2 – 53 *Strategy of Conflict,* Thomas Schelling, 309pp, 1960, Harvard, $6.95. A study of the nature of conflict, and of strategies to conduct it to win.

2 – 54 *Nuclear Weapons and Foreign Policy,* Henry Kissinger, Philip Quigg (ed.) 259pp, 1969 (1957), abridged, Norton, $3.95. Kissinger's call for a coherent strategic doctrine, which links the forces essential for deterrence to the need to limit conflict should deterrence fail, or to fight a limited war. Peace is a product of the wise manipulation of threat and the matching of one's aspirations with one's power.

2 – 55 *Security in the Nuclear Age: Developing U.S. Strategic Arms Policy,* Jerome Kahan, 351pp, 1975, Brookings, $5.95. A study of shifting strategic concepts from mutual assured destruction to parity. Develops a doctrine justifying a stable, affordable, nuclear deterrent.

2 – 56 *Nuclear Strategy and National Security,* Robert Pranger & Roger Labrie (eds.), 515pp, 1977, American Enterprise Institute, $10.25. Thirty-eight contributors discuss how to maintain a stable nuclear deterrent capacity through the year 2000.

2 – 57 *Strategic Power: Military Capabilities and Political Utility,* Edward Lutwak,

70pp, 1976, Sage, $3.50. Maintains strategic nuclear forces yield bargaining leverage, particularly if one side has a demonstrated superiority.

2 – 58 *Strategy of Survival,* Brian Crozier, 224pp, 1978, Temple Smith, $8.95. Crozier sounds an alarm that the Soviets are bent on world conquest and we are engaged in a life and death struggle; offers proposals for winning.

2 – 59 *Can America Win the Next War?* Drew Middleton, 265pp, 1975, Scribner's, $3.95. The author answers no because of the failure of the U.S. to equal the Soviet military's rate of growth and the fractured sense of community in the U.S. after Vietnam.

2 – 60 *Defending America, Toward a New Role in the Post-Detente World,* Institute for Contemporary Studies (eds.), 255pp, 1977, Basic, $16.00. Fourteen authors discuss why strategic and conventional military forces are important, and the public will critical in preventing either nuclear war or Soviet global domination. Detente has benefited only the USSR and should be rejected given Soviet military and political moves and human rights record.

2 – 61 *Soviet Strategy for Nuclear War,* Joseph Douglass, Jr. & Amoretta Hoeber, Richard Starr, (eds.), 160pp, 1979, Hoover, $5.95. Offers evidence that the Soviet Union is prepared to fight and win a nuclear war, and is constructing forces which make that possible both for the political bargaining leverage it provides short of war, and for war — if need be.

2 – 62 *Strategic Options for the Early Eighties: What Can Be Done?* William Van Cleave & W. Scott Thompson (eds.), 200pp, 1979, National Strategic Information Center, $4.00. Advocates building specific new weapons systems such as ABM's, and accelerating cruise missile developments and civil defense as essential in maintaining a credible deterrent against a Soviet first strike capability.

2 – 63 *Strategic Thought in the Nuclear Age,* Lawrence Martin (ed.), 233pp, 1980, Johns Hopkins, $18.50. Presents a concise summary of expert thought on military strategy. Included are essays by Klaus Knorr and Robert Osgood.

F. Arms Control and SALT

2 – 64 *Cold Dawn: The Story of SALT,* John Newhouse, 288pp, 1973, Holt, Rinehart & Winston, $7.95. A detailed and valuable analysis of the issues and the people at the origins of the SALT talks.

2 – 65 *SALT: The Moscow Agreements and Beyond,* Mason Willrich & John Rhinelander (eds.) 286pp, 1974, Macmillan, $5.95. An excellent introduction to the political setting for the nuclear arms race, attempts to control it (1945 – 1972), and the prospects for ending it.

2 – 66 *SALT: Implications for Arms Control in the 1970s,* William Kinter and Robert Pfatzgraff (eds.), 447pp, 1972, Pittsburgh, $19.95. Assesses the self-interest reasons why the U.S. and the USSR agreed to SALT I, and the political implications of the agreement in world politics.

2 – 67 *The SALT Experience,* Thomas Wolfe, 405pp, 1979, Ballinger, $18.50. A careful history of the process leading to SALT I and II, giving insight into the institutional setting in both Washington and Moscow.

Intro

2 – 68 *SALT II: Facts, Values, Choices,* Karen Minnice (ed.), 59pp, 1979, World Without War Council, $2.00. Offers a self-survey, contending perspectives on the treaty which is summarized, and an essay introducing how the arms limitation talks might actually limit arms.

2 – 69 *SALT II: Toward Security or Danger,* Foreign Policy Association, 32pp, 1979, Foreign Policy Association, $2.00. A clear summary of the treaty, the major points in the debate and contending viewpoints on them.

2 – 70 *Arms Control and SALT II, A Concise Presentation of the Central Issues Underlying the Current Debate over SALT II,* W. Panofsky, 88pp, 1979, U. of Washington Press, $2.95. Places SALT in the context of the twenty-year attempt to limit arms.

2 – 71 *Endgame: The Inside Story of SALT II,* Stobe Talbott, 288pp, 1980, Harper, $15.95. A detailed account of the Carter Administration's internal discussion of SALT II covering the options considered and rejected, plus the intricate tradeoffs which made agreement achievable. Unfortunately, similar information about the Soviets is not available.

2 – 72 *Shall America be Defended? SALT II and Beyond,* Daniel Graham, 267pp, 1979, Arlington, $10.95. A critique of the concept of mutual assured destruction, SALT II and strategic arms by a former director of the Defense Intelligence Agency on behalf of U.S. superiority.

2 – 73 *Negotiating Security, An Arms Control Reader,* William Kincade & Jeffrey Porro (eds) 321pp, 1978, Carnegie, $11.00. Seeks to clarify the relationship between limitations on arms and national defense to further progress in achieving greater national security through arms limitation. Offers a glossary, summary of arms control agreements in force, and an extensive bibliography.

2 – 74 *The Future of Arms Control: Part II, Arms Control and Technological Change, Elements of a New Approach,* Christoph Bertram, 584pp, 1978, International Institute for Strategic Studies, $4.00. Maintains that changes make arms control agreements more difficult by posing problems for verifying qualitative refinements; the multi-mission role of many new weapons also complicates matters.

See also Chapter 4, pp 100 to 101.

G. Deterrence: A Changing Concept?

2 – 75 *Deterrence: A Conceptual Analysis,* Patrick Morgan, 216pp, 1977, Sage, $6.00. An analysis and criticism of the literature defending the manipulation of violent threat to gain political objectives.

TEW

2 – 76 *Military Deterrence in History, A Pilot Cross-Historical Survey,* Raoul Naroll, Vern Bullough & Frada Naroll, 416pp, 1974, State U. of New York Press, $30.00. A fascinating study of twenty decades of warfare selected at random from the last 2,500 years. In each period one political community attempted to deter war with a rival through military preparedness. The conclusion:"the search for peace and security through armed force is in vain. Those who live by the sword may indeed expect to perish by the sword." (p.343). The absence of arms, however, does not mean peace either: "Hardly any people expect to be left in peace (the Moriori did, but a handful of warlike and cannibalistic Maori ate them)" (p. 2).

2 – 77 *The Deadly Logic: The Theory of Nuclear Deterrence,* Philip Green, 361pp, 1968, Schocken, $2.45. A critique of the logic of deterrence theory.

2 – 78 *Deterrence in American Foreign Policy: Theory and Practice,* Alexander George & Richard Smoke, 666pp, 1974, Columbia U. Press, $10.00. A thorough analysis of the concept, of how deterrence worked in specific crises and a contribution to the re-formulation of the doctrine. Defines deterrence as "the persuasion of one's opponent that the costs and/or risks of a given course of action he might take outweigh its benefits" (p. 11).

2 – 79 *The Use of Force: International Politics and Foreign Policy,* Robert Art and Kenneth Waltz (eds), 575pp, 1981 (2nd ed.), U. Press of America, $10.95. An anthology examining the role threatened or actual use of military power has played in international politics. Includes selections on different types of deterrence, case studies in the use of violence, and a discussion of MIRV and ABM weapons systems.

2 – 80 *The Private Nuclear Strategists,* Roy Locklider, 213pp, 1972, Ohio State, $11.00. Statistical analysis of data gathered from a substantial sample of civilian nuclear strategists indicates how they influence the public policy process.

2 – 81 *Theories of Peace and Security: A Reader in Contemporary Strategic Thought,* John Garnett (ed.), 272pp, 1970, St. Martin's, $6.95. An excellent reader on the role of force in international politics organized around four paths to peace and security: deterrence, disarmament, arms control, and limited war.

2 – 82 *From Superiority to Parity: The United States and the Strategic Arms Race, 1961 – 1971,* Harland Moulton, 333pp, 1973, Greenwood Press, $15.50. A historical survey of strategic doctrines and force levels from 1945 to 1971, which concludes that parity is necessary, but all that is necessary, to maintain a deterrent second strike capability.

2 – 83 *Grand Strategy for the 1980s,* Bruce Palmer, Jr. (ed.), 113pp. 1978, American Enterprise Institute, $5.25. Four retired generals and an admiral outline the military problems and challenges military strategists now face.

2 – 84 *U.S. Defense Policy, Weapons, Strategy and Commitments, Congressional Quarterly,* 220pp, 1980, Congressional Quarterly, $7.95. Surveys the existing circumstances as the Reagan Administration takes office.

H. Defensive War

2 – 85 *Nations in Arms, The Theory and Practice of Territorial Defense,* Adam Roberts, 288pp, 1976, Praeger, $18.50. Roberts argues that at least some European States should develop only ''armed national defence in depth against foreign attack'' — i.e. territorial defense as opposed to nuclear deterrence. Sweden and Yugoslavia are considered successful practioners of the concept.

2 – 86 *Disturbing the Universe: A Life in Science,* Freeman Dyson, 283pp, 1979, Harper & Row, $4.95. Since world government, international organizations, and nuclear deterrence have failed to keep peace, each State should arm adequately to defend itself and should insist that other States disarm all their offensive weapons also. The distinction between offensive and defensive weapons is clear enough, he maintains: There is a ''sharp moral distinction between offensive and defensive uses of all kinds of weapons. . . . Bombers are bad. Fighter airplanes and anti-aircraft missiles are good. Attack tanks are bad. Anti-tank missiles are good. Inter-continental missiles are bad. Anti-ballistic-missile systems are good.''

2 – 87 *Strategic Defense in Soviet Strategy,* Michael Deane, 119pp, 1980, Advanced International Studies Institute, $6.50. Argues that the Soviet Union will build whatever defense capability becomes technologically feasible.

2 – 88 *U.S. Arms Control Objectives and the Implications for Ballistic Missile Defense,* Symposium, 115pp, 1979, Harvard Center for Science and International Affairs, $6.50. Because of technological advances, cost factors, and the lack of arms control, ballistic missile defense is a hot issue. Its implications for deterrence theory are among the subjects considered here.

2 – 89 *U.S. Strategic-Nuclear Policy and Ballistic Missile Defense: The 1980s and Beyond,* William Schneider, Jr., Donald Brennan, William Davis & Hans Ruhle, 61pp, 1980, Institute for Foreign Policy Analysis, $6.50. Examines the implications of the Soviet military buildup, the increasing vulnerability of U.S. land-based strategic forces, technological advances, the China factor, the significance of strategic superiority and the growing importance of ballistic missile defense.

I. Nuclear Non-Proliferation

2–90 *Swords from Plowshares: The Military Potential of Civilian Nuclear Energy,* Albert Wohlstetter, et al, 228pp, 1979, Chicago, $5.95. Discusses nuclear proliferation incentives and restraints.

2–91 *Nuclear Policies: Fuel without the Bomb,* Albert Wohlstetter & Victor Gilinsky, 128pp, 1978, Ballinger, $16.50. An introduction to the basic issues concerning nuclear energy as a servant of weapons proliferation, and what can be done to limit proliferation.

2–92 *Destruction of Nuclear Energy Facilities in War,* Bennett Ramberg, 203pp, 1980, Lexington, $19.50. Maintains that nuclear power facilities are inadequately protected against radioactive leakage if bombarded in war, and offers proposals to reduce the hazards.

2–93 *Nonproliferation and U.S. Foreign Policy,* Joseph Yager (ed.), 400pp, 1980, Brookings, $7.95. A study of likely new members of the nuclear club and U.S. policy choices in pursuing nonproliferation of nuclear weapons.

2–94 *The Last Chance: Nuclear Proliferation and Arms Control,* William Epstein, 341 pp, 1976, Macmillan, $14.95. A detailed study by a former U.N. official of how international organizations could help limit the threatened nuclear proliferation.

2–95 *Nuclear Arms in the Third World: U.S. Policy Dilemma,* Ernest Lefever, 154pp, 1979, Brookings, $3.95. Considers fear of abandonment by the U.S. as the central incentive to acquire nuclear weapons. Taiwan and South Korea are considered prime candidates.

2–96 *Postures for Non-Proliferation: Arms Limitation and Security Policies to Minimize Nuclear Proliferation,* Stockholm Institute for Peace Research (SIPRI, hereafter), 168pp, 1979, Crane, Russak, $19.50. A study of both the technical and political issues addressed at the Non-Proliferation Treaty (NPT) Review Conference (1975).

2–97 *Internationalization: An Alternative to Nuclear Proliferation?* Eberhard Meller (ed.), 192pp, 1980, Oelgeschlager, Gunn & Hain, $22.50. The head of the International Atomic Energy Agency here discusses how international control of recycling could help limit proliferation risks.

J. Tactical Weapons

2–98 *Tactical Nuclear Weapons; European Perspectives,* SIPRI, 371pp 1978, Crane, Russak, $29.95. Describes the tactical nuclear weapons inventories of NATO and the Warsaw Pact, the danger that the "neutron bomb" and other tactical weapons will lower the nuclear "threshold" and proposals for arms control.

2 – 99 *Tactical Nuclear Weapons: An Examination of the Issues,* W.R. Van Cleave and S.T. Cohen, 119pp, 1978, Crane, Russak, $10.90. A hard look at the role of tactical weapons particularly given the Soviet preponderance of conventional forces in Europe.

2 – 100 *Illusions of Choice: Robert McNamara, the F-111, and the Problem of Weapons Acquisition Reform,* Robert Coulam, 432pp, 1977, Princeton, $27.50. Offers a theoretical explanation why the attempt to build one plane for both the Navy and Air Force resulted in a weapons system suited to neither.

2 – 101 *Jane's All the World's Aircraft, 1977 – 78,* John Taylor (ed.), 1977, Watts, $72.50. An authoritative description of aircraft, published regularly since 1909.

K. Sea Power

2 – 102 *Jane's Fighting Ships, 1977 – 78,* John Moore (ed.), 1977, Watts, $72.50. An indispensable, regular assessment of naval vessels.

2 – 103 *The Future of United States Naval Power,* James Nathan and James Oliver, 248pp, 1979, Indiana, $15.00. Emphasizes the many uncertainties in planning U.S. forces.

2 – 104 *Sea Power in the 1970s,* George Quester (ed.), 248pp, 1975, Kennikat, $17.50. Provides a comparison of the Soviet and U.S. naval forces and budgets over fourteen years, and concludes that the Soviet Navy is becoming an offensive force. Different opinions are offered about the implications of this.

2 – 105 *The Future of the Sea-Based Deterrent,* Kosta Tsipis and others (eds.), 266pp, 1974, MIT Press, $4.95. Argues that nuclear submarines will remain invulnerable (hence a stable deterrent to war) "very far in the future."

2 – 106 *The Sea Power of the State,* S.G. Gorshkow, 290pp, 1978, Pergamon, $39.00. The Commander-in-Chief and leading Soviet advocate of a powerful U.S.S.R. naval force here outlines how such forces can aid a super-power achieve its objectives.

2 – 107 *Securing the Seas: The Soviet Naval Challenge and Western Alliance Options,* Paul Nitze, Leonard Sullivan, Jr., and the Atlantic Council working group, 464pp, 1979, Westview, $12.00. A comparison of Soviet and Western naval strategies and military capabilities, offers force-building proposals for meeting the Soviet threat.

2 – 108 *The Unnoticed Challenge: Soviet Maritime Strategy and the Global Choke Points,* Robert Hanks, 64pp, 1980, Institute for Foreign Policy Analysis, $6.50. Examines the bid for naval hegemony by the Soviet Union, its acquisition of naval forces capable of controlling the world's shipping lanes and the strengths and weaknesses of Western naval forces.

L. Conventional Arms Transfers

2 – 109 *Arms Transfers and American Foreign Policy,* Andrew Pierre (ed.), 331pp, 1979, New York U. Press, $22.50. An assessment of the Carter Administration's attempt to curtail conventional arms transfers — the shipment of weapons from one country to another — examining the political, military and economic benefits and costs involved. Sympathetic to arms control imposed among suppliers through negotiated agreements.

2 – 110 *Arms Across the Sea,* Philip Farley, Stephen Kaplan & William Lewis, 134pp, 1978, Brookings, $2.95. Presents the pro and con arguments concerning U.S. conventional arms transfers.

2 – 111 *Arms Transfers in the Modern World,* Stephanie Neuman & Robert Harkavy (eds.), 400pp, 1980, Praeger, $29.95. Seventeen authors assess contemporary arms transfers. The volume of transfers is increasing, the size of developing countries' arsenals is now awesome, and bargaining position of importing countries strengthened. The political implications of arms transfers are emphasized throughout.

2 – 112 *The Arms Bazaar: From Lebanon to Lockheed,* Anthony Sampson, 352pp, 1978, Bantam, $2.95. A journalistic treatment arguing that private profit is a major reason for the rise of U.S. arms transfers.

M. Military Expenditures

2 – 113 *The Soviet Military Buildup and U.S. Defense Spending,* Barry Blechman and others, 61pp, 1977, Brookings, $2.95. Compares Soviet and U.S. military expenditures from 1964 to 1976 and concludes that if inflation is discounted the military spending of the U.S. is down 20% while the Soviets has grown 40 to 70%. The authors conclude that the result is a "low but not negligible" possibility of military confrontation with an unfavorable result to the U.S.

2 – 114 *World Military Expenditures and Arms Transfers, 1967 – 1976,* U.S. Arms Control and Disarmament Agency, 168pp, 1978, U.S. Gov. Printing Office, $4.95. A study of trends in military spending, which compares each country's military expenditures, GNP, social expenditures, with a brief discussion of arms control and extensive statistical tables.

2 – 115 *World Military Expenditures and Arms Transfers, 1969 – 1978,* U.S. Arms Control and Disarmament Agency, 116pp, 1980, U.S. Gov. Printing Office, $2.50. Updates the above.

2 – 116 *New Technology and Military Power: General Purpose Military Forces for the 1980s and Beyond,* Seymour Deitchman, 315pp, 1979, Westview, $24.00. Designed to

help pick new weapons systems to be built since increased defense spending now is considered likely for the 1980s.

2– 117 *Arms, Men and Military Budgets: Issues for Fiscal Year 1979*, Francis Hoeber, David Kassing and William Schneider, Jr., 154pp, 1978, Crane, Russak, $5.95. A survey of defense budgets, which underlines the steady Soviet military buildup and concludes that the U.S. forces will soon be inadequate to their missions unless more resources are provided.

2– 118 *The Economics of Third World Military Expenditure*, David Whynes, 165pp, 1979, Texas, $13.50. A British economist asks why third world countries have demanded transfers of wealth to aid development while their military budgets have grown twice as fast as GNP. There is a relationship, the author claims, between military spending and slow growth.

(See also section B,"Weapons and Budgets")

N. Regions of the World

2– 119 *European Security and the Atlantic System*, William Fox and Warner Schilling (eds.), 276pp, 1973, Columbia, $16.00. Essays addressing the economic, technological, and strategic problems related to achieving arms control agreements in Europe.

2– 120 *Europe Without Defense? 48 Hours that Could Change the Face of the World*, Gen. Robert Close, 250pp, 1979, Pergamon, $19.50. Maintains that the Soviet Union could overrun West Germany in 48 hours in a war fought with conventional armaments; calls for a build-up of NATO forces.

2– 121 *Arms Control and European Security, A Guide to East-West Negotiations*, Joseph Coffey, 271pp, 1977, Praeger, $24.95. The London Institute for Strategic Studies assesses force levels, and concludes that conventional and nuclear mutual force reductions would provide better security.

2– 122 *The United States, China and Arms Control*, Ralph Clough, A. Doak Barnett, Morton Halperin and Jerome Kahan, 153pp, 1975, Brookings, $3.95. A study of nuclear strategy as developed in China, and the implications of Chinese nuclear programs for the U.S., the Soviet Union, Japan, and China's close neighbors.

2– 123 *NATO: The Next Thirty Years*, Kenneth Myers (ed.), 469pp, 1980, Westview, $35.00. Includes papers written at the Georgetown Center for Strategic and International Studies, the foremost of which are by Henry Kissinger and Alexander Haig.

2– 124 *Force Reductions in Europe: Starting Over*, Jeffrey Record, 92pp, 1980, Institute for Foreign Policy Analysis, $6.50. Argues that the Mutual Balanced Force Reduction Talks (MBFR) should be reopened with forces restructured to blunt fears of surprise attack as the first goal.

O. Weapons Acquisition

2 – 125 *The Genesis of New Weapons: Decision-Making for Military R & D,* Franklin Long & Judith Reppy (eds.), 224pp, 1980, Pergamon $22.50. Describes the weapons acquisition process in the United States and in the Soviet Union. Indicates the roles played by technology, industry, military, civilian officials, and Congress in the U.S.

2 – 126 *The Economy of Death: A Hard Look at the Defense Budget, the Military Industrial Complex, and What You Can do About Them,* Richard Barnet, 201pp, 1969, Atheneum, $2.95. Argues the complex is a reality and a "serious and immediate threat to national survival."

2 – 127 *The Defense Industry,* Jacques Gansler, 432pp, 1980, MIT, $19.95. Describes in a measured fashion the role of defense industries in shaping defense policies.

2 – 128 *The Military-Industrial Complex,* Carroll Pursell (ed.), 320pp, 1973, Harper & Row, $3.95. An anthology tracing the development of the military-industrial complex from World War I to the present through a combination of documents, analysis, and viewpoints ranging from those of Senator Proxmire to Senator Goldwater.

2 – 129 *Defense Policy Formation: A Comparative Analysis of the McNamara Era,* Clark Murdock, 209pp, 1974, State U. of New York, $16.50. A comparison of weapons acquisition policies under Eisenhower, Kennedy, Johnson and Nixon, which focuses on McNamara's "management revolution" designed to permit rational evaluation of expenditures not bargaining between and within military services.

P. Requirements of Military Organizations

2 – 130 *Military Conflict, Essays in the Institutional Analysis of War and Peace,* Morris Janowitz, 319pp, 1975, SAGE, $20.00. Studies the institutions of the military to determine ways they are used to avoid and pursue military conflict.

2 – 131 *The Political Economy of War and Peace,* Richard Ashley, 384pp, 1980, Nichols, $26.50. Points up the costs as well as the uses of organization for war.

2 – 132 *War, Economy and Society, 1939 – 1945,* Alan Milward, 395pp, 1977, U. of Calif., $5.95. Denies that war is becoming obsolete, more deadly or economically unrewarding, as he presents a detailed economic study of World War II. Some of the results are surprising — Germany's industrial capacity was little damaged by aerial bombardment: changes required by the war were not very dislocating; some are not surprising — full employment aided the poor, and provided high levels of income for blacks and women in the U.S.; developing societies benefited.

2 – 133 *Strategic Implications of the All-Volunteer Force, the Conventional Defense of Central Europe,* Kenneth Coffey, 210pp, 1980, U. of North Carolina, $9.00. A judicious assessment that concludes the American component of NATO has a reduced ability to defend Central Europe.

2– 134 *The Future Global Challenge, A Predictive Study of World Security, 1977 – 1990,* Neville Brown, 402pp, 1977, Crane, Russak, $26.50. A survey based on the belief that progress on arms control will remain "cosmetic rather than substantial." Security is to be sought by achieving economic growth, addressing urban problems, and by maintaining nuclear and conventional forces with well-defined missions.

2– 135 *American Military Commitments Abroad,* Roland Paul, 237pp, 1973, Rutgers, $15.00. Seven types of military commitments are defined and the means for fulfilling them considered.

2– 136 *The Pentagon Papers,* Neil Sheehan & E.W. Kenworthy, 816pp, 1971, Bantam Books, $2.25. Traces the development of the U.S. commitment to South Vietnam through four administrations.

2– 137 *U.S. Intelligence and the Soviet Strategic Threat,* Lawrence Freedman, 235pp, 1977, Westview, $22.50. A study of the U.S. intelligence community concludes that it has been "socialized into a particular worldview which is shared by the main consumers of their work."

2– 138 *Soldiers, Statesman, and Cold War Crises,* Richard Betts, 292pp, 1977, Harvard, $15.00. A careful study of "military advice and influence on the use of force." Betts concludes that military leaders are no more aggressive than civilian advisors until military forces are engaged, and that military advice since 1945 has neither overridden civilian control nor been rejected out of hand.

2– 139 *The Soldier and the State: The Theory and Politics of Civil Military Relations,* Samuel Huntington, 534pp, 1957, Harvard, $18.50. A classic study of the military profession, mind, and ideology, and its relationship to the society and the State; focuses on the interaction between the professional officer corps and civilian departments of government.

2– 140 *Plowshares into Swords: Managing the American Defense Establishment,* Jacob Stockfish, 328pp, 1973, Mason and Lipscomb, $10.00. An analysis of the interplay of changing technology, bureaucratic politics and analytical tools (such as cost-effectiveness analysis), and how they have affected weapons' procurement and shaped defense policy.

2– 141 *America's Army in Crisis: A Study in Civil-Military Relations,* William Hauser, 256pp, 1973, Johns Hopkins, $8.50. A survey of the contemporary problems of the U.S. army with a suggestion for a dual force: one devoted to spartan discipline and training, and the other more lax but relegated to support functions.

2– 142 *The Modern Military in American Society,* Charles Ackley, 400pp, 1972, Westminster Press, $10.95. A study of the modern military after the Vietnam war, which assesses the impact of the ending of the draft and the public disenchantment with the military.

2– 143 *The Professional Soldier: A Social-Political Portrait,* Morris Janowitz, 464pp, 1971, (1960) (rev. ed.), Macmillan, $6.95. A study of the military establishment as a social organization. Analyzes the way authority is exercised, the external relations and pressure tactics of the military, and the role of ideology and political beliefs.

2– 144 *The War Game, A Critique of Military Problem Solving,* Garry Brewer and Martin Shubik, 1979, Harvard, $18.50. Argues that a new profession has arisen committed to applying the results of computerized "war games" to decisions made in world politics.

2– 145 *The Military and Politics in Modern Times: Professional, Praetorians and Revolutionary Soldiers,* Amos Perlmutter, 335pp, 1977, Yale, $6.95. Depicts modern armies as both guardians of the existing order and in some societies, as instruments of revolutionary change.

2– 146 *War, Business, and American Society: Historical Perspectives on the Military-Industrial Complex,* Benjamin Cooling (ed.), 205pp, 1977, Kennikat, $15.00. From the old "munition-makers" and "merchants of death" to the current "military-industrial complex," the association between self-interested economic forces and war has been discerned. Yet, public opinion polls suggest the public supports an American military establishment equal, if not superior, to that of the Soviet Union.

Q. Political Uses of Military Force

2– 147 *Diplomacy of Power, Soviet Armed Forces as a Political Instrument,* Stephen Kaplan, 752pp, 1981, Brookings, $14.95. Assesses 190 post-World War II incidents in which a Soviet show or use of force influenced a political decision.

2– 148 *Strategy & Politics, Collected Essays,* Edward Luttwak, 340pp, 1980, Transaction, $16.95. A collection of papers by a strategist convinced that military power readily translates into political leverage if it is backed with the will to use it.

2– 149 *Limited War Revisited,* Robert Osgood, 124pp, 1979, Westview, $16.50. Updates a 1957 work, studying Vietnam and the ability of the Soviet Union to exploit conflicts in the Third World. Asks whether our ability to fight limited war is not an essential political bargaining weapon.

2– 150 *Understanding the Soviet Military Threat, How CIA Estimates Went Astray,* William Lee, 73pp, 1977, Transaction, $3.95. Argues that the CIA has been systematically optimistic about "Soviet intentions and capabilities," and that if you look at the military purposes of their new weapons, their intent is plain: "The Soviet Union is bent on indefinite political expansion and is shaping a military force to determine the direction of world political development."

2– 151 *Force Without War: U.S. Armed Forces As a Political Instrument,* Barry Blechman & Stephen Kaplan, 584pp, 1978, Brookings, $9.95. A survey of 215 incidents in which the U.S. used military force since 1945, and an assessment of that force's utility.

R. Consequences of Military Organizations

2 – 152 *How Much War in History, Definitions, Estimates, Extrapolations and Trends,* Francis Beer, 60pp, 1974, Sage, $3.00. A comparative study of conventional war costs from 3600 B.C. to 1974 A.D., with estimates of casualties. Wars used to be more frequent than at present but with fewer casualties.

2 – 153 *The Wages of War, 1816 – 1965: A Statistical Handbook,* J. David Singer and Melvin Small, 419pp, 1972, Wiley, $16.50. A statistical overview of 149 years of warfare with a profile of each nation's "war proneness." Excludes civil wars and wars in which two states were not involved, and concludes that European States are the most war prone but that the incidence and duration of war is *not* increasing.

2 – 154 *The Warriors, Reflections on Men in Battle,* J. Glenn Gray, 242pp, 1959, 1970, Harper, $3.95. Based on the author's World War II experiences, these reflections explore the appeals of battle, the images of the enemy, and the effects of war on those who participate in it.

2 – 155 *War and Rumors of War,* Roger Shinn, 298pp, 1972, Abingdon, $5.95. An autobiographical account of the author's participation in World War II followed by reflections on war, violence, and peace influenced by New Testament texts: "And when you hear of wars and rumors of wars, do not be alarmed; this must take place, but the end is not yet" (Mark 13:7), and (Matthew 7:7) "Seek and you will find."

2 – 156 *War and Human Progress: An Essay on the Rise of Industrial Civilization,* John Nef, 464pp, 1968 (1950), Norton, $5.95. A general history of Europe which finds the sources of the industrial revolution in England's isolation from European wars; peace, not war, is the source of invention and creativity.

2 – 157 *Warfare in a Fragile World: Military Impact on the Human Environment,* SIPRI, 249pp, 1980, Cranek, Russak, $27.50. Third in a series of SIPRI books on warfare's impact on the environment.

2 – 158 *The Third World War: August 1985,* Gen. Sir John Hackett & others, 368pp, 1979, Macmillan, $12.95. Describes how NATO's conventional arms weaknesses could lead to war, escalate to a limited nuclear war and then end with the Soviet's backing down.

2 – 159 *War and Domestic Political Violence: The American Capacity for Repression and Reaction,* Michael Stohl, 153pp, 1976, Sage, $6.95. Examines the five wars since 1898 and their contribution to domestic violence, and finds that they had different consequences: domestic violence increased during W.W. I, Korea and the Vietnam wars, and decreased during the Spanish-American and Second World Wars.

2 – 160 *Violence in Our Time,* Sandy Lesberg, 256pp, 1977, Beekman, $19.95. All the dead, maimed, hanging, and butchered bodies you'll ever care to see; victims of all kinds of violence.

2 – 161 *The First Casualty – From the Crimea to Vietnam: The War Correspondent as Hero, Propagandist, and Myth Maker,* Phillip Knightley, 465pp, 1976, Harcourt, Brace and Jovanovich, $5.95. The first casualty may be truth or the war correspondent searching for the truth.

2 – 162 *War Survival in Soviet Strategy: USSR Civil Defense,* Leon Goure, 218pp, 1976, Advanced International Studies Institute (Miami), $6.95. More a discussion of the role of civil defense in strategic thought than about a consequence of war, but, nonetheless, suggests one implication: into what kind of world would the survivors emerge?

2 – 163 *War on the Mind: The Military Uses and Abuses of Psychology,* Peter Watson, 534pp, 1978, Basic Books, $17.50. Provides an overview of this century's most popular social science's application to problems of war from psychological warfare, combat psychiatry to ''brain-washing.'' The tone of the book is rational, limiting the claims made for military psychology and pointing up real and potential abuses.

2 – 164 *Overkill, Weapons of the Nuclear Age,* John Cox, 208pp, 1977, Crowell, $7.95. A lay person's introduction to the weapons, destructive capability, strategies, and alternatives to nuclear war.

2 – 165 *Chance and Circumstances, the Draft, the War and the Vietnam Generation,* Lawrence Baskin and William Strauss, 312pp, 1978, Vintage, $10.00. A comprehensive study of 53 million Americans who became of draft age during the Vietnam war years (1964 – 1973). Commissioned by those dissatisfied with Ford's clemency program, the study details statistically the different responses to military services. It concludes that low income families and low educational achievement were circumstances which greatly increased chances of being drafted and doing Vietnam duty.

2 – 166 *The Dangers of Nuclear War,* Franklyn Griffins & John Polanyi (eds). 224pp, 1979, U. of Toronto Press, $5.95. Papers presented at the Pugwash Conference, 1978, addressed to the dangers of nuclear war and the need to develop a new framework of peace.

CHAPTER 3

CAUSES OF WAR

THE bibliographies for Chapters 1 and 2 include works which assume that it is important to know when the threat or use of military power is appropriate or inappropriate; the central question in many such works is, ''How can the instruments of threat best be deployed?'' *To End War* is based on different assumptions. The central question here is, ''Can war be ended as a legitimate means for conducting and resolving international conflict?'' To answer that question requires a consideration of why wars occur. If a strategy of peace is based on a faulty analysis of the causes of war, it is sure to fail.

There are many different theoretical approaches to understanding the causes of war. Optimists believe that there is only one cause of war (though they differ on what that is), while the pessimists believe that there are many causes. Among the optimists are Thomas Paine, who thought wars would end with the destruction of monarchical forms of government; Marx and Engels, who thought wars would end with the destruction of capitalism; and Woodrow Wilson, who thought autocratic government was the cause of war. Curiously, optimists frequently argue that war itself is a means to end war.

The pessimists say that any peace movement aimed at eliminating one cause of war is bound to fail. The very multiplicity of the causes of war prove the wisdom of Plato's claim: ''Only the dead have seen the end of war.''

Yet we do not have to accept the pessimistic conclusion that all of the many

61

causes of war have to be eliminated to end war. Ending war requires that we identify first the causes of war — as many as we can. Then we can determine which of these causes can be eliminated, which modified or diverted into non-military forms of conflict resolution, and which will still remain to make peace precarious. Those seeking to end war and to develop a strategy of peace can accept Kenneth Waltz's challenging questions:

1. Can the final proposition be implemented, and if so, how . . .?
2. Does the prescription attack the assigned causes?
3. Is the image [of what causes war] adequate; or has the analyst simply seized upon the most spectacular cause or the one he thinks most susceptible to manipulation and ignored other causes of equal or greater importance?
4. How will attempts to fill the prescription affect other goals?[1]

Waltz refers to "images" but the term "cause" is used here. A cause is considered anything which increases the possibility of war. This broad definition is theoretically justifiable and practically useful in the study of war and its elimination. This chapter does not offer empirical evidence that each of the causes discussed increases the chance of war occurring. Instead, it summarizes the conclusions reached by others through their research and provides the references.

Waltz (Man, the State and War, 3 – 3) has examined the many theoretical treatments of war in Western Civilization, and finds three separate sources of war: 1) human nature (Augustine, Machiavelli, Hobbes, Niebuhr); 2) the organization or composition of particular States (Marx, Paine, Wilson); and 3) the society of States, or relations between States (Thucydides, Morgenthau). Each theorist's views may not exclude the other categories, but there is an emphasis within each which distinguishes it from others. In answer to the pessimists' challenge to list the many causes of war, as many causes will be listed as appear useful in each of the three sources which Waltz has set forth.

CAUSES OF WAR ARISING FROM HUMAN NATURE

Many note the regularity with which war occurs, note also that by one estimate,[2] there have been only 270 years of peace in the last 3,500 years, and argue that human nature accounts for this. How else can the prevalence of war be explained, given its devastation and costs? There is little agreement about what in human nature assures the continuance of war. Some believe that it is our

[1] Kenneth Waltz, Man, The State and War (New York: Columbia 1959).
[2] L. Montross, War Through the Ages.

sinful nature or original sin (Augustine, Niebuhr), others cite some instinctual drive toward death (Freud), or the preservation of territory (Ardrey), or the desire to dominate others (Lorenz). Still others argue that the trait is the drive for power (Morgenthau), greed (Plato), fear (Butterfield), or our unwillingness to learn from less deadly forms of feedback (e.e. cummings).

Those committed to ending war respond (as do many of the above theorists in other writings) that these traits of human nature do not of necessity produce war. Most individuals never participate in war and live out their lives without the psychological impediments that massive repression of instinctual drives would entail. Such traits would help account for aggressive behavior and conflict. Conflict *is* inevitably woven into any society in which economic resources are scarce; prestige or status limited or inaccurately perceived; or in which individuals misunderstand each other. In any societies we know, *conflict* is inevitable.

Conflict is also assured because of value disagreements, different conceptions of sex roles, and generational differences, to name only a few. Although non-violent resolution of those conflicts is preferable, the occasional use of violence may be unavoidable. Individuals and small groups may act out with violence feelings of aggression, desires for power, or fear of others. But there is a categorical difference between such personal or small-group violence and the indiscriminate, mass violence of war. War is an activity which governmental institutions decide. Governments hire strategists to plan war. People are trained to conduct it.

Those committed to ending war claim that there is good reason to believe that human failings can be prevented from finding an outlet in organized mass violence. Violence is considered an inappropriate means of resolving conflicts between groups within States. In every stable State today, it is illegal to use unauthorized mass violence. The occurrence of war can also be influenced by human decision-making and planning. If it can be avoided at one time or delayed at another, it, therefore, is at least possible that it can be eliminated altogether. In sum, the pessimists are not persuasive when making their case on human nature alone. They must add to their arguments about human nature a demonstration that human failings must find expression in State policy. If they do not, they have only identified traits that we all share in different degrees, and have not proved that human nature makes mass organized violence inevitable.

CAUSES OF WAR ORIGINATING WITHIN STATES

The pessimists may concede that *individuals* are capable of living their lives without aggression or other impulses finding expression in war, but they say that when one considers the history of States and the behavior of groups (particularly those controlling State power), one must conclude that war is inevitable. Those seeking to end war can respond by citing social groups that have not warred, such as the Quakers in Colonial Pennsylvania (1691 – 1756) and Eskimos (among whom war is unknown). Their experiences establish that social groups are not fated to wage war on others by their natures. Nonetheless, the causes of war should be examined to determine which are internal and which grow out of the interaction of States.

There are two distinct versions of the argument that wars arise from causes internal to the State. One version focuses on internal, civil, or revolutionary warfare: a segment of the society views some characteristics of the State as justifying warfare. This may lead to the division of the State in two through a violent change of leadership (for example, through a *coup d' état)* or by some fundamental economic, social or political change through revolutionary violence. These forms of conflict involve war (the organized use of mass violence), but because they are internal to a State, perhaps they should be excluded from a book focused on international conflict. Such internal conflicts today usually involve other States that either aid one faction or intervene directly, and, therefore, are included here. A second version of how internal causes lead to war does focus on war between States.

INTERNAL WAR

Those pessimists who argue that the causes of war found within States alone assure the continuance of war point to many reasons for this in a civil society. Among those frequently mentioned are:

1. *Right of revolution against tyranny.* The Declaration of Independence provides an argument for revolutionary warfare. When a government has become tyrannical, Jefferson wrote, "it is the Right of the People to alter or abolish it." Although rarely heard today on behalf of representative government and liberty, this argument found many adherents in the decolonization process, and continues as a warning against tyranny or foreign domination.

2. *Relative deprivation.* When things begin to improve, expectations rise disproportionately to what society can or does deliver; and rebellions and war are more likely.

3. *Class conflict — urban.* States that erect legal and social barriers to upward mobility may face class or revolutionary warfare. An example of this is the French Revolution (1789), which resulted in class and subsequent international warfare (1791 – 1815).

4. *Class conflict — rural.* Uprisings by rural groups have frequently produced wars, although such uprisings are usually quickly suppressed. While similar to class conflicts, the distinction between urban and rural internal wars is important.

5. *Right of self-determination.* Many States are composed of different ethnic, racial, linguistic, or other groups. A persistant source of conflict in the 20th Century has been the attempts of such groups to break away from existing States or to gain greater autonomy within States. Among wars influenced by this cause are World War I, the Nigerian Civil War, and the war in the Sudan, as well as those of the Croatians and South Moloccans. Separatist currents have many sources, among them the persistence of discrimination, persecution, or other violations of human rights.

6. *Irredentist movements.* Irredentist movements seek to unite in one State all people of a similar ethnic, national, or religious background, or to recover territory that was once part of an existing State. Tibet has been absorbed into China; Taiwan is claimed. The divided States of Korea, Germany, and Yemen produce irredentism; Palestinians seek to reclaim all or part of the land Israel now possesses. Part of Kenya is claimed by Somalia. The United Kingdom is threatened by demands that Northern Ireland be reunited with Ireland. And so on.

INTERNAL SOURCES OF INTERNATIONAL WAR

A common thesis is that a particular State has a flawed cultural tradition which makes it prone to go to war. Germany, the United States, and the Soviet Union have been the most frequently studied examples. Research into the authoritarian family structure, the philosophic traditions, and the cultural heritage of Germany was once popular. Today, attention focuses on the United States and its cultural isolation, deep-seated racial prejudices, or moralistic tendencies as underlying causes of the Vietnam war. Other researchers (Huxley, in 1 – 21), have argued that the commitment to rationality and technology, combined with territorial acquisitiveness, makes European States particularly bellicose. Thus, the following sources of war can be added to the pessimists' list:

1. *Flawed national tradition.* The national or cultural tradition is considered particularly likely to be expansionist, aggressive, or xenophobic and thus a source of international war.

2. *Internal cohesion through external conflict.* War is frequently sought by an elite wishing to maintain its dominance against an internal challenge. Conjuring up an external enemy unites the country under the existing leadership of the elite. Bismarck's unification of Germany under Prussian Junker leadership, through wars which Bismarck provoked between 1866 and 1871, is an example of this cause of war.

3. *Capitalism.* Countries in which the major means of production are in private hands are largely responsible for war in the 20th Century. This is held to be so for various reasons: capitalism needs new territory in which to invest (Lenin, *Imperialism, The Highest Stage of Capitalism,* 3 – 90); access to raw materials (Hobson, *Imperialism,* 3 – 83); access to markets (Marx, *Das Capital*[3]). Because capitalist production requires expansion and is based on self-interest, war ensues when these interests cannot be achieved on the desired terms through the use of bargaining or threat.

4. *State socialism.* Industrialization produces a desire to expand the economy, these theorists argue (Wright, *A Study of War,* 3 – 1). That is true whether the industries are managed by public officials or by private corporations. The dangers of war are greater when the affairs of the State and the management of the economy are in the same hands.

5. *Autocratic government.* The same arrogance and drive for power that lead to the suppression of opposition voices internal to a State, are expressed in warfare in conflicts between autocratic national leaders and others (Rummel, 17 – 24).

6. *Military-industrial complexes.* Government officials and private leaders benefit from the contemporary arms race, cold war atmosphere, and occasional wars. There is in the U.S. (and in some versions of the argument, in the U.S.S.R.), a small but powerful elite capable of manipulating governments into adopting pro-war policies. Each complex points to the other (or conjures up the other), and thus justifies its own military expansion.

7. *National ethnocentrism.* Groups naturally take pride in their accomplishments and attribute them to their national genius or heritage. Group pride can turn into arrogance and lead to war when it produces an unwillingness to compromise or resolve peacefully small quarrels with other states. Popular sentiments of nationalism require that leadership not compromise in conflict situations.

[3]Karl Marx, *Das Capital* (New York: Modern Library 1936).

CAUSES OF WAR ORIGINATING IN RELATIONS
BETWEEN STATES

Some theorists argue that the following external causes of war will remain, regardless of whether internal causes can be removed:

1. *Drives for hegemony*. In ancient Greece, later in Europe, and now on a global scale, a regular feature of inter-state relations is the attempt of one State to gain a preponderance of power and influence over the known world. The benefits to a State's pride as well as to its economic interests, territory, and the deference shown to its members, all contribute to these drives. The response is usually for other States to join together in a defensive military alliance to gain redress through war.

2. *Colonialism*. When a State seeks to establish a colony, war is usually necessary to displace or subdue the people already living there.

3. *Imperialism*. The rule of one State by another is usually possible only through the threat or actuality of war. Imperialistic States may govern directly by placing their own people in the positions of power, or indirectly, through intimidated or compliant indigenous leaders.

4. *Imbalance of power*. In a time of rapid technological innovation, the balance of power is particularly precarious. At any moment, one State may gain an advantage over its rival and may try either to exploit it politically or through war.

5. *Misperception*. Communication between States which have different cultural, national, religious, or ideological backgrounds is often difficult. Misunderstandings follow, and wars may result from such misperceptions. For example, in an arms race each side may be seeking only to defend itself. Perceiving that another State is also arming, it desires to stay ahead or, at least, remain equal. Considering itself defensive, and recognizing the advantage which an offensive power has, it requires more armaments. Each State sees the build-up of the other as an offensive threat, not a defensive requirement.

6. *Absence of law*. In the society of States, the legal instruments to resolve conflicts are weak, and sovereign States resist their being strengthened. Thus, when conflicts between States become intense, the absence of legal remedies makes war or the threat of war more possible.

7. *Real Differences*. A study of the world's creeds and national interests makes it clear why there is conflict. There are real interests and issues at stake, and a consensus exists that war or the threat of war are in many circumstances an

appropriate means to defend or advance them. These theorists often conclude with words such as:

> . . . most wars involve very real incompatibilities between the basic moral objectives of the two sides, and it is a historical fact that ordinarily the population of each side deliberately and without any element of crowd irrationality supports the carefully formulated policy of the leadership. In his zeal to eradicate war, the political scientist cannot ignore the nonconspiratorial and quite rational processes in social life that turn the peace-loving into warriors. It is the behavior of these people that is the core of the theory of war as a rational instrument of conflict resolution.[4]

CONCLUSION

The pessimists will say that the foregoing is by no means an exhaustive list of the causes of war but that it is adequate to prove their point. They consider the goal of ending war to be unrealistic, and say to the optimists, "While we approve your good intentions, your analysis of the causes of war is faulty and, thus, so will be your strategy of peace."

Those assessing this dispute with the desire to end war may well agree that the odds favor the pessimists' conclusion: we have not seen the end of war. But war is no longer what it was in Thomas Jefferson's day, and even he knew its costs. Today there is no distinction between the civilian and the soldier — whether the war is nuclear, conventional, or guerrilla, all people are targets. We must face the stark fact that nuclear war could destroy humanity. It makes sense to define war as a problem, and to work to abolish it even against formidable odds.

There are also changes in world circumstances which make possible an end to war. Contending creeds do not live in isolation from each other. They compete in a single world communication system. Each State is confronted with many problems which no State can solve alone. In the past, when political communities faced such circumstances, they joined with other political communities and abolished war among them. To create such a broader political community it is not essential that we first eliminate all the causes of war. What is required is that non-military ways to resolve conflicts should be created; that we identify the conditions essential to a world without war; that we locate the forces most likely to achieve those conditions; and that we identify the obstacles to be overcome, and learn how to overcome them. It is necessary to combine the optimist's faith that a world without war is possible with the pessimist's sense of

[4]Rosen & Jones, *The Logic of International Relations,* p. 313.

the obstacles. Both are needed — the realism of the pessimists, and the vision of the optimists.

BIBLIOGRAPHY

The bibliography covers the above causes of war, and, in addition, one other cause which is not discussed in the chapter, namely, the benefits which are supposed to result from war, such as "social progress" and "population control." The debate about the relationship between population control, social progress, and war is conducted in 3 – 3 and 3 – 5 below. See also 2 – 155. Other questions for which answers are offered in the bibliography include: 1) Why is it that traits in human nature which cause war do not find an outlet in war within a State? 2) If war is a product of human nature, why is war not constant? 3) How frequent has war been? 4) What past strategies of peace have had the most success? 5) Is there a basic pattern in which periods of peace alternate with periods of war? 6) Does the experience of war make a society more or less likely to wage war again? 7) Is war exciting, or is it that the descriptions of war are exciting when read at a distance from battle? 8) Do leaders act as a restraining influence on the public disposition to war, or do leaders manipulate the public into war? 9) Are some wars just and others unjust? 10) What shifts in power relationships (or perceptions of changes in power relations) would significantly increase the chances of war occurring?

A. Overviews

3 – 1 *A Study of War,* Quincy Wright, 451pp, 1965 (1942), abrd. ed., Chicago, $3.45. Argues that all the causes of war can be subsumed under "political-technological, juro-rational, socio-ideological, and psycho-economic" categories. Wright believed that world interdependence and a developing sense of world community would make possible world law which could eliminate war.

3 – 2 *The War System: An Interdisciplinary Approach,* Richard Falk & Samuels Kim (eds.), 500pp, 1980, Westview, $15.00. Twenty-seven essays from many disciplines held together by a common focus on the causes of war.

INF
3 – 3 *Man, the State and War: A Theoretical Analysis,* Kenneth Waltz, 263pp, 1959, Columbia, $5.00. Distinguishes between the causes of war originating in the nature of human beings (weakness, instinct, desire for power, boredom); in the nature of political

communities (the tendency to substitute foreign enemies for domestic ones); and in the nature of international relations (sovereign state in conflict without supranational means for resolving disputes and assuring compliance). An extremely useful categorization and introduction to the problem.

3 – 4 *The War Disease,* Norman Alcock, 238pp, 1972, Canadian Peace Research Institute Press, $5.00. An attempt to determine the sufficient conditions for war (those which, when present, always result in war) which identifies thirty candidates, and highlights territorial disputes between adjacent ideological rivals as the leading candidate. Concludes with an attempt to reconcile the view that "the onset of war is the automatic end product of an action-and-reaction Richardson process" and that it is also the "deliberate choice of national leaders." They lead us where we want to go.

3 – 5 *The Causes of War,* Geoffrey Blainey, 278pp, 1975, Macmillan, $5.95. A study and critique of many explanations of the origins of war and peace based mainly on European wars. Blainey concludes that most theories about the causes of war are flawed and that a principal consideration is "forgetfulness of the realities and sufferings ⟨ ⟩ war" (p. 246).

3 – 6 *War: Its Causes and Correlates,* Martin Nettleship (ed.), 813pp, 1975, Beresford Book Service, $53.50. A wide-ranging anthology.

B. Causes of War in Human Nature

INSTINCTUAL AGGRESSION

Classic
3 – 7 *Civilization and Its Discontents,* Sigmund Freud, 199pp, 1963, Norton, $1.95. Freud's attempt to translate individual psychoanalytic findings into a theory of social behavior in which civilization's survival is precarious because renunciation of instinctual drives is always necessary and never adequate; and one of those instincts is for death, another for aggression, both of which may find expression in war.

3 – 8 *Man's Aggression: The Defense of the Self,* Gregory Rochlin, 300pp, 1973, Gambit, $9.95. Argues that aggression is sublimated in the pursuit of excellence but turns violent if humiliation, thwarting or status anxiety occurs.

3 – 9 *The Psychoanalysis of War,* Franco Fornari, 248pp, 1975 (1966), Indiana, $12.00. Offers an interesting summary of the "psychoanalytic literature on war" and some reflections of war in primitive societies and on nuclear war. Does the threat of nuclear war breed alienation from the State?

3 – 10 *Psychiatric Aspects of the Prevention of Nuclear War,* Committee on Social Issues, 91pp, 1964, Group for the Advancement of Psychiatry, $2.00. A study of the psychological barriers contributing to the nuclear arms race and to conducting international conflict without violence.

3 – 11 *From Genesis to Genocide: The Meaning of Human Nature and the Power of Behavior Control,* Stephan Chorover, 256pp, 1980, MIT, $5.95. An exploration of the roots of violence and how the propensity can be redirected.

TERRITORIALITY

INF
3 – 12 *On Aggression,* Konrad Lorenz, 308pp, 1970, Bantam, $2.25. A study of aggression with animal and human groups which maintains aggression is an instinctual act that will find expression in war until substitute outlets are found or a new stage of evolution is reached.

3 – 13 *The Territorial Imperative, A Personal Inquiry into the Animal Origins of Property and Nations,* Robert Ardrey, 220pp, 1971 (1966), Bell, $1.95. A study of aggression and violence among animal species triggered when a concept of space, territory, or status is violated.

3 – 14 *The Human Zoo,* Desmond Morris, 256pp, 1970, Dell, $1.50. Argues that human beings are instinctually violent, or, so nearly so, that whatever alternative concept you offer would be a distinction without a difference.

3 – 15 *The Human Imperative,* Alexander Alland, Jr., 160pp, 1972, Columbia, $4.50. A response to Robert Ardrey, Konrad Lorenz and Desmond Morris, arguing that human capacities for aggression must be mobilized for war: "warfare cannot be explained in genetic terms, nor is a hypothetical instinct for aggression adequate." War has many causes, many functions. Also argues that war "does not appear to have long-range demographic or genetic effects, although in the early stages of evolution it may have played a role in selection" (p. 148).

3 – 16 *The Nature of Human Aggression,* Ashley Montagu, 336pp, 1976, Oxford, $4.95. Examines and argues against the popular argument "that human beings are inescapably killers — that because of their animal heritage, they are genetically and instinctively aggressive, and cannot be otherwise" (p. 3).

3 – 17 *Territoriality & Proxemics: Archaelogical and Ethnographic Evidence for the Use and Organization of Space,* Ruth Tringhon (ed.), 121pp, 1974, Mississippi, $2.95. Essays on how crowding, fighting, distancing, and designation as hollowed ground influence behavior.

3 – 18 *Man Adapting,* René Dubos, 527pp, 1965, Yale, $6.95. Human nature is much more resilient and capable of fashioning institutions and behavior patterns to meet contemporary circumstances than supposed. Otherwise we would not have made it so far.

3 – 19 *Cows, Pigs, Wars and Witches: The Riddles of Culture,* Marvin Harris, 276pp, Random House, $10.00. An anthropological look at war, its symbolic and ritualistic content, as well as its origins.

3 – 20 *The Biology of Peace and War: Men, Animals and Aggression,* Irenaus Eibl-Eibesfeldt, 294pp, 1979, Viking, $15.00. A review of the literature with some suggestions on how ''conflict control'' and ''harmony'' may be increased; argues that a world federal system of law is required to keep peace which is at least as detailed as civil law.

SIN

Classic

3 – 21 *Moral Man and Immoral Society: A Study in Ethics and Politics,* Reinhold Niebuhr, 1932, Scribner, $4.95. Human nature when expressed in group conflicts is likely to turn violent. Races, classes, nations, and religions are constantly in conflict; democracy can restrain the evil we may do, but it too has its limits.

POWER

Classic

3 – 22 *History of the Peloponnesian War,* Thucydides, ed. by Richard Livingstone, 230pp, 1960 (circa 510 B.C.), Oxford, $4.95. The true cause of war lay hidden: it was the growth of the power of Athens and the fear it aroused in others.

(See also Morgenthau, *Politics Among Nations,* 1 – 59.)

C. Causes of War in the Nature of Human Society

MONARCHICAL/AUTHORITARIAN/TOTALITARIAN GOVERNMENTS

3 – 23 *Common Sense,* Thomas Paine, 250pp, 1976 (1776), Penguin, $1.95. Argues that monarchical forms of government cause war; republican forms of government would abolish war because those who would fight them would have to authorize them.

3 – 24 *Totalitarianism,* Michael Curtis, 128pp, 1979, Transaction, $5.95. Studies the usefulness of the concept, and concludes that it is needed to distinguish traditional authoritarian systems from regimes like Nazi Germany, the Soviet Union under Stalin, and Fascist Italy. Authoritarian regimes control all things political but do not consider everything political; totalitarian regimes consider everything political.

REVOLUTION/COUP D'ETAT

3 – 25 *Revolutionary Violence, the Theories,* Anthony Burton, 147pp, 1978, Crane, Russak, $14.00. An analytical introduction to terrorist and revolutionary violence which traces much of it to Marxist-Leninist ideology: ''Lenin argued that war was the great opportunity for revolution; today terrorism is the closest the revolutionary can get to it'' (p. 144).

3 – 26 *Revolutions and Revolutionaries: Four Theories,* Barbara Salert, 161pp, 1976, Elsevier, $14.95. A summary of the literature focusing an Olson's, Gurr's, Johnson's and Marx's theories.

3 – 27 *Wars and Revolutions: A Comprehensive List of Conflicts, Including Fatalities,* Part One: 1820 – 1900, Part Two: 1900 – 1970, 1971, Hoover Institute, $5.00 each part. An attempt to compile a complete list of wars, revolutions, riots, and similar violent conflicts which result in more than twenty casualties.

INF

3 – 28 *The Anatomy of Revolution,* Crane Brinton, 310pp, 1965, Random House, $2.95. A study of four successful, none unsuccessful, revolutions which attempts to describe the stages through which every revolution must pass including the "ascension of the extremists" and the "themodorian reaction." Compares the English (1648 – 1660), American (1775 – 1789), French (1789 – 1815) and the Russian revolutions (1917 – 1921).

3 – 29 *Ideologies & Illusions: Revolutionary Thought from Herzen to Solzhenitsyn,* Adam Ulam, 288pp, 1976, Harvard, $16.00. Examines continuity in Russian intellectual history.

3 – 30 *Utopia and Revolution: On the Origins of a Metaphor, or Some Illustrations of the Problem of Political Temperament and Intellectual Climate and How Ideas, Ideals, and Ideologies have been Historically Related,* Melvin Lasky, 726pp, 1976, U. of Chicago, $10.95. Maintains that the poor may rebel, but utopian ideas embodied in unlimited rhetoric cause revolutions. This intellectual history of European thought concludes that reform and tradition are the agents of progress, not revolution.

3 – 31 *Fire in the Minds of Men: Origins of the Revolutionary Faith,* James Billington, 677pp, 1980, Basic, $25.00. Explores the dream of revolution as a spiritual thirst in the minds of European revolutionary leaders.

3 – 32 *The Declaration of Independence, A Study in the History of Political Ideas,* Carl Becker, 286pp, 1958, Random House, $2.45. Traces the key concepts in the Declaration to contract theory, and natural law traditions, and inalienable rights derived from them, which lead to a justification for revolution against tyranny.

3 – 33 *The Ideological Origins of the American Revolution,* Bernard Bailyn, 335pp, 1967, Harvard, $3.95. Finds in the pamphlet literature of the American revolution the ideas which made it a transforming event. Revolutions to advance liberty must aim to do so: this one questioned political authority, rejected social differences as incidental, and sought to distribute, not concentrate power.

3 – 34 *On Revolt: Strategies of National Liberation,* J. Bowyer Bell, 252pp, 1976, Harvard, $15.00. Based on interviews with participants in national revolts since 1945. This part-narrative, part-theorical study helps to understand the sources of violence.

3 – 35 *Coup d'Etat, A Practical Handbook,* Edward Luttwak, 214pp, 1979 (1968), Harvard, $3.95. Defines a coup as a seizure of the instruments of State power

without either mass support or significant military force, and, using examples, illustrates how to succeed at it. It is a common method for changing a government.

3 – 36 *Battlefront Namibia,* John Ya-Otto, 151pp, 1981, Lawrence Hill, $6.95. SWAPO's (Southwest Africa People's Organization) Labor Minister trades his personal odyssey into politics, conflict with South Africa, imprisonment, and exile.

3 – 37 *Background to Revolution, the Development of Modern Cuba,* Robert Smith, 256pp, 1979, (2nd ed.), Krieger, $6.95. Portrays both the circumstances and personalities involved.

3 – 38 *National Liberation Revolutions Today,* K. Brutents, 2 vols., 1977, Progress, $6.90. A survey.

RELATIVE DEPRIVATION

3 – 39 *Why Men Rebel,* Ted Robert Gurr, 421pp, 1970, Princeton, $5.95. An important contribution to thought about collective violence, which concludes that when a wide gap opens between what a group believes to be theirs by right and what they actually have, violence is likely.

3 – 40 *On War; Political Violence in the International System,* Manus Midlarsky, 229pp, 1975, Macmillan, $16.95. Argues statistically that wars originate most often when there is a "gap between ascribed and achieved status" and their duration or intensity are products of "domestic processes."

3 – 41 *The Pattern of Expectation, 1644 – 2001,* I.F. Clarke, 344pp, 1979, Basic Books, $16.50. A history of an idea: the future. How has the perception of what the future will be like influenced people at different times and places?

3 – 42 *The Age of Democratic Revolution, A Political History of Europe and America, 1760 – 1800,* 2 vols., Robert Palmer, 539pp, 584pp, 1968, Princeton, $6.95 ea. Places the American and French Revolutions in the mainstream of a democratic movement throughout the Atlantic region.

3 – 43 *French Revolution, From its Origins to 1793,* Georges Lefebvre, Vol. I, 366pp, 1962, Columbia, $5.45. An analysis of the class composition of France prior to and during the French revolution which argues that the three major classes were improving their economic positions prior to the revolution.

3 – 44 *The Civil War in the United States,* Karl Marx & Frederick Engels, 334pp, 1961, (1861), International Publishers, $3.25. Newspaper articles describing the civil war as a class conflict between the bourgeois North and the aristocratic South, fought over wage or the life-long form of slave labor.

Classic
3 – 45 *The Old Regime and the French Revolution,* Alexis De Tocqueville, 195pp, 1955 (1832), Doubleday, $2.50. Argues that much of the old regime survived in the new, particularly the tendency toward centralization of authority.

3 – 46 *Ideology and Popular Protest,* George Rudé, 176pp, 1980, Pantheon, $4.95. A historical assessment of ideas and mass movements written from a Marxist perspective with contemporary applications in mind.

3 – 47 *Revolutionary Marxism Today,* Ernest Mandel, 236pp, 1980, Schocken, $10.70. A synoptic view of socialism throughout the contemporary world.

(See also Chapter 9, "The Foundations.")

PEASANT REVOLTS

3 – 48 *Peasants, Politics and Revolution: Pressures Toward Political and Social Change in the Third World,* Joel Migdal, 301pp, 1975, Princeton, $15.95. A synthesis of the literature on peasant revolts which maintains that peasant revolts succeed when they provide practical benefits to peasants or when peasants form coalitions with urban revolutionaries. Peasant revolts are triggered by many things; the focus here is on the impact of external investment on social structures.

3 – 49 *The Moral Economy of the Peasant: Rebellion and Subsistence in Southeast Asia,* James Scott, 246pp, 1976, Yale, $4.95. Maintains that the modern State, capitalist and socialist industrialization, and political modernization intrude on the peasant already barely surviving and create uncertainty, leading to revolts.

3 – 50 *Peasant Nationalism and Communist Power: The Emergence of Revolutionary China, 1937 – 1945,* Chalmers Johnson, 256pp, 1962, Stanford, $3.45. Focuses on the subjective beliefs of peasants as the motivation for revolts which have occurred over widely separate places and times.

3 – 51 *Theory and Practice of Modern Guerilla Warfare,* Ka Wang Mei, 120pp, 1971, Asia, $5.75. How to win.

INF
3 – 52 *Peasant Wars of the Twentieth Century,* Eric Wolf, 328pp, 1970, Harper & Row, $4.95. A study of peasants' roles in five revolutions: the Mexican, Russian, Chinese, Algerian, and Cuban.

3 – 53 *Peasant Mobilization and Solidarity,* B.F. Galjart, 132pp, 1976, Humanities, $13.00. Studies the circumstances in which peasants revolt.

3 – 54 *Scarcity and Survival in Central America, Ecological Origins of the Soccer War,* William Durham, 1979, Stanford, $14.50. Argues that the cause of the 1969 war between El Salvador and Honduras was primarily a response to land pressure resulting from large holdings and the migration of 300,000 Salvadoreans to Honduras.

3 – 55 *The Rational Peasant, The Political Economy of Rural Society in Vietnam,* Samuel Popkin, 306pp, 1979, California, $4.95. Points up the rational motivation of peasants in both economic and political pursuits.

SELF-DETERMINATION

3 – 56 *Political Self-Determination and Terrorism; A Tragic Marriage We Could Help Decouple,* Janet Mackey (ed.), 64pp, 1980, World Without War Publications, $1.00. Introduces irredentist and separatist movements, their frequent use of terrorism to advance their cause and outlines ways to define, test and achieve self-determination without violence.

3 – 57 *The Quest for Self-Determination,* Dov Ronen, 144pp, 1979, Yale, $15.00. A critique of the State and its refusal to grant the right of self-determination to many ethnic, national, class, racial, and sectarian separatist currents.

3 – 58 *The Rules of Riot: Internal Conflict and the Law of War,* James Bond, 280pp, 1974, Princeton, $18.00. An attempt to define a line beyond which "government cannot go in its fight to survive" and thus where the international community has an obligation to uphold internal legal principals and conventions. Bond calls these norms inadequate to assure either basic human rights or the right of self-determination and proposes new rules aimed to protect such rights.

3 – 59 *Kings or People: Power and the Mandate to Rule,* Reinhold Bendix, 692pp, 1978, Calif., $9.95. A study of the change in legitimate political authority from monarchs to "the people," and the difficulty of establishing whether one speaks for "the people."

INTERNAL COHESION THROUGH EXTERNAL CONFLICT

3 – 60 *Bismarck & The Development of Germany,* Vol. 1: *The Period of Unification, 1815 – 1871,* Otto Planze, 510pp, 1971, Princeton, $4.95. Provides background and a discussion of the motives of the foreign wars around which Bismarck unified many German-speaking people.

CAPITALISM/SOCIALISM

3 – 61 *The Passions and the Interests, Political Arguments for Capitalism Before its Triumph,* Albert Hirschman, 153pp, 1977, Princeton, $3.95. Examines the hope and the reality which economic growth originally inspired in 18th and 19th Century political and economic theorists: capitalism would displace the passionate and harmful struggle for power with the distasteful but socially harmless pursuit of wealth.

3 – 62 *Capitalism: Sources of Hostility,* Ernest Van Den Haag (ed.), 206pp, 1979, Heritage Foundation, $9.95. Seven authors (including Peter Bauer, Lewis Feuer, Nathan Glazer, and the editor), ask why so many intellectuals despise capitalism, and find most of their reasons spurious.

MILITARY-INDUSTRIAL COMPLEXES

3 – 63 *Testing the Theory of the Military-Industrial Complex,* Steven Rosen, (ed.), 311pp, 1973, Lexington, $15.00. Seeks to define and empirically test the thesis that the

arms race is fueled primarily by domestic self-interested groups than by an adversary power system. Although the presented research limits extreme versions of the thesis that deny the reality of international conflict, it is clear that there are groups within both super-powers more committed to private than public objectives.

3 – 64 *The Military-Industrial Complex, A Historical Perspective,* Paul Koistinen, 186pp, 1980, Praeger, $18.95. Traces the development of the military and its industrial suppliers' growth of influence, and concludes that contrary to other theories, the complex continues "to be a strong, dangerous, and corrosive force in molding the policies of the national security state."

3 – 64A *The Iron Triangle: The Politics of Defense Contracting,* Gordon Adams, 465pp, 1981, Council on Economic Priorities/Transaction Books, $15.00. An updating of the military/industrial complex thesis which adds Congress to form a closed, "iron triangle."

NATIONALISM

3 – 65 *Nationalism, Opposing Viewpoints,* Bruno Leone (ed.), 135pp, 1978, Greenhaven, $4.60. Twenty-one essays giving contrasting views of nationalism in different settings and delineating its basic functions: to promote equality, to create a State for an ethnic or culturally homogenous group, to separate from an existing state, or to cultivate patriotism.

3 – 66 *Nationalism: Its Meaning & History,* Hans Kohn, 191pp, 1965, Princeton, $4.95. A brief introduction to the career of an idea.

3 – 67 *Nationalism & Social Communication: An Inquiry into the Foundations of Nationality,* Karl Deutsch, 248pp, 1953, MIT, $8.95. Introduces communications patterns as the basic indicator of when political institutions can be built.

3 – 68 *Nationalism in the 20th Century,* Antony Smith, 1979, NYU Press, $8.95. A history of the transformations of European nationalism and the emergence of nationalism in developing countries.

3 – 69 *The New Nationalism: Implications for Transatlantic Relations,* Werner Link & Werner Feld (eds.), 176pp, 1979, Pergamon, $7.95. Essays exploring the limits of European integration and the resilience of nationalistic feelings.

3 – 70 *Nationalism in Asia and Africa,* Elie Kedouri (ed.), 576pp, 1970, NAL, $4.95. Selections by Tom Mboya, Sun Yat-Sen, Damodar Hari Chapekar, and others, combining nationalism with revolutionary concepts illustrating the way in which nationalism helped end 19th-century imperialism.

3 – 71 *Nationalism & Communism in Asia: The American Response,* Norman Graebner (ed.), 204pp, 1976, Heath, $4.95. Contrasted selections clarifying nationalist, revolutionary socialist, traditional, and world political currents in Asia.

3 – 72 *The Nationalization of the Masses: Political Symbolism & Mass Movements in*

Germany from the Napoleonic Wars through the Third Reich, George Mosse, 252pp, 1977, NAL, $4.95. Nationalism as a substitute religion.

3 – 73 *Nationalism: A Trend Report and Bibliography,* Anthony Smith, 1975, Mouton, $19.50. Prepared for the International Sociological Association.

TENSION

3 – 74 *An Inter-Nation Tensionmeter for the Prediction of War,* Alan Newcombe & James Wert, 326pp, 1972, Canadian Peace Research Institute, $4.00. Identifies the causes of tension between States and finds the possession, building, and threat to use armaments as the key factor.

3 – 75 *International Crisis: The Outbreak of World War One,* Eugenia Nomikas & Robert North, 339pp, 1976, McGill – Queen U. Press, $23.00. An exhaustive study of the crisis which deepened into World War I in which mounting tension, national identity, the belief that the war would be short, and national rivalry for colonies in Asia and Africa culminated in the eclipse of European supremacy.

D. Causes of War Arising from the Nature of World Politics

BIDS FOR HEGEMONY

Classic
3 – 76   *The Prince*, Niccolo Machiavelli, Robert Adams (ed. & trans.), 283pp, 1977 (1515), Norton, $2.95. Includes the text of Machiavelli's portrayal of *raison d'etat* plus selections from his other writings and interpretations by contemporary scholars. Machiavelli advises the Prince to pursue the interests of the State by private vices, war, or treachery, or become the victim of those who do.

3 – 77   *The Reason of States: A Study of International Political Theory*, Michael Donelan (ed.) 1978, Allen & Unwin, $18.95. Discusses the many uses and abuses of the concept.

3 – 78   *The Law of Civilization & Decay: An Essay on History*, Brooks Adams, 343pp, Arno, $21.00. States expand to the extent their resources (and the divisions among their adversaries) permit.

3 – 79   *Nations in Conflict: National Growth and International Violence*, Nazli Choucri & Robert North, 356pp, 1975, Freeman, $21.50. A theoretical study of how "substantially growing state(s) are likely to generate expansion, competition, rivalry, conflict, and violence"; the period from 1870 to 1914 provides the setting.

COLONIALISM

3 – 80   *Spanish Seaborne Empire*, John Barry, 416pp, 1966, Knopf, $13.95. A history

of the displacement of the Inca and Aztec empires, the establishment of Spanish settler colonies in North and South America, and the history of the blending of those colonists with the original cultures.

(See also histories of the Portuguese, Dutch, French and English settler colonies established from 1515 to 1725.)

IMPERIALISM

3 – 81   *Theories of Imperialism,* Wolfegange Mommsen, 180pp 1981, Random House, $9.95. Presents Marxist, neo-Marxist and non-Marxist theories of imperialism, and finds them antiquated. The advocacy of anti-imperialism, not the thing itself, is the current dominant influence in Western intellectual circles.

3 – 82   *Imperialism in the Twentieth Century,* A. P. Thornton, 363pp, 1980, U. of Minn., $10.95. Counterposes the forces of "imperialism" — the government of one country by another — and those of "nationalism," and finds the end of imperialism is not yet. Both the United States and the Soviet Union are considered imperialistic today.

3 – 83   *Imperialism,* J.A. Hobson, 386pp, 1965 (1902), Michigan, $4.95. A pioneering and influential work maintaining that British imperialism originated from an embarrassment of excess capital which could not be reinvested at home because demand was too low; wages of workers needed to increase. A new introduction by Phil Siegelman summarizes criticisms of Hobson's thesis.

3 – 84   *Why War?,* Frederic Howe, 394pp, 1916, 1970, U. of Washington, $11.50. A study of the economic causes of war.

3 – 85   *Imperialism: From the Colonial Age to the Present,* Harry Magdoff, 279pp, 1978, Monthly Review Press, $5.00. A contemporary Marxist interpretation of capitalism.

3 – 86   *Imperialism and Revolution: An Essay for Radicals,* Bernard Morris, 81pp, 1973, Indiana, $1.95. A presentation of Lenin's view that capitalism causes one State to seek to govern another, and Liska's view that it is a product of a State system grown acute when one State's ideology is cast in universal terms and becomes a crusade.

3 – 87   *Colonialism in Africa, 1870 – 1960,* P. Duignan & L. Gann, 5 Volumes, 1975. Vol. 1, *History and Politics of Colonialism, 1870 – 1914*, $51.95; Vol. 2, *History and Politics of Colonialism, 1914 – 1960,* $51.95; Vol. 3, *Profiles of Change: African Society & Colonial Rule* (ed., V. Turner), $43.00; Vol. 4, *Economics of Colonialism,* $66.00, Vol. 5, *Bibliography,* $43.00.

3 – 88   *Imperialism, Intervention & Development,* Andrew Mack, et al, 393pp 1979, Biblio, Dist., $50.00. An attempt to assess the economic costs.

3 – 89   *Imperialism & Social Classes,* Joseph Schumpter, 221pp, 1951, Kelley, $15.00. A classic.

3 – 90 *Imperialism: The Highest Stage of Capitalism*, V.I. Lenin, 120pp, 1969, International Publishers, $1.25. The internal logic of capitalist production requires new markets to invest surplus capital; hence the expansion of Europe 1871-1914.

3 – 91 *Imperialist Revolutionaries: Trends in World Communism in the 1960s & 1970s,* Hugh Seton-Watson, Richard Starr (ed.), 157pp, 1978, Hoover, $6.95. Soviet expansionism is a product of ideological conviction and the absence of economic checks on governmental authority.

IMBALANCE OF POWER

3 – 92 *War and Politics*, Bernard Brodie, 514pp, 1973, Macmillan, $7.95. Argues that war is a constant because world government is required for peace, and it is impossible because people will not submit to a government of foreigners. Thus, what peace can be achieved should be sought through a balance of military power and through a wise military strategy and limited war.

3 – 93 *The Origins of Peace. A Study of Peacemaking and the Structure of Peace Settlements*, Robert Randle, 550pp, 1973, Macmillan, $14.95. A study of peace settlements after wars, which seeks to identify the common elements in both simple and complex wars and their resolution in European history. Although devoted to the aim to end a war once begun, Randle concludes that the settlement of one war sets the stage for the next.

3 – 94 *Long Term Projections of Power: Political, Economic and Military Forecasting,* Klaus Heiss, Klaus Knorr & Oskar Morgenstern, 256pp, 1973, Ballinger, $17.50. Suggests the utility of 20-year projections of trends for guiding research and technological developments and for maintaining the balance of power.

(See also Chapter 1, particularly 1-59 to 1-64.)

MISPERCEPTION

3 – 95 *Image and Reality in World Politics*, John Farrell and Asa Smith (eds.), 140pp, 1968, Columbia U. Press, $3.50. An anthology clarifies why students, "reflecting on the causes of war, cannot fail to be struck by the role of distorted images and misperceptions in compounding the objective conflicts of interest that are ever present between nations" (p.vi).

3 – 96 *Perception and Misperception in International Politics*, Robert Jervis, 445p, 1976, Princeton, $11.50. A detailed study of the varieties of ways misperception influences decision-makers, a listing of common misperceptions (attribution of a single motive or coherent plan to adversaries, exaggerated sense of the consequences of one's actions), and an application of the theory of "cognitive dissonance" to international politics.

3 – 97 *Communication in International Politics*, Richard Merritt (ed.), 461pp, 1972,

U. of Illinois, $20.00. An overview of the field asking with Harold Lasswell, ''Who says what, in which channel, to whom, with what effect?'' Included are the effects of cultural and other differences on agreement about the meanings of such words as communism, socialism, capitalism, and democracy, the influence of education in another country, exchange of populations, media reporting of events in other countries, and the impact of governments and cultures on each other.

3 – 98 *Why Nations Go to War*, John Stoessinger, 246pp, 1978 (2nd ed.), St. Martin's, $5.95. A study of six 20th-century conflicts in which States crossed the threshold between peace and war. The author concludes that economic issues were not the important cause but instead ''the most important single precipitating factor'' is leaders' misperceptions. These include a belief that the war will be ''a brief and triumphant campaign,'' and an underestimation of the adversaries' power (p. 231).

3 – 99 *Threat Perception in International Crisis*, Raymond Cohen, 229pp, 1979, Wisconsin, $17.50. Six case studies provide examples of how threats to use military force are intended and perceived, and the consequences of accurate and inaccurate perceptions.

ABSENCE OF LAW

3 – 100 *The Psychological Problem of Disarmament*, Philip Seed, 72pp, 1966, Housmans, $1.00. The effect of political identification with the State is described here as making effective international enforcement of arms control and disarmament agreements very difficult.

Classic
3 – 101 *The Anatomy of War*, Emery Reeves, 145pp, 1947, Viking. O.P. The classic statement of the view that wars cease when previously sovereign political units accept law to adjudicate their disputes.

RELIGIONS

3 – 102 *The Holy War,* Thomas Murphy (ed.), 214pp, 1976, Ohio State, $15.00. A study of justifications for aggressive violence based on divine will or the rectitude of one's human cause.

(See also Chapter 15, *''Religious and Ethical Thought on War.''*)

NATIONAL INTERESTS

(See Chapter 1, *''Introduction to World Politics,''* as well as Chapters 8, 9, and 10.)

CULTURAL DIFFERENCES

(See Chapter 10.)

IDEOLOGICAL DIFFERENCES

3 – 103 *Age of Ideology: Political Thought 1750 to the Present*, Isaac Kramnick & Frederick Watkins, 128pp, 1979, Prentice-Hall, $5.95. The focus is on contemporary ideologies labeled feminism, Marxism, neo-conservativism, neo-liberalism, and neo-Marxism.

3 – 104 *Democracy, Ideology and Objectivity*, Arne Naess and associates, 1956, Oslo University Press, O.P. Offers over 300 definitions of democracy (pp. 277 – 329) as a way of illustrating how ideologies have infused the key concepts of 20th-century world politics with their own specific messages.

3 – 105 *Ideology and the Ideologists*, Lewis Feuer, 220pp, 1975, Harper, $5.95. An analysis of the common elements in all ideologies, their emotional sources and an appeal for intellectuals to be scientists and scholars, not ideologists.

3 – 106 *Contemporary Political Ideologies; A Comparative Analysis*, L. T. Sargent, 177pp, 1975 (4th ed.), Dorsey, $2.95. Asks common questions of nationalism, democracy, communism, anarchism, fascism, and socialism.

3 – 107 *Political Ideologies: Their Origins and Impact*, Leon Baradot, 352pp, 1979, Prentice-Hall, $10.95. Traces their roots to the 19th Century.

3 – 108 *Ideologies of Violence*, Kenneth Grundy & Michael Weinstein, 117pp, 1974, Merrill, $6.95. Focuses on political justfications for violence.

3 – 109 *Ideologies of Politics*, Anthony De Crespigny (ed.), 160pp, 1976, Oxford U. Press, $6.75. Six authors expound on a definition and the basic principles of six ideologies: conservatism, liberalism, socialism, "democraticism," totalitarianism, and nationalism. The essays by Oakeshott, Hayek, Cole, and Kohn are outstanding.

3 – 110 *Ideologies and Modern Politics*, Rio Christensen, Alan Engel, Dan Jacobs, Mostafa Rejai and Herbert Waltzer, 280pp, 1975, Harper, $6.95. A concise introduction to the origins, purposes and limits of modern ideologies, makes the essential distinction between totalitarian and democratic ideologies, and presents both democratic socialism and democratic capitalism as forms of economic democracy. Nationalism, communism, guerrilla communism, and fascism are also presented.

3 – 111 *Ideals and Ideologies, Communism, Socialism, and Capitalism*, Harry Ellis, 240pp, 1968, 1972, Mentor, $1.25. A description of the gap between contemporary ideologies and practices, making the case for the irrelevance of current ideologies and implying a new synthesis may be forthcoming. Includes over 100 pictures.

3 – 112 *Modern Political Ideologies*, Alan Grimes and Robert Horwitz, 542pp, 1959; Oxford, $11.00. 19th-century and contemporary theorists present their arguments for democracy, capitalism, socialism, communism, nationalism, and racial and political elitism.

3 – 113 *The War of Ideas in Contemporary International Relations*, George Arbatov, 317pp, 1973, Progress, $2.50. The refutation of "imperialist doctrine, methods and organization of foreign political propaganda."

3—114 *The Ideal Worlds of Economics, Liberal, Radical and Conservative World Views,* Benjamin Ward, Basic Books, $18.00. Compares three world views.

3—115 *Crooked Paths, Reflections on Socialism, Conservatism, and the Welfare State,* Peter Clecark, 206pp, 1977, Harper & Row, $3.95. Examines the above ideologies and finds they break down at critical points; offers a precarious existence in a mixed system as the best we should hope for.

3—116 *Why War? Ideology, Theory and History,* Keith Nelson & Spencer Olin, Jr., 201pp, 1979, California, $10.95. A study of the justifications for war in conservative, liberal, and radical political theories.

3—117 *-Ologies and -Isms: A Thematic Dictionary,* Howard Zettler, 277pp, 1978, Gale, $28.00. A variety of terms are defined and arranged under thematic headings. An alphabetical index is included.

LIBERALISM

3—118 *The Relevance of Liberalism,* Zbigniew Brzezinski (ed.), 233pp, 1978, Westview, $22.50. An intellectual defense of liberalism, tracing its basic ideas, distinguishing liberalism from revolutionary and democratic socialism and suggesting that despite the intellectually fashionable rejection of liberal political ideas and economic institutions, liberal values are sought where they do not exist. Marx's dictum that you cannot achieve liberty in States with capitalist economies is turned on its head; you won't find much liberty anywhere else.

3—119 *Human Nature & History, A Study of the Development of Liberal Political Thought,* Robert Cumming, Vol. I., 352pp, Vol. II., 457pp, 1969, Chicago, $30.00. Traces John Stuart Mill's crisis to his liberalism, and then delineates the elements of liberalism which make it crisis-prone in the setting of a broad history of Western liberal political thought.

3—120 *The Life and Times of Liberal Democracy,* C. B. MacPherson, 120pp, 1972, Oxford, $2.95. Maintains that liberalism is but the idealized self-interest of the middle class.

(See also Mill, *On Liberty;* Acton, *The Liberal Interpretation of History;* Adam Smith, *The Wealth of Nations;* and James Madison, Alexander Hamilton, & John Jay, *The Federalist Papers.)*

COMMUNISM

3—121 *Communism: Opposing Viewpoints,* Bruno Leone (ed.), 138pp, 1978, Greenhaven, $4.60. An introduction to the 20th-century debates on whether the Soviet Union promotes peace, economic freedom and conflict, or whether those concepts have been subverted and are better embodied in other Communist States or in non-Communist States.

3 – 122 *Leon Trotsky,* Irving Howe, 214pp, 1978, Penguin, $2.95. Howe assesses Trotsky's career as a Bolshevik, an advocate of repression outside the party and democracy within, and as a critic of Stalin and Stalinism.

3 – 123 *Barbarism with a Human Face,* Bernard-Henri Levy, 210pp, 1979, Harper, $3.95. A biting attack on glosses over the massive deaths and emigrations occasioned as a Communist party takes power, consolidates its power, and rules. Maintains that "Socialism with a Human Face" is a contradiction in terms.

(See also the writings of Marx & Engels, Lenin, Mao, Castro, and the varieties of Marxism now popular among intellectual elites in developing societies.)

DEMOCRATIC SOCIALISM

3 – 124 *Socialism,* Michael Harrington, 536pp, 1973, Bantam, $2.95. A defense of democratic socialism, its critique of democratic welfare states and its prescription for a poverty free, racism free, egalitarian society, if economic producing plants are democratically run.

3 – 125 *Socialism: Opposing Viewpoints,* Bruno Leone, 113pp, 1978, Greenhaven, $4.60. Conflicting statements concerning socialist theory and the moral and practical arguments for and against socialism.

3 – 126 *The Humanization of Socialism: Writings of the Budapest School,* Andras Hegedus, Agnes Heller, Maria Markus, and Mihaly Vajda, 177pp, 1977, St. Martin's, $17.95. A "neo-leftist alternative to orthodox Communism" which argues that advanced socialist societies need constructive criticism to check bureaucratization, avoid centralization, and need to "revolutionize" private life through "collective families" and "organic communes."

(See also the writings of Irving Howe, George Lichtheim, Willy Brandt, Harold Wilson, and others.)

CONSERVATISM

3 – 127 *Can Capitalism Survive?* Benjamin Rogge, 120pp, 1979, Liberty Fund Press, $3.50. The case that it should.

3 – 128 *Conservatism,* N. K. O'Sullivan, 173pp, 1976, St. Martin's, $5.95. A statement of the basic tenets.

(See also the writings of Edmund Burke, William F. Buckley, and Peter Vierek.)

FASCISM

3 – 129 *Fascism, A Reader's Guide, Analyses, Interpretations, Bibliography,* Walter Laqueur (ed.), 478pp, 1977, California, $6.95. A summing up of fifty years of research on fascism with ideological, national, social, and other intrepretations offered.

3 – 130 *Fascism,* Paul Hayes, 260pp, 1973, Free Press, $7.95. The basic ideas expounded.

(See also the writings of Benito Mussolini, Adolf Hitler, and Generalissimo Franco.)

ANARCHISM

3 – 131 *Contemporary Anarchism,* Terry Perlin (ed.), 294pp, 1979, Transaction, $12.95. Selections from the 1960s when anarchist ideas were found in both the New Left and the New Right. An analytic introduction explains the context for the revival of anarchism.

3 – 132 *Reinventing Anarchy: What are Anarchists Thinking These Days?* Howard Ehrlich, Carol Ehrlich, David DeLeon, Glendi Morris, 1979, Routledge & Kegan Paul, $10.95. Essays seeking to refresh the ideas.

3 – 133 *In Defense of Anarchism,* Robert Wolff, 118pp, 1979, 1976, Harper, $2.95. Maintains that State power cannot be justified; it must encroach on the autonomy of the individual. Advocates "a system of voluntary compliance with governmental directives."

3 – 134 *Anarchism: Nomos XIX,* J. Roland Pennock and John Chapman (eds.), 375pp, 1978, New York U. Press, $17.50. A philosophical look at the tenets of anarchism which clarifies the variety of ideas involved, including conflicting views within the tradition concerning political authority, economic production, and the optimum size of a society.

3 – 135 *The American As Anarchist: Reflections on Indigenous Radicalism,* David DeLeon, 255pp, 1979, Johns Hopkins, $15.95. Identifiies the decentralization trends of left and right wings in American politics as the central idea of anarchism.

THIRD WORLD IDEOLOGIES

3 – 136 *Revolution in the Third World,* Gerard Chaliand, 202pp, 1978, Penguin, $2.95. Considers the role of "diverse civilizations in the destruction of capitalism as a world system and the construction of socialism" in which Vietnam and China are considered successful because they are less bureaucratized than other 20th-century revolutions.

(See also the writings of Castro, Nehru, Nasser, Ataturk, Tito, Nkrumah, and Mao; selections in Chapters 1, 7, 10, and 12.)

PART II

CONDITIONS ESSENTIAL TO A WORLD WITHOUT WAR

IN THIS second part of *To End War* the building blocks essential to a world without war are identified. In each chapter a significant idea that could help end war is introduced. In Chapter 4, the idea of arms control and disarmament is presented. While arms control as a means of stabilizing the arms race was considered in Chapter 2, arms control is presented here as a step toward disarmament. General and complete disarmament is presented as one condition essential to a world without war. Subsequent chapters in this part introduce the other conditions: reforming and strengthening international organizations into instruments of a responsive world law (Chapter 5); developing the nascent sense of world community (Chapter 6); and achieving world economic and political development (Chapter 7).

A way in which one country could seek these conditions in the current system of adversary States, without unacceptable risk to itself, is presented in Chapter 19.

CHAPTER 4

ARMS CONTROL AND DISARMAMENT

ARMS control can limit the costs and risks of preparation for war by stabilizing force levels between adversaries. Arms control measures, however, can also be designed to break the momentum of the race and to open the way to arms reduction and eventual disarmament. Approaches to disarmament are considered in this chapter, including multilateral disarmament through negotiated agreement, unilateral disarmament, arms reduction to a plateau, and disarmament through independent, reciprocal peace initiatives.

THE ARMS RACE: A CAUSE OF WAR

For many reasons, advocates of arms control and disarmament reject primary reliance on deterrence and related military strategies for security. Such advocates argue that military deterrence entails a willingness to destroy another society, and that is not an eventuality in which anyone should acquiesce. There are risks involved in the manipulation of threat, including war by miscalculation, accident, or as a result of a third party triggering it. Arms control negotiations have not produced significant results despite over thirty years of effort. To be sure a number of agreements are in place, but the period can only accurately be characterized as one of armaments expansion, not limitations. The current course promises nuclear proliferation with even greater risks than the present moment. Deterrence and other military strategies absorb enormous economic resources, and promote psychological identification with the State in a time when those resources are needed to address cooperatively problems no State can solve alone. Finally, studies of contemporary war (Richardson, 17 – 2), and of war in history (Preston, 2 – 3), conclude that arms races and military deterrence generally end in war. Given the incredible destruction of nuclear war and the devastating consequences of modern conventional war, some arms controllers and all disarmament advocates maintain that general and complete disarmament is the only appropriate long-term goal.

ARMS CONTROL: TOWARDS ARMS REDUCTIONS

The most influential school of thought today which aims at stopping the arms race is focused on arms control. Disarmament, while desirable, is not achievable, most arms controllers argue. Instead, ceilings can be set on the arms build-up, and these will help stabilize the balance of power and maintain peace. In addition, ceilings would set a standard (and perhaps help create a political climate) from which reductions might later occur. Henry Kissinger, while Secretary of State, was one forceful advocate of this approach:

> We cannot expect to relax international tensions or achieve a more stable international system should the two strongest nuclear powers conduct an unrestrained strategic arms race. . . . Through SALT [Strategic Arms Limitation Talks] the two sides can reduce the suspicions and fears which fuel strategic competition. . . . Our specific objectives have been: 1) to break the momentum of ever-increasing levels of armaments; 2) to control certain qualitative aspects. . . . 3) to moderate the pace of new developments; and 4) ultimately, to achieve reductions in force levels.[1]

In 1972 the first SALT Agreement was signed. SALT II was signed (but not ratified by the United States) in 1979. Other arms control agreements have been reached which prohibit weapons on the seabed, in outer space, and in Antarctica. Nuclear testing is prohibited in the atmosphere and is limited underground. Negotiations on a comprehensive test ban and other arms control measures continue. In all, there are over fifteen bilateral and multilateral agreements in force.

[1] Henry Kissinger, *American Foreign Policy*, pp. 162 – 166 (8 – 148).

DISARMAMENT

Advocates of disarmament generally support these negotiated agreements, but maintain that they are woefully inadequate to achieve even the objectives of the arms controllers. The SALT process is a case in point. What began as an attempt to limit arms and thus to stabilize both the Soviet Union's and the United States' deterrent forces, has, in fact, been accompanied by a significant expansion of the arms race. The number of nuclear warheads, and "throw weight" (the destructive capability of the warheads), and the number and accuracy of the delivery systems, have all increased significantly during the SALT negotiations.

The negotiated SALT II agreement permits the building of new ballistic missile systems (one for each side). The shift in doctrine from a deterrent posture, emphasizing mutual assured destruction, to deterrence based on a counterforce capability follows from the increase in numbers of launchers and warheads and their improved accuracy. The existing aircraft and ICBM (Intercontinental Ballistic Missile) forces are now vulnerable to attack. If the consequence of either a SALT II Treaty or no treaty is the maintenance of forces at their current levels or enlarging them, both sides may reasonably fear the other is nearing a first strike capability (Moynihan, *Rescuing SALT*, 4 – 22). In short, disarmament advocates maintain, arms control has produced much of what it was designed to avoid: a continuing spiral of costs and armaments, an incentive for a first strike, and increased tension between the super-powers. Now more than ever, disarmament is the appropriate and desperately needed goal.

Arms controllers respond to such statements about disarmament in two ways. First, they argue, the United States will never launch a first strike. Our forces, they declare, are defensive in character. The force levels which disarmers rightly point out SALT II accepts, do make vulnerable land-based missiles. Ours are now vulnerable. That is the reason why the MX missile is needed — it makes it more difficult to launch a credible first strike, and it does not increase the number of U.S. launchers should they be limited by agreement. Second, arms controllers maintain that general and complete disarmament (GCD) was agreed to in 1962 in the McCloy-Zorin Accords between the Soviet Union and the United States, and has been reaffirmed in the Non-Proliferation Treaty, in the SALT II Treaty, at the U.N. Special Session on Disarmament (1978), and in other international agreements and conferences.

U.S. arms control advocates are particularly angry at disarmers who accuse them of responsibility for the armaments expansion of the 1970s. The truth is, they insist, that the U.S. built no new strategic systems in the decade. Until 1978, U.S. annual military spending did not increase with the rate of inflation, so there were real reductions. Throughout the decade, Soviet expenditures increased rapidly. Despite their verbal affirmation of the goal of disarmament, the Soviet Union continues to build up massively their strategic and conventional military forces. They apparently do not believe that war is obsolete today, just more deadly. In today's world one must make a choice between surrender to an adversary's will or countering its power with military might.

Advocates of disarmament reply that there are many forms of power other than the threat or use of military violence. The utility of violence is greatly exaggerated, for "violence can only subdue, it cannot reconcile antagonists" (Burke). In a world of thermonuclear weapons, we must find ways short of war or the threat of war to resolve conflict. Agreement on universal, enforceable, inspected disarmament is essential to the growth of world law — an alternative and nonviolent way of resolving conflict. Continued reliance on national military power for security is more risky than disarmament would be if both superpowers cooperate. The first problem is to reaffirm the right goal; the second is how to get one superpower to initiate progress toward it and how to get the other to reciprocate; a related problem is how, then, to get other powers to participate.

MULTILATERAL DISARMAMENT BY NEGOTIATED AGREEMENT

For a time in the 1950s and 1960s there was a clear response to the question of how to achieve disarmament. Disarmament proposals called for negotiated agreements among all States which would establish a timetable for moving steadily toward a disarmed world, kept so by agreement on inspection and enforcement procedures (Clark & Sohn, *Introduction to World Peace through World Law*, 5–120). Not all advocates of disarmament, however, consider world law as a corollary of disarmament today.

There are at least three current strategies for disarmament: 1) Significant and unilateral arms reductions to a plateau. This would dramatically break with the existing situation but, nonetheless, retain a significant nuclear or conventional war-making capacity — a view closely allied with the minimum or sufficient deterrent posture.[2] 2) Unilateral disarmament: perhaps a phased reduction of military forces, perhaps a precipitous drop, moving as rapidly as possible away from nuclear and conventional force reliance, with reciprocation by others hoped for, but not required as a condition of the movement toward disarmament; 3) Multilateral disarmament through independent peace initiatives designed to induce reciprocation from other powers.

[2]See Chapter 2.

ARMS REDUCTION TO A PLATEAU

One school of disarmers advocates significant changes in the force structure of the United States as a means toward disarmament. *The Price of Defense*, 4 – 49, advocates substantial reductions of U.S. conventional forces, particularly naval support for land-based operations. The book maintains that these forces are useful only for intervening in third world countries. If the U. S. would forego such a capability, it could unilaterally cut defense spending by 40 to 50 billion dollars annually and thus dramatically alter the U.S. participation in the arms race. The onus for military spending, for intervention in third world countries, and for blocking progress toward desirable economic development objectives would then fall on the Soviet Union. Skillful diplomacy could exert significant pressure on others to respond positively; but, in any case, the break of the U.S. with an interventionist foreign policy would be clear, great resources would be saved, and could be used to meet other urgent domestic and international needs.

A second version of this argument holds that substantial reductions of strategic forces is preferred and achievable. A single submarine, or at the most ten, provide all the deterrent needed, they claim. The only reasons for not disarming to that level of strategic armaments are domestic and international political pressures. Thus, the U. S. could make significant, unilateral reductions, without any undesirable consequences (Myrdal, *The Game of Disarmament*, 4 – 5).

A third version of the move to a new plateau of armaments maintains that nuclear weapons are different in kind from conventional weapons. Nuclear disarmament, but not general and complete disarmament, is thus the proper goal. It is achievable because plutonium is controllable, because nuclear weapons are so vastly more destructive, and because their possession prevents the emergence of a much more egalitarian political order. Richard Falk, among others, believes for such reasons that nuclear disarmament should be the first goal (*Nuclear Policy and World Order: Why Denuclearization*, 4 – 46).

A fourth version urges a shift from offensive to defensive weapons systems, maintaining that laser technology, anti-ballistic missile defenses, anti-tank forces, and other defensive weapons, make possible an adequate military defense. Offensive weapon disarmament could then take place and the prospects for GCD significantly improve (Dyson, *Disturbing the Universe*, 2 – 86).

Critics of these approaches point out that they are, in fact, arguments for conceding military superiority to the Soviet Union. With that, the critics argue, go many undesirable consequences including the danger of a first strike by the Soviet Union, increased Soviet intervention in the third world, attacks or threats to attack Japan, South Korea, Western Europe, Israel, and Taiwan, to name but five allies, and thus, the likelihood that all these will go nuclear. When the political advantages of being able credibly to threaten to do such things are considered, critics point out that these proposals for lowering the U. S. military posture to some new plateau combine the worst features of the arms race with few of the advantages of disarmament.

UNILATERAL DISARMAMENT

Unilateral disarmers reject the use of military force altogether. When one State unilaterally and irrevocably renounces the use of military force, it will be morally superior to other States, and the example of such an act could induce others to disarm also. To be sure, significant changes in world politics would follow — for one, unpopular governments would have to seek a popular base. In the worst possible situation, an invasion of the United States, we could respond through non-violent, civilian-based defense; that is, the socially organized non-military resistance of an entire society (Sharp, *Making the Abolition of War a Realistic Goal,* 4 – 62).

Critics point out that one's refusal to arm is just that. It is no guarantee that the other side will not wage war. No, say the unilateralists, whatever else it is, unilateral disarmament is a defense against war. "Aggressors may occupy our country," they say, "but we would rather deal with that evil than with nuclear war." Some unilateralists ridicule the suggestion that the Soviet Union or others have aggressive intentions, arguing that Soviet armaments are a response to our own.

Critics concede the point that one country could withdraw from world politics if it is willing to leave the shaping of the world's future to others who are willing to use force, like Hitler, Stalin, Mao, Brezhnev, Pinochet, Khomeini or Pol Pot. But the withdrawal of one country will not end war, which will continue among the other States.

Once a highly visible point of view in the public arena (cf. Britain's Campaign for Nuclear Disarmament or the San Francisco to Moscow Walk, *The Power of the People,* 16 – 52), it may become so again. For many years this current has been muted after decades of living with the bomb. Pacifist organizations have attacked particular weapons systems (the B-1 Bomber or MX Missile campaigns), thus appearing to be drifting into the "Arms Reduction to a Plateau" position outlined above. But with the renewed concern about nuclear war, this case could again gain national public visibility. The core value underlying this position is an appealing one, for it rejects all violence and does so in a public and forceful way. Like other values, it is frequently corrupted in practice, in that its political impact is largely felt within democratic States.

The strength of unilateralist and "arms reductions to a plateau" positions is in their recognition that disarmament through negotiations is unlikely. By calling for dramatic changes in force postures they act on their conviction. But in assessing the political consequences of their advocacy, many doubt their ideas will produce progress toward a disarmed world. The expansion of Soviet influence is the more likely consequence, some critics conclude.

**MULTILATERAL DISARMAMENT THROUGH INDEPENDENT
PEACE INITIATIVES**

There is a synthesis of the above views that aims at first reversing the arms race and then working step by step toward universal, inspected, enforced disarmament. Such a policy aims at the multilateralist goal of universal agreement but shares the unilateralists' and arms reduction to a plateau advocates' willingness to make the first move. The difference is that a peace-initiatives strategy combines such first moves with a thought-through approach to gain the reciprocation of others.

Peace initiatives are, in this approach, actions taken outside of negotiations which make negotiated agreement more likely. Advocates of peace initiatives call on the U.S. government to take very specific steps toward disarmament, such as inaugurating the use of a standardized, military accounting system, and calling on other powers to adopt a similar system, then turning over the results for verification, to the U.N. or another international agency. This action would then make easier the negotiation of reductions. An answer would be available to the first question asked those advocating a five or ten percent reduction of forces: "Ten percent of what?" The actions taken would be small at first, larger later. They would be steps that would reduce the physical threat to adversaries while not seriously weakening the initiating power's military strength. They would be steps toward the stated goal of general and complete disarmament. Peace initiatives would be taken without any advance agreement or commitment to reciprocate, but it would be made clear that they would continue and increase in size only if there were appropriate and continuing responses from the other side. The idea would be for U.S. unilateral, non-military actions to generate pressures within adversary societies, and pressures from other States, to induce them to respond.

There are several versions of the initiatives idea. The pioneer in developing the idea, Charles Osgood *(An Alternative to War or Surrender,* 4–67), maintains that initiatives would reduce tension and dispel misperceptions, but doubts that they would be useful in forcing an adversary to alter its basic objectives. Robert Johansen *(Toward a Dependable Peace,* 8 – 160), has argued that significant unilateral reductions could be initiated by the U.S. without a significant response from the Soviet Union. Many within the World Without War Council *(Peace, Security, and the 1980 Elections,* 4 – 71), have argued that a peace initiative strategy should begin slowly, should be made toward a set of interrelated goals, and could move from intention clarifying to force reduction, to punitive, but non-military, acts. The latter could well increase tensions and could alter the basic objectives of an adversary.[3]

Critics question the kind of reciprocation which could be expected and whether either adversaries or allies would understand the initiating power's intention. Might they instead perceive any force reduction as a sign of weakness in the case of an adversary, or, in the case of an ally, as a sign of abandonment (Jervis, *Perception and Misperception in International Relations,* 3 – 96, and Ziegler, *War, Peace, and International Politics,* 1 – 79)? If so, might adversaries become more demanding and allies more inclined to go their own way?

Advocates of this reciprocated initiatives strategy agree that single initiative acts could be misread, especially if no long-term goals are clarified by the initiative action. What makes this a promising strategy is the invitation to reciprocate and the offer of further action if there were reciprocation. Once the other side responded, the charge of ''weakness'' would not apply, and both sides would be able to take other actions of increasing significance toward disarmament. Since reciprocation is of great importance in this approach, thinking through all the non-military ways to induce reciprocation is a critical first step. To succeed, such a policy would need to be accompanied by moves to strengthen international peace-keeping machinery. Here, too, progress might come through step-by-step initiatives that invite reciprocation if negotiations bog down. These initiatives should also be combined with steps toward other conditions essential to a world without war.

Disarmament initiatives, which understand the need to gain adversary States reciprocation, are offered as a realistic disarmament strategy. They reject the naivete and sentimentality that have characterized so many approaches to disarmament. In calling for U.S. leadership they also reject acceptance of the existing dangerous level of armaments and negotiations as the only means to move toward disarmament.

The fundamental positions in the disarmament discussion have been summarized above. These broader judgments underlie the complex arguments that attend every change in weapons technology and military strategy. Much of

---

[3] See Chapter 19.

the discussion in the U.S. gathers around specific choices, such as whether to build or reject a specific weapon system, or what level of military spending to approve. These choices are best followed in the periodicals listed in Section C, Resource H. Work on specific issues is discussed in Chapter 14.

BIBLIOGRAPHY

The books listed cover general approaches to arms control and disarmament as well as the discussion of specific problems such as nuclear proliferation, conventional arms trade, the safeguarding of disarmament agreements, and the economics of disarmament. Some explore the relationship of disarmament to the problems of world economic development, of world community, and of world law. They offer an introduction to each of the contending approaches to disarmament. These books are helpful in exploring further the ideas introduced above, and to consider questions such as these: 1) How are arms control efforts designed to stabilize the arms race related to, and how are they different from, arms control efforts designed to make possible significant arms reductions? 2) What negotiated agreements have been achieved? How well have they been lived up to? What enforcement measures are available and needed? 3) How are violations or suspected violations of arms control agreements now detected? 4) Why have the Strategic Arms Limitation Talks (SALT) not achieved arms reductions, but instead been accompanied by significant arms expansion? 5) What is the role of technological innovations in undermining the significance of arms control agreements? 6) In a disarmament strategy, does yielding strategic nuclear superiority to an adversary also yield significant political bargaining leverage? 7) How are nuclear and conventional armaments related in various regions of the world? Can they be uncoupled in a disarmament strategy? 8) What are the strengths and weaknesses of the ''arms reduction to a lower plateau'' and the ''unilateral disarmament'' positions? 9) What are the main characteristics of peace initiative acts? How are they different from statements of intentions? 10) What peace initiative acts are most likely to clarify the U.S. intention to disarm? How can the U.S. clarify to adversaries that these initiatives are not a sign of weakness, and how is the U.S. likely to gain the needed response from adversaries? How can the cooperation of allies be secured? 11) How can peace initiative acts in the disarmament field be linked to peace initiatives toward other conditions essential to a world without war? How would such an initiatives strategy differ from isolated initiative acts?

A. Overviews

4 – 1 *Armaments and Disarmament in the Nuclear Age: A Handbook,* Stockholm International Peace Research Institute (hereafter, SIPRI), $14.95. A brief overview of the arms race, including sections on the state of armaments, nuclear momentum, new weapons systems, economic and social consequences of armaments, and disarmament efforts. Includes a brief section on peace initiatives.

4 – 1A *World Military and Social Expenditures*, 1981, Ruth Leger Sivard, 38pp, 1981, World Priorities, $4.00. An annual survey. This edition graphically portrays the information in the title and "military-dominated governments in the third world" and the effects of one megaton nuclear bombs dropped on Washington and Moscow.

INF

4 – 2 *World Armaments and Disarmament, The SIPRI Yearbook 1981,* SIPRI, 500pp, 1981, Oelgeschlager, Gunn & Hain, $50.00. The fourteenth edition describing the growth of military expenditures, technological innovations, the major trends in strategy, and an analysis of arms control efforts. Indispensable.

4 – 3 *World Armaments and Disarmament: SIPRI Yearbooks 1968 – 1979, Cumulative Index,* SIPRI, 90pp, 1980, Crane, Russak, $16.50. An index to the twelve volumes previously published.

4 – 4 *Arms Control: Readings from Scientific American,* Herbert York (ed,), 427pp, 1973, W.H. Freeman, $8.95. Articles published from 1949 to 1973 analyze the arms race and trace its progress. Includes discussion of atomic bombs, the hydrogen bomb, the fallout controversy, inspection, ABM, SALT, MIRV, nuclear fusion, and lasers. A painful reminder of progress not made.

4 – 5 *The Game of Disarmament: How the United States and Russia Run the Arms Race,* Alva Myrdal, 397pp, 1978, Pantheon, $5.95. Places the blame for the arms race on the two superpowers, offers a long list of disarmament proposals, and endorses a posture of minimum deterrence as the best way to get disarmament.

4 – 6 *Arms and Politics, 1958 – 1978: Arms Control in a Changing Political Context,* Robin Ranger, 288pp, 1979, NYU, $19.95. A study of negotiations and conferences including the SALT talks, with an emphasis on the interaction of world leaders.

B. Arms Control

Intro

4 – 7 *Arms Control and Disarmament Agreements, Texts and Histories of Negotiations,* U.S. Arms Control and Disarmament Agency, (hereafter, ACDA), 239pp. 1980, U.S. Government Printing Office, $2.50. Offers a brief history of arms control and

disarmament efforts and presents the texts of current agreements with brief summaries of the negotiating processes.

4 – 7A *Armaments or Disarmament?* SIPRI Brochure, 36pp, 1981, Stockholm International Peace Research Institute, $1.00. A valuable, introductory overview of strategic and conventional arms races with a summary of the status of arms control negotiations.

4 – 8 *The Politics of Arms Control, the Role and Effectiveness of the U.S. Arms Control and Disarmament Agency,* Duncan Clark, 280pp, 1979, Free Press, $15.95. An intimate look at the people, policies, and work of the agency, charting its shift from a focus on disarmament to work exclusively on arms control.

4 – 9 *Arms Control: A Survey and Appraisal of Multilateral Agreements,* SIPRI, 238 pp., 1978, Crane, Russak & Co., $27.50. A thorough review of existing agreements from the Declaration of St. Petersburg (1868), to the Guidelines for Nuclear Transfers (1977). Included are U.N. General Assembly resolutions and a record of voting on disarmament issues in the 1970's.

4 – 10 *Chemical Weapons and Chemical Arms Control,* Matthew Meselson (ed.), 128 pp., 1978, Carnegie Endowment for International Peace, $3.00. Report of a weekend conference discussing strategic uses of, defense against, and problems of, controlling chemical weapons. Control requires a definition of chemical weapons, as distinguished between military and non-military uses, verification, and destruction or control of banned substances.

4 – 11 *The Future of Arms Control: Part II, Arms Control and Technological Change: Elements of a New Approach,* Christoph Bertram, 584pp, 1978, International Institute for Strategic Studies, $6.50. Maintains that changes make arms control agreements more difficult, such as the difficulty in verifying qualitative restraints; the multi-mission role of many new weapons and the impact of new technologies. Offers modest change in policies to constrain armaments.

4 – 12 *Negotiating Security, An Arms Control Reader,* William Kincade & Jeffrey Porro, 321pp, 1979, Carnegie, $11.00. Seeks to clarify the relationship between limitations on arms and national defense to further progress in achieving international security through arms control. Offers a glossary, summary of arms control agreements in force, and an extensive bibliography.

4 – 13 *International Arms Control: Issues and Agreements,* John Barton & Lawrence Weiler, 444pp, 1976, Stanford, $12.95. Compiled by twenty professors for use in their interdisciplinary arms control course, the focus is on using arms control to eliminate some wars and to make those that are unavoidable less destructive. The concluding chapters place arms control in the setting of changing international institutions and politics.

4 – 14 *The Missile Defense Controversy: Strategy, Technology and Politics, 1955 – 1972,* Ernest Yanarella, 236 pp., 1977, University Press of Kentucky, $18.00. A detailed analysis of the Anti-Ballistic Missile (ABM) controversy. Yanarella concludes

that much of the momentum of the arms race during the 1960's was generated within the U.S. government, and that SALT I closed off arms competition in defense weapons systems which should lead to "thinking beyond SALT I and the policy of mutual assured destruction toward the genuine goal of disarmament" (p. 204).

4 – 15 *Arms, Defense Policy, and Arms Control,* Franklin Long and George Rathjens, 215 pp., 1976, Norton, $5.95. Assesses the many political, economic, and social obstacles to arms control, and offers little hope that meaningful agreements can be reached.

4 – 16 *The Soviet Union and Arms Control: A Superpower Dilemma,* Roman Kolkowiez and others, 212 pp., 1970, Johns Hopkins Press, $12.00. An informative analysis of the composite influences affecting Soviet participation in arms control negotiations. The authors argue that there was strenuous domestic opposition to Soviet participation in SALT which had to be overcome.

4 – 17 *Force Reductions in Europe,* SIPRI, 105 pp., 1974, Humanities Press, $12.00. Summarizes recent proposals on force reductions, strategic military doctrines of NATO, and the Warsaw Treaty Organization (WTO). Provides an analysis of specific issues — balanced, symmetrical and asymmetrical reductions — conventional and nuclear forces, geographical areas to be covered, and associated measures.

4 – 18 *China as a Nuclear Power in World Politics,* Leo Yueh-Yun Liu, 125 pp., 1972, Taplinger, $5.95. Looks at the nuclear weapons capacity of the People's Republic of China, and foresees these consequences: the vigor with which Chinese foreign policy goals are pursued will increase; the U.S. and the USSR will accelerate their own programs to defend against two potential opponents; India probably and Japan possibly will develop their own nuclear weapons; alliances will break, and the international order will become increasingly unstable.

4 – 19 *The United States, China and Arms Control,* Ralph Clough, A. Doak Barnett, Morton Halperin and Jerome Kahan, 153 pp., 1975, Brookings Institution, $3.95. A study of nuclear strategy as developed in China and the implications of China's nuclear programs for Japan, the Soviet Union and the U.S.

C. SALT (Strategic Arms Limitation Talks)

4 – 20 *SALT, Nonproliferation and Nuclear Weapons-Free Zones: An Introduction,* Richard Burns, 62pp, 1978, Center for the Study of Armaments and Disarmament, $1.00. Offers an introduction to the terms, distinguishes arms control and disarmament, and outlines approaches to nuclear disarmament.

4 – 21 *Doubletalk: The Story of the First Strategic Arms Limitations Talks,* Gerard Smith, 552pp, 1980, Doubleday, $17.95. An American negotiator of SALT I offers his memoir; he pushed for limiting MIRV's, resented Kissinger's role, and is critical of the outcome.

TEW

4 – 22 *Rescuing SALT,* Daniel Patrick Moynihan, 23pp, 1979, World Without War Publications, $1.00. Maintains that the SALT process combined with a shift in weapons and strategic doctrine has led to a situation which SALT was designed to avoid: both super-powers are nearing, or can fear the other is nearing, a first strike capability.

See also Chapter 2, F. Arms Control and SALT and I. Nuclear Non-Proliferation.

D. Nuclear Non-Proliferation

4 – 23 *Nuclear Arms Control Agreements: Process and Impact,* G.W. Rathjens, Abraham Chayes and J.P. Ruine, 72 pp., 1974, Carnegie Endowment for International Peace, $1.00. This work argues that partial arms control agreements can be an impetus to new weapons programs in areas not covered by the agreement. A section on verification and compliance with agreements is also valuable.

TEW

4 – 24 *NPT: Paradoxes and Problems,* Anne Marks (ed.), 102 pp., 1975, Arms Control Association and Carnegie Endowment for International Peace, $1.50. Participants in the Divone Conference concluded that nuclear weapons parties to the Non-Proliferation Treaty should "begin to fulfill their obligations under Article VI of the NPT, to pursue negotiations in good faith on effective measures relating to the cessation of the nuclear arms race at an early date and to nuclear disarmament, including a treaty on general and complete disarmament."

4 – 25 *NPT: The Review Conference and Beyond,* UNA of the USA and the Association for the UN in the USSR, 36 pp., 1975, United Nations Association, $2.00. The two reports, prepared after joint discussion, reveal areas of agreement as well as differences concerning goals. The specific Soviet proposals — a world disarmament conference, a 10% reduction in the military budget of all permanent members of the U.N. Security Council, the allocation of a part of the savings to development assistance — could be initiated by either superpower.

4 – 26 *The Politics of Nuclear Proliferation,* George Quester, 260 pp., 1973, Johns Hopkins Press, $16.50. Examines how seventeen nations have reacted to the Non-Proliferation Treaty. Warns against assuming that agreement by the U.S. and USSR will resolve the problem of proliferation. Emphasizes the domestic bureaucratic aspects of nuclear politics.

4 – 27 *The De-nuclearization of Latin America,* Alfonso Robles, 167 pp., Carnegie Endowment, $1.95. One of the leading proponents of declaring Latin America a nuclear-free zone describes the process by which that result was initiated through the Treaty of Tlatelolco.

4 – 28 *Peaceful Uses of Atomic Energy, Vol. 1,* International Atomic Energy Agency, 877 pp., United Nations, $15.95. A U.N. conference report on how to meet the demand for nuclear energy, and how to safeguard against diversion of spent fuels for making nuclear weapons.

4 – 29 *To Avoid Catastrophe: Toward a Future Nuclear Weapons Policy,* Michael Hamilton (ed.), 240 pp., 1978, Eerdmans, $4.95. Four authors maintain that the spread of nuclear reactors for energy makes likely the proliferation of nuclear weapons. They offer scenarios of how the present course can lead to disaster. A few practical arms control suggestions are offered in a concluding essay.

4 – 30 *Nuclear Politics: The British Experience with an Independent Strategic Force 1939 – 1970,* Andrew Pierre, 388 pp., 1972, Oxford University Press, $20.00. Surveys the pro and con arguments concerning Britain's nuclear force, with implications for other nations. Issues discussed include whether nuclear force is a deterrent against or a trigger for nuclear war, and the possible status it provides for Britain.

4 – 31 *Nuclear Weapons and World Politics: Alternatives for the Future,* David Gompert, Michael Mandelbaum, Richard Garwin, and John Barton, 370 pp., 1977, McGraw-Hill, $6.95. The authors speculate about four possible accommodations between world politics and nuclear weapons: 1) the continuance of the existing system without any central authority, based on a nuclear equilibrium between two powers, 2) a limit on the number and types of nuclear weapons, 3) nuclear disarmament, 4) an increase in the numbers, distribution, or quality of nuclear weapons.

4 – 32 *Internationalization to Prevent the Spread of Nuclear Weapons,* SIPRI, 220 pp, 1980, Crane, Russak, $24.50. Maintains that the critical portions of the nuclear-fuel process should be internationalized to prevent weapons proliferation and offers detailed suggestions for how that might be done.

4 – 32A *The NPT: The Main Political Barrier to Nuclear Weapons Proliferation,* SIPRI, 64pp, 1980, SIPRI, $10.00. Indicates that the States most likely to acquire nuclear weapons are not signatories to the non-proliferation treaty and suggests how the NPT might be strengthened to be more effective.

E. Arms Control: Conventional Armaments

4 – 33 *Arms Control II, A New Approach to International Security,* John Barton & Ryukichi Imai (eds.), 352pp, 1980, Oelgeschlager, Gunn & Hain, $27.50. The new approach is more sober; it wants to "reduce weapons increases." The essays here focus on regional conflicts and arms limitations in each region.

4 – 33A *Controlling Future Arms Trade,* Anne Cahn & Joseph Kruzel, Peter Dawkins & Jacques Huntzinger, 210pp, 1977, McGraw-Hill, $5.95. An overview of the problem with proposals for limiting the transfers.

4 – 34 *Arsenal of Democracy: American Weapons Available for Export,* Tom Gervasi, 240pp, 1978, Grove Press, $7.95. A description of 500 weapons exported by the U.S. The justification for doing so (deterrence) is briefly stated and rejected. The author calls for a halt to these shipments, recognizing that others will then ship similar weapons. The requirements necessary for arms control are not considered.

4 – 35 *Supplying Repression; U.S. Support for Authoritarian Regimes Abroad,* Cynthia Arnson & Michael Klare, 56pp, 1980, Institute for Policy Studies, $4.95. Argues against U.S. involvement in the affairs of other States, and calls particularly for ending military assistance and police training programs.

(See also Chapter 2.)

F. The United Nations and Disarmament

4 – 36 *Basic Problems of Disarmament,* United Nations, 264 pp., 1970, United Nations, $2.50. Presents three U.N. studies: 1) On the Economic and Social Consequences of Disarmament, 2) The Effects of the Use of Nuclear Weapons, 3) Effects of the Use of Chemical and Biological Weapons.

4 – 37 *The United Nations and Disarmament, 1945 – 1970,* United Nations, 515 pp., 1970, United Nations, $8.50. A history of the United Nations' attempt to prevent, limit and reverse the arms race, which includes both the U.S. and USSR treaties designed to achieve general and complete disarmament, plus texts of General Assembly resolutions.

4 – 38 *The United Nations and Disarmament, 1970 – 1975,* United Nations, 267pp., 1976, United Nations, $12.00. Presents the efforts of the various United Nations entities on behalf of disarmament. Includes General Assembly resolutions, new issues, and the economic and social consequences of the arms race and disarmament.

4 – 39 *The United Nations Disarmament Yearbook, 1976,* 1978, United Nations, $15.00. Prepared by the U.N. Centre for Disarmament, this is the first edition of the new annual publication. It includes a summary of negotiations inside and outside the U.N.

4 – 40 *United Nations Disarmament Yearbook 1977,* 1979, United Nations, $15.00. Summarizes the year's activity on nuclear and conventional disarmament measures, includes resolutions adopted and proposals offered, plus texts of treaties and conventions under consideration.

4 – 41 *United Nations Disarmament Yearbook, 1978,* $22.00.

4 – 42 *United Nations Disarmament Yearbook, 1979,* $22.00.

4 – 43 *Opportunities for Disarmament: A Preview of the U.N. Special Session on Disarmament,* Jane Sharp (ed.), 156pp, 1978, Carnegie, $3.00. Offers six proposals for sharply reducing armaments for presentation at the 1978 Special Session.

TEW

4 – 44 *Disarmament Workbook, The U.N. Special Session and Beyond,* Homer Jack, 136pp, 1978, World Conference on Religion and Peace, $4.95. Assesses the results of the Special Session, and presents guidelines for building a disarmament constituency.

4 – 45 *U.N. Special Session on Disarmament,* World Without War Issues Center, 16pp, 1978, World Without War Publications, $.25. Includes background on the Special Session, the "Speech the President should give to the Special Session," and an essay on the obstacles posed by non-governmental organizations pretending to be for disarmament but only addressing one nation's armaments.

G. Disarmament to a Plateau

4 – 46 *Nuclear Policy and World Order: Why De-nuclearization,* Richard Falk, 30pp, 1978, Institute for World Order, $1.50. A broad brush theoretical treatment advocating nuclear disarmament and the abolishment of nuclear power as steps toward general and complete disarmament.

4 – 47 *The Last Chance: Nuclear Proliferation and Arms Control,* William Epstein, 341pp, 1976, Macmillan, $14.95. An overview of the arms race since 1945. Focuses on nuclear proliferation as the greatest danger, but also looks at zonal disarmament and arms reduction.

4 – 48 *The Day Before Doomsday. An Anatomy of the Nuclear Arms Race,* Sidney Lens, 274pp, 1978, Beacon, $6.95. Argues that the U.S. needs a defense against its own leaders more than the Soviet Union, blames the arms race on the U.S. Argues that a single submarine, ten at most, are all the deterrent capacity one needs.

4 – 49 *The Price of Defense. A New Strategy for Military Spending,* Boston Study Group, 359pp, 1979, New York Times, $15.00 Argues that by changing the U.S. objectives from an interventionist capacity in third world conflicts to deterrence in Europe, some 50 billion dollars could be saved without any loss.

H. Disarmament

4 – 50 *Documents on Disarmament,* 1980, Arms Control and Disarmament Agency, U.S. Government Printing Office, $8.50. This a rich collection of official statements from many countries, reports, texts of treaties and statements of policy, which is published annually.

4 – 51 *Arms Control Impact Statements,* ACDA, Prepared and published annually by ACDA as required by Congress. These statements are supposed to describe the effect of arms control agreements in one area, on agreements being negotiated in another, and to survey the implications of proposed agreements.

4 – 52 *The First World Disarmament Conference, 1932 – 1933, and Why it Failed,* Philip Noel-Baker, 147pp, 1979, Pergamon, $15.00. A brief history by a participant.

Classic
4 – 53 *The Arms Race: A Program for World Disarmament,* Philip Noel-Baker, 603pp, 1959, Oceana, $15.00. An historical analysis of the 1945 – 1958 period with specific recommendations, now dated.

TEW
4 – 54 *Approaches to Arms Control and Disarmament,* Betty Goetz Lall, Chairperson, 75pp, 1976, Commission to Study the Organization of Peace, $2.50. The result of a two-year study by a working group, this report offers a variety of unilateral peace initiative acts designed to reverse the arms race.

4 – 55 *National Disarmament Mechanisms,* Larry Ross & John Redlick, 23pp, 1980, Stanley Foundation, free. Offers information on how disarmament could proceed if there was the will to do so.

4 – 56 *Nuclear Disarmament,* A. Yefremov, 313pp, 1980, Progress, $6.40. The Soviet view on how its efforts at nuclear disarmament have been thwarted by the United States.

4 – 57 *Disarmament: The Human Factor; Proceedings of a Colloquium on the Social Context for Disarmament,* E. Laszlo & Donald Keys (eds.), 200pp, 1981, Pergamon, $25.00. Concludes that the ''absence of global identification'' is a major obstacle to disarmament.

I. Unilateral Disarmament

4 – 58 *Unilateral Disarmament,* W.H. Ferry, 32pp, 1980, Fellowship, $.50. Makes the case for unilateral disarmament.

4 – 59 *Approaches to Disarmament: An Introductory Analysis,* Nicholas Sims, 180pp, 1978, Quaker Peace and Service (England), $2.95. Argues that only unilateral disarmament is truly moral and likely to be effective.

4 – 60 *Nuclear Disarmament for Britain: Why We Need Actions, Not Words,* Betty England, 23pp, 1980, Campaign for Nuclear Disarmament, $1.00. Argues for unilateral nuclear disarmament by Britain as a first step.

4 – 61 *European Nuclear Disarmament,* Ken Coats, 26pp, 1980, Bertrand Russell Peace Foundation, $1.00. Argues for Western European acts.

J. Civilian-Based (Non-Military) National Defense

4 – 62 *Making the Abolition of War a Realistic Goal,* Gene Sharp, 15pp, 1981, Institute

for World Order, $1.50. Selected the best essay out of over 500 entries in the Wallach Peace Prize Competition (1981), this essay first identifies twelve "hard facts which most peace workers rarely face," and then outlines how civilian-based defense might be created as an auxiliary to military defense, how it might be used when military defense is clearly unworkable (i.e. in Poland), and how it might augment disarmament processes.

4 – 63 *War Without Weapons: Nonviolence in National Defense,* Anders Boserup and Andrew Mack, 194pp., 1975, Schocken, $2.95. The authors argue that a nation trained in nonviolent techniques would be more secure and less vulnerable to destruction than a nation trained in the techniques of nuclear deterrence. The authors are waiting for advocates of nuclear deterrence to begin the discussion of risks.

4 – 64 *The United States in a Disarmed World: A Study of the U.S. Outline for General and Complete Disarmament,* Arnold Wolfers and others, 236 pp., 1966, Johns Hopkins Press, $2.95. Seven scholars criticize the U.S. 1962 plan for general and complete disarmament. Their criticisms challenge those taking this approach to overcome their objections.

K. Multi-lateral Disarmament through Independent Peace Initiatives

Intro

4 – 65 *World Disarmament Kit,* Robert Woito (ed.), 88 pp., 1977, World Without War Publications, $2.50. Provides a concise introduction to the arms race and to disarmament. The kit includes a self-survey, a summary of facts, contending perspectives, obstacles, proposals for reversing the arms race, and the outline of a peace initiatives approach.

4 – 66 *Policy Statement on Arms Control and Disarmament,* World Without War Issues Center – Midwest, $.35. Presents a brief statement of the peace initiatives approach with 31 specific peace initiatives.

INF

4 – 67 *An Alternative to War or Surrender,* Charles Osgood, 183 pp., 1962, University of Illinois Press, $1.45. A pioneer work by the originator of the Graduated Reciprocation in Tension Reduction (GRIT) Strategy.

4 – 68 *The ABM and a World Without War,* Robert Pickus, 86 pp., 1969, World Without War Council, $.95. Valuable for its background information on the ABM decision, this book's primary focus is on the contextual framework within which any war/peace issue is considered.

4 – 69 *GRIT I,* Alan Newcombe (ed.) 88pp, 1979, Peace Research Reviews, $5.00. Reprints key essays by Amitai Etzioni and Charles Osgood, the former describing "The Kennedy Experiment" with initiatives, the latter introducing the Graduated Reductions in Tension (GRIT) concept.

4 – 70 *GRIT, II.* Alan Newcombe, (ed.), 104pp, 1979, Peace Research Reviews, $5.00. Offers six essays applying GRIT to historical conflicts (China vs Tibet in the 8th Century B.C.), to MBFR, and to reducing military expenditures generally.

TEW
4 – 71 *Peace, Security, and the 1980 Elections,* World Without War Issues Center – Midwest, 16pp, 1980, World Without War Publications, $.50. Offers a political analysis of the post-Afghanistan circumstances, and outlines a series of peace initiative acts through which the United States could, without unacceptable danger to itself, initiate progress toward a disarmed world under law. Some of the proposals would increase tension; all seek reciprocation by others.

L. Specific Proposals

4 – 72 *The Negotiations on Mutual and Balanced Force Reductions: The Search for Arms Control in Central Europe,* John Keliher, 240pp, 1980, Pergamon, $25.00. Suggests ways the deadlocked talks could become fruitful.

4 – 73 *Chemical Weapons, Destruction and Conversion,* SIPRI, 201pp, 1980, Crane, Russak, $19.50. Identifies the problem of destroying chemical weapons as one of the obstacles to a successful treaty, and then considers how to solve the problem.

4 – 74 *A New Design for Nuclear Disarmament,* William Epstein and Toshiyuki Toyoda, 338pp, 1977, Spokeman, $8.95. Papers from a Pugwash Conference of scientists from different parts of the world (an annual event since 1959) marking the 30th anniversary of the first use of nuclear weapons and the 20th anniversary of the Russell-Einstein pledge to seek their abolishment.

4 – 75 *Military Expenditures Limitations for Arms Control: Problems and Prospects,* Abraham Becker, 348pp, 1977, Ballinger, $18.50. A history and analysis of why efforts to limit military expenditures have failed.

TEW
4 – 76 *The Latin American Nuclear Weapon-Free Zone,* Alfonso Robles, 31pp, 1979, Stanley Foundation, free. The author played a critical role in negotiation of the agreement, and summarizes here the provisions of the Treaty now in force.

4 – 77 "Nuclear Free Zones," William Epstein, *Scientific American* Reprint, November 1975, $.50. Describes the concept of zonal disarmament and its largely successful application in Latin America.

4 – 78 *Napalm and Other Incendiary Weapons and All Aspects of Their Possible Use,* 63pp., 1973, United Nations, $1.50. As a consequence of a U.N. General Assembly resolution, this work was prepared to study the effects of these weapons. The report concludes with a recommendation for their prohibition.

4 – 79 *Weapons of Mass Destruction and the Environment,* SIPRI, 99pp, 1978, Crane,

Russak, $2.95. Discusses nuclear weapons, chemical and biological weapons and their implications for arms control, and provides a twenty-one-page bibliography.

4 – 80 *Ecological Consequences of the Second Indochina War,* SIPRI, 119pp, 1976, $21.75. Studies the impact and implications of environmental weapons used by the U.S. in Vietnam.

M. Safeguarding Agreements

4 – 81 *Verification: The Critical Element of Arms Control,* 32 pp., 1976, U.S. Arms Control and Disarmament Agency, $.55. Surveys forms of verification: national technical means (satellites, electronic eavesdropping, espionage), technical data sharing, and international inspection. Makes the case for verifying compliance with any arms control agreements.

4 – 82 *Arms Control Agreements: Designs for Verification and Organization,* David Wainhouse and others, 220pp., 1968, Johns Hopkins Press, $15.95. This book addresses the problems in moving from arms control toward general and complete disarmament. The analysis of the U.S. and Soviet disarmament proposals, of Stage I (in the three stage plan), and of verification techniques and the handling of violations make it an extremely useful, though dated, introduction to the means for safeguarding agreements.

4 – 83 *Strategic Disarmament Verification and National Security,* SIPRI, 174 pp., 1977, Crane, Russak & Co., $16.50. Examines the conditions which make verification necessary and the forms of verification which are appropriate for different agreements.

N. Economic and Social Consequences

Intro
4 – 83 *World Military and Social Expenditures,* 1982, Ruth Leger Sivard, 38pp, 1981, World Priorities, $4.00. An annual survey of the abundance of funds available for war (over $500 billion in 1982), and the limits of funds for social programs.

4 – 84 *Economic and Social Consequences of the Arms Race and of Military Expenditures,* United Nations, 90pp, 1978, United Nations, $6.00. An updated analysis of a periodic UN assessment.

4 – 85 *Disarmament and World Development,* Richard Jolly (ed.), 206pp, 1978, Pergamon, $15.00. Introduces the objective of disarmament and presents a study of the economic consequences.

O. Bibliography

4 – 86 *Arms Control and Disarmament: A Bibliography,* Richard Burns (ed.), 430pp, 1978, ABC-Clio, $39.75. 8,847 entries categorized into subject areas including: overviews, international organizations, proposals and treaties, limitations, outlawry of war, the arms trade, proliferation, and stabilizing the international environment.

CHAPTER 5

INTERNATIONAL ORGANIZATION
AND WORLD LAW

Wars between groups . . . forming social units always take place when these units — tribes, dynasties, churches, cities, nations — exercise unrestricted sovereign power.

Wars between these units cease the moment sovereign power is transferred from them to a larger or higher unit.

EMERY REVES' statement succinctly defines one cause of war and identifies the reason world law is usually considered one condition for a world without war. There is a long-held belief that an overarching authority is essential to keep sovereign political units from warring (Newcombe, *World Unification Plans and Analyses*, 5-117). Pierre Dubois (1307), Dante Alighieri (1309), Erasmus (1517), Sully (1595), Emeric Cruce (1623), William Penn (1693), Hugo Grotius (1625), and Abbé de Saint-Pierre (1716), among others, developed ideas of international law, binding arbitration between States and world government, and it is sobering to study the fate of these early plans for peace. The more recent history of the Hague Conference conventions of 1899 and 1907, the League of Nations, and our current experience with the United Nations and the International Court of Justice are not much more encouraging.

Many believe that the achievement of peace through the transfer of ''sovereign power to a larger or higher unit'' is no more than an enduring illusion. There are, however, good reasons for believing that international

110

institutions can become effective agents of international, if not world, law. While in the past there have been ideas and plans, in the twentieth century there are in fact existing international organizations and an impressive list of functional agencies working on problems that require cooperation.

The current, most prominent embodiment of this tradition is the United Nations. Opinion in the United States is divided over the U.N.'s performance in the 1970s and about ways to make it (or another international organization) an effective keeper of the peace.

THE U.N. OF THE 1970s: A DANGEROUS PLACE?

Many informed Americans, once enthusiastically supportive of the U.N. and still in some ways committed to it, changed their minds in the 1970s. They came to regard the United Nations as a "dangerous place" (Moynihan, *A Dangerous Place*, 5 – 72).[1] For them the problem became not how to make the U.N. more nearly match someone's formula for world government, but how to prevent the U.N. from damaging existing international law. Those making this case cite various "shocks":

> . . . aggressive challenges and opposition to Israeli legitimacy and policies, including the equating of Zionism with racism, the recommendation that states halt economic aid to Israel and action in the U.N. Educational, Scientific, and Cultural Organization (UNESCO) to exclude Israel from the European group; support for national liberation movements . . . demands for redistribution of global economic wealth [as a matter of right] . . . a general conversion of UN forums into platforms for vitriolic attacks on the West in general and the United States specifically. . . .[2]

The fear was expressed that even the accepted morality which condemns aggression and massacre was being distorted and subverted. A double standard enabled condemnation of the West and its allies, while leaving most other countries immune to criticism. Such a double standard was clearly evident in sessions of the U.N. Human Rights Commission when human rights violations in Israeli-occupied territories, in South Africa, and in Chile were condemned while violations in Uganda, Kampuchea, and in Arab and Communist States were generally ignored. Apparently countries considered allied to the West, and open enough to have their human rights violations reported, were condemned; but closed societies went unreproached despite evidence of even more flagrant violations.

[1] See also Abraham Yeselson and Anthony Gaglione, *A Dangerous Place* (Grossman: New York, 1974) and Shirley Hazzard, *Defeat of an Ideal* (Boston: Little, Brown, 1973).
[2] David Kay, *The Changing United Nations* (5 – 73).

Another disillusioning experience with the U.N. in the 1970s was the defining of aggression in international law. The consensus reached was so vague that it is more likely to condone than condemn one country's forceful deployment of military forces inside another country (Stone, *Conflict through Consensus*, 5 – 102).[3]

But, despite disillusionment about the effectiveness and purpose of the U.N., public support for U.S. participation remained constant. In the 1970s, polls indicated that only 15% to 18% of the American public wanted the U.S. to withdraw — approximately the same as in the 1950s.

Critics of the U.N. who want the U.S. to continue participating find fault with more than specific policies. They see the prospect for international organizations to become instruments of world law countered by the most emotionally powerful force in world politics today: nationalism. Nationalistic feelings tie people to States, not to international or global institutions. The attempt to strengthen international institutions by transferring tasks to them, despite the lack of a supporting constituency, is bound to fail and to lead to a loss of credibility. Agreement about policies within the current U.N. structure is difficult to reach because of the diversity of interests. Ambiguous and vague policies are pronounced, and these cannot be administered. When agreements are reached, they often express the desire of the majority of small and weak States for sacrifices by the minority of large and powerful States. The U.N. structure is cumbersome at best and raises many bureaucratic problems — for example, how many nationalities must be members of each agency? Since State leaders are accountable to domestic rather than international or global constituencies, is it any wonder that they use U.N. forums primarily for domestic purposes? Given these realities in present international organizations, those who argue that State actions are bad and international actions are good may be asking for the transfer of functions from effective to ineffective political organizations.

The U.N. has political as well as structural problems since most member States are dictatorships, and their leaders did not come to power through persuasion and compromise. The politics of the U.N. are understood by some as motivated by a desire to cripple democracies (Moynihan, *A Dangerous Place*, 5 – 72), and by others as a form of trade-union bargaining (with the third world cast as the unions and the developed, industrial democracies as management (Cleveland, *The Third Try at World Order*, 5 – 74). But whatever the motivation, the result is an arena in which the U.S. must defend its own legitimacy and interests and seek allies committed to defending international

---

[3]For a favorable assessment of the U.N.'s defining of aggression, see Benjamin Ferencz, ''Defining Aggression,'' *American Journal of International Law,* July, 1972, pp. 491 – 508.

law, not one that can be expected to become an effective world political institution capable of resolving conflict without war.

STRENGTHS OF THE CURRENT U.N.

Defenders of the U.N. respond to both specific and general charges by agreeing that the U.N. *is* no better than its membership. How could it be otherwise? The problem is that the U.N. does not have real power to resolve conflicts or carry out policies. The real test of international organizations will come when they have the authority to act on their own (Clark & Sohn, *Introduction to World Peace through World Law,* 5 – 120). Give the U.N. more power and its members will act more responsibly. One of the current problems is the sense of powerlessness felt by leaders of developing countries. They want a larger share of the decision-making power over decisions that deeply affect them. They attack the West because of its resources and because the West, unlike the Soviet Union, responds to rhetoric. The U.N. will become more responsible, these defenders conclude, when the authority to make recommendations is combined with the power to implement them.

Whenever the U.N. has been given specific peacekeeping functions it has been effective. It significantly aided in the nonviolent resolution of conflict in Iran (1946), Indonesia (1947), Egypt (1956), Cyprus (1968 – 1974), the Middle East (1948, 1956, 1967, 1973 —), and it limited violence in the Congo (1960). Given the logistic, cultural, and political complexities of U.N. peacekeeping operations, this is a remarkable record ("Peacekeeping," 5 – 81 to 5 – 92). In addition, the U.N. has served as a forum for the clarification of objectives and goals, and has, through a series of conferences, focused attention on economic development, food, environment, technology transfer, women's rights, disarmament, and other problems. Through its specialized agencies, the U.N. has impressive achievements to its credit, such as the elimination of smallpox. There are very few ten-mile square areas on earth that have not benefited directly from U.N. activities.

Much of the criticism of the U.N. during the 1970s resulted from actions by its General Assembly. The General Assembly has changed from a forum led by the U.S. to one in which other voices set much of the tone, agenda and results (Newcombe, *National Patterns in International Organizations,* 5-60, Vincent, *Empirical Studies of Behavioural Patterns at the United Nations,* 5-59, Jacobsen, *The General Assembly of the United Nations,* 5-55). A new majority of developing States, called the Group of 77 (actually now over 120 States) can easily pass resolutions over U.S. opposition. But while the U.S. has opposed and lost on a few highly publicized resolutions in the General Assembly, it has supported most of those passed. Indeed, the U.N. has shifted from a forum for U.S. policy to the world arena which it was intended to be. Harlan Cleveland calls this result a ''victory for pluralism'' — a traditional U.S. objective. The United States is the principal member of the U.N. today able to help it improve. This is because of its size, the openness of its society (which makes it possible for new ideas to be developed), and its resources. It is so frequently attacked because its policies matter. Those making this case concur with John Stoessinger:

> . . . a new United Nations is emerging. It has a different agenda and different priorities. . . . North-South tensions have begun to supersede old East-West rivalries. . . . The struggle for power continues unabated. And yet, there is a new emphasis on the problems that we face as fellow passengers on Planet Earth. . . . It is this new slow dawning of compassion and of global consciousness that I begin to sense in the United Nations of tomorrow.[4]

Stoessinger calls for a renewal of our commitment, combined with a more compassionate response to the ''New International Economic Order'' proposed by the Group of 77.

THE SETTING FOR INTERNATIONAL INSTITUTION-BUILDING

Despite, or perhaps because of the limits of the current U.N., many people still believe that institutions with supranational authority are desperately needed and that their creation should be an urgent goal of policy-makers (*Elements of U.N. Reform*, 5 – 112). They point out the progress made since 1940 in the creation of new institutions and ask, ''Who can be sure what might be achieved in the next forty years or so?'' There are many changed realities in the contemporary world which make supranational authority more necessary and more likely then in previous eras. Paramount among these are nuclear weapons and interdependence.[5]

---

[4]Stoessinger, *The United Nations and the Superpowers*, 5 – 57.

[5]Interdependence has several meanings. As used here it means mutual dependence between two or more States. Other related concepts include convergence — the tendency of separate States to become more socially and economically alike; integration — the forming of one political authority where before there were two or more; and interpenetration — the cultural or technical impingement of one society upon another.

Some form of supranational authority[6] is required to control weapons of mass destruction. Even as the two superpowers' arsenals have grown, the number of States with nuclear capability has increased. Unless the superpowers begin serious arms reductions, the number of nuclear powers will continue to increase (Epstein, *The Last Chance*, 2 – 94), and arms control will be even more difficult. Nuclear arms control and non-proliferation require supranational authority.

There is now greater interdependence among States than ever before. One indication is the growing volume of transactions between States. Some of these transactions are by heads of State, others by non-State actors (such as international non-governmental organizations (INGOs)) and some by transnational corporations (TNCs). These activities include world trade, the transfer of technological innovations and aesthetic tastes, tourist travel, conferences and correspondence among member of professional associations. Careful study of these trends indicates that States' social structures are converging.[7] Such convergence, however, does not necessarily lead to political integration or the formation of regional or world governmental structures.

BEYOND THE STATE: ALTERNATIVE APPROACHES TO WORLD ORDER

All proponents of global institutions agree that existing international structures need to be strengthened or changed if they are to help end war. They do not agree on which institutions are needed and which are achievable, and what the power of these should be. The present situation is comparable to past settings in which common institutions were possible: there is a vast array of problems which no existing political organization can solve alone. But there is not agreement on a single formula for new global structures, and for the foreseeable future the prospect is for a wide range of institutions. This range is likely to include supranational global authorities with narrow responsibilities, such as inspecting nuclear fuel handling or verifying arms control and disarmament agreements; regional bodies acting to resolve conflict within a geographical or cultural region; international institutions, in which each government retains the decisive say, regulating common activities, such as currency exchange.

A diffusion of power may help to control war. However, this approach raises some perplexing questions: (1) Is a world of, say, 250 States safer than one of 170?; (2) Is it both feasible and desirable to break up the larger States? It

---

[6]Supranational here means a new, sovereign authority capable of imposing binding sanctions upon those violating its rules; transnational authority refers to actions across State lines, without implying sovereignty; international refers to inter-governmental activity.

[7]Alex Inkels, "The Emerging Social Structure of the World," *World Politics*, July 1975.

can be argued that war would be more frequent but less deadly in a world composed of smaller States; but given existing technologies, wars could be more frequent *and* more deadly than World War II. While some may want to explore how the problem of war might be resolved in a world of many small States, our focus here is on the idea that strengthening international institutions can help prevent war between the existing political communities. While a complex array of international regimes, regional bodies, and governmental and non-governmental agencies are possible (Falk, *Future Worlds*, 5 – 113), only five specific institutional settings address the problem of controlling the threat of war. The institutions needed could be achieved by 1) changing State policies toward the present United Nations; 2) continuing the development of functional and regional international institutions (and thus creating a web of relationships that would make supra-national peace-keeping organizations possible later); 3) revising the U.N. Charter to give the U.N. binding authority in the security area; 4) creating a new world organization in cooperation with the U.N.; and 5) writing a new world constitution at a world constitutional convention (thus by-passing States).

CHANGE NATIONAL GOVERNMENTAL POLICIES, NOT INTERNATIONAL STRUCTURES

Proponents of achieving world law within the presently constituted U.N. system argue that the key to effective international institutions is agreement among the great powers. When the great powers agree, the United Nations is effective; when they do not, any international organization powerful enough to stand in their way would be the creature of one of them. The current U.N., in this view, reflects political reality with the veto in the Security Council and the absence of legislative authority in the General Assembly. If States would use the existing institutions, these could restrain the military policies of States. It is unwise, in this view, to press for structural change in the U.N. because such changes would violate the realities of power in a world dominated by two antagonistic superpowers. Before stronger international institutions can be built, there must be a change in policies of the superpowers and in public attitudes. If the U.S., for example, would consistently use the U.N. as it is now constituted, the U.N. would be greatly strengthened. Besides, the Soviet Union has always made it clear that it would veto any proposals for altering the U.N. Charter; so we should make the best use of what now exists.

An influential voice within this school of thought argues that existing international law is much more significant than is generally realized. Advocates of this view (McDougal & Feliciano, *Law and Minimum World Public Order*, 5 – 11) point out that existing treaties, customary law, judicial opinions, and the great works of scholars provide the substance of international law; the components of any legal sanctioning process are all in place: prevention, deterrence, restoration, rehabilitation, and reconstruction. These five processes can be set up concerning any issue on the global agenda. Those who want to further the rule of law should, in this view, insist on the use of existing judicial processes.

REGIONAL AND FUNCTIONAL APPROACHES TO WORLD LAW

Another approach to strengthening international organizations into instruments of world law agrees with the central contention of the first: agreement about structural changes in global international institutions cannot now be achieved. But, the functionalists argue, that there are many practical problems faced by all States for which cooperation is both needed and agreement possible. These matters have been assigned to what are called "functional," international organizations, because they are focused on a specific task, such as the World Health Organization's focus on the problem of eradicating small pox. The accomplishments of this and similar international organizations are impressive. People divided by national, religious, ideological, and other differences can nonetheless cooperate to ease common problems. Out of this experience, the functionalists assert, could come the will to build similar institutions to address the problem of war.

Related to the functionalist approach is one which seeks to build regional international organizations into effective peacekeeping institutions. Its proponents argue that people in geographic proximity and sharing common cultural heritages are far more likely to accept common political institutions. Here, too, the emphasis is on narrow functions, not on broad agreement across ideological divisions. Advocates of regionalism see in the Council of Europe, the Organization of American States, and the Organization of African Unity, embryonic regional governments. Europe's steps toward political integration are, in this view, the best example of how national rivalries can be transcended.

U.N. CHARTER REVISION OR CREATION OF A WORLD SECURITY ORGANIZATION

Those who believe that world law is possible today feel an overriding urgency brought on by the threat of nuclear war, by pollution, by population growth, and by a scarcity of resources. The central problem is to achieve a world authority capable of addressing these problems, with the legal right and economic resources capable of resolving them. The best way to achieve these ends is to revise the U.N. Charter, and what is required to accomplish that purpose is leadership in a sufficient number of countries.

However, there are many different approaches to achieving world law through U.N. Charter revision. The most prestigious and widely discussed one was developed by Grenville Clark and Louis Sohn (*Introduction to World Peace through World Law*, 5 – 120). It features a constitutional model, a weighted voting system, and an extensive peacekeeping, conflict-resolution authority superseding that of sovereign States. But in most respects, the authority of existing States is left intact. The central idea is that of a world federal authority in which power is divided between a central world government and existing States. Such a system of world federalism accepts a great deal of diversity in the world and offers an institutional solution to the problem of resolving conflict.

In response to critics who suggested that this looks like the U.S. Constitution writ large, the Institute for World Order launched the World Order Models Project (Mendlovitz, *On the Creation of a Just World Order*, 5 – 129). They solicited from teams of scholars representing various regions and world views their conception of a preferred world order which might be achievable by the 1990s. In response to other critics who said that agreement on Charter revision was not likely (the Soviet Union argued that world government was impossible in a world of different, competing economic systems), they recommended a parallel organization which would address the security question and perhaps sponsor economic development programs. Participation would be by consent and would be viewed as a demonstration of sincerity of peaceful intent.

WORLD CONSTITUTIONAL CONVENTION AND EXTRANATIONAL APPROACHES

Some advocates of world law disagree with the Federalist approach. They argue that world law cannot be built on top of the existing State system; the States are the main obstacle to world law, not its base. The world is sufficiently interrelated to sustain a world government or a functioning world court; it is the States that hinder clear perception of the existing reality of world community.

One extranational approach to world law advocates the formulation of a world constitution at a special convention of delegates elected by people throughout the world. Since no State can be expected voluntarily to yield control of its crucial powers to tax and wage war, that obstacle can be circumvented in the same way the Founding Fathers of the United States circumvented the sovereign States that made up the Confederation (1781-1789). A convention could draft a world constitution (*A Constitution of the Federation of Earth*, 5-126), and submit it directly to conventions held in each State for the purpose of adopting or rejecting world law. Out of this would come a world government representing people, not States. The U.S. Constitution, after all, begins, "We, the people . . . " not "We, the States . . . "

A related approach seeks to create international institutions and practices without waiting for the approval of States. Advocates maintain that the resources available to international lawyers are even now adequate; existing treaties, norms of behavior, the U.N. Charter, and case law provide an adequate tradition. Gerald Gottlieb has advocated the creation of a "Court of Man," for example, based on Medieval examples of courts which successfully challenged the monopoly of empires or feudalities over the process of law. Such "courts of community" have functioned in the past without State authorization in several regions of the world. A similar idea is simply to hold State leaders judicially accountable for violation of, for example, international human rights treaties. Luis Kutner sought to prosecute Idi Amin, has filed suits against Fidel Castro, and has sought to enforce *habeas corpus* rights in international courts which can be created if existing courts decline jurisdiction. Such proposals would require an extranational judiciary, independent of States, which would render judgment on those who misuse State power.

CONCLUSION

Every approach to world law is confronted by skepticism: of course we should participate in the U. N. and in functional and regional organizations, but these are basically intergovernmental organizations; they operate only when they help countries discover where their self-interests coincide. When they work, they do so effectively; when they do not work, no international organization can override them. The basic reality of modern world politics remains psychological loyalty to the State. Contemporary ideological divisions make it extremely unlikely that there will be any voluntary yielding of sovereignty to a body capable of enforcing world law. Nationalism is a growing force in Asia,

Africa, and Latin America. Interdependence has brought with it an increase in transactions between States and thus the ability of one State to influence another. This may produce a desire for cooperation, but it can as well produce conflict or a desire for isolation from other States. Thus, the precondition for effective world political institutions — a politically effective sense of world community — does not now exist. Until it does, skeptics believe, peace will be kept as it has been kept for a long time: by a realistic assessment of the national interest, by the maintenance of an adequate military deterrent, and by careful diplomacy.

The central issue between proponents of these divergent views is the extent to which there now exists a sense of world community. The possible rewards for those who succeed in overcoming the obstacles are eloquently stated as the goals of the United Nations:

1. To save succeeding generations from the scourge of war.
2. To reaffirm faith in fundamental human rights.
3. To establish conditions under which justice and respect for the obligations arising from treaties and other sources of international law can be maintained.
4. To promote social progress and better standards of life in larger freedom.

BIBLIOGRAPHY

Among the questions the reader may want to pursue in the books that follow are these: 1) What purposes were previous international organizations designed to fulfill? How well did they succeed? 2) What makes law possible? 3) How are States formed? 4) Does a sense of community precede the creation of a State or follow from the creation of a State? 5) Can organizations with opposing ideologies agree to cooperate on rules so that they can conduct their conflict politically within one institution? Opposing religions? 6) What types of international organizations exist today at the regional and global levels? 7) How successful have they been? 8) Are their failings the result of their having too much or too little power? 9) When and where has the U. N. acted successfully to keep the peace? 10) What level of international or supranational organization is possible and needed today? What are the tasks such an organization would address?

A. Introductions

Intro

5 – 1 *International Organizations, An Introductory Kit,* 30pp, 1977, World Without War Publications, free. Identifies contending perspectives, indicates choice points between them, and outlines U. N. reform proposals.

5 – 2 *International Organization, A Conceptual Approach,* Paul Taylor & A. J. R. Groom, 466pp, 1978, Nichols, $25.00. Offers a 200-year perspective on the emergence of international organizations.

5 – 3 *International Organizations: Principles and Issues,* A. LeRoy Bennett, 530pp, 1980, 2nd ed., Prentice-Hall, $14.95. A systematic introduction to the origins and development of the 20th Century's contribution to world politics: international organizations. A judicious assessment.

5 – 4 *The Strategy of World Order,* Richard Falk and Saul Mendlovitz (ed.), 2,298pp, 1966, Institute for World Order, Volumes I-IV, $14.00. An attempt to develop an academic discipline oriented toward the principal policy questions of world affairs: how to achieve world order. Each volume is an anthology of carefully selected materials, with connecting notes and discussion questions. Volume I presents the plan of this systematic study and gathers articles on the various theoretical problems involved in the prevention of war. Vol. I *Toward a Theory of War Prevention,* 394pp, 1966, $3.50. Selections by Kenneth Boulding, Herman Kahn, Quincy Wright, Harold Lasswell, and others. Vol. II *International Law,* 382pp, 1966, $3.50. Selections by Falk and Mendlovitz, Louis Henkin, Inis Claude, Stanley Hoffmann, and others. Vol. III *The United Nations,* 848pp, 1966, $4.50. Selections on the League of Nations, the International Court of Justice, peacekeeping, financing, and proposals for a world police force. Vol. IV *Disarmament and Economic Development,* 672pp, 1966, $4.50. Articles by Jerome Wiesner, Thomas Schelling, Charles Osgood, Richard Barnet, Emile Benoit and others.

Intro

5 – 5 *The United Nations: The World's Last Chance for Peace,* Winthrop and Frances Neilson, 276pp, 1975, NAL, $1.75. A brief introduction to the structure and functioning of many parts of the U. N. system.

Classic

5 – 6 *Swords into Plowshares: The Problems and Progress of International Organization,* Inis Claude, Jr. 514pp, 1971, 4th ed., Random House, $15.95. A classic in the field; includes historical background of contemporary international organizations, constitutional problems, approaches to peace through international organization, and the future of world order.

B. International Law

5 – 7 *A Modern Introduction to International Law,* Michael Akehurst, 283pp, 1978, (3rd ed.) Allen & Unwin, $13.75. Discusses succinctly the sources, nature, and uses of international law.

5 – 8 *Contemporary International Law: A Concise Introduction,* Werner Levi, 391pp, 1978, Westview, $11.00. Maintains that law is part of politics and is useful in clarifying communications but is not an effective control on power.

5 – 9 *The Future of Law in a Multicultural World,* Adda Bozeman, 229pp, 1971, Princeton, $5.95. Points out the role and limits of law in adjudicating disputes between States with different cultures and different notions of law.

5 – 10 *International Law in a Changing World: Cases, Documents and Readings,* Edward Collins, Jr., 493pp, 1970, Random House, $17.95. Characterizes international law as an ''instrument whereby States may achieve tentative reconciliations between their simultaneous urges for freedom of action and for predictable patterns of behavior.'' This text describes the important uses and current limits of international law.

5 – 11 *Law and Minimum World Public Order,* Myers McDougal & Mendoza Feliciano, 1961, O.P. A classic introduction to the effectiveness of existing international law.

5 – 12 *Toward World Order and Human Dignity: Essays in Honor of Myers McDougal,* Michael Reisman & Burns Weston (eds.), 603pp, 1976, Macmillan, $20.00. Essays honoring a leading advocate of international law as a ''policy-oriented jurisprudence'' in which values are pursued rather than rules applied.

5 – 13 *The Bases of International Order, Essays in Honour of C.A.W. Manning,* Alan James (ed.), 218pp, 1973, Oxford, $11.25. Essays honoring a revered teacher, examining the attitudinal and structural requirements of order with an emphasis on inter-state relationships.

5 – 14 *Principles of Public International Law,* Ian Brownlie, 772pp, 1980 (3rd ed.), Oxford, $27.50, Covers both the technical content of international law and its specific applications.

5 – 15 *The Creation of States in International Law,* James Crawford, 500pp, 1979, Oxford, $48.00. A comprehensive account of the international law of statehood.

5 – 16 *International Law and World Order,* Burns Weston, Richard Falk, Anthony D'Amanto (eds), 1266pp, 1980, West Publishing, $23.95 (Supplementary *Documents in International Law and Order,* 460pp, 1980, $5.95). A problem-oriented course book designed for introductory international law students.

5 – 17 *International Law and National Behavior, A Behavioral Interpretation of Contemporary International Law and Politics,* Ahmed Sheikh, 352pp, 1974, Wiley, $12.95. Examines the broadening scope and acceptance of international law including

chapters on the attitude toward law of the Soviet Union and of selected third world countries.

5 – 18 *The Price of International Justice,* Philip Jessup, 82pp, 1971, Columbia, $10.00. Jessup cites five cases when States submitted disputes to international arbitration, and defines the price of peace as accepting international arbitration, and calls each arbitrated dispute an advance of a few inches on the long road to peace.

5 – 19 *International Environmental Law,* Ludwik Teclaff and Albert Utton, 270pp, 1974, Praeger, $18.95. Covers a wide range of areas from U. N. programs to specific problems such as air pollution and outer space.

5 – 20 *International Law and the Movement of Persons Between States,* Guy Goodwin-Gill, 324pp, 1978, Oxford, $34.95. A study of the rights of foreign nationals in a country, when they may be expelled, when they must be permitted to enter, and the application of the "principle of non-discrimination."

5 – 21 *The Law Relating to Activities of Man in Space,* S. Houston Lay & Howard Taubenfeld, 360pp, 1970, U. of Chicago, $25.00. An analysis of the national laws relating to the use of outer space, and a consideration of the need for internationally recognized laws controlling space activities.

5 – 22 *Seeking World Order: The United States and International Organizations to 1920,* Warren Kuehl, 320pp, 1969, Vanderbilt, $10.00. Describes the background to Wilson's proposal for a League of Nations and its rejection in the U.S.

5 – 23 *Great Britain and the Creation of the League of Nations, Strategy, Politics, and International Organization, 1914 – 1919,* George Edgerton, 273pp, 1978, North Carolina, $17.50. Provides a useful background on the formation of the first world institution.

5 – 24 *Office Without Power, Secretary-General Sir Eric Drummond 1919 – 1933,* James Barrios, 448pp, 1979, Oxford, $41.00. The chief officer of the League of Nations used his influence behind the scenes, much like the U.N. Secretary General.

5 – 25 *Collective Insecurity: The United States and the League of Nations During the Early Thirties,* Gary Ostrower, 288pp, 1979, Bucknell, $19.50. Traces the existence of an "international impulse" particularly toward the Far East in an era of isolationist sentiments.

5 – 26 *The World Court and the Contemporary International Law-Making Process,* E. McWhinney, 227pp, 1979, Sijthoff & Noordhoff, $35.00. Describes the law-making process under international law as it applies to the International Court of Justice.

5 – 27 *The Law of Armed Conflicts,* Dietrich Schindler & Jiri Toman, 904pp, 1980, Sijthoff & Noordhoff, $105.00. Presents international conventions, resolution, and conferences concerning the law in war along with a list of who is party to what conventions.

5 – 28 *World Treaty Index and Treaty Profiles,* Peter Rohn, ed., six volumes, 5300pp,

1975, ABC-Clio, $510.00. Lists over 20,000 treaties and offers a statistical analysis of national, regional and global treaty patterns.

5 – 29 *Uncertain Judgment, A Bibliography of War Crimes Trials,* John Lewis, 251pp, 1979, ABC-Clio, $25.75. Lists 3,352 books and articles related to war crimes; included are historical works as well as an exhaustive bibliography of the trials at the end of World War II.

5 – 30 *Social Science Literature: A Bibliography for International Law,* Wesley Gould and Michael Barkun, 641pp, 1972, Princeton, $15.00. Nearly 3,000 annotated entries of articles and books covering such areas as the dynamics and evolution of international law, inter-governmental organization, war crimes, human rights, decision-making, sovereignty and nationalism, and natural resources.

5 – 31 *Bibliography of International Law,* Ingrid Delupis & Nee Nettor (eds.), 670pp, 1975, Bowker, $37.50. For the specialist.

For an extensive list of international law publications, write Oceana Publications, Dobbs Ferry, N. Y. 10522

C. Regional Organizations

5 – 32 *Regional Politics and World Order,* Richard Falk and Saul Mendlovitz (eds.), 475pp, 1973, Freeman, $5.95. Continues the format of *The Strategy of World Order,* and asks whether regional organizations can transcend national sovereignties; and if so, how such regional organizations might aid or prevent the emergence of a world order capable of preventing war. Contributors include Emest Haas, Joseph Nye, Inis Claude, Kay Boals and Hedley Bull.

5 – 33 *Regionalism and the United Nations,* Berhanykun Andemicael (ed.), 603pp, 1979, Oceana, $50.00. Prepared for UNITAR, this volume provides largely favorable views of the workings of regional organizations.

Intro
5 – 34 *Regional International Organizations: Structures and Functions,* Paul Tharp, Jr., (ed.), 1971, St. Martin's, $8.95. A valuable introduction to the world's regional organizations.

(See also Chapter 10.)

D. International Organizations

5 – 35 *Yearbook of International Organizations, 1978 – 79,* Union of International Associations, 1,200pp, 1978 (17th ed), International Publications Service, $80.00.

Lists 8,200 governmental and non-governmental organizations and provides a brief history and description of each.

5 – 36 *Moderation from Management: International Organizations and Peace,* Robert Butterworth, 140pp, 1978, Pittsburgh, $4.95. Studies 166 conflicts in which international organizations played a role, and argues their effectiveness is directly related to their willingness to aid States reach agreement rather than to impose solutions.

5 – 37 *Multinational Cooperation: Economic, Social and Scientific Development,* Robert Jordan (ed.), 392pp, 1972, Oxford, $4.95. Essays on international organizations including UNESCO, the World Bank and International Monetary Fund, and the Organizations of American States.

5 – 38 *Organizing Mankind: An Analysis of Contemporary International Organizations,* Lynn Miller, 365pp, 1972, Holbrook, $5.95. An introduction to the field of international organization which here includes not only the U.N., but also economic blocs, multilateral alliances, and regional organizations.

5 – 39 *The Future of International Economic Organizations,* Don Wallace, Jr. and Helga Escobar (eds.), 184pp, 1977, Praeger, $18.95. Considers the type of organizations and their functions in the areas of international trade, food supply, and natural resources except oil. Diverse views are presented.

5 – 40 *The Anatomy of Influence: Decision Making in International Organization,* Robert Cox, *et al,* 520pp, 1973, Yale, $37.50. Applies general theoretical concepts about influence to International Labour Organization decision-making.

E. The United Nations

Intro
5 – 41 *Basic Facts about the U.N.,* United Nations, 131pp, 1980, United Nations, $1.95. A factual introduction to the organization and function of each part of the U.N. system.

Intro
5 – 42 *Issues Before the 36th General Assembly of the United Nations,* 1981 – 82, Donald Puchala (ed.), Frederic Eckhard, Project Editor, 150pp, 1980, United Nations Association of the U.S.A., $7.00. An annual assessment of the issues expected to be brought before the fall session, published in September.

5 – 43 *Charter of the United Nations and Statute of the International Court of Justice,* United Nations, 57pp, 1945, United Nations, $1.50. The texts.

5 – 44 *Reference Guide to the United Nations,* UNA of the USA, 100pp, 1978, United Nations Association, $7.50. A looseleaf notebook with basic factual information on every U.N. body, specialized agency and program; up-dated annually.

5 – 45 *The Challenge of Peace,* Kurt Waldheim, 224pp, 1980, Rawson Wade, $9.95. Offers a brief autobiographical sketch and an account of the Secretary General's role in resolving conflicts.

5 – 46 *Building the Future Order, The Search for Peace in an Interdependent World,* Kurt Waldheim, Robert Schiffer (ed), 224pp, 1980, Free Press, $12.95. A selection of the Secretary General's speeches designed to illustrate how he is using his office to further the purposes stated in the U.N. Charter.

5 – 47 *Your Man at the U.N.: People, Politics & Bureaucracy in the Making of Foreign Policy,* Seymour Finger, 368pp, 1980, NYU Press, $26.50. A handbook on how the U.S. mission operates, a sketch of its leaders, and a description of the political influences on the mission.

5 – 48 *Soviet & American Policies in the United Nations: A Twenty-Five Year Perspective,* Alvin Rubinstein & George Ginsburgs (eds.), 211pp, 1971, New York U. Press, $12.00. Examines the different approaches to the U.N. of the superpowers during a period when peacekeeping, conflict resolution, and decolonization were the major issues.

5 – 49 *UN Law-Fundamental Rights: Two Topics in International Law,* A. Cassese (ed.), 268pp, 1979, Sijthoff & Noordhoff, $38.00. Discusses legal and political issues concerning the law of the United Nations and the international protection of human rights.

5 – 50 *An Idea and Its Servants: UNESCO from Within,* Richard Hoggart, 1978, Oxford, $13.95. A critical examination of the UN Agency.

5 – 51 *Sovereign Equality Among States: The History of an Idea,* Robert Klein, 198pp, 1974, Toronto, $15.00. Describes the origins of the principle underlying the U.N. General Assembly and consequences to it for limiting the authority powerful States are willing to grant it and other similarly structured international bodies.

5 – 52 *The United Nations, How it Works and What it Does,* Evan Luard, 190pp, 1979, St. Martin's, $18.95. Offers a hopeful assessment of the U.N.'s problem-solving capacity.

5 – 53 *Nations on Record: United Nations General Assembly Roll-Call Votes* (1946– 1973), Lynn Schopen, Hanna Newcombe, Chris Young, and James Wert, 534pp, 1975, Canadian Peace Research Institute, $17.00. A record of how each country voted on each General Assembly roll call vote during the first twenty-eight sessions.

5 – 54 *The United Nations System, Coordinating its Economic and Social Work,* Martin Hill, 252pp, 1978, Cambridge, $37.50. Notes the shift from peacekeeping to economic concerns, and is a penetrating analysis of the current functioning of the U.N. system in the economic field.

5 – 55 *The General Assembly of the United Nations, A Quantitative Analysis of Conflict, Inequality, and Relevance,* Kurt Jacobsen, 300pp, 1978, Columbia, $15.00.

After a study of the resources and actions of member States in the first 24 sessions, he concludes that despite their voting strength, few developing countries have the resources to fully participate in General Assembly activities.

5 – 56 *Organizing for Peace: A Personal History of the Founding of the United Nations*, Clark Eichelberger, 317pp, 1977, Harper, $17.95. Covers the period from the rejection of the League of Nations by the U.S. to the establishment of the U.N. in New York, and provides insight into U.S. policy in seeking to create the United Nations.

5 – 57 *The United Nations and the Superpowers; China, Russia, and America*, John Stoessinger, 245pp, 1977, 4th ed., Random House, $5.95. A valuable analysis of recent trends in U.N. activity, and a partial response to those now making the case that it is a dangerous place: most resolutions have not been against U.S. interests.

5 – 58 *China, the United Nations, and World Order*, Samuel Kim, 581pp, 1979, Princeton, $12.50. Details China's approach to international law and to participation in the U.N.

5 – 59 *Empirical Studies of Behavioural Patterns at the United Nations*, Jack Vincent, 120pp, Vol. I, 130pp, Vol.II, 1978, Peace Research Reviews, $5.00 per vol. Presents data on delegate attitudes and General Assembly voting patterns.

5 – 60 *National Patterns in International Organizations*, Hanna Newcombe, 367pp, (3 vols.), 1975, Peace Research Reviews, $5.00 each. A search for quantitatively verified patterns of voting in multilateral, parliamentary settings.

F. The United Nations Publications

5 – 61 *Everyone's United Nations, A Handbook on the United Nations, Its Structure and Activities*, 477pp, 1980, United Nations, $7.95. Describes the structure and activities of the United Nations and the seventeen intergovernmental agencies related to it; focuses on the years 1966 to 1978. Among the other series published by the United Nations are: United Nations Documents, United Nations Documents Index, Annual Report of the Secretary General, United Nations Demographic Yearbook, United Nations Statistical Yearbook, United Nations Treaty Series, Yearbook of the United Nations, United Nations Disarmament Yearbook. Write United Nations Publications, New York, N.Y. 10017. Ask for a free catalogue.

5 – 62 *World Statistics in Brief, United Nations Statistical Pocketbook*, United Nations, 90pp, 1981, U.N., $2.50. Provides brief statistical profiles of member States including area, population, products, and social indicators.

5 – 63 *World Economic Survey*, 1977, United Nations, $10.00. Provides information on world trade, production, inflation, employment, monetary reserves, debts, and rates of exchange.

5 – 64 *Apartheid, A Select Bibliography on the Racial Policies of the Government of the*

Republic of South Africa, 1970 – 1978, 50pp, 1979, United Nations, $5.00. Traces the development of apartheid and the attempts to end it.

5 – 65 *The United Nations and Human Rights,* United Nations, 89pp, 1973, United Nations, $3.00. A survey of U.N. human rights activities.

5 – 66 *The Realization of Economic, Social and Cultural Rights: Problems, Policies, Progress,* Monouchehr Ganji, 326pp, 1975, United Nations, $14.00. Primarily an assessment of economic development.

5 – 67 *Transnational Corporations in World Development: A Re-Examination,* 1978, United Nations, $12.00. A comprehensive view of the effects of TNC's on governmental policies as well as on legal, economic, and social circumstances in host countries.

5 – 68 *The Work of the International Law Commission,* United Nations, 325pp, 1980, United Nations, $16.00. Describes the purposes of the commission, the background to its work, and work accomplished.

5 – 68A *Directory of United Nations Information Systems*, UN, 1981, United Nations, Vol. I $22.00, Vol, II $13.00. Describes over 300 UN information systems, publications and several thousand addresses of sources of information within countries.

5 – 69 *The United Nations Disarmament Yearbook,* United Nations, 481pp, 1980, United Nations, $28.00. A summary of U.N. work on disarmament in 1979 including the follow-up to the Special Session, General Assembly resolutions, and work on specific issues like strategic arms limitations and nuclear-weapons-free zones.

5 – 70 *Yearbook of the United Nations* 1977, United Nations, 1,302pp, 1980, United Nations, $50.00. An annual overview of events throughout the U.N. system related to political and security questions, disarmament, economic and social questions, international law, special programs, and relations to other intergovernmental agencies.

G. Assessments and Policy Recommendations

5 – 71 *U.S. Policy in International Institutions: Defining Reasonable Options in an Unreasonable World,* Seymour Finger and Joseph Harbert (eds.), 489pp, 1978, Westview, $13.50. Thirty-five scholars and diplomats present specific recommendations for policy changes and a few reforms to make the current structure more effective.

5 – 72 *A Dangerous Place,* Daniel Patrick Moynihan & Suzanne Weaver 297pp, 1980, Berkley, $2.75. A collection of essays and reflections on the dangers posed for democratic societies by international bodies dominated by authoritarian and totalitarian governments, and on the central role that international law must play if democracy is to survive.

5 – 73 *The Changing United Nations, Options for the United States,* David Kay (ed.), 226pp, 1978, Praeger, $20.95. Emphasizes the changes in the U.N. in the 1970s, the

challenge of the third world, politization of specialized agencies, but argues that the need for U.N. peacekeeping activities is greater now than ever.

5 – 74 *The Third Try at World Order, U.S. Policy for an Interdependent World,* Harlan Cleveland, 119pp, 1976, Aspen Institute $3.95. Calls for a planetary bargain to establish functional regimes for common problems but without overarching authority.

5 – 75 *The Future of the UN, A Strategy for Like-Minded Nations,* Charles Yost, Chairman, 58pp, 1977, Westview, $7.50. Calls for a new pragmatism in U.S. participation in coalitions of democratic states, flexibility in response to social change movements, and hard bargaining concerning the new interdependence issues — food, trade, technology transfer, energy, commodity pricing, and environmental issues.

5 – 76 *The United Nations in Perspective,* E. Berkley Tompkins (ed.), 155pp, 1972, Hoover Institution, $7.50. Eight essays commemorating the 25th anniversary of the UN, addressing a wide range of problems.

5 – 77 *The Paralysis of International Institutions and the Remedies: A study of Self-Determination, Concord Among the Major Powers, and Political Arbitration,* Istvan Bibo, 152pp, 1976, Krieger, $17.50. Maintains that existing international institutions lack the constituencies essential to effective operation.

5 – 78 *The New Nations in the United Nations, 1960 – 67,* David Kay, 254pp, 1979, Columbia, $15.00. A study of the influence of newly independent States prior to their dominance in the General Assembly.

5 – 79 *Defeat of an Ideal: A Study of the Self-Destruction of the United Nations,* Shirley Hazzard, 286pp, 1973, Little, Brown, $8.50. A former member of the U.N. Secretariat claims that the structure and competence of the U.N. have been hopelessly corrupted — initially by yielding to U.S. security practices, then by neglect, and finally by advanced bureaucratic paralysis. Her conclusion: Start over again.

5 – 80 *UNESCO and World Politics, Engaging in International Relations,* James Sewell, 384pp, 1975, Princeton, $18.50. A study of the workings of UNESCO and its policization.

H. Peacekeeping & Sanctions

TEW
5 – 81 *The Power to Keep Peace, Today and in a World Without War,* Lincoln Bloomfield, and others, 250pp, 1971, World Without War Publications, $2.95. A revised edition of the basic study of international peacekeeping. This book is indispensable to any student or citizen interested in seeing the international community develop a strengthened peacekeeping capability. Includes contributions by Hans Morgenthau, Stanley Hoffmann, Thomas Schelling, and others, plus policy proposals, U.N. documents and proposals of private organizations, all focused on achieving a standby U.N. police force.

5 – 82 *Peacekeeper's Handbook,* International Peace Academy, 339pp, 1978, International Peace Academy, $10.00. A practical handbook on the problems of U.N. peacekeeping forces prepared by experienced practitioners of the craft.

5 – 83 *The Thin Blue Line: International Peacekeeping and its Future,* Indar Jit Rikhye, Michael Harbott and Bjorn Egge, 353pp, 1974, Yale, $18.50. Case studies of U.N. peacekeeping operations and other attempts at multinational conflict control set the background for thoughtful proposals for the future.

5 – 84 *The Sinai Blunder,* Major General Indar Jit Rikyhe, 240pp, 1980, Biblio, $24.00. A first-hand account of the events leading to the withdrawal of the U.N. Emergency Force from the Sinai in 1967 by its then Commander, now head of the International Peace Academy.

5 – 85 *The United Nations Operation in the Congo 1960 – 1964,* Georges Abi-Sabb, 206pp, 1978, Oxford, $4.95. Examines the U.N. decision to deploy a peacekeeping force in the Congo, and the decisions after deployment as a contribution to evolving a legal basis for conflict mediation. One of five books in the American Society of International Law's series ''International Crises and the Role of Law''; others are *Cyprus,* 1958-67, Thomas Ehrlich; *The Cuban Missile Crisis,* 1962, Abram Chayes; *Suez,* 1956, Robert Bowie, and *Points of Choice,* Roger Fisher.

5 – 86 *Points of Choice, International Crises and the Role of Law,* Roger Fisher, 89pp, 1978, Oxford, $4.95. Indicates how law can help resolve international disputes involving conflicting goals, provided mediators, arbitrators, elections or courts are accepted and each side is prepared to lose some of its objectives.

5 – 87 *International Peacekeeping at the Crossroads, National Support Experience and Prospects,* David Wainhouse, with Frederick Bohannon, James Knott and Anne Simons, 640pp, 1973, Johns Hopkins, $30.00. Presents case studies of past United Nations peacekeeping forces, and asks under what conditions they are desirable.

5 – 88 *Soldiers Without Enemies: Preparing the United Nations for Peacekeeping,* Larry Fabian, 315pp, 1971, Brookings, $4.95. A comprehensive treatment of the history, evolution, and structure of U.N. peacekeeping operations, national attitudes toward them, and recommendations for improving the U.N.'s capability in this field.

5 – 89 *An Inter-American Peace Force within the Framework of the Organization of American States,* James Jose, 334pp, 1970, Scarecrow Press, $7.50. The author finds unlikely the creation of an often discussed peacekeeping force.

5 – 90 *Economic Sanctions and International Enforcement,* Margaret Doxey, 160pp, 1980, (2nd ed.). Oxford, $22.00. A survey of the cases where sanctions have been imposed and an assessment of their effectiveness.

5 – 91 *Sanctions, The Case of Rhodesia,* Harry Strack, 318pp, 1978, Syracuse, $15.00. Examines the effect of external sanctions on internal developments within Rhodesia from 1965 to 1977, and assesses their effectiveness.

5 – 91A *Economic Sanctions*, Robin Renwick, 140pp, 1981, Harvard, $7.95. Examines the use of sanctions in the Italian-Ethiopian war in 1935 – 36 and against Rhodesia in the 1960s and 1970s and suggests what sanctions can and cannot do.

5 – 92 *The Implementation of International Sanctions*, P.J. Puyper, 372pp, 1978, Sijtoff & Noordhoff, $37.50. A case study of U.N. sanctions against Rhodesia as carried out by the Netherlands, and the legal and bureaucratic constraints which limited their effectiveness.

5 – 92A *Managing the Risks of International Agreement*, Richard Bilder, 302pp, 1981, Wisconsin, $22.50. Lists the ways in which non-compliance can be minimized.

I. International Organizations and Internal War

5 – 93 *The International Regulation of Civil Wars*, Evan Luard (ed.), 244pp, 1972, NYU Press, $12.00. An important study of how international organizations might aid in the resolution of essentially domestic conflicts.

5 – 94 *The International Law of Civil War*, Richard Falk (ed.), 226pp, 1971, Johns Hopkins, $25.00. Applies international law to the question.

5 – 95 *World Order and Local Disorder: The United Nations and Internal Conflict*, Linda Miller, 235pp, 1967, Princeton, $10.00. An analysis of the role the United Nations has played and failed to play in internal wars.

5 – 96 *Nonintervention and International Order*, R.J. Vincent, 457pp, 1974, Princeton, $20.00. Attempts to refute current Soviet and U.S. justifications for intervening in internal wars and thus to reestablish the principle of nonintervention as the rule in international law.

J. Specific Tasks and Activities

TEW
5 – 97 *International Mediation: A Working Guide*, Roger Fisher & William Ury, 159pp, 1978, International Peace Academy, $10.00. "From the UN peacekeeper on the local scene to the head of State mediating between two sworn enemies, all future go-betweens can benefit enormously from this goldmine of common-sense advice" (Lincoln Bloomfield).

5 – 98 *Referendums: A Comparative Study of Practice & Theory*, David Butler & Austin Ranney (eds.), 250pp, 1978, American Enterprise Institute, $7.25. Devoted primarily to domestic issues, but with reference to referendums as a means of deciding who should rule.

5 – 99 *The United Nations in Bangladesh*, Thomas Oliver, 231pp, 1978, Princeton,

$17.50. A comprehensive report on the relief operation run by the U.N. Secretariat.

5 – 100 *The United Nations and the Human Environment,* Louis Sohn, Chairperson, 72pp, 1972, Commission to Study the Organization of Peace, $1.00. Outlines specific proposals for improving the U.N.'s ability to deal with threats to the environment; includes Marion McVitty's "Declaration of the Rights and Responsibilities of Individuals with Respect to the Environment They Share," and Quincy Wright's "Draft Declaration on the Human Environment."

5 – 101 *To Keep the Peace: The United Nations Condemnatory Resolution,* William Orbach, 155pp, 1977, U. Press of Kentucky, $14.50. Maintains that condemnatory resolutions combine moral and political judgments but do little to keep the peace.

5 – 102 *Conflict through Consensus, United Nations Approaches to Aggression,* Julius Stone, 234pp, 1977, Johns Hopkins, $14.50. In 1974 the U.N. General Assembly reached a consensus definition of aggression. This book provides an analysis of how this was possible and concludes the agreement reached is a "Pyrrhic achievement." It won't help and may be harmful.

5 – 103 *The Concept of Aggression in International Law,* Ann Thomas & A.J. Thomas, Jr. 114pp, 1972, Southern Methodist University, $6.95. Provides an introduction to the issue.

5 – 104 *International Economic Sanctions: The Cases of Cuba, Israel, and Rhodesia,* Donald Losman, 156pp, 1979, U. of New Mexico Press, $12.95. Maintains that while economic sanctions brought significant economic hardship in these cases; they were not politically successful.

K. The Law of the Sea

5 – 105 *The United Nations and the Bed of the Sea* (II), Richard Swift, Chairperson, 45pp, 1970, Commission to Study the Organization of Peace, $.75. Seeks to achieve a U.N. resolution declaring the "sea-bed and ocean floor, and the subsoil thereof . . . the common heritage of mankind" and to assure that development of sea bed resources benefits all mankind.

5 – 106 *Pacem in Maribus,* Elizabeth Mann Borgese (ed.), 382pp, 1972, Dodd, Mead, $10.00. Considers the problems of planning and development for an Ocean Regime, harvesting sea resources, international controls, demilitarization of the seabed, and control of the growing threat of pollution. Includes recent specific proposals.

5 – 107 *Law of the Sea: Caracas & Beyond,* Francis Christy, Jr., et al (eds.), 416pp, 1975, Ballinger, $20.00. A report on the Law of the Sea Conference at mid-point, outlining the many areas of agreement — coastal waterways, the 200-mile economic zone, rights of innocent passage through international waterways — and areas of disagreement — the authority to mine deep sea bed resources.

5 – 108 *Ocean Yearbook,* Elisabeth Mann Borgese & Norton Ginsburg (eds.), 713pp, 1980, Chicago, $35.00. A timely collection of recent writings on the uses, wealth, and resources of the oceans, with an extensive, often confusing series of documents, tables, and reports from organizations involved in ocean issues.

5 – 109 *International Law of the Sea; A Bibliography,* N. Papadakis, 432pp, 1980, Sijthoff & Noordhoff, $85.00. A bibliographical guide to the literature.

(See Also Chapter 14.)

L. U.N. Reform

5 – 110 *Reform of the U.N. Security Council,* Hanna Newcombe, 104pp, 1979, Peace Research Reviews, $5.00. A wide-ranging description of numerous proposals for reforming the Security Council, with two criteria offered for evaluating them: Which are most "efficacious in producing true improvement, and acceptable to the world's national leaders."

5 – 111 *President Carter's Report on the Reform and Restructuring of the United Nations System,* Reprinted by the Campaign for U.N. Reform, 11pp, 1978, $.25. The Administration's response to the Baker-McGovern U.N. Reform Rider requesting clarification of the Carter Administration's approach to U.N. reform.

5 – 112 *Elements of U.N. Reform,* Walter Hoffman (ed.), 96pp, 1977, Campaign for U.N. Reform, $5.00. Seventeen papers advocating significant reform and restructuring of the U.N. system to make it capable of imposing settlements, producing change, and solving global problems.

M. World Order and World Law

5 – 113 *Future Worlds,* Richard Falk, 62pp, 1976, Headline Series, $1.40. An imaginative discussion of the various actors, their possible power relations and the form of world order possible.

5 – 114 *Alternative Approaches to World Government,* II, Hanna Newcombe, 94pp, 1974, Peace Research Reviews, $4.00. Describes briefly 16 approaches to a world government in which law is substituted for violence, also that law is an expression of the "essential unity of mankind." Law may be achieved through U.N. charter revision, a constitutional convention, regional federations, institutions built parallel to the U.N., through the gradual expansion of international law and through an initiative by the non-aligned who align themselves to accept law; unity can be achieved in many ways.

5 – 115 *Global Challenges,* Harry Blaney, 288pp, 1979, New Viewpoints, $6.95. Contending kinds of doom and institutional fixes are reviewed here; the proposals for

voting powers in international institutions which reflect numbers and power are of special interest.

5 – 116 *The Court of Man: Introduction and Invitation,* Gerald Gottlieb, 28pp, 1973, Court of Man Foundation, free. A proposal for a world judiciary consisting of extranational courts of community.

5 – 117 *World Unification Plans and Analyses,* Hanna Newcombe, 1981, Peace Research Institute, $15.00. A collection of over 500 summaries of proposals for world government, world order, world unity, world community, and/or world citizenship.

Classic

5 – 118 *The Federalist Papers,* Alexander Hamilton, James Madison and John Jay, 559pp, 1961, (1788), New American Library, $2.50. In another setting, three experts on government consider the problems of federalism: How to resolve conflicting, often hostile, interests without violence. What is the relationship between the size of a territory and the type of government? How can the consent of the governed be achieved and, once achieved, be continually reaffirmed? How can liberty be defended and territorial integrity preserved?

5 – 119 *World Federalism: What? Why? How?,* Lawrence Abbott, 54pp, 1976, World Federalists, $1.00. A statement of the case for world federal authority to achieve world peace and promote change without war.

INF

5 – 120 *Introduction to World Peace through World Law,* Grenville Clark and Louis Sohn (revised by Louis Sohn 1973), 128pp, 1973, World Without War Publications, $1.50. Outlines the institutional and constitutional changes needed to make the U.N. or other international organization an effective, but limited world government. Relates the need for world economic development, world community, and processes for peaceful change.

5 – 121 *Memoirs of a Man, Grenville Clark,* Collected by Mark Clark Dimond, Norman Cousins, and J. Garry Clifford (eds.), 319pp, 1975, Norton, $10.00. Papers of a leading advocate of world peace through world law, and co-author of the most detailed plan for world law published in this century.

5 – 122 *The Practical Way to End Wars and Other World Crises,* Mia Lord, 30pp, 1978, Association of World Federalists, $1.00. For every problem an institution can be spelled out, a legal remedy found.

5 – 123 *Stop Global Drift,* William Sheehan, 131pp, 1978, Center for the Future, $5.00. Describes the institutional drift of the present and calls for a world federal government capable of resolving world problems.

5 – 124 *Freedom in a Federal World,* Everett Lee Millard, 253pp, 1970, 5th ed., Oceana, $6.00. An exploration of issues of world federalism with a draft revision of the U.N. Charter.

5– 125 *A Feasibility Study of World Government,* Theodore Caplow, 29pp, 1977, Stanley Foundation, free. Concludes that a world federation adequate to prevent war by disarming States and arming itself is "probably feasible under existing international conditions."

5– 126 *A Constitution for the Federation of Earth,* World Constituent Assembly, Innsbruck, Austria, 50pp, 1977, World Constitution and Parliament Association, $5.00. A constitution complete with parliament, world executive, administrative structure, and courts; all that is wanting is consent.

5– 127 *The Growth of World Law,* Percy Corbett, 216pp, 1971, Princeton, $13.50. Traces the development of legal institutions transcending the State which constitute the beginning of a framework of world law.

5– 128 *A Constitution for the World,* Elisabeth Mann Borgese (ed.), 112pp, 1965, Center for the Study of Democratic Institutions, $1.00. An attempt to formulate a constitution for a government that would eliminate war and establish the preconditions of justice. Originally drafted in 1948 by a committee headed by Robert Hutchins with Rexford Tugwell, Stringfellow Barr, Mortimer Adler, and others as members.

N. Reference Works

TEW

5– 129 *On the Creation of a Just World Order: Preferred Worlds for the 1990s,* Saul Mendlovitz (ed.), 1977, Macmillan, $6.95. Introduces the Institute for World Order's Model World Orders Project.

5– 130 *International Organization: An Interdisciplinary Bibliography,* Michael Hass, 944pp, 1973, Hoover, $35.00. A comprehensive reference work on institutionalized cooperation among States from ancient times to the present.

UNITED NATIONS AGENCIES

Food and Agriculture Organization of the United Nations (FAO)
Via delle Terme di Caracalla, Rome, Italy
To help countries increase food production and improve distribution, to coordinate the
Freedom from Hunger Campaign, and to help administer the World Food Program.

General Agreement on Tariffs and Trade (GATT)
United Nations, New York, NY 10017
To establish and maintain a code of conduct for international trade, to assist in removing
trade barriers, and to promote assistance to developing countries.

Inter-governmental Maritime Consultative Organization (IMCO)
101-4 Piccadilly, London W1V OAE, England
"Facilitates cooperation and exchange of information among governments on technical
    matters affecting shipping, with special responsibility for the safety of life at sea, high
    maritime standard and efficiency in navigation, and the prevention and control of
    maritime pollution caused by ships."

International Atomic Energy Agency (IAEA)
Kaerntnerring 11, A-1010 Vienna, Austria
Seeks the peaceful use of atomic energy through research, exchange of information,
    publication, establishment of safety standards, and application of safeguards for
    nuclear materials in many countries to ensure they are used for peaceful purposes.

International Civil Aviation Organization (ICAO)
100 Sherbrooke St. West, Montreal P.Q., Canada H3A 2R2
Promotes all aspects of international civil aeronautics, including the technology,
    economics, and legal aspects of the development of aviation.

International Development Association (IDA)
1818 H St., NW, Washington, DC 20433
"The IDA was created to promote economic development in the poorest of the develop-
    ing countries. IDA makes loans on terms that are more flexible and bear less heavily
    on the balance of payments than those of conventional loans."

International Finance Corporation (IFC)
1818 H St., NW, Washington, DC 20433
Promotes private enterprise in less developed member countries by providing risk capital
    without governmental guarantees.

International Fund for Agricultural Development (IFAD)
Via del Serafico 107, EUR, Rome, Italy
The fund helps finance food production and rural development.

International Labor Organization (ILO)
4, route des Morillions, CH 1211 Geneva 22, Switzerland
Works to improve labor conditions through meeting of workers, management, and
    governments.

International Monetary Fund (IMF)
700 19th St., NW, Washington, DC 20431
"The IMF was established to promote international cooperation on economic problems
    and is the major international mechanism for stabilizing currency exchange rates and
    for providing additional resources for countries with balance of payment problems."

International Telecommunication Union (ITU)
Place des Nations, 1211 Geneva 20, Switzerland
Promotes international cooperation for the improvement and use of telecommunica-
    tions.

United Nations Children's Fund (UNICEF)
United Nations, New York, NY 10017
"UNICEF assists developing countries to improve their basic services for children in
    health, nutrition, and education."

United Nations Conference on Trade and Development (UNCTAD)
Palais des Nations, 1211 Geneva 20, Switzerland
"Coordinates economic/social development of low-income countries."

United Nations Development Programme (UNDP)
One United Nations Plaza, New York, NY 10017
World's largest source of international technical cooperation for development.

United Nations Educational, Scientific and Cultural Organization (UNESCO)
7, Place de Fontenoy, 75700 Paris, France
UNESCO's aim is to stimulate progress in education, science, culture, and communica-
    tion. It encourages international cooperation in these fields by bringing experts
    together, by serving as a clearinghouse for pertinent materials, and by providing
    assistance to member states.

United Nations Environment Program (UNEP)
P.O. Box 30552, Nairobi, Kenya
Works to protect the human environment by promoting environmentally sound
    economic and social programs.

United Nations Fund for Drug Abuse Control (UNFDAC)
Palais des Nations, 1211 Geneva 20, Switzerland
"Strengthens international control of narcotics by helping governments to exercise
    supervision over production of narcotic drugs, to take measures to combat illicit
    traffic, and to reduce the demand for illicit drugs."

United Nations Fund for Population Activities (UNFPA)
485 Lexington Ave., New York, NY 10017
"Projects/publications; largest multilateral population agency."

United Nations Institute for Training and Research (UNITAR)
801 United Nations Plaza, New York, NY 10017
Established to carry out research and training programs to help developing nations.
    Researches all aspects of UN operations and policy, especially peace, security, and
    development.

Universal Postal Union (UPU)
Weltpoststrasse 4, 300 Berne 15, Switzerland
Provides for the organization and improvement of postal services and promotes interna-
    tional cooperation.

World Bank
1818 H St., NW, Washington, DC 20433
"Loans, especially for comprehensive rural development programs aimed at small
    farmers."

World Food Program (WFP)
Via delle Terme di Caracalla, Rome, Italy
"Contributions of food, cash and services are used to assist nations in pre-school and
    school feeding and in economic and social development projects, and to relieve
    emergency needs."

World Health Organization (WHO)
20, Avenue Appia, 1211 Geneva 27, Switzerland
"WHO coordinates health action on a global [basis and aims] to integrate primary health
    care into an overall development effort."

World Intellectual Property Organization (WIPO)
34, Chemin des Colombettes, 1211 Geneva 20, Switzerland
Works to gain international cooperation in the protection of intellectual property includ-
    ing trademarks, copyrights, inventions, and designs.

World Meteorological Organization (WMO)
41, Avenue Giuseppe Motta, 1211 Geneva 20, Switzerland
Promotes international cooperation in meteorology to standardize, coordinate, and
    improve activities and encourage exchange of weather-related information.

CHAPTER 6

WORLD COMMUNITY AND HUMAN RIGHTS

THE CONCEPT OF COMMUNITY

The word "community" has several meanings in political discussion. It can mean a "group of people living in the same locality under the same government" (*The Concept of Community,* 6-1), or it can refer to the locality itself. It can mean an attitude among people such as a "vague yearning for a commonality of desire, a communion with those around us, an extension of the bonds of kin and friends to all those who share a common fate with us." These meanings are interrelated in that a sense of community (the attitude) is essential to enable a community (the people) to form political institutions based on consent to manage the affairs of even a small village (the place). Here, the focus is on attitudes. The basic question is "Can the nascent sense of world community become emotionally and politically powerful enough to sustain instruments of world governance?"

An attitude or sense of community is something that is valued. Robert Nisbet describes it as follows:

Community involves relationships among individuals that are characterized by a high degree of personal intimacy, of social cohesion or moral commitment, and of continuity in time. The basis of community may be kinship, religion, political power, revolution or race. . . .All that is essential is that the basis be of sufficient appeal and of sufficient durability to enlist numbers of human beings, to arouse loyalties, and to stimulate an overriding sense of distinctive identity.[1]

It is a small step from "an overriding sense of distinctive identity" to a willingness to create and sustain political institutions. That step can be taken once there is recognition of the need to accomplish basic societal tasks, to resolve problems, to promote change, or to resolve conflict without violence.

A SENSE OF WORLD COMMUNITY AND WAR

The concept of community can be rendered meaningless in at least two ways. First, the existence of community at any level can be denied. Those who do so argue that political institutions are established by violence or force, are run by coercion, and that the political process is primarily a mechanism for deciding who gets what. Politics exists to allocate wealth, status and power. In such a worldview, loyalties can be aroused, "a distinctive identity" created as the product either of economic self-interest or submission to coercion. Community as a positive value is not, in this view, a meaningful political idea.

Second, the concept of community can be rendered meaningless by empty rhetoric. While some form of spiritual unity embracing all humanity is meaningful, it must be given substance in politics if it is to help end war, hunger, or gross human rights violations — the negations of world community.

As used here, a sense of world community is an attitude through which one claims a right to participate in world politics. It means that one has a "distinctive political identity" not only as a participant in local, state and national politics, but also in world politics. A sense of community at the national level involves an implicit agreement that law, not violence, should resolve disputes. The use of violence by individuals or groups violates that sense of community and triggers the application of legal constraints, including the use of police powers. Resort to violence is held to be an attack on the political process itself. From a sense of world community can come the expectation that conflicts will be resolved and change achieved through legal and political processes, not through war.

A politically effective sense of world community does not now exist. Could one State or group of States lead in its creation? Could a State act to end world hunger and lead in arms control and disarmament to demonstrate its commit-

[1]Nisbet, *The Social Philosophers*.

ment to law? Could that State's action elicit a positive response from other States? The central test of political community is: Can one actor accept risks, make sacrifices, demonstrate willingness to settle disputes, and reasonably expect adversaries to do so as well? What type of punitive and security measures would indicate clearly to such adversaries that the risks taken are for a mutually beneficial end and not an indication of weakness? To have a chance of success, such leadership must be sustained over a period of time; be composed of actions, not statements of intentions; and be realistic in its appraisal of the need for change in others as well as in itself. In addition, the initiating State would have to be creative in developing strategies that induce reciprocation from both its adversaries and its allies.

A politically effective sense of community has been created in many ways. Sometimes a sense of community originates as diverse people unite against a common enemy. Common inspiration by new ideas, or functional cooperation to resolve problems, also make unity by consent possible. Sometimes unity comes from submission to force. Since today neither America, the Soviet Union, nor any other power appear capable of imposing a world order, world community must arise from consent.

NATIONALISM VERSUS SUPRANATIONALISM

The "nationalists" argue that we cannot expect to see global political institutions in this century. A sense of community, in this view, cannot be created — it must develop over a long period of time. Nationalism is the emotional bond which most effectively integrates political communities and gives most people their sense of political identification. Attempts to build political loyalties beyond the State will not produce stronger international or supranational institutions but will, instead, undermine the only political units capable of addressing current problems and resolving conflicts. For nationalists today, the critical issue is how to maintain or develop effective national communities.

Nationalism has arisen from many different sources and takes many different forms (Hans Kohn, *The Age of Nationalism*, 6-63). Its most obvious form, from which the name is derived, is an ethnic group or nation whose members intermarry, which has a common linguistic, historical, and cultural tradition, and for which the creation of common political institutions is but one more expression of their homogeneity. Most European States are such homogeneous "nations." Such States have either remained homogeneous, or the strongest ethnic group within them has assimilated the others and instilled its own linguistic, cultural, and political traditions.

According to Walter Connor, however, most of the world's States today are not homogeneous: " . . . of a total of 132 contemporary states, only 12 (9.1%) can be described as essentially homogeneous from an ethnic viewpoint."[2] Most African States today had their borders drawn by colonial powers without regard to linguistic, ethnic, or natural boundaries. Others States are composed of different ethnic groups which migrated from other places. Some States are the current embodiments of old empires or the result of the conquest of many diverse groups, as is the Soviet Union. Nationalism takes a variety of forms: it can exclude ethnic diversity and be xenophobic; it can be a defense against the imposition of external domination; it can be a weapon against separatist purposes and functions (Snyder, *Varieties of Nationalism*, 6-64). But in any case, it is at the State level that nationalism is likely to remain an effective political idea.

The supranationalists concede that the search for effective political organization begins with the different forms of nationalism in the world today, and that it is necessary to study how States have been formed in the past. They feel that there is a growing sense of global political identity, that a sense of world community develops as transactions across State lines increase. Trade, communications, and travel activity all indicate that people are reaching out across State barriers. Space exploration, and world ecological and food problems provide occasions for cooperative activities in which ideological and national interests are, or can be, subordinated to world interests. Each transaction across a State line provides an opportunity for strengthening the sense of unity essential to sustain legal and political authority on the world level. Such an authority, legitimized by freely given consent, is the central requisite of lasting peace.

A sense of world community can grow in many ways. It is strengthened by the image of the planet earth as shown in pictures taken from outer space. It is strengthened as satellite TV enables half the world to enjoy in common the experience of seeing, for example, the World Cup soccer finals. Scientists from many States strengthen it when they research common problems, and share their knowledge in ways which eclipse national and ideological boundaries. It is expressed in conferences addressing common problems and in student exchanges. It is present in a growing number of documents of international law — the Universal Declaration of Human Rights is one important example — addressed to all governments and affirming common standards for all States. The sense of world community has always been a product of those aesthetic and religious experiences that affirm our common humanity.

[2] "National Building or Nation-Destroying?", Walter Connor, *World Politics,* No. 24, April 1972, p. 320.

This sense of world community is emerging slowly, the supranationalist contends. It is set back by every act of war, for the sense of community is broken when violence, not law or other nonviolent processes of change, resolve conflicts. Perhaps the sense of community needed to sustain supranational institutions is growing too slowly to enable the timely development of political and legal structures which are capable of managing international conflict without violence. Without such structures, progress in economic development is hostage to the ever-present threat of war.

Exactly, respond the nationalists, because when vital issues are confronted, the State remains the only actor capable of providing security. Whatever degree of world community exists today, it is clearly ineffective as a political force in controlling the threat or use of the organized mass violence of war. Whatever measure of security we can achieve now, the nationalists insist, will be achieved through a balance of power between States.

The supranationalists respond that the existing armed truce, broken by intermittent warfare and overshadowed by the threat of a devastating nuclear war, should not be confused with security. A cataclysm has broken down old economic and social forms, and new levels of political organization are necessary. The technological changes which are transforming industry and society also force a new time-table for altering political structures. Despite the current withdrawal into national shells, there is a recognition that the new interconnections of States are both real and threatening. It is real in that new problems have arisen which no single State can solve alone. It is threatening because one State can now significantly influence another and may do so in detrimental ways. Community is built by positive and mutually beneficial interactions which are not assured by the fact of interdependence; that fact only makes community possible.

Thus, harsh disagreement remains between the nationalists and the supranationalists. These disagreements, as well as some areas of agreement, emerge if we look into the question of human rights promotion.

HUMAN RIGHTS

It is in the definition of human rights that the relationship between the individual and political authority is regulated. Thus, the attempt since World War II to define international human rights in the Universal Declaration of Human Rights (1948), two implementing Covenants (1965) and a series of conventions could be a major contribution to creating a sense of world community. There are, however, significant disagreements within the world community about these questions:

1. What is a human right?
2. Should some human rights be given precedence over others?
3. How should human rights be effectively enforced?
4. Has the international human rights movement succeeded in improving the enjoyment of human rights?

WHAT IS A HUMAN RIGHT?

There are a number of different ideas about what constitutes a human right. To some, human rights arise from the nature of human beings and are inherent in what it means to be truly free. In this view, the State's role is limited to defending the individual's rights against violation by others. Human rights define an area in which the individual, not the State, is sovereign. Thus, the fundamental rights of the individual are viewed as existing independently of the State and as superior to State power. This philosophy is expressed in the Bill of Rights of the U.S. Constitution. A second conception of human rights maintains that they are whatever is agreed to by the State, they are granted by the State, and are necessarily subordinated to the power of the State. In this conception, all good things can be rights; the most common, however, are the right to food and other economic necessities as well as rights of property, security, and political freedom. The contrast between these two types of rights is sometimes described as the difference between ''negative'' and ''positive'' rights, between ''procedural'' and ''substantive,'' or between ''natural'' and ''contractual'' rights.

This dispute about the nature of human rights finds expression in the discussion of whether ''economic rights'' complement or supersede ''civil and political rights,'' or whether they should be considered rights at all. Here are two statements expressing different views about the scope of human rights:

A. The language and concepts of human rights cannot be restricted to the traditional North Atlantic civil and political liberties, nor the question of government in its relationship to individuals. ''Human rights'' must include those fundamental claims to food, work, medical care, education, and culture that are primary requisites of a *human* life.

B. The language and concepts of human rights should be reserved to the arena of political and civil liberties. Other language and concepts will serve us better in seeking to meet other basic human needs. This is because there is a difference between the essential goals of any enlightened political community, and the identification of those goals as entitlements to be delivered primarily by governments under the rubric of ''human rights.'' Government may not be the best way to reach those goals, and the price of giving government this power may be a serious encroachment on the civil and political liberties that define a democratic society.[3]

The dispute concerning the nature of human rights is far from over.

WHICH HUMAN RIGHTS SHOULD BE GIVEN PRIORITY?

This disagreement about the nature of rights finds expression in the international human rights movement. In U.S. constitutional law, our courts generally rule in favor of civil and political rights; but in the Soviet Union and in many developing countries, priority is given to the achievement of economic rights or goals. These types of rights are segregated in the two international human rights Covenants. Their language reflects the disagreement about priorities by stating that the economic, social, and cultural rights are to be ''progressively realized'' while civil and political rights ''ought to be respected.''

HOW WELL ARE INTERNATIONAL HUMAN RIGHTS ENFORCED?

International agencies have weak enforcement authority to uphold the more than 100 principles now defined as international human rights. An individual must exhaust domestic remedies before submitting a human rights complaint to an international agency, such as the International Labour Organization, the Organization of American States, or a U.N. agency. Each organization has different enforcement procedures. A human rights complaint is heard by the U.N. Human Rights Commission only if there is a consistent pattern of gross human rights violations, and then only if the Commission agrees to hear the complaint. For years, human rights violations in Idi Amin's Uganda were not heard by the Commision despite the fact that the International Commission of Jurists had discovered over 50,000 murders by Uganda's soldiers. There is not, in short, a judicial remedy for human rights violations in the present interna-

---

[3]These two statements were formulated by Robert Pickus and George Weigel, and presented in the ''International Human Rights Quotient, an Organizational Assessment Tool,'' which is reprinted in its entirety as Resource for Action, Chapter 21, Resource F.

tional structures,[4] although human rights seminars, public hearings, charges of violations and publications may act as restraining influences *(International Human Rights Kit,* 6-110).

HAS THE ENJOYMENT OF HUMAN RIGHTS IMPROVED?

There are different criteria for assessing performance just as there are different judgments about the nature and priority of human rights. Annual assessments of each country's commitment to human rights began in the 1970s when non-governmental organizations (Amnesty International, Freedom House, and the Overseas Development Council) issued separate country-by-country reports. Freedom House noted modest overall progress in the enjoyment of civil and political rights during the 1970s. The Overseas Development Council developed a Physical Quality of Life Index (PQLI) to assess national economic performance (which is suggestive of a commitment to economic rights).[5] This index too measured modest progress in the 1970s. Given the prevalence of hunger, torture (Amnesty International, *Report on Torture,* 6-136), human massacre and widespread murder of political opponents, few indeed can argue that the current international institutions are effective promoters of human rights. No sustained positive trend is discernible for the period.

Those interested in human rights consider the ''right of self-determination'' as critical. One study in the late 1960s predicted that over 70% of the violent conflicts in the 1970s would be between groups (usually different ethnic groups), one of which claimed the right to use violence to achieve the ''right of self-determination.''[6]

Ethnic conflict may be of many different kinds: in some cases, the goal is broader assimilation into the community — as in the civil rights movement in the United States. In other cases, violence may be considered justified by groups seeking to separate themselves from an existing State, as in Canada (Quebec), Spain (Basques), and Ethiopia (Eritrea), among others. Irredentist movements also seek the right of self-determination, usually to unite members

---

[4]The European Human Rights Court is an exception, although here, too, domestic remedies must first be exhausted.

[5]The Overseas Development Council does not use the language of human rights in discussing the utility of the PQLI.

[6]Steven Rosen (ed.), *A Survey of World Conflicts* (Pittsburgh, Pa,: University of Pittsburgh Center for International Studies, 1969).

of a single ethnic group living in different countries. This uniting would be in an existing State (the Somalis) or by forming a new State out of parts of two or more existing States (the Kurds in Iran, Iraq, and Turkey).

Procedures for achieving the right of self-determination have rarely been discussed in inter-governmental forums, much less worked out. The Organization of African Unity (OAU), for example, is committed to the existing boundaries, and thus has not taken up issues of self-determination, despite gross violations of human rights. States in other areas of the world have been equally reluctant to consider claims to self-determination *(Terrorism and Political Self-Determination,* 6-108).

In short, there has been significant progress toward the definition of human rights, but little toward their enforcement. When vital issues, such as the control of territory, are considered, the nationalist case is stronger. The right of self-determination, for example, is usually championed only by those who want it for themselves or wish to use it against their enemies.

POLITICAL INTEGRATION

Is there any hope that an authority beyond the State will become effective in the enforcement of human rights or in other areas of public life? Those who wish to build new political communities maintain that there is, and point to a number of forces helpful to the formation of new States: a common ethnic or racial background, a common language, a common cultural and religious tradition, a shaping historical experience, and continuity over time (Karl Deutsch, *Nationalism and Social Communication,* 6-2). Each can help form the bond and commitment which constitute a sense of community.

While theorists of political integration agree that all these forces help create a sense of community, they disagree about the importance of each. The historical experience of World War II, for example, brought to fruition a sense of community adequate to gain acceptance of the United Nations. Many believed that the destructiveness of the war and the cooperation required to win it would override different religious, cultural, and political traditions and make possible political organization at the world level. The breakdown of the war-time alliance disappointed those who say that the United Nations is the first step toward global organization and the formation of a world government. Neither the historical experience nor the fear of nuclear war has been a sufficiently strong integrative force to offset ideological and national rivalry.

FUNCTIONAL POLITICAL INTEGRATION

When this hope for world government failed, a new approach was developed. The functional approach to political integration seeks to define:

> . . . the process whereby political actors in distinct national settings are persuaded to shift their loyalties, expectations, and political activities toward a new and larger center, whose institutions . . . demand jurisdiction over the pre-existing national states.[7]

Building a sense of community adequate to sustain supranational institutions is possible, in the functional view, by identifying in separate sectors (economic, social, political, or security), the tasks which different States can agree to undertake jointly. Successful cooperation in one sector is expected to spill over into others as the sense of community is strengthened. The Western European process of integration is the best example and illustrates the functional-integrationist theory.

STEPS TOWARD EUROPEAN POLITICAL INTEGRATION

The process of integrating Western Europe began with the Brussels Treaty of 1948, under which Britain, France, Belgium, the Netherlands, and Luxembourg agreed to consult with each other on mutual defense matters. In 1949, the United States led in forming NATO (North Atlantic Treaty Organization), which originally included twelve States. Later West Germany, Greece, and Turkey joined. Concurrently, the Marshall Plan reduced tariff barriers and currency controls among Western States, and called for the creation of a European Common Market. These effective economic measures established supranational supervisory agencies in France, Italy, Western Germany, Belgium, the Netherlands, and Luxembourg. Success there made possible the creation of the Common Market in 1957, which established free movement of labor and capital among members and a uniform tariff system for non-members. In addition, the Common Market was a deliberate step toward European economic integration and political unity. The Council of Europe, established in 1949, created a European Parliament whose representatives were originally elected by national parliaments, but now directly by the citizens of each member country. The Courts of the Council of Europe have the power to hear cases brought by individuals against States, and, in that respect, are supranational institutions.

[7]Ernst Haas, *Beyond the Nation-State.*

The steps toward Western European political integration have, however, slowed, and national decision-making remains the predominant reality. The time-table for developing a single currency has been abandoned. One of the developers of integration theory, Ernst Haas, has now concluded "the existing half-way house cannot last, for substantive as well as procedural reasons" (Haas, *The Obsolescence of Regional Integration Theory*, 6-73); either the momentum toward unification will be regained, or it will have to be recognized that integration in the military and economic sectors has not spilled over into the political sector.

Opinions vary about why this momentum toward integration has been lost. Some argue that the changed relationship with the Soviet Union has altered perceptions of Europe's role; others point out that without a secure energy source, Europe cannot itself be an independent political voice. Even so, the sense of community expressed as a political identification remains an important attitude among many Europeans; more than 50% believe that specific issues (negotiations, energy, economic issues . . .) could best be resolved by European, not national, authority *(Domestic Political Realities and European Unification,* 6-81).

Students of European political integration conclude that functional cooperation in one sector does not guarantee cooperation in other areas. What is essential is that a sense of world community be added to, and not substituted for, individual political identification with a State. Only then can the institutions needed to conduct and resolve conflicts without violence become effective. The stakes in doing so are high, as Hugh Seton-Watson recently wrote:

> The survival of human civilization depends on the recognition of both sets of truth: that neither absolute state sovereignty nor the abolition of national identities is possible; that there must be a balance between national cultures and interstate cooperation, no less than a balance between class interests and interclass cooperation within nations, if destructive civil wars and nuclear holocausts are to be avoided. It may be that the vast bulk of the human race care not for any of these things. That does not absolve those who do know and do care from making an effort. . . .[8]

BIBLIOGRAPHY

The bibliography in this section offers books about the concept of community and political integration. It includes assessments of nationalism, functional

[8]*Nations and States,* p.485 (6-66).

integration theory, and European integration practice. In addition, works on the international human rights movement and on ethnic conflict are presented. Among the questions the reader will want to explore further are the following: 1) Is the concept of a sense of community meaningful? 2) Have effective political institutions ever been created without a pre-existing sense of community? How? 3) Which experiences in world politics strengthen, and which weaken, the sense of community today? 4) What problems, besides war, hunger and torture, now exist in world politics which make a sense of community difficult, if not impossible, to sustain? 5) Could one State lead in overcoming those problems in such a way as to induce a supportive response from other States? 6) What is the nature of human rights? 7) What different conceptions of human rights are embodied in international human rights instruments? 8) Are these conceptions mutually reinforcing or incompatible? 9) Why is violence so frequently involved in ethnic conflicts? 10) Are the steps toward political integration in Europe suggestive of a process that could be duplicated at the world level or are they unique?

A. The Concept

6 – 1 *The Concept of Community, Readings with Interpretations,* David Minar and Scott Greer (eds.), 370pp, 1969, Aldine, O.P. An anthology which presents different forms of community: political, cultural, artistic, and utopian. The editors present works which answer these questions: What is the character of community in different settings? What is the relationship of politics to community? What is the prospect for community in today's changing world?

INF

6 – 2 *Nationalism and Social Communication, An Inquiry into the Foundations of Nationality,* Karl Deutsch, 345pp, 1966, (1953), MIT Press, $8.95. A pioneer in the study of nationalism, Deutsch examines here the resilience of the idea, its many contemporary forms and uses, the features which make possible and which inhibit the formation of new political communities.

6 – 3 *Peace in the Family of Man,* Lester Pearson, 104pp, 1968, Oxford University Press, O.P. Pearson succinctly argues that "the rationale for change from a military deterrence system of security to one based on a sense of world community sustaining international organizations has been established. The will to make it has not" (p. 54).

6 – 4 *Dynamics of International Relations,* Ernst Haas and Allen Whiting, 557pp, 1956, 1975, Greenwood Press, $31.50. An older text still useful for its focus on the means used to achieve objectives and for the emphasis given to integration.

6 – 5 *Power and Community in World Politics,* Bruce Russett, 372pp, 1974, W.H. Freeman, $4.95. The distinction between four types of world community is of special

interest: unification through 1) construction of common institutions, 2) a transference of loyalty, 3) acceptance of peaceful settlement of disputes, and 4) through a responsiveness to others expressed in joint problem solving.

6– 6 *The Global Community: A Brief Introduction to International Relations,* Andrew Axline & James Stegenga, 196pp, 1972, Harper & Row, $8.95. Introduces integration theory and assesses the prospect at the global level.

INF
6– 7 *A History of the Modern World,* Robert Palmer & Joel Colton, 2 vols, 1977 (5th ed.), Knopf, $19.95. European ideals (the State, bureaucracy, science, democracy, the alleviation of suffering, and progress) are considered basic to the formation of a global civilization.

6– 8 *Birthright of Man, An Anthology of Texts on Human Rights,* Jeanne Hersch (ed.), 590pp, 1969, UNESCO, $12.00. Thousands of fragments of thoughts from 3,000 B.C. to 1948 illustrate the many sources of the Universal Declaration of Human Rights.

6– 9 *The Political Community, A Study of Anomie,* Sebastian de Grazia, 258pp, 1978, (1948), Chicago, $10.00. The classic study of alienation and of the search for a sense of community: "men stand today in the twilight zone of a society uneasy, distressed, feeling joined to their fellows only in war or crises . . .they stand as 'individual,' which is all they can ever be in a society."

6– 10 *The Case for Modern Man,* Charles Frankel, 240pp, 1971 (1952), Beacon, $2.95. An optimist's reflections on the capacity of humans to transcend evil, a critique of Toynbee's pessimism and a suggestion of how to cope.

B. Forms of Community — Social

6– 11 *The Atlas of Man,* Andre Singer, 272pp, 1978, St. Martin's, $25.00. A detailed survey of human geography: some 400 societies, the tribal, ethnic, racial, and national groupings of humanity, illustrated with photographs, maps, and charts.

6– 12 *The Structure of Political Geography,* Roger Kasperson & Julian Minghi (eds.), 527pp, 1969, Aldine, $17.95. An anthology seeking common elements in the organization of States, patterns of integration, transfers of sovereignty, how States perceive each other, rankings, and communication patterns.

6– 13 *The Meaning of the Twentieth Century: The Great Transition,* Kenneth Boulding, 199pp, 1964, Harper & Row. $3.50. An examination of the transition from civilization to "post civilization" (technological society). Calls for research on the problems of war and overpopulation which are seen as the main obstacles to the successful transition.

6– 14 *The Social System of the Planet Earth,* Kenneth Boulding, Elsie Boulding, & Guy Burgess, 233pp, 1980 (1977), Addison Wesley, $10.95. Introduces social science concepts through the medium of an alien's report after visiting the planet.

6 – 15 *Progress for a Small Planet,* Barbara Ward, 305pp, 1979, Norton, $13.95. Progress requires "the application to the planetary community" of certain "basic principles which govern and harmonize domestic society."

6 – 16 *The Commonwealth of Man: An Inquiry into Power Politics & World Government,* Frederick Schuman, 1977 (1972), Greenwood, $27.00. Focuses on the power struggle and how it might be contained once diverted into political institutions.

6 – 17 *The Family of Man,* Edward Steichen, 1980 (1955), New American Library, $4.95. A compilation of photographs depicting things all people share — birth, youth, joy, suffering, aging, and death.

6 – 18 *The Family of Women,* A Ridge Press Book, 1979, Grosset and Dunlap, $14.95. Focuses on common experiences of women.

6 – 19 *The Human Connection,* Ashley Montagu & Floyd Matson, 228pp, 1981, McGraw-Hill, $4.95. Explores the universals in nonverbal communication and the provocative signals our bodies send.

6 – 20 *Kings or People, Power and the Mandate to Rule,* Reinhard Bendix, 692pp, 1978, Calif., $9.95. A historical introduction to the shifting basis of legitimate political authority.

6 – 21 *A World Federation of Cultures: An African Perspective,* Ali Mazrui, 508pp, 1976, Macmillan, $14.95. Argues that the emergence of a world culture stimulates the design of separate sovereignties; offers speculation on the origins and nature of religion, government, and society in a pluralistic world society.

6 – 22 *World Communications: A 200-Country Survey of Press, Radio, Television, and Film,* UNESCO, 533pp, 1975, Gower Press, $21.00. A brief summary of the types, numbers and audiences of different communications media in each country, without discussion of quality or control of content.

6 – 23 *Operating Manual for Spaceship Earth,* R. Buckminister Fuller, 127pp, 1977, Dutton, $3.95. A diagnosis of the causes of environmental stress and a query whether humanity can adapt.

6 – 24 *Constructing Alternative World Futures: Reordering the Planet,* Louis Beres & Harry Targ, 264pp, 1977, Shenkman, $6.95. Identifies the elements of a universal culture and considers the institutions that are desirable and possible in it.

6 – 25 *The Everyman Project: A World Report on the Resources from Humane Society,* Robert Jungk, 1977, Liverright, $10.95. Argues that alternatives to fossil fuel energy resources exist and should be exploited.

6 – 26 *World Society,* John Burton, 250pp, 1972, Cambridge, $7.50. A definition of a field of inquiry — the make-up of world society.

6 – 27 *Superpowers and Victims: The Outlooks for World Community,* Charlotte Waterlow, 181pp, 1974, Prentice-Hall, $2.95. Discusses the massive problems that

developing States face and the aids and obstacles put in their way by industrialized countries. Calls for semi-supranational global institutions, an international police force, world economic planning, and the development of more functional agencies.

C. Forms of Community: Ideas and Values

6 – 28 *Goals in a Global Community,* Ervin Lazlo & Judah Bierman, Vol, I, *Studies on the Conceptual Foundation,* 349pp, 1977, Pergamon, $27.50, Vol. II, *The International Values and Goals Studies,* 566pp, 1978, Pergamon, $44.00.

6 – 29 *In the Minds of Men,* UNESCO, 1946-71, 319pp, 1972, UNESCO, $5.30. Fifteen contributors reflect on the contribution of UNESCO in its first twenty-five years to the life of the mind.

6 – 30 *Ideological Differences and World Order: Studies in the Philosophy and Sciences of the World's Cultures,* Filmer Northrop, 1971 (1949), Greenwood $20.25. A search for the universal in the particular.

6 – 31 *The Inner Limits of Mankind: Historical Reflections on Today's Values, Culture and Politics,* Ervin Laszlo, 79pp, 1978, Pergamon, $7.50. Suggests that deeper values may underlie current commitments and thus unite diverse traditions.

6 – 32 *Earth at Omega: Passage to Planetization,* Donald Keys, 1981, Branden Press, $9.95. A collection of articles seeking a "paradigm shift" from national to planetary consciousness with great expectations that the global political institutions then possible will be more humane and efficient than those currently commanding allegiance.

6 – 33 *The Revolt of the Masses,* Jose Ortega Y Gasset, 190pp, 1957, Norton, $2.25. An analysis of a time which considers itself "modern" and thus the culmination of the past; every political faction claims to meet the needs of the people; that is an inadequate moral standard.

6 – 34 *Goals for Mankind, A Report to the Club of Rome on the New Horizons of Global Community,* Ervin Laszlo, 374pp, 1978, Signet, $2.50. Identifies the goals of major States and regions as well as international and transnational actors. The concluding section seeks a grand synthesis.

6 – 35 *Humankind,* Peter Farb, 528pp, 1980, Bantam, $3.95. An anthropological look at what we know about our species — human nature, adaptability, variety, mind, and society.

6 – 36 *The Human Quality,* Aurelio Peccei, 216pp., 1977, Pergamon Press, $6.95. An optimist's credo which analyzes the human condition in universal terms and closes with a ringing call for mankind to undertake six missions to escape from the current predicament (see Club of Rome, "Limit of Growth" argument). Peccei calls for exploring the 1) outer limits, for example, the carrying capacity of the environment, 2) the inner limits of biological and psychic stress, 3) the cultural heritage, 4) world community, 5) the human habitat, and 6) the production establishment.

6–37 *Men and Nations,* Louis Halle, 228pp, 1962, Princeton Univ. Press, $5.95. A philosophical search for the basis of community, which concludes by identifying as essential ingredients, tolerance, progressive revelation, and the continuing search for the ultimately unknowable truth.

6–38 *Twilight of Authority,* Robert Nisbet, 287pp, 1975, Oxford Univ. Press, $4.95. Maintains that people once naturally sacrificed for the State, but that now authority appears arbitrary, bureaucratic and militaristic. The trends toward local and ethnic identity, and to voluntary associations, are welcome precursors to the establishment of legitimate authority.

6–39 *World Prehistory in New Perspective,* John Grahame Clark, 1977, Cambridge, $11.95. Presents the common origins of humankind.

6–40 *The Ascent of Man,* Jacob Bronowski, 448, 1974, Little, Brown, $8.95. A cultural, pictorial overview of the evolution of human society with emphasis on human ingenuity and intelligence. Sees the idea in the artifact.

6–41 *Modernization and the Transformation of International Relations,* Edward Morse, 203pp, 1976, Macmillan, $14.95. Argues that the current era in international relations is unique because of ''the great upheavals that international society has witnessed in recent years.'' Among the upheavals are population growth, secularization, scientific thought, technological innovation, economic interdependence, fragmentation of systems of ideas, rapid change, (fostered more by the Western than the Soviet impact on developing societies), growth of transnational activities, and a changed sense of geography of one's place. While rapid evolution of international relations is considered certain, the goals one should seek remain an enigma amidst this upheaval.

6–42 *Civilization in Crisis: Human Prospects in a Changing World,* Joseph Camilleri, 303pp, 1976, Cambridge, $9.95. A global reform strategy based on a new life-affirming ethos, which combines ''civilian defense'' (nonviolent, national defense) and planetary reorganization made possible by an emerging, unitary world culture.

6–43 *The Quest for World Order,* Robert Angell, 186pp, 1979, U. of Michigan, $4.95. A progress report on the ''new internationalism.''

6–44 *The Development of the Democratic Idea, Readings from Pericles to the Present,* Charles Sherover (ed.), 587pp, 1974, rev. ed, Mentor, $2.50. Unified by the theme that democracy is the only political alternative to repression. Classical and modern essays make the case for democracy.

6–45 *Power Maps: Comparative Politics of Constitutions,* Ivo Duchacek, 252pp, 1973, ABC-CLIO, $5.95. A study of 130 national constitutions which finds them alike in maintaining that power originates with the people and that authority should be divided among legislative, judicial and executive branches of government. Duchacek maintains that a constitution is ''the official blueprint for the use of public power'' and identifies that constitutional provisions which permit authoritarian executives to usurp the powers of the other branches; nonetheless, the form of constitutional government is now universal, he maintains.

D. Functional Tasks

6– 46 *The Seventh Enemy,* Ronald Higgins, 1979, McGraw Hill, $12.50. Assesses the cumulative impact of six global crises — population, food resources, environment, nuclear power, and technological innovation — but calls the seventh the most deadly: institutional inertia.

6– 47 *Guide on the Global Observing System,* World Meterological Association, 1978, UNIPUB, $42.00. A detailed discussion of how an international agency accomplishes a task beneficial to all countries: weather forecasting.

6– 48 *Refugees: A Problem of our Time, The Work of the United Nations High Commissioner for Refugees; 1951 – 1972,* Louis Holborn, 1525pp, 1975 (2 vols.), Scarecrow Press, $50.00 (set). Describes one consequence of war, famine, and human rights violations: refugees, and the role of the UN High Commissioner acting on behalf of the world community to ease the problem.

6– 49 *Disaster Assistance, Appraisal, Reform and New Approaches, UNA – USA,* 337pp, 1979, New York University Press, $8.95. Aims to make multilateral responses more effective.

6– 50 *The Politics of Natural Disaster, The Case of the Sahel Drought,* Michael Glantz, 340pp. 1976, Praeger, $22.50. Emphasizes the shortcomings and political motivation of relief efforts in the Sahel, but, nonetheless, indicates the natural and human contributions to help the victims of drought and famine.

6– 51 *The Politics of Starvation,* Jack Shepherd, 101pp, 1975, Carnegie Endowment for International Peace, $3.00. Details the widespread famine in Ethiopia from 1973 – 1975, and condemns the governments, the U.N., and other relief agencies for the initial cover-up. It also deplores the meager response both to the immediate crisis and to the resulting long-term consequences. A postscript by Steven Green offers reforms of the international relief agencies.

E. World Communications

6– 52 *World Communications, Threat or Promise: A Socio-Technical Approach,* Colin Cherry, 229pp, 1978, Wiley, $14.50. Assesses the influence of the rapidly expanding global communications network on international relations.

6– 53 *A Free and Balanced Flow, Report of the Twentieth Century Task Force on the International Flow of News,* 296pp, 1978, Lexington, $5.75. An assessment of Western dominance of world news sources and of proposals for reform.

6– 54 *Propaganda, Towards Disarmament in the War of Words,* John Whitton and Arthur Larson, 305pp, 1964, Oceana, $15.00. Maintains that most propaganda is disseminated by States and concludes that the antidote is greater freedom of information, a code of ethics, the right of reply, and a U.N. broadcasting system.

6 – 55 *Mass News Media and the Third World Challenge,* Leonard Sussman, 80pp, 1977, Sage, $3.50. An assessment of the complaints of Western press agencies, a description of the Soviet effort to get government control of news sanctioned by UNESCO and some suggestions.

6 – 56 *American Communication in a Global Society,* Glen Fisher, 161pp, 1979, Ablex, $17.50. Argues that the world is an interdependent, global society that is greatly influenced by media originating in the U.S.

6 – 57 *National Sovereignty and International Communication: A Reader*, Kaarle Nordenstreng & Herbert Schiller (eds), 304pp, 1979, Ablex, $27.50. Readings presenting Western and third world views on communication. The third world viewpoints maintain Western methods violate their sovereignty.

6 – 58 *The Geopolitics of Information: How Western Culture Dominates the* World, Anthony Smith, 192pp, 1980, Oxford, $13.95. Maintains that cultural differences underlie the imbalance between what first and third world leaders believe constitutes news.

6 – 59 *The Politics of East-West Communication in Europe,* 180pp, 1979, Renouf, $27.00. Explores how Basket Three of the Helsinki Final Act has influenced non-official communication between East and West. Modest changes at best have resulted.

F. The Creation of Community

TEW
6 – 60 *The Sahara Forest and Other Superordinate Goals,* Gene Keyes & Scott Seymour, 62pp, 1975, Canadian Peace Research Reviews, $4.00. A superordinate goal is one which two or more groups want but neither can obtain alone; this work identifies how the achievement of superordinate goals can build a sense of community. The first task: forest the Sahara desert.

6 – 61 *Caribbean Integration, The Politics of Regional Negotiations,* Andrew Axline, 225pp, 1979, Nichols, $23.50. Introduces political integration theory and applies it in the Caribbean.

6 – 62 *A History of Thought on Economic Integration,* Fritz Machlup, 323pp, 1977, Columbia, $20.00. More like a dictionary than a text; the author defines terms and the main ideas concerning economic integration, and then provides annotated lists of the contributions to the ideas made by scholars, diplomats, and organizational leaders.

G. Nationalism

6 – 63 *The Age of Nationalism: The First Era of Global History,* Hans Kohn, 172 pp, 1976 (1962) Greenwood, $14.50. A basic introduction.

6 – 64 *Varieties of Nationalism, A Comparative Study,* Louis Snyder, 326 pp, 1976, Holt, Rinehart & Winston, $9.95. A valuable introduction to the origins, history, types and persistence of nationalism. It indicates how the same idea has aided in the creation of as well as the destruction of States, and has both led to war and prevented it. Includes a twenty-three page bibliography on nationalism.

6 – 65 *The Nationalization of the Masses: Political Symbolism and Mass Movements in Germany, from the Napoleonic Wars through the Third Reich,* George Mosse, 252pp, 1975, Fertig, $18.50. A study of the myths and symbols which have proved effective in manipulating people in modern politics.

6 – 66 *Nations and States: An Inquiry into the Origins of Nations and the Politics of Nationalism,* Hugh Seton-Watson, 563pp, 1977, Westview, $32.50. A study of the "formation of nations, the activities of nationalist movements, and the ways in which these have influenced and been influenced by the emergence, creation and dissatisfaction of states." While States come and go, Seton-Watson concludes, "nations . . . with their own speech and culture and belief and institutions . . . are virtually indestructible" (p. 482).

6 – 67 *The New Nationalism, Implications for Transatlantic Relations,* Werner Link & Werner Feld (eds.), 165pp, 1979, Pergamon, $7.95. The new nationalism, "contrary to classical nationalism, which is usually of an aggressive nature, . . . tends to be rather defensive and inward-looking in character" (p. 2). Coordination, not integration, is, therefore, the only feasible objective.

6 – 68 *Nationalism in the Twentieth Century,* Anthony Smith, 257pp, 1979, NYU Press, $8.95. Traces the various forms and politics of nationalistic feeling in European history, notes the resurgence of ethnic identities, and considers the future of inter-nationalism and supranationalism. But since nationalism provides internal cohesion and since world politics provides losses for those who break with nationalism, Smith sees little hope of limiting nationalism.

6 – 69 *The Problem of Partition: Peril to World Peace,* Thomas Hachey (ed.), 259pp, 1972, Rand McNally, O.P. An anthology analyzing the strengths and weaknesses of the partition solution to the problems of Ireland, Korea, Germany, India/Pakistan/ Bangladesh, Vietnam and Palestine/Israel.

H. Regional Integration

Intro

6 – 70 *Getting Nations Together, A Case Study of the European Community,* William Nesbitt, 74pp, 1979, Council on International and Public Affairs, $3.00. A description of successful economic integration which suggests that some form of political integration is likely and concludes that "the step-by-step, functional approach . . . may offer the best hope for bringing nations closer together" (p. 72).

6 – 71 *International Theory and European Intergration,* Charles Pentland, 283pp, 1973, Free Press, $14.95. Identifies various forms of integration and maintains that for the foreseeable future modern States will continue to exist within a community of States.

6 – 72 *Divided Loyalties: British Regional Assertion and European Integration,* Martin Kolinsky & D.S. Bell (eds.), 216pp, 1978, Humanities, $32.25. Assesses the relationship of devolution of power to the regional assemblies and European integration.

6 – 73 *The Obsolescence of Regional Theory,* Ernst Haas, 123pp, 1975, California, $3.00. Argues that the spill-over effect did not occur, as the theory would lead you to expect.

6 – 74 *The Nordic Council and Scandinavian Integration,* Erik Salem, 197pp, 1977, Praeger, $18.50. A test of theories of political integration applied to four countries.

6 – 75 *Decision Making in the European Community,* Christoph Sasse (ed.), 352pp, 1977, Praeger, $33.95. Traces the evolution of the European Coal and Steel Community (1950) into the nine-member European Community of today. The focus of the essays is on how to improve existing structures.

6 – 76 *Integration and Disintegration in NATO: Processes of Alliance Cohesion and Prospects for Atlantic Community,* Francis Beer, 330pp., 1969, Ohio State University Press, $10.00. A study of the influence of a largely military alliance on political integration, which concludes that "binding institutional procedures remained weak and there was limited task expansion."

6 – 77 *The New Politics of European Integration,* Ghita Ionescu (ed.) 278pp, 1973, St. Martin's Press, $17.95. Officials of the European Community, as well as British and continental political scientists, examine the history of movement toward European integration, British attitudes, and the political processes involved in integration.

6 – 78 *Quest for Peace Through Diplomacy,* Stephan Kertezy 192pp, 1967, Prentice-Hall, $2.45. Emphasizes the role a unified Atlantic Community could play in strengthening international institutions.

6 – 79 *The European Challenge,* Louis Armund and Michel Drancourt, 256pp, 1970, Atheneum $5.95. Describes what a united Europe could do to respond to the cultural and economic challenges of contemporary technology.

6 – 80 *Towards One Europe,* Stuart de la Mahotiers, 332pp, 1970, Pelican, $1.95. A study of the political organization of Europe, the Common Market, NATO, and European agricultural, industrial and transportation policies.

6 – 81 *Domestic Political Realities and European Unification, A Study of Mass Publics and Elites in the European Community Countries,* Werner Feld and John Wildgen, 188pp, 1976, Westview, $16.50. A study of Europe's faltering integration with the rejection of a common currency. Discovers that public support among the original Common Market countries remains persuaded that most public issues could best be

handled by European, not national institutions. The economic set-backs of the 1970s and the lessening fear of Soviet expansionism have stalled the pace of political integration.

6 – 82 *The European Parliament and the European Community,* Valentine Herman and Juliet Lodge, 199pp, 1978, St. Martin's, $19.95. A careful study of European federalist and nationalist attitudes and ideas, the powers of the European parliament and how it may influence opinion in Europe.

6 – 83 *The European Parliament,* John Fitzmaurice, 190pp, 1979, Praeger, $19.95. Asks how the direct election of members affected the institution.

6 – 84 *The European Community and the Third World, The Lomé Convention and its Impact,* Ellen Frey-Wouters, 304pp, 1980, Praeger, $23.95. Assesses how the 1975 convention between the EEC and African, Caribbean and Pacific countries has facilitated mutually beneficial relationships. Defines a major role for the EEC in North-South negotiations.

6 – 85 *Devolution,* Vernon Bogdanor, 192pp, 1979, Oxford, $8.95. Examines the growing demand for regional autonomy in Britain and the experience of Northern Ireland, which possessed its own parliament from 1921 to 1972.

6 – 86 *Policy-Making in the European Communities,* Helen Wallace, William Wallace & Carole Webb, 341pp, 1977, Wiley, $28.95. Offers case studies of European States in their national policy-making, and relates this evidence to theories of European integration.

6 – 87 *The European Alternatives, An Inquiry into the Policies of the European Community,* Ghita Ionescu, (ed.), 538pp, 1979, Sijthoff & Noordhoff, $30.00. Articles on a variety of European wide problems which the elected European Parliament might address. Edited by the chairman of the Research Committee on European Unification, International Political Science Association.

6 – 88 *Uniting the Democracies: Institutions of the Emerging Atlantic-Pacific System,* James Huntly, 393pp, 1980, NYU Press, $29.50. Argues that the existing web of functional relationships between Japan, North America and Western Europe foreshadows political integration.

6 – 89 *European Communities Yearbook,* 1978, Europa, 701pp, 1979, UNIPUB, $35.00. A guide to the structure and activities of the European Community, including the composition of the European Parliament, economic and monetary integration, and non-governmental associations' activities.

I. Ethnic Conflict

6 – 90 *The Quest for Self-Determination,* Dov Ronen, 144pp, 1979, Yale, $15.00. Traces the search for self-determination to the 18th century's democratic ideologies, and finds five modern expressions: ethnic, national, minority group, class, and anti-colonial.

6 – 91 *The Future of Cultural Minorities,* Antony Alcock, Brian Taylor & John Welton (eds.), 220pp, 1979, St. Martin's, $19.95. Comparative essays in the search for a comprehensive theory of cultural minorities.

6 – 92 *Intergroup Accommodation in Plural Societies,* Nic Rhoodie (ed.), 512pp, 1979, St. Martin's, $22.50. Studies conflict regulation, political and social structures, and policy options in pluralistic societies.

6 – 93 *The Pity of It All: Polarization of Ethnic & Racial Relations,* Leo Kuper, 302pp, 1977, Minnesota, $19.50. Presents studies of Algeria, Burundi, Rwanda, and Zanzibar, and identifies common elements leading to violent massacres in each: social structures which accentuate divisions, polarizing ideologies, reciprocal violence, driving out mediating groups, and the ending of conciliating relationships. Ethnic and racial conflict is influenced by other divisions but also supersedes their impact.

6 – 94 *Small States and Segmented Societies. National Political Integration in a Global Environment,* Stephanie Neuman (ed.), 238pp., 1976, Praeger, $18.95. In a context set by the editor's attack on the concept of integration as developed by its theorists, the eight authors emphasize forces, external to a state in influencing the cohesion of Zaire, Yugoslavia, Cyprus, Pakistan, the German Democratic Republic, Philippines, and Malaysia.

6 – 95 *Ethnic Groups and Boundaries: The Social Organization of Culture Difference,* Fredrik Barth (ed.), 153pp, 1969, Little, Brown $4.95. A social anthropological study which concludes: ''ethnic distinctions do not depend on an absence of social interaction and acceptance . . . cultural differences can persist despite inter-ethnic contact and interdependence.'' Thus, ethnic groups may have natural boundaries rendering political boundaries unnecessary if the aim is to maintain ethnic group identity. Mexico, Ethiopia and Laos are among the countries studied.

6 – 96 *Ethnic Conflict in International Relations,* Astri Suhrke and Lela Noble (eds.), 246pp, 1978, Praeger, $27.50. Addressed to the question ''does ethnic conflict within a state lead to foreign intervention or, since all states are vulnerable, does ethnic conflict lead to cooperation among national leaders?'' Seven case studies — Kurds, Northern Ireland, Lebanon, Cyprus, Eritrean-Ethiopia, the Kazakhs in China, and the Muslims in the Philippines and Thailand — are framed by two analytic essays.

6 – 97 *The Politics of Division, Partition and Unification,* Ray Johnston (ed.) 98pp, 1976, Praeger, $17.50. The introduction surveys the literature about how States are formed and divided; faults the tendency to see partition as a desirable way to avoid conflict; and states empirically, answerable questions. Case studies of Berlin, Pakistan, Germany, Korea, and China follow.

6 – 98 *Nationality Group Survival in Multi-Ethnic States, Shifting Support Patterns in the Soviet Baltic Region,* Edward Allworth (ed.), 299pp. 1977, Praeger, $29.50. A study of the resilience of nationalities under pressure from the Soviet state and of their support mechanism, accounting for the desirability of ethnicity in the Baltic region, particularly among Lithuanians, Estonians, Jews, Ukranians and Poles.

6–99 *Ethnic Conflict and Political Development,* Cynthia Enloe, 282pp, 1973, Little, Brown, and Co. $5.95. Maintains that ethnic identity is not so much a security mechanism against discrimination as against impersonal specialized relationships with a remote, centralized, bureaucratic government. Ethnicity is frequently strengthened even as the power and wealth of the group increases.

6–100 *Ethnicity and U.S. Foreign Policy,* Abdul Said (ed.), 180pp, 1978, Praeger, $18.95. The introduction calls the rise of ethnicity a fundamental change in world politics: ethnic identity supersedes national identity, the national interest loses meaning, the mass media revolution fosters separatism not community. The essays then explore the influence on U.S. policy of American blacks, Greeks, Jews, and others.

6–101 *Ethnic Conflict in the Western World,* Milton Esman, 399pp, 1977, Cornell, $19.50. Traces the development of heightening ethnic identities.

6–102 *Ethnic Autonomy – Comparative Dynamics, the Americas, Europe and World,* Raymond Hall, 400pp, 1979, Pergamon, $10.95. Compares separatist currents and their expression in proposals for federation.

6–103 *The Right to Self-Determination: Implementation of United Nations Resolutions,* Hector Espiell, 86pp, 1980, United Nations, $8.00. Outlines UN resolutions and actions designed to implement them.

6–104 *The Politics of Pluralism, A Comparative Study of Lebanon and Ghana,* Audrey & David Smock, 369pp, 1975, Elsevier, $14.95. Introduces the problem of ethnic tension and conflict in two States.

6–105 *Nationality and the Pursuit of National Independence,* T.W. Moody (ed.) 175pp, 1978, Humanities, $16.25. A historical survey of the link between consciousness of nationality and the desire for an independent State.

6–106 *The Question of Separatism: Quebec and the Struggle over Sovereignty,* Jane Jacobs, 134pp, 1980, Random House, $8.95. Without committing herself, the author argues that most of the economic and political problems of a separate Quebec could be overcome.

6–107 *Secession, The Legitimacy of Self-Determination,* Lee Buchheit, 260pp, 1978, Yale, $17.50. Attempts to establish criteria for calculating the legitimacy of claims to self-determination.

TEW
6–108 *Terrorism & Political Self-Determination, A Tragic Marriage We Could Help Decouple,* Janet Mackey (ed), 64pp, 1980, World Without War Publications, $1.00. Introduces the relationship between terrorism and the pursuit of self-determination, offers standards for evaluating and testing claims, and suggests how they might apply in specific situations.

J. Human Rights: Overviews

6 – 109 *Basic Documents on Human Rights,* Ian Brownlie (ed.), 450pp, 1981, Oxford $24.95. Includes the basic texts plus the Final Act of the Helsinki Conference, the United Nations Declaration on Protection from Torture, and the judgment of the European Court of Human Rights in *The Sunday Times* case.

Intro

6 – 110 *International Human Rights Kit,* Robert Woito (ed.), 192pp, 1982 (1977) World Without War Publications, $6.00. Offers a self-survey, contending perspectives, the basic human rights in Declarations, Covenants and Treaties, and proposals for reform with suggestions for action.

6 – 111 *The Human Rights Reader,* Walter Laqueur & Barry Rubin (eds.), 375pp, 1979, NAL, $6.95. Offers seventy major statements on human rights drawn from over eight centuries, plus an extensive bibliography.

6 – 112 *Basic Documents on International Protection of Human Rights,* Louis Sohn & Thomas Buergenthal, 244pp, 1973, Bobbs-Merrill, $4.25. In addition to basic UN Declarations, Convenants and Conventions, this book provides the texts of the European and Inter-American Conventions on Human Rights.

6 – 113 *Human Rights: A Compilation of International Instruments of the United Nations,* United Nations, 106pp, 1978, UN, $9.00. Includes the complete texts of forty-one Human Rights statements by the UN from 1948 to 1973.

6 – 114 *The Moral Imperative of Human Rights: A World Survey,* Kenneth Thompson, 254pp, 1980 Univ. Press of America, $8.75. Assesses the state of human rights observance, and maintains that political interests, as well as moral imperatives, must be weighed by those wishing to improve performance.

6 – 115 *Essays on Human Rights: Contemporary Issues and Jewish Perspectives,* David Sidorsky, 359pp, 1979, Jewish Publication Society of America, $12.00. A significant collection of essays by Jewish scholars.

K. The Nature of Rights Dispute

6 – 116 *What Are Human Rights?* Maurice Cranston, 170pp, 1978, Taplinger, $4.95. A discussion of the conflict between natural law and constitutional law justifications of human rights, with a detailed analysis of specific rights.

6 – 117 *Essays in the Liberal Interpretation of History,* Lord Acton, William McNeil, ed., 427pp, 1967, Chicago, $4.50. Includes Acton's famous essays on "The History of Freedom in Antiquity" and "The History of Freedom in Christianity." These essays conclude that the following are conducive to liberty: the modern State, the idea of

conscience, a multi-racial, ethnic, religious or social society, a system of law which transcends particular interest, a standard of morals higher than State authority, and a working compromise between equality and reward for achievement.

6– 117A *Basic Rights: Subsistence, Affluence and U.S. Foreign Policy*, Henry Shue, 231pp, 1980, Princeton, $4.95. Although committed to rights of liberty and security also, "the purpose of this book is to present the reasons why the most fundamental core of the so-called 'economic rights' . . . ought to be among those that receive priority." (Author's introduction)

6– 118 *Human Rights, The United States and World Community,* Vernon Van Dyke, 292pp, 1970, Oxford, $5.95. An especially valuable assessment of the post-World War II human rights movement, the implications of human rights convenants and conventions: the arguments for and against the U.S. accepting additional international obligations in this field; and the case for accepting civil and political, economic, social, and cultural rights.

6– 118A *The Rights of Man Today*, Louis Henkin, 1978, Westview, $17.50. Offers a careful statement of the historical origins of both types of rights.

6– 119 *Human Rights and World Public Order,* Myres McDougall, Harold Lasswell, & Lung-chu Chen, 1,015pp, 1980, Yale, $45.00. A general treatment of existing, non-constitutional, international law, and how it can be effective in defending human rights.

6– 120 *Freedom in the World: Political Rights and Civil Liberties, 1978,* Raymond Gastil, 320pp, 1978, Transaction Books, $8.95. The first edition of what has become an annual yearbook; each edition includes the annual survey of freedom in each country; this year's argues that only civil and political rights are inalienable; includes essays on self-determination.

6– 121 *Four Essays on Liberty,* Isaiah Berlin, 213pp, 1979, Oxford, $3.95. Carefully distinguishes between kinds of rights, between human rights and the conditions within which their enjoyment is more likely, and explores other distinctions related to human rights issues.

6– 122 *On Liberty,* John Stuart Mill, David Spitz (ed.), 260pp, 1975, Norton, $3.95. The classic text defending pure tolerance, the open exchange of ideas, and intellectual freedom as the only way to secure individual liberty and approximate the truth; reprinted here with critical comments.

6– 123 *Democracy in Plural Societies: A Comparative Exploration,* Arend Lijphart, 248pp, 1980, Yale, $5.95. A study of legitimate opposition.

6– 124 *International Law Perspectives of the Developing Countries: The Relationship of Law and Economic Development to Basic Human Rights,* Charles Okolie, 420pp, 1975, Nok, $8.00. A discussion and assessment of the relevance of law to human rights concerns focusing on economic development.

6 – 125 *Internationul Protection of Human Rights,* Louis Sohn & Thomas Buergenthal, 1,402pp, 1973, Bobbs Merrill, $25.00. Written for lawyers, this volume presents a comprehensive introduction to human rights protection under international law.

See also Human Rights section of Chapter 15.

L. The United Nations and Human Rights

6 – 126 *The United Nations and Human Rights,* UN, 89pp, 1973, UN, $3.00. A useful summary of the range of UN activity in the field.

6 – 127 *Yearbook of Human Rights for 1973 – 1974,* UN, 327pp, 1978, UN, $15.00. A concise account of legislative and other developments in implementing the rights defined in the Universal Declaration of Human Rights.

M. Regional Human Rights Activity

6 – 128 *The OAS and the Promotion and Protection of Human Rights,* Lawrence LeBlanc, 179pp, 1977, Klvwer, $31.00. A study of the Inter-American human rights' institutions and their role in promoting human rights.

6 – 129 *European Human Rights Reports,* European Law Centre, Elm Hause, $135. Quarterly report on human rights violations, and the institutional efforts to prevent and correct them.

6 – 130 *The European Convention on Human Rights,* Frede Castberg, 230pp, 1974, Oceana, $24.00. Describes the function of the European system and the procedures by which individuals file human rights claims.

6 – 131 *International Protection of Human Rights: The World of International Organizations and the Role of U.S. Foreign Policy,* Donald M. Frazer, Chairman, House Subcommittee on International Organizations and Movements, 987pp, 1974, $6.95. A wealth of material.

6 – 132 *Report on a Negotiation: Helsinki-Geneva-Helsinki, 1972 – 73,* Luigi Ferraris, 430pp, 1979, Institute Universitarie de Hautes Etudes Internationales, $46.00. Provides detailed background information on the negotiations that led to the Helsinki Accords.

6 – 133 *European Protection of Human Rights,* Laurids Mikaelsen, 280pp, 1980, Sijhoff & Noordhoff, $42.50. Describes the European system since 1974, focusing on the function of the now-operating European Court of Human Rights, and the Commission of Human Rights. Of the 200 individual applications for redress received, ninety-seven were returned because the applications have not fulfilled various conditions.

N. Human Rights Assessments

6– 134 *Freedom in the World, Political Rights and Civil Liberties, 1979,* Raymond Gastil, 321pp, 1979, Transaction, $8.95. In addition to the annual "Comparative Survey of Freedom," this year's edition focuses on "liberalization in the Soviet Union."

6– 135 *Freedom in the World, Political Rights and Civil Liberties, 1980,* Raymond Gastil, 331pp, 1980, Transaction $8.95. Focuses on press freedom, trade union rights, the elections in Zimbabwe, and the struggle for democracy in Iran against the Shah, by the totalitarian left and the authoritarian right.

6– 135A *Freedom in the World, Political Rights and Civil Liberties 1981*, Raymond Gastil, 331pp, 1981, Transaction Books, $8.95. In addition to updating the annual survey of freedom and noting trends, this volume discusses freedom of the press and the prospects for freedom in Muslim Central Asia.

6– 136 *Report on Torture,* Amnesty International, 285pp, 1975, Farrar, Straus and Giroux, $4.95. A country-by-country assessment of torture in 1975.

6– 137 *Amnesty International Report,* 1980, Amnesty International, 408pp, 1980, $5.45. An annual assessment of prisoners of conscience — people imprisoned for their beliefs or acts of non-violent advocacy of their views.

6– 138 *Victims of Politics, The State of Human Rights,* Kurt Glaser and Stefan Possony, 584pp, 1979, Columbia, $35.00. An encyclopedic documentation of human rights violations and a number of constructive recommendations for change.

6– 139 *The New Politics of Human Rights,* James Joyce, 256pp, 1979, St. Martin's $19.95. A history of the human rights movement from 1948 to 1978, which argues that we are on the edge of a new era of human freedom.

6– 140 *Murder of a Gentle Land,* John Barron and Anthony Paul, 240pp, 1977, Crowell, $9.95. A preliminary assessment of the deaths caused by the Pol Pot regime from 1975-1977 with estimates ranging up to four million.

6– 141 *The Fourth World: Victims of Group Oppression,* Ben Whitaker (ed.), 342pp, 1973, Schocken Books, $10.00. A report by the Minority Rights Group (London), on oppression of a dozen minorities including Asians in central and eastern Africa, Eritreans in Ethopia, Blacks in Rhodesia and Brazil and religious groups in Ireland and the Soviet Union. The purpose of the book is to develop an international conscience about the rights of minorities.

6– 142 *Indonesia —1965: The Coup that Backfired,* CIA, Directorate of Intelligence, 1968, Gov. Printing Office, O.P. Argues that the Communist Party of Indonesia initiated a coup d'etat which provoked a counter-coup and massacre.

6– 143 *Taking Lives, Genocide and State Power,* Irving Louis Horowitz, 199pp, 1980, 3rd ed., Transaction, $5.95. A thoroughly revised study of genocide, which is viewed as a "totalitarian technique for achieving national solidarity, ultimately resulting in a state without compassion and law without justice."

6 – 144 *Voices from the Holocaust,* Sylvia Rothchild (ed.), 456pp, 1981, New American Library, $14.95. Transcripts of a few of the "two hundred and fifty survivors of the Holocaust," detailing their lives before, during, and after, and their feeling of abandonment.

6 – 145 *Witness to the Holocaust,* Azriel Eisenberg, 649pp, 1981, Pilgrim, $17.95. In addition to documents of survivors, this collection includes historical and other interpretations.

6 – 146 *Sourcebook on the New Immigration,* Roy Bryce-LaPorte, 511pp, 1979, Transaction, $29.95. A collection of essays on the implications of the new immigration on sending and host countries, particularly the U.S. Included too are transition and adjustment problems for immigrants, and the extent to which human rights violations prompt immigration to be considered.

6 – 147 *Human Rights and the South African Legal Order,* John Dugard, 470pp, 1978, Princeton, $12.50. A detailed study, by a South African jurist, of apartheid legislation and the judicial system that interprets it.

O. U.S. Human Rights Policy Assessments

6 – 148 *The United States, the United Nations, and Human Rights, The Eleanor Roosevelt and Jimmy Carter Eras,* A. Glen Mower, Jr., 215pp, 1979, Greenwood, $17.50. A study of the two personalities that contributes to an understanding of how the U.S. has sought to promote human rights with a discussion on whether an increased role for the UN would help.

6 – 149 *Human Rights and U.S. Foreign Policy, Principles and Applications,* Peter Brown & Douglas MacLean, 352pp, 1979, Lexington, $16.95. Introduces the principles underlying a sustained commitment to promote human rights in world politics.

6 – 150 *Toward a Humanitarian Diplomacy,* Tom Farer (ed.), 288pp, 1980, New York University, $15.00. A critique by experts of the Carter Administration's human rights policy combined with case studies and advice.

6 – 151 *Global Evangelism Rides Again: How To Protect Human Rights Without Really Trying,* Ernst Haas, 46pp, 1978, California, $2.00. Haas fears human rights rhetoric will build a domestic constituency for military intervention on behalf of human rights; and calls, instead, for a recognition of the obstacles to the promotion of human rights in another country, to the possibility of trade-offs, and to the unintended consequences of human rights promotion. He then offers a number of constructive suggestions.

INF

6– 152 *American Dream, Global Nightmare, the Dilemma of U.S. Human Rights Policy,* Sandy Vohelgesang, 1980, Norton, $13.95. A foreign service officer studies the human rights initiative of the Carter Administration and asks what went wrong.

6– 153 *The Politics of Human Rights,* Paula Newberg (ed.), 256pp, 1980, New York University, $8.95. An analysis of the trade-offs in human rights issues: Are political stability, cultural diversity, or social justice more important?

6– 154 *Human Rights and World Order,* Abdul Aziz Said (ed.), 170pp, 1978, Praeger, $18.95. A wide range of political perspectives and issues are presented from Kissinger's foreign goals, children's rights, and terror.

P. Proposals for Reform

6– 155 *Implementing a Human Rights Commitment in United States Foreign Policy,* International League for Human Rights, 75pp, 1977, World Without War Publications, $3.00. At the beginning of the Carter Administration, a group of fifty human rights professionals outlined specific and valuable policy recommendations for making human rights concerns a continuing feature of the U.S. engagement in world politics.

6– 156 *Implemention of the Final Act of the Conference on Security and Cooperation in Europe: Findings and Recommendations Five Years After Helsinki,* Commission on Security and Cooperation in Europe, 341pp, 1980, U.S. Gov. Printing Office, $3.50. An assessment of the implementation of the Helsinki Accords with suggestions for fulfillment of the intention of the Accord.

6– 157 *Toward an Integrated Human Rights Policy: A Commentary on the Interrelationship of Economic, Social, Cultural, Civil and Political Rights,* 14pp, 1979, International Commission of Jurists, $1.00. Describes how these can be implemented together.

6– 158 *Due Process of Rebellion,* Luis Kutner, 169pp, 1974, Bardian, $7.95. An attempt to apply judicial procedures to issues usually contested with violence.

6– 159 *Individual Rights & the State in Foreign Affairs: An International Compedium,* Elihu Lauterpact & John Collier (eds.), 743pp, 1977, Praeger, $45.95. Papers from an international symposium where problems of national implementation of international human rights treaties were considered by lawyers from Chile, Uganda, Egypt, and other countries.

TEW

6– 160 *New Aspects of the International Protection of Human Rights,* Margaret Galey, Chairwoman, 40pp, 1977, Commission to Study the Organization of Peace, $2.50. A wide ranging study of the existing international system with specific recommendations for changes. Special chapters are included on women's rights, torture and terrorism.

6– 161 *Enhancing Global Human Rights,* Jorge Dominguez, Nigel Rodley, Bryce Wood, and Richard Falk, 268pp, 1979, McGraw Hill, $6.95. Four essays united by the title and focused on conditions essential for human rights, Latin America, monitoring violations, and severe abuses of human rights. A variety of proposals for reform are offered.

6– 162 *The Realization of Economic, Social and Cultural Rights: Problems, Policies and Progress,* Manouchehr Ganji, Special Rapparteur of the Commission on Human Rights, 326pp, 1975, United Nations, $14.00. A report on a U.N. sponsored congress designed to advance economic, social, and cultural rights.

6– 163 *The Road to Madrid: Recommendations for United States Human Rights Policy,* Aspen Institute, 9pp, 1979, $3.50. Recommendations for U.S. policy, at the November 1980 review of the Helsinki Accords.

G. Resources

6– 164 *How to File Complaints of Human Rights Violations, A Practical Guide to Inter-Governmental Procedures,* Glenda Da Fonseca, 152pp, 1975, World Council of Churches, $4.00. Outlines the procedures of the U.N., International Labour Organization and the European and Inter-American Commissions on Human Rights.

6– 165 *International Human Rights: A Bibliography, 1870 – 1976,* William Miller, 123pp, 1977, U. of Notre Dame Law School, $2.00. One in a continuing series of reference bibliographies on human rights.

CHAPTER 7

WORLD ECONOMIC AND POLITICAL DEVELOPMENT

DISARMAMENT, world law, and a sense of world community have been identified as conditions essential to a world without war. Such goals, however, must be pursued in conjunction with a fourth: world economic and political development. A sense of world community, for example, cannot exist if more than one billion people live in dire poverty in the midst of comparative affluence. Overcoming poverty, promoting economic development, and facilitating change through responsive political institutions and social processes are necessary for world economic development.

In this chapter the gaps between the North (the industrialized countries in the Northern Hemisphere) and the South (the remaining countries, most in the Southern Hemisphere) are described,[1] as are gaps within countries in the South. Different approaches to improving the economic circumstances of the poor within the South are outlined, as is the politics of achieving change within developing societies.

---

[1]These two sides are also frequently called the "developed" and the "developing" countries, but the geographical designation is less evaluative and admits of greater diversity, and is therefore preferred here.

THE NORTH-SOUTH GAP

World politics in the post-World War II era is dominated by the East-West conflict, with political and security concerns overshadowing economic issues. Only more recently has the economic gap between the North and the South also claimed significant attention.

The stark contrasts between the North and the South are revealed by the economic indicators. Most of the South's people are hungry. Per capita income in the thirty-five poorest countries is only about $176 per year.[2] The rate of illiteracy is about 65 percent. Life expectancy averages forty-nine years. Basic medical needs are unmet. Opportunities for useful employment are severely limited. Population growth is about 2.4 per cent per year, while economic growth is about .9 per cent a year. Whatever the measure — gross national product (GNP), life expectancy, infant mortality, the physical quality of life index (PQLI) — the North enjoys a significant advantage. In 1978 the gap between the per capita GNP was $5,871 ($6,468 for the North, $597 for the South). The gap has widened since 1960, when it was $1,275 ($1,407 for the North, $132 for the South) (Ward, *The Widening Gap*, 7-6).

In considering the distinction between the North and the South there are a number of qualifications to keep in mind. The countries of the South have quite varied economic resources, political and economic systems, traditions, and population. North Korea has a socialist economy; Argentina, a capitalist one. Tanzania is seeking to insulate itself from external influences; Brazil has encouraged external investment. The oil-exporting countries now have vast economic resources; Mali and Chad have very few. In fact, twenty-four out of fifty-six high income countries in the world are in the South with an average per capita income of over $2,000. Brazil, Iran, Argentina, Taiwan, Mexico, and Venezuela also have significant resources. They do not fit neatly into the dichotomy of North/South, and rich/poor countries.

There is a second dramatic gap within most States in the South between the moderately wealthy and rich minorities, as well as the newly educated elites, and the chronically poor and illiterate majority. Aid programs developed by the North may not reach the poor, if the elites in the South prevent it. The language of egalitarianism is used in international forums to justify a redistribution of wealth among States, but such redistribution within States is rarely mentioned.

There is another contrast between the North and the South: in the North, democratic forms of political organization are the rule, with the Soviet Union (and its allies) being the outstanding exceptions. In the South, authoritarian

[2]Statistics in this chapter are from *U.S. and the Developing World, Agenda, 1980*, 7-3.

forms of political control are the norm, with India, Nigeria and Costa Rica being among the exceptions.

The concept of North/South dichotomy is of limited usefulness given the economic variations within the South. It has greater strength in capturing the lack of access to the decision-making institutions of the North, which have, in the past, established the rules of world economic transactions. North-South tensions remain as political obstacles to a sense of world community.

THE GAP AND WAR

The economic circumstances of those living in chronic poverty within the South provide a powerful justification for violence. We cannot expect people to turn away from war, revolution, or similar forms of violence if doing so means acceptance of chronic poverty. Once, of course, such conditions were accepted as being inevitable, a product of nature or of other forces beyond human influence. Today, as a result of world communications, nearly everyone knows that such circumstances can be changed. Many people experience great suffering, but there are now expectations that it can be alleviated. Even when local resources are available and even when the effort is made, they are inadequate to fulfill such expectations *(Peasants, Politics and Revolution, #*3-47*)*. The modest results that are achieved frequently raise expectations for more rapid improvement, thus creating an explosive situation. The widening gap between perceptions of what ought to be and the reality of what is builds frustration. The identification of the dominant political force as responsible for such deprivation results in a powerful justification for violence.[3]

The argument about closing the gap or aiding the poor is largely about how, not whether, to do so, since there are few who justify such circumstances. However, the motivation for change varies. One is the belief that such conditions shame and disgrace those who live in affluence, for not doing everything possible to alter them. Another motivation is to remove a cause of war by removing a reason for insurrection and civil war, or by eliminating a fertile field for external powers to influence the domestic politics of dependent States. But change and development will not automatically produce a world without war. *Development is not another word for peace.* Developing societies, like developed ones, may continue to resolve their conflicts through the threat or fact

[3]See Chapter 3.

of war. Japan's industralization in the 1920s and 1930s suggests that development may even increase the likelihood of war. Most of the wars in world politics
since 1945 have been between or within developing States *(World Disarmament Kit,* 4-65). Expansionist tendencies in the newly-developed States is as
likely a result as peace, if nothing else changes. Success in development could
provide more reasons for war. Thus, political development, combined with
progress toward the conditions described in earlier chapters, can provide at least
some assurance that economic development occurs without the organized mass
violence of war.

PROBLEMS IN DEVELOPMENT

The gap between the North and the South, the gaps within the South, and the
gap between rising expectations and their fulfillment, pose separate but interrelated problems. First, some 1.3 billion of the earth's four billion people have
incomes of less than $150 per capita per year. In most countries such circum-
stances indicate that emergency measures are needed, even if they are historically normal. People and groups and States with differing ideologies and
interests might be convinced to cooperate to eradicate such abject poverty.

Second, many have argued that given a small, educated elite and large,
illiterate populations, and given the desire for a sudden, dramatic improvement
in economic circumstances, political and civil rights should be abandoned in
favor of some form of authoritarianism.

Third, there are questions concerning how to fashion a more equitable global
economic order which limits environmental damage, while generating and
distributing wealth to meet rising expectations. The questions concerning the
changing world economic order and the environment are addressed in Part IV.

Those working for world economic development must understand alternative
approaches and related problems involved in the politics of development. How
are the developing States to meet the human economic needs of their people,
who are now aware that ''it doesn't have to be like this''? The world is
dominated by nationalist and ideological passions, but made ever more inter-
connected by modern technological, communications, and economic realities.
As we confront overwhelming and pressing economic deprivations, how are we
to achieve that recognition of interdependence that would make enforceable law
possible? Can a sense of community grow out of the specific steps taken by the
many different actors to eradicate such problems? How, then, can we best act to
change circumstances of terrible deprivation?

CAUSES AND CURES OF WORLD POVERTY

There are two important schools of thought concerning the origins of mass poverty in the South: one, the conventional or classical liberal school, the other, the radical or Marxist school (Rosen and Jones, *The Logic of International Relations,* 1-78), Blake and Walters, *The Politics of Global Economic Relations,* 12-93). The teachings of the conventional school prevail in Western governmental circles and in the policies of such inter-governmental organizations as the International Monetary Fund and the World Bank, as well as in the leadership of transnational corporations (TNCs) based in Western countries. The radical school has proponents in the academic communities of Western countries, although the conventional theory has its advocates there as well. The leadership of developing countries tends to rally around the radical view in international organizations. The two schools disagree about the basic motives of the decision-makers in Western industrialized countries, about whether the West or the leadership of developing countries is responsible for the widening gap, and about who or what the obstacles are to economic development in the developing countries.

THE CONVENTIONAL OR CLASSICAL LIBERAL SCHOOL

Those in this school are not in agreement about the causes of the gap. Some argue that the wonder is that one corner of the world achieved affluence, not that most of the world is poor (Rostow, *The Stages of Economic Growth,* 7-21). Others maintain that the colonial period of Western history (1450 – 1750) and the imperialist period (1870s to the 1950s) were characterized by the Western countries' pursuit of economic advantage. Slavery, the displacement or subjugation of indigenous populations, the exploitation of mineral resources, and the conversion of agricultural land to crops needed in the home country, all took their toll. Cuba became a sugar plantation, the Congo (now Zaire), a rubber plantation. Other countries became tea, coffee, banana, oil or other mineral or commodity-producing centers for the Western powers. Many within the conventional camp, however, also point out that there were economic advantages to the colonies as well. These advantages included railroads, medical knowledge, Western conceptions of political organization and science; in short, modern institutions were transferred and benefited the colonized. Life expectancy increased (Bauer, *Dissent on Development,* 7-22), and unprecedented economic growth took place. All classical liberals deplore the fact that two-thirds of the States in the modern world were created in opposition to the Western powers' colonial rule; however, some point out that independence was more frequently granted than won in war.

The conventional theory maintains that, whatever the origins of the gap prior to World War II, it has widened in the subsequent era largely because of *obstacles within developing societies.*

One such obstacle was the absence of an infra-structure prior to colonialism or imperialism. Also, leadership in developing countries has been largely ineffectual in checking excessive population growth; and economic resources that might have aided development have gone elsewhere. Developing countries spent over $97 billion in 1978 for armaments; also, foreign aid and new resources generated internally have too often enriched elites rather than the poverty stricken masses. Whether through corruption or mismanagement, profit has rarely been reinvested in labor-enhancing technology. To this list might be added the building of prestigious athletic facilities or showcase investments, such as airlines, instead of investment in basic industries that benefit many people. In addition, many from developing countries who study in the West do not return to aid their own countries, thus constituting a serious "brain drain." All this places responsibility for the slow pace of economic development in the emerging countries on the countries themselves.

THE CONVENTIONAL CURE

Four types of programs are offered to close the gap: direct foreign assistance, investments by multinational corporations, the transfer of technology, and the education of third world leaders in developed countries. Foreign aid can provide the capital, the credit, and the educational skills which developing countries need badly. The classical liberals maintain that whatever the subsidized activity, contact with the Western world is beneficial. If put to productive use, the skills learned can provide a significant resource for development. Thus, when transnational investments are made in developing countries, jobs are created, technology transferred, the tax base enlarged, the balance of payment problem improved, and access to markets increased. Transnational corporations provide demonstrations of effective management and examples of good work habits to the host country. The conventional theory contends that none of these resources from developed countries can help unless the developing country is politically stable, economically prudent, and prepared to reorganize itself.

THE RADICAL THEORY OF DEVELOPMENT

While the conventional theory of development holds that forces internal to developing countries are largely responsible for their economic backwardness, the radical theory fixes blame on external forces. These external forces are often the very forces seen as helpful by the liberals. In the radical view (Wallerstein, *The World System of Capitalism*, 7-38), the external economic and political forces, centered in the U.S., Japan and Western Europe, have made economic and political dependencies of the developing countries of Asia, Africa, and Latin America. The instruments of this dependency today are transnational corporations, foreign aid, and the economics of developing countries tied to a single commodity, such as coffee, cocoa, or rubber.

Some 80 per cent of developing countries' exports in 1973 were primary products such as minerals, fuels, or crops. By contrast, 80 percent of the industrialized countries' exports were in manufactured goods. When prices are primarily set by market forces, the prices of industrial goods rise while those of primary products fluctuate widely. In the long run, prices of such commodities (with the exception of oil) have been far below those of industrial goods. Thus, the terms of trade between the North and South are not equally beneficial, for the market prices of industrial goods rise to cover costs, while the prices of primary products are fixed by supply and demand factors (Harrington, *The Vast Majority*, 7-30). This frequently means low prices for commodities like cocoa, bananas, and rice because the market for such products is not easily expanded and a bumper crop can result in dramatically lowered prices.

In the conventional view, transnational corporations add resources to developing States. In the radical view, however, they deplete them. TNCs take out more money than they invest, insist those who hold the radical view, although this is not inherently incompatible with increasing the capital available. For example, if the research costs of developing a computer are borne in the United States, the manufacture of the computer in another country may well return more dollars to the United States than were invested in that country. In another case, however, the capital flow may inhibit rapid economic development and distort the host country's economy. This occurs when a TNC helps finance its operation by borrowings from local banks, thus drying up available local capital. In addition, TNCs may take advantage of their transnational status to shift assests and liabilities on their ledgers. Thus, they avoid taxes and royalty payments, and gain a bargaining advantage concerning the terms of their operation. TNCs can also distort the local productive process by introducing inappropriate technology which requires costly energy, and unavailable skills where there is usually a surplus of local labor available.

Foreign aid is considered a similar drain by the radical school of thought.

While aid looks like a gift, it is usually tied to the recipients' purchase of products from the donor countries or to specific projects. Moreover, equipment purchased continues to require replacement parts and support services from the developed countries *(Rich Against Poor,* 7-78). Much aid is in the form of loans, the repayment of which is increasingly difficult, particularly since the cost of oil imports has grown dramatically since 1973. From 1970 to 1978, Pakistan's oil import costs rose more than the foreign aid it received. Aid, in effect, strengthens dependence on the developed countries.

THE RADICAL CURE

If external forces do keep the developing countries poor, the cure is to break sharply with the international economic system, as well as with the domestic elites which benefit from that system. This was once the Chinese model, widely heralded before Mao's death, and now being altered by his successors. Still, China's economic gains should not be dismissed, unless disproven; and Tanzania appears bent upon a similar course of isolation from international economic forces. The development of regional common markets offers an alternative to dependence upon markets of the developed countries, and gives governments and corporations the ability to gain negotiating advantage by playing one off against another. Regional economic experiments have been tried (the Andean Common Market, for example), and are frequently recommended as part of the radical cure for economic backwardness.

The most effective cure has been the development of a producers' cartel: the Organization of Petroleum Exporting Countries (OPEC). The members of this cartel, having significant oil production capacity, are now among the richest countries in the world. The hope that other countries with primary products could form similar cartels, and thus gain significant leverage to offset price fluctuations, has not materialized. There are, it now appears, few other products as essential as oil to the industrialized States, and for these, substitutes or sacrifice often remain preferable to paying drastically higher prices.

THE POLITICS OF DEVELOPMENT

The conventional theory of development tends to separate economic and political issues. It maintains that if we engaged in economic exchanges only with those with whom we agree, we would all be much poorer. While the theory supports democracy, it also accepts a wide variety of forms of government capable of modernizing a country.

The radical theory maintains that political choices are encountered everywhere in the economic system. Current practices outside the Communist bloc are seen as a result of coercion, past or present. The liberal economic measures (aid, transnational corporation investment, technology transfer, and education) are considered means of maintaining in power autocratic and repressive elites which benefit from current arrangements and (with the aid of their external supporters) prevent change.

After surveying the economic conditions of backwardness, some (e.g. Robert Heilbroner, *An Inquiry into The Human Prospect,* 13-10) abandon their normal opposition to political violence and their preference for democratic institutions. Their justification for totalitarian or authoritarian governments is roughly as follows: the pitiful circumstances of two billion or more people justify the use of mass political violence, if this will produce needed change. Only an elite committed to ruthless action, backed by a political organization motivated by an ideological commitment, is capable of mobilizing the resources, overcoming cultural inertia, and coercing the population into a dictated development drive. The acts of such a revolutionary elite, though bloody and hateful, are necessary if the human potential of most people on this earth is to be fulfilled.

For a time, the argument that some form of authoritarian government was needed, if not desirable, was widely accepted. Democracy was considered possible only when certain pre-conditions existed: it was urban, industrial, middle class, literate societies which made democratic governments possible (Apter, *The Politics of Modernization,* 7-43). Traditional societies would have to be modernized before such governments could come into being. Political modernization was defined as the creation of bureaucratic procedures; the development of rational scientific habits of thought; the application of technology to agricultural and industrial production; and the creation of stable, national political institutions able to execute nationally-made decisions. Only then would democratic values, such as the right to participate in politics, respect for the dignity of the individual, and freedom of information be truly applicable. In a traditional society, it was argued, the government must master the society to bring it into the 20th century.

THE ROLE OF DEMOCRACY IN DEVELOPMENT

The various lines of argument sustaining this anti-democratic stance include Marxist-Leninist, Maoist, liberation theology and the economic modernization advocates (*The Cruel Dilemmas of Development* 7-42). The register of those who would be the masters of their society turns out to be rather long. In fact, once in power, these new leaders frequently have turned the instruments of State coercion against ethnic or political rivals for power, as well as against the economic or cultural survivals from traditional societies. The toll in Burundi, Uganda, China, Cambodia, Iran, and Iraq has been appallingly high.

The anti-democratic argument has now been attacked at a variety of points. Some within each of the authoritarian camps, and many urgently committed to economic development, now reject mass violence as the best means to change developing States. War and violence do not feed, clothe, educate, or build. They kill. Mass violence may bring new elites to power and in fact has done so; however, their performance has not been good. Mass violence itself creates chaos, the motive for revenge, political instability, and economic disruption.

A ruling elite's commitment to modernization is not enough; it must also be held accountable. This is possible only when new ideas can circulate throughout the society, when access to information permits an assessment of performance, and when the political opposition can gain power without violence. India's return to democratic government, the commitment to elections in many developing States, Nigeria's democratic constitution, the attempts of authoritarian governments to retain democratic forms while robbing them of their substance, all suggest that democratic values and political institutions retain an intrinsic attraction and importance.

PATHS TO DEVELOPMENT

Careful examination of the differences in the development of a modern industrial base in Puerto Rico and Cuba, in Taiwan and China, in Brazil and Yugoslavia, in Nigeria and Tanzania, lead many to doubt that all the wisdom is found in either the conventional or the radical view. Behind the ideological disagreement about violence, aid, transnational corporations, trade, the transfer of technology, and education are the terrible facts of deprivation. Can such deprivation be eliminated? Belief swings widely from despair about inflation, burgeoning population, corruption and political instability to hope, when one realizes that for the first time in history, the resources are available to eradicate starvation, malnutrition, and illiteracy. Many share the sense of despair, for despite unprecedented economic growth in the developing countries since World War II, many are worse off than before. But there have also been some noticeable successes. The poor have economically benefited in Taiwan, South Korea, Yugoslavia, and no doubt elsewhere. Both successes and failures have stimulated the search for new economic development and resource transfer strategies.

THE GROWTH OF INTERNATIONAL APPROACHES

One of the new strategies has been the increase in multi-national approaches to development problems. In the first twenty-five years of aid, some 90 per cent of available economic assistance was administered on a bilateral basis, involving only a granting and a receiving country. The remaining 10 percent was multilateral with a number of countries planning and administering aid programs together *(The Charity of Nations, 7-71)*. In the last few years of the 1970s the shift was increasingly to multilateral forms of assistance, such as the UN Development Program.

The criteria for allocating funds by the UN Development Program commits the greatest amounts of aid to the eighty-four countries with annual per capita GNPs under $500. The World Bank's former president as well as major U.S. congressional advocates have consistently called for strategies aimed at the poorest of the poor. Governments at the World Food Conference in Rome (1974) expressed concern about the food crisis occasioned by successive bad harvests, climatic changes, increased food consumption, and population growth. Over thirty specific measures designed to build a floor under the world's poverty stricken were developed *(World Hunger Crisis Kit, 7-81)*. Thus, governments joined what previously had been a preponderance of nongovernmental organizations in the World Food Congresses of 1963 and 1970.

Additional multi-national approaches to economic development are being debated. The developing States of the South have proposed the New International Economic Order (NIEO). These proposals (see Chapter 12) have brought developed and developing States into a series of forums and produced sometimes heated, and sometimes constructive, discussion of the rules and procedures necessary to accommodate the interests of all States.

Many international organizations have picked up ideas developed in the conferences. These include the United Nations Development Program, the International Bank for Reconstruction and Development, the UN Food and Agricultural Organization (FAO), General Agreement on Tariff and Trade (GATT), the International Monetary Fund, and the UN Conference on Trade and Development.

Most individuals, who recognize State rivalries as a cause of war and who believe that a world economy has emerged, prefer the multilateral over the bilateral approach. Multilateral aid programs — governmental or private —

reduce the chances of a powerful State's misusing an assistance program or making the recipient State dependent upon it. This kind of aid can also help strengthen international institutions, and promote cooperation on a regional basis. There has been an increasing recognition of the value of multilateral assistance, but the politics of international organizations also pose obstacles (*The Politics of Starvation*, 7-108).

Given the realities of political and bureaucratic life within the UN., one may view multilateral activity with considerable skepticism. For example, while the term "heritage of mankind" was originally applied to much of the ocean resources, it is now attached only to the resources to which developing States do not have access. The extension from a U.S. proposed fifty-mile economic zone to a 200-mile economic zone for coastal States has divided among coastal States, an estimated twenty-seven trillion dollars worth of resources. For landlocked States, this decision could result in a permanent gap between them and developed coastal States.

ELEMENTS IN A NEW CONSENSUS

There are many obstacles to an effective development strategy, including limited aid, rapid population growth, and the absence of non-military security systems. When one adds attitudes in the U.S. toward taxation, the politics of the UN, the aid patterns of OPEC countries, and the Soviet Union (which chiefly aids its allies) to the other internal and external obstacles considered earlier, one begins to see why the poorest of the poor have not yet made it. Despite these, the international community persists in emphasizing a basic needs strategy. Criteria have been established to measure progress: Does aid alleviate the plight of the poorest of the poor? Is the technology to be transferred appropriate? Will the rural sector be strengthened?

Land reform in Taiwan and Pakistan has strengthened the rural sector by developing small, productive agricultural units. Minimal international cooperation could make available appropriate technology adjusted to each local situation. Agricultural research is overcoming many different barriers to increased production in various soil and climatic conditions. Thus, there is significant agreement on a variety of new approaches to overcome hunger at the supply end: land reform (*Land Reform*, 7-93), transfer of appropriate research, improved nutritional information and a new awareness of the critical role of women (*Women and Development*, 7-52 & 53), have all been brought into prominence recently.

Leadership trained to guide development programs now exists, as do a range of international agencies and representative international forums. The UN General Assembly's Special Session on Development (1980) is a recent example of a long series of conferences, focused, at least in part, on aiding development.

Non-governmental organizations such as CARE and the International Red Cross, have often cut red tape and channeled a very high proportion of their resources to people in need *(Beyond Charity,* 7-118). After some thirty years of effort, there is an accumulated wisdom about what will not work and, to a lesser extent, about what will. In the United States, the Overseas Development Council and a host of other voluntary organizations, has kept the issue before the public, as has ''Walks for Development.''

Thus, in the midst of despair about development, it is still possible to aid the poorest of the poor and to provide the changes essential to restore and to increase agricultural productivity in developing countries. Imaginatively conceived land-reform programs have increased farm yields and reduced the burdensome rural to urban migration which has clogged the cities. An effective world economic and political development effort possibly can resolve the remaining problems and establish one condition essential to a world without war.

BIBLIOGRAPHY

The annotated books describe the developing countries, and present differing views of the paths to economic and political development. They assess the successes and failure of aid and technology transfer; describe the debate between conventional and radical theorists, and between advocates of bilateral and multilateral aid; present problems such as population growth; cultural, religious, and social restraints on growth; and consider what form of political organization is needed and possible. The reader will find these works useful in answering questions such as these: 1) What percent of the world's population lives in conditions of chronic poverty? 2) How many of the world's children live in poverty? What percent go to school? 3) Are conditions in the developing countries better or worse than during the decade before World War II? Than in the pre-colonial era? 4) What are the causes and the cures for these conditions? 5) Why are revolts more likely to occur when conditions begin to improve than when they remain steadily bad? 6) How can economic growth include the poorest of the poor? 7) What measures have apparently worked in some States? Which failed? Is there any one formula for success? 8) What is the record of multilateral aid programs? 9) Why is the economic health of the rural sector of the economy essential to successful development? 10) How can democratic government in developing States help hold leaders accountable to economic development goals?

A. The North-South Gap: Overviews

7 – 1 *The Economic History of World Population,* Carlo Cipolla, 128pp, 1972, Prentice-Hall, $1.25. For nine-tenths of humanity's existence, we have been predatory hunters. Cipolla explains how the agricultural and industrial revolutions have made possible a better life.

7 – 2 *The Economic Handbook of the World — 1981,* Peter DeWitt, Jr. & Arthur Banks, 1981, McGraw-Hill, $29.95. The first edition of what is intended to be an annual survey of international financial organizations, regional economic issues, global trends, and macro- and micro-economic data for national economies.

7 – 3 *Encyclopedia of the Third World,* George Kurian (ed.), 1,700pp, 1978, 2 vols,. Facts on File, $85.00. Provides basic facts on 114 States in Asia, Africa, and Latin America, including information on the population, ethnic groups, religion, constitution, government, foreign policy, and economic conditions of the country.

7 – 4 *The Great Ascent: The Struggle for Economic Development in Our Time,* Robert Heilbroner, 160pp, 1973, Harper & Row, $3.50. Argues that democracy is a luxury only the developed countries can afford and that totalitarian socialism is the most human way to achieve industrialization in the developing States. "Communism may well be the quickest possible way out of underdevelopment and the desperate fact is that in many areas of the world the present non-communist effort looks like the slowest possible way" (p. 138).

TEW

7 – 5 *The U.S. and World Development: Agenda 1980,* John Sewell (ed.), 237pp, 1980, Praeger, $6.95. An annual summary of development issues with statistical annexes portraying economic accomplishments and circumstances in each country.

7 – 5A *U.S. Foreign Policy and the Third World: Agenda 1982,* John Sewell and others, 272pp, 1982, Praeger, $7.95. Updates the annual statistical portrayal of economic achievement and provides specific essays on trade, food and aid policies.

7 – 6 *The Widening Gap: Development in the 1970s,* Barbara Ward et al (ed.), 372pp, 1971, Columbia, $17.50. A variety of essays portraying the faster rate of economic growth in the developed than in the developing countries with ways suggested to close the gap or at least, to accelerate the growth of the developing countries.

7 – 7 *Asian Drama: An Inquiry into the Poverty of Nations,* Gunnar Myrdal, abridged by Seth King, 464pp, 1972, Random, $3.95. Critical of both Marxist and Keynesian

economics, Myrdal offers an in-depth analysis of South Asia's struggle toward economic modernization and political democracy. He rejects any single model of development, and portrays the complexity and difficulties of development in the world's most populous region.

7 – 8 *The Developing Nations: A Comparative Perspective,* Robert Gamer, 651pp, 1976, Allyn, $10.95. Points up the diversity within the third world.

7 – 9 *Economic Development: An Introduction,* Clarence Zuvekas, 433pp, 1979, St. Martin's, $14.95. An overview of the field designed for an introductory college level course.

7 – 10 *Economic Development: Past and Present,* Richard Gill, 160pp, 1973, 3rd ed., Prentice-Hall, $8.95. An introduction to contending theories, to basic economic terminology, and to how development has occurred in industrialized and developing countries.

7 – 11 *Income Distribution Policy in Developing Contries, A Case Study in Korea,* Irma Adelman & Sherman Robinson, 346pp, 1978, Stanford, $12.50. Based on the conviction that development policy must shift from "economic growth and industrialization toward an explicit concern with equity and the alleviation of poverty" the authors suggest two strategies likely to succeed; one aims at the urban poor, the other at the rural poor. "An intensification of the policy South Korea has pursued, particularly in the 1964 – 73 decade" is recommended.

7 – 12 *Redistribution with Growth, An Approach to Policy,* Hollis Chenery, et al, 304pp, 1974, Oxford, $6.95. Papers from a conference offering proposals to act on and to research.

7 – 13 *Economic Growth & Social Equity in Developing Countries,* Irma Adelman & Cynthia Morris, 257pp, 1973, Stanford, $2.95. A "quantitative investigation of the interactions among economic growth, political participation and the distribution of income in noncommunist developing nations." Concludes that the growth of the 1950s and 1960s did not, in fact, usually reach the poorest of the poor.

7 – 14 *Measuring the Condition of the World's Poor, The Physical Quality of Life Index,* Morris Morris, 173pp, 1979, Pergamon, $5.95. Offers a major new tool for assessing the life chances of individuals in different countries; the PQLI is based on a composite of life expectancy, infant mortality, and literacy.

7 – 15 *Portraits of Poverty,* Edythe Shewbridge, 107pp, 1972, Norton $1.25. A case by case study of poverty in the United States.

7 – 16 *Five Economic Challenges,* Lester Thurow & Robert Heilbroner, 140pp, 1981 Prentice-Hall, $10.00. Emphasizes the importance of political choice in "coping with inflation, overcoming recession and unemployment, facing up to the realities of taxing and government spending, finding our place in the world economy, adjusting our way of life to the energy sources available to us."

7 – 17 *Development Reconsidered, Bridging the Gap Between Government and People,* Edgar Owens and Robert Shaw, 190pp, 1972, Lexington, $12.00. An argument for decentralized development through aid aimed at the urban and rural poor, and designed to make them self-sufficient entrepreneurs as well as participants in the political processes.

7 – 18 *The Advanced Developing Countries: Emerging Actors in the Changing World Economy,* John Mathieson, 72pp, 1979, Overseas Development Council, $3.00. Six ADCs — Brazil, Mexico, Hong Kong, South Korea, Singapore, and Taiwan — are called the economic miracles of the 1970s. Their impact on the world economy and the need for international institutional changes to accommodate them, are considered here.

7 – 19 *The Nature of Mass Poverty,* John Kenneth Galbraith, 150pp, 1979, Harvard, $8.95. Maintains that capitalism is more likely to eliminate mass poverty in developing countries than socialism because socialism requires administrators which it lacks.

7 – 20 *Food Policy, The Responsibility of the United States in the Life and Death Choices,* Peter Brown and Henry Shue, 352pp, 1978, Macmillan, $16.95. Deals with the full range of specific choices, policy alternatives and their practical and moral implications.

B. Development: Conventional View

7 – 21 *The Stages of Economic Growth,* W.W. Rostow, 253pp, 1971 (1958), Cambridge, $6.95. The pioneer study which emphasizes the ability to reinvest earnings in technology which decreases the per unit cost of the product, increases the productivity of labor and which makes possible the accumulation of capital and the take-off into self-sustained economic growth.

7 – 22 *Dissent on Development, Studies and Debates in Development Economics,* P.T. Bauer, 550pp, 1972, Harvard U. Press, $6.95. A carefully reasoned critique of how popular attitudes toward economic development issues are formed, and a rebuttal of the currently popular ideas such as "the allegation that the rich countries have caused the poverty of the underdeveloped world, the belief that forces external to poor countries today are responsible for low levels of growth, and the practice of discussing economic issues without regard to the effects of price on supply and demand."

7 – 23 *Why the Poor Get Rich and the Rich Slow Down,* W.W. Rostow, 456pp, 1980, Texas, $19.95. Provides an overview of the world economy with a focus on North – South questions.

7 – 24 *Critical Food Issues of the Eighties,* Marilyn Chou and David Harmon (eds.), 420pp, 1979, Pergamon, $32.50. A wide-ranging set of results derived from a Hudson Institute program.

7 – 25 *Challenges to Interdependent Economies: The Industrial West in the Coming*

Decade, Robert Gordon & Jacques Pelkmans, 147pp, 1979, McGraw-Hill, $6.95. Discusses the politicization of world economic issues and policies designed to protect the industrial West in the 1980s through adjustments to external changes.

7 – 26 *A Bias for Hope, Essays on Development and Latin America,* Albert O. Hirschman, 374pp, 1971, Yale U. Press, $3.45. Collected essays by the author over a ten-year period of problems of development, aid, technology. Stresses political dimensions of economic phenomena and processes of social change.

7 – 27 *The Challenge of World Poverty, A World Anti-Poverty Program in Outline,* Gunnar Myrdal, 530pp, 1970, Random House, $2.95. The noted Swedish economist outlines the changes needed in the developing nations to make substantial increases in aid useful, and calls for a significant multilateral world attack on poverty financed by the developed nations. Mydral contends that aid should be seen both as a moral requirement and as a socially and practically desirable objective.

7 – 27A *Equality, the Third World, and Economic Delusion,* P.T. Bauer, 312pp, 1981, Harvard, $17.50. A staunch defense of the conventional approach to development and a harsh refutation of its critics.

7 – 28 *The Politics of Food, Producing and Distributing the World's Food Supply,* D. Gale Johnson (ed.), 218pp, 1980, Chicago Council on Foreign Relations, $3.50. Offers the editor's plan for a worldwide "grain insurance program" that would make it possible to eliminate all deaths due to the direct effects of food production variability." Also provides evidence that agricultural production has increased 50 percent in twenty years, that a similar growth rate can be expected, and that population growth is slowing down.

7 – 29 *World Economic Development,* Herman Kahn, 519pp, 1979, Morrow, $7.95. Argues that rapid growth has occurred and will continue if the developed countries continue to consume, new energy sources are found, and environmental strain is monitored — all doable tasks in the author's judgment.

C. Development: Radical View

7 – 30 *The Vast Majority, A Journey to the World's Poor,* Michael Harrington, 281pp, 1978, Simon & Schuster, $3.95. Argues that "intricate economic mechanisms . . . subvert the innate generosity of Americans and perpetuate misery around the globe," largely because the U.S. is not leading in aiding the "poorest 30 percent of humanity which has 3 percent of the income, while the top 20 percent has 66 percent," of the resources and because transnational corporations are harmful to the poor.

7 – 31 *Food First, Beyond the Myth of Scarcity,* Francis Lappe & Joseph Collins, 466p, 1979, Ballantine, $2.75. A question-and-answer book which states a claim and then marshals the evidence against it. The central argument is that the poor in developing societies will be better off the less they are engaged in transactions with other countries. China and Cuba are considered models.

7 – 31A *World Hunger, Ten Myths,* Frances Moore Lappé & Joseph Collins, 72pp, 1979, Institute for Food and Development Policy, $2.95. Argues that adequate food exists, but land tenure systems prevents it being locally distributed.

7 – 32 *Fear in the Countryside, The Control of Agricultural Resources in the Poor Countries by Non-Peasant Elites,* Evans Vallianatos, 310pp, 1976, Ballinger, $16.00. Argues that the green revolution is one of a number of mechanisms by which the poor are being driven off small plots of land and made destitute.

7 – 33 *Appropriate Technologies for Third World Development,* Austin Robinson, 417pp, 1979, St. Martin's, $32.50. Offers empirical evidence in an effort to establish a relationship between small-scale technology and economic efficiency.

7 – 34 *Alternative Development Strategies and Appropriate Technology; Science Policy for an Equitable World Order,* Romesh Diwan & Dennis Livingston, 255pp, 1979, Pergamon, $25.00. Concentrates on what constitutes appropriate technology and on a critique of the conventional theory of development.

7 – 35 *Agrarian Revolution, Social Movements and Export Agriculture in the Underdeveloped World,* Jeffery Paige, 435pp, 1975, Free Press, $8.95. Offers a theory of agrarian revolution based largely on the issue of whether the upper class's only source of wealth is in land.

INF
7 – 36 *The Pillage of the Third World,* Pierre Jalee, 115pp, 1968, Monthly Review Press, $2.95. Makes the case for the West's dependence on third world raw materials and its exploitation of them.

7 – 37 *African Labor History,* Peter Gutkind, Robin Cohen and Jean Copans (eds.), 280pp, 1978, SAGE, $9.95. Case studies from nine areas of Africa on the impact of European created jobs on those who took them or were forced into them. The focus here is on situations in which uprisings or strikes resulted between 1897 and 1975.

INF
7 – 38 *The World System of Capitalism: Past and Present,* Walter Goldfrank (ed.), 300pp, 1979, SAGE, $8.95. Theoretical and case studies of capitalism from 1700 to the present using the "world-systems" approach, formulated by Immanuel Wallerstein. The argument is that the developed countries took their wealth from the developing ones and that is why the developing countries are poor.

7 – 39 *Nationalization of Multinationals in Peripheral Economics,* Julio Faundex & Sol Picciotto (eds.), 238pp, 1979, Holmes & Meier, $27.50. Multinationals as instruments of exploitation.

7 – 40 *Hunger for Justice: The Politics of Food and Faith,* Jack Nelson, 230pp, 1980, Orbis, $4.95. Attempts to demonstrate that the American economic system "victimizes the poor" (p. 202), and offers an eight-point program to stop it including organic gardening and debt relief.

7 – 41 *Beyond Ujamaa in Tanzania: Underdevelopment and an Uncaptured Peasantry,* Goran Hyden, 280pp, 1980, California, $8.50. A critique of dependency theory arguing that the peasants in the periphery have largely escaped the core; a Leninist solution is suggested.

7 – 42 *The Cruel Dilemmas of Development: 20th Country Brazil,* Sylvia Hewlett, 243pp, 1980, Basic, $15.00. Using Brazil as an example, Hewlett maintains growth can be achieved only at the cost of widespread political repression and widespread income differentials.

D. Modernization: Overviews

INF
7 – 43 *The Politics of Modernization,* David Apter, 481pp, 1965, U. of Chicago Press, $2.95. An important study of the modernization process which focuses on the development of political values and loyalties, professionalism, innovation, and ideology.

INF
7 – 44 *Political Order in Changing Societies,* Samuel Huntington, 488pp, 1977 (1968), Yale, $6.45. Maintains that serious conflicts can be institutionalized if the stakes in the conflict are power or wealth, not life.

7 – 45 *Revolution and the Transformation of Societies, A Comparative Study of Civilization,* S.N. Eisenstadt, 348pp, 1978, Macmillan, $15.95. "A study of what types of traditional societies are and are not likely to undergo revolutionary change, and about those aspects of modernization that are particularly likely to produce abrupt political and social transformation."

7 – 46 *World Modernization: The Limits of Convergence,* Wilbert Moore, 192pp, 1979, Elsevier, $12.95. Maintains that modernization is a universal process leading to an attempt to rationalize social life.

7 – 47 *Modernization and Bureaucratic Authoritarianism: Studies in South American Politics,* Guillermo Donnell, 219pp, 1973, Institute of International Studies, U. of Calif, Berkeley, $5.50. Argues that either left or right wing authoritarianism is likely because of South American social and cultural traditions.

7 – 48 *Nation Building: A Review of Recent Comparative Research & A Select Bibliography of Analytical Studies,* Stein Rokkan, et al., 219pp, 1973, Mouton, $10.00. A valuable introduction.

7 – 49 *Crises and Sequences in Political Development,* Leonard Binder & Joseph Lapalombara, 344pp, 1974, Princeton, $8.50. This study labels crises in political development — identity, legitimacy, penetration, and distribution — and maintains that they occur in that sequence.

7 – 50   *From Peasant to Farmer: A Revolutionary Strategy for Development,* Raanan Weitz, 292pp, 1971, Columbia, $15.00. A Twentieth Century Fund study stresses the human factor in rural development. Argues that traditional attitudes and values must be preserved, and offers guidelines for applying this principle.

7 – 51   *Women and National Development: The Complexities of Change,* Wellesley Editorial Committee of Nine, 346pp, 1977, Chicago, $10.00. Papers from a conference of over 500 people on two pressing problems: women's role in society and economic development. Some twenty-three of eighty papers are presented by women from Asia, Africa and Latin American on specific problems, such as participation in the labor force, sex role, societal attitudes, and legal standing, among others.

7 – 52   *Women and World Development,* Irene Tinker and Michele Bramsen (eds.), 240pp, 1976, Praeger, $2.50. A wide-ranging anthology on the contribution of women to development and how the disparities can be narrowed between men's and women's access to education, employment and other forms of equal participation in the society.

7 – 53   *Women and World Development: An Annotated Bibliography,* Mayra Buvinic, 176pp, 1976, Praeger, $2.50. A companion volume to 7-52 above. Both volumes are available in a hard cover edition from Praeger for $24.95.

7 – 54   *Third World Women Speak Out, Interviews in Six Countries on Change, Development, and Basic Needs,* Perdita Huston, 152pp, 1979, Praeger, $4.95. Direct interviews provide simple yet eloquent descriptions of practical problems faced by women in developing states.

7 – 55   *Asian Development: Problems and Prognosis,* John Badgley, 210pp, 1971, Free Press, $2.95. Most Asian peoples live in societies where the idea of a nation has no organic meaning, where political authority usually lacks legitimacy, and where political conflict is a continuing probability. Calls for U.S. involvement, yet concludes that effective development is more likely to occur through local and parochial structures than at the national level.

7 – 56   *Modernizing Peasant Societies; A Comparative Study in Asia and Africa,* Guy Hunter, 324pp, 1969, Oxford, $4.50. Seeks to discover a more humane way to change agricultural societies into industrial ones, peasants into farmers and urban workers, largely illiterate populations into literate ones, than the painful process of industrialization in Western Europe or the Soviet Union.

7 – 57   *Political Development and Social Change,* Jason Finkle and Richard Gable (eds.), 685pp, 1966, 1971 (2nd ed.), Wiley, $16.50. An anthology of articles by political scientists addressed to the problems and prospects of achieving political institutions which are capable of facilitating rapid change in developing countries.

Intro

7 – 58   *The Developing Nations: What Path to Modernizaion?* Frank Tachau (ed.), 243pp, 1972, Harper & Row, $10.95. Twenty-three selections cover a range of development problems: traditionalism, nationalism, communications, education, political

elites, bureaucracy, and political integration. Various paths to modernization — pluralism, authoritarianism, communism, democracy — are delineated by theorists and practitioners such as Nehru, Nyerere, Piao, Fanon, C.E. Black, Horwitz, Pye and Halpern.

7 – 59 *The Dynamics of Modernization: A Study in Comparative History,* Cyril E. Black, 253pp, 1967, Harper and Row, $3.95. Outlines seven different paths which nations have followed to modernization. Argues that violence is not essential to economic progress and may in fact retard the accumulation of capital, the emergence of centralized bureaucracies, and the sense of common purpose needed for development.

7 – 60 *The Political Consequences of Modernization,* John Kautsky, 286pp, 1980, Krieger, $11.50. Characterizes modernization as ''a belief in the rational and scientific control of man's physical and social environment and the application of technology to that end'' (p. 20). Kautsky believes that there are as many paths to political modernization as there are paths to industrialization. The basic difference in developing societies is whether they developed from within or in response to external influences.

E. Modernization: Democracy vs. Authoritarianism

7 – 61 *Politics and the Stages of Growth,* W.W. Rostow, 410pp, 1971, Cambridge, $9.95. The author of *The Stages of Economic Growth* argues that the '70s ought to be the Decade of Political Development as the '60s were a Decade of Economic Development.

7 – 62 *Crises of Political Development in Europe and the United States,* Raymond Grew (ed.), 434pp, 1978, Princeton, $6.95. Maintains there are five crises in political development; this theory is then applied to ten case studies drawn from the European and U.S. experience.

7 – 63 *A World of Nations: Problems of Political Modernization,* Dankwart Rustow, 306pp, 1967, Brookings Institution, $4.95. Places democratic government at the center of the ''how best to modernize'' debate and concludes that it is both possible and desirable but not likely, given the fragmented character of the new States' societies.

7 – 64 *The State of the Nations: Constraints on Development in Independent Africa,* Michael Lofchie (ed.), 305pp, 1971, California, $17.50. A study of the political constraints on economic progress in six African countries. Includes an essay on the prospects for constitutionalism in Africa.

7 – 65 *Aspects of Political Development,* Lucian Pye, 205pp, 1966, Little, Brown, $6.95. A pioneering definition of the issues in political development.

7 – 66 *Small is Politics: Organizational Alternatives in India's Rural Development,* Marcus Franda, 296pp, 1979, Wiley, $14.95. Argues that the Janata (then the ruling Party) shifted to rural development strategies and produced a 12% increase in food production the first year although the landless, the urban poor, and the marginal peasants did not immediately benefit because of their lack of political participation.

7 – 67 *Politics and Policy Implementation in the Third World,* Merilee Grindle (ed.), 310pp, 1980, Princeton, $7.95. A study of the gap between policy and its implementation in seven third world countries.

7 – 68 *Social Origins of Dictatorship and Democracy,* Barrington Moore, Jr., 559pp, 1966, Beacon, $6.95. A comparative study of England, the U.S., India, Russia, and Japan, which examines the conditions for the emergence of democratic institutions and makes the case for violence and tyranny over democracy in situations requiring rapid social change.

F. Development Assistance

7 – 69 *Inside Foreign Aid,* Judith Tendler, 140pp, 1977, Johns Hopkins U. Press, $3.45. A summary of recent aid criticisms, such as aid for large projects requires sophisticated technology, and also that aid helps most the donor country; recommended changes are also presented: multilateral aid, appropriate technology, liberalized trade, and greater sensitivity to the developing countries' special circumstances. She concludes that bureaucratic administration of aid produces a need for quick, visible results and becomes self-defeating.

7 – 70 *We Don't Know How: An Independent Audit of What They Call Success in Foreign Assistance,* William and Elizabeth Paddock, 331pp, 1973, Iowa State U. Press, $4.95. This title summarizes the authors' conclusion about efforts by the U.S. to aid poor countries. How should development be financed? Easy, they answer, the U.S. should give its aid to create a U.N. peacekeeping force to guarantee third world borders, and the third world countries should devote the twenty-six billion spent by them on armaments in 1972 to development.

7 – 71 *The Charity of Nations: The Political Economy of Foreign Aid,* David Wall, 181pp, 1973, Basic Books, $8.95. Argues that the need for aid is greater than the world economy can provide, but substantial aid ought to be administered by multilateral agencies (e.g. the World Bank).

7 – 72 *Alliance for Progress: A Social Invention in the Making,* Harvey Perloff, 253pp, 1969, John Hopkins U. Press, $8.50. Analyzes the reasons for the Alliance's shortcomings and proposes a program of human resource investment, social reform, and agricultural development to bring it "up to a plane of excellence and effectiveness."

7 – 73 *The Alliance That Lost Its Way: A Critical Report on the Alliance for Progress,* Jerome Levinson and Juan de Onis, 381pp, 1970, Quadrangle, $2.95. A thoughtful study which finds that the Alliance attempted too much, and concludes that development efforts, divorced from security considerations, should be directed to the assistance of countries willing and able to pursue economic and social reforms by democratic means.

7 – 74 *Mobilizing Technology for World Development,* Jairman Ramesh & Charles Weiss, Jr., 229pp, 1979, Praeger, $6.95. Twenty essays offered at a conference in

Jamaica are tied together by two concerns: how to combine industrialization with overcoming poverty, and how to facilitate the transfer of technology from developed to developing countries.

7 – 75 *The Uncertain Promise, Value Conflicts in Technology Transfer,* Denis Goulet, 318pp, 1977, IDOC/North America, $5.95. While rejecting technological determinism, Goulet maintains that developing countries can manage to incorporate new technologies *and* maintain cultural continuities if they limit what they accept through increased self-reliance and even autonomy.

7 – 76 *Technology for Developing Nations, New Directions for U.S. Technical Assistance,* Rutherford Poates, 225pp, 1972, Brookings Institution, $10.95. An AID (Agency for International Development) official assigns priority to agricultural research, job creating industrial technology, and education, as fields where U.S. assistance can best help.

7 – 77 *International Aid and National Decisions, Development Programs in Malawi, Tanzania, and Zambia,* Leon Gordenker, 190pp, 1976, Princeton U. Press, $16.50. International organizations now provide development assistance to more than 100 countries. This is a study of the impact of these programs on three countries.

7 – 78 *Rich Against Poor, The Reality of Aid,* C.R. Henman, 293pp, 1975, Penguin Books, $3.95. An attack on aid as reinforcing oligarchical elites when the solution to hunger, alienation, and powerlessness is readily available in the China model which "has enough food to eliminate not merely starvation and chronic hunger, but even malnutrition" (p. 277).

7 – 79 *The Lending Policy of the World Bank in the 1970s: Analysis and Evaluation,* Bettini Hurni, 173pp, 1980, Westview, $20.00. Evaluates the shift from traditional capital intensive projects to "growth with equity" and "rural development" strategies by the Bank, and evaluates the success of the new approaches sympathetically.

7 – 80 *The World Bank and the Poor,* Aart van de Laar, 269pp, 1980, Nijhoff, $15.00. A critical assessment of the World Bank's performance, which argues that the developing countries themselves should be more directly involved in deciding bank policies.

G. Food Policy

TEW
7 – 81 *World Hunger Crisis Kit; Hope for the Hungry,* Robert Woito, (ed.), 96pp, 1975, World Without War Council, $1.50. Provides an overview of world hunger through a self-survey highlighting choice points, statements of contending perspectives, a summary of obstacles and a wide range of proposals for overcoming them as well as resources for action.

7 – 82 *Focal Points, A Global Food Strategy,* George Borgstrom, 320pp, 1971, Macmillan, $8.95. Calls for a restructuring of world trade and a massive assault on waste and spoilage as part of a successful strategy.

7 – 82A *Basic Needs and Development*, Danny Leipziger (ed.), 223pp, 1981, Oelges-chlager, $25.00. Seeks to establish "securing access to minimum levels of consumption" as the first task of a development strategy and to indicate how that goal could be best accomplished.

7 – 83 *Food and Agriculture in Global Perspective, Discussions in the Committee of the Whole of the United Nations,* Toivo Miljan (ed.), 285pp, 1980, Pergamon, $20.00. A discussion and papers following up the World Food Conference (1974), recommendations to see how well they have worked, and what is needed.

7 – 84 *Food for War —Food for Peace,* Mitchell Wallerstein, 312pp, 1980, MIT, $30.00. Offers a balanced assessment of American foreign aid and multilateral food aid.

7 – 85 *Ho-ping: Food for Everyone, Strategies to Eliminate Hunger on Spaceship Earth,* Medard Gabel, 272pp, 1979, Doubleday, $9.95. A global perspective and historical portrayal of famines, resources available, and techniques, along with strategies for success including new sources of food.

INF
7 – 86 *To Feed This World: The Challenge and the Strategy,* Sterling Wortman & Ralph Cummings, Jr., 454pp, 1978, Johns Hopkins, $6.95. Maintains that new techniques are enabling farmers to increase production some 30% and that successful drives to accelerate food production have occurred in many countries. Also includes a useful survey of the literature from Malthus to 1977.

7 – 87 *India's Green Revolution, Economic Gains and Political Costs,* Francine Frankel, 232pp, 1972, Princeton U. Press, $12.50. A district-by-district study of India's utilization of new seeds and the impact of India's politics prior to the "emergency."

7 – 88 *Local Response to Global Problems: A Key to Meeting Basic Human Needs,* Bruce Stokes, 64pp, 1978, Worldwatch Institute, $2.00. A hit-and-miss survey of how gardens in urban areas, family plots in China, and other individual activity can help meet food and shelter needs when permitted by governments.

7 – 88A *Villages,* Richard Critchfield, 408pp, 1981, Doubleday, $17.95. Surveys changes in villages in Asia, Africa, and Latin America and suggests that village industrialization and modernization will stem the rural to urban flow of people.

7 – 89 *The World Food Situation and Prospects to 1985,* Economic Research Service, U.S. Dept of Agriculture, 90pp, 1974, U.S. Gov. Printing Office, $1.70. In the aftermath of the World Food Conference (1974), this study concludes that world food production can be expanded to meet the growth needs of that world's population through 1985; that the most efficient way to do this is not through diverting grain from livestock feedlots to overseas distribution, but through a grain reserve, increased production in developing countries, and better utilization of fertilizers to increase yields.

7 – 90 *Food for Peace: Hope and Reality of U.S. Food Aid,* Robert Stanley, 355pp,

1972, Gordon and Breach, $10.95. Explains the nature and magnitude of the world food shortage and the role the U.S. has played in meeting it.

7 – 91 *The Rural World, Education and Development,* Louis Malassis, 128pp, 1976, UNESCO Press, $12.90. Points out that "half the population of school-going age in the LDC's will be members of the farming community" in 1985, and that the total rural population of the world is expected to increase until 2050; the author then offers proposals for effective rural education as part of a development strategy.

7 – 92 *The Nutrition Factor: Its Role in National Development,* Alan Berg, 290pp, 1972, Brookings Institution, $4.95. Assesses the role of an inadequate diet in productivity, literacy, politics, and many other implications, and concludes with specific policy recommendations.

7 – 93 *Land Reform, A World Survey,* Russell King, 446pp, 1977, Westview Press, $28.75. A thorough study of the motives for and types of land reform, plus a world survey of land reform programs in Asia, Africa, and Latin America.

7 – 94 *Land Reform and Politics, A Comparative Analysis,* Hungo-chao Tai, 565pp, 1965, U. of Calif., $28.50. A survey of land reform efforts in developing countries which concludes "that land reform has a definite and positive contribution to make to these aspects of political development" — rural political participation, national integration, institutionalization of rural organization, and rural stability.

H. Population

7 – 95 *Population in Perspective,* Louise Young (ed.), 460pp, 1968, Oxford U. Press, $6.50. Past population surges resulted from discovery of some new forms of subsistence; the current surge is propelled by decreasing death rates and thus no new natural equilibrium is likely; human beings themselves must limit their population. Forty-five essays discuss themes such as these, and why and how to limit population.

7 – 96 *In the Human Interest, A Strategy to Stabilize World Population,* Lester Brown, 190pp, 1974, Norton, $3.95. Brown maintains that the planet can sustain only a finite number of people and must therefore limit population growth through education, economic development, and a new concept of citizenship.

7 – 97 *Women and Population Growth, Choice Beyond Childbearing,* Kathleen Newland, 32pp, 1977, Worldwatch Institute, $2.00. Addresses the question "what needs to be done to make it possible for women in developing societies to have small families?"

7 – 98 *World Population and Development: Challenges and Prospects,* 704pp, 1979, Syracuse, $9.95. Seventeen experts assess current population growth and economic development problems and seek coordinated policies related to both.

7 – 99 *Resource Trends and Population Policy: A Time for Reassessment,* Lester Brown, 55pp, 1979, Worldwatch, $2.00. UN projections expect world population to

stabilize at about twelve billion people about 100 years from now. Brown says basic energy, food and other natural resources required to sustain them will not be available. He offers a way to halt growth at about six billion people.

7 – 100 *Six Billion People: Democratic Dilemmas and World Politics*, George Tapinas and Phyllis Pitrow, 218pp, 1978 McGraw-Hill, $5.95. Projects problems in the 1980s and 1990s such as unemployment, migration and social upheaval; and worries how third world governments and international institutions will react.

7 – 101 *The Population Bomb*, Paul Ehrlich, 222pp, 1971, Ballantine Books, $1.95. An intentionally, and some would say unwarranted, alarmist prediction of the consequence of continued uncontrolled population growth: global famines, wars, social disruption, and 500 million deaths in the 1970s.

I. Toward a New Consenus

7 – 102 *Can the North-South Impasse be Overcome?*, Robert Hansen, 44pp, 1979, Overseas Development Council, $3.00. Calls the North-South negotiations a "dialogue of the deaf," suggests changes in both sides to meet basic needs.

7 – 103 *Can Health and Nutrition Interventions Make a Difference?*, Davidson Gwatkin, Janet Wilcox, & Joe Wray, 88pp, 1980, Overseas Development Council, $5.00. A study of the ten pilot projects explaining how to make the answer "yes,"

7 – 104 *Structural Change and Development Policy*, Hollis Chenery, 526pp, 1980, Oxford, $5.95. An empirical assessment of contending development strategies.

7 – 105 *Peasant Mobilization and Solidarity*, B.F. Galjart, 132pp, 1976, Van Garcum, $13.00. Studies 264 rural communes in Chile to discover what makes for success.

7 – 106 *Dependency Approaches to International Political Economy, A Cross-National Survey*, Vincent Mahlet, 336pp, 1980, Columbia, $22.50. Offers cross-national data from 70 less-developed countries to test the dependency theorists' hypothesis.

7 – 107 *Economic Development, Poverty, and Income Distribution*, William Loehr and John Powerson (eds.), 307pp, 1977, Westview, $22.00. A study of ways to achieve economic development and income distribution so that the poorest in developing countries benefit. Included are assessments of the unreliable data currently available, the role of technological transfers, land reform, rural industrialization, population growth, and aid as policies which are more likely to aid the poorest rather than capital intensive aid or investments.

7 – 108 *The Politics of Starvation*, Jack Shepherd, 101pp, 1975, Carnegie Endowment for International Peace, $3.00. A critique of the way UN officials responded to drought in Ethipia.

7 – 109 *Policies for Industrial Progress in Developing Countries*, John Cody, Helen

Hughes & David Wall, 316pp, 1980, Oxford, $5.95. Twelve economists introduce the central issues in deciding good policies.

7— 110 *Toward a New Strategy for Development,* Rothko Chapel, 365pp, 1979, Pergamon, $8.95. A report on a colloquium with twelve economists from eight countries reflecting different perspectives.

7— 111 *Land Reform and Politics, A Comparative Analysis,* Hung-chao Tai, 565pp, 1965. U. of California Press, $28.50. A survey of land reform efforts in developing countries which concludes "that land reform has a defiinite and positive contribution to make to these aspects of political development" — rural participation, national integration, institutionalization of rural organization, and rural stability.

7— 112 *An Alternative Road to the Post-Petroleum Era: North-South Cooperation,* James Howe & James Tarrant, 80pp, 1980, Overseas Development Council, $5.00. Argues that developing countries can skip the petroleum era and go directly to alternative, renewable forms of energy utilization.

7— 113 *International Indebtedness and the Developing Countries,* George Abbott 308pp, 1979, Sharpe, $25.00. Sees similarities between the debts of third world countries now and Weimar Germany in the 1920s and fears similar results. He offers an ingenious plan for recycling debt payments.

7— 114 *Developing Country Debt,* Lawrence Franko & Marilyn Seiber, 306pp, 1979, Pergamon, $29.50. Provides a background, case studies and current policy choices on this issue.

J. Non-Governmental Organizations

7— 115 *Who's Involved With Hunger, An Organizational Guide,* Patricia Kutzner & Timothy Sullivan (eds.), 35pp, 1979, American Freedom from Hunger Foundation and World Hunger Education Service, $3.00. Provides the names, addresses, and a brief description of more than 250 governmental and private agencies acting to eliminate hunger at both the global and domestic level.

7— 116 *Bread for the World,* Arthur Simon, 177pp, 1975, Paulist Press, $1.50. An attempt to isolate hunger from politics and consider trade, aid, and investments as potentially helpful to developing countries. This book launched the largest citizens' lobbying organization on hunger issues drawn mainly from the religious community and aimed specifically at hunger legislation.

7— 117 *Growing out of Poverty,* Elizabeth Stamp (ed.), 165pp, 1977, Oxford U. Press, $4.95. After an introductory chapter establishing the context in which the projects occur, subsequent chapters describe Oxfam's (a private aid organization) efforts to demonstrate ways to overcome rural poverty.

7— 118 *Beyond Charity, U.S. Voluntary Aid for a Changing Third World,* John Sommer, 180pp, 1977, Overseas Development Council, $3.95. In 1975, U.S. private assistance to developing countries was about one billion dollars. This book assesses the impact of past non-governmental aid, analyzes the direction in which aid is moving, and offers recommendations for increasing he effectiveness of this form of aid.

7 – 119 *Foreign Assistance: A View from the Private Sector,* Kenneth Thompson, 144pp, 1972, U. of Notre Dame Press, $7.95. A former Vice President of the Rockefeller Foundation argues the superiority of private to governmental efforts because of clearer goals and better concentration of resources.

K. Keeping-Up and Reference

7 – 120 *World Hunger, A Guide to the Economic and Political Dimensions,* N. Nicole 1981, ABC-Clio, $30.00. Over 3,000 entries, with an introduction discussing "the worldwide phenomenon of hunger as a political problem."

Write Overseas Development Council, 1717 Massachusetts Ave. N.E., Washington, D.C. 20036, for its current publications list.

Write World Bank, 1818 H Street N.W., Washington, D.C. 20433, for its "Catalog — World Bank Publications."

PART III

ACTORS IN WORLD POLITICS

PART III introduces the actors that might initiate progress toward the conditions essential to a world without war. Their decisions will determine whether progress takes place.

Of all the actors in world politics, States predominate. And among the 170 States, the Soviet Union and the United States are clearly the most powerful. Although the bi-polar division of power that characterized the 1950s has ended, the two superpowers remain in a class by themselves. They alone possess enormous nuclear arsenals and the ability to deliver them anywhere on earth. They possess massive conventional forces and an airlift capacity. In addition, each has an industrial base and at least a minimum supply of energy sources. Each also embodies, though imperfectly, ideologies and ideals which attract followers in other countries. For these reasons, the United States and the Soviet Union are treated in separate chapters.

Since 1960, many new centers of policy initiative and political action have emerged. These include regional powers like Japan, China, Saudi Arabia, Nigeria, and Brazil, which possess a high degree of independence from the superpowers, and can initiate new politics in their regions without regard for superpowers' wishes. In time, they could become superpowers themselves. But today each lacks one or more of the characteristics of the superpowers: an industrial base, a significant energy source, or an attractive ideology or ideal. Such regional powers are discussed in Chaper 10.

While international organizations today generally reflect the policies of leading States and blocs of States, they and other non-State actors can be independent sources of ideas and action. International non-governmental or-

197

ganizations within States also play increasingly significant roles. Transnational corporations have likewise emerged as significant actors in world politics, weaker than most States, but nonetheless capable of exercising considerable influence.[1]

States, intergovernmental organizations, and non-State actors are each introduced in this Part III. Differing assessments of their abilities, goals and performance are presented, as well as their present or potential roles in initiating progress toward a world without war.

---

[1] A corporation's gross receipts may be larger than many States' GNP, but these are not comparable figures, since a corporation cannot control its receipts in the same way. Much of a corporation's revenue is spent in earning the income. In addition, a corporation's income within any State is bound to be far less than that State's GNP.

CHAPTER 8

THE UNITED STATES AND WORLD POLITICS

A WORLD POWER WITH A SENSE OF FAILURE

Two general themes prevail in the literature assessing the role of the United States in world politics from 1945 to the present. The first stresses its enormous resources — military, economic, political, and moral — which can be brought to bear on foreign policy objectives. Its military power is similar to that of the Soviet Union in size and superior in technical quality. Its economic resources remain the largest of any State. For over one hundred years, its democratic political system has accommodated change and, against internal and external challenges, has retained the overwhelming support of the electorate. Its attempt to confront and resolve the problems of an urban, industrialized, multi-racial, multi-ethnic society make it a leader in the world for addressing these problems. Religious institutions remain a vital part of its societal life, clarifying values and asserting their relevance to world politics.

But the second theme elaborates on the paradoxical fact that its foreign policy has failed. Today there are few champions of U. S. achievements in world politics since 1945.

THE ORTHODOX AND REVISIONIST EXPLANATIONS

An intense debate rages as to *why* U. S. policy has failed. Those like Arthur M. Schlesinger, Jr., generally supportive of U. S. motives and the main thrust of our post– World War II foreign policy, maintain that the public's understanding of the U. S. as a well-meaning power is generally correct. He and other defenders of our motives maintain that U. S. foreign policy in 1945 was properly oriented toward achieving peace through international organization. The creation of the UN and our participation in it, even the hope that the UN would evolve into an effective world government, drew support from many in this orthodox camp. Some, to be sure, saw the veto power in the Security Council as an essential requisite for U. S. participation and in conformity with power realities. All agreed that the U. S. must participate in world politics, and should and could do so with benefit to itself, to others, and to democratic values.

The UN could be effective in resolving major security issues only so long as the United States and the Soviet Union were in agreement, and each had a veto power in the Security Council. Thus, when Stalin refused to abide by the Yalta agreements concerning elections in East Europe, put pressure on Turkey and Greece, and sought to subvert governments elsewhere, the U. S. did what it had to do. It created a series of military alliances, the foremost of which was NATO, to prevent overt aggression. It funded the Marshall Plan and other economic assistance programs to prevent internal subversion, promote development, and rebuild Europe.

According to the orthodox view, the dominant driving force in the post– World War II era was an expansionist Soviet Union. From the Berlin Blockade (1948) to the Cuban Missile Crisis (1962), the initiative in world politics lay with the Soviet Union. It was the Soviet Union that provided the military supplies and political approval which enabled the North Koreans to launch the Korean War (1951), and which sought to place revolutionary socialists (aligned to the Soviet Union) in power wherever they could. The U. S. response was measured. It kept ahead in the arms race, thus deterring nuclear war; it sought to promote trade as an essential ingredient in achieving economic assistance to numerous States around the world; and it sought to promote political democracy in Europe and in the newly emerging countries. In Korea, a collective military response was required. In all of this, the orthodox school of thought seldom questioned U. S. motives. Military commitments were made only if there was a clear-cut instance of aggression by a major power and if a collective response could be entered into through the constitutional processes of government. Thus, in summary, the orthodox viewpoint supported the bi-partisan consensus for a U. S. foreign policy aimed at a limited and appropriate response to Soviet expansionism and at a defense of democratic and Western values against onslaught by a totalitarian power.

All these conclusions were challenged incthe 1960s by the revisionists, who sought to reverse every judgment in the orthodox interpretation. Where, in the orthodox view, the Soviet Union originated the Cold War, the revisionists saw the United States as the primary instigator. With different emphases, a variety of scholars (Williams, 8-57; Kolko, 8-54; and Alperovitz, 8-60) argued that U. S. business leaders (either by extensive lobbying or by holding government positions) sought to control world trade. These business leaders feared the return of a depression after World War II, and so sought to secure overseas markets for American products, to gain access to inexpensive raw materials, and to find new outlets for investments. The Soviet Union, far from being expansionist, had legitimate security concerns in its sphere of influence and acted in Eastern Europe as the U. S. itself would have, had it been attacked twice in thirty years. It was the United States, through the United Nations, which sought to impose its conception of world order on the rest of the world. Far from enjoying genuine public support, U. S. foreign policy objectives gained support only by whipping up anti-communist hysteria through scare tactics and control of the media.

In both the orthodox and the revisionist camps there are significant internal disagreements. Many who hold the orthodox view have accepted some of the revisionist points to supplement their own perspective. Many now argue that the United States is also responsible for the Cold War because it missed many opportunities to reduce mutual antagonisms. The Soviet Union did have security and economic needs which the United States ignored; as the Cold War developed, the United States, through the doctrine of containment, acquired bases and stationed soldiers in other countries; it supported allies wherever they could be found, whether or not they had democratic governments.

The two views coincide in explaining many areas of United States foreign policy in the 1960s and 1970s. But there remains a fundamental difference as to what motivated, and still motivates, that policy. Among the revisionists, some (e.g. Kolko) argue that a capitalist elite is pursuing its self-interest in world politics through the avenue of U. S. foreign policy. The Vietnam war was not a mistake, but rather the logical conclusion of this policy influence. The orthodox respond that not business interests but power politics led to Vietnam. They argue that the U. S. commitment of 500,000 combat soldiers in Vietnam violated all of the earlier criteria for military engagements: it was not decided upon by constitutional procedures as a collective response to a clear-cut act of aggression by a major power. Instead, "the best and the brightest" (the young scholars and academics) John F. Kennedy had brought to Washington, and Lyndon Johnson, misapplied the containment doctrine of the 1950s.

LESSONS AND "UN-LESSONS" OF VIETNAM

For a long time, the divisive legacy of the Vietnam war invaded every discussion of U. S. foreign policy. A study of the impact of Vietnam on leaders and the public concluded:

> Of the thirteen lessons of Vietnam all but four represent the antithesis of the postwar axioms. To be sure, an overwhelming majority of the respondents in the study continued to regard the Soviet Union as an expansionist power, and two-thirds of them considered the domino theory to be valid. But beyond that, change and disagreement are much more evident than continuity and consensus. . . .

The study goes on to identify competing belief systems and to conclude:

> . . . these differences appear to be embedded within and sustained by well-defined clusters of supporting beliefs that extend from conceptions of the international system to the most effective means by which the U. S. should pursue its foreign policy goals. . . . these competing conceptions of international politics are unlikely to change soon or casually.[1]

The sources of this division in the public, which undermines any constructive foreign policy, can be traced to different interpretations of the Vietnam war.

After a period of silence, a new series of books, articles, and public discussion of the Vietnam war interpreted and reinterpreted the Vietnam lesson. The discussion remained focused on the same questions. Were the United States presidents right or wrong in committing American troops in Vietnam? Was the best military strategy adopted for fighting the war? Was the conduct of the war within the rules of warfare, or did it violate them in so fundamental a way that charges of war crimes should be made? Could a non-military strategy have succeeded in gaining what was lost militarily: a political process capable of enabling the South Vietnamese people to choose their form of government? Was the National Liberation Front just a facade for North Vietnam? How much support did it have? What is the primary lesson for the U.S.?

A consensus concerning the Vietnam experience exists in the conclusion "never again," but disagreement as to *why* never again is as broad now as it was at the height of the war. The mistake, many argue, was to escalate the war slowly. That failed to persuade the leadership in Hanoi to negotiate for appropriate political processes through which to decide who should rule in South

---

[1]James Rosenau and Ole Holsti, *Vietnam Consensus and the Belief Systems of American Leaders* (Los Angeles: University of Southern California, 1980)

Vietnam. It also failed to take into account the difficulty for a democratic society to wage a long war, and to sustain high casualties, when its vital interests did not appear to be at stake. Once a military commitment is made, the full use of military power should be employed. Many in this camp felt betrayed by U. S. leadership, seeing in the Panama Canal Treaties, the SALT II Treaty, the Iranian seizure of the U. S. Embassy, and the Soviet invasion of Afghanistan continuing instances of a weak America failing to protect its national interests. They applaud the new assertiveness of the Reagan Administration.

Others argue that the lesson to be learned from Vietnam is that, as Jospeh Buttinger (*Vietnam* 8-78) puts it, the U.S. should "never again try to save reactionary dictatorships whose survival is threatened by popular uprisings." Those who argue that Vietnam policy flowed from the economic and political structures of the United States still maintain that view. Both conclude that in Iran, the U. S. had it coming.

Events following the end of the Vietnam war have been less kind to the critics of American involvment than to the supporters. The National Liberation Front did not survive the end of the war by one week, thus indicating it was hardly the autonomous political organization many considered it to be. Those who championed the NLF as a popular democratic movement, likely to pursue a neutralist foreign policy once in power, found instead Hanoi's leaders imposing repressive mechanisms of totalitarian control, and a base for Soviet influence in Southeast Asia. One opponent of American military policy in the 1960s, Robert Pickus, now concludes that the aftermath of the war may have been worse, for the Vietnamese people, than the war itself. During the war, no one preferred the risks of dying on the South China Seas to the risks of survival on land. Since 1975, over 500,000 Indochinese "boat people" have tested the roughly 50 percent odds of survival. Pickus goes on to underline the need for a genuine anti-war movement capable of challenging the military policies of the U. S. *and* its adversaries, while developing non-military ways to conduct and resolve conflict (Pickus, preface to *Neither Victims Nor Executioners,* 20-134).

The lesson of America's abuse of power in Vietnam was a prevailing theme in our foreign policy discussion in the 1970s. That theme was applied by Congress to what was described as the imperial presidency (Schlesinger, 8-140). The institutions within the executive branch held primarily responsible for the war (the Presidency, the CIA, and the military) were subjected to prolonged scrutiny and attack. Studies of the battles between the executive and legislative branches of government over control of foreign policy find in thirty skirmishes betwen 1969 and 1973, thirty victories for Congress. The CIA (Colby, *Honorable Men,* 8-138) was the target of the most devastating attack ever launched on a U. S. intelligence agency. The military could no longer count on its requests for new weapons systems to be honored, despite a significant, even alarming, increase in Soviet military expenditures. By 1973, Congress was in a position to cut off funding for the Vietnam war and to block U. S. military aid to a faction fighting in Angola against the Cuban-backed faction; and did so *(Foreign Policy by Congress,* 8-105). The Carter Administration came to office advocating a lower American profile in world politics, detente with the Soviet Union, reduction of military spending and of conventional arms transfers, the advocacy of human rights observance by allies, strategic arms limitation, and non-intervention in third world countries. All this suggested a shift from a military and unilateral engagement, toward a non-military, and even a multi-lateral, approach to world politics.

SNAPPING

The sudden reversal of attitudes in the American public, brought about by the Vietnam war, suggests a concept used by the human potential movement — "snapping," the sudden change of personality. Is the United States, as the consensus of the 1950s had it, the leader of the free world, sacrificing its wealth and youth in a protracted conflict against the insidious forces of totalitarianism? Or, is the United States, as the revisionist historians and others would have it, the enemy (8-47 to 66)? As the 1980s began, the seizure of the U. S. Embassy in Teheran and the Soviet invasion of Afghanistan brought a new U. S. personality into public view. The withdrawal of American influence from Southeast Asia, and the lowered profile everywhere but in the Middle East, was not the victory for liberation for which some had hoped; rather, it had produced a power vacuum from which emerged regimes profoundly disappointing to everyone with democratic values and not blinded by the lessons of Vietnam. Soviet military power or Soviet-aided national forces not only came to power in Vietnam, but by 1980 influenced Laos, Cambodia, Afghanistan, South Yemen, Ethiopia, and Angola. The Soviet invasion of Afghanistan overthrew a head of State previously installed by the Soviets and placed, in his stead, someone not even in the country when the invasion began. The Soviet invasion tested the independence of its friends and allies, and the French Communist Party joined the PLO, Cuba, the new third world clients, and the Eastern European States in approving aggression. Several Western European Communist Parties opposed, as did the rest of the third world countries. The lowered U. S. profile in world politics, détente, the reduction of military spending, and non-intervention did not deter the Soviet Union from aggression.

But what will be the new U. S. personality? Most likely it will be a new containment strategy composed of new military alliances; lines drawn on a map which, if crossed, will trigger war; and spiraling of military expenditures. This is called a "new assertiveness" of American interests in world politics. It is hailed by those who learned the costs of appeasement in the 1930s and of a misnamed detente in the 1970s. Advocates of this view argue that a get-tough policy will demonstrate that international support for American objectives pays off, and this will draw new allies to the U. S., provided one of those objectives is the independence of allies. Alliances are sought with authoritarian governments on the grounds that they may evolve into democratic governments while left-wing totalitarian governments never do. The American assertiveness is largely military, with its supporters divided over how much (or how little) to emphasize as conditions of support, human rights concerns, internal economic reforms, and honesty in government.

This new, largely military, assertiveness is challenged by those opposed to American military power and by those who doubt the Soviet Union has ambitious strategic objectives. These latter believe that the Soviet invasion of Afghanistan was a form of "defensive aggression" designed to warn the Soviet's Muslim minority so that the "Islamic revival" will never become an effective political force within the Soviet Union. The opposition in America will be sizable: drawing strength from those who remember Vietnam as a terrible abuse of American military power, from those who know the financial and human costs, and the drain away from resources for domestic programs, as well as from those who are subject to the draft.

But neither the new containment strategy nor the challenge to American military power speaks adequately and effectively to the problems which this country now faces: Soviet military power, the agenda of a threatening interdependent world, gross violations of human rights, the lack of positive economic and political alternatives suited to third world countries, the lack of moral credibility — to name but a few. When the proposed alternatives appear inadequate to the challenges, when the country's foreign policy personality appears to be "snapping," the best course may be to re-examine the perennial questions of world politics, to clarify and apply democratic values to the challenges of the 1980s.

THE PERENNIAL QUESTIONS

The questions which students of world affairs and of America's role in them usually ask are these:

1. What level of engagement in world politics is appropriate and desirable for the United States?

2. What purposes should the U.S. pursue — national security, economic advantage, human rights, containment, building a sense of world community — to make possible conflict resolution and constructive change?

3. Should the national interest or moral and legal concepts provide the evaluative principles for deciding policies?

The appropriate level of engagement cannot be debated meaningfully in time-honored terms of isolationism versus internationalism. An awareness of interdependence (see Chapter 12), in a world with nuclear weapons and without enforceable law, alters the consequences of following either course. To reach a consensus necessary to sustain a new U. S. engagement in world affairs, we must in some way progress toward all the goals listed in the second question above — security, economic self-interest, human rights, containment, world community, conflict resolution, and constructive change. None of the goals can be achieved in isolation from the others. The national interest, when offered as a preferred substitute for moral abstractions, may not be of much use. Different perceptions of the national interest quickly emerge, rooted in conflicting moral premises. Many people, even some who admire the aristocratic age of European statecraft, consider pursuit of world community as the course most in the national interest in today's interdependent world.

Those who argue that self-interest is an appropriate motive for foreign policy assert that there is no possibility of escape from power politics "into a realm where action is guided by moral principles rather than by consideration of power" (Morgenthau). Nevertheless, many of them argue that both moral purposes and today's power realities dictate a wider definition of the national interest. The new definition would acknowledge the need for supporting moral and legal principles that are demonstrably in the interests of all countries, not only of one.

WHAT GOALS?

Building consensus around a constructive engagement by the U. S. requires agreement about the goals to be sought, and an understanding of how to pursue such goals in the face of Soviet military policies. No society other than that of the U.S. has greater influence on its leaders' choice of goals, and no other State's decision about what goals to seek is of greater importance. U. S. goals could be defined as "blocking Soviet expansionism," "avoiding nuclear war," or "ignoring Soviet expansionism," or "no more Vietnams," but these are basically negative objectives. In a world being shaped and reshaped by swift currents of change, such a negative stand is not adequate, appropriate, or effective in eliminating war from international conflict.

Our country's policies have a definite impact upon world politics. The withdrawal of power has consequences; so does the misuse of power. A creative alternative to either withdrawal or the abuse of military power is to work to reach agreement with adversaries on the next steps toward the conditions essential to a world without war. Agreements are needed concerning the goals which all parties should pursue; the specific steps that will help move this and other societies toward those goals; the international or supranational institutions, procedures and actions needed for resolving conflicts without violence; and the procedures to be used in resolving common problems and to facilitate change. Gaining agreement on these objectives would return the U. S. to the goals which the State Department articulated (but did not find the appropriate means to pursue) in the Truman, Eisenhower, and Kennedy Administrations: 1. Universal and complete disarmament under international controls; 2. strengthening the United Nations and its agencies into instruments of world law; 3. economic and other assistance for Africa, Asia, and Latin American countries in their revolution of modernization; 4. communication, exchange, and peaceful settlement with the Communist world, so that those countries would join the U. S. in pursuing the above goals.

It is, however, no longer enough to offer positive goals; it is also necessary to demonstrate how they can be pursued. Progress toward these goals is not likely in the midst of the present escalating arms race. It is not likely at all unless the kinds of agreements indicated above can be achieved with the Soviet Union, with regional powers, and with other States.

The setting within which these goals can be pursued and within which agreements must be sought is complex and changing. The web of relationships imperfectly captured in the concept of interdependence suggests that there are many levers of influence besides those afforded by military force. In many ways, the attempt to use military force is counter-productive, even in practical terms. In other ways, and at different times and places, military force is clearly what decides many issues in today's world politics. The U. S. has yet to apply its full resources to the non-military pursuit of the goals essential to a world without war. The U. S. has yet to test whether it can bring adequate non-military incentives and pressures to bear on the Soviet Union and on others to gain their agreement. Given the widespread yearning for economic development and constructive change, the superpower which leads in the direction of the goals that can produce those results will have a powerful advantage over the other. Those who agree that U. S. policy has failed, still know that it is the only democratic superpower which can offer the necessary leadership. Only if such leadership is forthcoming can we make significant progress in this century toward a world without war.

BIBLIOGRAPHY

The bibliography will help the reader to answer questions such as these: 1) Is world politics a constant struggle for power and advantage which must be carried out with violence? 2) Could a sense of world community be created through the leadership of one State and by the response of others? 3) Is the United States a functioning democracy, or does a closed elite make the basic decisions without having to account to the electorate for its judgments? 4) Is the American economic system responsible for a bellicose post-World War II engagement of the U. S. in world politics, or did it respond in an appropriate way to Soviet expansionism? 5) What goals should this country now pursue? 6) What means are appropriate to use in pursuit of those goals? 7) Does a democratic country which is deeply influenced by Judaic and Christian values have a particular responsibility to seek non-military conflict resolution in world politics? 8) What lessons should U. S. leaders learn from World War I? The isolationism of the 1920s? The attempt to keep America out of war in the 1930s? World War II? The Cold War? The Vietnam War? The post – Vietnam era? 9) What is the combined impact of all of those lessons? 10) What are the strengths and weaknesses of the U. S. as it engages more deeply in world politics in the 1980s?

A. Documents & References

8 – 1 *News Dictionary 1978,* Donald Paneth, 390pp, 1979, Facts on File, $9.95. An annual, alphabetized, brief summary of national and international news.

8 – 2 *The Dynamics of World Power: A Documentary History of U. S. Foreign Policy, 1945 – 1973,* Arthur M. Schlesinger, Jr. (ed.), 5,075 pp, 1980, Chelsea House, $80.00. Each volume is devoted to a geographic region and includes documents on both the formulation and execution of foreign policy. A valuable reference work.

8 – 3 *American Foreign Relations, 1976: A Documentary Record,* Elaine Adam (ed.), 559pp, 1978, New York University Press, $28.50. Contains both analytical essays and documents.

8 – 4 *Makers of American Diplomacy, From Benjamin Franklin to Alfred Thayer Mahan,* Vol. I, *From Theodore Roosevelt to Henry Kissinger,* Vol II, Frank Merli & Theodore Wilson (eds.), 672pp, 1974, Scribner., $9.95 each. Essays describing U.S. Secretaries of State.

8 – 5 *Encyclopedia of American Foreign Policy, Studies of the Principal Movements and Ideas,* Alexander DeConde (ed.), 1,201pp, 1978, Scribner, $130.00. Comprises ninety-five essays covering the political spectrum, from 1776 to the 1970s. Essays are arranged by topics with an excellent cross-reference system.

8 – 6 *U. S. Federal Official Publications: The International Dimension*, J. A. Downey, 352pp, 1978, Pergamon, $52.00. A guide to the mountains of governmental publications, some quite valuable.

8 – 7 *United States Foreign Relations: A Guide to Information Sources*, Elmer Plischke (ed.), 1980, Gale, $24.00. A useful reference.

8 – 8 *A Guide to American Foreign Relations Since 1970*, ABC-Clio. An annotated bibliography with introductions to each section. (Forthcoming.)

B. Diplomatic History

8 – 9 *The American Diplomatic Experience*, Daniel Smith, 491pp, 1972, Houghton-Mifflin, $7.95. A survey of the U. S. international relations from independence to the 1970s. Examines the fundamental continuities, and highlights the controversies of interpretation surrounding specific events.

8 – 10 *History of American Foreign Policy*, Alexander DeConde, 490pp, 1978 (3rd ed.), Scribner, 2 vol., $9.95 each. Each volume provides an overview of the period and then a narrative. Essays focus on different issues and areas and are only loosely connected.

8 – 11 *American Foreign Policy: A History*, Thomas Paterson, J. Gary Clifford, Kenneth Hagan, 607pp, 1977, Heath, $14.95. A survey of American diplomatic history from 1789 to the present.

8 – 12 *Major Problems in American Foreign Policy: Documents and Essays*, Thomas G. Paterson, (ed.) Vol. I (to 1914) $7.95, 360pp, 1978, Vol. II (since 1914)., 525pp, 1978, Heath, $8.95. Combines documents with interpretations of the major problems by contemporary scholars.

8 – 13 *American Diplomacy, 1900 – 1950*, George F. Kennan, 127pp, 1952, Mentor, $.95. A history of the U. S. rise to global power, sympathetic to U. S. motives but critical of the influence of moralistic and legalistic concepts in a world dominated by national interest diplomacy.

8 – 14 *Two Hundred Years of American Foreign Policy*, William Bundy (ed.), 251 pp, 1977, N. Y. Univ. Press, $15.00. Bi-centennial reflections by eight men who helped conceptualize or carry out U. S. foreign policy. Essays provide both an overview of the period and specific studies of the last ten years.

8 – 15 *Rendezvous with Destiny, A History of Modern American Reform*, Eric Goldman, 372pp, 1978, Random House, $3.95. A broad social history of the 20th century America, describing the isolationalist-internationalist debate of the 1930s.

8 – 16 *Walter Lippmann and the American Century*, Ronald Steel, 640pp, 1980, Little, Brown, $22.50. A judicious political biography of the influential columnist and intellec-

tual. Lippmann was a realist who understood the measured use of military force as necessary to secure nationalist interests. He opposed the use of force outside America's sphere of influence except in concert with many others.

8 – 17 *American Appeasement, United States Foreign Policy and Germany 1933-1938,* Arnold Offner, 328pp, 1976, Norton, $3.95. Details U. S. role in appeasing Hitler as it sought the moderator's role in European politics.

8 – 18 *Franklin D. Roosevelt and the World Crisis, 1937 – 1945,* Warren Kimball (ed.), 297 pp, 1973, D. C. Heath, $4.95. Conflicting interpretations of U. S. policies and the origins, conduct, and wartime diplomacy of World War II; for example, FDR is seen both as an anti-Communist crusader (Kolko) and as a Communist dupe (Kubek).

8 – 19 *Franklin Roosevelt and American Foreign Policy, 1932 – 1945,* Robert Dallek, 657pp, 1979, Oxford, $25.00. A detailed and largely sympathetic treatment of Roosevelt, arguing that the constraints of public opinion and Congress limited Roosevelt's effectiveness. Mistakes are recognized but are placed in the larger perspective of winning World War II and the creation of the United Nations.

8 – 20 *20th Century American Foreign Policy, Security and Self-Interest,* Ronald Caridi, 388pp, 1974, Prentice-Hall, $11.50. An historical reassessment ''stressing the interpretations of the revisionists'' and giving ''emphasis to domestic influences on foreign policy.'' It includes evidence supporting other interpretations and influences.

C. Overviews Since World War II: Theory and Anthologies

8 – 21 *Ideals and Self-Interest in America's Foreign Relations, The Great Transformation of the Twentieth Century,* Robert Osgood, 491pp, 1963, Chicago, $10.00. Argues that neither national self-interest nor utopian idealism offers an intelligent context for foreign policy decision-making. The trick is to relate ideals to political realities.

8 – 22 *The Isolationist Impulse: Its Twentieth Century Reaction,* Selig Adler, 538pp, 1974 (1957) Greenwood, $26.00. Examines the roots and different expressions of isolationist sentiment in the U. S. since World War I. Argues that both a withdrawal from foreign affairs and a militant crusading spirit spring from a single root: a self-conscious fear of differences.

8 – 23 *American Foreign Policy: A Contemporary Introduction,* Thomas Brewer, 302pp, 1980, Prentice-Hall, $9.95. Introduces the major concepts and points of view.

8 – 24 *Readings in American Foreign Policy,* Robert Goldwin and Harry Clar (eds.), 721pp, 1971 (2nd ed.), Oxford, $7.95. Probably the best anthology on the crucial concepts and persistent tendencies of American foreign policy. Presents classic and contemporary readings from a variety of perspectives on American expansionism, the relationship between democracy and foreign policy, the U.S. role in international organizations, and the principles that should guide American foreign policy.

8 – 25 *The Western Alliance: European – American Relations Since 1945,* Alfred Grosser, 416pp, 1980, Continuum, $19.05. Traces the complex web of interests, actors, and purposes over the period when America's role was preeminent.

8 – 26 *Reflections on the Cold War: A Quarter Century of American Foreign Policy,* Lynn Miller & Ronald Pruessen (eds.), 224pp, 1974, Temple, $15.00. A collection of essays offering different interpretations of America's role in the cold war.

8 – 27 *Successful Negotiation: Trieste 1954: An Appraisal by the Five Participants,* John Campbell (ed.), 225pp, 1975, Princeton, $14.50. A study of diplomacy.

8 – 28 *The Lessons of the Past: The Use and Misuse of History in American Foreign Policy,* Ernest May, 238pp, 1975, Oxford, $3.95. Describes policy-makers' attempts to learn a single lesson from history as well as the consequences: backing into the current war by avoiding the errors which led to the previous one.

8 – 29 *The Imperial Republic: The United States and the World, 1945 – 1973,* Raymond Aron, 339pp, 1975, Prentice-Hall, $7.95. An important study of the U.S.'s troubled role in world politics since World War II and its effects on America.

8 – 30 *American Foreign Policy, Opposing Viewpoints,* David Bender & Gary McCuen (eds.), 88 pp, 1972, Greenhaven, $4.60. Brief opposed selections highlight the choices between self-interest and idealism, between goals and about communism.

D. The Orthodox Interpretation

8 – 31 *American Foreign Policy and the Blessings of Liberty and other Essays,* Samuel Flagg Bemis, 423pp, 1975 (1962), Greenwood, $21.25. A famous diplomatic historian's best essays.

8 – 32 *Liberal America and the Third World: Political Development Ideas in Foreign Aid and Social Science,* Robert A. Packenham, 395pp, 1973, Princeton Univ. Press, $5.95. Accepts Hartz's thesis that the U.S. is a unique country having become democratic without a revolution, and then argues that government officials and social scientists have been wrong in stressing liberal values in relations with third world countries. "Autocratic" governments are considered more likely, instead, to "achieve the most salient objectives of their peoples."

8 – 33 *The Ordeal of World Power: American Diplomacy Since 1900,* Samuel Wells, Jr., Robert Ferrell and David Trask, 366pp, 1975, Little Brown, $6.95. Features personalities and issues interwoven with the changing setting of American diplomacy; few criticisms are offered, motivation is rarely questioned: preventing the domination of Europe by any hostile power is a permanent worthy objective.

8 – 34 *The Inequality of Nations,* Robert W. Tucker, 214pp, 1979, Basic Books, $4.95. Argues that given the inherent inequality of states, the challenge of the developing states to the existing system in the name of equality, will produce a new hierarchy. The basic

thrust of the new egalitarianism is toward the sovereign equality of states, not to the elimination of the economic disparities within states.

8 – 35 *Realities of American Foreign Policy,* George F. Kennan, 120pp, 1966, Norton, $2.95. A discussion by one of America's most thoughtful and experienced diplomats of the principles which he believes should underlie U.S. foreign policy. A critique of inappropriate uses of moralistic and legalistic approaches to foreign policy problems.

8 – 36 *The Devil and John Foster Dulles, The Diplomacy of the Eisenhower Era,* Townsend Hoopes, 562pp, 1973, Atlantic – Little, Brown, $4.95. Condemns Dulles' tendency to see the Cold War as a clash between good and evil, while recognizing that Dulles avoided actual war; critical of most elements of Dulles' policies, particularly those concerning the third world.

8 – 37 *The United States in World Affairs,* Paul Seabury, 124pp, 1972, McGraw – Hill, $5.95. An introduction to the basic concepts in national interest diplomacy.

8 – 38 *America and the World, From the Truman Doctrine to Vietnam,* Robert Osgood, et al, 434pp, 1970, Johns Hopkins Press, $5.95. "What are America's vital interests and how should it use its power to support them? This is the fundamental foreign policy question facing the U.S. after two decades of the Cold War." This question sets the framework within which seven authors assess U.S. foreign policy including its impact on domestic issues.

8 – 39 *Imperial America: The International Politics of Primacy,* George Liska, 115pp, 1967, Johns Hopkins Press, $2.95. A reasoned argument for American use of military power throughout the world as a means of preserving peace.

8 – 40 *Retreat From Empire?, The First Nixon Administration,* Robert Osgood (ed.), 350pp, 1973, Johns Hopkins Press, $4.95. An anthology tracing the retrenchment of American power from what the editor believes was an overextended posture. The result, he says, will be a safer international order.

8 – 41 *A World Elsewhere: The New American Foreign Policy,* James Chace, 108pp, 1973, Scribner, $5.95. A brief survey of post – World War II foreign policy rationales. Argues for a balance between pursuit of transnational interdependence and balance-of-power politics; neither alone is adequate.

8 – 42 *American Foreign Policy Since World War II,* John Spanier, 273pp, 1960, 1980 (8th ed), Praeger, $9.95. Based on the premise that a nation's foreign relations "are largely determined by the requirements of maintaining a balance of power," and rejects the views that focus solely on domestic factors. Spanier argues that the U.S. is ill-prepared by tradition or experience to play the role the state system requires of it . . . a counterweight to expansionist Communist states.

8 – 43 *Beyond Containment: U.S. Foreign Policy in Transition,* Robert W. Tucker and William Watts (eds.), 212pp, 1973, Potomac Associates, $3.50. Commentaries on U.S. foreign policy — past, present, and future — by the men involved in formulating it.

Addresses the question: Are we still guarantors of a global order now openly identified with the status quo?

8 – 44 *Caging the Bear: Containment and the Cold War,* Charles Gati (ed.), 228pp, 1974, Bobbs-Merrill, $5.50. Essays by Truman, Fulbright, Spanier, Brzezinski, and others, evaluate the policy of containment and its effects on U.S. relations with the Soviet Union and China.

8 – 45 *The Origins of the Cold War,* J. Joseph Huthmacher and Warren Susman (eds.), 122pp, 1970, Ginn-Blaisdele, $9.95. Essays by Lloyd Gardner, Arthur Schlesinger Jr., and Hans Morgenthau re-define the orthodox view of the origins of the cold war. Gardner stresses the expansionist character of Soviet Communism; Schlesinger, the personality of Stalin; and Morgenthau, the inevitable power struggle between two incompatible political systems.

8 – 46 *A Thousand Days,* Arthur M. Schlesinger, Jr., 967pp, 1977, Fawcett, $2.95. A sympathetic chronicle of the Kennedy Administration of particular interest for its description of Kennedy's peace intitiative strategy which led to the signing of the partial test-ban treaty.

E. The Revisionist Interpretation

8 – 47 *Rise to Globalism, American Foreign Policy, 1938 – 1980,* Stephen Ambrose, 464pp, 1980 (Rev. Ed.), Penguin Books, $4.95. A revisionist work which explains the difference between the U.S. military budget of 1939 ($500 million) and 1976 ($80 billion) as a product of choices by U.S. leaders during a depression (1945 – 1950), as well as the resultant building of a global system of markets and raw material sources. Little hope is offered for a change. The Soviet Union is seen as largely a defensive power acting in response to U.S. initiative.

8 – 48 *Pax Americana: The Cold War Empire and the Politics of Counterrevolution,* Ronald Steel, 365pp, 1977 (rev. ed.), Penguin Books, $4.50. Effectively contrasting John Adams' call for the U.S. to be "the well-wisher to the freedom and independence of all . . . but the champion and vindicator only of her own" with John F. Kennedy's call to be the "watchman on the walls of world freedom," calls for a return from global commitments to an acceptance of global pluralism and an effort to achieve U.S. ideals here at home.

8 – 49 *The Elusive Enemy; American Foreign Policy Since World War II,* Simon Serfaty, 241pp, 1972, Little, Brown & Co., $5.95. Attempts "to narrate and to interpret the growth of American interventionism after World War II," and concludes that the U.S. has acted as a great power should be expected to act, no better and no worse.

8 – 50 *Cold War and Counterrevolution: The Foreign Policy of John F. Kennedy,* Richard J. Walton, 250pp, 1972, Penguin, $2.95. A critique of the Schlesinger and

Sorenson histories of "Camelot" which argues Kennedy's anti-communism prevailed over his sympathy for the oppressed. "It did not seem to occur to Kennedy or his advisers that there might be circumstances when a people, through revolution, might validly choose Communism as offering the best path to economic and social development" (Richard Walton, p. 207), or to Walton how a people under Communism might change their minds.

8 – 51 *Intervention and Revolution: America's Confrontation with Insurgent Movements Around the World,* Richard Barnet, 302pp, 1972 (Rev. Ed.), New American Library, $1.75. An analysis of U.S. intervention in Greece, Lebanon, the Dominican Republic, and Vietnam, which concludes that the U.S. cannot and should not attempt to suppress revolutionary movements. Recommends a multilateral (United Nations) approach to international conflict resolution.

8 – 52 *Readings in U.S. Imperialism,* K.T. Fann and Donald C. Hodges (eds.), 397pp, 1971, Porter Sargent $4.95. The title of the introductory essay by Bertrand Russell, "Peace Through Resistance to American Imperialism," summarizes the theme of this collection. Other contributors include Williams, Castro, Piao, Che, and Carmichael.

8 – 53 *The Origins of the Cold War,* Thomas Paterson (ed.), 274pp, 1974, D. C. Heath, $4.95. An anthology which presents the main revisionists' arguments, plus several orthodox views which adequately introduce major points in the debate although only one speech by Stalin suggests Soviet objectives.

8 – 54 *The Roots of American Foreign Policy: An Analysis of Power and Purpose,* Gabriel Kolko, 166pp, 1969, Beacon Press, $3.95. Kolko's thesis is that American foreign policy has been motivated by the only thinly veiled or rationalized economic self-interest of U.S. business. U.S. capitalism has been saved by projecting its failure beyond the U.S. to the globe. "The elimination of . . . American hegemony is the essential precondition for the emergence of a nation and a world in which mass hunger, suppression, and war are no longer the inevitable and continuous characteristics of modern civilization."

8 – 55 *The Arrogance of Power,* J. William Fulbright, 264pp, 1967, Random, $1.95. The title summarizes the former Senate Foreign Relations Committee Chairman's criticism of a decade of U.S. foreign policy. Few of Fulbright's constructive ideas show here.

8 – 56 *Containment and Change: Two Dissenting Views of American Society and Foreign Policy in the New Revolutionary Age,* Carl Oglesby and Richard Shaull, 248pp, 1967, Macmillan, $1.45. A New Left analysis and rejection of the Western political tradition. U.S. foreign policy is seen as part of the Westernization of the globe which is opposed, peculiarly enough, on the grounds of that distinctively Western concept-individual conscience.

8 – 57 *The Great Evasion: An Essay on the Contemporary Relevance of Karl Marx and on the Wisdom of Admitting the Heretic into the Dialogue about America's Future,* William Appleman Williams, 187pp, 1968, *New Viewpoints,* $2.45. An American

Marxist historian argues that U.S. foreign policy is interventionist because the U.S. is capitalist. Therefore, the only way to change U.S. foreign policy is to change the economy from which it springs.

8 – 58 *The Best and the Brightest,* David Halberstam, 831pp, 1972, Fawcett, $2.95. The best-selling indictment of the intellectuals whom Kennedy brought to Washington, arguing that they were blinded by anti-Communism and the legacy of the McCarthy era and were filled with a misplaced enthusiasm for effort, technology, and persistence as the keys to success.

8 – 59 *The United States, Communism & the Emergent World,* Bernard Kierman, 248pp, 1972, Indiana Univ. Press, $10.00. Argues that authoritarian socialism is the only path to modernization in the third world, and therefore, that the U.S. should aid in the creation of a world of national Socialist dictatorships — each economically powerful enough to resist either Russian or Chinese influence.

8 – 60 *Atomic Diplomacy,* Gar Alperovitz, 317pp, 1965, Simon and Schuster, O.P. Argues that the Cold War began in 1945 as a result of Truman's attempt to reverse Roosevelt's policies toward the Soviet Union.

8 – 61 *Containment and Revolution,* David Horowitz (ed.), 252pp, 1968, Beacon, $2.45. An anthology of writings opposing U.S. intervention in revolutions. The authors either justify revolutions *per se* or argue from isolationist premises. Explain the origins of the Cold War and subsequent U.S. foreign policy as a result of American fears of Communist revolutions.

8 – 62 *Corporations and the Cold War,* David Horowitz (ed.), 249pp, 1970, Monthly Review Press, $4.50. Essays by a number of Marxist and revisionist historians argue that U.S. foreign policy during the Cold War was shaped in response to the needs of a tiny corporation-based oligarchy.

8 – 63 *Beyond Conflict and Containment: Critical Studies of Military and Foreign Policy,* Milton J. Rosenberg (ed.), 341pp, 1972, Transaction Books, $3.95. An anthology of essays critical of current U.S. foreign policy. Argues generally that the U.S. has been too preoccupied with the Cold War and has over-reacted to the "threat" of Communist power.

8 – 64 *At War with Asia,* Noam Chomsky, 1971, Vintage, O.P. A collection of essays by a leading New Left critic of American policy in Southeast Asia.

8 – 65 *America's Asia: Dissenting Essays in Asian – American Relations,* Edward Friedman and Mark Selden (eds.), 480pp, 1971, Vintage, $2.45. A series of essays challenging American policies in Asia since World War II. The editors charge that American intellectuals have uncritically accepted and perpetuated Cold War myths.

8 – 66 *American Empire: The Political Ethics of Twentieth-Century Conquest,* John Swomley, 250pp, 1970, Macmillan, $1.95. Argues that U.S. policy has aimed to thwart political and social change "in the interest of military and financial circles . . . quite as

much for the expansion of American control as for the distraction of Fascism or the containment of Communism.''

F. Revisionist Revised

8 – 67 *The New Left and the Origins of the Cold War*, Robert Maddox, 182pp, 1974, Princeton Univ. Press, $4.95. Examines the writings of William Appleman Williams, Gabriel Kolko, Gar Alperovitz, David Horowitz, and other revisionist historians of the Cold War, and concludes that their interpretations are based on ''misused quotations, jumbled figures, and distortions of documentary material.''

8 – 68 *The Radical Left and American Foreign Policy*, Robert W. Tucker, 168pp, 1971, Johns Hopkins Press, $2.95. Distinguishes the differences between economic determinist, dialectic materialist, cultural imperialist and power madness schools of revisionism, and seeks to refute their basic underlying theme: that American foreign policy emerges out of America's social structure.

8 – 69 *The Impact of the Cold War, Reconsiderations*, Joseph Siracusa & Glen Barclay St. John (eds.), 208pp, 1977, Kennikat Press, $7.95. Assesses the impact of the cold war between the U.S. and the Soviet Union on Australia, Nigeria, Argentina, Yugoslavia, China, Indochina, and other countries. The emphasis is on finding the truth beyond the interests or condemnation of either superpower, e.g., the essay on Nigeria points out how the rhetoric of the cold war obscured the fact that the British colonial administration saw independence as its goal in 1945.

8 – 70 *On Every Front: The Making of the Cold War*, Thomas Paterson, 210pp, 1979, Norton, $3.95. As the title indicates, this work finds both sides initiating actions which lead to the cold war.

8 – 71 *The United States and the Origins of the Cold War, 1941 – 1947*, John Gaddis, 448pp, 1972, Columbia, $6.50. Gaddis rejects the economic determinism of the revisionist, accepts most of the thesis that the U.S. significantly contributed to the origins of the cold war. Both Stalin and U.S. leaders wanted peace, neither would make the concessions essential to achieve it: Stalin because of his personality and need to dominate and to drain Eastern Europe for rebuilding the Soviet Union; the U.S. leaders because of domestic constraints, primarily public opinion.

G. The Vietnam War

8 – 72 *The Vietnam Trauma in American Foreign Policy, 1945 – 1975*, Paul Kattenburg, 354pp, 1980, Transaction, $19.95. An analysis of ten policy decisions made between 1961 and 1975, on the domestic impact of the war, and of the lessons to be learned.

8 – 73 *A Turning Wheel: Three Decades of the Asian Revolution as Witnessed by a Correspondent for The New Yorker,* Robert Shaplen, 397pp, 1979, Random, $15.00. A veteran correspondent's reflections based on personal interviews.

8 – 74 *Vietnam: A History in Documents,* Gareth Porter (ed.), 490pp, 1981, Meridian, $9.95. A collection of American and North Vietnamese/NLF documents designed to show that "American leaders failed to see the longer and broader sweep of history, in which the Vietnamese revolution could not be denied its place." There are no documents from South Vietnamese, social, political, or religious leaders.

8 – 75 *Why Vietnam?* Archimedes Patti, 612pp, 1980, California, $19.50. Describes and analyzes the U.S. role in Vietnam from 1945 to 1954. Suggests that U.S. policy options were limted even then.

8 – 76 *When Governments Collide: Coercion and Diplomacy in the Vietnam Conflict, 1964 – 1968,* Wallace Thies, 465pp, 1980, California, $20.00. Focuses on the Johnson Administration's failure to understand the political forces that the U.S. faced in Vietnam.

8 – 77 *America in Vietnam,* Guenter Lewy, 540pp, 1980, Oxford, $7.95. Lewy uses newly available military archives to compile a war history, covering the years 1965 – 1973. Clarifies for the benefit of a new generation, how and why the war was fought.

8 – 78 *Vietnam: The Unforgettable Tragedy,* Joseph Buttinger, 191pp, 1977, Horizon, $8.95. A brief history by a one-time advisor of the Diem regime, then a critic of U.S. policy. He concludes the U.S. should "never again try to save reactionary dictatorships whose survival is threatened by popular uprisings."

8 – 79 *America's Longest War: The United States and Vietnam, 1950 – 1975,* George Herring, 298pp, 1979, Wiley, $8.95. A broad survey of the secondary literature and summary of the debated points.

8 – 80 *History of Vietnamese Communism, 1925 – 1976,* Douglas Pike, 181pp, 1978, Hoover, $5.95. Traces the party's development back to the anti-French struggle. Discusses the "party's operational trinity: organization, mobilization, motivation."

8 – 81 *The Indochina War, Why Our Policy Failed,* David Bender & Gary McCuen, 122pp, 1975, Greenhaven, $4.65. Defenders and critics here argue the broad choices; the nuances are left out.

8 – 82 *The Wound Within, America in the Vietnam Years, 1945 – 1974,* Alexander Kendrick, 432pp, 1974, Little Brown, $4.95. Not likely to heal any wounds; maintains that "like Vietnam, Watergate was not an aberration but the logical extension of authority, indeed the political form of Vietnam."

8 – 83 *Dispatches,* Michael Herr, 288pp, 1980, Avon, $2.50. Letters and ideas of American servicemen in Vietnam.

8 – 84 *Fire in the Lake: The Vietamese and the Americans in Vietnam,* Frances Fitzgerald, 491pp, 1973, Random, $4.95. An attempt to portray the human tragedy of the war.

8 – 85 *Sideshow: Kissinger, Nixon and the Destruction of Cambodia,* William Shaw-cross, 467pp, 1979, Simon & Schuster, $13.95. Assigns historical responsibility for the abuses of power by the Pol Pot regime to Kissinger and Nixon who sought to prevent him from coming to power.

8 – 86 *P.O.W.: A Definitive History of the American Prisoner-of-War Experience in Vietnam, 1964 – 1973,* John Hubbell, et al, 633pp, 1976, Reader's Digest, $15.00. First person accounts of prison life, torture, and abuse.

8 – 87 *All Quiet on the Eastern Front: The Death of South Vietnam,* Anthony Bouscaren (ed.), 1976, Devin-Adair, $5.95. An anthology including essays by William F. Buckley, Ambassador Graham Martin, General Westmoreland, and others, largely conservative critics of U.S. policy.

8 – 88 *The My Lai Inquiry,* Lt. Gen. W.R. Peers, 306pp, 1979, Norton, $12.95. Much of the official testimony plus a commentary by the officer who conducted the government's investigation.

8 – 89 *A Soldier Reports,* General William Westmoreland, 446pp, 1976, Doubleday, $12.95. Suggests that the U.S. could have honorably pulled out in 1964 and that Lyndon Johnson manipulated the U.S. command staff into becoming, in effect, spokesmen for the Administration's policy.

8 – 90 *A Peace Denied: The United States, Vietnam, and the Paris Agreement,* Gareth Porter, 416pp, 1976, Indiana, $15.00. Makes the case that the U.S. supported Thieu's sabotage of the Paris Agreements signed in January 1973 and that this prevented a political solution to the conflict.

8 – 91 *The Lost Peace: America's Search for a Negotiated Settlement of the Vietnam War,* Allan Goodman, 298pp, 1978, Hoover, $22.50. An assessment of the 1963-1973 negotiations which concludes that there was, in fact, no basis for a negotiated settlement: Hanoi refused to recognize any South Vietnamese force as legitimate; it wanted only victory, and would not negotiate anything other than U.S. withdrawal.

8 – 92 *War Comes to Long An: Revolutionary Conflict in a Vietnamese Province,* Jeff Race, 300pp, 1971, California, $5.95. A detailed and compassionate study of one Vietnam province, the origins of the military conflict, the different strategies of war, and the objectives of the parties involved.

8 – 93 *Elections in South Vietnam,* Howard Penniman, 246pp, 1973, Hoover, $7.50. Describes seven elections in South Vietnam between 1966 and 1971 and concludes: "South Vietnam was in the process of developing viable institutions that reasonably approach the norms of a democratic system" (p. 183).

8 – 94 *Big Story: How the American Press and Television Reported and Interpreted the Crisis of Tet 1968 in Vietnam and Washington,* Peter Braestrup, 1000pp, 1977 Westview, $65.00. A detailed critique of how the media misinterpreted the Tet offensive as a defeat for Saigon and the U.S when it resulted, in fact, as all observers now agree, in a massive military defeat for the Viet Cong and North Vietnam.

8 – 95 *War, Presidents, and Public Opinion,* John Mueller, 288pp, 1973, Wiley, $10.95. Among other things, gives answers to questions about the American public attitudes: What kept the public supportive of the war so long? Indicates that in the early stages of the war, youths, Democrats, and the college-educated were more supportive of the war than were the conservatives.

8 – 96 *Delusion and Reality: Gambits, Hoaxes and Diplomatic One-Upmanship in Vietnam,* Janos Radvanyi, 1978, Gateway, $12.95. Brings to light evidence concerning the Soviet Union, China, and Eastern European countries' roles in Vietnam.

8 – 97 *Many Reasons Why: The American Involvement in Vietnam,* Michael Charlton & Anthony Moncrieff, 1978, Hill & Wang, $5.95. Restates the reasons for involvement in view of the aftermath of disengagement.

8 – 98 *Summons of the Trumpet: U.S. – Vietnam in Prospective,* Dave Palmer, 277pp, 1978, Presidio Press, $12.95. Col. Palmer traces the slowly increasing U.S. commitment, describes the war as arising because of aggression from the North, depicts the brutality on both sides, and underlines what is, for him, the main lesson: slow escalation does not work; once military force is committed, it should be used to achieve military objectives.

8 – 99 *The Lessons of Vietnam,* W. Scott Thompson & Donaldson Frizzell (eds.), 288pp, 1977, Crane, Russak, $19.50. A wide-ranging reassessment discussing both the military and political failures of American policy, but emphasizing the military failures.

8 – 100 *The Irony of Vietnam: The System Worked,* Leslie Gelb, 387pp, 1979, Brookings, $6.95. Chops down many assumptions dearly held by "hawks" and "doves"; concludes the historical evidence about Vietnam is "still alive, being shaped by bitterness and bewilderment, reassurances and new testimony."

8 – 101 *A Guide to the Vietnam Conflict,* Richard Burns & Milton Leitenberg, 300pp, 1981, 2nd ed., ABC-Clio (not set). Contains approximately 5,000 annotated listings of works about the first, second, and third Indochinese wars.

H. The Policy-Making Process: Congress vs. the Presidency

8 – 102 *The Executive, Congress, and Foreign Policy, Studies of the Nixon Administration,* John Lehman, Jr., 247pp, 1974, Praeger, $19.95. Traces the rise of congressional displacement of executive leadership in foreign affairs through some thirty battles fought between 1969 and 1973 which were all won by Congress. The consequences of an inability of friend or foe to know U.S. policy are lamented.

8 – 103 *The Formulation and Administration of United States Foreign Policy,* H. Field Haveland, Jr., and eleven collaborators, 191pp, 1974, 1960, Greenwood Press, $12.75. A summary of the internal structure deemed appropriate when "international communism" was considered a "continuing threat," with executive leadership, a large

defense establishment and well-financed intelligence-gathering, and covert operation capability as the essential requisites needed to cope.

8 – 104 *Presidents, Secretaries of State, and Crises Management in U.S. Foreign Relations: A Model and Predictive Analysis,* Lawrence Falkowski, 173pp, 1978, Westview, $9.50. A study of leadership ability to change foreign policy objectives and goals, which focus on the personality and perceptions of the leaders, and not the domestic or international constraints.

8 – 105 *Foreign Policy by Congress,* Thomas Franck & Edward Weisband, 357pp, 1979, Oxford, $15.95. Describes the "revolution" which made Congress, not the Presidency, the manager of American foreign policy, and suggests that while Congess has changed, it cannot provide the continuity, intelligence, strategy, or tactics necessary to safeguard the national interest.

8 – 106 *Congress and the Politics of U.S. Foreign Economic Policy, 1929 – 1976,* Robert Pastor, 416pp, 1981, California, $24.50. Traces the executive/legislative battles over trade policy.

8 – 107 *Presidential Decisionmaking in Foreign Policy: The Effective Use of Information and Advice,* Alexander George, 267pp, 1980, Westview, $10.00. An informed analysis of how Presidents can organize an advisory system in order to produce sound decisions, and on how others might influence that process.

8 – 108 *The Politics of Policy-Making in Defense and Foreign Affairs,* Roger Hilsman, 198pp, 1971, Harper & Row, $9.50. Argues that there are significant built-in limits on Executive Branch authority and that additional limits could be crippling.

I. The Policy-Making Process: The Public

8 – 109 *The Domestic Context of American Foreign Policy,* Barry Hughes, 240pp, 1978, H.W. Freeman, $7.95. Do public opinion, interest groups, the press, attitudes of policy makers, political parties all influence foreign policy decisions? Hughes says yes and suggests the circumstances under which each is decisive.

8 – 110 *The Public Impact on Foreign Policy,* Bernard Cohen, 240pp, 1973, Little Brown, $6.95. A significant study of how perceived public opinion influences governmental decision-makers and concludes with a discussion on increasing governmental responsiveness.

8 – 111 *Politics and Government, How People Decide Their Fate,* Karl Deutsch, 607pp, 1980, 3rd ed, Houghton Mifflin, $17.95. A study of "the making of decisions by public means" — a growing field since custom and private decision-makers now decide less and more people and groups push their way into decision-making processes. Presents an interesting comparison of the nature, degree of participation, stakes, and performance of the political processes in the U.S., the USSR, France, England, China,

West Germany, and the "emerging nations." Deutsch concludes, "Perhaps the first emergency task will be to *abolish war*. Either we abolish all-out war or it will abolish us" (p. 572). Civil war he considers likely, however.

8 – 112 *Cold War and Detente, The American Foreign Policy Process Since 1945,* Paul Hammond, 320pp, 1975, Harcourt, Brace and Jovanovich, $10.95. A survey of U.S. foreign policy which is especially attentive to the role of public opinion. Hammond believes that the public impact on foreign policy has been great with both good and bad results; he believes a major concern now is how to gain public support for foreign policy.

8 – 113 *The Public and American Foreign Policy, 1918 – 1978,* Ralph Levering, 1978, William Morrow, $3.95. Discusses the role of the general public, foreign policy activists, and the mass media on decision-makers in Congress and the Executive Branch, and concludes with the current search for a new consensus.

8 – 114 *Domestic Sources of Foreign Policy,* James Rosenau (ed.), 340pp, 1967, Macmillan, $12.95. Ten authors study many non-governmental sources of foreign policy: personality traits, public attitudes, social position, the mass media, interest groups, and national politics, among others.

8 – 115 *The Politics of War,* Walter Karp, 416pp, 1979, Harper, $15.00. Argues that party politics is the source of foreign policy, not world political systems.

8 – 116 *The Politics of American Foreign Policy, The Social Context of Decisions,* Morton Berkowitz, P. Bock & Vincent Fuccillo, 310pp, 1977, Prentice-Hall, $9.95. Studies eleven post-World War II foreign policy decisions to determine how influential various groups are in deciding outcomes.

8 – 117 *American Opinion and the Russian Alliance, 1939 – 1945,* Ralph Levering, 255pp, 1976, U. of North Carolina, $18.00. How could the U.S. launch the cold war when even the DAR referred to Stalin as "Uncle Joe" during this period?

J. The Policy-Making Process: Government

8 – 118 *The Essence of Decision: Explaining the Cuban Missile Crisis,* Graham Allison, 338pp, 1971, Little, Brown, $7.95. An attempt to describe the conceptual frameworks within which political scientists explain international events. Allison distinguishes the "rational actor" model (the researcher must learn how possibly the people involved acted the way they did, given their assumptions, information and objectives), the "organizational process" model (the researcher must weigh various organizational pressures seeking different outputs), and the "governmental process" model (in which the researcher must determine not who won the internal fight but what bargain was struck between contenders).

8 – 119 *How American Foreign Policy is Made,* John Spanier and Eric M. Uslaner, 180pp, 1978, Krieger, $8.95. A study of "the actors and elements in the foreign policy

decision process'' and of ''the analytic approaches most useful in understanding and criticizing it.'' Included among the actors are the Executive and Congressional branches of government, special interests, the media, public opinion, and non-governmental organizations.

8 – 120 *The Making of United States International Economic Policy, Principles, Problems and Proposals,* Stephen Cohen, 236pp, 1977, Praeger, $9.95. An urgent call for recognizing that ''external events increasingly determine the fate of our domestic economy. Economic considerations increasingly dictate the focus of our foreign policy.'' Cohen provides a detailed study of how policies of trade, monetary exchange, investment, aid, and resources are determined. He recommends the creation of a Department of International Commercial Policy to coordinate dispersed decision-makers while maintaining diversified inputs and viewpoints on what constitutes good policies.

8 – 121 *A Pretty Good Club: The Founding Fathers of the U.S. Foreign Services,* Martin Weil, 313pp, 1978, Norton, $12.95. Studies the social background (wealthy New England), education (prep school — Ivy League), and outlook of the professional foreign service (1900). Weil argues that their focus on Europe made them unsympathetic to the Soviet Union and thus an influence on the origins of the cold war. In addition, the study traces the continuing tensions between the foreign policy elite and popular attitudes.

8 – 122 *Foreign Affairs and the Constitution,* Louis Henkin, 573pp, 1975, Norton, $5.95. A careful study of the provisions of the U.S. Constitution that relate to foreign affairs, its powers, responsibilities, and limits on each branch of government as well as the implications of international treaties and organizations for U.S. law.

8 – 123 *The Constitution and the Conduct of Foreign Policy,* Francis O. Wilcox and Richard Frank, 166pp, 1976, Praeger, $8.95. An inquiry by a panel of the American Society of International Law. The panel focuses on Legislative versus Executive branch prerogatives concerning secrecy, public participation in decision-making processes, war-making powers, and making international agreements; also offers recommendations in each area.

8 – 124 *Industrial Policy as an International Issue,* William Diebold, Jr., 320pp, 1980, McGraw-Hill, $6.95. Examines how governments shape their economies and the consequences of these decisions for international economic relationships.

8 – 125 *Bureaucratic Politics and Foreign Policy,* Morton Halperin et al, 340pp, 1974, Brookings Institutions, $5.95. A former Deputy Asst. Sec. of Defense assesses the decision-making processes related to military affairs. Actors in the process and the tactics available to them to influence the outcome are described. Halperin concludes '' . . . the impact of an action by one government on another depends on the nature of the internal debate in that government on which participants are strengthened or disheartened by the action and on the common interpretation which comes to be given to it in the second government'' (p. 312).

8 – 126 *Understanding Foreign Policy Decisions: The Chinese Case,* David Bobrow, et al. Steve Chan and John Kringer, 320pp, 1979, Free Press, $16.95. Uses a complex model to predict foreign policy choices and tests it against past behavior.

8 – 127 *Making Foreign Economic Policy,* I.M. Destler, 256pp, 1980, Brookings, $4.95. A detailed study of how food and trade policy is made and carried out.

8 – 128 *Readings in American Foreign Policy, A Bureaucratic Perspective,* Morton Halperin and Arnold Kanter (eds.), 434pp, 1973, Little Brown and Co., $6.95. Includes a classification of the participants in decision-making within the government and many analyses of how decisions are reached.

8 – 129 *The Making of the Diplomatic Mind: The Training, Outlook, and Style of United States Foreign Service Officers, 1908 – 1931,* Robert Schulzinger, 260pp, 1975, Columbia, $17.50. Demonstrates that elite grooming for Department of State posts once existed and worked well in European diplomatic relations.

8 – 130 *Remaking Foreign Policy: The Organizational Connection,* Graham Allison & Peter Szanton, 238pp, 1976, Basic, $12.00. Suggests how organizations can influence bureaucratic decision-making processes.

K. The Policy-Making Process

8 – 131 *Secrecy and Foreign Policy,* Thomas Franck & Edward Weisband (eds.), 453pp, 1976, Oxford, $5.95. A study of the control of classified information within the U.S., Canadian, and British governments, which seeks the principles for reconciling the need for secrecy in the conduct of certain policies with the possible abuse of power that can result.

8 – 132 *The Man Who Kept the Secrets: Richard Helms and the CIA,* Thomas Powers, 393pp, 1979, Knopf, $12.95. Maintains that the CIA's policies were always shaped and under the watch of the President.

8 – 133 *U.S. Intelligence and the Soviet Strategic Threat,* Lawrence Freedman, 235pp, 1977, Westview, $22.50. A study of how estimates of Soviet nuclear weapons capabilities are made, with suggestions why they are usually exaggerated.

8 – 134 *The CIA and the Security Debate: 1975 – 1976,* Judith Buncher (ed.), 280pp, 1977, Facts on File, $19.95. A collection of facts and newspaper clippings about the CIA and the re-evaluation of it in 1975 – 1976.

8 – 135 *CIA: The Myth and the Madness,* Patrick McGarvey, 240pp, 1973, Penguin Books, $2.50. Dispels the myth of the CIA as an efficient omnipresent specter and maintains that reorganization and re-definitions of its task are essential to its carrying out its vital intelligence-gathering functions.

8 – 136 *The Lawless State: The Crimes of the U.S. Intelligence Agencies,* Morton H. Halperin, Jerry J. Berman and others, 328pp, 1976, Penguin Books, $3.95. A scathing indictment of the intelligence agencies which compiles the revelations of the past ten years; offers little evidence concerning other countries' intelligence operations in this and other countries, and thus creates the impression that the only enemies of democracy are the abuses of these agencies.

8 – 137 *Hidden Terrors, the Truth About U.S. Police Operations in Latin America,* A.J. Langguth, 345pp, 1979, Pantheon, $3.95. Alleges the CIA planted agents in South American countries to aid military coups and to sanction the use of torture by Latin American security forces (in fact training them) against political enemies.

8 – 138 *Honorable Men: My Life in the CIA,* William Colby and Peter Forbath, 493pp, 1978, Simon and Schuster, $12.95. A candid account of Colby's earlier years in the CIA and an attempt to defend the agency against its harsher criticisms by putting them in context.

L. Kissinger & Detente Diplomacy

8 – 139 *Detente or Debacle, Common Sense in U.S. – Soviet Relations,* Fred Warner Neal & nine others, 108pp, 1979, Norton, $3.95. The American Committee on East-West Accords makes the case for detente — the Soviet Union, while repressive, is considered conservative; in any case, the danger of war requires silence concerning Soviet human rights violations.

8 – 140 *The Imperial Presidency,* Arthur M. Schlesinger, Jr., 505pp, 1973, Popular Library, $2.50. An historian who celebrated the exercise of Presidential authority by Andrew Jackson, Franklin Delano Roosevelt and John F. Kennedy, has second thoughts when Richard Nixon is in the White House. Schlesinger argues that Nixon saw the presidency as accountable only every four years.

8 – 141 *Detente: Prospects for Democracy and Dictatorship,* Aleksandr Solzhenitsyn, 134pp, 1980, Transaction, $3.95. Reprints three major speeches and offers commentaries on them.

8 – 142 *White House Years,* Henry Kissinger, 1,521pp, 1979, Little, Brown, $22.50. Kissinger's account of the years from 1969 – 1973, presented in great detail, along with an appeal for Americans to see foreign policy as he does and scorn for those who do not. The central lesson, he suggests, is that "diplomatic skill could augment but never substitute for military strength. In the final reckoning weakness has invariably tempted aggression and impotence brings abdication of policy in its train."

8 – 143 *The Necessity for Choice: Prospects of American Foreign Policy,* Henry Kissinger, 370pp, 1961, Harper, $12.50. A comprehensive study of American foreign policy prior to Kissinger's holding public position.

8 – 144 *Kissinger: Portrait of a Mind,* Stephen Graubard, 288pp, 1973, Norton, $3.45. An appreciative, perceptive biography which traces Kissinger's intellectual history, especially his concern to relate the hard choices posed by political realities to concepts of the present international system.

8 – 145 *The Diplomacy of Detente: The Kissinger Era,* Coral Bell, 278pp, 1977, St. Martin's, $14.95. Assesses detente as "an American diplomatic strategy consciously deployed with a triangular power balance, vis-a-vis both China and the Soviet Union." Bell is guardedly optimistic about the future of detente in maintaining peace.

8 – 146 *Uncertain Greatness, Henry Kissinger & American Foreign Policy,* Roger Morris, 312pp, 1977, Harper, $10.95. Morris is a National Security Council staff member who resigned over the violent incursion of the U.S. into Cambodia in 1970. He argues that Kissinger's true accomplishment is detente, which Morris says indicates the U.S. "has come to terms at last with the Russian and Chinese revolutions."

8 – 147 *Henry Kissinger: The Anguish of Power,* John Stoessinger, 234pp, 1976, Norton, $8.95. An informative well-written discussion of Kissinger's attempt to construct a realistic world order. Kissinger's reliance on the 19th century balance-of-power model and his later efforts to build bridges to developing States and to move toward a stable peace in the Middle East are sympathetically portrayed.

8 – 148 *American Foreign Policy,* Henry Kissinger, 445pp, 1977 (3rd ed.), Norton, $6.95. An anthology of Kissinger's writings including three essays written before entering government plus his major foreign policy addresses as Secretary of State. The key concepts as well as the shifting emphasis are both well-documented by this collection.

8 – 149 *Beyond Kissinger, Ways of Conservative Statecraft,* George Liska, 159pp, 1975, Johns Hopkins, $2.95. A study which places Kissinger in the tradition of Machiavelli, Metternich, and Bismarck. It pleads for a "State-centered" balance of power, national interest, approach to foreign policy, and limits Kissinger's contribution to such a policy.

8 – 150 *The Crises of Power, Foreign Policy in the Kissinger Years,* Seyom Brown, 194pp, 1979, Columbia, $10.95. A balanced assessment of the Kissinger era, of the new forces shaping international relations and the role of the U.S. in world politics.

8 – 151 *Detente and Dollars, Doing Business with the Soviets,* Marshall Goldman, 337pp, 1975, Basic Books, $18.50. Investments by U.S. corporations in the USSR totalled over $2 billion between 1972 and 1974. This book is cautiously optimistic in believing that trade and investment can, if realistic, be mutually beneficial.

8 – 152 *Dimensions of Detente,* Della Sheldon (ed.), 219pp, 1978, Praeger, $21.95. Seven contributors agree that detente is preferable to great power confrontation in the nuclear era, and examine the implications of cooperation for other powers, the Middle East conflict, and Soviet – U.S. economic relationship.

M. Cautious Internationalism & World Order

8– 153 *Primacy or World Order, American Foreign Policy Since the Cold War,* Stanley Hoffmann, 252pp, 1978, McGraw-Hill, $5.95. A critical assessment of American primacy through international organizations in the 1945-1968 period and a biting critique of Kissinger's "neo-Bismarckian" view of the world. Calls for a new world order based on working with allies and smaller States and an acceptance of pluralism in economic and political systems.

8– 154 *In Search of American Foreign Policy: The Humane Use of Power,* Lincoln Bloomfield, 192pp, 1974, Oxford, $4.95. An analysis of the breakdown of the traditional foreign policy consensus in this country, and a thoughtful prescription for a new direction. Emphasizes the need to recognize persisting realities (e.g. the balance of power keeps the peace) while seeking new, more humane means to alter them (e.g. purposeful steps toward world order through functional international organizations).

8– 155 *The Third Try at World Order, U.S. Policy for an Interdependent World,* Harlan Cleveland, 140pp, 1975, World Affairs Council of Philadelphia, Aspen Institute, $3.95. The League of Nations was the first, the United Nations the second try. The third try includes bargaining between sovereign States and between non-national actors; a pluralism of forums, issues and agreements. In short, many actors, many tasks, many forums . . .

8– 156 *After Afghanistan: The Long Haul: Safeguarding Security and Independence in the Third World,* The Atlantic Council's Working Group on Security Affairs et al., 71pp, 1980, Westview, $6.00. Recommends a coordinated Western approach to conflicts in the third world.

8– 157 *Diplomacy for a Crowded World: An American Foreign Policy,* George Ball, 356pp, 1976, Little, Brown, $4.95. Conceding little to critics of U.S. policy, Ball faults Kissinger only for a lack of a grand design. Ball calls for U.S. support for democratic governments, rejects the current form of detente and too close ties with China, and calls for new U.S. leadership in promoting liberty and equality of economic opportunity in world politics.

8– 158 *Robert Kennedy and His Times,* Arthur Schlesinger, Jr., 1066pp, 1979, Ballantine 3.50. A sympathetic assessment by a distinguished historian and friend of the family.

8– 159 *Foreign Policy for a New Age,* Robert Wesson, 462pp, 1976, Houghton Mifflin, $17.50. Seeks to chart a new path for American foreign policy: that of building a new world order.

8– 160 *Toward a Dependable Peace: A Proposal for an Appropriate Security System,* Robert Johansen, 58pp, 1978, Institute for World Order, $1.50. Argues that the arms race is too dangerous and that a new security system is needed based on strengthened international organizations and disarmament.

TEW

8 – 161 *Peace, Security and the 1980 Elections,* World Without War Issues Center, 16pp, 1980, Issues Center, $.50. Outlines the goals and the strategy which could answer these two questions with a thoughtful yes: 1) Given the realities of Soviet policy and the present international system, is it possible for one country to intitiate progress toward a world which resolves international conflict without mass violence? 2) Could the United States, without unacceptable danger to our own political community, become that country?

8 – 162 *United States Foreign Policy and World Order,* James Nathan & James Oliver, 598pp, 1981 Little Brown, $10.95. A detailed history of post– World War II policies focused on policy makers and the prevailing attitudes in the American public. The importance of public attitudes is underlined in the concluding chapter which studies public opinion during the 1970s and finds it neither isolationist nor badly misinformed. The public, according to Nathan and Oliver, are far ahead of leadership in wanting to pursue non-military international relations objectives.

8 – 163 *The Conduct and Misconduct of Foreign Affairs, Reflections on U.S. Foreign Policy Since World War II,* Charles Yost, 234pp, 1972, Random House, $7.95. The Yost thesis is roughly that national interest diplomacy leads to conflict, that without supranational organizations and a sense of world community, we can expect war, little joint problem-solving efforts, and an endless striving after power and influence. But a qualitative change imposed by science and technology now makes our globe "smaller" than Rhode Island in the 18th century while our politics is more explosive than Italy's in the 14th century. In short, the State-system must go.

8 – 164 *The National Interest and the Human Interest, An Analysis of U.S. Foreign Policy,* Robert Johansen, 511pp, 1980, Princeton, $6.95. Defines values and offers an analysis suggesting that a "global humanistic" approach to world politics is more in the national interest than promoting national interest by military power.

N. The Superpower Rivalry

8 – 165 *Thirteen Days, A Memoir of the Cuban Missile Crisis,* Robert Kennedy, 184pp, 1971 (1968), Norton, $2.95. A description of how the deadliest of games was played to gain changes in an adversary's policies.

8 – 166 *The Real War,* Richard Nixon, 341pp, 1980, Warner, $12.50. It began when WW II ended and is a struggle to the death between the Soviet Union and the United States. ". . .if we resolve to accept no substitute for victory, then victory becomes possible."

8 – 167 *Facing Reality: From World Federalism to the CIA,* Cord Meyer, 416pp, 1980, Harper, $15.00. A leader in the World Federalist movement, following WW II, found his ideas inadequate to the Soviet challenge: Are they still?

8 – 168 *The Present Danger,* Norman Podhoretz, 109pp, 1980, Simon & Schuster, $2.95. Defines the 1970s as a period of passivity in American foreign policy now demonstrably bankrupt. A new nationalism has arisen in the U.S., auguring a re-assertion of American interests; Podhoretz laments that containing the Soviet Union, not defending democracy against the assault by totalitarian Communism, is the current motive.

8 – 169 *Munich: The Price of Peace,* Telford Taylor, 1004pp, 1980, Doubleday, $17.50. Compares Munich with Vietnam to provide guidance for those who would be neither appeasers nor military interveners.

8 – 170 *The Rivals: America and Russia Since World War II,* Adam Ulam, 405pp, 1972, Penguin, $4.50. A thoughtful study of the Cold War which finds the main threat to peace to be "the irrational impulses that underlie the policies" of both the U.S. and the USSR.

8 – 171 *Soviet – American Rivalry: An Expert Analysis of the Economic, Political, and Military Competition which Dominates Foreign Relations,* Thomas Larson, 320pp, 1981, Norton, $6.95. Examines the strength and weakness, the rhetoric and behavior of both superpowers, at home and abroad, focusing on the years from 1945 to 1975.

8 – 172 *The Giants; Russia and America,* Richard Barnet, 175pp, 1977, Simon & Schuster, $10.95. Barnet argues that the "elites which manage" the two superpowers depend upon each other; but the greatest danger is that the dynamics of the arms race will lead each elite to misunderstand the other's basically peaceful intentions. The most urgent security threats "facing the giants come not from each other but from the systematic crisis each faces at home" (p. 175).

8 – 173 *Nations in Darkness: China, Russia & America,* John Stoessinger, 223pp, 1978, Random House, $4.95. An analysis of the misperceptions of each power, and an appeal to face reality — but little indication of what that entails.

O. New Domestic Priorities/A Perimeter Defense

8 – 174 *The Cloud of Danger, Current Realities of American Foreign Policy,* George F. Kennan, 234pp, 1977, Little, Brown, $8.95. The best statement of the "New Priorities" context. Kennan argues that the very nature of a democratic society fore-closes an effective role as a superpower. Secrets are not kept; persistence in adversity is impossible. Domestic needs, the military-industrial complex, the environment require our attention; the U.N. and other international bodies do not; the world food-population crisis is too large, the North – South dialogue empty; the Soviet Union acting with restraint, aiding, as any great power can be expected to aid, factions sympathetic to it in other countries. Western Europe, Japan, and Israel should alone be defended.

8 – 175 *Never Again: Learning from America's Foreign Policy Failures,* Earl Ravenal,

153pp, 1978, Temple, $10.00. Calls for a new isolationism in the wake of Vietnam and spiraling defense costs, if that means former allies are to be dominated by Soviet power, so be it.

8 – 176 *Encounters with Kennan: The Great Debate,* George F. Kennan et al, 218pp, 1979, Cass, $19.50. Kennan counters his critics who doubt "defensive" is the best word with which to describe Soviet intentions.

8 – 177 *Beyond the Water's Edge: America's Foreign Policies,* Howard Bliss & Glen Johnson, 272pp, 1975, Harper & Row, $6.50. Describes the shattering of the Cold War consensus and the need to face four questions to rebuild a consensus: 1) Is nationalism or Communism the force making for change in world politics? 2) Does the U.S. have a responsibility to aid other States? 3) Under what circumstances should the U.S. intervene in other countries? 4) Who should make foreign policy?

8 – 178 *Prophets on the Right, Profiles of Conservative Critics of American Globalism,* Ronald Radosh, 345pp, 1978, Free Life Editions, $5.95. Profiles of Senator Robert Taft, John Flynn, Oswald Villard, Lawrence Dennis, and Charles Beard.

8 – 179 *Policy Makers and Critics, Conflicting Theories of American Foreign Policy,* Cecil Crabb, Jr., 322pp, 1976, Praeger, $6.95. A valuable statement of seven contexts for considering U.S. policy which seeks to subject them to the "same logical and objective scrutiny applied to governmental policies." Crabb succeeds in highlighting the diversity of U.S. thought about foreign policy and in restoring the credibility of the isolationist heritage.

8 – 180 *The Political Psychology of Appeasement, Finlandization and Other Unpopular Essays,* Walter Laqueur, 283pp, 1980, Transaction, $16.95. Essays on European accommodation to growing Soviet power and Eurocommunism, terrorism, and the loss of nerve, traced to oil dependence in the Middle East.

P. The 1980s: Containment without Consensus?

8 – 181 *Setting National Priorities, Agenda for the 1980s,* Joseph Pechman (ed.) 550pp, 1980, Brookings, $8.95. Nineteen contributors analyze foreign and domestic issues in the 1980s and offer their prognosis.

8 – 182 *The United States in the 1980s,* Peter Duignan & Alvin Rabushka (eds.), 868pp, 1980, Hoover, $20.00. Essays by Reagan advisors outlining the "stand tall" policies the Reagan Presidency may initially follow.

8 – 183 *America and the World 1981,* Foreign Affairs, 1982, Pergamon, $6.95. An annual reprinting of the magazine's assessment of the state of America's involvement in world affairs; it is designed for the classroom and highlights the main challenges, themes, and opportunities for American policy makers.

8 – 184 *Trilateralism, The Trilateral Commission and Elite Planning for World Man-*

agement, Holly Sklar, (ed.), 604pp, 1980, South End Press, $8.00. Self-described as a "tool in understanding ruling class strategy and action, it can be a tool for organizing resistance."

8 – 185 *America and the Third World: Revolution and Intervention,* John Girling, 276pp, 1979, Routledge, Kegan Paul, $25.00. Maintains that third-world countries and the United States have many common concerns and interests. American intervention may be necessary to balance Soviet intervention and to maintain a regional balance of power.

8 – 186 *Intelligence Requirements for the 1980s: Analysis and Estimates,* Roy Godson (ed.), 223pp, 1980, Transaction Books, $7.50. A critical assessment of the Government's current intelligence capability.

8 – 187 *A New Foreign Policy Consensus,* Herbert Spiro, 72pp, 1979, Sage, $3.50. Maintains that to achieve a new consensus, a much broader foreign-policy attentive public must be engaged in the discussion.

Intro

8 – 188 *Great Decisions 1981,* Foreign Policy Association, 60pp, 1981, $7.00. An annual introduction to critical foreign policy decisions to be made each year; this edition introduces as the great decisions, "America's Basic Options," plus the Middle East, the UN, Eastern Europe, Vietnam, Brazil, Energy, and Migration. A bibliography and leader's discussion guide are available.

8 – 189 *Challenges to America, United States Foreign Policy in the 1980s,* Charles Kegley, Jr., and Patrick McGowan, 300pp, 1979, Sage, $9.95. An annual "International Yearbook of Foreign Policy Studies" focused this year on the strategic arms balance, other perceptions of the U.S., and the relationship between the U.S., Europe, and Japan.

8 – 190 *Politics and the Oval Office,* Arnold Meltsner (ed.), 332pp, 1981, Institute for Contemporary Studies, $7.95. Maintains the Presidency is manageable; suggests how the public, the media, Congress, the Courts, and the bureaucracy limit the power but do not control the Presidency.

8 – 191 *The Hovering Giant, U.S. Response to Revolutionary Change in Latin America,* Cole Blasier, 315pp, 1976, Pittsburgh, $6.95. A study of U.S. interventions from 1900 to 1961 and from 1961 to 1975, which offers various explanations (economic, bureaucratic, and geo-political interests), and seeks to draw lessons of history.

8 – 192 *The Dynamics of Human Rights in United States Foreign Policy,* Natalie Hevener (ed.), 305pp, 1981, Transaction, $19.95. Fourteen essays address the question of how U.S. foreign policy can advance universal human rights; contending perspectives are presented.

8 – 193 *U.S. Policy and Low-Intensity Conflict: Potentials for Military Struggles in the 1980s,* Sam Sarkesian & William Schully (eds.), 224pp, 1981, Transaction, $8.95. Debates the circumstances under which the U.S. should commit military forces.

Q.The Changing U.S.

8 – 194 *America in Our Time: From World War II to Nixon, What Happened and Why,* Godfrey Hodgson, 564pp, 1976, Vintage, $4.95. What happened is that a liberal ideological consensus which prevailed until the 1960s broke under the impact of the Vietnam war and the civil rights movement. The alternative ideology, which the author favors, was developed by the New Left in the 1960s but it failed to offer anything to low-income whites.

8 – 195 *The American Vision: An Essay on the Future of Democratic Capitalism,* Michael Novak, 60pp, 1979, American Enterprise Institute, $2.75. A spirited endorsement of the economic, political, and cultural pluralism of the United States, and a call for an intellectual offensive against the contending views.

8 – 196 *The Silent Revolution: Changing Values and Political Styles Among Western Publics,* Ronald Inglehart, 1979, Princeton, $9.95. Argues that a "post-materialist" segment of the Western world now exists on someone else's earnings which seeks "self-actualization." Albeit a minority, Inglehart believes it to be a growing one for whom "What life styles?" is the central political question.

8 – 197 *The Foreign Affairs Kaleidoscope, Changing American Perceptions of the Nation and the World,* William Barnds, 109pp, 1974, Council on Religion and International Affairs, $2.00. Written during the last days of the Nixon Administration, this book seeks to recover a positive, optimistic, if limited engagement, by the U.S. in world politics.

R. A Changing World

8 – 198 *Between Two Ages, America's Role in the Technetronic Era,* Zbigniew Brzezinski, 334pp, 1970, 1977, Penguin, $3.50. Maintains that the industrially advanced countries, especially the U.S., are emerging from the industrial age and passing into an age shaped by technology and electronics — i.e., the technetronic age. Brzezinski is optimistic about the impact of the U.S. global involvement, provided it aims to build "a community of the developed nations," concentrates on disseminating scientific and technological knowledge, and encourages the spread of a "more personalized, rational, humanist" outlook.

8 – 199 *United States National Interests in a Changing World,* Donald Neuchterlein, 203pp, 1973, U. Press of Kentucky, $10.00. Motivated by a belief that the Vietnam war required the U.S. to rethink what was in its vital national interests, the author appraises alternative definitions of the concept and concludes that defense, private investment abroad, and world order, including the promotion of democracy, are goals which are in the national interest during a time of great change.

8 – 200 *World Power Trends and U.S. Foreign Policy for the 1980s,* Ray Cline, 200pp,

1980, Westview, $8.95. Using a mathematical model of what constitutes power, Cline profiles each nation. The U.S. has declined by 30%; the Soviet Union has gained by 20%. He offers a partial remedy: an "All-Oceans Alliance" to protect the sea lanes.

S. Specific Policy Studies

8 – 201 *Water's Edge: Domestic Politics and the Making of American Foreign Policy,* Paula Stern, 265pp, 1979, Greenwood, $19.95. A detailed account of the Jackson-Vanik Amendment, its conception and eventual passage, which led to the linkage of trade with the USSR liberalization of emigration policy.

8 – 202 *The Panama Canal: The Crisis in Historical Perspective,* Walter La Feber, 334pp, 1979, Oxford, $4.95. The first Carter Administration foreign policy battle here assessed and placed in broader perspective.

8 – 203 *Communist Indochina and U.S. Foreign Policy: Postwar Realities,* Joseph Zasloff and MacAlister Brown, 221pp, 1978, Westview, $20.00. An attempt to summarize events in Indochina from 1975 to 1978, which calls for a recognition of the Communist regimes and treatment of them as centers of power, not ideological adversaries or client States.

8 – 204 *U.S. Strategy in the Indian Ocean, The International Response,* Monoranjan Bezboruah, 268pp, 1977, Praeger, $25.95. Focuses on the U.S. decision to build a naval base at Diego Garcia as the pivotal event which required the Soviet to respond, and aroused fears among countries bordering on the Indian Ocean.

8 – 205 *US-Soviet Relations: A Strategy for the '80s,* UNA – USA Policy Panel, 102pp, 1981, United Nations Association, $4.00. Argues that the Soviet Union has changed from a Eurasian giant to a world power, and that some new formula for sharing political power is the best means of containing it.

8 – 206 *Nonproliferation and U.S. Foreign Policy,* Joseph Yager, 438pp, 1980, Brookings, $8.95. A regional analysis of each country's choices; doubts U.S. policy can limit proliferation.

8 – 207 *U.S. Policy Toward Korea,* Nathan White, 231pp, 1979, Westview, $17.00. A careful analysis of U.S. policy options toward the two Korean States which sees no basis for reunification.

8 – 208 *About Face: The China Decision and Its Consequences,* John Tierney, Jr. (ed.), 444pp, 1979, Arlington House, $14.95. Essays attacking the withdrawal of U.S. recognition of Taiwan, including one by Barry Goldwater on the constitutional issues.

8 – 209 *Toward a Humanitarian Diplomacy: A Primer for Policy,* Tom Farer, 288pp, 1980, NYU Press, $15.00. A realistic assessment of obstacles to the promotion of human rights in Iran, South Korea, Brazil, and South Africa.

8 – 210 *United States Foreign Policy and Human Rights, Principles, Priorities, Practice*, Paula Newburg, 86pp, 1980, UNA – USA, $3.00. Describes the national and international laws regarding human rights, defines them, and describes how they can become a continuing feature of U.S. foreign policy.

8 – 211 *China Scapegoat, The Diplomatic Ordeal of John Carter Vincent*, Gary May, 370pp, 1979, New Republic Books, $15.95. A sympathetic biography of a China hand in the critical years up to 1948, who advised encouraging "liberal elements" in both the Kuomintang and Maoist forces, in the hope that an alternative "liberal China" would emerge. His accurate assessment of the forces in the war (and his inaccurate assessment of the alternative) led to accusations that he was sympathetic to Communism and he was dismissed on those grounds. Here he is exonerated from that charge.

8 – 212 *The United States and China in the Twentieth Century*, Michael Schaller, 208pp, 1980, Oxford, $2.95. A perceptive overview focused primarily on the period from 1945 to 1955.

8 – 213 *The Neglected Aspect of Foreign Affairs, American Educational and Cultural Policy Abroad*, Charles Frankel, 156pp, 1965, Brookings, $8.95. Attempts to clarify the principles underlying the Government's cultural and educational activities in other countries by re-stating and re-formulating the ends of that policy and then arguing for its significance.

8 – 214 *The United States and Western Europe: The Political, Economic and Strategic Perspectives*, Wolfram Hanrieder, (ed.), 320pp, 1974, Winthrop, $6.95. Original essays on current problems in the relationships between European states and the United States.

BIBLIOGRAPHY & RESEARCH AIDS

8 – 215 *The National Archives and Foreign Relations Research*, Milton S. Gustafson (ed.), 292pp, 1974, Ohio U. Press, $15.00. A guide to Presidential and Departments' records, as well as neglected sources, and an assessment of current research.

CHAPTER 9

THE SOVIET UNION AND
WORLD POLITICS

A SUCCESSFUL SUPERPOWER?

THE SOVIET UNION today possesses the economic, military and other resources of a superpower. Its gross national product (GNP) exceeds $720 billion (1976), ranking it among the wealthier countries. It is the world's second largest oil producer, with significant reserves, although some forecast that it will switch from an oil exporting to an oil importing country sometime in the 1980s (Klinghoffer, *The Soviet Union and International Oil Politics,* 9-108). It has significant iron ore and an abundance of coal. More than sixty years of continuous rule by one party provide the seemingly stable government (see below) important for the conduct of world affairs. The proportion of its GNP spent for military purposes is the highest in the world except for the Middle East and nearly equals that of Germany in the 1930s. Its military arsenal is numerically superior to any other. Although some experts doubt the qualitative capabilities of its forces, no one denies that it has awesome military forces. A large industrial base, significant scientific achievements, and an educated population of 260 million people constitute additional resources.

In addition to such geopolitical components of power, the Soviet Union claims to be the only legitimate successor to the revolutionary socialist tradition of Marx and Engels and applied in Russia by Lenin (*The Lenin Anthology* 9-11).

234

That claim, acknowledged today by all but two Communist States, China and Yugoslavia, retains an attraction to Communist Parties in Western European States and to many non-Communist educated elites in developing countries, as well as a few in American academic circles (Wesson, *Why Marxism?*, 9-21). The Soviet Union has sympathizers in every country and the support of at least one government on every continent except Australia. The Soviet Union is in every sense a world power.

Anyone concerned with world affairs must study Marxist – Leninist ideology, the Soviet Union's political and economic system, the history of Soviet foreign policy and current Soviet objectives in world politics. Those seeking a world without war will need to consider also the prospects for change, how best to gain the agreement of the Soviet Union on the goals essential to ending war, and what next steps are most helpful in advancing toward them. But two schools of thought in American politics urge that we forego a careful consideration of Soviet policy.

SHOULD SOVIET POLICY BE STUDIED CAREFULLY?

Nearly everyone accepts the facts presented in the opening paragraph of this chapter, but it is often difficult to discuss their implications. Passionate reactions to Communism dominated world affairs discussion in America from 1947 until well into the 1960s. For much of that period, the U.S. approach was shaped by a perception of Communism as a monolithic force directed from Moscow. It ignored the fact that Marxism held great appeal to economically backward countries, promising a short-cut to the modern world via a planned, controlled, economy. It thought that superiority in the arms race and nuclear deterrence were the best available strategies for peace. Anyone challenging such ideas was often considered to be either consciously or unconsciously aiding the Soviet Union and assisting the spread of Communism. In such a climate it was difficult to pursue a careful study of Soviet policy and practice, of alternative routes to economic development in the third world, and of related international issues.

In some sectors of the liberal, left, academic and peace communities – especially after Senator Joseph McCarthy's indiscriminate use of the label "Communist" had intimidated holders of views divergent from his own – an "anti-anti-Communism" grew in strength. This reaction still poses a serious obstacle to a balanced examination of the implications of Soviet power and purpose. Although fed to some extent by those who favor the expansion of revolutionary socialist regimes, this current drew its primary strength from other sources. Among the reasons given for not discussing Soviet policy were these: it will strengthen "the Right"; the U.S. should put its own house in order first; any discussion of differences will increase tensions and perhaps create a climate in which war is more likely. Others argued that the Soviet leadership, like Russian history, needed to be understood as a product of different cultural traditions and that Western concepts did not apply. Whatever the reasons, the refusal to consider Soviet objectives posed a serious obstacle to thoughtful consideration of policy alternatives.

It is now evident that unless there is a better understanding of Soviet policy and objectives, the U.S. will be groping in the dark as to the nature, extent and need for military expenditures; trade relations with the Soviet Union; the measures which might be taken to promote universal human rights; what measures might be taken to promote international organizations with binding authority; and the specific policies the U.S. should adopt with respect to any country which the Soviets seek to influence.

There are three central questions that have divided those who do consider Soviet policies:

1. Is the current regime stable or might rapid change in the near future be expected?

2. Given the facts of Soviet power, military build-up, and success in intervening in third world countries, what are its overall objectives?

3. Can actions by the United States or others significantly influence the Soviet leadership and its policies?

Contending views on each of these questions will be considered below and their relevance assessed for work to end war.

IS THE CURRENT REGIME STABLE?

The arrival in recent years of over 150,000 Russian émigrés in Western countries has provided new information and has promoted renewed speculation about internal opposition within the Soviet Union. The stability of the regime is questioned for four reasons. First, during the 1970s, Soviet economic performance, in foodstuffs and industrial goods, had been woefully poor. Khrushchev's confidence that the Soviet Union would surpass the United States by 1970 or at least by 1980, proved to be wishful thinking. Soviet economic growth rates continue to lag behind the West; the 1970s saw dramatic attempts to import Western capital and technology so as not to fall behind even farther. Second, the economic failures further undermine the Soviet rationale for domestic repression — i.e., that religious and political liberties were impediments to economic progress and therefore must be sacrificed. Third, most of those currently in power are over seventy, and Brezhnev's consolidation of power has meant that new leaders have not been prepared. Thus the transition to new leadership, when it comes, may be abrupt, even disruptive. Fourth, the nationalism sweeping the third and fourth worlds has had its impact on the Soviet Union, especially among those nationalities absorbed into the Russian empire as recently as the 19th century. Particularly in Central Asia, where population growth rates are very high, the cultural, ethnic, religious, and traditionally separate populations are not immune to the nationalist passions sweeping other colonized areas. Similar separatist and nationalist feelings exist in Soviet Georgia, Armenia, and the Ukraine, as well as in the Baltic States annexed during World War II, and the Eastern European States occupied in its aftermath. Some see the invasion of Afghanistan as a form of "defensive aggression" to prevent militant Islamic nationalism from spreading into the Soviet Muslim population in Central Asia.

The debate on Soviet stability or instability is based on such considerations. In his summary of the literature, George Breslauer (*Five Images of the Soviet Future*, 9-75) describes the current regime as "welfare-state authoritarianism." In this system a single party rules on the ground that its doctrine and apparatus permit it to guide the State, providing basic necessities and, by increments, consumer goods and eventually luxury items. Is this form of government stable? Is the justification plausible enough to provide legitimacy for Soviet power? Those making the case for its stability (Breslauer, Hough, *The Soviet Union and Social Science Theory*, 9-66) maintain that under Brezhnev the government of the Soviet Union has changed. Consumer welfare, a campaign against rural poverty, the de-emphasis on ideology, greater regional autonomy, and a degree of public participation in the decision-making process are developments cited by Hough. The Soviet military, industrial, and scientific establishments assure the continuation of the Communist Party's dictatorship in the Soviet Union. The party is supported by a large public constituency whose welfare is tied to perpetuation of the current regime.

Those making the case against stability (Yanov, *Detente After Brezhnev*, 9-116), argue that the Soviet government has lost its legitimacy and must either reform or face crippling domestic disorder. Such severe instability could result from the failure to provide consumer goods after raising the people's expectations. Basic foodstuffs are scarce. Health care is poor. Employment in most cases is menial with little or no participation in decision-making. The flexibility needed in the face of technological innovation is missing from the Soviet system of centralized control. Police repression against dissidents remains nearly as fierce as ever, with exile more frequent than before and imprisonment and executions continuing as well. Brezhnev has consolidated his power so that when he leaves the scene no successor can quickly control the apparatus of State power.

Is change possible? That change will come seems likely. The question is its nature and direction. Yanov identifies six major constituencies within the Soviet Union which are likely to contend for power in the 1980s: 1) elitist liberal intellectuals; 2) new managers (technocrats, intermediaries now between Moscow and local administrators); 3) the aristocratic elite — current party officials, a privileged new class that wants to maintain its prerogatives such as travel in the West, access to exclusive State-run stores where Western consumer goods are sold, and their privileged access to information, wealth and status; 4) the military-industrial complex — the greatly expanded military hierarchy and the domestic production facilities that feed it by means of nearly unhindered access to State funds; 5) local party officials; 6) neo-Stalinist intellectuals. In Yanov's analysis the odds favor the maintenance of the current "welfare authoritarianism" because of the power and influence of the new managerial class, the military-industrial establishment, and the local party officials. For any other alternative to become possible requires that the United States and Western European countries change their policies. Current practices of open trade, investments, credit, and technology transfer aid the "welfare authoritarians." A U.S. – China alliance, a series of U.S. ultimatums, or the ever present threatening of war, would strengthen the military, the local party officials, and the new Stalinist intellectuals. The U.S., however, could also aid the other three groups through limited economic help, acceptance of the Soviet Union as a co-equal world power, and skillful uses of incentives and restraints.

Other scenarios have emerged in the Soviet dissident literature: Adam Amalrik's of the emergence of a Slavophile, anti-Western Russian regime; Roy Medvedev's view that a Democratic Socialistic regime will emerge *(On Socialist Democracy* 9-160); Andrei Sakharov's belief in a liberal, constitutional government *(Sakharov Speaks* 9-149); and Alexander Solzhenitsyn's *Gulag Archipelago* (9-146), in which a Christian, authoritarian basis of government is suggested.

ASSESSMENT

It is difficult to evaluate these possible alternatives to Communist Party rule in the Soviet Union. The Soviet Union remains a closed society; accurate information is not available, even to many within the government. Figures on the Soviet Union's gross national product, military spending, health care, and political prisoners, for example, are usually estimates with a wide range of variance. Who can actually say what segments of the leadership, of the urban or rural public, of the diverse ethnic groups, or of the religious leadership might combine to form a new basis of power if they were permitted (or could find the opportunity) to do so? What is known, however, is that the current leadership maintains operational control of the Soviet Union, its bureaucracy and people. It commands great industrial and military power. In an interdependent world, the policies of the United States and other countries may influence the internal changes and power struggles within the Soviet Union, but cannot control them. The degree of domestic stability or instability may not be an accurate clue to Soviet intentions in world politics. For example, a stable regime can usually command sufficient resources to apply toward its objectives, but an unstable regime may feel it necessary to command even greater resources. The projection of Soviet power through military and economic assistance and military force could be, in part, a consequence of internal instability. An expansionist foreign policy provides a rallying cry for the "welfare-authoritarians" who excuse domestic failures on the grounds of external necessities and who justify their power on the basis of national security. (See Chapter 3, "Causes of War")

IS THE SOVIET UNION SEEKING WORLD HEGEMONY?[1]

A second debate continues over Soviet intentions in world politics. Those who argue that the Soviet Union is seeking world hegemony (the consensus assumption of the 1950s), are today in the minority but are rapidly regaining attention. They can marshal impressive facts to support their view. Since 1973, when the U.S. ended its direct military engagement in Vietnam, Soviet military forces, Cuban forces dispatched at Soviet request, or Soviet-aided forces have had a significant part in deciding the fate of seven countries: Vietnam, Angola, Ethiopia, South Yemen, Afghanistan, Cambodia, and Laos. Soviet military forces have expanded so much in the last fifteen years that they are now equal, if not superior, to those of the United States. The Soviet lead in conventional forces has widened and is useful in applying political leverage. This leverage has long been evident in Soviet relations with Finland and has been described as the process of "Finlandization":

> Those who believe in Finlandization see a country losing its independence in policy-making in two stages. In the first stage the country concerned, while

---

[1]Hegemony is the "preponderant influence of one state over others."

retaining its traditional institutional forms, adapts both the personnel of its government and its decisions of external policy either to the dictates of the Soviet Union or to what it feels Russia really wishes. In the second stage the process of adaptation has gone so far as to divide or sap the energies of the nation, which then becomes unable to resist further pressures.[2]

Those who claim that the Soviet Union is bidding for world hegemony argue that something very like this is now happening in Western Europe. Specifically, according to George Ginsburg and Alvin Rubinstein (9-117), Finlandization has the following characteristics:

1. Responsiveness in foreign policy to Soviet preferences; 2. avoidance of alliance with countries deemed by the Soviet Union to be competitors or rivals; 3. acceptance of neutrality in peace or war; 4. abstention from membership in regional and international groupings considered unfriendly by Moscow; 5. restraint over the media in one's country to muffle or minimize criticism of the USSR, so as to avoid possible provocation; 6. compensatory gestures in commercial and cultural contacts with the USSR, extending to treaties and diplomatic consultations, to offset disparities in the relationship with the USSR, on the one hand, and West European countries, on the other; 7. openness to penetration by Soviet ideas and media.[3]

While most would deny that these characteristics now describe Soviet influence over the NATO countries, there are a number of trends that are suggestive.

All these analyses were published before the Soviet invasion of Afghanistan. With Soviet military forces now less than 300 miles from the straits through which pass two-thirds of the Western world's oil supply, fears that the Soviet Union is gaining world hegemony are now confirmed for many observers.

George F. Kennan (*The Cloud of Danger*, 8-174), among others, remains unalarmed by Soviet moves in world politics. Kennan argues that the Soviet Union has "problems enough in Eastern Europe. . . . and that it is enough of a strain on Russia to try to hold this great area together without increasing those responsibilities by trying to take areas further afield." Soviet judgment of the domestic forces within third-world countries has put them on the winning side in each of the seven countries mentioned above, although it is unclear if the regimes in Ethiopia and Angola would survive the departure of Cuban troops. (Afghanistan now appears to be an exception, in that the Soviet-client regime had been losing control, hence the Soviet invasion.) In this view, a Soviet invasion need not necessarily be feared by Iran or Pakistan. Kennan maintains that the Soviet Union aids those who are sympathetic to it, or even the enemies

---

[2]George Maude, *The Finnish Dilemma* (9-101), p. 45.
[3]*Soviet Foreign Policy Toward Western Europe,* (9-117).

of their enemies. "But doesn't every great power?" Kennan asks. When one looks at the force requirements needed to hold Poland and Czechoslovakia, to protect the Sino — Soviet border, to prevent or quell domestic uprisings, one can conclude that the Soviets have more than enough to manage. Asian, African, and Latin American countries could hardly be expected to submit to Soviet domination, having recently thrown off Western domination or emerged from colonialism. Western Europeans are similarly resilient.

In addition to the debate about whether the Soviet Union is seeking world hegemony, there are two other schools of thought in American politics concerning Soviet power. One such view, not widely shared in the United States, welcomes the expansion of Soviet power and influence. It sees the Soviet Union as an expression of an egalitarian way of life which meets the basic economic and social needs of its people and which, in time, will evolve toward greater political freedom. In the meantime, the Soviet Union has, in this view, a higher degree of democracy than the U.S., because economic rights are more meaningful than civil or political human rights. (Trotsky, *My Life,* 9-13). Another view, also limited in its impact on foreign policy decision-making, responds to this adulation with complete incredulity. Nobody was ever shot trying to get into the Soviet Union, they scoff. The Soviet leadership has as much legitimacy in Russia as it might have in Ethiopia. How can a government which has executed from twenty to fifty million people in the sixty years since it seized power be described as legitimate? It is completely inconsistent to support a Soviet leadership which has killed millions of people, and to say in the next breath that the Soviets do not want war because they lost twenty million lives in World War II. They conclude that the Soviet Union is perfectly capable of launching a nuclear first strike, even at the cost of millions of lives, if it will help them achieve domination. Of course, like any aggressor, the Soviets would prefer to achieve their enemies' demise by peaceful means, but we must be mindful of the precedent that the Soviets have taken millions of lives to consolidate and extend their power (Conquest, *The Great Terror,* 9-155).

THE SOVIET UNION'S OWN STATEMENT OF OBJECTIVES

Lost in this debate is the Soviet leadership's own statement of objectives. In President Brezhnev's speeches before the 25th and 26th Congresses of the Communist Party of the Soviet Union (CPSU) and from a recent work written by the head of the Moscow State Institute for International Relations (Lebedev, *A New Stage in International Relations,* 9-103) a common theme is evident. According to these sources, a fundamental change has taken place in world political relations:

The main factor that determined the switch from confrontation and cold war to detente and the worldwide assertion of the principles of peaceful coexistence was the shift in the balance of power in the world in favor of socialism.[4]

Brezhnev, in his address to the 25th Congress of the CPSU, noted the "changes in the correlation of world forces." Lebedev said, "the notable changes in the alignment of forces in the world in favor of socialism . . . demonstrate the indisputable advantage of socialism over capitalism . . . They have given the Socialist community an incomparably greater opportunity than ever before for effectively influencing the entire course of world development" (p. 1). From both sources, four specific objectives can be paraphrased:

1. *Detente and peaceful coexistence:* Between States with different economic and political systems, there can be peaceful coexistence. The devastation of nuclear war renders peaceful coexistence a practical necessity.

2. *Support national liberation movements:* Military and economic aid is justified to help allies struggling within other countries.

3. *Support the working class:* Soviet economic and other support is available for working class movements within capitalist countries although the national resources should be decisive.

4. *Socialist bloc unity:* The Soviet leadership proclaims the right to intervene in any socialist bloc country that begins to experiment with capitalist innovations or democratic political institutions as in Czechoslovakia (1968).

Persons who have traveled to the Soviet Union or who have met with Soviet citizens find a much more open dialogue than is suggested in such a listing of objectives. One attempt to open such a dialogue is the Models World Order Project of the Institute for World Order. N.I. Lebedev responds directly as well as indirectly to the statement in Part II of this book of the conditions considered essential to a world without war. In criticizing the World Order Models Project, Lebedev states:

The authors' method of approach to the problems concerned does not stand up to criticism. They set out to represent world events from "non-class" positions and reject the "political, economic, and ideological dimensions of foreign policy" as criteria in the analysis of present-day international relations . . . .This standpoint is, therefore, practically the same as that of other bourgeois philosophers and sociologists studying the motives and character of the transformation of capitalist

[4]*A New Stage in International Relations*, p. 35.

society (Kahn, Bell, Brzezinski, and others). For them capitalism as a socio-economic system is indestructible. By attributing the crisis phenomena of capitalism to the world as a whole, portraying them as the "growing pains" of civilization, they close their eyes to the objective existence of different social systems and depreciate the success of the socialist world system. The ways and means suggested by the World Order Models Project to "improve" the modern world are divorced from the facts and neglect the chief motivator of world events — the confrontation of the two socio-economic systems in which socialism is continuously gaining ground and exercising a decisive influence on the development of the contemporary system of international relations.

The profoundly scientific Marxist-Leninist concept of the development of the whole system of present-day international relations formulated by the 25th CPSU [Congress] and extended in the decisions of the 26th CPSU Congress, is the only constructive answer to the imperatives of the present period. It is being put into effect by the Soviet Union together with the other countries of the socialist community. . . .[5]

These paraphrases and quotations are presented as authoritative statements of Soviet objectives. The Soviet Union is the disinterested agent of peace, progress and disarmament, although when what it considers to be the forces of progress can be aided by military violence, it is prepared to go to war.

Many knowledgeable students of Soviet affairs, however, doubt that much is to be gained by taking seriously such Leninist proclamations at ceremonial occasions. The sources of Soviet intentions, such students maintain, are to be found in the Russian national tradition, its geopolitical position, its cultural heritage, and isolation from Europe, as well as its expansionist tendencies. Such students can even quote Churchill's oft-repeated statement: "Russian foreign policy is a mystery, wrapped in an enigma, inside a puzzle. But perhaps there is a key: the Russian national interest."

Whether Soviet objectives result from ideological commitments or from national interest, their pursuit includes the threat or use of mass organized violence. Thus, Soviet foreign policy must, like that of the United States, be considered as a cause of war. The hope, once widely held in peace circles, that Socialism would bring peace, at least between Socialist States, has not materialized. With Vietnam's invasion of Cambodia, China's invasion of Vietnam, the continuing conflicts along the Sino-Soviet border, Soviet occupation of Eastern European countries, and the Soviet invasion of Afghanistan, it is now clear that neither domination by Communist powers nor State ownership of the means of production brings an end to war.

[5]*A New Stage in International Relations*, pp. 238–239.

CAN EXTERNAL POWERS INFLUENCE SOVIET POLICIES?

Whatever the United States does affects Soviet policy; American passivity has its effects, military responses theirs. For example, the Cuban Missile Crisis included threats to attack Soviet missile sites there. Throughout the 1950s and 1960s the building of new weapons systems was considered necessary as influences on Soviet decision-makers not to go to war. The lack of a response to the Soviet military build-up and interventions encourages further expansion. Soviet dissidents insist that publicity in the West affects decisions concerning Soviet political prisoners.

What persistent, long-term American strategy is most likely to induce the changes needed to develop peaceful competition, to bring about a world capable of resolving conflict without mass violence? What acts could we initiate that would coerce the Soviet Union into reciprocation? How can Soviet agreement be achieved on institutions of world law, universal and enforceable disarmament, a common commitment to world economic development, and a sense of world community?

For those working toward a world without war, the problem is first to determine what policies and what initiative acts would achieve such agreement and then to take concrete steps toward implementation of such policies and acts. Such policies must open the channels of communication, enhance mutual understanding, and build a sense of community across national and ideological boundaries. These policies must find supporters within the Soviet Union and must increase their influence. The peace-seeker's central problem is to identify influences — benefits and losses, external and internal — that could move leaders of the Soviet Union away from the arms race and toward disarmament, away from mass political violence and toward world institutions capable of promoting needed change and resolving conflict without violence.

BIBLIOGRAPHY

The bibliography for this chapter is devoted to understanding the Soviet Union. The books in this chapter introduce the basic works of the Marxist tradition. They examine the Bolshevik seizure of power in Russia, the questions of stability, Soviet foreign policy objectives and possible allies there in the search for a world without war. The books will assist in answering questions such as these: 1)What are the main concepts of Marxism? 2)What did Lenin (or Leninism) add to or subtract from Marxism? 3) Is Marxism a scientific philosophy of history? Or merely a set of useful but unrelated concepts? Or concepts which obscure more than they illuminate? 4) Is Russia rightly regarded as a Marxist State? 5) What is the relationship between the Russian people and their Soviet rulers? 6) How well does the Soviet economic system work? 7) What are the real objectives of the Soviet Union's foreign policy? 8) What means do the Soviet leaders consider legitimate to achieve those objectives? 9) What actions by the United States and others are most likely to influence Soviet leaders? 10) What could Western individuals and organizations do to influence leaders and the public within the Soviet Union in the direction of a world without war?

A. The Foundations: Marxism and Its Revisions

9 – 1 *The Marx-Engels Reader,* Robert C. Tucker (ed.), 686pp, 1978, 2nd ed, Norton, $6.95. Includes selections from the young Marx, the critique of political economy, and revolutionary strategy.

9 – 2 *Basic Writings on Politics and Philosophy, by Karl Marx and Friedrich Engels,* Lewis Feuer (ed.), 497pp, 1959, Peter Smith, $7.50. A selection of the major political writings of the founders of modern Communism.

9 – 3 *The Communist Manifesto,* Karl Marx and Frederick Engels, Samuel Moore (tr.), 32pp, 1977, 1848. C.H.Kerr, $.50.

9 – 4 *Early Writings,* Quintin Hoare (ed.), Rodney Livingston & Gregor Benton (trs.), 1975, Random House, $4.95. Stresses Marx's concept of alienation from work in modern production.

9 – 5 *Eastern Question,* Karl Marx, Eleanor & Edward Aveling (eds.), 1897, 1968, Kelley, $29.00. Marx's analysis of Slavic peoples.

9 – 6 *Karl Marx – Frederick Engels: Collected Works,* 9 volumes, 1835 – 1849, published 1975 – 1977, International Publishers, $8.50. Includes all of Marx's and Engels' writings from 1835 – 1849.

9 – 7 *The Marxian Revolutionary Idea,* Robert C. Tucker, 240pp, 1969, Norton, $3.95. An analysis of Marxism applied to the modernization of backward economies, distributive justice, and revolution. Tucker traces the de-radicalization of the Soviet Union and the contemporary impact and importance of the Marxian vision.

9 – 8 *To the Finland Station,* Edmund Wilson, 502pp, 1973, (1940), Noonday, $7.95. A study of the rise of modern socialist thought which is sympathetic to the idea that socialism, not Stalinism, is the logical outcome of Western European history.

9 – 9 *Karl Marx,* Isaiah Berlin, 228pp, 1939, 1978, 4th ed., Oxford, $4.50. A brief intellectual history of Marx combined with an introduction to current controversies about Marx and Marxism, and a fourteen-page guide to further reading.

9 – 10 *Karl Marx,* David McLellan, 110pp, 1976, Penguin, $2.95. A brief summary of his life, ideas and influence.

9 – 11 *The Lenin Anthology*, Robert C. Tucker (ed.), 764pp, 1975, Norton, $8.95. A collection built around the concept of revolution.

9 – 12 *The Class Struggle,* Karl Kautsky, 217pp, 1892, 1971, Norton, $3.95. Written as a general statement of the articles of belief of the Social Democratic Party of Germany at the time when it was the largest and most influential Marxist party in Europe. Kautsky's call for seeking power through democratic political processes foreshadowed the split between the Social Democrats and Bolsheviks, between Democratic Socialists and Communists.

9 – 13 *My Life*, Leon Trotsky, 1970, Pathfinder, $6.95. A key figure in the Bolshevik Revolution (1917), founder of the Red Army, and antagonist of Stalin's "socialism in one country," Trotsky remains a symbol of world revolution.

9 – 14 *Terrorism and Communism*, Leon Trotsky, 191pp, 1961, U. of Michigan $6.95. Trotsky defends terror in the Russian Revolution on the grounds that it was necessary to the defense of Socialism. He argues that the Party can permit no opposition and that terrorism is a necessary means for the highest moral end of humanity: the Socialist state. Trotsky himself became a victim of the police state which he helped to create.

9 – 15 *The Social and Political Thought of Leon Trotsky*, Baruch Knei-Paz, 656pp, 1980, Oxford, $19.95. A survey of the entire corpus of Trotsky's writings with a critical assessment.

9 – 16 *An Introduction to Marxist Economic Theory*, Ernest Mandel, 78pp, 1974, Pathfinder, $2.25. A "Trotskyite" seeks to demonstrate the continued relevance of Marxist economic theory to explain the workings of the American economy.

9 – 17 *Socialist Thought, A Documentary History*, Albert Fried and Ronald Sanders, 544pp, 1964, Doubleday, $3.95. Brief selections form the many strands of socialist thought — utopian, rational, communal, anarchistic, Marxian, revisionism, and Bolshevik.

9 – 18 *Toward a Humanist Marxism: Essays on the Left Today,* Leszek Kolakowski, 200pp, 1968, Grove, $3.95. A re-interpretation of Marxism by a Polish intellectual who is branded a "revisionist" by the Soviet Union.

9 – 19 *Main Currents of Marxism, Its Rise, Growth and Dissolution,* Leszek Kolakowksi, Vol. I, *The Founders*, 480pp, Vol. II, *The Golden Age,* 592pp, Vol. III., *The Breakdown,* Oxford, $26.50 each. A survey of the varieties of Marxism and of the broadening current of thought called Marxism.

9 – 20 *Three Faces of Marxism, The Political Concepts of Soviet Ideology, Maoism and Humanist Marxism*, Wolfgang Leonhard, 497pp, 1970, 1974, Paragon, $5.95. Surveys the career of the main political concepts of Marxism from the Communist Manifesto (1848) to the present, with special attention to change brought by Lenin and Stalin; the second part of the book describes three varieties of Marxism today.

9 – 21 *Why Marxism? The Continuing Success of a Failed Theory,* Robert Wesson,

281pp, 1976, Basic Books, $12.95. Succinctly describes the failure of Marx's Marxism to 19th or 20th century change, and suggests that its success is traceable to the addition of new ideas and its refusal to describe what should replace the old order.

9 – 22 *Marxism in the Modern World*, Milorad Drachkovitch (ed.), 292pp, 1965, Stanford, $3.25. An anthology highlighted by Ramond Aron's examination of the argument for a dictatorship of a minority and Richard Lowenthal's essay on pluralistic Communism.

9 – 23 *Marx's Theory of Politics*, John Maguire, 251pp, 1978, Cambridge, $24.95. After a careful reading of the texts, Marx's view of politics is described, criticized, and appreciated; while economic motivation remains the key to Marx's thought, this work denies that there is any "overarching metaphysical predetermination" involved and finds it possible to consider the "abolition of politics."

9 – 24 *The Origins of Totalitarian Democracy,* J.L. Talmon, 366pp, 1970, Norton, $5.95. Introduces both liberal and totalitarian sources of democracy, tracing the latter to Rousseau's concept of the "general will" and Babeuf's "conspiracy of the equals" during the French Revolution.

9 – 25 *Marxism in Our Time*, Isaac Deutscher, Tamara Deutscher (eds.), 312pp, 1971, Ramparts, $7.95. An analysis and apppreciation of contemporary Communist States by an anti-Stalinist Marxist.

9 – 26 *Stalinism: Essays in Historical Interpretation*, Robert C. Tucker (ed.), 332pp, 1977, Norton, $5.95. A description of the intellectual foundations of totalitarian, expansionist Communism.

9 – 27 *Marx's Theory of History*, William Shaw, 202pp, 1978, Stanford, $3.95. A reinterpretation of Marx's theory of history attempting to accommodate non-economic forces as well as the unforeseen.

9 – 28 *Marxism-Leninism and the Theory of International Relations*, V. Kubalkova & A.A. Cruickshank, 424pp, 1980, Routledge, Kegan Paul, $40.00. Summarizes the theories of international relations of Marx, Engels, Lenin, Stalin, and the current leadership; compares their theories with selected Western theories, to the advantage of the former.

B. Russian and Soviet History

9 – 29 *Russia: A History & Interpretation*, Michael Florinsky, 628pp, Vol I; 1,511pp Vol II, 1969, 2nd ed., Macmillan, $16.95. A widely respected history to 1917.

9 – 30 *Russia: A History,* Sidney Harcave, 787pp, 1968, 6th ed., Lippincott, $9.95. A widely used and useful textbook.

9 – 31 *The Making of Modern Russia*, Lionel Kochan, 335pp, 1974, Penguin, $3.95. A

survey of Russian history from the 10th century to the present, with an emphasis on the post-1917 period.

9—32 *The Russians*, Hedrick Smith, 509pp, 1976, Quadrangle, $12.50. A popular overview with a contemporary, journalistic assessment.

9—33 *The Russian Revolution, 1917—1921*, Volumes 1 & 2, W.H. Chamberlin, 511pp, 556pp, 1965 (1935), Grosset & Dunlop, $4.95 each. Still considered the best history of the Revolution by those unsympathetic to the Bolsheviks.

9—34 *The Russian Revolution: From Lenin to Stalin*, E.H. Carr, 191pp, 1979, Macmillan, $10.00. A distillation of the main ideas, analysis, and conclusions of Carr's ten-volume history written from the winner's perspective.

9—35 *The October Revolution*, Roy Medvedev, 232pp, 1979, Columbia, $14.95. A Russian Democratic Socialist reinterprets the events leading to the establishment of a totalitarian form of government.

9—36 *The Debate on Soviet Power, Minutes of the All-Russian Central Executive Committee of Soviets Second Convocation, October 1917—1918*, John Keep (ed.), 480pp, 1979, Oxford, $39.00. Minutes of meetings after the Bolsheviks seized power in which advocates of democratic forms of political organization are consigned by Lenin & Trotsky to the "dustbin of history."

9—37 *World Communism, A History of the Communist International*, Franz Borkenau, 442pp, 1962, U. of Michigan Press, $4.95. A study of the failure of the Communist Internationale, headquartered in Moscow, successfully to inspire, engineer, and aid Communist parties come to power in Western Europe.

9—38 *The Soviet Union Since Stalin*, Stephen Cohen, Alexander Rabinowitch, and Robert Sharlet (eds.), 352pp, 1980, Indiana, $7.95. Themes of continuity and change in Soviet politics, society and foreign affairs are examined by scholars.

9—39 *World Communism, The Disintegration of a Secular Faith*, Richard Lowenthal 296pp, 1964, Oxford, $4.95. Identifies a series of ideological crises in keeping doctrine in conformity to events since 1950.

9—40 *Russia's Failed Revolutions, From the Decembrists to the Dissidents*, Adam Ulam, 1981, Basic $18.95. Makes the case that nationalism may yet spark a successful series of liberal reforms in the Soviet Union.

C. Soviet Leaders

9—41 *Plekanov, The Father of Russian Marxism*, Samuel Baron, 400pp, 1963, Stanford, $17.50 A Menshevik, a leader of a rival faction, who rejected Lenin's view that you could skip stages of history.

9– 42 *Lenin, A Biography*, David Shub, 496pp, 1948, 1976, Penguin, $2.95. A personal history of Lenin's career and achievement which concludes; "Leninism lives on, but with each passing year it becomes increasingly an anachronism — not least in Russia."

9– 43 *The Bolshevik Tradition, Lenin, Stalin, Khrushchev, Brezhnev,* Robert McNeal, 210pp, 1975, 2nd ed., Prentice-Hall, $2.95. Maintains that the tradition is an imposing force in the world today.

9– 44 *Stalin: Man of History, A Biography*, Ian Grey, 547pp, 1979, Doubleday, $14.95. Tries to see the person behind the deeds which are attributed to Stalin: "He gave positive leadership and transformed a vast, backward agrarian nation into a modern industrial power. . . . He was also ruthless and inhuman in his methods." A sympathetic portrayal.

9– 45 *Stalin's Successors*, Seweryn Bialer, 416pp, 1980, Cambridge, $19.95. A study of the evolution of the Soviet system and the generational conflict expected in the 1980s.

9– 46 *Khrushchev Remembers*, Nikita Khrushchev, Strobe, Talbot (ed. & tr.), 639pp, 1971, Little, Brown, $15.00. The first volume of the former Soviet Premier's recollections of life under Stalin: his own ascent to power: domestic and world affairs, including the Cuban missile crisis, and his speech denouncing Stalin's excesses.

9– 47 *Khrushchev, A Career*, Edward Crankshaw, 311pp, 1971, Penguin, $3.95. A biography focused on the years before he became head of state, including a chapter entitled "more Stalinist than Stalin."

9– 48 *Khrushchev: The Years in Power*, Roy Medvedev & Zhores Medvedev, 198pp, 1978, Norton, $2.95. A sympathetic portrayal of the limited domestic and foreign policy changes instituted by Khrushchev (1953 – 1964), as well as criticism of his domestic failures.

9– 49 *Leonid Brezhnev: Pages from His Life*, Soviet Academy of Sciences, 320pp, 1978, Simon & Schuster, $11.95. A book of empty glorifications; "underscores the depressing sterility of Soviet writings on their own political system."

9– 50 *Brezhnev, The Masks of Power*, John Dornberg, 317pp, 1974, Basic, $14.95. A biography focused on the Soviet head of State as a politician carrying out Lenin's heritage and expanding Soviet power.

9– 51 *Soviet Leadership in Transition,* Jerry Hough, 175pp, 1980, Brookings, $4.95. Provides generational profiles of Soviet political, administrative, and foreign policy elites and emphasizes the ways that the impending succession may affect Soviet policies.

D. The Soviet Economy

9– 52 *The Industrialization of Soviet Russia*, R.W. Davies, Vol. I, *The Socialist*

Offensive, 576pp, 1980, Harvard, $35.00; Volume II, *The Soviet Collective Farm, 1929 – 1930*, 256pp, 1980, Harvard, $18.50. These are the first two in a multi-volume series which "will demonstrate how, during the crucial period from 1929 to 1937, the most rapid and broadest industrial development in modern times was undertaken in the USSR."

9 – 53 *The Soviet Economy*, Constantin Krylov, 255pp, 1979, Lexington, $17.95. Offers a history of the Soviet economy and concludes that "the Soviet economic system is the fruit of an ill-considered, . . . crudely conducted experiment. In the beginning it was entirely natural [*sic*] to have some hopes for it, despite all the brutality of its measures. These hopes are now groundless" (p.244). But change is impossible: If the economic controls are lossened, how will the political controls be maintained?

9 – 54 *Political Economy and Soviet Socialism*, Alec Nove, 249pp, 1979, Allen & Unwin, $8.95. A collection of essays written in the 1970s which attempt to define what was possible to achieve under Soviet Socialism, but to limit criticisms and praise within those limits.

9 – 55 *Socialist Economic Integration*, Jozef Van Brabant, 375pp, 1980, Cambridge, $29.50. An analysis of the Council of Mutual Economic Assistance.

9 – 56 *Distribution of Income: East and West*, Peter Wiles, 136pp, 1975, Elsevier $22.00. Argues that income is better distributed in Britain than in the Soviet Union.

9 – 57 *Soviet Economic Policy: Income Differentials in USSR*, Vinod Mehta, 134pp, 1977, Humanities Press, $8.50. A study of Soviet income differentials, based on data made available by the government, concluded that income differentials have narrowed although an "aura of secrecy" surrounds the salaries and living styles of Party leaders.

9 – 58 *Comparative Communism, The Soviet, Chinese, and Yugoslav Models*, Gary Bertsch and Thomas Granschow (eds.), 463pp, 1976, Freeman, $8.95. Includes articles by authorities on each country addressed to common problems: form of political organization, strategy of development, decision-making, participation in world affairs.

9 – 59 *Environmental Misuse in the Soviet Union*, Fred Singleton (ed.), 100pp, 1976, Praeger, $17.95. Four authors consider why "the Soviet Union appears to have no better record than other countries in its treatment of the environment."

9 – 60 *Soviet Foreign Trade*, William Turpin, 172pp, 1977, Heath, $16.95. Discusses the organization and operation of Soviet trade with developed Western countries.

9 – 61 *Soviet-Type Economic Systems: A Guide to Information Sources*, Edward O'Reilly, 228pp, 1978, Gale, $22.00. A useful reference.

E. The Soviet Political System

9 – 62 *The Government and Politics of the Soviet Union*, Leonard Shapiro, 192pp,

1978, Vintage, $2.95. An authoritative study of the origins of the Soviet State, and the constitutional, administrative, and political structure through which the society is controlled.

9– 63 *The Constitutions of the Communist World,* William Simons (ed.), 640pp, 1980, Sijthoff & Noordhoff, $92.50. Includes the constitutions of each Communist State and an index systematically presenting the provisions of each.

9– 64 *Soviet Communism: The Socialist Vision,* Julius Jacobson (ed.), 363pp, 1972, Transaction, $4.95. Articles from *New Politics* on Soviet dissidents, anti-Semitism in the USSR, the manipulative function of law, the corruption of Communist Party bureaucrats, and the socio-political bases of Czech liberalization.

9– 65 *Public Policy and Administration in the Soviet Union,* Gordon Smith (ed.), 240pp, 1980, Praeger, $9.95.

9– 66 *The Soviet Union and Social Science Theory,* Jerry Hough, 336 pp, 1977, Harvard, $16.50. Explores how social science methodologies can increase our understanding of the Soviet government, and through those methodologies explains State-society relations, the political party, and the bureaucracy.

9– 67 *Communist Local Government: A Study of Poland,* Jaroslaw Piekalkiewicz, 282pp, 1975, Ohio U. $15.00. Describes the impact of industrialization and urbanization on local government in Poland from 1958 to 1969. Argues that the degree of centralization and single party elections is both inefficient and stifling although the forms of public participation are maintained.

9– 68 *Contemporary Soviet Politics, An Introduction,* Donald Barry and Carol Barner-Barry, 406pp, 1978, Prentice-Hall, $10.95. Identifies the fundamental principles, outlines the structures, and discusses how they operate — while lamenting the lack of verifiable information.

9– 69 *Russian Peasants and Soviet Power, A Study of Collectivization,* Moshe Lewin, 539pp, 1975, Norton, $5.95. A detailed account of Soviet policy toward peasants from 1917 to 1930, the collectivization of landholdings, and the massive peasant response in the destruction of livestock and machines. The number of peasants killed can only be guessed.

9– 70 *The Russian Dilemma: A Political and Geopolitical View,* Robert Wesson, 240pp, 1974, Rutgers, $3.95, Argues that the Soviet Union increasingly needs the West for technology and quality consumer goods, but that such contact acerbates inequalities of wealth and power in the Soviet Union; to enter the modern world requires changing the relations of people to the State and of Russians to non-Russians.

9– 71 *Communism and Communist Systems,* Robert Wesson, 227pp, 1978, Prentice-Hall, $9.95. Identifies the elements which all Communist States have in common, which give the label its utility, and discusses the particular circumstances in each Communist State as of 1975.

9 – 72 *The Unperfect Society, Beyond the New Class*, Milovan Djilas, 267pp, 1970, Harvest, $2.35. A dissenter in Tito's Yugoslavia argues that the Communist Party has become a new, privileged class and will remain so as long as it maintains exclusive control of the political process.

9 – 73 *How the Soviet Union is Governed*, Jerry Hough, 679pp, 1979, Harvard, $18.50. A rewriting of Merle Fainsod's *How Russia Is Ruled* that argues against Fainsod's thesis; Hough believes there is wide participation in Soviet decison-making; Fainsod called it a totalitarian State.

9 – 74 *The Soviet Union: Looking to the 1980s*, Robert Wesson (ed.), 288pp, 1980, Hoover Inst. $25.00. A variety of perspectives on the future from the official optimism to Andrei Amalrik's doubts that the dictatorship will survive until 1984.

9 – 75 *Five Images of the Soviet Future: A Critical Review and Synthesis*, George Breslauer, 78pp, 1978, U. of Calif., $2.50. Describes five different images of rule in Russia by the Communist Party in the future, and suggests that an overthrow is unlikely but that change from within will happen. The outcome of that change is uncertain.

F. The Soviet Society

9 – 76 *Socialist Population Politics: The Political Implications of Demographic Trends in the USSR and Eastern Europe*, John Besemeres, 371pp, 1980, Sharpe, $25.00 Suggests the declining size of the Russians compared with the over 100 other ethnic groups.

9 – 77 *Soviet Asian Ethnic Frontier*, William McCagy & Brian Silver, 280pp, Pergamon, $32.50. Discusses the rapid growth of the Asian population and the prospects for its increased self-consciousness as a major force in Soviet society.

9 – 78 *Muslim National Communism in the Soviet Union: A Revolutionary Strategy for the Colonial World*, Alexandre Bennigsen & S. Enders Wimbush, 268pp, 1980, Chicago, $7.95. Explains how Marxist ideas were transformed into the doctrine of National Communism.

9 – 79 *Man, State, and Society in the Soviet Union*, Joseph Nagee (ed.), 599pp, 1972, Praeger, $7.95. Detailed and scholarly criticisms of the internal workings of Soviet society confirm the totalitarian nature of governmental control and its permeation of social life.

9 – 80 *The Jews in Soviet Russia Since 1917*, Lionel Kochan (ed.), 431pp, 1978, Oxford, $5.95. Seventeen essays on the legal, cultural, religious, social, and political life of a minority in the Soviet Union. The tone is scholarly, concerned, and critical of the State.

9 – 81 *Socialism, Politics, and Equality: Hierarchy and Change in Eastern Europe and*

the USSR, Walter Connor, 488pp, 1980, Columbia, $10.00. Using available quantitative data and other information, the author assesses the impact of Communism on social structures.

9–82 *Women Under Communism: A Cross-National Analysis of Women in Communist Society,* Barbara Jancar, 301pp, 1978, Johns Hopkins, $16.00. Studies the economic, social, and political rights of women in the Soviet Union, Eastern Europe, China, and Cuba, and concludes that more gains have been made in economic and educational objectives than political.

9–83 *Women in Soviet Society: Equality, Development and Social Change,* Gail Lapidus, 381pp, 1978, California, $4.95. Assesses women's drive for equality in general and in the Soviet Union in particular, and concludes that great progress has been made but that a "time lag" prevents women from being visible at the top.

9–84 *Social and Economic Inequality in the Soviet Union, Six Studies,* Murray Yanowitch, 197pp, 1977, Sharpe, $6.95. Attempts to apply social science research techniques to the problem of inequality.

9–85 *Privilege in the Soviet Union,* Mervyn Mathews, 1978. Allen Unwin, $7.95. Finds many forms of privilege in the Soviet Union, one form of which is the opportunity to know the facts on which the government bases policy, not the untruths offered to the public.

9–86 *Religion and Modernization in the Soviet Union,* Dennis Dunn (ed.), 442pp, 1978, Westview, $27.50. Suggests that religious institutions were never a hinderance to economic modernization; just to the totalitarian quest for power by the Bolsheviks.

9–87 *Soviet Legal System and Arms Inspection: A Case Study in Policy Implementation,* Zigurds Zile, et al, 394pp, 1972, Irvington, $12.95. Explores how Soviet legal institutions could help inspect arms control agreements.

G. Soviet Foreign Policy Objectives

9–88 *Soviet Foreign Policy Since World War II: Imperial and Global,* Alvin Rubinstein, 354pp, 1981, Winthrop, $9.95. An overview of the Soviet Union's objectives finds them generally expansionist although cautious when challenged, relentless when not.

9–89 *Soviet Foreign Policy: Its Social and Economic Foundations,* Egbert Jahn, 160pp, 1978, St. Martin's, $16.95 The domestic sources of Soviet policy.

9–90 *Peace, Detente and Soviet-American Relations: A Collection of Public Statements,* by Leonid Brezhnev, 1979, Harcourt, Brace & Jovanovich, $12.95 A trend toward bolder statements of objectives is discernible.

9–91 *Soviet Perceptions of the United States,* Morton Schwartz, 216pp, 1978,

California, $4.95. Suggests the screens through which Soviet leaders filter information about the United States as they calculate their own policies.

9 – 92 *The USSR and Global Interdependence, Alternative Futures*, Walter Clemens, Jr., 113pp, 1978, American Enterprise Institute, $5.25. Cautiously advances the possibility that strategic, economic, technological, and ecological mutual vulnerabilities open the prospect for greater cooperation between the superpowers with liberalization expected to take place in the Soviet Union.

9 – 93 *Soviet – Asian Relations in the 1970s and Beyond: An Interperceptual Study*, Bhabani Sen Gupta, 368pp, 1976, Praeger, $27.95. A study of the Soviet Union's "presence building in the 1970s" from Iran to Japan, which concentrates on the leaders' image of their country, the Soviet Union's image of other countries in terms of itself, and the similarities and differences between the various images.

9 – 94 *The Sino – Soviet Territorial Dispute*, Tai Sung An, 254pp, 1973 Westminister, $8.95. Examines the history, current developments, and the potential for full-scale war.

9 – 95 *War Between Russia and China*, Harrison Salisbury, 224pp, 1969, Norton, $4.95. The author believes that Sino-Soviet differences may well lead to war. He suggests ways the U.S. could help prevent such a war and the possible consequences of U.S. failure.

9 – 96 *Readings in Russian Foreign Policy*, Robert Goldwin (ed.), 751pp, 1964, Oxford, $5.95. A still interesting anthology raising important questions about the role of national character, ideology, geography, and leaders in deciding foreign policy objectives.

9 – 97 *The Twenty-Fifth Congress of the CPSU: Assessment and Context*, Alexander Dallin (ed.), 121pp, 1977, Hoover, $5.95. A description of the Congress and of its importance in signaling the confidence that a "new correlation of forces" between East and West had been achieved in favor of the East.

9 – 98 *Survey of the Sino-Soviet Dispute: A Commentary and Extracts from the Recent Polemics 1963 – 1967*, John Gittings, 410pp, 1968, Oxford, $22.00. Traces Soviet-Chinese relations from the Russian Revolution (1917) to 1967 and examines the origins of the world's most intense hatred.

9 – 99 *Soviet Foreign Policy, 1962 – 1973, The Paradox of Superpower*, Robin Edmonds, 197pp, 1975, Oxford, $4.95. Describes a period of Soviet failures in world politics, particularly in the Middle East.

9 – 100 *The Soviet Union in World Affairs, A Documented Analysis, 1964 – 1972*, W.W. Kulski, 526pp, 1973, Syracuse, $12.00. A wide-ranging analysis of Soviet relations with the U.S., China, various parts of the third world, and its attempt to direct the Communist International.

9 – 101 *The Finnish Dilemma: Neutrality in the Shadow of Power*, George Maude, 153pp, 1976, Oxford, $17.50. Underlines the concessions made and the independence granted in Finland's efforts to remain neutral.

9 – 102 *Soviet Strategy for the Seventies, From Cold War to Peaceful Coexistence*, Foy Kohler and three others, 241pp, 1977, Center for Advanced Studies, U. of Miami, $4.95. Charts a shifting use of "peaceful coexistence" to become consistent with a global strategy. Argues that the changed military posture confirms that shift in policy.

9 – 103 *A New Stage in International Relations*, N.I. Lebedev, 253pp, 1976, Pergamon Press, $20.00. The rector of the Moscow Institute for International Relations describes the "scientific" application of Leninist principles as they guide Soviet policy-makers today.

9 – 104 *The Soviet Triangle: Russia's Relations with China and the West in the 1980s*, Donald Shanor, 288pp, 1980, St. Martin's, $13.95. Describes the Soviet Union's geopolitical viewpoint and its efforts to avoid a Chinese – Western alliance against it.

9 – 105 *Prospects of the Soviet Power in the 1980s*, Christoph Bertram, (ed.), 128pp, 1980, Shoestring, $19.50. Western experts maintain that despite formidable challenges, few changes in Soviet expansionism or domestic repression are likely.

9 – 106 *Soviet Propaganda, A Case Study of the Middle East Conflict*, Baruch Hazan, 293pp, 1976, Transaction, $12.95. Studies the instruments, purposes, techniques, and significant success of Soviet propaganda efforts — both direct and through front organizations.

9 – 107 *Politics and Oil: Moscow in the Middle East*, Lincoln Landis, 201pp, 1973, Dunellen, $5.95. A discussion of the mixture of national self-interest and ideological conviction guiding Soviet Middle East policy with a "world energy delivery system" for Socialist states as the ultimate objective.

9 – 108 *The Soviet Union and International Oil Politics*, Arthur Klinghoffer, 399pp, 1977, Columbia, $20.00. Surveys Soviet domestic and international energy policies and concludes that the Soviet Union may have to choose between exports to Eastern Europe (and elsewhere) and domestic consumption.

9 – 109 *Soviet Military Strategy in Europe*, Joseph Douglass, Jr., 270pp, 1980, Pergamon, $30.00. Based on Soviet sources, the authors conclude that the Warsaw Pact countries are developing an "effective, usable, preemptive, offensive nuclear war-fighting capability."

9 – 110 *The Many Faces of Communism*, Morton Kaplan (ed.), 366pp, 1978, Free Press, $16.95. A study of the fragmentation within the world Communist movement and within Communist States, as well as Communist movements in non-Communist States.

9 – 111 *Russia and the United States: U.S. – Soviet Relations from the Soviet Point of View*, Nikolai Sivachev & Nikolai Yakovlev, 301pp, 1979, Chicago, $12.95. A well written but predictable castigation of American imperialism on the one hand and Soviet practice of peaceful coexistence on the other.

9 – 112 *Soviet – American Relations in the 1980s: Superpower Politics and East – West Trade*, Lawrence Caldwell & William Diebold, Jr., 320pp, 1981, McGraw-Hill,

$7.95. Foresees a new generation of Soviet leaders with changed attitudes toward strategic thought and toward the role of the Soviet Union in the world economy.

9 – 113 *Russia and World Order, Strategic Choices and the Laws of Power in History*, George Liska, 194pp, 1980, Johns Hopkins, $14.00. Argues for inclusion of the Soviet Union in an enlarged North to combat the ''economic aggression'' of the South.

9 – 114 *The USSR and Africa: New Dimensions of Soviet Global Power*, Morris Rothenberg, 280pp, 1980, Advanced International Studies Institute, $8.95. A summary of Soviet expansionist intentions in Africa based largely on Soviet sources.

9 – 115 *The Soviet Union and Africa: The History of the Involvement*, Charles Lanbam, 250pp, 1980, U. Press of America, $7.50. A history of Soviet perceptions of African politics.

9 – 116 *Detente after Brezhnev: The Domestic Roots of Soviet Foreign Policy*, Alexander Yanov, 87pp, 1977, Institute of International Studies, Berkeley, $3.00. Calls for a subtle mixture of economic and political incentives to aid Russia's liberal intelligencia and the current technocrats as well as other moderating forces rather than the military after Brezhnev.

9 – 117 *Soviet Foreign Policy Toward Western Europe*, George Ginsburg & Alvin Rubinstein (eds.), 295pp, 1978, Praeger, $20.00. A variety of essays whose preponderant conclusion is that ''congenial neutralization'' not ''communication'' is Moscow's aim.

9 – 118 *Soviet Perspectives on International Relations, 1956 – 1967*, William Zimmerman, 338pp, 1969, Princeton, $5.95. Introduces international relations theory as developed in Soviet journals — the definition of the actors, U.S. policy objectives, and of the role of the Party are of particular interest.

9 – 119 *The American Image of Russia: 1917 – 1977*, Benson Grayson, 388pp, 1978, Ungar, $14.50. A valuable collection of American opinions about the Soviet Union beginning with Woodrow Wilson's welcoming the February revolution (and his opposition to the October Revolution) to Carter's 1977 speech on Human Rights and the Cold War. Fascinating, diverse views.

9 – 120 *World Communism at the Crossroads, Communist Military Ascendancy, Political Economy, and Human Welfare*, Steven Rosefielde (ed.), 336pp, 1980, Martinus Nijhoff, $19.95. Asks how the projection of Soviet power through military superiority effects the achievement of economic objectives.

H. Means of Conducting Foreign Policy

9 – 121 *The Soviet View of War, Peace, and Neutrality*, P. Vigor, 256pp, 1975, Rutledge & Kegan, $19.95. An interpretation of these concepts in the conduct of Soviet policy.

9 – 122 *The Evolution of Soviet Security Strategy 1965 – 1975*, Avigdor Haselkorn, 1978, Crane & Russak, $4.95. Traces the shifting Soviet objectives as military power grows and the U.S. suffers in Vietnam.

9 – 123 *The Conduct of Soviet Foreign Policy*, Erik Hoffmann & Frederick Fleron, (eds.), 478pp, 1980 (2nd ed.), Aldine, $19.95. Thirty-seven contributors reflect different political perspectives as they assess Soviet policy.

9 – 124 *Peaceful Coexistence, International Law in the Building of Communism*, Bernard Ramundo, 262pp, 1967, Johns Hopkins, $17.00. A detailed study of how Soviet jurists view international and world law as instruments in the triumph of Soviet communism. Offers little hope that this view has changed or will change.

9 – 125 *Diplomacy of Power: Soviet Armed Forces as a Political Instrument*, Stephen Kaplan, 800pp, 1980, Brookings, $14.95. A detailed analysis of 190 incidents since World War II in which the Soviet Union used or threatened to use military force to influence diplomatic outcomes.

9 – 126 *The Armed Forces of the USSR*, Harriet Scott & William Scott, 439pp, 1979, Westview, $12.50. Describes the origin, strategies, chain of command, political influence, and training of the Soviet army.

9 – 127 *The Political Implications of Soviet Military Power*, Lawrence Whetten (ed.), 183pp, 1977, Crane & Russak, $16.95. Surveys fifteen meanings of ''detente'' (from intense competition short of war to convergence) and finds that ''more than ever before, influence-competition is based on military balances, either on global or regional levels'' and that ''States will continue to seek political influence achieved in the past by exploiting a rival's vulnerability on the entire spectrum of contentious issues'' (p. 17).

9 – 128 *Soviet Strategy for Nuclear War*, Joseph Douglass, Jr., and Amorette Hoeber, 160pp, 1979, Hoover $5.95. Maintains the Soviet Union's strategic doctrine accepts the possibility of fighting and winning a nuclear war, and suggests the Soviet build-up of the 1970s has that end in mind.

9 – 129 *Soviet Naval Policy, Objectives and Constraints*, Michael McGwire, Ken Booth & John McDonnell (eds.), 350pp, 1975, Praeger, $39.95. Presents a detailed analysis of Soviet naval doctrine and of changes in Soviet ship acquisition. The relationship of expanding political influence through naval deployments is the focus.

9 – 130 *The Soviet Navy, 1941 – 78, A Guide to Sources in English*, Myron Smith, Jr., 210pp, 1980, ABC-Clio, $23.75. Provides 1,741 citations of works written during the period, with an introduction assessing the change from a coastal navy to a ''blue-water'' navy.

9 – 131 *Analyzing Soviet Strategic Arms Decisions*, Karl Spielmann, 184pp, 1978, Westview, $19.00. Advocates a ''multiple approach analysis'' including strategic doctrine, vested interests, nationalist leaders, and policy objectives to infer Soviet motives for armament policies.

9 – 132 *The Soviet Union and SALT*, Samuel Payne, Jr., 224pp, 1980, MIT, $22.50. Depicts two contending groups within the Soviet leadership disagreeing about whether arms control or arms increases best advance Soviet interests.

9 – 133 *The Soviet Invasion of Czechoslovakia: Its Effects on Eastern Europe*, E.J. Czerwinski and Jaroslaw Pielkalkiewicz (eds.), 210pp, 1972, Praeger, $14.00. Eleven assessments of the impact of the 1968 invasion on other Eastern European States.

9 – 134 *Peaceful Coexistence: International Law in the Building of Communism*, Bernard Ramundo, 260pp, 1967, Johns Hopkins, $17.00. Introduces the Soviet conception of international law.

9 – 135 *Soviet Diplomacy and Negotiating Behavior: Emerging New Context for U.S. Diplomacy*, Congressional Research Service for the House Committee on Foreign Affairs, 573pp, 1979, GPO. A comprehensive survey of negotiating experience, and the conclusions American diplomats have drawn, with suggestions for negotiations in the 1980s.

9 – 136 *Soviet Bargaining Behavior, The Nuclear Test Ban Case,* Christer Jonsson, 266pp, 1979, Columbia, $13.50. A careful review of negotiations concludes there was "continuous bargaining of the test ban issue within the Soviet Union," and that "negotiating behavior at Geneva seems to be correlated with changes in the success and influence of the different groupings" which bargain internally.

9 – 137 *Strategy & Tactics of Soviet Foreign Policy*, J. Mackintosh, 353pp, 1962, Oxford, $8.75. A history of Soviet policy from 1944 to 1960 which illustrates the twin goal of strengthening the Soviet Union and aiding to power groups sharing its ideology.

9 – 138 *Russia's Road to the Cold War, Diplomacy, Strategy, and the Politics of Communism, 1941 – 1945*, Vottech Mastny, 384pp, 1980, Columbia, $9.00. A carefully researched assessment of Stalin's post-World War II expansionist designs.

9 – 139 *Uncertain Detente*, Frans Alting von Geusau, 310pp, 1979, Alphen aan den Rijn, Sijhoff & Noordhoff, $47.50. Contributors from East and West discuss detente; the editor's essay on the Belgrade follow-up to the Helsinki accords foresees the end of detente.

9 – 140 *Yearbook on International Communist Affairs: 1980*, Richard Staar (ed.), 520pp, 1980, Hoover Institute, $35.00. The annual survey of Communist movements which are in power in sixteen countries, and contending for power or operating in eighty-two more. Information is given on members, percent of votes or seats in legislature, position on Sino-Soviet dispute, and current activities.

9 – 141 *World Communism, A Handbook, 1918 – 1965*, Witold Sworakowski (ed.), 592pp, 1973, Hoover Institute, $25.00. Supplements the Institution's yearbook by providing similar country-by-country information on Communist Party activity and policies.

I. Dissidents

9 – 142 *Detente and the Democratic Movement in the USSR*, Frederick Barghoorn, 229pp, 1976, Macmillan, $12.95. After a survey of democratic dissident criticism of Soviet foreign policy, the author concludes that the West can help through hard bargaining over the conditions of even cultural exchange programs.

9 – 143 *Manipulated Science: The Crisis of Science and Scientists in the Soviet Union Today*, Mark Popovsky, 242pp, 1979, Doubleday, $10.95. A former Soviet scientist, now living in the United States, depicts the subordination of the pursuit of knowledge to official orthodoxy and with the consequences for science and for the Soviet Union.

9 – 144 *Progress, Coexistence & Intellectual Freedom*, Andrei Sakharov, 158pp, 1968, Norton, $3.95. The original plea for coexistence, convergence, and ultimate world government by the "Father" of the Russian H-Bomb, now a dissident.

9 – 145 *History's Carnival: A Dissident's Autobiography*, Leonid Plyushch, 430pp, 1979, Harcourt, Brace, Jovanovich, $14.95. A Ukrainian scientist turned dissident and in exile, describes his intellectual and personal odyssey.

9 – 146 *The Gulag Archipelago*, Aleksandr Solzhenitsyn, 3 Volumes, 1979, Harper, $7.50. A relentless portrayal of the failure of a judicial system to restrain political power, of how, in fact, the law is an instrument of State power and of the sources of the system under Lenin, not Stalin.

9 – 147 *Kronstadt*, 1921, Paul Avrich, 288pp, 1974, Norton, $4.95. Uses the revolt to describe the Bolsheviks' attitude toward Socialist opposition.

9 – 148 *The Unknown Civil War in Soviet Russia: A Study of the Green Movement in the Tambov Region 1920 – 1921*, Oliver Radkey, 1976, Hoover Institution $12.95.

9 – 149 *Sakharov Speaks*, Harrison Salisbury (ed.), 245pp, 1974, Vintage, $1.65. A selection of writings on the need for de-Stalinization of Russia, for the establishment of intellectual freedom, and for peaceful competition between socialism and capitalism.

9 – 150 *Soviet Psychoprisons*, Harvey Fireside, 201pp, 1979, Norton, $12.95. Details the use of psychiatry in the Soviet Union to punish and isolate those who disagree with Soviet policies.

9 – 151 *The Mortal Danger: Misconceptions about Soviet Russia and the Threat to America*, Aleksandr Solzhenitsyn, 71pp, 1980, Harper, $8.95. Reprinted from *Foreign Affairs*, Spring 1980, this article argues that the Soviet leaders are as alien to Russia as they are to Afghanistan. Until the West understands that political control does not indicate public support, the danger posed by Soviet control of Russia will remain.

9 – 152 *A World Split Apart*, Aleksandr Solzhenitsyn, 298pp, 1979, Harper, $2.95. The complete Russian and English text of the Harvard commencement address, June 8, 1978.

9 – 153 *The Challenge of the Spirit*, Boris Shragin, 262pp, 1978, Knopf, $10.00.

Describes the crushing weight of totalitarian societies (in this case, the Soviet Union) on human beings: "good . . . does not die but lives, even in a single free idea that is independent of human authority."

9— 154 *Kolyma: The Arctic Death Camps*, Robert Conquest, 254pp, 1979, Oxford, $4.95. Details life and death in the arctic region camps, based on seventeen eyewitness accounts. Estimates three million people were killed there between 1932 and 1954.

9— 155 *The Great Terror: Stalin's Purge of the Thirties*, Robert Conquest, 733pp, 1968, Macmillan, $4.95. A well-documented account of the purges of the thirties which emphasizes the immense scale (over ten million perished), the methods, and the secrecy.

9— 156 *A Question of Madness: Repression by Psychiatry in the Soviet Union*, Zhores & Roy Medvedev, 223pp, 1979, Norton, $3.95. A description of the abuse of psychiatry to imprison political opponents, and of the response of Soviet intellectuals and others.

9— 157 *The Soviet Cage: Anti-Semitism in Russia*, William Korey, 384pp, 1973, Viking, $12.50. Discusses and documents Russian anti-Semitism. Takes its title from Andrei Sakharov's statement: "A free country cannot resemble a cage."

9— 158 *To Defend These Rights, Humans Rights, and the Soviet Union*, Valery Chalidze, 340pp, 1975, Random House, $10.00. A description of the human rights movement within the Soviet Union, the legal and political barriers, and how Western support can help.

9— 159 *The Grigorenko Papers, Writings by General P.G. Grigorenko and Documents on His Case*, Peter Grigorenko, Introduced by Edward Crankshaw, 187pp, 1976, Westview, $16.00. The chilling account of an important World War II Soviet General who was arrested for indicating publicly his belief that Stalin was responsible for the ill-prepared State of the Soviet army in 1941. He was forced to undergo psychiatric imprisonment, and has been a rallying point for the human rights movement.

9— 160 *On Socialist Democracy*, Roy Medvedev, 405pp, 1977, Norton, $5.95. The case for the Soviet Union's evolution from totalitarian to democratic socialism.

9— 161 *Dissent in the USSR, Politics, Ideology, and People*, Rudolf Tokes, 453pp, 1975, Johns Hopkins, $4.95. A thorough description.

9— 162 *Psychiatric Terror, How Soviet Psychiatry Is Used To Suppress Dissent*, Sidney Bloch, Peter Reddiway, 510pp, 1977, Basic Books, $12.95. A detailed history, analysis, and condemnation of the sentencing of dissenters to mental institutions in the Soviet Union. The effect of opposition from external psychiatric associations is also considered.

9— 163 *Alarm and Hope*, Andrei Sakharov, 200pp, 1978, Vintage, $2.95. Recipient of the Nobel Peace Prize for his defense of human rights; these selections include his acceptance lecture, his analysis of "totalitarian-socialist" regimes, the costs of social services and his belief in arms control and disarmament.

J. Eastern Europe

9 – 164 *Communist Systems in Comparative Perspective*, Leonard Cohen and Jane Shapiro (eds.), 520pp, 1974, Doubleday, O.P. Compares the emergence of Communist governments in Russia, China and East Europe; the role of the Party once in power; and the resulting politics in each case. For example, Jerry Hough distinguishes three views of the Soviet leadership: 1) a sect in control of a State and directing its activities; 2) a conservative, oligarchic elite managing affairs in their own interest and 3) a pluralistic model exercising influence, with public interest groups as well as factions within the leadership.

9 – 165 *Communist Reformation: Internationalism, and Change In The World Communist Movement*, G.R. Urban (ed.), 335pp, 1979, St. Martin's, $19.95. Interviews with Czechoslovakian, British, and American diplomats and scholars, focused on the degree to which a Communist State can liberalize without antagonizing the Soviet Union.

9 – 166 *Since the Prague Spring, Charter 77 and the Struggle for Human Rights in Czechoslovakia*, Hans-Peter Riese (ed.), 208pp, 1979, Random House, $4.95. Details the continuing struggle and repression of the human rights movement in Czechoslovakia.

9 – 167 *Communism in Eastern Europe*, Teresa Rakowska-Harmstone and Andrew Gyorgy (eds.), 338pp, 1979, Indiana U. Press, $7.95. Emphasizes the diversity of the regions.

9 – 168 *Soviet Intervention in Czechoslovakia, 1968: Anatomy of a Decision*, Jiri Valenta, 208pp, 1979, Johns Hopkins, $12.95. A case study of Soviet decision-making.

9 – 169 *Opposition in Eastern Europe*, Rudolf Tokes (ed.), 306pp, 1979, Johns Hopkins, $22.50. An anthology depicting the many and various forms of opposition in Eastern Europe, some based on opposition to Soviet domination, some on changing economic and social relationships.

9 – 170 *The Kremlin's Dilemma: The Struggle for Human Rights in Eastern Europe*, Tufton Beamish and Guy Hadley, 280pp, 1979, Presidio, $12.95. Surveys the violations of human rights in Eastern Europe and argues that the Helsinki accords provide an excellent occasion to challenge the Soviet Union.

9 – 171 *Yugoslavia: Self-Management Socialism and the Challenges of Development*, Martin Schrink, Cyrus Ardalan and Nawal El Tatowy, 392pp, 1979, Johns Hopkins, $9.50. A World Bank report on Yugoslavian economic development.

9 – 172 *Communism in Eastern Europe*, Teresa Rakowska-Harmstone & Andrew Gyorgy, 384pp, 1980, Indiana, $7.95. Overview of each country with an emphasis on events in the mid- and late-1970s.

9 – 173 *Perspectives for Change in Communist Societies*, Teresa Rakowska-Harmstone (ed.), 194pp, 1979, Westview, $21.50. Distinguishes between societies whose political

culture is congruous with the Communist system (USSR, German Democratic Republic, and Bulgaria) and those whose culture is not (Poland, Czechoslovakia, and Hungary), and predicts the greatest change in the latter.

9– 174 *The Alternative in Eastern Europe*, Rudolf Bahro, 460pp, 1979, Schocken, $19.50. A critique of East European and Soviet governments from within the Marxist categories which, nonetheless, got the author imprisoned.

9– 175 *The Intellectuals on the Road to Class Power*, George Konrad & Ivan Szelenyi, 252pp, 1979, Harcourt, Brace & Jovanovich, $10.00. Maintains that in Eastern Europe and the Soviet Union the intellectuals have coalesced into the dominant class, imposing their will on the weaker societies of "the East"; in the West, social institutions resist the State.

9– 176 *East European Integration and East-West Trade*, Paul Marer & John Montias (eds.), 432pp, 1980, Indiana, $32.50. Articles assessing political integration among centrally planned economies.

K. The Soviet Union and the Third World

9– 177 *Revolutionary Cuba in the World Arena*, Martin Weinstein (ed.), 166pp, 1979, Institute for the Study of Human Issues, $13.50. A study of the projection of Cuban political and economic values in world politics through Soviet assistance.

9– 178 *Model or Ally? The Communist Powers and the Developing Countries*, Richard Lowenthal, 400pp, 1976, Oxford, $16.95. Assesses the appeal of Marxist ideology and the Soviet, Chinese, and Cuban models in developing countries; and, once a client is in power, the success of Soviet imperialism through the rejection of ideology.

9– 179 *Soviet-Third World Relations*, Charles McLane, Volume 1, 126pp, 1973, Columbia, $17.50; Volume 2, *Soviet-Asian Relations*, 150pp, 1974, Columbia, $17.50; Volume 3, *Soviet-African Relations*, 130pp, 1975, Columbia, $17.50. A survey providing columns of data with a brief introduction.

9– 180 *Soviet and Chinese Aid to African Nations*, Warren Weinstein & Thomas Henriksen (eds.), 184 pp, 1980, Praeger, $27.95. Describes the amount of aid and assesses its long-range impact.

9– 181 *The Soviet Union and the Developing Nations*, Roger Kanet (ed.), 314pp, 1974, Johns Hopkins, $3.95. Essays by specialists on Soviet policy since 1977 in five regions and in the UN.

9– 182 *Soviet and Chinese Influence in the Third World*, Alvin Rubinstein (ed.), 231pp, 1976, Praeger, $9.95. Assesses what constitutes "influence," and how the two Communist states now view it for developing countries.

9– 183 *The USSR and the Cuban Revolution: Soviet Ideological and Strategic Perspec-*

tives, 1959-1977, Jacques Levesque, 215pp, 1978, Praeger, $19.95. Discusses the shifting end of the relationship, and suggests that Castro is seeking foreign circuses to bolster sagging popular support and to hide domestic scarcity.

9–184 *The Economic Transformation of Cuba*, Edward Boorstein, 303pp, 1969, Monthly Review, $5.95. An American economist, who assisted in the socialization of Cuban industry from 1960-1963, comments favorably on the results.

L. Research Aids

9–185 *The Soviet Air and Strategic Rocket Forces, 1939-1980: A Guide to Sources in English*, Myron Smith, Jr., 321pp, 1981, ABC-Clio, $45.00. A list of 3,350 books and articles, divided into seven categories, including "Reference Works," and "Soviet Aerospace Arms and Assistance around the Globe."

9–186 *Current Research in Comparative Communism, An Analysis and Bibliographic Guide to the Soviet System*, Lawrence Whetten, 159pp, 1978, Praeger, $17.50. A forty-six page introduction identifies the major categories for analysis: Soviet internal development, political change, the role of law, the role of the Party, economic reforms, and minorities. The bibliography includes English works published between 1965 and 1975.

CHAPTER 10

REGIONAL POWERS AND ORGANIZATIONS

THE number of "worlds" within the international system has increased steadily since World War II. Immediately after the war, the hope of "One World," undivided by nationalist and ideological antagonisms, dissolved. The Cold War reflected a bipolar division of power between the East and the West. War, if it were to occur, would happen between these two "worlds." The emergence of a "third world" of countries with less developed economies and not aligned to either the Eastern or Western bloc, was given rhetorical currency at the Bandung conference (1955), and at succeeding meetings of those States. In 1971 the third-world countries formed a "Group of 77" (grown now to over 120) countries which often vote as a bloc in the UN General Assembly, particularly on economic issues (see Chapter 12). Within the third world, however, there are many divisions, one now being called the fourth world — the poorest of the poor countries, usually defined as those countries with a GNP below $200 per capita per year. For the purposes of this chapter, this further division will not be used.

Differences and divisions are now so significant that policy-making is fragmented within each world. Even decisions to go to war are made in separate centers of power. In fact, most of the recent wars have occurred within these worlds, not between them. Zacher *(International Conflict and Collective Security, 1946 – 77,* 10-14) lists 116 post-World War II wars, over 100 of them originating within regions of the third world. On the basis of such evidence, one important school of thought looks to the regions of the world as the main actors in world politics: it is within the regions that the decisions for war and for peace are most frequently made.

THE SUPERPOWER CONNECTION

While most wars occur within the third world, it can be argued that many of them are influenced by one or both of the superpowers. The ability of many States to wage war — Syria, Israel, South Yemen, North Yemen, Somalia, and once North and South Vietnam — is dependent upon military or financial assistance by one of the superpowers. If one power intervenes or provides massive assistance in a civil war, and the other does not similarly respond, that may tip the balance between the domestic factions contending for power. Economic, political, and military decisions made in Washington and Moscow can influence every country, and its overt or covert support can make all the difference.

But the bipolar division of power has now clearly ended and many other States, coalitions of States, and regional organizations are playing increasingly significant roles. Japan, for example, has the world's third largest economy and may well have the largest output (per capita) by the year 2000 *(Japan as Number One,* 10-148). Japan's economic influence is clear. Its decision today to remain a defensive military power is unique, but subject to change. A decision by Japan to ''go nuclear'' or to build up its military force could bring a crucial change in world politics (Scalapino, *The Foreign Policy of Modern Japan,* 10-151).

China's role in the post-Mao era is another uncertainty. It has emerged as the leading advocate of a coalition of States to block Soviet expansionism; it is already seeking to influence Asian and African countries and is aiding factions to struggle against Soviet-backed forces in Africa. China has invested in Malta to limit Soviet influence there, provided aid to Afghanistan forces fighting Soviet troops, invaded Vietnam to punish that country for the Soviet-backed invasion of Cambodia, and periodically clashed with Soviet troops along their 3,000-mile common border. In addition, China is a strident voice in international forums, denouncing the Soviet Union and rallying third-world support. The Sino – Soviet dispute, within what was once the second world, is now one of the more intense hostilities in world politics. Within the Communist world, China challenges the Soviet claim to the right to intervene in other socialist countries in the interest of the Socialist world as a whole. The geopolitical resources China brings to these tasks are meager by comparison to those of the Soviet Union, but if its modernization drive succeeds and the new energy discoveries pan out, China could well be a superpower in the not too distant future.

WESTERN EUROPE

Western Europe, because of its economic might and its intellectual and cultural traditions, has re-emerged as an independent actor — and sometimes as several independent actors. The attempt by the European Economic Community (EEC) to speak as one voice in world forums through the European Council (1974) has met with only modest success. While the EEC is a considerable power in the international economic order, national decision-making concerning foreign policy remains the dominant reality. France has long pursued an independent course in its development of a nuclear capability and in its political dealings with Communist States and others. West Germany, despite objections from the U.S., opened new relationships with Eastern Europe and the Soviet Union. The United Kingdom's special role within the British Commonwealth of Nations gives it a focus outside the EEC, and its tradition of engagement in world affairs makes it a significant and independent actor.

ORGANIZATION OF PETROLEUM EXPORTING COUNTRIES

Policy initiative in the pricing of oil does not now reside in either the East or the West. The Organization of Petroleum Exporting Countries (OPEC) was formed in 1960, and by the start of the 1980s had the power to redistribute much of the wealth on the planet. Its decision to raise crude oil prices from about $2.50 per barrel in early 1973 to over $30 per barrel in 1980 affected the economic development plans of every other country.

The political leverage that results from control over so much of a needed raw material was suggested during the Middle East war in 1973. How much such leverage can accomplish is unclear. Many third-world leaders first celebrated the oil price increase, seeing in it a transfer of wealth from the first world to the third. Later, however, the industrial countries recovered part of their losses as prices of food and industrial products rose, with devastating effects on third-world economies.

While there are non-Arab State members of OPEC (Venezuela, Indonesia, and Nigeria) the principal effect of its action has been to increase greatly the wealth available to the Middle East at the expense of other regions of the world. Western economies have been badly hurt; developing States have been devastated.

EASTERN EUROPE

The Soviet Union retains overwhelming influence within Eastern Europe, though Yugoslavia has long been considered an independent maverick. Eastern Germany's industrial growth and national traditions have provided it with a slight degree of independence (*Perspectives for Change in Communist Societies,* 9-173). The Pope's visit to Poland in 1979 and the general strike in 1980, and the emergence of an independent political force in Solidarity, suggest that religious and Polish national movements, not imposed political ones, reflect the aspirations of the Polish people. Romania has on occasion initiated policies not approved by Moscow and other East European States have tried, with varying degrees of success, to establish new relationships with the rest of the world. But the reality in Eastern Europe remains Soviet domination.

REGIONAL POWERS

There are other major new centers of power and policy initiative within each region of the world. In South Asia both India and Pakistan could soon be nuclear weapons states. In the Middle East, Israel, Saudi Arabia, Iraq, Egypt, Libya, and Kuwait all bring significant resources to bear on their objectives. In sub-Saharan Africa, Nigeria, Ethiopia, Angola, and Tanzania now offer new leadership in resolving regional problems. Once the United States was the only hemispheric power; today Brazil, Venezuela, Mexico, Chile, and Argentina initiate policies which are strongly opposed from time to time in Washington. Vietnam, Indonesia, Taiwan, and South Korea exercise influence within Southeast Asia; and Taiwan and South Korea, through their own transnational enterprises, contribute to development efforts in Africa and Latin America as well.

These regional powers suggest another dimension of the divided world. Significant new economic, political, and moral resources are now available to States reflecting all the cultural diversity of the world. There are then, not just three or four ''worlds'' but nine to eleven, depending upon one's definition of culture *(Regional Geography of the World,* 10-2). This reality has often been ignored; but the cultural divisions of the world "are important to an understanding of the problems of public policy." *(One World Divided,* 10-3, p. 4). Understanding regional powers within different cultural settings is thus one new and significant feature of world politics that can influence the chances for a warless world. Understanding the culturally-based sources of misperception, the impact of cultural traditions on forms of government, conceptions of human rights, family, work and social change efforts, as well as the potential for war and for conflict resolution within regions, is an important task for those entering the world affairs arena.

CULTURES

While cultural anthropologists differ, the list of cultures, identified largely by geographical regions, usually includes the following: 1) European, 2) Russian, 3) Anglo-American, 4) Latin American, 5) North African – Southwest Asian, 6) South Asian, 7) Southeast Asian, 8) East Asian, 9) African, 10) Australia – New Zealand, 11) Pacific.

The first three cultures have already been touched on. A full survey of each area is out of place here, but the uniformity and diversity of cultural traditions will be introduced and a few specific policy implications indicated for two regions, Africa and Latin America. All the regional powers are represented in the bibliography, and research centers specializing in regions and providing bibliographies are listed on pages 619 to 628.

According to Cara Richards, *(People in Perspective,* 10-4) each region of the world has evolved many different cultural patterns, each accomplishing a number of common tasks or functions. Each culture has: 1) a system of internal and external order; 2) a method of producing and distributing food, goods, and services; 3) a system of education; 4) a family structure, essential for reproduction; and 5) religious institutions that interpret the purpose or meaning of life. The ways in which these tasks are accomplished differ widely, particularly when the Western European influences on Russian, American, and Australian-New Zealand cultures are contrasted with non-Western cultures. Although contemporary technological, communications, travel, commercial, and social practices penetrate cultural barriers, cultural traditions and differences persist. Yet elements of commonality can be drawn upon as the cultures of the world interact and change in response to each other.

LATIN AMERICA

The twenty-five States of Latin America share cultural traditions derived from a blending of Spanish or Portuguese influences with Indian (particularly Aztec and Inca) and West African cultures. One analysis, reflecting the European component of this blend, maintains that the cultures of Latin American States assure authoritarian governments, an aristocratic life style for a few, and slow rates of economic growth *(The Centralist Tradition of Latin America, 10-27).* Proponents of this theory cite the inequalities of wealth which originated in the colonial era, are retained today, and are expressed through large landholdings. The military, the church, and the large landowners form a power elite which is arrayed against the poor majority. Such arguments, however, have been called into question by Portugal's and Spain's movement from authoritarian to democratic government; by Costa Rica's democratic institutions; and by Venezuela's and Colombia's multiparty political systems. *(Venezuela: The Democratic Experience, 10-51).* Although it has an authoritarian regime, Brazil has industrialized rapidly in the last fifteen years, and Mexico's one-party democracy governs an expanding economy. Thus, the diversity of the political and economic systems in Latin America indicates that cultural traditions have not imposed any insuperable barriers to the emergence of democratic political organization.

Despite the fact that most Latin American States gained their independence in the early 19th century, they have today joined the newly independent States of Asia and Africa in international forums. *(Latin America: The Search for a New International Role, 10-38).* The former President of Mexico, Luis Echeverria, was a primary drafter of the New International Economic Order proposals (see Chapter 12), and Venezuela initiated the formation of OPEC *(Contemporary Venezuela and Its Role in International Affairs, 10-50).* Brazil has recently forged new links with Japan and some African States, primarily Angola *(Brazil's Multilateral Relations, 10-47).* In the closing decades of the 20th century, the Latin American States share a common desire to reduce their dependence on the United States, to assert themselves in world politics and to achieve economic growth.

Although the Organization of American States (OAS) is now a more important and credible multilateral forum than it was when the United States could count on it for automatic approval of its proposals, there is a critical need for more effective multilateral regional organizations. Founded in 1948, the OAS was designed to accomplish four purposes: to contain Communism, to promote non-intervention, to promote economic development and to promote human rights. Zacher *(International Conflict and Collective Security, 10-14)* maintains that conflict resolution is essential to non-intervention. There have been, by his count, "19 wars, crises, and military interventions involving OAS members since 1948." They fall into three categories: conflicts among non-Communist members, conflicts between non-Communist and Communist States in which the Communist State was the victim, and conflicts between Communist and non-Communist States in which the non-Communist State was the victim.

The record of the OAS for dealing with these conflicts varies: it did not come to the aid of Guatemala (1954) or Cuba (1961), but it did condemn Cuban military intervention in Venezuela in 1963 and 1967. In the fourteen cases of conflict between non-Communist States, the OAS authorized multilateral intercession and was successful in limiting the conflict. The record of the OAS in the promotion of human rights is promising, yet somewhat inconsistent (LeBlanc, *The OAS and the Promotion and Protection of Human Rights,* 6-128).

AFRICA

The sub-Saharan region of Africa is divided politically into forty-one States, and is geographically, ideologically, and ethnically differentiated into many additional subdivisions *(Africa,* 10-74). In a recent survey *(Africa in the 1980s,* 10-81) the particular features which shape conflict in this region were identified as: 1) The tribal or ethnic-group basis of society; 2) The boundaries of the existing States imposed by European powers; 3) The common experience of elites in the decolonization process.

This suggests the impinging of cultures. European concepts such as States, nationality, and bureaucracy have been superimposed on ethnic or tribal groups, many of whose members live in different States. These features of contemporary African politics point to a common agenda for the new leadership:

1. *National integration* — the creation of viable institutions and new value systems that can win the loyalty and cooperation of individuals and groups

2. *Economic development* — in some cases against formidable natural obstacles (Mali, Chad) and in others with important natural resources (Nigeria, Angola)

3. *Defense of the new State* — both from internal disintegration and from external intervention

Intertwined with these features and the common agenda are issues, such as ocean politics (The Law of the Sea Conference), white minority rule in Southern Africa *(South Africa's Options,* 14-61). Sino – Soviet rivalry for influence in Africa, Afro-Arab politics and the North – South Agenda (Okolie, *International Law Perspectives of Developing Countries,* 6-124).

But the common tasks the leaders in African States now face should not obscure the rich diversity of the continent. Nigeria, the most populous State, has re-established civilian authority under a constitution similar to that of the United States; it has new oil revenues and is open to external investment; and it has achieved peace after a devastating civil war. This contrasts strikingly with the continued tribal conflict in Burundi, the national socialist experiment in Tanzania (*Toward Socialism in Tanzania*, 10-87) and the influence of the Soviet Union in Angola and Ethiopia (*Ethiopia: Empire in Revolution*, 10-95, *Communism in Africa*, 10-86).

THE ORGANIZATION OF AFRICAN UNITY

The Organization of African Unity (OAU), as the name implies, was originally intended to be a vehicle for the federation of sub-Saharan African States. During the formation of the OAU, Nkrumah of Ghana pushed for federation but failed to gain acceptance. The OAU has accepted the boundaries drawn in the colonial era, and resists secessionist movements. At an annual meeting of the heads of State or their delegates, the OAU can, by a two-thirds majority vote, endorse a policy but cannot impose it. Membership in the OAU does not oblige a State to accept the will of the majority. The OAU has recommended action when conflicts arose over attempts to alter boundaries or to secede, but not in other kinds of conflicts. In summarizing the first fourteen years of its existence, Zacher states:

> . . . it is obvious that its effectiveness peaked during the first three years. Since 1965 it has not intervened (that is, passed a resolution calling for a cessation of a military action) in a single conflict. . . . For the most part it was conflicts between radical, nonaligned, and moderate pro-Western states that dominated this era, but those between Moslem and non-Moslem states also caused serious cleavages among Africans in several cases. There is also little prospect of such cleavages dissipating so as to support an expanded role for the OAU as an African collective security agency in coming years.[1]

The conclusion suggests a bleak prospect for the non-military resolution of conflict in a continent torn by sectional and religious strife. There exists now only a weak international organization to aid in the resolution of conflict. Leadership by a regional power could, however, alter that situation.

[1] International Conflicts and Collective Security, (10-14), p. 155.

CONCLUSION

Regional differences pose challenges to those seeking an end to war. In some cases, conflicts within regions can be resolved only by regional organizations. In other cases, the UN or other peacekeeping, mediation, and conflict-resolution institutions may be required. A regional organization benefits from cultural similarities among its members; it is continuously involved in the politics of the region; and it may be better situated than the United Nations to gain the consent of the parties to the conflict (Falk and Mendlovitz, *Regions and World Order,* 5-32). World organizations, however, may appear more nearly neutral; be better equipped to sustain the effort when those in proximity to the conflict have lost the will; and may have more resources available or more coercive sanctions to aid in achieving the necessary objective.

It is open to dispute whether regional organizations are the forerunners of integrated political communities or whether they are destined to remain the instruments of government. But as Haas, Butterworth, and Nye have said: "These organizations are little more than governments linked in permanent conclave. They have no power and personality beyond the collective will of governments and no capacity to grow apart from the ability of governments to learn" (*Conflict Management by International Organizations,* p. 215). Nonetheless, regional organizations and programs have proliferated in recent years and can provide a needed resource in the management of conflict, the promotion of change, the acceptance of human rights standards, and the accomplishment of other common purposes.

BIBLIOGRAPHY

The bibliography in this section provides an overview of the cultural map of the world, and then divides the world accordingly. A section of the bibliography is devoted to regional organizations, another to coalitions, and a third to conflict resolution. Books are presented on the regions and the major powers within them. These books will be helpful in answering questions such as these: 1) What is the underlying influence that shapes cultures: the environment? stage of evolution? religion? or something else? 2) What are the basic functions that every culture must perform to survive? What are the ways these functions have been accomplished? 3) Is cultural homogeneity a likely result of the industrial and technological revolutions? Or, do those revolutions just provide more resources to build walls between cultures? 4) What problems do cultural differences pose for the enforcement of human rights? for resolving conflict?

for creating a sense of world community? 5) What are the primary policy concerns in each region? 6) Which State is the most powerful in each region? the most likely to aid in the non-military resolution of international conflict? 7) What are the records of the OAS and of the OAU in resolving conflicts? How are they similar and dissimilar from the EEC? the Arab League? 8) How are regional organizations best related to global international organizations? 9) What are the strengths and weaknesses of regional and global international organizations for resolving conflicts within a region? 10) Would the formation of strong regional organizations provide building blocks for the growth of strong global conflict-resolution organizations, or would they become the new powers destined to struggle militarily for hegemony?

A. Overviews

10 – 1 *Geography and Development, A World Regional Approach,* Don Hoy, 728pp, 1978, Macmillan, $18.95. Outlines the environmental and human features which distinguish the regions of the world.

10 – 2 *Regional Geography of the World,* Jesse Wheeler, Jr., Trenton Kostbade & Richard Thoman, 798pp, 1975, rev. ed., Holt, Rinehart & Winston, $18.95. Provides an introductory overview of the different cultures of the world and their geographical settings.

10 – 3 *One World Divided: A Geographer Looks at the Modern World,* Preston James and Kempton Webb, 1980, Wiley, $6.95. Emphasizes the uniformities underlying the differences.

Intro
10 – 4 *People in Perspective: An Introduction to Cultural Anthropology,* Cara Richards, 413pp, 1976 (2nd ed.), Random House, $8.95. Introduces the basic tasks every society must perform to survive (produce and distribute food, goods and services; maintain internal and external order; reproduce; educate; find meaning through religious experience); and the diverse ways in which these tasks have been accomplished.

10 – 5 *Atlas of World Cultures,* George Murdock, 152pp, 1981, Pittsburgh, $9.95. Offers a selection of 563 societies for cross-cultural research.

B. Regions and Regional Organizations

10 – 6 *Comparative Regional Systems: East Europe, North America, the Middle East and Developing Countries,* Werner Feld, 426pp, 1980, Pergamon, $12.95. Suggests the importance of culturally conditioned values in sustaining international activity.

10 – 7 *Conflict and Intervention in the Third World,* Mohammed Ayoob (ed.), 272pp, 1980, St. Martin's $27.50. Nine case studies explore the persisting conflicts in selected regions of the third world, and the intermittent character of superpower intervention.

10 – 8 *Regional Integration; Theory and Research,* Leon Lindberg & Stuart Scheingeld (eds.), 427pp, 1971, Harvard, $4.95. A study of non-coercive attempts to create political community in regions.

10 – 9 *The OAU and the UN, Relations Between the Organization of African Unity and the United Nations,* Berhanykun Andemicael, 331pp, 1976, Holmes & Meier, $27.50. A legalistic interpretation of the interaction between the two intergovernmental organizations.

10 – 10 *Organization of African Unity, After Ten Years: Comparative Perspectives,* Yassin El-Ayouty, 262pp, 1975, Praeger, $22.95. A study of the first ten years of the OAU, the understandings underlying its existence (the acceptance of the existing boundaries, non-intervention, unanimous decision-making, and a focus on development).

10 – 11 *The League of Arab States and Regional Disputes,* Hussein Hassouna, 512pp, 1975, Oceana, $30.00. Describes the origins of the League's system for settling regional disputes, and evaluates its effectiveness in ten conflicts.

10 – 12 *The Future of the Inter-American System,* Tom Farer (ed.), 315pp, 1979, Praeger, $20.95. Proposes major revisions of the OAS, given the increased importance of Latin American States, when compared to the United States.

10 – 13 *Organization of American States: A Handbook,* 1977, OAS, $1.00. A factual introduction to the tasks, accomplishments, and purposes of the OAS.

TEW
10 – 14 *International Conflicts and Collective Security, 1946 – 77, The United Nations, Organization of American States, Organization of African Unity, and Arab League,* Mark Zacher, 297pp, 1979, Praeger, $21.95. Provides a summary of 116 post-World War II wars, and offers hypotheses concerning what makes for success in UN or regional international organization conflict-resolution efforts.

See also Chapter 5, especially "Regional Organizations."

C. Alliances

10 – 15 *Alliance Politics,* Richard Neustadt, 167pp, 1970, Columbia, $3.50. An important study of what holds alliances together and what drives them apart.

10 – 16 *Unity and Disintegration in International Alliances: Comparative Studies,* Ole Holsti, P. Terrence Hopmann & John Sullivan, 293pp, 1973, Krieger, $19.50. Examines among other things, the way an external threat can build a fragile sense of

community that leads to limited cooperation; disintegration follows when the enemy is defeated, withdraws, or is no longer perceived as a threat.

10– 17 *The Non-Aligned Movement: The Origins of a Third World Alliance,* Peter Willetts, 310pp, 1978, Nichols, $23.50. A statistical and interpretative study of U.N. voting patterns, the "non-aligned" stand on North– South, and East– West issues.

See also Chapter 3, especially on military alliances.

D. North American Regional Powers: Canada

10– 18 *Canada as an International Actor,* Reyton Lyon & Brian Tomlin, 232pp, 1979, New York University Press, $10.95. An assessment of the strengths, weaknesses, and potential of Canada in world politics.

10– 19 *The Shaping of Peace: Canada and the Search for World Order 1943 – 1957,* John Holmes, 368pp, 1979, Toronto, $25.00. A member of the Department of External Affairs describes the Canadian efforts to shape the San Francisco Conference where the UN was created. A second volume is planned to describe the evolution of Canadian policy in NATO, during the Korean War, and in the 1950s.

10– 20 *Canada – United States Relations,* H. Edward English (ed.), 180pp, 1976, Praeger, $18.95. Explores misperceptions of both sides, Canadian concerns, and the problems of both neighbors in an interdependent world.

10– 21 *The Future of North America: Canada, the United States, and Quebec Nationalism,* Elliot Feldman & Neil Nevitte, (eds.), 378pp, 1979, Harvard, $6.95. An exploration of contending perspectives on U.S.-Canadian relations with presentations by Canadians and responses by Americans.

10– 22 *Trudeau and Foreign Policy, A Study in Decision-Making,* Bruce Thordarson, 231pp, 1972, Oxford, $6.50. Upon taking office in 1968, Trudeau conducted an extensive review of Canada's role in economic development assistance, the UN, Europe and military matters. This book examines the process and the conclusions.

10– 23 *Quebec and the Constitution 1960 – 1978,* Edward McWhinney, 170pp, 1979, Toronto, $5.95. Describes the constitutional requests made by Quebec as a condition for remaining part of Canada, and the response.

E. Latin America

10– 24 *Latin America's Emergence, Toward a U.S. Response,* Abraham Lowenthal & Albert Fishlow, 80pp, 1979, Foreign Policy Association, $1.40. A survey of Latin America, common themes in all countries, as well as diversity, is noted with a focus on the new wealth, power, and position in world politics of Latin America. Latin America's wealth in 1980 equals Europe's in 1960.

10 – 25 *The Epic of Latin America,* John Crow, 1,000pp, 1980, California, $9.95. A history including introductory chapters on the Inca, Mayan, and Aztec, Spanish and Portuguese fusion of European and West African culture and concluding chapters on current problems and prospects.

10 – 26 *The United States and the Latin American Sphere of Influence,* Vol. I, *The Era of Caribbean Intervention, 1898 – 1930;* Vol. 2, *The Era of Good Neighbors, Cold Warriors and Hairshirts, 1930 – 1980,* Robert Smith, 1982, Krieger, forthcoming.

10 – 27 *The Centralist Tradition of Latin America,* Claudio Veliz, 355pp, 1980, Princeton, $9.75. Since Latin America did not have the same historical experience as Western Europe, it cannot be expected to adopt European political and social forms. Its own traditions are "bureaucratic centralism, pre-industrial and non-egalitarian in character."

10 – 28 *The Continuing Struggle for Democracy in Latin America,* Howard Wiarda (ed.), 311pp, 1980, Westview, $24.50. Argues for an indigenous form of democracy as preferable to the authoritarian regimes of left or right.

10 – 29 *Political Participation in Latin America,* John Booth & Mitchell Seligson, (eds.), 260pp, 1978, Vol. I, 262pp, 1979, Vol. II, Holmes & Meier, $9.50 each. A multi-disciplinary perspective on how citizen participation is stimulated, controlled, or manipulated.

10 – 30 *Armies and Politics in Latin America,* Abraham Lowenthal (ed.), 356pp, 1976, Holmer & Meier, $9.50. One supposed support for oligarchic rule is the army. It is studied here to determine whether reality fits the theory.

10 – 31 *Land and Power in Latin America,* Benjamin Orlove & Glynn Custard (eds.), 260pp, 1980, Holmer & Meier, $34.50. A study of rural economic and social organization in the Andean countries.

10 – 32 *Inflation and Stabilization in Latin America,* Rosemary Thorp & Lawrence Whitehead, (eds.), 304pp, 1980, Holmes & Meier, $34.50. A study of six countries' attempts to manage inflation and balance of payments problems in today's international economic setting.

10 – 33 *The New Authoritarianism in Latin America,* David Collier (ed.), 424pp, 1980, Princeton, $5.95. Explores why authoritarian models of government appear more effective in achieving development than democracies.

10 – 34 *Revolution of Being, A Latin American View of the Future,* Gustavo Lagos & Horacio Godoy, 226pp, 1977, Macmillan, $14.95. Emphasizes the need for Latin American countries to overcome dependence and domination by other countries (primarily the U.S., but also the USSR in the case of Cuba), as a step toward a world order characterized by strong regional organizations.

10 – 35 *Problems of Economic Growth in Latin America,* Bela Kadar, 267pp, 1979, St. Martin's, $37.50. A Hungarian economist's critique of capitalism in Argentina, Brazil, Mexico, Peru, and Colombia.

10 – 36 *Regional Development in a Global Economy: The Multinational Corporation, Technology and Andean Integration,* Lynn Mytelka, 233pp, 1979, Yale, $17.50. A judicious assessment of the economic integrative process among the Andean countries, and the role of multinational corporations in transferring technology and aiding development.

10 – 37 *The Mature Neighbor Policy: A New United States Economic Policy for Latin America,* Albert Fishlow, 56pp, 1977, Calif., $2.00. A short survey of the U.S. relationship with Latin America, and an outline of a "mature neighbor" policy in which the U.S. accepts as equals the States of Latin America.

10 – 38 *Latin America: The Search for a New International Role,* Ronald Hellman & H. Jon Rosenbaum, 297pp, 1975, Sage, $15.00. Essays on domestic factors, inter- and intra-American relations, and the new role sought by Latin American States in world politics.

10 – 39 *Latin America, the Cold War, and the World Powers, 1945 – 1973,* F. Parkinson, 288pp, 1974, Sage, $8.95. Describes the period of superpower, particularly American, hegemony as coming to an end.

10 – 40 *Latin America in the International Political System,* G. Pope Atkins, 448pp, 1977, Free Press, $15.50. A valuable introduction which presents the role of non-state actors, regional and global institutions, non-hemispheric powers, and the States.

10 – 41 *Latin America, the United States, and the Inter-American System,* John Martz & Lars Schoultz (eds.), 272pp, 1980, Westview, $24.50. Nine essays on U.S. policy, human rights, and other countries' fears of U.S. hegemony.

10 – 42 *Latin American Foreign Policies: An Analysis,* Harold Davis, Larman Wilson, 488pp, 1975, Johns Hopkins, $5.95. Over sixteen authors review country-by-country, the foreign policy goals of Latin American countries, the resources they bring to the achievement of those goals, and their participation in international organizations.

10 – 43 *U.S. – Mexico Economic Relations,* Barry Poulson & T. Noel Osborn (eds.), 442pp, 1979, Westview, $33.50. Thirty essays covering a wide range of economic issues.

10 – 44 *Mexico in Crisis,* Judith Hellman, 229pp, 1979, Holmes & Meier, $7.95. A history of Mexico since 1910 reflecting much of the pessimism about Mexico current in the mid-1970s.

10 – 45 *Brazil, Politics in a Patrimonial Society,* Riordan Roett, 189pp, 1978, rev. ed., Praeger, $8.95. While focused on the military government since 1964, this book provides a broad introduction to Brazilian politics and concludes that little change is likely although as development continues, new groups will come to the fore and Brazil will seek to enlarge its role in world politics.

10 – 46 *Foundations of Brazilian Economic Growth,* Donald Syvrud, 295pp, 1974, Hoover, $12.00. Between 1968 and 1972 the Brazilian economy averaged nearly 10% growth in GNP per year. This book explores the basis of the boom.

10–47 *Brazil's Multilateral Relations Between First and Third Worlds*, Wayne Selcher, 301pp, 1978, Westview, $23.50. Identifies twenty points of disagreement in the third world, as Brazil uses multilateral organizations to advance its bid for recognition as a world power.

10–48 *Brazil: Foreign Policy of a Future World Power*, Ronald Schneider, 236pp, 1978, Westview, $21.00. Brazil's economic growth in the last decade is such that it has become a regional power. This book suggests influences shaping how that power will be used.

10–49 *Politics in Venezuela*, David Blank, 293pp, 1973, Little, Brown, $6.95. Traces the origins of democratic procedures in a non-democratic culture, and maintains democracy will survive as long as no single elite can eliminate the others.

10–50 *Contemporary Venezuela and Its Role in International Affairs*, Robert Bond (ed.), 288pp, 1977, NYU Press, $6.95. Examines Venezuela's role in OPEC, in regional and North-South politics and its rare domestic achievement: "substantial socio-economic progress with widespread political participation and political stability."

10–51 *Venezuela: The Democratic Experience*, John Martz & David Myers (eds.), 406pp, 1977, Praeger, $9.95. A study of the problems and prospects of democracy in Venezuela, which suggests that oil revenue has been important but not crucial; the foreign policy of Venezuela is also discussed.

10–52 *The Challenge of Venezuelan Democracy*, Jose Yepes, 275pp, 1981, Transaction, $19.95. Explores the political bargaining and policy-making institutions of a third-world democracy.

10–53 *Chile: The Legacy of Hispanic Capitalism*, Brian Loveman, 384pp, 1979, Oxford, $5.95. A history of Chile including the overthrow of Allende, which emphasizes the influence of Western capitalism, liberalism, Marxism, and the United States on the Hispanic tradition.

10–54 *Allende's Chile*, Philip O'Brien (ed.), 296pp, 1976, Praeger, $20.00. All of the authors are either sympathetic to Allende or are critics from the left; here, they examine the failure of Allende's economic policy, and conclude that the causes of the overthrow were more internal to Chile than external.

10–55 *Chilean Voices: Activists Describe Their Experiences of the Popular Unity Period*, Colin Henfrey & Bernardo Sorj, 196pp, 1979, Humanities, $13.00. Supporters of the Popular Unity coalition, Allende's base, discuss their conflicting aims and evaluations of three years in power.

10–56 *Chile's Days of Terror, Eyewitness Accounts of the Military Coup*, Judy White (ed.), 124pp, 1974, Pathfinder, $2.45. Fifteen eyewitness accounts of the Junta's terror which followed the overthrow of Allende on September 11, 1973.

Intro
10–57 *The Overthrow of Allende and the Politics of Chile, 1964–1976*, Paul Sig-

mund, 326pp, 1978, Pittsburgh, $5.95. A study of Chilean politics which argues that democratic values were served by neither Allende nor the Pinochet regime which overthrew him; U.S. involvement is considered far less significant than many liberals believe, but far from insignificant.

10 – 58 *Politics of Compromise: Coalition Government in Colombia*, Albert Berry, Ronald Hellman & Mauricio Solaun, 488pp, 1980, Transaction, $7.95. From the Center for Inter-American Relations, this study analyzes the extent and limits of Colombian democracy.

10 – 59 *Peru: The Authoritarian Tradition*, David Palmer, 156pp, 1980, Praeger, $8.95. Traces the practice of authoritarian government to Spanish and Inca traditions and doubts that it can be altered.

10 – 60 *Peasants and Poverty: A Study of Haiti*, Mats Lundahl, 699pp, 1979, St. Martin's, $37.50. Finds the government is the villain, not the rural economic forces.

10 – 61 *Political Forces in Argentina*, Peter Snow, 183pp, 1979, (rev. ed.), Praeger, $8.95. The military, political parties, the Church, labor, and university students are the actors; the failure to compromise, a problem, as are polarization, terror, and extra-legal "disappearances."

10 – 62 *Diary of the Cuban Revolution*, Carlos Franqui, 546pp, 1980, Viking, $16.95. A member of the Cuban government provides records of the years preceding Castro's obtaining power and the first years of the Castro regime.

10 – 63 *Cuban Communism,* Irving Horowitz (ed.), 688pp, 1981 (4th ed.), Transaction, $9.95. Twenty-eight essays on the political, economic, and international implications of the Cuban experience, measured both in praise and in criticism.

10 – 64 *The Economic Transformation of Cuba*, Edward Boorstein, 303pp, 1969, Monthly Review, $5.95. An American economist, who assisted in the socialization of Cuban industry from 1960 – 1963, comments favorably on the results.

Intro
10 – 65 *Cuba, Order and Revolution*, Jorge Dominquez, 683pp, 1978, Harvard, $27.50. The author, a Cuban who "never belonged either to an organization seeking to overthrow the (Castro) government or to one supporting it," strives to describe impartially the politics and government of 20th-century Cuba, its international role, and the changes wrought by the revolution — some favorable, some not.

10 – 66 *The Cuban Revolution*, Hugh Thomas, 755pp, 1971, Harper & Row, $9.95. A detailed, sympathetic history of a revolution that lost its way. Provides a balanced assessment of economic achievements; is sharply critical of the continuing dictatorship.

10 – 67 *Secret Report on the Cuban Revolution*, Carlos Montaner, 292pp, 1980, Transaction, $6.95. Finds Cuba the most dependent State in Latin America, and argues that domestic repression and foreign intervention are the price paid for Soviet patronage.

10 – 68 *Cuba in the World,* Cole Blasier & Carmelo Mesa-Lago (eds.), 343pp, 1979, Pittsburgh, $5.95. Fifteen essays concerning the emergence of Cuban troops as a major military force in third-world conflicts; and the economic, political, and social settings within which they are used.

10 – 69 *The Latin American Political Dictionary,* Ernest Roosi & Jack Plano, 261pp, 1980, ABC-Clio, $12.95. Provides paragraph-length definitions of key terms, events, organizations, and movements.

10 – 70 *Bibliography of Books & Articles on the Organization of American States,* Organization of American States, 22pp, 1977, $1.00.

F. Africa

10 – 71 *Basic Documents on African Affairs,* Ian Brownlie (ed.), 556pp, 1971, Oxford, $19.25. Includes the Charter of the OAU and other documents of African international organizations, plus charters, agreements, commission reports, and UN Declarations from the 1961 – 1969 period.

10 – 72 *African Boundaries: A Legal and Diplomatic Encyclopaedia,* Ian Brownlie, 1,391pp, 1979, U. of Calif, $130.00. A massive reference work details the boundaries, problems, and disputes of forty-eight African States.

10 – 73 *The Boundary Politics of Independent Africa,* Saadia Touval, 645pp, 1973, Harvard, $16.50. Describes the origins of the current boundaries and attempts to maintain and change them; lists twenty-seven post-independence disputes.

10 – 74 *Africa,* Phyllis Martin & Patrick O'Meara (eds.), 482pp, 1979, Indiana, $7.95. A wide-ranging, scholarly introduction to African societies, politics, and international affairs.

10 – 75 *Alternative Futures for Africa,* Timothy Shaw, 325pp, 1981, Westview, $27.75. Offers a range of views concerning the perimeters of Africa's future; the recurring theme is the prospect of dependence unless development strategies are successful.

10 – 76 *Atlas of African History,* Colin McEvedy, 140pp, 1980, *Facts on File,* $8.50. Provides a concise history which focuses on people, empires, tribes, and the present division into States; covers from 175 million B.C. to the 21st century.

10 – 77 *Africa Contemporary Record:* Vol, XI, 1978 – 79, Colin Legum (ed.), 1980, Holmes & Meier, $95.00. An annual assessment by experts of current issues. This edition focuses on the Organization of African Unity, Southern Africa and foreign intervention, with country-by-country reviews and documents.

10 – 78 *African Realities,* Kenneth Adelman, 192pp, 1980, Crane, Russak, $16.50. Places African politics in the wider context of global international affairs, focuses on security concerns, and political and economic issues.

10–79 *The Press of Africa: Persecution and Perserverance,* Frank Barton, 304pp, 1979, Holmes & Meier, $35.00. An informal study of Africa's journalists and their maneuvering in a largely state-controlled media.

10–80 *Socialism in Sub-Saharan Africa: A New Assessment,* Carl Rosberg and Thomas Callaghy, (eds.), 426pp, 1979, Institute of International Studies (Berkeley), $8.50. A contemporary review of African socialist regimes.

10–81 *Africa in the 1980s: A Continent in Crisis,* Colin Legum, I. William Zartman, Steven Langdon, & Lynn Mytelka, 229pp, 1979, McGraw-Hill, $6.95. A summary of key issues in the 1980s, including the questions of whether stable nation-states will emerge, development take place, authoritarian or democratic governments prevail, and how African States will participate in world politics.

10–82 *Africa and the United States, Vital Interest,* Jennifer Whitaker (ed.), 200pp, 1978, N.Y.U. Press, $6.95. Includes diverse essays on what U.S. foreign policy objectives in Africa should be.

10–83 *The Theory and Practice of African Politics,* Christian Potholm II, 304pp, 1979, Prentice-Hall, $8.95. A study of the second generation of post-colonial leaders, and the major political forms in Africa described as the ''polyarchal spectrum and the authoritarian spectrum.''

10–84 *Analyzing Political Change in Africa, Applications of a New Multidimensional Framework,* James Scarritt (ed.), 360pp, 1980, Westview, $27.75. Studies eight States and the influence of political instability, class conflict, and prolonged economic dependency on them for national integration.

10–85 *Cuba's Policy in Africa, 1959 – 1980,* William LeoGrande, 82pp, 1980, Institute for Policy Studies, $3.25. A survey of Cuban military and political involvement in Africa.

10–86 *Communism in Africa,* David Albright (ed.), 288pp, 1980, Indiana, $12.95. A variety of authors trace the rise of Soviet influence in Africa, as well as the indigenous appeal of Marxism to an educated elite: Marxism explains why Africa is economically underdeveloped, assigns a key role to an educated elite in modernizing, and offers an explanation for current slow growth patterns. All of this appeals to an educated elite.

10–87 *Towards Socialism in Tanzania,* Bismarck Mwansasu & Cranford Pratt (eds.), 243pp, 1979, Toronto, $20.00. A debate between ''Marxist socialism'' and ''democratic socialism,'' about Tanzania's experiment with Socialism and how it has affected the public welfare.

10–88 *Politics and Public Policy in Kenya and Tanzania,* Joel Barkan & John Okumu, 316pp, 1979, Praeger, $9.95. A comparison by eleven scholars of capitalist vs socialist development in East Africa.

10–89 *Senegal,* Sheldon Gellar, 128pp, 1981, Westview, $16.50. One of the ''Nations of Contemporary Africa'' series which offers a brief historical, political, economic, and international relations introduction of each country.

10 – 90 *Zambia's Foreign Policy: Studies in Diplomacy and Dependence*, Douglas Anglin & Timothy Shaw, 453pp, 1979, Westview, $26.50. An important study of the forces shaping Zambia's foreign policy, particularly that of Zambia and the Angolan Civil War.

10 – 91 *War Clouds on the Horn of Africa: The Widening Storm*, Tom Farer, 196pp, 1979, Carnegie Endowment, $5.00. Introduces the conflict between Ethiopia, Somalia and Eritrea, and discusses the interests of the U.S. & USSR in the war.

10 – 92 *The Story of Nigeria*, Michael Crowder, 365pp, 1978, 4th ed., Merrimack, $9.95. An introduction to social and political history of Africa's most populous and richest State.

10 – 93 *Nigeria and the World: Readings in Nigerian Foreign Policy*, A. Bolaji Akinyemi (ed.), 152pp, 1979, Oxford, $28. An anthology which assesses from different perspectives, Nigeria's initial pro-Western leanings, the strains which developed during the Civil War, and Nigeria's independent and powerful role in African affairs today.

10 – 94 *Zaire: The Political Economy of Underdevelopment*, Guy Gran, 352pp, 1979, Praeger, $22.95. Documents the exploitation of Zairian people by national and international forces, but offers few policy alternatives.

10 – 95 *Ethiopia: Empire in Revolution*, Marina & David Ottaway, 224pp, 1978, Holmes & Meier, $27.00. A history of the overthrow of Haile Selassie and a sympathetic portrayal of the military council's rule, particularly, the land reform program. Russian and Cuban troops, massacre, murder within the Council, are described as the costs of Africa's "first real revolution."

10 – 96 *Africa's International Relations: The Diplomacy of Dependency and Change*, Ali Mazrui, 310pp, 1979, Westview, $13.50. An informative and wide-ranging assessment of Africa's search for an independent role in world politics.

10 – 97 *African International Relations: An Annotated Bibliography*, Mark DeLancey, 366pp, 1980, Westview, $27.75. Includes English, French, German, and several other language books and articles focused on the post-independence period. Includes a section on "Inter-African Conflicts and Refugees."

10 – 98 *Bibliography for the Study of African Politics*, Alan Solomon, 1978, African Studies Association, $15.00.

See also "Crisis Areas" concerning South Africa, Nambia, Angola, Ethiopia.

G. Western Europe

10 – 99 *The Making of Europe*, Christopher Dawson, 274pp, 1956, NAL, $3.95. Argues that European civilization was decisively influenced by Christianity.

10 – 100 *Europe 2000*, Peter Hall (ed.), 274pp, 1977, Columbia, $15.00. Over 200

experts from ten countries were engaged in research to identify European educational, industrial, urban and agricultural policy. The results are summarized here.

10–101 *A Continent Astray: Europe 1970–1978,* Walter Laqueur, 293pp, 1979, Oxford, $16.95. A pessimistic assessment of Europe's cultural health, derived from a careful evaluation of political polarization, economic recession, and social problems.

10–102 *Europe Between the Superpowers: The Enduring Balance,* A.W. Deporte, 272pp, 1980, Yale, $6.95. A historical perspective on Europe's current position, which maintains that the current degree of autonomy and dependence will continue.

10–103 *Ideology and Politics: The Socialist Party of France,* George Codding, Jr., & William Safran, 280pp, 1979, Westview, $25.75. A history of the Party prior to the election of its head as Premier.

10–104 *In Defense of Decadent Europe,* Raymond Aron, 297pp, 1979, Regnery/ Gateway, $14.95. Contrary to the title, Aron maintains that Western Europe is a vital, innovative society because it is politically open.

10–105 *Eurocommunism and Eurosocialism: The Left Confronts Modernity,* Bernard Brown, (ed.), 408pp, 1979, Cyrco Press, $9.95. Essays examining the impact of advanced industrialization on the European left and the hesitant response of the Left.

10–106 *Eurocommunism Between East and West,* Vernon Aspaturian, Jiri Valenta & David Burke (eds.), 384pp, 1980, Indiana, $9.95. Emphasizes the international effects on Eastern Europe, China, and Japan.

10–107 *The Political Transformation of Spain After Franco,* John Coverdale, 176pp, 1979, Praeger, $17.95. Describes the transition from authoritarian to democratic rule.

10–108 *The Federal Republic, Europe, and the World: Perspectives on West German Foreign Policy,* Martin Saeter, 120pp, 1980, University, $15.00. Maintains that West Germany needs broad European support to be a regional power.

10–109 *The German Problem Reconsidered: Germany and the World Order,1870 to the Present,* David Calleo, 208pp, 1978, Cambridge, $13.95. An introductory history.

10–110 *Dilemmas of the Atlantic Alliance, Two Germanys, Scandinavia, Canada, NATO and the EEC,* Peter Ludz, H. Peter Dreyer, Charles Pentland, & Lother Ruhl, 253pp, 1975, Praeger, $19.95. Profiles of seven countries, each independent, two overshadowed by larger neighbors, and five Western European states integrating into the Common Market. The strains within the alliance are considered.

10–111 *Eurocommunism: A New Kind of Communism?* Annie Kriegel, 131pp, 1978, Hoover, $12.00. Denies that Eurocommunism combines freedom with Communism, and argues that it is rather a regional strategy for the conquest of State power.

10–112 *The Communist Parties of Western Europe,* Neil McInnes, 224pp, 1975, Oxford, $19.95. An empirical study asking what groups belong to or vote for the Communist Parties, what are their attitudes toward democracy, how independent are they of Moscow, and once in office, what would be the consequences of their failure.

10–113 *"Eurocommunism"; Implications for East and West,* Roy Godson, Stephen Haseler, 144pp, 1979, St. Martin's, $6.95. An assessment of the goals and strategies of the European Communist parties.

10–114 *European Security: Prospects for the 1980s,* Derek Leebaert, (ed.), 302pp, 1979, Lexington, $15.00. Treats energy and Eurocommunism, as well as military issues, introduces specific choices in each field.

H. Mediterranean

10–115 *Cyprus, War and Adaptation: A Psychoanalytic History of Two Ethnic Groups in Conflict,* Vamik Volkan, 192pp, 1979, Univ. Press of Virginia, $13.50. A study of how the Turkish and Greek Cypriot populations perceive each other.

10–116 *The Turkish Experiment in Democracy* 1950-1975, Feroz Ahmad, 492pp, 1977, Westview, $27.75. A study of the emergence of multiparty rule, role of the military, and the prospect for democracy.

10–117 *U.S. Relations with Greece and Turkey,* Theodore Couloumbis, 200pp, 1981, Praeger, $8.95. A study of decision-makers, how U.S. influence in Greece and Turkey has declined, while the influence of Greek and Turkish decision-makers over U.S. policy increased.

10–118 *The Government and Politics of the Middle East and North Africa,* David Long & Bernard Reich (eds.), 480pp, 1980, Westview, $13.50. A study of the region and a forecast of change.

See also "Crisis Areas," Chapter 14.

I. The Middle East

10–119 *A History of Israel: From the Rise of Zionism to our Time,* Howard Sachar, 883pp, 1979, Knopf, $9.95. A comprehensive history by an American Jewish scholar who is sympathetic to the establishment of Israel.

10–120 *The Zionist Idea: A Historical Analysis and Reader,* Arthur Hertzberg (ed.), 638pp, 1969, Atheneum, $5.95. A collection of writings of the Zionist movement from its inception until its success in establishing a Jewish State.

10–121 *The History of Egypt, From Muhammad Ali to Sadat,* P.J. Vatikiotis, 528pp, 1980 (2nd ed.)., Johns Hopkins, $9.50.

10 – 122 *Palestinian Society and Politics,* Joel Migdal, 290pp, 1980, Princeton $6.95. Provides an overview of the major 20th-century changes in Palestinian society and politics with an emphasis on social life.

10 – 123 *Islam and Development: Religion and Sociopolitical Change,* John Esposito (ed.), 292pp, 1980, Syracuse, $9.95. Eleven essays, each focused on a different Islamic country or on a region, which asks: "How are Islamic teachings applied to political and economic questions?"

10 – 124 *On the Sociology of Islam,* Ali Shari'ati, 125pp, 1979, 2nd ed., Mizan, $3.95. Explores the key concepts in Islam, such as that of an ideal society; not an empirical study.

10 – 125 *Arab Politics: The Search for Legitimacy,* Michael Hudson, 434pp, 1977, Yale, $8.95. Describes the cultural pluralism of the Arab world, which poses the difficulty of achieving and maintaining political legitimacy. The prospects for democracy are not good.

10 – 126 *The Persian Gulf States, A General Survey,* Alvin Cottrell (ed.), 736pp, 1980, Johns Hopkins, $37.50. Offers an historical, cultural, economic, and political background on Iran, Iraq, Saudi Arabia, Kuwait, Bahrain, Qatar, the United Arab Emirates, and Oman.

10 – 127 *Social and Economic Development in the Arab Gulf,* Tim Niblock (ed.), 242pp, 1980, St. Martin's, $25.00. Disconnected essays providing valuable information but no general thesis.

10 – 128 *Arabia, the Gulf, and the West, A Critical View of Arabs and Their Oil Policy,* John Kelly, 530pp, 1980, Basic Books, $25.00. A critical assessment of the leaders, outside governments, oil companies, etc.

10 – 129 *North Yemen,* Manfred Werner, 128pp, 1981, Westview, $16.50. One of the "Nations of the Contemporary Middle East" (*South Yemen,* Robert Stookey, forthcoming) provides a geographical and economic background for current political choices.

10 – 130 *Iraq, International Relations and National Development,* Edith Penrose and E.F. Penrose, 569pp, 1978, Westview, $39.75. Provides background on the physical setting and history, plus Iraq's purposes in world politics.

10 – 131 *Middle East Foreign Policy, Issues and Process,* R.D. McLaurin, Mohammed Mughisuddin & Don Peretz, 320pp, 1981, Praeger, $8.95. An in-depth analysis of foreign policymaking in Egypt, Iraq, Israel, Syria, and Saudi Arabia.

10 – 132 *U.S. Strategy in the Indian Ocean, The International Response,* Monoranjan Bezboruah, 1977, 288pp, 1977, Praeger, $27.95. Describes the Soviet – American rivalry in this Ocean.

See also Crisis Areas

J. Central Asia

10 – 133 *Countercoup: The Struggle for the Control of Iran*, Kermit Roosevelt, 217pp, 1979, McGraw Hill, $12.95. A detailed account of the forces which overthrew the Mosaddeq regime in 1953 — the Shah, key Iranians, elements of the armed forces, segments of the population with CIA financial assistance. CIA aid was considered justified because the Tudeh (Iranian Communist) Party was being aided by the KGB and was similarly planning a coup.

10 – 134 *Iran: Dictatorship and Development*, Fred Halliday, 386pp, 1979, Penguin, $3.95. A survey of the social, political, and cultural background, with a new chapter discussing the overthrow of the Shah and the programs of the new regime.

10 – 135 *Paved with Good Intentions: The American Experience and Iran,* Barry Rubin, 320pp, 1980, Oxford, $15.95. Describes critically but fairly U.S. policy since 1945, including the attempts to cope with the revolutionary situation of 1978/79.

10 – 136 *The Rise and Fall of the Shah*, Amin Saikal, 294pp, 1980, Princeton, $14.50. This measured assessment acknowledges Iran's significant economic achievements under the Shah while underlining the failure to establish a constituency or to redress rural poverty.

10 – 137 *Marxism and other Western Fallacies, An Islamic Critique*, Ali Shari'ati, 122pp, 1980, Mizan, $3.95. Maintains that "Islam and Marxism . . .are two diametrically opposed ideologies," and that Islam did not need to await the invention of the steam engine to have a sense of justice.

10 – 138 *Militant Islam,* Godfrey Jansen, 160pp, 1980, Harper, $3.95. Offers sketches of the politics of a dozen Muslim countries and their common resistance to Western influence.

10 – 139 *Islam in the Modern World, and Other Studies*, Elie Kedourie, 256pp, 1981, New Republic, $16.95. Identifies key issues confronting Islamic political leaders today.

10 – 140 *India's Political Economy, 1947 – 1977: The Gradual Revolution*, Francine Frankel, 600pp, 1972, Princeton, $12.50. Addresses the problems of the Indian economy.

10 – 141 *India: Emergent Power?*, Stephen Cohen & Richard Park, 91pp, 1978, Crane Russak, $4.50. Makes the case for India's emergence as a regional power.

10 – 142 *Food Trends and Prospects in India*, Fred Sanderson & Shyamal Roy, 162pp, 1979, Brookings, $4.95. Argues that India's agricultural production has increased at an annual rate of 2.8 percent, which is considered high but only slightly higher than India's population growth rate. High yield grains can help, but double-cropping, and greater use of fertilizers and irrigation could enable India to feed one billion people by the year 2000.

10 – 142A *The Emergence of Modern India*, Arthur Lall, 288pp, 1981, Columbia, $16.95. An historical interpretation of modern India, its strengths and weaknesses.

10 – 143 *India at the Polls: The Parliamentary Elections of 1977,* Myron Weiner, 150pp, 1978, American Enterprise Institute, $6.25. The massive endorsement of democracy in the defeat of Indira Gandhi's "emergency" is described in this account of the campaign and the result.

10 – 144 *India's Political System,* Richard Park, Bruce Bueno De Mesquita, 208pp, 1979, Prentice-Hall, $8.50. Studies the electoral process before and after Indira Gandhi's emergency and the replacement of the Congress Party with the Janata Party.

10 – 145 *India's Nuclear Option, Atomic Diplomacy and Decision Making,* Ashok Kapur, 280pp, 1976, Praeger, $24.95. Although the focus is on how India decided to become a nuclear power, this study also explores much of the post-World War II setting: India's non-aligned policy, relations with Pakistan, China, and the Soviet Union, as well as NPT.

K. The Far East

10 – 146 *Constitutionalism in Asia: Asian Views of the American Influence,* Lawrence Beer (ed.), 210pp, 1979, U. of Calif., $18.75. Considers the impact of American Constitutionalism on diverse Asin states and the current preference for other forms of law and government.

10 – 147 *The Japanese Challenge: The Success and Failure of Economic Success,* Herman Kahn & Thomas Pepper, 162pp, 1980, Morrow, $6.95. Argues that the U.S. should maintain its military force levels in the Pacific because of the mutual benefits to Japan and the U.S.

10 – 148 *Japan as Number One, Lessons for America,* Ezra Vogel, 272pp, Harper & Row, $4.95. The continuing miracle of the Japanese economy is examined, its preponderance in the future forecast, and changes in American economic relationships recommended.

10 – 149 *United States-Japanese Economic Relations: Cooperation, Competition and Confrontation,* Diane Tasca (ed.), 135pp, 1980, Pergamon, $16.50. A candid assessment of the problems and a suggestion that things might get worse.

10 – 150 *Japan and the United States: Challenges and Opportunities,* William Barnds, 286pp, 1979, N.Y.U. Press, $6.95. A careful analysis of future areas of conflict.

10 – 151 *The Foreign Policy of Modern Japan,* Robert Scalapino (ed.), 426pp, 1977, California, $5.95. Thirteen American scholars assess Japanese interests, perceptions of the U.S., and the debate within Japan about Japan's foreign goals.

10 – 152 *A Theory of Japanese Democracy,* Nobutaka Ike, 178pp, 1980, Westview, $8.50. A study of the role played by unprecedented economic success, localism, low correlation between social class and voting patterns, and the decline of the Liberal Democratic Party in maintaining Japanese democracy.

INF

10 – 153 *The United States and China,* John King Fairbank, 606pp, 1979 (1949), 4th ed., Harvard, $6.95. Revised and updated to include the establishment of diplomatic relations in the post-Mao era.

10 – 154 *Chinese Communism and the Rise of Mao,* Benjamin Schwartz, 258pp, 1979, Harvard, $3.95. The setting in which China became a Communist State is described.

10 – 155 *China's Role in World Affairs,* Michael Yahuda, 298pp, 1978, St. Martin's, $18.50. Outlines Maoist conceptions, traces the origins of the Sino-Soviet split, and considers alternative foreign policy goals.

10 – 156 *Sino-American Normalization and Its Policy Implications,* Gene Hsiao & William Feeney (eds.), 352pp, 1981, Praeger, $9.95. Provides background on normalization and then assesses congruence and disparity between the countries' national interests.

10 – 157 *China's Global Role: An Analysis of Peking's National Power Capabilities in the Context of an Evolving International System,* John Franklin Cooper, 181pp, 1980, Hoover, $7.95. An attempt to forecast China's power potential, which concludes that China will never be more than a regional power.

10 – 158 *The Chinese,* David Bonavia, 288pp, 1980, Lippincott & Crowell, $12.95. Describes both Chinese culture and the Communist system, and concludes with an assessment of China's likely role in world politics — expansionist as the Soviet Union.

10 – 159 *Broken Images: Essays on Chinese Culture and Politics,* Simon Leys, 156pp, 1979, St. Martin's, $17.50. A collection of essays exposing Maoism as a fraud, while pointing out the strengths of traditional Chinese culture.

10 – 160 *Chinese Encounters,* Inge Marath & Arthur Miller, 255pp, 1979, Farrar, Straus, Giroux, $25.00. A post-Maoist travellers' assessment of a reviving artistic tradition and the freeing of the human imagination in the brief interval when public expression was permitted. Over 100 pictures illustrate the texts.

10 – 161 *China's Future, Foreign Policy and Economic Development in the Post-Mao Era,* Allen Whiting and Robert Dernberger, 202pp, 1977, McGraw-Hill, $5.95. A study of the likely course of China's foreign policy.

10 – 162 *Mao: A Biography,* Rose Terrill, 481pp, 1980, Harper, $17.50. An attempt to get at Mao Zedong, the person. Mao is considered "among the half dozen or so most consequential rulers in the entire three thousand years of China's recorded history."

10 – 163 *The People's Emperor: A Biography of Mao Tse-tung,* Dick Wilson, 552pp, 1980, Doubleday, $17.50. The editor of the *China Quarterly* offers a detailed portrayal of Mao, who Wilson believes "invented for China a completely new system of life, economy, and government." Mao is praised for his flexibility when he ended the "100 Flowers Bloom" episode with wide-scale executions.

10 – 164 *Chinese Shadows,* Simon Ley, 220pp, 1978, Penguin, $2.50. Argues that Mao imprisoned the genius of the Chinese people, hindered their economic development and, in fact, contributed no new ideas to economic development.

10 – 165 *20th Century China,* O. Edmund Clubb, 554pp, 1978 (1964) Columbia, $9.00. A history and overview updated with a section on post-Maoist China.

10 – 165A *China's Economy in Global Perspective,* A. Doak Barnett, 752pp, 1981, Brookings, $16.95. A detailed study of the post-Mao economy which suggests that there are enormous obstacles to success and yet a reasonable expectation that significant results will be available by 1985.

10 – 166 *Encyclopedia of China Today,* Frederic Kaplan, Julian Sobin & Stephen Andors, 336pp, 1980, Harper & Row, $27.50. Advertised as the only current guide including information on all aspects of social, political, commercial and artistic life.

10 – 167 *The Duel of the Giants, China and Russia in Asia,* Drew Middleton, 241pp, 1978, Scribner, $10.95. The great game in Asia is played with both new and old weapons.

10 – 168 *The Coming Decline of the Chinese Empire,* Victor Louis, 188pp, 1979, Times Books, $12.50. A Soviet author with KGB connections describes China as exploiting its poor, repressing minorities, and out to conquer the Soviet Far East, Siberia and Central Asia. Some consider it part of the war of nerves; others claim it lays the ground for a Soviet preemptive nuclear strike against China.

10 – 169 *China in the Global Community,* James Hsiung & Samuel Kim (eds.), 288pp, 1980, Praeger, $27.95. Ten scholars examine the methodological problems involved in studying China's foreign policy, and that policy's aims and methods.

10 – 170 *Indonesia,* Donald Fryer and James Jackson, 313pp, 1977, Westview, $29.75. One of the "Nations of the Modern World" series surveys the land, people, recent history, economic prospects, foreign affairs, and future of each country.

10 – 171 *The Army and Politics in Indonesia,* Harold Crouch, 377pp, 1978, Cornell, $22.50. Provides background on the coup that failed, the bloody aftermath, and how the army filled the void created by the discrediting of Sukarno and the destruction of the Communist Party of Indonesia.

10 – 172 *Indonesia and the Philippines: American Interests in Island Southeast Asia,* Robert Pringle, 296pp, 1980, Columbia, $8.00. Focuses on six specific policy areas to define American interests in each country.

10 – 173 *Marcos and Martial Law in the Philippines,* David Rosenberg (ed.), 315pp, 1979, Cornell, $19.50. An assessment of the dictatorship in a once democratic country.

10 – 174 *The Security of Korea: U.S. and Japanese Perspectives on the 1980s,* Franklin Weinstein and Fuji Kamiya (eds.), 276pp, 1980, Westview, $8.50. Teams of scholars from the U.S. and Japan discuss Korean security: both the controversy and the conclu-

sion are of interest. Called by *Foreign Affairs* a "model for future studies of important international security issues."

10– 175 *The Future of the Korean Peninsula,* Young Kim and Abraham Halpern (eds.), 193pp, 1977, Praeger, $21.95. Eleven authors assess South Korea's economic successes and North Korea's failures, plus the political future and the role of the U.S., USSR, China, and Japan in that future.

10– 176 *Economic Development of South Korea, The Political Economy Of Success,* L.L. Wade & B.S. Kim, 284pp, 1978, Praeger, $23.95. Describes South Korea's economic development since the 1950s, its success in promoting diversified growth with reduced income differences, and a prediction that South Korea will be the "first third world nation to attain broad, accelerated, and self-sustained economic modernization."

10– 177 *The Security of Korea: U.S. and Japanese Perspectives on the 1980s,* Franklin Weinstein & Fuji Kamiya, 276pp, 1980, Westview, $8.50. Argues that security prospects are brighter and suggests alternative policy choices.

10– 178 *Economic Growth and Structural Change in Taiwan: The Postwar Experience of the Republic of China,* Walter Galenson (ed.), 519pp, 1979, Cornell, $29.50. Describes the rapid rate of growth, with improved distribution providing a more egalitarian social base.

10– 179 *The Economic and Social Modernization of the Republic of Korea,* Edward Mason, et al, 552pp, 1981, Harvard, $20.00. During the 1970s South Korea's economic growth rate (9.6 percent) surpassed that of Japan after World War II. The assessment offered here credits U.S. aid, the investments of multinational corporations, plus the policies of Park Chung Hee (1961 – 79). They question whether as much growth would have been achieved under democracy: "Would a democratic polity have accepted quadruple gasoline prices overnight?" they ask. They conclude, whatever the verdict on democracy, South Korea is "a prime example of how growth can be achieved with equity."

CHAPTER 11

NON-STATE ACTORS

States, singly or in groups, are the most powerful actors in the international arena. It is States that wage war and collect taxes. Ending war will require fundamental changes in States policies, and neither the deeper spiritual sources which move people without regard to national boundaries nor a vision of a nascent world community should make us lose sight of that reality. But non-State actors can play a significant role in helping to achieve constructive changes in world affairs.

The number of non-State actors is very large, and they vary significantly in nearly every characteristic. Some have existed longer than any State — for example, the Catholic Church. More typically, they survive only a few years. Transnational corporations have significant economic resources; other non-State actors operate on shoestring budgets. Some non-State actors aspire to control States; some seek to supersede States; others want to abolish them. While most non-State actors reject the use of violence, one class (non-State nations) has frequently been the instigator of terrorist acts. Defining the types of non-State organizations is difficult but helpful. We will first distinguish the types of non-State actors, provide examples of each, and then describe selected non-State actors engaged directly in conflict-resolution activities. The bibliography covers a wide range of additional functions that non-State actors perform.

Among the important categories of non-State actors (some now exist, some are only potential) are the following:

291

I. *Supranational organizations:* organizations or agencies empowered to perform a function of government without the permission of a State, and, if necessary, against the wishes of the State

    A. Global supranational organizations

        1. Multi-purpose: (none)

        2. Single-purpose: International Atomic Energy Agency (IAEA) (The IAEA possesses a supranational responsibility for monitoring the disposition of spent atomic fuel rods among States which have previously agreed to permit such monitoring.)

    B. Regional supranational organizations or agencies

        1. Multi-purpose: European Economic Community (Common Market)

        2. Single-purpose: Human Rights Court of the Council of Europe

None of these non-State actors are truly autonomous; their supranational character is more potential than real. They are dependent upon State governments for their continued operation.

II. *Intergovernmental organizations:* an organization in which State representives meet to accomplish agreed upon tasks that do not supersede State prerogatives

    A. Global intergovernmental organizations

        1. Multi-purpose (United Nations)

        2. Single purpose or functional (components of the UN and others)

            a. Economic (UN Conference on Trade and Development — UNCTAD)

            b. Security (Security Council)

            c. Food (Food and Agricultural Organization — FAO)

            d. Decolonization (Trusteeship Council)

            e. Transportation, air (International Civil Aviation Organization); sea (International Maritime Consultative Organization)

            f. Judicial (International Court of Justice)

            g. Human Rights (UN Commission of Human Rights)

            h. Disarmament (UN Centre for Disarmament)

            i. Communication, mail (International Postal Organization), telegraph (International Telegraphic Organization)

    B. Regional intergovernmental organizations

        1. Intra-bloc organizations

            a. Economic (European Monetary System)

            b. Security (NATO and Warsaw Pact)

        2. Regional organizations

            a. Economic (European Economic Community, Common Market)

b. Security (Organization of American States; Rio Pact)

c. Cultural (Organization of American States; Bogotá Pact)

3. Integrating organizations

    a. Economic (European Coal and Steel Community)

    b. Political (Parliament of Europe)

III. *International non-governmental organizations* (INGOs): An organization which seeks to influence world political or social life in two or more countries. This category includes very diverse organizations. Examples are

1. Business: General Motors (a transnational corporation), United Automobile Workers
2. Communications: International Telephone and Telegraphy
3. Transportation: Airline Pilots Association
4. Travel: AFS International
5. Finance: Bank of America
6. Agriculture: Rockefeller Foundation
7. Arts: International Association of Art
8. Media: International Press Institute
9. Sciences: World Psychiatric Association
10. Technology: World Association of Industrial and Technological Research Organizations
11. Medicine: International Council of Nurses
12. Nutrition: International Union of Nutritional Sciences
13. Education: Institute for World Order
14. Religion: World Council of Churches
15. Social Welfare: YMCA, YWCA
16. Sports: International Olympic Committee
17. Law: Institute of International Law
18. Politics: Western European organizations of Christian Democratic, Liberal, and Democratic Socialist parties
19. Human Rights: International Commission of Jurists
20. Disaster Relief: International Red Cross
21. Economic Development: Oxfam, CARE
22. Conflict-Resolution: Pugwash and Dartmouth Conferences, International Peace Academy, American Friends Service Committee
23. International Organizations: World Federation of United Nations Associations
24. Peace Research: Stockholm International Peace Research Institute
25. Youth: Scouts, International Student Exchange

26. Police: International Federation of Senior Police Officers

IV. *Non-governmental organizations* (NGOs): Organizations that seek to
influence attitudes or policies within one country

Nearly all the above tasks and many others are on the agenda of NGOs
within a single country. A typology of such organizations, an introduction to their activities, and tools for assessing their work, are provided
on pages 535 – 538.

V. *Non-State nations:* Organizations that claim the right to exercise State
authority on behalf of people or territory controlled by an existing State
   A. Secessionist movements, seeking to split off a portion of an existing
      State and to establish a new independent State.
   B. Irredentist movements, seeking to unite in one country people of a
      similar ethnic group living in several countries, e.g., Kurds.
   C. Federation movements, seeking a greater degree of autonomy within
      a State: Navaho Indian groups, Scotch and Welsh nationalist
      movements.
   D. Liberation movements, seeking to overthrow foreign domination,
      now broadened to include movements seeking State power in the
      name of the poor or oppressed: SWAPO (South West African
      Peoples Organization).
   E. Revolutionary movements, seeking to overthrow an existing gov-
      ernment by extra-legal, usually violent means: Spartacist League.
   F. Terrorist organizations, using violence and terror but expecting other
      organizations to form a new government: Baader-Meinhof gang.

VI. *Individuals*
Men and women of many countries personally seek to influence world
affairs. Their activities include creating and staffing organizations,
taking membership in organizations, declaring themselves conscientious objectors to war, devoting their lives to peace research, serving as
liaison between people or groups in conflict, contributing time, talent,
wisdom, and/or wealth to aid world affairs organizations and seeking to
influence organizations engaged in any of the above.

The examples indicate that non-State actors are alike only in the lack
of State power. Their number and their impact on world affairs have
increased significantly in the last twenty-five years. Non-State actors,
particularly INGOs and NGOs, can act in ways not open to States. They
can create new options and opportunities which State leaders are unlikely to develop — for example, non-military security strategies. Not
all non-State actors are oriented toward ending war, and those that are

may not be effective. They tend to separate themselves from the larger political organizations, and even from each other. Those which justify violence (especially the non – State nations) in effect usurp a State function without being subject to public accountability and control.

SUPRANATIONAL ORGANIZATIONS

In Chapter 5 ("International Organizations and World Law"), current efforts to create supranational institutions were discussed. Chapter 6 ("World Community and Human Rights") presents the steps toward the political integration of Western Europe as steps toward supranational organization. These global and regional efforts could lead to supranational organizations capable of acting without the consent of States. Efforts to provide the United Nations, or agencies set up through the UN, with independent sources of revenue (from sea-bed mining, for example), autonomous powers (to monitor spent nuclear fuel reprocessing), or independence of action (a UN Human Rights Commissioner) also are steps toward supranational authority.

INTERGOVERNMENTAL ORGANIZATIONS

Existing international organizations are most accurately characterized as intergovernmental organizations. The United Nations and its agencies, the World Court, regional organizations such as the Organization of American States (OAS), and functional international organizations such as the World Health Organization (WHO), reflect primarily national governmental policies. To date, these organizations have not been capable, except in very limited ways, of acting independently of States. They are forums for expressing or achieving nationally determined purposes; they are rarely effective in constraining war-making or other security-related functions of the State. Peacekeeping activity by international organizations, with the unusual exception of the UN-authorized military action in the Korean War, is based upon the consent of States which are parties to the conflict.

Perhaps as important as the agencies for international political action are the functional international organizations which have proliferated at an astounding rate since World War II. Growing world interdependence has made necessary and possible the development of international structures that are somewhat removed from political and ideological conflict and are capable of dealing with specific functional problems. Some pre-date World War I (the International Postal Union and the International Labour Organization) but most post-date World War II.

INTERNATIONAL NON-GOVERNMENTAL ORGANIZATIONS (INGOs)

In 1951, Lyman White wrote:

> The time has come to realize that the unofficial side of world affairs has developed to the point where it should be given consideration as an important aspect of international life. In particular, the students of international organizations should recognize the immense contribution of these organizations, composed of unofficial groups in different countries, which have come together to promote common interest through international action.[1]

These organizations, as White points out, are referred to in the UN Charter (Article 71) as "international non-governmental organizations"(INGOs) and have since been defined by the UN Economic and Social Council as "any organization which is not established by intergovernmental agreement."

International non-governmental organizations link people in different countries without using governmental channels. Being less dependent upon governments, such organizations have a greater capacity for independent action and are therefore significant non-State actors. With few exceptions, they have modest economic resources and no military forces; their influence is through persuasion, service, or skills and they depend upon their ability to sustain the interest of their supporters. In 1978 there were over 75,000 such organizations working in the twenty-six fields listed above (*International Non-Governmental Organization*, 11-44) and others. These organizations vary greatly as to resources, functions, purposes, and membership. Here we will describe briefly a few categories of INGOs.

Religious Organizations

Each of the major religions has a division which seeks to influence world affairs. For example, the International Affairs Committee of the World Council of Churches provides Protestants with an office, programs, and financial

[1] Lyman White, *International Non-Governmental Organizations* (New York: Greenwood 1968)

resources to enable them to apply the values of their tradition to world affairs. The Catholic Church and other major religions of the world — Islam, Buddhism, Judaism, Hinduism, and Confucianism also have decison-making centers where their respective values are applied to world affairs issues and crises.

The relationship between religious organizations and governments varies considerably from region to region. In Arab countries, a commitment to Islam is often written into their constitutions; in the Soviet Union, the role of religious institutions is carefully circumscribed. One consequence is that when religious leaders of the Eastern and Western blocs gather, Westerners are free to challenge their own government policies while Eastern leaders rarely do so.

Professional Associations

Professional, scientific, and scholarly associations (e.g. physicists, geneticists, historians, anthropologists, journalists, doctors) constitute another set of transnational linkages. Through their common interests and concerns about professional standards and values, many of these groups are led to active efforts directed at influencing people and governments in other countries. The abuse of psychiatry to silence dissidents in the Soviet Union, for example, was a major issue before the 1977 World Psychiatric Association Convention. The international media play an especially important role (*Big Story,* 8-94) in providing information and shaping attitudes toward world events. The legal profession's international associations are another with special importance for the development of world law and common definitions of human rights.

The Military Profession

Surprisingly, the military is a profession that is becoming a transnational actor in the resolution of political conflict without violence. More than 200,000 soldiers from many States have participated in United Nations peacekeeping operations in the past twenty-five years. More conventional assignments in international military alliances and in training and assistance programs make the military a critical and potentially constructive actor in the international arena (*The Professional Soldier,* 2-143).

Transnational Corporations

International commercial enterprises have long played an important role in relations between States. According to some, the dramatic proliferation in recent years of transnational corporations (TNCs) represents a challenge to the sovereignty of the State as the primary actor in world politics. They are capable of creating and transferring wealth, of encouraging technological innovation, of managing scarce resources efficiently, and of distributing the benefits of such activities, however inequitably. Particularly because of this last capability, they remain controversial. However, TNCs are subservient to State power, since they operate under the laws of the host State and because their resources can be taken over by such States. As the size of the resources controlled by TNCs has grown, there has been a concern for formulating a code of conduct for their activity and for imposing some form of regulation. Whether TNCs will be phased out of host countries or will be allowed to perform functions that these do badly, depends in part on the assessment of their impact on development programs and on the alternatives available. The heavy investments welcomed in the Soviet Union and China in the 1970s suggest that TNC's life expectancy may be longer than their critics have indicated.

Conflict-Resolution Organizations

Among the many tasks INGOs now perform, none is more critical for achieving a world without war than conflict-resolution. Many organizations have undertaken the task of resolving conflicts within consensual communities but the task is far more difficult when the conflict is between ideological, religious, or national antagonists. In a summary of INGO activity focused on this latter task, Maureen Berman and Joseph Johnson state:

> [INGOs seek] to help prevent, resolve, or reduce the costs of major social conflict. [The tools available include] . . . pure conceptual work, both normative (e.g. theory of justice) and analytic (e.g. game theory); computerized conflict data analysis (e.g. the CASCON experiment); exercises simulating specific conflicts and negotiations; workshops; Burton's controlled communication; third party mediation and arbitration; and, of course, the various forms of traditional, two-party negotiation.[2]

Among the different efforts to reduce and resolve international conflict,

[2] *Unofficial Diplomats*, (11-1) p.220

only a few have aimed at conflict-resolution between the superpowers. Three continuing series of conferences are the Pugwash Conference, the Dartmouth Conference, originally suggested by President Eisenhower *(The Improbable Triumvirate,* 11-104), and the meetings between the United Nations Association of the U.S. and the U.S.S.R. *(NPT,* 11-62).

Such conferences are, however, rarely meetings between private citizens, as they may appear to be. As one regular participant put it:

> Often times the Russians who are sent abroad are, I imagine, either officials or certain people who are under official instructions. Yet, the faith that keeps one going is that some small corner of a contact may have some utility, and that even though there are carefully chosen and carefully briefed people on the Soviet side, you may nevertheless have some little change in values.[3]

The same observer, however, could report a degree of progress six years later, particularly when American participants rejected the prepared ideological diatribes as unhelpful:

> While the range of independence among Soviet participants in non-governmental contacts is obviously restricted, it has nevertheless been widening with experience and the growth of confidence. An important consequence of this is that American participants are able to go beyond the limited printed sources of information on Soviet positions and to become aware of the richer and complex oral levels of discussion of policy issues.[4]

INGOs have also tried to lessen regional conflicts by arranging conferences, using communication opening techniques *(Unofficial Diplomats,* 11-1), acting as intermediaries *(Quaker Experience in International Conciliation,* 11-63), floating ideas that governments want discussed but are unwilling to announce publicly, and conducting simulations of conflicts for decision-makers and for others concerned. While assessments of the effectiveness of this type of activity vary (see 11-68 and 11-69 on the Stirling, Scotland Conferences with fifty-six Protestant and Catholic residents of Belfast, Northern Ireland), there is a need for enabling government officials, non-governmental leadership, and citizens to meet and to know each other as well-intentioned individuals.

---

[3]Marshall Shulman, "Observations on International Negotiations: Transcript of an Information Conference" Academy for Education Development, 1971.
[4]Marshall Shulman, "On Learning to Live with Authoritarian Regimes," *Foreign Affairs,* Jan. 1977.

NON-STATE NATIONS AND MOVEMENTS

There are, at any given time, many movements which aspire to the prerogatives of Statehood — territory, sovereignty, the right to collect taxes, and to make war. Such movements are called non – State nations *(Nonstate Nations in International Politics*, 11-81). They are not identical with ethnic groups (although ethnic groups may aspire to such status). They include secessionist, national independence, irredentist, and other movements. They differ in at least one important respect from INGOs and NGOs by claiming the political right to use violence and to establish themselves as authorities with State power. Among such organizations are the Palestine Liberation Organization (PLO), which has diplomatic relations with many countries and observer-status at the United Nations. Others are organizations of South Moluccans, Croatians, and Armenians, each seeking an independent State, as well as the American Indian Movement (AIM), Aztlan, and others seeking greater autonomy within the United States. Some nonstate nations initiate terrorist violence.

When they act on behalf of ethnic minorities living in multi-ethnic States (most States have one or more ethnic minorities living within them) and assert the "right of self-determination," they pose a fundamental problem for any system of world order. A world reorganized around ethnic lines would be a world in which nearly every State boundary would be redrawn.

INDIVIDUALS

Individuals can be — and have been — significant international actors. Abie Nathan, an Israeli citizen, preceded Anwar Sadat's historic trip by ten years, when he went from Tel Aviv in Israel to Port Said in Egypt to focus attention on the need for starting peace talks. Nathan then worked for five years to organize and finance a ship which broadcast peace proposals to Egypt and Israel and to any others who would listen. He sought to create a climate in which leaders could negotiate a comprehensive settlement, and he now thinks, rightly or wrongly, that he was partially successful. Another individual, Cyrus Eaton, organized and financed the original Pugwash Conference in his hometown in Nova Scotia, and then went on to promote trade between the Soviet Union and the U.S. as a means of lowering barriers.

At different levels and in different ways, actors in the world arena — individuals and States, the United Nations, and the Catholic Church, the International Congress of Geneticists, and literally thousands of others — offer a multiplicity of channels for new ideas and approaches to progress toward an end to war. The individual, who seeks to bring his or her best thought and effort to bear on problems of war and peace, will find opportunities to link work in the domestic political arena with work in the nascent world community so that people may one day live free from the threat of war.

BIBLIOGRAPHY

The bibliography in this chapter will be useful in exploring answers to questions such as these: 1) What are the special capabilites of various types of non – State actors? 2) What are the differences between supranational, transnational, and international organizations? 3) What supranational organizations exist? What conditions make their formation possible? 4) Why have so many intergovernmental or international organizations been created in this century? Why so few before? 5) What is the difference between international non-governmental organizations (INGOs) and non-governmental organizations (NGOs)? 6) What are the aims and means which characterize non – State nations? 7) What are the accomplishments and limitations of non – State actors in resolving conflicts between States? 8) Why have transnational corporations (TNCs) gained prominence recently? 9) Are TNCs more or less powerful than States? 10) Can individuals influence world politics?

A. Overviews[4]

TEW
11 – 1 *Unofficial Diplomats*, Maureen Berman & Joseph Johnson (eds.), 268pp, 1977, Columbia, $5.95. An extremely valuable assessment of ways individuals have tried to aid the non-violent resolution of international confiict.

11 – 2 *The Web of Politics: Nonstate Actors in the Global System,* Richard Mansbach & Yale Ferguson, 336pp, 1976, Prentice-Hall, $10.95. A survey of the multitude of non-State actors seeking to influence national and international decision-makers.

11 – 3 *Toward a Politics of Planet Earth*, Harold Sprout & Margaret Sprout, 500pp, 1971, Van Nostrand, $10.95. Calls for an ecological approach to world politics, emphasizing environmental deterioration, economic interdependence, and the declining

---

[4]Because of the limited number of books in print in some subsections of this chapter's bibliography, a few out-of-print books (marked O.P.) and articles are included.

utitlity of military force; the politics of planet earth must be conducted through non-national actors for any hope of success.

11 – 4 *Peace on the March: Transnational Participation*, Robert Angell, 203pp, 1969, Van Nostrand, O. P. Argues that the growing number of transnational linkages will reduce the chances of war.

11 – 5 *Conflict Resolution and the Structure of the State System: An Analysis of Arbitrative Settlements*, Gregory Raymond, 128pp, 1980, Allanheld Osumn, $22.50. Makes clear that States are the primary participants in world politics, but that the role of intergovernmental organizations and non-State actors are important in resolving conflicts.

11 – 6 *Europe and the United States: The Future of the Relationship*, Karl Kaiser, 146pp, 1973, Columbia, $2.50. Describes the growth of transnational relations between the two continents, particularly the movement of capital, people, and goods.

11 – 7 *International Politics: Foundations of the System*, Werner Levi, 320pp, 1974, Minnesota, $12.50. Doubts that NGOs (Non-Governmental Organizations) or INGOs (International Non-Governmental Organizations) can ever effectively constrain State power.

11 – 8 *Making Peace*, Adam Curle, 301pp, 1971, Tavistock, O.P. Emphasizes the positive contribution of organizations which challenge State power and thus restrain it.

11 – 9 *Transnational Relations and World Politics*, Robert Keohane & Joseph Nye (eds.), 428pp, 1972, Harvard, $6.95. Includes "The Growth of International Non-governmental Organizations in the Twentieth Century," and other essays on world political issues without focusing on national leaders or security issues.

11 – 10 *State and Society in Contemporary Europe,* Jack Hayward & R.N. Berki (eds.), 288pp, 1979, St. Martin's, $22.50. Offers an analysis of the political makeup of East and West European polities.

B. Supra-National Organizations

11 – 11 *Supranationalism and International Adjudication,* Forest Grieves, 266pp, 1969, Illinois, $14.00. Suggests ways in which State conflicts might be adjudicated.

11 – 12 *The European Convention on Human Rights,* Francis Jacobs, 298pp, 1975, Oxford, $29.95. Describes the areas in which the individual, not the State, is sovereign and how, under the European Convention, the individual can appeal against the State to a supranational, judicial arena.

11 – 13 *International Arrangements for Nuclear Fuel Reprocessing,* Abraham Chayes & Bennett Lewis (eds.), 1977, Ballinger, $18.50. Suggests ways in which the reprocessing could be monitored to prevent diversion for nuclear weapons.

11 – 14 *The International Civil Services, Changing Role and Concepts,* Norman Graham & Robert Jordan (eds.). 244pp, 1980, Pergamon, $24.00. A study of the charges that the civil service of UN agencies are politicized and unevenly distributed among the regions, ideologies, and countries of the world; considers also the extent to which this bureaucracy has acquired decision-making discretion of its own.

C. Intergovernmental Organizations

11 – 15 *New International Actors: The United Nations and the European Economic Community,* Carol Cosgrove & Kenneth Twitchett, 272pp, 1970, St. Martin's, $6.95. Thirteen essays on the two most successful new actors in world politics, and an assessment of their performance.

11 – 16 *Networks of Interdependence, International Organizations and the Global Political System,* Harold Jacobson, 486pp, 1979, Knopf, $15.95. Explores the role of intergovernmental and non-governmental international organizations in the world political system. The typology of organizations and the assessment of their performance are particularly valuable.

11 – 17 *Global Bargaining: UNCTAD and the Quest for a New International Order,* Robert Rothstein, 280pp, 1979, Princeton, $4.95. Blames the failure of NIEO negotiations to gain agreement between 1974 and 1977 on both sides; suggests how an intergovernmental organization can aid governments to explore controversial issues.

See also Chapter 5, "International Organization and World Law."

D. Transnational Enterprises

11 – 18 *World Directory of Multinational Enterprises,* John Dunning & John Stepford, 1,500pp, 1980, Facts on File, $195.00. Two volumes of information on the 600 largest multinational corporations, including profit tables, products, main offices, subsidiaries, and other information. Included are 250 American companies, 100 Japanese, plus British, French, German, Italian, and others.

11 – 19 *Storm over the Multinationals: The Real Issues,* Raymond Vernon, 260pp, 1977, Harvard, $15.00. Identifies the major issues concerning the economic, political, and social roles of multinationals.

11 – 20 *Transnational Corporations in World Development: A Re-Examination,* United Nations, 343pp, 1979, United Nations, $12.00. A report of the UN Commission on Transnational Corporations, assessing their political, legal, economic, and social effects.

11 – 21 *Quest for Survival and Growth: A Comparative Study of American, European*

and Japanese Multinationals, Anant Negandhi & B.R. Baliga, 180pp, 1979, Praeger, $27.95. Compares multinational corporation activities in six developing countries — Brazil, India, Malaysia, Peru, Singapore, and Thailand. Conflicts between the host government and the businesses are explored.

11 – 22 *Foreign State Enterprises: A Threat to American Business,* Douglas Lamont, 272pp, 1979, Basic Books, $12.95. Maintains that State enterprises that invest in the U.S. and which compete on world markets have unfair advantages, such as access to nearly unlimited capital, subsidies to gain entree to markets, and scientific, and technological research funds.

11 – 23 *Distortion or Development? Contending Perspectives on the Multinational Corporation,* Thomas Biersteker, 199pp, 1979, MIT, $17.50. A summary of the dependence-producing consequence of TNCs and their role as engines of development, to see if they contradict each other.

11 – 24 *The Sovereign State of ITT,* Anthony Sampson, 373pp, 1980, Stein & Day, $7.95. A study of the International Telephone & Telegraph Company (ITT) from its origin to the present. The author maintains ITT influences many governments, including the U.S. and the USSR, but controls none.

11 – 25 *Bribery and Extortion in World Business,* Neil Jacoby, Peter Nehemkis & Richard Eells, 294pp, 1977, Free Press, $12.95. A summary of the extent to which bribery by governmental officials is a custom and how business officials respond.

11 – 26 *Merchants of Grain,* Daniel Morgan, 387pp, 1980, Penguin, $3.95. A critical assessment of large companies which sell grain abroad. Provides significant information on how grain gets from American farms to foreign consumers.

11 – 28 *Government Controlled Enterprises: International Strategic and Policy Decisions,* Ranato Mazzolini, 400pp, 1979, Wiley, $34.50. Based on extensive interviews with leading executives, governmental officials, and union leaders throughout the nine ECC countries, this study is focused on how policy decisions are made.

11 – 29 *Multinationalism, Japanese Style: The Political Economy of Outward Dependence,* Terutoma Ozawa, 289pp, 1979, Princeton, $16.50. A study of the fast growing multinational enterprises.

11 – 30 *The Japanese Company,* Rodney Clark, 282pp, 1979, Yale, $20.00. A sociological study of the organization of Japanese corporations, the labor-management relationship, and the corporation's place in Japanese society.

11 – 31 *Multinational Corporations and U.N. Politics: The Quest for Codes of Conduct,* Werner Feld, 173pp, 1980, Pergamon, $18.50. A detailed description of the issues in the negotiations and what blocks agreement on a code.

11 – 32 *Multinationals Under Fire, Lessons in the Management of Conflicts,* Thomas Gladwin & Ingo Walter, 689pp, 1980, Wiley, $32.95. Focuses on the non-economic problems multinationals face such as terrorism, governmental policies, and other day-by-day matters.

11 – 33 *Multinationals, Unions, and Labor Relations in Industrialized Countries,* Robert Banks & Jack Stieber, 208pp, 1977, N.Y. State School of Industrial and Labor Relations, $10.00. Brings business and labor leaders together with scholars to consider the impact of multinationals on unions and industrial relations.

11 – 34 *The Economics of Multinational Enterprise,* Neil Hood & Stephen Young, 412pp, 1979, Longman, $19.95. A thorough, empirical and cautious study which concludes "from both theoretical and empirical standpoints . . . the MNE may have negative as well as positive effects on world welfare." The contending views are well-stated, and research confirming and refuting each view summarized.

11 – 35 *The Multinational Corporation, the Nation State, and the Trade Unions; An European Perspective,* Gunnar Hedlund & Lars Otterbeck, 168pp, 1977, Kent State, $15.00. A study of Swedish MNCs, public attitudes about them; and how, given the internationalization of business, conflict can be diminished between management, unions, and the State.

11 – 36 *The Wealth Weapons, U.S. Foreign Policy and the Multinational Corporations,* Ben Wattenberg & Richard Whalen, 350pp, 1980, Transaction, $6.95. Discusses the relevance of non-military economic influence in protecting American vital interests and considers it an important resource if used in "close coordination with U.S. allies and trading partners."

11 – 37 *Alternatives to the Multinational Enterprise,* Mark Casson, 116pp, 1979, Holmes & Meier, $26.00. Why not license technology instead of encouraging direct investment, asks this British economist.

11 – 38 *Functioning of the Multinational Corporation: A Global Comparative Study,* Anant Megandhi (ed.), 294pp, 1980, Pergamon, $29.50.

11 – 39 *Foreign Enterprise in Developing Countries,* Isaiah Frank, 199pp, 1980, Johns Hopkins, $5.95. A report on a survey of ninety multinational corporations with head-quarters in eleven countries. Many interesting questions are raised, and the survey indicates . . . most business leaders are prepared to adapt themselves to the rules imposed by third-world countries.

11 – 40 *Multinationals in Latin America: The Politics of Nationalization,* Paul Sigmund, 426pp, 1980, U. of Wisconsin, $6.50. With the emergence of powerful States, MNCs can be true partners, Sigmund maintains: the cost, dislocations, and other results of nationalization are frequently very high. Cuba, Chile, Peru, and Venezuela are used as examples for this thesis.

11 – 41 *Survey of Research on Transnational Corporations,* United Nations, 533pp, 1979, United Nations, $20.00. An indexed listing of researchers, topics, institutions, and countries plus information on TNCs operation, all of which is designed to help formulate a code of conduct.

11 – 42 *Bibliographical Notes for Understanding the Transnational Corporations and*

the Third World, Harry Strharsky & Mary Riesch (eds.), 237pp, 1975, Cooperation in Documentation & Communication, $3.95. A collection of largely unsympathetic works.

11 – 43 *Bibliography of Multinational Corporations and Foreign Direct Investment* Eric Browndorf, Scott Reimer, & Kenneth Simmonds, 1979, Oceana, $75.00. A collection of largely sympathetic works.

E. International NonGovernmental Organizations

11 – 44 *International NonGovernmental Organizations, Their Purposes, Methods and Accomplishments,* Lyman White, 325pp, 1968, (1951), Greenwood, $16.25. A valuable introduction, typology, and analysis of INGOs, their relations to "intergovernmental organizations," and a listing of these INGOs recognized by the United Nations in 1951.

11 – 45 *Yearbook of International Organizations, 1978 – 79,* Union of International Associations, 1978, International Publications Service, $80.00. Lists 8,200 governmental and nongovernmental organizations, and provides a brief history and description of each.

11 – 46 *Yearbook of International Organizations: Latest Edition,* 1979, Adler, $119.00. This is the latest edition listed in the 1980 – 81 edition of *Books in Print.*

11 – 47 *In Search of a Responsible World Society; the Social Teachings of the World Council of Churches,* Paul Bock, 1974, Westminister $10.00. The focus is on WCC statements from 1925 – 1970; their nature and purpose, and the shifting emphasis from containing Communism to race relations, treatment of ethnic minorities, and relations with third world countries.

11 – 48 *The World Council of Churches in International Affairs,* Darrill Hudson, 336pp, 1977, Royal Institute of International Affairs, O.P. The WCC spends over $16 million per year — its activities in the 1970s are described here. The chapter on South Africa is titled "White Devils"; the WCC's work on race, development and disarmament is in general lauded.

11 – 49 *Amsterdam to Nairobi: The World Council of Churches and the Third World,* Ernest Lefever, 114pp, 1979, Georgetown, $5.00. A critical assessment of the Protestant Church body's endorsement of a "theory of revolution," which supports antidemocratic and often anti-religious political movements.

11 – 50 *The Politics of the Olympic Games,* Richard Espy, 224pp, 1979, U. of Calif. Press, $10.95. Traces the mixture of politics and sports involved despite the wish of the International Olympic Committee that they be kept separate.

11 – 51 *Scientists and World Order : The Uses of Technical Knowledge in International Organizations,* Ernst Haas, Mary Williams & Don Bahai, 378pp, 1976, U. of Calif.,

$17.50. An empirical study of the "roles scientists play in molding international institutions in areas of high technical content (environment, energy, development, health, agriculture, and so forth)" — Foreign Affairs.

11 – 52 *A Voice Crying in the Wilderness: Essays on Problems of Science and World Affairs,* B.T. Feld, 320pp, 1979, Pergamon, $25.00. The Secretary-General of the Pugwash Conferences since 1973 offers a selection of essays on arms control issues discussed at the conferences.

11 – 53 *A Flame in Barbed Wire, the Story of Amnesty International,* Egon Larsen, Norton, O.P. Tells the story of Amnesty International, its work on behalf of prisoners of conscience, and the internal organization as well as effectiveness of the organization.

11 – 54 *Humanitarian Politics, the International Committee of the Red Cross,* David Forsythe, 298pp, 1977, Johns Hopkins, $17.95. A detailed study of how the ICRC operated between 1945 and 1975; the system of control, national affiliation, action on behalf of individuals in war or in other countries, and its role in the development of international law.

11 – 55 *The Foreign Policies of West European Socialist Parties,* Werner Feld (ed.), 149pp, 1978, Praeger, $16.50. Assesses foreign policy changes likely if the French Socialist party comes to power as well as the foreign policies of other Western European Socialist and Communist parties in and out of power.

11 – 56 *The Media Are American, Anglo-American Media in the World,* Jeremy Tunstall, 1979, Columbia, $7.50. A carefully researched study of the effects of U.S. media exports on other countries.

11 – 57 *Whose News? Politics, the Press and the Third World,* Rosemary Righter, 272pp, 1978, Times Books, $12.50. A balanced assessment of international news which maintains that it is neither as biased or unfair as third world leaders claim nor as objective as Westerners might think.

11 – 58 *International News: Freedom under Attack,* Dante Fascall, 320pp, 1979, Sage, $15.00. Four essays on the politics of international broadcasting, the challenge to Western news services, the barring of Western reporters, the move to create government monopolies on the distribution of information in third-world countries and the quality of the existing flow of information.

11 – 59 *Human Factors in International Negotiation,* David Druckman, 1974, Sage O.P. Surveys theories of the role misperception plays and the contribution of INGOs and NGOs to it.

11 – 60 "Transnational Political Interest and the Global Environment," Anne Feraru, 1974, *International Organization.* Offers an analysis of the role of transnational groups at the Stockholm Conference On the Environment, referring to INGOs as international pressure groups within international organizations.

F. NonGovernmental Organizations

11 – 61 *Nongovernmental Forces and World Politics, A Study of Business, Labor and Political Groups,* Werner Feld, 284pp, Praeger, O.P. Offers a useful introduction.

11 – 62 *NPT, The Review Conference and Beyond, Reports of the UNA of the U.S.A. and the Association for the United Nations in the USSR,* 32pp, 1975, UNA of the U.S.A., $2.00. An assessment of a common worry by the two associations.

11 – 63 *Quaker Experiences in International Conciliation,* Mike Yarrow, 308pp, 1979, Yale, $10.00. A brief background statement of Quaker values and reflection on how nongovernmental efforts work to conciliate governments, bracket case studies of Quaker work in the Berlin Crisis (1961), Kashmir (1965), and Nigerian Civil War (1967-70).

11 – 64 *Conflict and Communication: The Use of Controlled Communication in International Relations,* John Burton, 1969, Macmillan, O.P. Describes how Greek and Turkish Cypriot leaders were brought together with six social scientists to discuss possible solutions to the conflict in 1966.

Intro

11 – 65 *Deviance, Terrorism and War, The Process of Solving Unsolved Social Problems,* John Burton, 240pp, 1979, St. Martin's, $22.50. A developer of controlled communication, as a means of discovering solutions to conflict, outlines the technique and its uses in a variety of specific conflicts.

11 – 66 "The Belfast Workshop: An Application of Group Techniques to a Destructive Conflict," Leonard Dobb & William Foltz, *Journal of Conflict Resolution* (Sept. 1973). Fifty-six Belfast Catholics and Protestants gathered for ten days in Scotland in 1972 to explore the attitudes, feelings, politics, and group dynamics that make the conflict in Northern Ireland irreconcilable – a sense of mutual trust develops by the end of the workshop.

11 – 67 "The Impact of a Workshop upon Grass-Roots Leaders in Belfast," Leonard Doob & William Foltz, *Journal of Conflict Resolution* (1974). Describes the effect of several weeks away from Belfast in a controlled setting in which Catholics and Protestants get to know each other, then the impact when they return home.

11 – 68 "Stirling: The Destructive Application of Group Techniques to a Conflict," G. H. Boehringer, V. Zeruolis, J. Bayley & K. Boehringer, *Journal of Conflict Resolution* (June 1974). A critique of the Belfast workshop techniques.

11 – 69 "Rationale, Research, and Role Relations in the Stirling Workshop," Daniel Alevy, Barbara Bunker, Leonard Dobb, William Foltz, Nancy French, Edward Klein, & James Miller, *Journal of Conflict Resolution* (June 1974). A response to the above.

11 – 70 "The Fermeda Workshop: A Different Approach to Border Conflicts in Eastern Africa," Leonard Dobb, William Foltz & Robert Stevens, *Journal of Psychology* (Nov.

1969). Six Somalis, six Ethiopians and six Kenyans gathered with the authors of this article and with several social psychologists to open communications, gain a sense of the good intention of each other and finally to discuss the border conflict.

11 – 71 "The Impact of the Fermeda Workshops on the Conflicts in the Horn of Africa," Leonard Dobb, *International Journal of Group Tensions* (1971).

11 – 72 *The Institute of Pacific Relations, Asian Scholars and American Politics,* John Thomas, 178pp, 1973, U. of Washington Press, $10.95. Founded in 1925, the Institute became a center of controversy when Mao's forces won the Chinese Civil War. This work details both the controversy within the Institute and the "hounding" of its leading scholars.

11 – 73 *Death of a Utopia, The Development and Decline of Student Movements in Europe,* Gianni Statera, 294pp, 1975, Oxford, $13.95. Identifies "perceived power-lessness" as the motives behind student movements, and traces their decline since 1968 to the inability of the ideologists of student power to gain a mass constituency.

11 – 74 *American Students, A Selected Bibliography on Student Activism and Related Topics,* Philip Altbach & David Kelly, 537pp, 1973, Lexington, $25.00. A sixty-page introductory essay is followed by 437 pages listing books and articles on student politics. Neither annotations nor an index is provided, but the works are grouped by subjects.

11 – 75 *The Trade Union Movement in Africa: Promises and Performance,* Wogu Ananaba, 248pp, 1979, St. Martin's, $19.95. A Nigerian describes the restrictions on trade unions in Africa, and calls for rethinking the OAU's condemnation of international affiliation.

11 – 76 *American Religious Groups View Foreign Policy: Trends in Rank-and-File Opinion, 1937 – 1969,* Alfred Hero, Jr., 552pp, 1973, Duke, $19.75. Compares American Protestant, Catholic, and Jewish responses to foreign affairs surveys over a thirty-two year period. Hero laments that U.S. churches have so many ill-prepared to apply their values to foreign policy issues.

11 – 77 *The American Movement to Aid Soviet Jews,* William Orbach, 1979, U. of Mass. Press, $15.00. The origins, history, and tactics of American non-governmental organization efforts to aid Soviet Jewry.

11 – 78 *American Labor in a Changing World Economy,* Ward Morehouse (ed.), 340pp, 1978, Praeger, $12.50. Thirty-three short essays which discuss the impact of trade on American jobs, the Adjustment Assistance Act, the AFL-CIO's work in other countries, multinational corporations, labor standards, and much more.

11 – 79 *Catholic Radicals in Brazil,* Emanuel De Kadt, 304pp, 1970, Oxford, $17.95. A case study of the Movement for Basic Education (MEB) in Brazil, "a small minority among Brazil's committed Catholics" who seek social change.

11 – 80 *The Political Transformation of the Brazilian Catholic Church,* Thomas

Bruneau, 302pp, 1974, Cambridge, $9.95. Traces the changes in social doctrine of the Brazilian Catholic Church.

See also Chapters 20 and 21.

G. Non-State Nations and Terrorism

11 – 81 *Nonstate Nations in International Politics, Comparative-System Analyses,* Judy Bertelsen (ed.), 263pp, 1977, Praeger, $20.00. Presents seven case studies of ethnic groups exercising the authority of States when they request greater autonomy; it concludes with a consideration of various kinds of non-State actors' impact on world politics.

Intro
11 – 82 *The Terrorism Reader, A Historical Anthology,* Walter Laqueur (ed.), 291pp, 1978, NAL, $5.95. Advocates of terrorism from Aristotle on the murder of tyrants to the Baader-Meinhoff Gang present their cases here; Laqueur and others give their analysis. The editor demonstrates that terror is not new, that it has limited effectiveness, is aided today by many governments (Algeria, Libya, East Germany, the Soviet Union . . .), and that terrorists today are often wealthy, from middle to upper income homes, and highly educated.

11 – 83 *A Time of Terror, How Democratic Societies Respond to Revolutionary Violence,* J. Bowyer Bell, 292pp, 1978, Basic Books, $10.95. Bell maintains nationalist movements (Croatian, IRA, South Moluccan, and Palestinian) have a certain legitimacy, while the ideologists (Red Brigade, SLA, and Weather-people) do not. Bell rejects that democratic societies must adopt the tactics of terrorists to succeed in reducing terrorism. Nothing can prevent terrorism.

11 – 84 *War and Terrorism in International Affairs,* Gerado Schamis, 100pp, 1980, Transaction, $3.95. Argues that terrorism is a new form of war against democratic societies and that once recognized as such, it significantly alters our view of international relations.

11 – 85 *Calling a Truce to Terror: The American Response to International Terrorism,* Ernest Evans, 180pp, 1979, Greenwood, $19.95. Assesses the political motives behind much contemporary terrorism, and argues that a successful strategy for dealing with terrorism is to understand its motivation.

11 – 86 *Never Again Without a Rifle; The Origins of Italian Terrorism,* Alessandro Silj, 233pp, 1979, Karx, $11.95. Describes Italian terrorists as indigenous, leftist revolutionaries, not youth gone astray.

11 – 87 *International Terrorism, National, Regional and Global Perspectives,* Yonah Alexander (ed.), 392pp, 1976, Praeger, $5.95. Twelve scholars from different perspec-

tives offer conflicting views on terrorism. Terrorism is considered in the U.S., Latin America, the Middle East, and South Asia.

11 – 88 *Terrorism: Theory and Practice,* Yonah Alexander, David Carlton, Paul Wilkinson (eds.), 280pp, 1979, Westview, $20.00. A search for causes, motives, and the purposes of terrorist movements.

11 – 89 *Ten Years of Terrorism: Collected Views,* Jennifer Shaw, E.F. Gueritz & A.E. Younger, 196pp, 1979, Crane, Russak, $14.95. A collection of papers addressed to terrorism as a problem of the 1970s.

11 – 90 *Terrorism: Threat, Reality, Response,* Robert Kupperman, & Darrell Trent, 450pp, 1979, Hoover, $14.95. Addresses the role of modern technology in aiding and combating terrorism.

Intro
11 – 91 *Self-Determination: National, Regional, and Global Dimensions,* Yonah Alexander & Robert Friedlander (eds.), 392pp, 1980, Westview, $28.75. Authors from different regions of the world examine the principle of self-determination, consider its legal standing, and ask what must change to make the principle both limited and capable of being implemented.

11 – 92 *Insurgency in the Modern World,* Bard O'Neill, William Heaton, & Donald Alberts, 291pp, 1980, Westview, $27,75. Offers case studies of insurgency in Thailand, Oman, Angola, Guatemala, Uruguay, Iraq (Kurds), the PLO, and Northern Ireland. Different conceptions of self-determination provide a portion of the rationale or motivation for terrorism.

11 – 93 *The Terror Network,* Claire Sterling, 357pp, 1981, Holt, Rinehart & Winston/Reader's Digest Press, $13.95. Provides substantial evidence that the Soviet Union sponsors much of the world's politically motivated terrorism with the intention of polarizing non-Communist societies.

11 – 94 *International Terrorism and Political Crimes,* M. Cherif Bassiouni, 624pp, 1975, Thomas, $25.00. An international lawyer offers a definition of terrorism, condemns nonstate nations and State-sponsored terrorism, and seeks to bring both under judicial constraints.

11 – 95 *International Terrorism: An Annotated Bibliography and Research Guide,* Augustus Norton & Martin Greenberg, 218pp, 1980, Westview, $20.00. Offers over 1,000 English language references, a useful categorization of the types of terrorism and of ways to combat it.

H. Individuals

11 – 96 *Individuals and World Politics,* Robert Isaak, 322pp, 1975, Wadsworth, $7.95. At least individuals like Gandhi, Hitler, Lenin, Mao, Wilson, and Kissinger

count. This work traces the impact of such leaders on institutions and on social change.

11 – 97 *Participation and Political Equality, A Seven Nation Comparison,* Sidney Verba, Norman Nie & Jae-on Kim, 1978, Cambridge, $9.95. Provides survey data on political participation in Nigeria, Austria, Japan, India, the Netherlands, Yugoslavia, and the United States.

11 – 98 *Governments and Leaders, An Approach to Comparative Politics,* Edward Feit (ed.), 552pp, 1978, Houghton Mifflin, O.P. A study of the lives of six leaders and their efforts, sometimes successful, to change the societies within which they lived.

11 – 99 *Roger Baldwin: Founder of the ACLU, A Portrait,* Peggy Lamson, 220pp, 1976, Houghton Mifflin, $12.60. A life committed to advancing civil liberties primarily within the United States, but in world politics as well.

11 – 100 *Mission to Hanoi: A Chronicle of Double-Dealing in High Places,* Harry Ashmore & William Baggs, 1968, Putnam, O.P. An attempt to open negotiations in the Vietnam war through private diplomacy.

11 – 101 *The John Doe Associates, Backdoor Diplomacy for Peace, 1941,* R.J.C. Butow, 468pp, 1974, Stanford, $16.95. Study of two Japanese citizens who sought to prevent war but complicated communications between Secretary of State Cordell Hull and Japanese Ambassador Nomura.

11 – 102 *Employment, Growth and Basic Needs: A One-World Problem,* International Labour Organization, 217pp, 1976, Praeger, $3.95. Based on statistics which indicate that basic needs will not be met even by the year 2000 unless significant changes are made. The report outlines the need for employment as a means of overcoming abject poverty and offers a variety of economic and political reforms designed to increase employment.

11 – 103 *New Age Politics, Healing Self and Society,* Mark Satin, 349pp, 1979, Dell, $4.95. The human potential movement's contribution to world politics.

11 – 104 *The Improbable Triumvirate: Kennedy – Khrushchev – Pope John, an Asterisk to the History of a Hopeful Year,* 1962 – 3, Norman Cousins, 1972, Norton, O.P. Personal diplomacy on the verge of reward?

11 – 105 *Tourism – Passport to Development? Perspectives on the Social and Cultural Effects of Tourism on Developing Countries,* Emanuel Kadt (ed.), 320pp, 1979, Oxford, $5.95. Thirteen papers designed to show the maximum benefits for the host country from the tourist trade.

PART IV

NEW PROBLEMS

IN PART I the major concepts and principles of world politics were introduced, as presented by the realist school of thought. The realists say that the State is the central actor in world politics, and security and economic self-interest are the basic motives. The management of military power is seen as the central mechanism for keeping the peace. The balance of power and armament races create a process by which power re-distribution may occur if one country improves significantly its economic or political position as compared with others. War is the ultimate arbiter of conflict and is seen as a continuation of the political struggle by military means.

In Part II the concept of world community and the interrelated goals of arms control and disarmament, of reformed and strengthened international institutions, of world economic and political development, are introduced. The concepts are important in any approach to world politics and are crucial to seeking an end to war. Upon that achievement rests the possibility of a world without war.

In Part III the actors in world politics were introduced. The superpowers, regional powers, and other States were presented as the largest "beasts in the jungle" of world politics. The full range of non-State actors was considered as current contributors to world politics and potentially critical agents in restraining the violent propensities of States.

In this part of *To End War,* world politics is presented from a third standpoint. Here, the overarching concept is not political power or community but "complex interdependence" (Keohane and Nye, *Power and Interdependence*, 12-21). Power intrudes, to be sure, but the complexity of the many issues and the number of actors involved prevent any single concept, such as the national interest or world community, from becoming the single standard for

313

evaluating policies. Domestic constituencies influence different issues. The watchwords are "transnational," not "international," and "regimes," not "governments."

There are many forums in which the issues in a complex interdependent world are negotiated. They include the United Nations Law of the Sea Conference and the UN General Assembly. They include institutions in which the industrialized countries predominate, such as the International Monetary Fund and the Organization for Economic Cooperation and Development (OECD). They include organizations in which developing countries prevail, such as the UN's Conference on Trade and Development (UNCTAD) and the Organization of Petroleum Exporting Countries (OPEC). But the approaches introduced in Parts I and II still intrude: How do these many institutions, bargaining processes, and actors relate to the distribution of power in the world? How do they relate to building a sense of world community?

Two new problems in a world of complex interdependence are considered here. Chapter 12 introduces the pro and con arguments concerning the proposals for a New International Economic Order (NIEO) advocated by the developing States. The implicit assumption of these proposals and the explicit commitment to them by the developing States is clear: world economic development, growth, industrialization, urbanization, and the meeting of consumer demands are acceptable, desirable objectives. In Chapter 13 these objectives are called into question. Chapter 13 presents the idea that there may be "limits to growth" and that those limits may require significant adjustments (e.g. of population growth, consumption patterns, and the utilization of fossil fuel as energy). If not, global catastrophe looms. These elements are examined, as are the contrary arguments which are made on behalf of development.

The crises of the world economic order and of the environment broke into widespread public consciousness in the 1970s. Each problem launched many new organizations and re-shaped the international affairs agenda. In the preceding section of *To End War,* we have tried to identify the perennial elements of world politics. Here we focus on two problems which produced a crisis atmosphere in the 1970s. In the concluding chapter of this Part we turn to a consideration of regional crises and specific issues.

Each of the problem areas or issues which are introduced, pose new challenges to those who seek a world without war. Mutually acceptable and workable agreements must be found, if that sense of community is to be achieved which will sustain global instruments of government.

CHAPTER 12

THE CHANGING WORLD ECONOMIC ORDER

THE OLD ECONOMIC ORDER

In the aftermath of World War II, the United States was the only major industrial power not devastated by the war. As the cold war progressed, the Communist bloc of countries and the Western powers became economically insulated from each other. In such circumstances, the United States and the other industrialized market countries evolved a series of measures that constituted a world economic order. This order was based on the principles of free trade (although there were many exceptions); on the free flow of capital to wherever rewarding investments could be made; and on an international division of labor designed to permit each State to take advantage of its resources. States with climatic conditions and terrain particularly suited to the growth of one commodity concentrated on it, hoping to gain in international trade the revenue for importing food and industrial products. International monetary exchange was handled outside the Communist bloc by the International Monetary Fund (IMF) established at Bretton Woods (1944), and based on the convertibility of other currencies into dollars.

Each of these specific policies concerning trade, investment, commodity and raw material prices, and international monetary exchange, has recently been called into question, as has the intention of those who created the system *(The*

New International Economic Order, 12-45). Such questions arise because of both successes and failures. Japan and Western Europe recovered economically, and indeed, West Germany and Japan grew faster than did the United States. By the 1970s, the Japanese yen and the West German deutschmark were stronger than the dollar, in part because the United States was experiencing large trade deficits. A number of developing countries also became strong competitors of the industrial powers: Taiwan, South Korea, Singapore, Israel, Brazil, Argentina, Mexico, and others. But the more modest economic development of the majority of developing countries has led to demands for a new world economic order. In many international forums, for nearly a decade, questions about the purpose of the existing economic order and the objectives of a new order have been debated.

AN ECONOMIC ORDER: WHAT OBJECTIVES? WHAT SPECIFICS?

The debate concerning what new economic order is desired and needed involves a very wide range of economic issues. There are to be considered what rules, norms, or principles should govern economic transactions between States, as well as what should be the overall objectives. For example, should the new international economic order seek to: 1) Close the economic gap between the developed and developing States? 2) Aid the poorest of the poor within developing States? 3) Make current performance in the market the primary determinant of price or value? Or: 4) Develop mutually beneficial rules modifying the workings of the market and, in addition, provide aid for those who cannot compete in the market?

Among the many questions discussed are the following:

1. *World trade:* Should trade between countries be "free," restricted to protect domestic or new industries, or based on specific, negotiated agreements between countries?

2. *Monetary exchange:* Should trade imbalances be paid by currencies valued at floating exchange rates, or at rates "pegged" to key currencies? Or should the gold standard be reintroduced? Should the International Monetary Fund also be a credit-creating institution and, if so, should developing countries receive credit according to need or financial prudence, or as reimbursement for past exploitation?

3. *Commodities:* Should the price of commodities be tied to the price of industrial goods? Should reserves of commodities be established to stabilize the fluctuation of prices within agreed limits?

4. *Raw materials:* Should the price of oil, bauxite, copper, and raw mate-

rials be set by the producers, by the consumers, by demand, or by political authority?

5. *Investment:* Under what conditions should transnational corporations or States invest in other States? Who should regulate their taxation, operation, and trade? Under what conditions is "nationalization" of foreign investments appropriate? Who should decide the compensation?

6. *Aid:* Should aid be considered a charitable act and thus closely controlled by the donors, or a right of developing countries and thus an automatic transfer payment? At what level should assistance be provided?

7. *Technology transfer:* Should patent restrictions be ended or modified, making it easier to transfer or copy new technological innovations? Should developed countries establish research facilities in developing countries which are devoted to the production of technological innovations appropriate to the host country?

8. *Debt:* Should the debts of existing developing countries be forgiven, refinanced or maintained?

9. *Authority:* Should the decisions concerning all such issues be decided in forums, conferences, and institutions based on the sovereign equality of States, or should significant discretion be given to those States with the largest stakes in the decision?

General and specific answers to each of these questions, as well as others, have been agreed on by some 120 developing countries. These answers are called the proposed New International Economic Order (NIEO).

ORIGINS OF THE NIEO

During the 1950s and 1960s a number of countries remained independent of both the Communist and Western blocs. Under the leadership of Nehru (India), Nasser (Egypt), Tito (Yugoslavia), Nkrumah (Ghana), and Sukarno (Indonesia), the non-aligned countries focused on decolonization and independence of Asian and African States. Leaders from many developing States joined these non-aligned countries in 1970 at Lusaka, Zambia. There the focus turned from political issues to economic concerns. At a subsequent summit meeting in 1973, an "Economic Declaration" and an "Action Program for Economic Co-operation" were affirmed. These statements were then presented to the Sixth Special Session of the UN General Assembly (1974), where they were adopted nearly verbatim as the "Declaration on the Establishment of a New International Economic Order" and the "Programme of Action on the Establishment of a New International Order." At the subsequent regular session of the General Assembly, a "Charter of Economic Rights and Duties of States" was adopted. At the Seventh UN General Assembly Special Session (1975), a resolution on "Development and International Economic Cooperation" was adopted, reaffirming the NIEO proposals. Virtually all international gatherings since 1974 have focused on questions relating to the establishment of a New International Economic Order or on obstacles to doing so, such as the arms race.

The impetus for the NIEO thus comes from third- and fourth-world developing States. It expresses the consensus judgment that the rules and procedures of the economic order established by the developed market States after World War II are responsible for the widening gap between developed and developing States (see Chapter 7). The leaders of the developing countries assert that the goal of an economic order should be to close the economic gap, and this has not happened.

The demand for the NIEO indicates a change in mood in the leadership of the developing countries. It expresses a shift from a perception of the old economic order as at least well-intended to a view of the malign intent of the developed countries. Thus, what was previously seen as a result of economic forces is now considered as imposed by political power. Economic development issues have become politicized, and the developing countries have organized themselves into an economic pressure group demanding greater participation in decision-making, as well as insisting on profound changes in the rules governing world economic transactions. At the very least, they have succeeded in placing economic issues before the international community.

Economic issues might have moved up on the international agenda even if the developing countries had not insisted upon it. By the early 1970s the economy of the United States no longer predominated in the world, although it was still the largest. The dollar was no longer the "bench-mark" on which the value of other national currencies could be fixed. Throughout much of the 1970s, the United States experienced persistent deficits in balance of payments, particularly with Japan and West Germany. Thus, change within the industrialized world required altering the monetary exchange system. Indeed, by the 1980s, a system of complex economic independence had emerged in many areas. There is now widespread agreement on the need to reassess world economic relations, though little consensus exists on what changes should be made.

COMPLEX ECONOMIC INTERDEPENDENCE

Many regions of the world have long been economically interrelated (a price rise in 16th-century Spain caused inflation throughout Europe), and the number of international transactions (exchanges of goods, communications, or people across national frontiers) is now doubling every ten years. These interrelationships, however, do not necessarily bring about dependence of States on each other. The important new feature is that many segments of State economies are heavily dependent upon resources controlled by another State. In turn, the dependent State may possess resources which make the dependence mutual.

There are many reasons why one State may be dependent upon another. A change in the marketing patterns of cereal grains, for example, may push marginal farmers into insolvency. An increase in the price of fuel may require vast alterations of consumption patterns. A population increase without an increase in employment creates widespread joblessness with all its attendant ills. A transnational corporation, whatever its economic impact, brings with it vastly different social mores; industrialization creates new jobs and displaces old ones. New wealth is created, together with more difficult choices about how it should be utilized. Shifts in prices of goods, commodities, and raw materials have an impact throughout the global web of economic relationships. A setback in one sector may force back into absolute poverty those who were just beginning to inch their way out. Thus, the world social situation and the complexity and impact of world economic relationships provide an explosive mixture which may increase political conflict and tensions. Rapid technological innovation and broadly based economic transformations touch and disrupt many lives in ways we scarcely understand.

Such examples of interrelatedness, however, are not identical with interdependence. Some States are more dependent on others rather than interdependent. The United States is dependent upon other countries for energy resources. It currently imports nearly 50% of its domestically consumed oil. In addition, the United States depends on other countries to provide access to raw materials such as bauxite and copper. We import many foods and raw materials from other countries. Other countries, in turn, depend upon the United States for exports of wheat and other cereal grains, or for technology. It is not surprising that the 1970s was the decade in which international economic issues moved to the forefront on the agenda in international organizations, nor is it surprising that so few agreements have been reached, considering the complexity of the issues, the diversity of the States' economic resources and capabilities, the number of contending principles involved, and the number of States involved in the debate over the NIEO.

AIMS OF THE NIEO

The NIEO proposals seek to "eliminate the widening gap between developed and the developing countries and insure steadily accelerating economic and social development. . . ." and claim that the existing order "perpetuates inequality" and "is in direct conflict with current development in international political and economic relations." Politically, the NIEO calls for the "active, full, and equal participation of the developing countries in the formation and application of all decisions that concern the international community," a doctrine often summarized as the "sovereign equality of States."

The text of the "Declaration of the Establishment of a New International Economic Order" assures each State of "full permanent sovereignty . . . over its natural resources and all economic activities . . ." and assures "restitution and full compensation for the exploitation, depletion of, and damages to the natural and all other resources of those States, previously under foreign occupation, alien and colonial domination or apartheid." Restitution for past exploitation is one theme of the NIEO documents, the supremacy of national sovereignty is another.

The NIEO documents refer occasionally to the economic needs of developed countries and they call for cooperation in meeting common development objectives. Among the specific proposals in the NIEO program are:

1. *Trade:* to remove tariff and non-tariff barriers and restrictive business practices; to repay custom duties to the country which was charged duty on its product, to limit expansion of the production of synthetic products when developing countries' products can fulfill the demand.

2. *Food:* to increase food production in developing countries and to decrease the price or provide subsidies for food imported.

3. *Raw Materials:* to facilitate the formation of producer cartels capable of setting prices.

4. *Monetary exchange:* to use the IMF for creating additional credit to developing countries.

5. *Debt reduction:* to reduce debt by obtaining agreement on debt cancellation, a moratorium on payments, a re-scheduling of payments, and a subsidization of interest.

6. *Industrialization:* to promote foreign, public and private investment in developing countries so that they would provide 25 percent of the world's industrial production by the year 2000.

7. *Technology transfer:* to give access on improved terms to modern technology through changing the patent system.

8. *Transnational corporations:* to formulate an international code of conduct for transnational corporations.

9. *Self-reliance:* to promote economic integration at the regional and sub-regional level.

10. *Commodity prices:* to increase stabilization of commodity prices through the creation of buffer stocks purchased by developed countries.

Proposals such as these have been discussed since 1974 in many different North – South forums, such as UNCTAD conferences, GATT, the Tokyo rounds of trade negotiations, the UN Committee of the Whole, and the Conferences on International Economic Cooperation — with agreements on a few matters. A summary of development in three areas — international monetary reform, trade, and transnational corporations — follows with an assessment of obstacles to broader agreement about the changing international economic order.

ISSUE 1: INTERNATIONAL MONETARY EXCHANGE

Any international monetary system must accomplish three purposes: it must provide a mechanism for setting the rates at which more than 100 currencies will be exchanged; it must supply the money to use in payments between central banks in different countries when a trade deficit cannot be erased through a currency transfer; and it must create credit for use in expanding trade if expansion is desired.

As economic transactions between States have increased, it has become more essential that each of these purposes be accomplished. In 1978, the total volume of world trade exceeded $800 billion. Tourist travel, troops stationed on foreign soil, and direct investment by one country in another added to the need for an orderly international monetary exchange. For example, in 1977 the United States, with imports of twenty-nine billion and exports at only ten billion, had a trade deficit with Japan of nineteen billion. How that deficit is paid is a function of how the international monetary system sets the rate at which dollars are exchanged for Japanese yen, or how it provides credit or some other form of payment (such as gold).

History of Monetary Exchange Regime Change

Before World War I (roughly from 1890 to 1914) these transfers were accomplished through an exchange of gold. Gold was not only exchangeable for valued products, it was salable in its own right and possessed the key property which an international monetary or credit system requires: relative stability of value. Directly after World War I and until 1946, a different international monetary regime existed, based on the "gold exchange standard." Under this system, a credit could, but need not, be changed for gold. During World War II the rules, procedures, and norms of the international monetary regime changed again. The International Monetary Fund (IMF) was created and the medium of exchange became the United States dollar. From 1946 to 1971, the dollar remained the standard against which the value of other currencies was decided. The dollar was desired by other countries because it had a stable value and because the United States agreed to exchange it for gold at a fixed $35 per ounce.

In 1971, President Nixon unilaterally initiated a new international regime when he ended the U.S. commitment to exchange dollars for gold at the fixed price. As a consequence, the dollar and other currencies, as well as gold, "floated," their values set by what buyers and sellers were willing to pay for them. Economists differ about what forces were most influential in the ending of convertibility: the diminishing of United States gold reserves, the U.S. trade imbalances with West Germany and Japan, the inflation which resulted in part from the Vietnam war, and the accumulation of dollars held by other countries. Whatever the decisive reason, negotiations began almost immediately among ten industrialized countries within the IMF, and were later broadened to include ten developing countries. From these negotiations emerged proposals for a new international monetary system.

Current Monetary Issues

From 1971 to 1976, discussions continued concerning how to change the charter of the IMF, and agreement on a series of amendments was reached in 1976 at Jamaica (the Jamaica Agreement). These amendments permit the major currencies to float while others have the choice of floating or being "pegged" to the dollar or to SDRs (Special Drawing Rights). The value of a pegged currency varies over a range set by that country's government. Should market conditions push the value of the currency above or below the peg (the middle point of the range), the government buys or releases some of its own currency, to bring its value back within the range. SDRs are a reserve asset or credit issued by the IMF to members in accordance with quotas based on the members' contributions to the IMF.

The 1976 Jamaica Agreement called for the sale of the IMF gold holdings. This effectively de-monetarized gold. The revenue realized has been placed in a trust fund to aid developing countries. In addition, the SDRs are suggested as the Fund's principal reserve asset. The value of the SDRs equals the average worth of the currencies of the sixteen countries, each of which has a volume of world trade exceeding 1% of the total.

These reforms in themselves do not fulfill the NIEO proposal that the IMF become a development agency. However, in addition to the trust fund, the IMF has created three facilities of particular value to developing countries: an extended fund facility, to which credits need not be repaid for three years and which may exceed the quotas allocated to a country by 140 percent; a compensatory-financing facility and a buffer-stock facility. The last two are both set-up to aid countries which have been hurt by commodity price fluctuations.

The combined resources of these facilities, however, do not equal the thirty billion-plus deficit experienced annually by the developing countries. Thus, in the continuing negotiations, developing countries have agreed that the "basis of SDRs allocation should be changed to allocate a greater proportion of newly created SDRs to developing countries than they are entitled to on the basis of quotas" (*The New International Economic Order,* 12-45). The developed countries are unwilling to grant the amount of credits sought by the developing countries. In addition, little consideration is being given to make the base of the IMF regime a one-State, one-vote base or other more egalitarian principle. To do so would, of course, give decisive voice to those who ask that the IMF become an aid-granting institution. Those opposed to the use of the IMF as such a resource-transfer mechanism, cite the dangers of inflation which result from the creation of credit without substantial backing. In addition, they fear that domestic inflationary policies would affect the world economy unless the IMF continues to exercise, as its charter requires of it, "firm surveillance over the exchange rate policies of its members."

In sum, the IMF has been modified both in its economic mechanisms and in the number of members with voices in its decision-making process. The one-State, one vote proposals have been rejected. Some progress has been made in insuring the NIEO request that "one of the main aims of the reformed international monetary system shall be the promotion of the development of the developing countries." Little has been done or even agreed to, however, to assure "the adequate flow of real resources to them."

ISSUE 2: TRADE

The NIEO proposals have been addressed to areas concerning trade, price of agricultural commodities, and access to markets of developed countries for manufactured goods of developing countries. The goal for the developing countries is a significant increase in their share of world trade, which dropped from 25.5 percent in 1963 to 18.6 percent in 1972. Although the OPEC oil price increases swelled the volume of developing countries' trade to 27 percent in 1973, the non-OPEC developing countries' share of trade has not increased.

The Communist countries' share of world trade since 1945 has fluctuated between about eight and twelve percent of the total.

Agricultural Commodities

There are ten "core" commodities which developing countries export to developed countries: coffee, cocoa, tea, sugar, cotton, rubber, jute, sisal, copper, and tin. Seven other commodities combine with the core to account for 75 percent of the exported commodities: wheat, rice, bananas, beef and veal, wool, bauxite, and iron ore. Five of the core ten are now covered by some kind of agreement. Coffee prices, for example, have risen substantially, in part as a result of an agreement among producers. But other commodities are not yet covered, or are covered by agreements which neither stabilize nor raise the price. The index of prices of about forty commodities traded fell from 1952 to 1972. Because many developing countries are heavily dependent upon a single commodity, any fall in prices in that commodity has had a severe impact on export earnings. But the prices on industrial products and minerals which they must import have increased.

To aid those countries with economies tied to the export of one commodity, UNCTAD has developed five basic elements of an integrated commodity program:

1. The establishment of internationally-owned stocks of a wide range of commodities.

2. The establishment of a common financing fund that will make resources available for the acquisition of stocks.

3. The institution, when justified, of a system of medium to long-term commitments to purchase and sell commodities at agreed prices.

4. The institution of more adequate measures to provide compensatory financing to cover shortfalls in export earnings.

5. The initiation of an extensive program of measures to further the processing of commodities by the producing countries themselves.

Some Northern economists who have examined these proposals question whether they will work *(The New International Economic Order,* 12-45). They point out that past schemes have failed because the producing countries lacked the unity to abide by fixed prices, particularly when market conditions forced the prices up. They also point out that the cost of such common stock arrangements might be three to six billion dollars per commodity. They doubt that it is politically feasible to ask the developed countries to increase their taxes to pay for such stocks when doing so will also increase food prices (particularly if oil prices remain high or continue to rise). While agreement in principle has been reached to establish buffer stocks, at this writing there are widely differing views of how the agreement should be implemented.

In short, commodity prices, with few exceptions, remain subject to market conditions. The IMF now lends small amounts to offset cyclical patterns of lost export revenues, and negotiations have reached agreement in principle on establishing buffer stocks. The harder question of who will pay for such buffer stocks, how they will be controlled, and under what circumstances they will be released all remain for further discussion.

In addition to stabilizing or raising the prices of exported commodities, developing countries have sought to gain easier access to markets for their industrial goods. The World Bank estimates that if all tariff and non-tariff restrictions on imports were lifted, developing countries would increase their trade revenues by about $24 billion by 1985. About $21 billion of this would go to middle-income developing countries, and $3 billion to the low-income developing countries whose GNP is under $200 per capita *(The United States and World Development: Agenda 1980,* 7-5).

Some developing countries already have strong markets in the United States. Indeed, in 1977, the United States imported more goods than it exported to the developing countries. Increases of the size that the World Bank estimates are needed, however, would have to be offset by increased exports to developing countries. The case for the NIEO proposals rests on the assumption that significant resource-transfers to developing countries would increase their purchasing power. They would then provide an improved market for United States exports, just as our "New Deal" legislation increased purchasing power, thus stimulating demand and permitting the expansion of production.

Significant domestic opposition can be expected from industries, union, and others threatened by competition from imports. Under UNCTAD rules some imports can be legitimately restricted but the United States actually restricts only a few imports. It can be argued that U.S. regulations are more effective in intimidating potential importers than they are legally successful in excluding them. The Trade Act of 1974 provides for adjustment to industries hurt by imports but in the first years of its operation relatively little was paid to those who claimed adjustment assistance.

There are, in short, many difficult trade-offs to be considered in determining United States trade policy. In a country already running a trade deficit of billions of dollars, it will be very difficult to absorb more imports unless exports also increase. While there is much that could be done to increase U.S. exports, there is also the need to consider measures to increase the purchasing power of developing countries.

ISSUE 3: TRANSNATIONAL CORPORATIONS (TNCs)

Transnational corporations are frequently defined as corporations with manufacturing facilities in two or more countries. Viewpoints on TNCs vary. Some see them as basically exploitative and harmful to the developing countries within which they establish manufacturing facilities (Barnet & Muller, *Global Reach,* 12-66): others see them as vehicles for economic assistance, transferring a great productive, wealth-producing asset to another country. The NIEO proposals fall between these views, calling not for TNC's expropriation but for a code of conduct which would regulate their operations. This implies that developing countries receive some benefits from TNC's operations. But some of the NIEO proposals concerning transnational corporations might be implemented in ways that would lessen the willingness of TNCs to invest in developing countries. These proposals include: 1) regulations preventing interference in the internal affairs of the host countries; 2) regulations to eliminate restrictive business practices and revise previously concluded arrangements to conform to the national development plan; 3) assistance in the transfer of technology on equitable and favorable terms; 4) repatriation of the profits and promotion of reinvestment of profits in developing countries.

These proposals in themselves may seem fair, but their implementation may not be. For example, the NIEO has ruled that compensation for nationalized firms is a matter of domestic rather than international law. In the case of Chile, this led not to compensation for the corporate assets nationalized but to a bill for past "exploitation".

The arguments over a code of conduct for TNCs turn primarily on how one views their past activities. One viewpoint maintains that no code is really needed; the corporation in any case must conform to the rules of the host country and must continue to act as a good citizen of that country. The finance minister of Brazil urges transnational corporations to invest in developing countries. He cites many advantages, including new jobs, enlarging the tax base and the creation of an efficiently-run model production facility. Critics counter that regulations are needed to prevent corporations from shifting their liabilities around to take advantage of different States' taxes, customs, or other laws. In addition, the critics contend that the TNCs drive out local business, dry up credit needed for other investments, export their profits, control technology unfairly through patents, and use their economic influence to affect the politics of the host country. Other critics argue against foreign investment on non-economic grounds: it damages the national morale to accept dependence on foreign investment by implying that neither domestic talent nor resources could produce equivalent benefits. Still other critics argue that in some cases TNCs are of major benefit to the host country — which is considered a problem in South Africa.

At present, each corporation bargains with each host country concerning the arrangements under which it will operate. Although some standardized principles may be helpful, the varied circumstances of developing States will probably prevent the negotiation of a uniform precise code.

OBSTACLES TO AGREEMENT ABOUT A CHANGED WORLD ECONOMIC ORDER

While there is an understandable urgency in the South to achieve a successful resolution of these issues, there is an understandable caution in the North. Some proposals that could severely hurt Northern economies (such as an international monetary exchange system which generates inflation in every currency) would also be harmful to the South. Even those States in the South which have sought to insulate themselves from the world economy would be severely damaged. The North's caution, however, appears to the South to be a delaying tactic. This raises again the question of whether the North's intent is ''malign'' or ''benign.'' The North questions the feasiblity of negotiating with a group of countries with vastly different economic systems, needs, and resources, all lumped together as the ''South.'' A number of NIEO proposals, which help some Southern countries, will hurt others. For example, producer cartels such as OPEC hurt the non-oil exporting Southern countries. Debt cancellation for newly industrialized countries might damage their credit standing even though it might be feasible for the ''poorest of the poor.'' It is those countries which lack raw materials, commodities, or riches in the 200-mile coastal economic zones (created by the Law of the Sea Conference) which are most in need of re-scheduling their debts. Doubts about one another's intentions, the difficulty of negotiating with a group of more than 120 countries, the complexities of the issues and hence the disagreements about the consequences of any specific policies, and the weakness of Northern as well as Southern economies, all pose serious obstacles to successful North-South dialogue.

Such obstacles have been considered in the many forums in which the North–South dialogue now occurs. The South has pushed proposals seeking assured transfers of resources, greater political influence, and has made many proposals to limit the full operation of ''free-market'' principles. The North has sought to negotiate parts of the NIEO package; to link negotiations of their own access to the South's raw materials and to human rights observations. In addition, the North has sought assurances that any automatic transfers will reach those poor whose plight is offered as the justification for such transfers.

Negotiations have not produced satisfactory results from the point of view of developing countries. To be sure, some changes have been made concerning the Internationl Monetary Fund. Commodity price stabilization schemes have been agreed to in principle, although not in detail, and the specific proposals outlined in the NIEO have not been accepted. That in itself is not as damaging to the sense of world community as the fact that very few counter-proposals have been offered by the North. Further negotiations are scheduled.

AT STAKE IN WORLD ECONOMIC ORDER NEGOTIATIONS

The stakes in the dialogue are very high. They include the quality of life for the 800 million to two billion people who live in developing countries in varying degrees of poverty and destitution. They also include many issues directly of interest to the economies of the North: high inflation, unemployment, and slow growth rates, all of which are influenced by the slow rate of growth in most developing countries. Population growth probably will not level off unless and until successful economic development removes the incentive to have a large family as "old-age insurance." The extent to which human rights are respected and to which democratic governments replace authoritarian ones are also likely to be influenced by the outcome of these dialogues. The arenas in which these dialogues take place provide an opportunity to help build a sense of world community; they could also result in permanent divisions, along which continuing, mutually counter-productive conflicts would take place.

BIBLIOGRAPHY

The bibliography in this chapter introduces economic concepts and theories, presents the theoretical arguments for viewing the issues presented here as those inherent in a world of complex interdependence, and provides arguments about the NIEO proposals and the specific issues which they raise. A list of questions which the following books seek to answer is provided on pp. 316-317.

A. Background

12 – 1 *The Growth of the International Economy* 1820 – 1960, A.G. Kenwood & A.L. Lougheed, 328pp, 1971, St. U. of N.Y., $23.00. Provides a history of the totally

unprecedented resources at the disposal of national leadership in nearly every country, and concludes that "trade between countries provides the opportunity for an international division of labour that lead to a better allocation of economic resources and greater productive efficiency in every country."

12 – 2 *The Evolution of the International Economic Order*, W. Arthur Lewis, 81pp, 1978, Princeton, $3.45. Assesses the operation of existing economic orders over the last century and concludes that developing countries do not require transfers of wealth to get rich and that the NIEO proposals are a serious threat to the industrialized-market economies.

12 – 3 *The World Economy: History and Prospect*, W.W. Rostow, 876pp, 1980, U. of Texas, $34.50. Uses theory, perspective, and facts in an attempt to capture the broad sweep.

12 – 4 *The World System of Capitalism: Past and Present,* Walter Goldfrank (ed.), 300pp, 1979, Sage, $8.95. Theoretical and case studies of capitalism from 1700 to the present in the world-systems approach formulated by Immanuel Wallerstein.

12 – 5 *Economic Imperialism,* Kenneth Boulding and Tapan Mukerjee (ed.), 338pp, 1972, U. of Michigan, $4.95. A variety of interpretations of the impact of industrialized countries on developing ones; includes an argument that British rule was economically beneficial to India.

12 – 6 *The Economists,* Leonard Silk, 294pp, 1976, Basic Books, $10.95. Five sketches of the lives and thoughts of U.S. economists (Samuelson, Friedman, Galbraith, Leontief, and Boulding). An informative and useful introduction.

12 – 7 *An Introduction to International Economics,* Chris Milner & David Greenaway, 264pp, 1979, Longman, $13.95. An introductory yet technical description of trade, monetary and development problems.

12 – 8 *The Contemporary International Economy, A Reader*, John Adams (ed.), 501pp, 1979, St. Martin's, $7.95. An anthology introducing economic issues from the perspective of their impact on American personal and national interests.

12 – 9 *Free to Choose: A Personal Statement*, Milton & Rose Friedman, 338pp, 1980, Harcourt, Brace & Jovanovich, $9.95. The case for less governmental coercion and more market place coercion in our lives.

12 – 10 *Asset Markets, Exchange Rates, and Economic Integration,* Polly Allen & Peter Kenen, 585pp, 1980, Cambridge, $55.00. A review of current economic theory, a detailed assessment of the loss of national control over national economic policy; cautious concerning policy.

12 – 11 *Perspectives on Inflation, Models and Policies*, David Heathfield (ed.), 238pp, 1979, Longman, $9.95. Offers an historical overview and monetary, labor cost, oil price, international, Keynesian, and Communist leader's views of the causes of inflation. The competing models are designed to "clarify and weaken prejudices" about the subject.

12 – 12 *OPEC Oil*, Loring Allen, 320pp, 1979, Oelgeschlager, Gunn & Hain, $20.00. An admiring report on OPEC, arguing they have managed oil better than the companies or consumers before them.

12 – 13 *Trading Blocs, U.S. Exports, and World Trade*, Penelope Hartland Thunberg, 197pp, 1980, Westview, $22.00. Describes the influence of the European Community and other blocs on U.S. trade, investment and licensing policy.

B. The Current Situation

12 – 14 *Encyclopedia of the Third World*, George Kurian (ed.), 1,700pp, in two volumes, 1979, *Facts on File*, $85.00. Provides basic facts on 114 nations in Asia, Africa and Latin America, including information on the population, ethnic groups, religion, constitutions, government, foreign policy, economy, defense, food, media, and physical quality of life index.

12 – 15 *1978 Report on the World Social Situation*, 120pp, 1979, United Nations, $5.00. "Analyzes living conditions currently prevailing in developed and developing countries; compares basic aspects of urbanization, employment, the role of women, working conditions," also participation in decision-making.

12 – 16 *World Development Report*, 1978, World Bank, 1978, Oxford, $5.95. Surveys the economic advances made by the less developed countries from 1950-1975, and concludes that "the development progress of the past twenty-five years has exceeded early expectations in many respects." Although average growth rates exceed 3.4 percent, still 800 million or more live in absolute poverty.

12 – 17 *World Economic Survey* 1979-80: *Current Trends in the World Economy*, United Nations, 116pp, 1980, International Pub. Service, $10.00. A valuable compilation of national statistics.

12 – 18 *The Future of the World Economy: A United Nations Study*, Wassily Leontief, et al, 110pp, 1977, Oxford, $6.95. An assessment of the carrying capacity of the environment and the availability of raw materials to sustain industrialization on a world scale. Concludes optimistically: "accelerated development is the only way to feed the world's population and meet other basic economic needs, and the limits to growth are not physical but rather political, social, and institutional in character."

12 – 19 *Catalog, World Bank Publications*, World Bank, 178pp, 1979, World Bank, free. A listing of over 200 publications, some free, some for sale through publishers on the full range of economic development subjects and country-by-country analyses. Write World Bank for current catalogues, 1818 H Street N.W., Washington, D.C. 20433.

12 – 20 *Economic Response: Comparative Studies in Trade, Finance and Growth*, Charles Kindleberger, 308pp, 1978, Harvard, $16.50. A comparison of the effects of

the same economic processes on different areas of Europe during the 19th and early 20th centuries.

C. Analysis

12 – 21 *Power and Interdependence: World Politics in Transition*, Robert Keohane & Joseph Nye, 273pp, 1977, Little, Brown, $6.95 Argues that economic interdependence is far from benign, and power between States far from obsolete: analyzes how international regimes are created by States to regulate and control transnational and interstate relations.

12 – 22 *Power and Money: The Politics of International Economics and the Economics of International Politics*, Charles Kindleberger, 246pp, 1970, Basic Books, $5.75. A good introductory overview of past economic history and current arguments with chapters on the economics of war and of peacekeeping. Both the "conventional" and "radical" arguments are presented. The author's conclusions tend toward the conventional side.

12 – 23 *Politics and Markets: The World's Political-Economic Systems*, Charles Lindblom, 403pp, 1980, Basic Books, $15.95. Methods, values, and the performance of political-economic systems. The author points out that "not all market-oriented systems are democratic, but every democratic system is a market-oriented system"; that "large private corporations" do not fit into democratic theory.

12 – 24 *The Three Worlds of Economics*, Lloyd Reynolds, 344pp, 1971, Yale, $5.95. A study of economic theory (how much is empirical, how much value based) and of capitalist, socialist and developing countries' economic systems. Concludes that "Western" economic theory has limited relevance to the other worlds.

12 – 25 *The Politics of International Economic Relations*, Joan Spero, 324pp, 1977, St. Martin's, $6.95. Rejects the separation between political and economic concerns basic to classical (19th Century) liberals and maintains that "international economic relations, in and of themselves, are political relations," e.g. the dominant political power or powers have always set the economic rules. Explains why the developing countries want an increased voice in economic institutions.

12 – 26 *Development Co-operation 1979 — Review*, Organization for Economic Cooperation and Development, 292pp, 1979, OECD, $10.00. An annual review of North-South issues such as trade, concessional and non-concessional transfer, and monetary exchange with statistics on each.

12 – 27 *The Developing Countries and the World Economic Order*, Lars Anell & Birgitta Nygren, 230pp, 1980, St. Martin's, $22.50. Challenges both the North and South views of the NIEO.

12 – 28 *Crisis In the World Economy*, Andre Frank, 366pp, 1980, Holmes & Meier,

$9.75. A Marxist analysis of the crises in the democracies, with criticisms of the Soviet Union for helping ease the situation by participating in the world economy, and of the developing countries for negotiating terms of access.

12 – 29 *The Third World Reassessed*, Elbaki Hermassi, 230pp, 1980, California, $15.00. Argues that Western and contemporary non-Western approaches to understanding the third world are heavily dependent upon concepts derived from European experience and thus the reality of third world life goes largely unnoticed.

12 – 30 *Analyzing Global Interdependence*, Hayward Alker, Jr., Lincoln Bloomfield, Nazli Chourci, 4 volumes, 1974, MIT, O.P. A detailed description of forms of interdependence.

12 – 31 *Beyond Boom and Crash*, Robert Heilbroner, 111pp, 1978, Norton, $2.95. Maintains that the environment and energy crises call for planning to permit growth, and thus socialism of some sort is necessary.

12 – 32 *Vain Hopes, Grim Realities: The Economic Consequences of the War*, Robert Stevens, 229pp, 1976, Franklin Watts, $4.95. Estimates the total economic costs of the Vietnam war to the U.S. at $842 to $875 billion (1969) dollars, maintains that post-war inflation, devaluation of the dollar, stagflation, and reduced domestic and international assistance programs are unrecognized consequences of the war.

12 – 33 *A World Divided, the Less Developed Countries in the International Economy*, Gerald Helleiner (ed.), 289pp, 1976, Cambridge, $14.95. Describes the origins and depth of the divide.

12 – 34 *The Weak in the World of the Strong, The Third World Countries in the International System*, Robert Rothstein, 384pp, 1977, Columbia, $16.50. Accepts that the developing countries share a "strongly felt sense of deprivation and resentment against the developed countries and a growing conviction that the rules of the international system are deliberately rigged against them," and concludes that as the developing countries put their own economic and political systems in order, the developed countries should be more responsive.

12 – 35 *The Power of Nations, The Political Economy of International Relations*, Klaus Knorr, 353pp, 1975, Basic Books, $6.95. A general survey and analysis of concepts concerning international relations which concludes that relationships between capitalist States and developing States are so complex that they are exploitative.

12 – 36 *Analyzing the Third World: Essays from Comparative Politics*, Norman Provizer (ed.), 510pp, 1978, Schenkman, $8.95. Seventeen essays reprinted from "Comparative Politics" focus on modernization in the third world.

12 – 37 *Third World Urbanization*, Janet Abu-Lughod & Richard Hay (eds.), 395pp, 1977, Methuen, $7.95. A wide-ranging anthology on urbanization, including selections from Ibn Khaldun, Machiavelli, Marx, and Engels, and contemporary authors. Among the subjects discussed are migration from rural areas, inequality, and dependency on other societies, as well as the UN declaration on "Human Settlements."

12 – 37A *The Political Economy of Income Distribution in Turkey*, Ergun Ozbudun & Aydin Ulusan, 625pp, 1980, Holmes & Meier, $45.00. The first in a series of books on developing countries prepared as a joint project with the Woodrow Wilson School of Public and International Affairs and a group of scholars from developing countries.

D. The New International Economic Order (NIEO)

12 – 38 *The Objectives of the New International Economic Order*, Ervin Laszlo, Robert Baker, Jr., Elliot Eisenberg, Venkata Raman, 288pp, 1978, Pergamon, $17.60. Traces the original formulations of twenty-five NIEO proposals (1970 – 1975), their development by UN sources (1975 – 78), the contribution of international bodies (1974 – 78), and a summary of national proposals in 1978.

12 – 39 *An International Redistribution of Wealth and Power: A Study of the Charter of Economic Rights and Duties of States*, Robert Meagher, 301pp, 1979, Pergamon, $27.50. A hopeful assessment of the first years (1974 – 1977) of North – South negotiations which concludes that redistribution will be successful.

12 – 40 *Alternative Views of the New International Economic Order, A Survey and Analysis of Major Academic Research Reports*, Jorge Lozoya, Jaime Estevez & Rosario Green, 146pp, 1980, Pergamon, $17.50. A publication prepared by the United Nations Institute for Training and Research (UNITAR) and the Center for Economic and Social Studies of the Third World (CEESTEM), summarizing divergent views and providing a forty-two page bibliography.

12 – 41 *The Obstacles to the New International Economic Order*, Ervin Laszlo, et al., 170pp, 1980, Pergamon, $17.50. One of seventeen books in a series prepared by UNITAR and CEESTEM, this one defining social, economic, and political obstacles which can be overcome.

12 – 42 *The Structure of the World Economy and Prospects for a New International Economic Order*, Ervin Laszlo & Joel Kurtzman, (ed.) 117pp, 1980, Pergamon, $15.00. Offers Northern and Southern perspectives on the obstacles to the creation of an NIEO and assesses the role of international law in its creation.

12 – 43 *Latin America and the New International Economic Order*, Jorge Lozoya & Jaime Estevez (eds.), 112pp, 1980, Pergamon, $15.00. A group of Latin American scholars assess the impact of NIEO objectives on their region.

12 – 44 *The Financial Issues of the New International Economic Order*, Jorge Lozoya & A.K. Bhattacharya (eds.), 256pp, 1980, Pergamon, $20.00. Examines the mechanisms for transferring wealth through banks, IMF, debt cancellation, and aid, plus the use of OPEC funds to promote self-reliance among developing countries.

The above seven books are among over fifty volumes in "The New International Economic Order (NIEO) Library." Complete list is available from Pergamon Press, Maxwell House, Fairview Park, Elmsford, N.Y. 10523

Intro

12 – 45 *The New International Economic Order: The North – South Debate*, Jagdish Bhagwati (ed.), 390pp, 1977, MIT, $9.95. The editor's introduction provides an exceptionally clear and concise presentation of the contending points of view. Thirteen articles with comments and a concluding panel report provide information and perspective on the proposals.

12 – 46 *Global Bargaining: UNCTAD and the Quest for a New International Economic Order*, Robert Rothstein, 286pp, 1979, Princeton, $4.95. An attempt to spell out the existing, informal and formal rules for bargaining over non-security issues and how they might be reformed.

12 – 47 *Legal Aspects of the New International Economic Order*, Kamal Hossain, 300pp, 1980, Nichols, $32.50. Identifies the legal requirements of the NIEO proposals, such as laws regarding sovereignty, economic rights and duties of States, transfer of technology, and the law of the sea.

12 – 48 *A New International Economic Order: Toward a Fair Redistribution of the World's Resources*, Jyoti Singh, 135pp, 1977, Praeger, $18.95. Maintains that "problems of economic and social development" have replaced war and peace as "the focal points" of international relations, and traces the origins of the NIEO proposals to a desire for economic independence.

12 – 49 *Issues and Prospects for the New International Economic Order*, William Tyler (ed.), 195pp, 1977, Lexington, $18.95. A concise introduction to the agenda of the NIEO and an examination of the specific issues.

12 – 50 *Economic Issues and National Security*, Klaus Knorr & Frank Trager (eds.), 330pp, 1978, Regents Press of Kansas, $7.50. Recognizes that an interdependent world is one in which new forms of threat and counter-threat to a nations's security and welfare are encountered and considers who obtains advantage from oil, trade, and monetary institutions.

12 – 51 *Beyond Dependency, The Developing World Speaks Out,* Guy Erg & Valeriana Kallab (eds.), 259pp, 1975, Overseas Development Council, $3.95. Official and non-governmental statements plus essays by scholars (all from developing countries) reflect on interdependence, ocean issues, North – South bargaining, population and multnational corporations.

12 – 52 *Moving Toward Change: Some Thoughts on the New International Economic Order*, UNESCO, 135pp, 1976, UNESCO, $4.00. Presents background on the NIEO proposals and defines UNESCO's contribution to the formulation and possible implementation of the proposals.

2 – 53 *Economics and World Order: From the 1970s to the 1990s*, Jagdish Bhagwati (ed.), 365pp, 1972, Macmillan, $5.95. A variety of world order problems analyzed from a Democratic Socialist perspective.

12 – 54 *Equality of Opportunity Within and Among Nations*, Khadija Haq (ed.), 223pp,

1977, Praeger, $24.95. A report of a conference which maintains that a new economic order is needed to achieve equality of opportunity. The consensus of the conference is that equality of opportunity, not result, is the goal; closing the gap within developing countries is urgent; market mechanisms are not helpful when the poor have little purchasing power; political participation in decisions is essential both within and between States.

12 – 55 *Partners in Tomorrow: Strategies for a New International Order*, Antony Dolman and Jan Van Ettinger (eds.), 266pp, 1978, Dutton, $9.95. Twenty-seven scholars assess the status of the North – South dialogue. Contributors are from over fifteen countries.

12 – 56 *The New Economics of the Less Developed Countries, Changing Perceptions in the North-South Dialogue*, Nake Kamrany (ed.), 346pp, 1978, Westview, $27.50. Theoretical articles about the range of NIEO proposals are contrasted with empirical studies on Taiwan, South Korea, Brazil and Mexico.

12 – 57 *RIO, Reshaping the International Order*, Jan Tingerben, 432pp, 1976, Signet, $2.50. Twenty-one specialists call for "fundamental structural change, not marginal reform" of the old economic order.

12 – 58 *The New International Economic Order, A U.S. Response,* David Denoon (ed.), 256pp, 1979, N.Y.U. Press, $8.95. A balanced assessment of alternative policy strategies for the U.S. in response to the NIEO proposals.

12 – 59 *Policy Alternatives for a New International Economic Order, An Economic Analysis*, William Cline (ed.), 392pp, 1979, Praeger, $7.95. An attempt to assess quantitatively the impact of such NIEO issues as commodity agreements, grain reserves, food aid, international trade, external debt obligations; an accumulative assessment by the editor of all the proposals.

12 – 60 *Sovereignty over Natural Resources*, M.S. Rajan, 176pp, 1978, Humanities, $8.75. Argues that national sovereignty over national resources provides the answer to who will control them.

E. Transnational Corporations

12 – 61 *Sovereignty at Bay, the Multinational Spread of U.S. Enterprises*, Raymond Vernon, 326pp, 1971, Basic Books, $12.95. An introduction to the spread of multinational production which argues that in time a multi-lateral agency must regulate the MNCs to derive the social benefits MNCs can help to provide.

12 – 62 *The Multinational Corporation and Social Change*, David Apter & Louis Goodman (eds.), 235pp, 1976, Praeger, $10.95. Socialists and capitalists consider the role which the MNCs play in internationalizing production. Raymond Vernon, Ronald Muller and Harry Magdoff join the editors and others in conflicting assessments.

12 – 63 *The International Corporation: A Symposium*, Charles Kindleberger (ed.), 415pp, 1970, MIT, $9.95. Eighteen economists and political scientists examine the theory of direct foreign investment, the legal, political, and economic implications, and the prospects for the future.

12 – 64 *People-Profits, The Ethics of Investment*, Charles Powers (ed.), 214pp, 1972, CRIA, $2.95. Business leaders and critics discuss the ethical responsibilities of multinational business leaders, stockholders, and investors, such as churches, to determine the consequence of MNCs activity.

12 – 65 *Taming the Giant Corporation, How the Largest Corporations Control Our Lives*, Ralph Nader, Mark Green, Joel Seligman, 312pp, 1976, Norton, $3.95. A biting assessment of corporations' record in product safety, control of markets, and in circumventing regulations. Makes the case for federal incorporation rather than state.

12 – 66 *Global Reach: The Power of the Multinational Corporations*, Richard Barnet & Ronald Muller, 508pp, 1975, Simon & Schuster, $5.95. A study of MNCs which sets out to answer this question: "Is the global corporation mankind's best hope for producing and distributing the riches of the earth . . . or . . . is their vaunted rational integrated world economy a recipe for a new stage in authoritarian politics, an international class war of huge proportions, and, ultimately, ecological suicide?" They conclude that the "global corporation aggravates the problems of mass starvation, mass unemployment, and gross inequality."

12 – 67 *Nationalization of Multinationals in Peripheral Economies*, Julio Faindez & Sol Picciotto, 1979, Holmes & Meier, $27.50. Argues for nationalization.

12 – 68 *The Multinational Corporation and Social Policy, Special Reference to General Motors in South Africa*, Richard Jackson (ed.), 113pp, 1974, Praeger, $2.50 A summary of a conference bringing together corporate managers and their critics to analyze the economic, political, and ethical implications of corporations which operate in developing countries, and in this case, South Africa.

12 – 69 *Transfer Pricing and Multinational Enterprises*, OECD, 100pp, 1979, Organization for Economic Cooperation and Development, $9.00. "Concerns the determination of acceptable prices for establishing taxable profits when transfers of goods, services and technology take place, or when loans are made, between associated enterprises situated in different countries."

12 – 69A *Private Power: Multinational Corporations for the Survival of Our Planet*, Axel Madsen, 258pp, 1980, Morrow, $12.95. The case for multinationals as pragmatic organizations. far more capable than governments of effectively producing goods and services.

12 – 70 *International Investment and Multinational Enterprises*, OECD, 69pp, 1979, OECD, $6.00. Review of the 1976 Declaration and Decisions. Guidelines and Code of Conduct, 28pp, 1979, $3.00.

F. Monetary Exchange

12 – 71 *Money in International Exchange: The Convertible Currency System*, Ronald McKinnon, 294pp, 1979, Oxford, $7.95. A largely non-technical analysis of how the current monetary exchange system resolves imbalances in trade between countries.

Intro
12 – 72 *Organizing the World's Money, The Political Economy of International Monetary Relations*, Benjamin Cohen, 310pp, 1977, Basic Books, $11.95. A useful analysis for the layperson, introducing the history, current issues, and principle alternative systems.

12 – 73 *The Origins of International Economic Disorder: A Study of United States International Monetary Policy from World War II To The Present*, Fred Block, 282pp, 1977, California, $4.95. Seeks to clarify "the ways in which specific international monetary arrangements both reflect and influence the distribution of political economic power among the major capitalist countries." Makes the case that the Bretton Woods system was designed to subordinate Western Europe to the U.S., both economically and politically.

12 – 74 *The International Money Game*, Robert Aliber, 312pp, 1976, 3nd ed., Basic Books, $6.95. Introduces the history and current ways in which countries, which use monetary policies primarily for domestic purposes, must seek to regulate the exchange of currencies and the supply of international monies.

12 – 75 *The International Monetary System: History, Institutions, Analyses*, Robert Carbaugh and Liang-Shing Fan, 176pp, 1976, U. Press of Kansas, $12.00. A brief history of the Bretton Woods gold system of International Monetary Exchange, a description of subsequent reforms, and an assessment of proposals for further reforms.

12 – 76 *Quest for World Monetary System: Gold-Dollar System and Its Aftermath*, Milton Gilbert, 255pp, 1980, Wiley, $19.95. Argues that the price of gold has to increase to help stabilize the international monetary system.

12 – 77 *Money and Monetary Policy in Interdependent Nations*, Ralph Bryant, 600pp, 1980, Brookings, $12.95. Stresses the ways that national and international decision-making institutions affect each other.

G. Transfer of Technology

12 – 78 *Appropriate Technologies for Third World Development*, Austin Robinson (ed.), 417pp, 1979, St. Martin's, $32.50. An empirically based assessment of what scale of technology is most efficient in developing countries.

12 – 79 *Mobilizing Technology for World Development*, Jairam Ramesh & Charles Weiss, Jr., 240pp, 1979, Praeger, $16.95. A report of a Jamaica symposium discussing how technology transfer can benefit both North and South.

12 – 80 *Soft Technologies, Hard Choices*, Colin Norman, 48pp, 1978, Worldwatch, $2.00. Significantly broadens the definition of what constitutes appropriate technology; highlights the crucial choices in deciding.

H. Population

12 – 81 *World Population and Development, Challenges and Prospects*, Philip Hauser (ed.), 704pp, 1979, Syracuse, $9.95. Seventeen experts assess current population growth and economic development problems in an effort to seek coordinated population and development policies.

12 – 82 *Population and Development*, Yves Bizien, 202pp, 1979, Praeger, $21.95. An overview of the relationship which finds a correlation between fertility and socio-economic variables.

12 – 83 *The Poverty of Nations: The Political Economy of Hunger and Population*, William Murdoch, 382pp, 1981, Johns Hopkins, $7.50. Argues that poverty underlies population growth and that aid, trade, and technology can help; encourages, or at least not blocks, the path to power for revolutionary Socialist organizations as the preferred prescription.

I. Food

12 – 84 *People and Food Tomorrow: The Scientific, Economic, Political, and Social Factors Affecting Food Supply in the Last Quarter of the 20th Century*, Dorothy Hollingsworth & Elizabeth Morse, (eds.), 1976, International Ideas, $39.60. A comprehensive overview.

12 – 85 *Food for the Future: How Agriculture Can Meet the Challenge*, Keith Campbell, 188pp, 1979, Nebraska, $12.50. Advocates a research effort in developing countries similar to that which succeeded by dramatically increasing U.S. farm yield since 1945.

See also Chapter 7.

J. Trade

12 – 86 *The New Protectionism, the Welfare State and International Trade*, Melvyn Krauss, 115pp, 1978, N.Y.U. $4.95. Studies the attempt to defend jobs threatened by imports.

12 – 87 *International Inequality and National Poverty*, Keith Griffin, 191pp, 1979, Holmes & Meier, $32.00. Argues that world trade and investment patterns exaggerate inequality.

12-88 *The Tokyo Round of Multilateral Trade Negotiations*, Report by the Director General of GATT, 196pp, 1979, UNIPUB, $10.00. A detailed analysis of the then-just-completed round of negotiations which describes the negotiating positions and the results.

12-89 *International Trade Under Communism; Politics and Economics*, Franklyn Holzman, 235pp, 1976, Basic Books, $15.00. Both theory and practice.

12-90 *The Theory of Dumping and American Commercial Policy*, William Wares, 118pp, 1977, Heath, $15.95. Defines "dumping" as price discrimination in international trade, e.g., selling a product at a lower price in a foreign market rather than a domestic one. Studies U.S. policy designed to regulate the practice and offers policy recommendations.

K. Politics

12-91 *Access to Power: Politics and the Urban Poor in Developing Nations*, Joan Nelson, 463pp, 1979, Princeton, $6.95. A study of the political role of the urban poor in third world cities; violent and reform movements are studied as are class, social, and ethnic economic development.

12-92 *Legislatures in Development: Dynamics of Change in New and Old States*, Joll Smith and Lloyd Musolf (eds.), 407pp, 1979, Duke, $19.75. An assessment of the role of legislatures in political and economic development.

INF
12-93 *The Politics of Global Economic Relations*, David Blake, Robert Walters, 240pp, 1976, Prentice-Hall, $8.50. Describes the threat of interdependence and a result: The U.S. is now "of necessity engaging itself with the rest of the world . . . as opposed to maintaining freedom of action by either avoiding formal multilateral commitments or shaping them unilaterally."

12-94 *Race and State in Capitalist Development*, Stanley Greenberg, 489pp, 1980, Yale, $11.50. Assesses racism and economic self-interest as motivating forces in South Africa, Israel, Northern Ireland, and Alabama; combines Marxist categories, facts, and enough open-mindedess to qualify, if not change, the categories.

L. Specific Countries

12-95 *The Political Economy of Underdevelopment: Dependence in Senegal*, Rita O'Brien (ed.), 288pp, 1979, Sage, $8.95. Includes both Marxist and "structuralist" analysis of Senegal's economic history from 1600 to 1973. Primary responsibility for Senegal's economic backwardness is placed on external forces, not on its climate or internal cultural or political traditions.

12 – 96 *The Long Transition: Building Socialism in Tanzania*, Idrian Resnick, 416pp, 1980, Monthly Review, $18.50. Provides a sympathetic history of the effort to promote Socialism in the face of ''the difficulties of managing the social transition with people who have little commitment to the ideology'' (Publishers' blurb).

12 – 97 *Bangladesh: The Test Case for Development*, Just Faaland and J. Parkinson, 203pp, 1976, Westview, $26.50. Estimates that in excess of $1.5 billion is needed per year for a decade to meet minimum economic needs.

12 – 98 *The Political Economy of Distribution: Equality Versus Inequality*, Michael Ward, 208pp, 1978, Elsevier, $16.95. Seeks to identify the determinants of inequality inside and outside a country.

12 – 99 *Growth with Equity, The Taiwan Case*, John Fei, Gustav Ranis, & Shirley Kuo, 300pp, 1980, Oxford, $5.95. Indicates how Taiwan achieved rapid growth and a more equitable distribution of income.

12 – 100 *Reducing Global Inequities*, Howard Wriggins & Gunnar Adler-Karlsson, 191pp, 1978, McGraw-Hill, $5.95. Emphasizes changes needed in both developed and developing countries to eliminate abject poverty.

12 – 101 *Economic Growth and Structural Change in Taiwan, The Postwar Experience of the Republic of China*, Walter Galenson (ed.), 519pp, 1979, Cornell, $29.50. Seven economists assess how Taiwan achieved the NIEO goals without the NIEO.

12 – 102 *Unequal Development, An Essay on the Social Formations of Peripheral Capitalism*, Samir Amin, 440pp, 1977, Monthly Review, $6.50. Transposes Marxist terms from class to international conflict, and concludes that the third world is poor because the first world is rich.

12 – 103 *Economic Growth and Distribution in China*, Nicholas Lardy, 244pp, 1978, Cambridge, $24.95. Maintains that China has achieved rapid growth with equitable distribution of income.

12 – 104 *Guyana Emergent:The Post-Independence Struggle for Nondependent Development*, Robert Manley, 158pp, 1979, G.K. Hall, $14.50. In praise of non-dependent (i.e. self-sufficient) development and the political base which made the experiment possible.

12 – 105 *Latin America and World Economy: A Changing International Order*, Joseph Grunwald (ed.), 320pp, 1978, Sage, $9.95. Different writers describe the emergence of Mexico and Brazil as economic middle-weights, discuss Latin America's economic relations with non-hemispheric States; present regional integration issues with problems of financing development and regulating the role of TNCs.

12 – 106 *China and the World Food System*, N. Doak Barnett, 128pp, 1979, Overseas Development Council, $5.00. Offers statistical evidence that Chinese food production increases have barely kept ahead of population growth and that increases ''lagged behind the average for Asia (including that of India).'' In the 1980s, Chinese imports of food will probably increase from about five million tons to ten to twenty million tons.

12 – 107 *Diversity and Development in Southeast Asia; The Coming Decade,* Guy Pauker, Frank Golay & Cynthia Enloe, 190pp, 1977, McGraw Hill, $5.95. Written before the Vietnamese invasion of Cambodia and therefore at best premature; the focus is nonetheless on Vietnam as a regional economic and military power.

12 – 108 *India's Political Economy, 1947 – 1977, The Gradual Revolution,* Francine Frankel, 1978, Princeton, $12.50. A study of the tension between seeking to reduce economic disparities between the rich and the poor and a desire to avoid disruptive violence in attacking the rich.

12 – 109 *The Impact of International Economic Disturbances on the Soviet Union and Eastern Europe,* Egon Neuberger & Laura Tyson, 501pp, 1980, Pergamon, $60.00. Studies the impact of inflation, energy shortages, and other economic disturbances on economies which are considered immune to them.

12 – 110 *Britain's Economic Performance,* Richard Caves & Lawrence Krause, (eds.), 388pp, 1980, Brookings, $7.95. Describes the slow growth, unemployment, inflation, and the impact of the North Sea oil; but concludes that productivity, not oil, is the key to better performance.

M. Assessing Performance

12 – 111 *Measuring the Condition of the World's Poor, The Physical Quality of Life Index,* Morris Morris, 173pp, 1979, Pergamon, $5.95. Describes the need for an indicator of economic conditions of the poor other than GNP and why the PQLI fills the need.

12 – 112 *Income Distribution Policy in Developing Countries: A Case Study in Korea,* Irma Adleman & Sherman Robinson, 346pp, 1978, Stanford, $12.50. Based on the conviction that development policy must shift from ''economic growth and industrialization toward an explicit concern with equity and the alleviation of poverty.'' The authors suggest two strategies are needed, one aimed at the urban, another at the rural poor. South Korea has done best in this.

N. Policy Proposals

12 – 113 *Beyond the North – South Stalemate,* Roger Hansen, 320pp, 1979, McGraw – Hill, $12.95. Calls for a constructive U.S. and developed countries' response to the NIEO proposals, adopts those which appear mutually beneficial, and offers counter-proposals to those considered unacceptable.

12 – 114 *U.S. Foreign Policy and the New International Economic Order,* Robert Olson, 184pp, 1981, Westview, $20.00. A detailed account of the NIEO negotiations from 1974 to 1980 and a consideration of an appropriate response by the U.S. Concludes that rapid change during the period has rendered obsolete most of the proposals.

12 – 115 *Trilateral Commission, Task Force Reports:* 9-14, Trilateral Commission, $13.50. Offers advice on managing the problems of a complex interdependent world.

12 – 116 *The Global Economic Challenge: Trade, Commodities, Capital Flows,* 1978, UNA Policy Panel, UNA of the USA, $3.00. First in a series dealing with economic issues.

12 – 117 *The Global Economic Challenge: Trade Policy, Energy and Jobs, and Technology Transfer,* UNA Policy Panel, UNA of the USA, $3.00.

12 – 118 *America and the World Political Economy: Atlantic Dreams and National Realities,* David Calleo and Benjamin Rowland, 384pp, 1973, Indiana, $3.95. Argues that only national cultures exist now and for the foreseeable future, and maintains that the nation-State is the only viable political unit. Main concern is to reorientate national economic policy to establish a "liberal world economic system, i.e., one based on free trade, investment across national boundaries,and economic self-sufficiency.

12 – 119 *Interfutures, Facing the Future: Mastering the Probable and Managing the Unpredictable,* OECD, 425pp, 1979, Organization for Economic Cooperation and Development, $20.00. Offers alternative scenarios for long-term world development addressing population, energy, raw material and social constraints on growth.

12 – 120 *Sharing the World's Resources,* Oscar Schachter, 172pp, 1977, Columbia, $10.00. Seeks to give "equitable sharing" a specific and politically acceptable meaning, and examines the utilization of ocean resources, technology, and food as areas where contending moral and practical claims can be reconciled. The focus is on "equity in distribution not reward for labor as achievement."

INF

12 – 121 *North-South, A Program for Survival, A Report of the Independent Commission on International Development Issues Under the Chairmanship of Willy Brandt,* 320pp, 1980, MIT, $4.95. An analysis of the next twenty years with both immediate and long-range policy recommendations. The members of the Commission reflect diverse views, but all agree on the specifics.

CHAPTER 13

THE ENVIRONMENT:
A LIMIT TO GROWTH?

THE possibility of an ecological crisis has led many people to realize that this world is characterized by complex interdependence. As our natural environment deteriorates, many revise their thinking about economic growth (was Thomas Malthus right after all?), and ethics (who is to survive in a time of scarcity?). Can national institutions resolve the problems or are new international or transnational agencies required? The contending schools of thought about the ecological crisis and its implications for international conflict are presented in this chapter.

THE NEO-MALTHUSIAN TRAP

By the late 1960s the impact of the post-World War II economic boom was being felt around the world. Issues, such as the spread of pesticides (DDT), oil spills from tankers (Torrey Canyon) and boom drilling platforms (Santa Barbara Channel), severe river pollution (Rhine, Volga, Ohio, Danube), and pollution of the oceans were being noticed in many States, particularly those industrialized. When such problems were seen as linked to industrial growth, the population explosion, a global food crisis, and to "quality of life" concerns, there seemed genuine cause for alarm.

Those sharing the sense of alarm revitalized an old science — ecology — and began to develop a coherent body of thought analyzing and offering solutions to environmental concerns. Others noted the similarity in the contemporary mood and analysis to that of Thomas Malthus. Malthus (1766 – 1834) had argued that, because population grows exponentially (2, 4, 16...) and food supply grows only arithmetically (1, 2, 3, 4 ...), population would some day outstrip food supply. He feared that violent conflicts over basic necessities would then result between the "have" and "have not" countries. This thesis earned for economics the name "the dismal science." Now, 200 years later, a new dimension has been added: the rising expectations of a growing world population can apparently be met only by burning fossil fuels which may do irreparable damage to the environment.

The titles of many books published in the 1970s indicate the alarm over the ecological crisis: *This Endangered Planet* (13-4), *Planet in Peril, Mankind at the Turning Point* (13-3), etc. What led to this sense of alarm? Is there a moral imperative to limit consumption, and if so, by how much? Or is the change in life styles calling for just that: a matter of preference?

THE TRAP DEFINED

A popular definition of the Neo-Malthusian trap is *The Limits to Growth* (13-2), a study funded by the Club of Rome. This projects five trends into the future: increase in food production, availability of non-renewable resources, ability of the environment to absorb pollution, population growth, and the rate of industrialization. The effect of each trend upon the others is simulated with a computer model. The central questions is "what is the carrying capacity of the earth's environment? how many people will it sustain and at what level of affluence?" The authors conclude that, if present trends continue, the combination of rapid population growth and increased industrialization will put intolerable strains on the environment, food supply, and available energy resources. Once the biosphere (the part of the earth's environment where living organisms can subsist) reaches a certain level of stress, it does not return to equilibrium. The dismal future foreseen can be averted only by acting now while the early warnings are all around us. The solution offered in *The Limits to Growth* is a "state of global equilibrium" (later modified in a second Club of Rome report, *Mankind at the Turning Point*, 13-3, to a call for a rejection of "undifferentiated growth" in favor of "organic" or planned growth).

Questions raised by this analysis are stated in *Mankind at the Turning Point:*

1. Are the crises — food, energy, raw materials, etc. — persistent, or are they aberrations due, possibly, to oversight or neglect?

2. Can the crises be solved within local, national or regional boundaries, or must truly lasting solutions be effected within a global framework?

3. Can the crises be solved by traditional measures which have always been confined to an isolated aspect of social development, such as technology, economics, politics, — or must the strategy for solution be more comprehensive, involving all aspects of social life simultaneously?

4. How urgent is the resolution of the crises? Will delay buy time and make the implementation of solutions less painful? Or are solutions made more elusive by delay?

5. Is there a way to solve the total crisis by cooperation without undue sacrifice on the part of any of the constituents of the world system; or is there the danger that some could gain permanently by seeking confrontation with their partners in the global context?

The Club of Rome answers that the crisis is persistent and can be solved only by a cooperative, comprehensive, and global strategy.

ONE RESPONSE

The prediction of the Neo-Malthusian trap quickly found a favorable response among many in the United States. Actually, a wide variety of movements had preceded *The Limits to Growth*, and these were greatly encouraged by the analysis. The most influential is the environmentalist movement which rapidly succeeded in bringing about protective legislation, including endangered species, and made the environment an international issue (Ward & Dubos, *Only One Earth*, 13-124). A widespread interest also developed in small-scale or appropriate technology *(Small Is Beautiful,* 13-109) and in non-fossil fuel energy sources. Some found in the analysis a renewed reason to criticize corporations, urban sprawl and nuclear energy. Others looked to U.S. fuel consumption and population data (the U.S. consumes over 30% of the world's natural resources used each year, with only 6% of the population) and concluded that Americans are ''energy drunkards'' *(Energy We Can Live With,* 13-30). They were countered with the argument that personal consumption did not produce the apparent imbalance *(Conservation and the Changing Direction of Economic Growth*, 13-45). Serious thought was given to the optimum size of the world's population, of urban areas, and of the economy. The possibility of a steady state (no growth) economy was explored (*Toward a Steady-State Economy*, 13-21). In short, a sense of peril emerged, lending impetus to proposals for conservation, environmental protection, and social reorganization.

THE NEO-FAUSTIAN REPLY

A thorough critique of limits to growth was prepared by a group of English scientists at Sussex University (*Models of Doom*, 13-33). They carefully analyzed the "limits" assumptions, pointing out, among other things, that variance permitted in the projections includes both a rapid demise of industrial growth and a very long lifeline.

Much of the reply focused on fossil fuel reserves. The amount of known energy reserves has always been limited, but the rate of discovery of new deposits and improved methods of recovery can increase what is available (*The Next 200 Years*, 13-44). Since 1970, new oil reserves have been found in Mexico, China, Peru, and under the North Sea. More new finds are likely. The new (but expensive and energy-costly) ways to increase production also promise the availability of a long transition time from fossil fuels to other energy sources. That promise may not be fulfilled if supplies are withheld from the market or if consumption increases dramatically. Research must go forward on solar, thermal, nuclear-fusion, methane, and many other energy sources. Should none of these prove feasible, there is still enough coal available in the U.S. for 150 to 350 years — enough to avoid an abrupt transition. Other critical minerals are also in larger supply, and thus subject to less rapid depletion than the original Club of Rome estimate. In short, even with increasing world demand, if we are willing to pay the monetary and environmental price, there are enough fossil fuels available now to last well into the 21st century. The search for alternatives should go forward, but without the sense of panic suggested by the "limits" arguments.

For reasons such as these, the Club of Rome has backed away from its original view of impending doom. Its third study, *Restructuring the International Order* (RIO), reports

. . . recent analyses have shown that the fears expressed in recent years concerning the exhaustion of natural resources may well be exaggerated, at least in some cases. . . .There is reason to believe that new technologies can be developed which will help solve problems of exploitation, extraction, substitution, and environmental degradations.[1]

RIO then turns to the NIEO proposals for increasing industrialization in developing countries and the related measures for transferring wealth. Despite the many unknowns, there are three certainties in the energy problem: the costs of fossil fuel energy will increase; the countries which control scarce resources will gain economic leverage and political influence; and conservation measures will be increasingly important.

THE POLITICS OF ECOLOGICAL INTERDEPENDENCE

The long-term impact of increased industrialization on the environment poses still other problems. There is a wide range of scientific opinion concerning what levels of environmental stress are acceptable, and the agreement on the effects of thermal (heat) pollution, the breaking down of the oxygen and nitrogen cycles, the depletion of the ozone, and pollution of fresh water, air and the oceans. These problems are pervasive and do not respect national borders. A number of countries also face deforestation and soil erosion. Can the quality of life in developing countries be improved without these by-products of industrialization? A country might, for example, achieve significant agriculture yield improvement per acre through biological controls (insect predators, crop rotation, compost, new seeds) rather than chemical fertilizers and pesticides. Extensive research is now in progress to determine pollution-tolerance levels and to develop biological controls for agricultural production. But who will bear the costs or be empowered to enforce rules against pollution?

The original Club of Rome report called for a global solution to a global problem. In a more recent study, (*Ecology and the Politics of Scarcity*, 13-26), William Ophuls calls for a "world government with enough coercive power over fractious nation states to achieve what reasonable men would regard as the planetary common interest." He, like Hardin (13-14), argues that "mutual coercion" should be "mutually agreed upon." Ophuls is also keenly aware that the ". . . clear danger is that instead of promoting world cooperation, ecological scarcity will simply intensify the Hobbesian war of all against all and cause

[1]pp.41-42.

armed peace to be replaced by overt international strife." He believes that the need is not widely enough felt to provide the impetus for cooperation. By the time it is, the scarcities will already be critical and each group may turn inward to defend or take care of its own. Others scoff at proposals for creating powerful, bureaucratic, and global organizations as an "institutional fix." How would such institutions come into being or be controlled, they ask. Some persons who are deeply committed to international institutions in other fields have even concluded that "for the most part environmental problems can best be dealt with at the national level" *(World Eco-Crisis,* 13-122).

International institution-building and cooperation in response to shared environmental problems have not progressed very far. The UN Conference on the Environment *(The Message from Stockholm,* 13-121), with the Soviet Union and the Eastern bloc absent in protest over a procedural matter, did endorse a variety of measures to provide early warning of environmental stress. Even while the Conference was in progress, however, a group of scientists from developing countries strongly dissented:

> We strongly reject models of stagnation, proposed by certain alarmist Western ecologists, economists, industrialists and computer fans, and assert that holding economic growth per se responsible for environmental ills amounts to a diversion of attention from the causes of the problem which lie in the profit motivation of the systems of production in the capitalist world. . . .

Others replied by pointing out that the Socialist, industrialized countries have problems similar to those with industries privately owned *(The Economic Superpowers and the Enviroment,* 13-110).

Despite the difficulties such issues had in getting international attention, by the end of the 1970s the United Nations Environment Program had eighty participating States and a budget in excess of $4 million. The fifty-eight member governing council seeks to implement the mandate to protect the human environment by acting as a catalyst for other UN agencies, governments, and nongovernmental organizations. The agency has established a monitoring system called Earthwatch, with 110 stations comprising a Global Environmental Monitoring System. It also maintains a register of potentially toxic chemicals and provides a computerized referral system on technical environmental questions. Some 400 projects aimed at decreasing marine pollution, preventing desertification, and other similar problems, have been financed through a UN Environmental Fund. However, work on an enforceable enviromental law is still in the drafting stage.

THE GLOBAL COMMONS

Given the continuing problems no State can solve alone, such as pollution, ocean resource exploitation and the use of outer space, the need remains high for creating international organizations with effective rule-making powers which might acquire significant authority after the members found participation to be mutually beneficial. Such organizations become visibly necessary when countries deplete an unregulated resource. As resources become overutilized, the "tragedy of the commons" occurs (Hardin, *Managing the Commons*, 13-14).

The concept of a "commons" is taken from the common land on which herdsmen once grazed their cattle in England. Each herdsman had an economic incentive to increase the size of his herd but this led to overgrazing; eventually access to the commons and the size of each herd had to be regulated.

Today, as resources become scarce, access becomes an issue. The oceans, oceanlife, the air, outer space, the forests, fresh water and other natural resources have long been treated as "commons." Now they are threatened by depletion beyond their restorative capacity. In this era of ecological interdependence, when complex and critical environmental choices must be faced, should ocean fishing, air pollution and ozone depletion be subject to regulation by intergovernmental regimes? Should participation in each regime be limited to those States which have physical access to the common resource? Should political influence within the regimes be tied to utilization, through a weighted voting system? Or should depletion be permitted to continue until the resource is exhausted?

ELEMENTS IN A COMMON APPROACH

The problems created by ecological interdependence cannot be solved by military force or its threat. Indeed, environmental issues have given impetus to arms-limitation agreements, particularly chemical and biological weapons. Those seeking to preserve the environment must resolve difficult political issues as well as complex technical questions. International regime-building requires the reconciliation of conflicting claims while demonstrating that there are benefits in voluntary participation. Self-interest must be seen as tied to the maintenance of a regime capable of defending the interest of all. This gives rise to questions such as these:

1. Are technical matters best studied by competing teams of specialists, to limit national, cultural, and scientific biases? Will the resulting information be acceptable for deciding issues?

2. What is the environmental impact of each new technology?

3. What are the social implications of technological change?

4. When commons are in danger, what regimes should be created to monitor depletion, to regulate use, and to fine or restrain those violating the regulations?

5. Should regimes be global, regional, or local in scope?

IMPLICATIONS FOR CONFLICT

The limits to growth argument has led to renewed recognition of likelihood of conflict within and between societies in times of scarcity. E.F. Schumacher *(Small Is Beautiful,* 13-109) has maintained that industrial growth, the domination of nature, and the danger to the environment that result from acquisitive motives, can lead to bellicose postures that can end in wars. In his view, a sustainable way of life is one in harmony with nature, with self-restraints on consumption, decreasing materialist and increasing aesthetic motivation. Such moral constraints aid in achieving peace within oneself, within a society, and among States.

Robert Heilbroner, however, rejects this view. He foresees conflicts becoming more acute in a world of finite resources which requires a steady state economy composed of competing political claims on the right to utilize such resources: "In a growthless economic system, the contest over incomes becomes a conflict over rights." Heilbroner goes on to forecast terrible "wars of redistribution" erupting along North – South lines or through nuclear terrorism.

Whether terrorism of this kind would provide leverage on these issues is questionable. What is clear is that scarcity without a sense of world community will increase the chances of intense conflict and war. New attitudes, new regimes, new understandings must be created if we are indeed entering a time of scarcity.

BIBLIOGRAPHY

The environmental crisis thus provides a new arena in which potentially serious conflicts are likely to erupt. The bibliography in this section explores the diversity of scientific, economic and political opinion on the nature of the crises and their possible resolution. The books will be of aid in answering questions such as those asked by the Club of Rome (see page 345) and those concerning technological innovation (see page 350). Books on energy are included, as are works on technological innovation and international approaches to resolve such problems and the conflicts which arise from them.

A. Definition of the Problem and Overviews

Classic
13 – 1 *An Essay on the Principle of Population,* Thomas Malthus, Philip Alleman (ed.), 256pp, 1976 (1798), Norton, $3.95. The original alarmist works of population outstripping food supply, reprinted with selections from the Neo-Malthusians and their critics.

INF
13 – 2 *The Limits to Growth, A Report for the Club of Rome's Project on the Predicament of Mankind,* Donella Meadows, Dennis Meadows, Jorgen Rangers and William Vehrens III, 205pp, 1974 (2nd ed.), University Books, $3.50. This influential book argues that our current reliance on fossil fuels for energy, plus the deterioration of the environment, pose limits on industrial growth.

13 – 3 *Mankind at the Turning Point, The Second Report to the Club of Rome,* Mihajlo Mesarovic and Eduard Pestel, 210pp, 1976, New American Library, $2.95. Based on computer projections of current trends, this report reaffirms the global character of the ecological crunch.

13 – 4 *This Endangered Planet, Prospects and Proposals for Human Survival,* Richard Falk, 495pp, 1972, Vintage Books, $2.95. Bridges the concepts of world order and "finite resources" with an analysis of the first planetary crisis. Both ecocide and war require a new world order. First steps, such as a world political party, are suggested toward "transformation in the 1990s."

INF
13 – 5 *The Global 2000 Report to the President, Entering the Twenty-First Century,* Gerald Barney, Study Director, 47pp, Vol. I, 1980, $3.50, 766pp, Vol.II, 1980, 401pp, 1980, $14.00. The product of a three-year effort "to discover the long-term implications of present world trends in population, natural resources, and the environment and to assess the Government's foundation for long-range planning." Concludes that "the world will be more vulnerable both to natural disaster and to disruptions from human causes" by 2000 rather than now. Volume I summarizes the findings, Volume II presents the study in detail, and Volume III provides technical documentation.

13 – 6 *The Ultimate Resource,* Julian Simon, 336pp. 1981, Princeton, $14.50. A response to Global 2000 and other reports and contends that the world's food supply is improving, farmland increasing, natural resources and energy getting less scarce, and that population growth has long-term benefits that outweigh short-term costs. Human imagination can overcome all the obstacles.

13 – 7 *Progress without Poverty, Socially Responsible Economic Growth,* Peter Albin, 229pp, 1978, Basic Books, $13.95. Denies that there is a conflict between economic growth and commitments to preserve the environment, and doubts that even existing wealth, redistributed, is enough to eradicate poverty.

13 – 8 *Ecoscience: Population, Resources, Environment,* Paul and Anne Ehrlich, John Holdren, 1051pp, 1977, (1970), W.H. Freeman, $22.00. Population growth and rising demands for goods place intolerable strains on the environment and on social institutions. War is feared as the poor "seek to relieve their frustrations aggressively" and the rich fear "denial of external resources."

13 – 9 *The Ecology Controversy: Opposing Viewpoints*, Gary McCuen, David Bender (ed.), 113pp, 1973, Greenhaven Press, $4.60. Succinct statements of pro and con arguments about environmental stress, energy supplies, nuclear power, and the trade-offs between energy utilization and pollution.

13 – 10 *The Economic Growth Debate, An Assessment,* E.J. Mishan, 277pp, 1977, George Allen & Unwin, $8.95. States the essential issue is whether "we are ready seriously to recognize that the collective pursuit of economic growth, which depends, in the main, on scientific advance and technological progress, has begun to have complex and far-reaching consequences both on the biosphere and on the 'sociosphere,' consequences that are by no means entirely benign." This book focuses on the human and social consequences.

13 – 11 *The Rise and Fall of Economic Growth, A Study in Contemporary Thought,* H. Arnolt, 161pp, 1978, Longman, $8.95. A history of attitudes about economic growth from 1945 to 1975, and of changing policy ends — stability, equality, freedom, national power and no growth.

13 – 12 *Where the Wasteland Ends, Politics and Transcendence in Postindustrial Society,* Theodore Roszak, 451pp, 1973, Doubleday, $2.95. Maintains that the religious sources of our culture have been displaced by science and industrialization which lead to "technocratic elitism, affluent alienation, environmental blight, nuclear suicide." The remedy lies in recognizing "that all the resources of the spirit human beings have ever needed to work out their destiny, have always been with them . . . in them . . ."

13 – 13 *Natural Resource Economics,* Charles Howe, 350pp, 1979, Wiley, $25.95. Offers an intelligent introduction to the lay person, demonstrates how markets have strengths and weaknesses in allocating scarce resources, and offers six criteria for intelligent resource management.

13 – 14 *Managing the Commons,* Garrett Hardin and John Baden (eds.), 294pp, 1977 Freeman, $8.50. Eight essays by Hardin, five by Baden, and twelve others explore the new concepts — "the commons," "lifeboat ethics," and "carrying capacity" and their economic, political, and ethical implications.

13 – 15 *Entropy: A New World View,* Jeremy Rifkin, 305pp, 1980, Viking, $10.95. Defines "entropy" as a measure of the capacity of a system to undergo spontaneous

change in our current utilization of the earth's resources and suggests we have gone too far.

13 – 16 *The Disaster Lobby, Prophets of Ecological Doom and Other Absurdities,* Melvin Grayson and Thomas Shepard, Jr., 256pp, 1973, Follett, $7.95. Argues that a measured assessment of dangers in nuclear power, population growth, supersonic transportation, and pollution does not justify the current mood of panic.

13 – 17 *Creating Alternative Futures, The End of Economics,* Hazel Henderson, 403pp, 1978, Berkley, $4.95. A work in the Schumacher vein, by the co-director of the Princeton Center for Alternative Futures. Clarifies choices within the "limits" perspective and advocates public interest groups to seek a greater role in implementing appropriate technology projects and broader social/economic change.

13 – 18 *An Incomplete Guide to the Future,* Willis Harman, 160pp, 1976, San Francisco Book Co., $4.95. Maintaining that the "present social system of the industrialized world" is illegitimate, Harman introduces "strategies for a viable future." The tone is pragmatic once the assumption is established that a "transformation" is inevitable. Includes many lists.

13 – 19 *Fundamentals of Ecology,* Eugene Odum, 1971, Holt, Rinehart & Winston, $17.95. Called by Ophuls an "indispensable work on ecology as a science."

B. Limits to Growth: The Response

13 – 20 *Blueprint for Survival,* Editors, *The Ecologist,* 144pp, 1972, Signet, $1.50. Based on the limits of growth's projections, it outlines a "new philosophy of life, whose goals can be achieved without destroying the environment, and a precise and comprehensive program for bringing about the sort of society in which it can be implemented." The basic change called for is decentralization "of polity and economy at all levels."

13 – 21 *Toward a Steady-State Economy,* Herman Daly, 332pp, 1973, W.H. Freeman, $8.95. Sixteen selections making the case that a steady-state economy is compatible with overcoming poverty, is essential to preserving the environment, and is morally preferable to the alternatives; the primary costs are certain matters previously considered up to individual discretion, e.g. how many children to have, how much energy to utilize, and what occupation to select.

13 – 22 *The Sustainable Society, Implications for Limited Growth,* Dennis Pirages (ed.), 342pp, 1977, Praeger, $24.95. Covers a wide range of issues in the "limits to growth" debate, and focuses on the economic reasons for limiting growth and the political difficulties in doing so.

13 – 23 *The Limits of Altruism: An Ecologist's View of Survival,* Garrett Hardin, 154pp, 1977, Indiana, $10.00. Explores the ethical implications of life in an environment with a

limited "carrying capacity" and considers the State as the permanent political unit whose survival "under emotionally satisfactory conditions is possible only if we set limits to the practice of altruism."

13 – 24 *Progress as if Survival Mattered, A Handbook for a Conserver Society,* Hugh Nash (ed.), 319pp, 1978, Friends of the Earth, $6.95. An anthology calling for a "soft energy economy" based on solar and coal energy sources, decentralized production, a steady state economy strictly enforced, very tough environmental protection laws, and a world government derived from a world constitutional convention. Only arguments for such objectives are presented.

13 – 25 *The Feeding Web: Issues in Nutritional Ecology,* Joan Gussow, 457pp, 1978, Bull Publishing, $11.95. An anthology of short articles on "limiting growth in a finite world" so that everyone gets fed.

13 – 26 *Ecology and the Politics of Scarcity, Prologue to a Political Theory of the Steady State,* William Ophuls, 303pp, 1977, W.H. Freeman, $8.50. Argues that the current environmental crisis is an overwhelming new fact, that scientific and technological ingenuity can only provide stop-gap measures; and discusses the international political implications of this.

13 – 27 *Soft Energy Paths, Toward a Durable Peace,* Amory Lovins, 231pp, 1979, Harper & Row, $8.95. Argues that the soft energy path is both socially more attractive and also cheaper and easier than the current reliance on fossil fuels. The subtitle refers to the benefits in reducing nuclear proliferation and in making available to the poor lower cost soft energy systems.

13 – 28 *Ecotopia,* Ernest Callenbach, 167pp, 1977, Bantam, $2.75. An ecologically sound, steady-state society is depicted.

C. Limits to Growth: The Response — Simplified Lifestyles

13 – 29 *99 Ways to a Simple Lifestyle,* Albert Fritsch, 381pp, 1976, Doubleday, $3.50. "How to" information presented to "teach us to make more responsible decisions" than those shaped by the "multinational corporate structure and commercial pressure."

13 – 30 *Energy We Can Live With: Approaches to Energy that are Easy on the Earth and Its People,* Daniel Wallace (ed.), 150pp, 1976, Rodale Press, $3.95. Praises the "home garden as a more important (and more liberating) energy source than the ultra high technology generating plants," offers practical suggestions for using solar energy, wind, methane gas, and geothermal energy, and gives information on how to recycle just about everything.

13 – 31 *The Dome Builders Handbook,* John Prenis (ed.), 144pp, 1973, Running Press, $5.00. For love of domes — with a few pages about their structural advantages.

13 – 32 *The Next Whole Earth Catalog,* Stewart Brand (ed.), 1980, Random House,

$12.50. In case the larger society disintegrates, you can survive provided you prepare for self-sufficient living.

D. Refined Growth

13 – 33 *Models of Doom: A Critique of the Limits to Growth,* H.S.D. Cole, *et al.* (ed.), 252pp, 1973, Universe Books, $3.50. A rebuttal to the Club of Rome's "limits to growth" thesis which criticizes its methods, techniques, and conclusions while recognizing problems posed by population growth, environmental decay, and technology.

13 – 34 *Social Limits to Growth,* Fred Hirsch, 208pp, 1976, Harvard U. Press, $3.95. Argues that modern economies faces three issues: "1) the paradox of affluence, 2) the distributional compulsion, and 3) the reluctant collectivism." Argues that all three have a single source: the social (not physical) limits to growth after basic wants are satisfied. Calls for refined growth.

13 – 35 *The Closing Circle,* Barry Commoner, 352pp, 1971, Bantom, $3.50. Recommended by Consumer Reports as "not only of the best but one of the most constructive books on ecology yet written."

13 – 36 *The Context of Environmental Politics,* Harold & Margaret Sprout, 216pp, 1979, Kentucky, $9.75. An assessment of U.S. ability to manage its environmental problems.

13 – 37 *The Global Economic Prospect: New Sources of Economic Stress,* Lester Brown, 56pp, 1978, Worldwatch Institute, $2.00. Growing global problems influence economic issues and offset traditional theory and practice.

13 – 38 *Technology and the Environment: A Reappraisal,* Amylya Reddy, 1979, United Nations, $5.40. Suggests guidelines to determine "whether or not a technology is either environmentally sound or appropriate."

13 – 39 *Reconciling Man with the Environment,* Eric Ashby, 104pp, 1978, Stanford, $7.95. Maintains that humanity's attitude toward the environment has evolved from seeking to extract a living from the environment, to domination over it, to harmony with it because sciences say that now we must.

13 – 40 *The Picture of Health: Environmental Sources of Disease,* Erik Eckholm, 256pp, 1977, Norton, $3.95. A review of the "major environmental influences on health today," both in economically developing and in industrialized countries.

13 – 41 *Energy, Ecology, Economy, A Framework for Environmental Policy,* Gerald Garvey, 235pp, 1972, Norton, $2.75. A study of the waste of natural resources characteristic of frontier America and early industrialization, with suggestions for restrained use and replenishment of remaining resources.

13 – 42 *Ark II: Social Response to Environmental Imperatives,* Dennis Pirages and Paul Ehrlich, 344pp, 1974, Freeman, $8.95. Argues we need now to build a new Ark — a society "that nurtures improvement of human beings and a spirit of unity rather than one that embraces the cult of the machine" (p. 282).

13 – 43 *Losing Ground, Environmental Stress and World Food Prospects,* Erik Eck-holm, 223pp, 1976, Norton, $3.95. Studies a neglected part of the ecological problem: environmental strains on land, forest, and fish, primarily in developing countries.

INF

13 – 44 *The Next 200 Years, A Scenario for America and the World,* Herman Kahn, *et al,* 241pp, 1976, Morrow, $3.95. A guardedly optimistic projection of current trends contending that continued growth is possible, environmental stress manageable, and what is more, such growth in the industrialized sectors is essential to the development of other sectors.

13 – 45 *Conservation and the Changing Direction of Economic Growth,* Bernhard Abrahamsson (ed.), 151pp, 1978, Westview, $16.95. A conference report concludes that for the next two centuries solutions to production, urban and other social problems are not tied to availability of raw materials.

13 – 46 *Earth, Inc.,* R. Buckminster Fuller, 179pp, 1973, Anchor Press, $2.95. Argues that the scientific design revolution gives all humans access to affluence if we abolish nation-States and create a world, democratic government.

13 – 47 *Ecological Principles for Economic Development,* Raymond Dasmann, *et al.,* 252pp, 1973, Wiley, $18.95. An anthology reconciling ecological principles and development.

13 – 48 *Industrial Policy as an International Issue,* William Diebold, Jr., 320pp, 1980, McGraw-Hill, $6.95. Describes the need for international coordination among States of their domestic industrial policies, and obstacles to it.

13 – 49 *Growth Policies and the International Order,* Lincoln Gordon, 183pp, 1980, McGraw-Hill, $6.95. Maintains that shifts in attitudes and social factors, not physical constraints, are effecting attitudes toward growth, and describes policies for resolving the food, energy and environmental problems.

E. Environmental Problems

13 – 50 *Sea in Danger,* Jacques Cousteau, 1975, Abrams, $9.95. Describes various dangers to the sea.

13 – 51 *The Twenty-Ninth Day, Accommodating Human Needs and Numbers to the Earth's Resources,* Lester Brown, 363pp, 1978, Norton, $5.95. Adds stresses to the four major biological systems — oceanic fisheries, grasslands, forests, and croplands — on the list threatened by population growth, etc.

Intro

13 – 52 *The Environment, From Surplus to Scarcity,* Allan Schnaiberg, 464pp, 1980, Oxford, $9.95. Although recognizing that the environmental concern has fallen, and the condition of the environment improved, the author believes that this is an interlude. Offers a summary of the literature.

13—53 *Environment, Technology and Health,* Merrill Eisenbud, 384pp, 1979, N.Y. Univ. Press, $19.50. Maintains that environmental improvement is significant and increasing; cancer deaths have remained consistent through industrialization except for those linked to smoking, and are not traceable to environmental deterioration.

13—54 *State of the Environment, 1979,* United Nations Environment Programme, United Nations, 1979. Focuses on four topics: schistosomiasis, resistance to pesticides, noise pollution, and tourism.

13—55 *The Environment as Hazard,* I. Burton, R. Kates, G. White, 240pp, 1978, Oxford, $6.95. A study of natural disasters (cyclones, drought, earthquakes) and why the number of lives lost is declining while property loss mounts.

F. Old and New Sources of Energy

13—56 *The World Energy Book, An A—Z Atlas and Statistical Source Book,* David Crabbe & Richard McBridge, 259pp, 1981, Nichols, $27.50. A comprehensive reference guide covering nearly every active and potential energy source.

Intro
13—57 *World Energy Survey,* Ruth Sivard, 42pp, 1981, World Priorities, $5.00. A graphic summary of the changes and the resulting choices, written for lay people. The focus is on conservation measures and renewable energy sources which, if adopted, would permit economic growth.

13—58 *Energy in a Finite World,* Wolf Hafele, et al, Vol. I, *Paths to a Sustainable Future,* 296pp, 1981, Ballinger, $14.95; Vol. II, *A Global Systems Analysis,* Ballinger, $42.50. Volume I states the conclusions, Volume II offers the findings of the International Institute for Applied Systems Analysis with experts from fifteen Institutes participating. The team represents twenty-five countries, including the U.S. and USSR and seeks to project energy consumption and source discovery.

13—59 *Energy and Security,* David Deese and Joseph Nye (eds.), 520pp, 1980, Ballinger, $14.50. A Harvard research project report with recommendations on how industrialized States can reduce their vulnerability.

INF
13—60 *Energy Future: Report of the Harvard Business School Energy Project,* Robert Stobaugh & Daniel Yergin, 353pp, 1979, Random House, $12.95. A prestigious assessment of all major energy sources and a plea for conservation.

13—61 *Energy in America's Future, The Choices Before Us,* Sam Schurr & four others, 1979, Johns Hopkins, $10.95. A clear, lay portrayal of the energy choices including the future of synthetic fuels, coal, the environment, nuclear waste disposal, and energy costs.

13—62 *The Solar Energy Timetable,* Denis Hayes, 40pp, 1978, Worldwatch Institute, $2.00. Advocates a "solar powered world . . . within fifty years" and thus considers ways of overcoming the obstacles.

13 – 63 *Energy for Development: Third World Options,* Denis Hayes, 43pp, 1977, Worldwatch, $2.00. Makes the case against nuclear and for solar energy.

13 – 64 *Rays of Hope, The Transition to a Post-Petroleum World,* Denis Hayes, 240pp, 1977, Norton, $3.95. We are running out of cheap energy, but solar energy can limit the environmental costs.

13 – 65 *Politics, Minerals and Survival,* R.W. Marsden (ed.), 86pp, 1975, U. of Wisconsin Press, $4.45. Noting the $24 billion dollar trade deficit in minerals, this conference report maintains that the U.S. can maintain its current levels of affluence if it is willing to pay the price.

INF

13 – 66 *A Time to Choose, America's Energy Future,* S. David Freeman, Director, 511pp, 1974, Ballinger, $9.95. Results of a two-year, four million dollar Ford Foundation study which offers a "technical fix": A conservation-oriented energy policy which will avoid shortages, protect the environment, avoid intense conflict with other nations, and keep real social costs as low as possible. Thus the "fix" will permit growth of GNP, full employment and no greater governmental interference with the market than under historical growth. Improved pollution control technology must be developed.

13 – 67 *U.S. Energy Policy: A Primer,* Edward Mitchell, 103pp, 1974, American Enterprise Institute, $3.00. Maintains the U.S. has never had more than twelve years of proven oil reserves: government policies, not market principles or consumption patterns, account for the current scarcities.

13 – 68 *The Mineral Position of the United States, 1975 – 2000,* Eugene Cameron (ed.), 96pp, 1973, U. of Wisconsin Press, $4.25. A symposium of papers by government, industry, and university specialists forecasting contribution of the U.S. to the world's mineral resources.

13 – 69 *Perspectives on Energy Issues, Ideas and Environmental Dilemmas,* Lon Ruedisili and Morris Firebaugh, 591pp, 1978, Oxford U. Press, $10.95. A scholarly anthology defining the boundaries of the energy problem and the related environmental issues, and includes selections on the search for non-fossil fuel energy resources and the pros and cons of nuclear energy.

13 – 70 *New Policy Imperatives for Energy Producers,* Conference Report, 300pp, 1980, International Research Center for Energy & Economic Development, $16.50.

13 – 71 *Food or Fuel: New Competition for the World's Cropland,* Lester Brown, 43pp, 1980, Worldwatch, $2.00. Explores how agricultural wastes can become a source of fuel; fears competition for land use between food products and fuel.

G. The Nuclear Power Controversy

13 – 72 *The Nuclear Power Controversy,* Arthur Murphy (ed.), 184pp, 1976, Prentice-Hall, $3.95. Largely a response to the case against nuclear energy by those who

believe its advantages outweigh the disadvantages. Sheds light on the safety, spent fuel storage, and proliferation issues.

13 – 73 *Nuclear Power Issues and Choices, Report of the Nuclear Energy Policy Study Group,* Ford Foundation, Spurgeon Keeny, Jr., Chair, 418pp, 1977, Ballinger, $7.95. Maintains that the real energy problem is not the supply but the high costs now and possibly in the future. Nuclear power and coal are compared to oil and natural gas; a commitment to both is recommended while solar, thermal, and nuclear fusion sources are pursued.

13 – 74 *The Future of Nuclear Power: A Conference Report,* Institute for Foreign Policy Analysis, 47pp, 1979, $1.00. Summarizes the findings of the Conference on the Future of Nuclear Power which gathered fifty participants from government, business and scientific communities in West Germany, Japan, and the United States.

13 – 75 *Atomic Energy: A New Start,* David Lilienthal, 124pp, 1980, Harper, $8.95. A lifetime advocate of nuclear energy reaffirms his commitment after the Three Mile Island accident but calls for safer technology, reduced energy consumption, and a new effort to prevent nuclear proliferation.

13 – 76 *Secret Fallout, Low-Level Radiation from Hiroshima to Three-Mile Island,* Ernest Sternglass, 300pp, 1980, McGraw-Hill, $5.95. A Professor of Radiology at the University of Pittsburgh challenges the governmental figures on acceptable levels of radiation; finds cumulative results and serious consequences from low level exposure.

13 – 77 *The New Tyranny, How Nuclear Power Enslaves Us,* Robert Jungk, 204pp, 1976, 1979, Grosset & Dunlap, $10.00. A broadside adding imaginative dangers to the real ones. Foresees a police State.

13 – 78 *Nuclear Madness, What You Can Do!,* Helen Caldicott, 120pp, 1979, Autumn Press, $3.95. Gathers those viewpoints maintaining that nuclear power is dangerous, and concludes "nuclear technology threatens life on our planet with extinction" not through nuclear war but through contamination by "radioactive pollutants" from power plants and nuclear tests.

13 – 79 *Plutonium, Power and Politics: International Arrangements for the Disposition of Spent Nuclear Fuel,* Gene Rochlin, 410pp, 1979, Calif., $22.95. A thorough study of why and how an international regime could manage spent fuel rods and reprocess nuclear waste, and reduce the risks of unintended nuclear proliferation.

13 – 80 *Proliferation, Plutonium and Policy: Institutional Technological Impediments to Nuclear Weapons Propagation,* Alexander DeVolpi, 384pp, 1979, Pergamon, $25.00. Introduces the constraints in existence and needed without attempting to make a convincing case that they are, or will become, adequate.

13 – 81 *Nuclear Disaster in the Urals,* Zhores Medvedev, 214pp, 1979, Norton, $12.95. A detective-like account tracking down what apparently was the worst nuclear reactor accident. The conclusion: "hundreds of people were killed, thousands more

evacuated and hospitalized, and hundreds of square miles contaminated near the city of Chlyabinsk during 1957–58." The U.S. Nuclear Regulatory Commission has concluded that procedures prohibited here were responsible and thus "the accident is not relevant to anything now done in this country."

13–82 *Of Acceptable Risk, Science and the Determination of Safety,* William Lawrence, 180pp, 1976, Kaufman, $4.95. Argues that risk is involved in everything, from nuclear power plants, to coal mining, to military strategies, to disarmament, and then outlines ways to compare the risks in each.

H. Oil

13–83 *The Future of Oil, A Simulation Study of the Interrelationships of Resources, Reserves and Use 1980–2080,* Peter Odell & Kenneth Rosing, 300pp, 1981, Nichols, $47.50. Contends that an oil supply crunch could be headed off for at least thirty years, maybe longer.

13–84 *The Future of Synthetic Materials: The Petroleum Connection,* Christopher Flavin, 55pp, 1980, Worldwatch, $2.00. Argues that the "production of synthetic materials is perhaps the major ingenious" use of petrochemicals in a time of scarce oil and natural gas resources.

13–85 *International Oil Policy,* Arnold Safer, 192pp, 1980, Lexington, $13.95. Predicts OPEC will weaken by the mid-1980s because there is no world-wide oil shortage "nor is there likely to be one for many decades to come." This statement is based on limited growth in consumption and the finding of new sources.

13–86 *Oil Politics in the 1980s: Patterns of International Cooperation,* Oystein Noreng, 192pp, 1980, McGraw-Hill, $5.95. Advocates a negotiated international energy agreement involving commitments of oil supplies and prices.

13–87 *Energy Issues and Alliance Relationships: The United States, Western Europe and Japan,* Robert Pfaltzgraff, Jr., 71pp, 1980, Institute for Foreign Policy Analysis, $6.50. Outlines the issues from a State-centered perspective: energy scarcity, Western oil dependence, Soviet energy needs, political instability in the Persian Gulf, and nuclear power, are all considered.

13–88 *Oil Crisis Management, Strategic Stockpiling for International Security,* Edward Krapels, 1980, John Hopkins, $15.00. Discusses the reserves needed for crisis by the United States, Japan, Germany, France, Italy, and the Netherlands.

13–89 *The Dependence Dilemma: Gasoline Consumption and America's Security,* Daniel Yergin (ed.), 174pp, 1980, Harvard, $4.95. Examines the political implications of importing nearly 50% of the U.S. energy and considers whether rationing or taxation is the preferred way to cut U.S. consumption.

13–90 *The Oil Crisis,* Raymond Vernon (ed.), 301pp, 1976, Norton, $4.95. Anthology on the 1973 oil crisis, the role of corporations, countries, consumers, international organizations, and politics.

13 – 91 *Oil Resources, Who Gets What How?* Kenneth Dam, 193pp, 1976, U. of Chicago Press, $4.95. Discusses the advantages of auctioning oil and by implication other mineral producing rights over the current discretionary allocation system. Favors market mechanisms.

13 – 92 *The Brotherhood of Oil, Energy Policy and the Public Interest,* Robert Engler, 338pp, 1977, Mentor, $2.50. A brief history of the oil industry which suggests a "new beginning" with public ownership.

13 – 93 *Myth, Oil and Politics, Introduction to the Political Economy of Petroleum,* Charles Doran, 226pp, 1977, Macmillan, $12.95. Debunks most of the conventional wisdom and calls for increased domestic oil production and conservation.

13 – 94 *The Control of Oil,* John Blair, 441pp, 1978, Vintage Books, $3.95. Calls for anit-trust action to restore competition in the production of domestic oil; calls dependence upon the Middle East for the energy essential to the U.S. transportation system, cause for immediate action.

13 – 95 *Oil and World Power, A Geographical Interpretation,* Peter Odell, 245pp, 1970, 1974, 2rd ed., Taplinger, $9.95. Traces the declining influence of the oil companies to 1974.

I. Technology

13 – 96 *Introduction to Appropriate Technology, Toward a Simpler Lifestyle,* R.J. Congdon, (ed.), 205pp, 1977, Rodale Press, $6.95. Anthology of writings on small-scale and intermediate technology developing criteria for selecting what is appropriate.

13 – 97 *Technology and Man's Future,* Albert Teich, (ed.), 284pp, 1977 (2nd ed), St. Martin's Press, $6.95. An anthology, surveying basically favorable views of technological innovation, concludes calling for new, more stringent standards to assess the impact of any particular innovations.

13 – 98 *Technology, World Politics and American Policy,* Victor Basiuk, 409pp, 1977, Columbia U. Press, $20.00. Examines the likely impact of military and non-military technological innovation on world politics in the next seventy-five years, and calls for exploiting technological advance to increase production while turning into a limited growth society.

13 – 99 *Appropriate Technology Sourcebook,* Ken Barrow and Rick Pam, 304pp, 1976, Volunteers in Asia, $4.00. Includes books, periodical and brief descriptions of hundreds of mechanical devices useful in rural development or energy-efficient urban projects, plus a philosophical argument for "appropriate technology."

13 – 100 *Science and Human Values,* J. Bronowski, 119pp, 1956, 1972, Harper and Row, $1.95. Explores the role of science in Western culture, and finds it equal to art but not superior to it.

INF
13 – 101 *Future Shock,* Alvin Toffler, 561pp, 1970, Bantam, $1.95. A best-selling assessment of the impact of technological innovations on how we lead our lives, on social institutions, on attitudes, and on how we might cope better in the future.

J. Urbanization

13 – 102 *The Urban Prospect,* Lewis Mumford, 255pp, 1968, Harcourt, Brace and World, $2.75. Argues for a change in our pattern of life, a movement toward regional organizations, and increased attention to the needs of people at various life stages.

13 – 103 *The Unheavenly City Revisited,* Edward Banfield, 358pp, 1974, Little, Brown, $4.95. A class analysis of urban problems which are not yet important enough to call for the effort to solve them.

13 – 104 *The City in History, Its Origins, Its Transformation and Its Prospects,* Lewis Mumford, 657pp, 1961, Harcourt, Brace & World, $6.95. A survey of the roles cities have played in human history and of the emergence of modern megalopolis.

13 – 105 *Anthropopolis, City for Human Development,* C.A. Doxiadis and others, 398pp, 1975, Norton, $5.95. An ''anthropopolis'' is the ''city that we need.'' This speculation seeks to balance five major elements of urban life.

13 – 106 *Ecumenopolis, The Inevitable City of the Future,* C.A. Doxiadis and J.G. Papaioannou, 469pp, 1974, Norton, $15.95. Based on models and computer simulations, it maintains that ''the container'' i.e. earth, can sustain twenty-two billion people by using only 7.5% of the total land surfaces.

13 – 107 *Marxism and the Metropolis,* William Tabb and L. Sawers (eds.), 376pp, 1978, Oxford U. Press, $6.95. Acknowledging their debt to ''Marx, Engels, and later thinkers in that tradition,'' fifteen authors address questions such as ''how do class relations manifest themselves in the city?'' and ''how do regional differences in class structure affect the process of urbanization?''

13 – 108 *The Home of Man,* Barbara Ward, 297pp, 1976, Norton, $3.95. Prepared for the UN Conference on Human Settlements, 1976, as a synthesis of many many concerns: urban problems, environmental stress, finite resources, economic interdependence, and world interrelatedness.

K. Implications for Conflict

13 – 109 *Small Is Beautiful, Economics as if People Mattered,* E.F. Schumacher, 305pp, 1973, Harper & Row, $2.95. Rejects large scale industrialization (''a system of

production that ravishes nature and a type of society that mutilates man''), and argues ''pollution must be brought under control and mankind's population and consumption of resources must be steered towards a permanent and sustainable equilibrium.'' War is caused by expansion, peace is to be found in permanence.

13 – 110 *An Inquiry into the Human Prospect,* Robert Heilbroner, 150pp, 1974, Norton, $2.25. Forecasts increased tension between nations, given finite resources, and wonders if authoritarian government might better resolve the problems of weapons of mass destruction, population growth, and nationalism.

13 – 111 *The Geopolitics of Energy,* Melvin Conant and Fern Gold, 224pp, 1978, Westview, $20.00. Studies the impact of East – West and North – South conflict on Western countries' dependence on others for energy. Threats and the possible response are discussed.

13 – 112 *Beyond Malthus, Population and Power,* Neil Chamberlain, 214pp, 1970, Prentice-Hall, $1.95. Identifies population growth when it is combined with effective social organizations and with belligerency, even war.

13 – 113 *The Zero-Sum Society,* Lester Thurow, 230pp, 1980, Basic, $12.95. Discusses the implications for policy in a pluralistic society in which no significant group will accept either a loss or reduction of one's share.

13 – 114 *The Politics of Environmental Concern,* Walter Rosenbaum, 311pp, 1977, 2nd, ed., Praeger, $8.95. A survey of movement, governmental, business, and other interests; and how they get reconciled in the political process.

13 – 115 *The Lean Years: Politics in the Age of Scarcity,* Richard Barnet, 349pp, 1980, Simon & Schuster, $12.95. Asks whether conservation can avoid a time of scarcity and if not, how conflicts over scarce resources will then be resolved.

13 – 116 *Energy/War, Breaking the Nuclear Link,* Amory & Hunter Lovins, 168pp, 1981, Friends of the Earth Books, $10.00. The case for non-fossil fuel energy sources, and against nuclear power emphasizing the danger of nuclear proliferation.

13 – 117 *Energy Politics,* David Davis, 278pp, 1978, 2nd end., St. Martin's, $5.95. Traces the influence of three variables — physical characteristics, the market, and the general political environment — to produce the ''politics of the fuel.'' This edition includes the politics of solar and thermal energy.

13 – 118 *Nuclear Energy and Nuclear Weapons Proliferation,* SIPRI, 462pp, 1979, Crane Russak, $32.50. A scientific, comprehensive study.

See also Nuclear Proliferation, ''Chapter 2, pp, 52 to 47.

L. National Responses: Comparative Perspectives

13 – 119 *The Economic Superpowers and the Environment: The United States, the*

Soviet Union, and Japan, Donald Kelley, Kenneth Stunkel and Richard Wescott, 335pp, 1976, Freeman, $5.95. The book examines "capitalist, communist, [and] a regulated economy" and finds that "a similar pattern of environmental deterioration" exists in each.

13 – 120 *Conservation in the Soviet Union,* Philip Pryde, 301pp, 1972, Cambridge, $21.50. A detailed and judicious assessment of the meaning of conservation in the Soviet Union, and how conservation may conflict with plan fulfillment; centralized control with popular understanding of the need for renewable utilization.

13 – 121 *The Energy Crisis and the Environment, An International Perspective,* Donald Kelley, 245pp, 1977, Praeger, $27.95. An examination of the ways in which the energy crisis set back environmental concerns in the United States, the Soviet Union, Eastern and Western Europe, Iran, Japan, and Brazil.

M. International Responses

13 – 122 *The Message from Stockholm, The U.N. Conference on the Human Environment,* Carol Leimas, 8pp, 1973, UNA of the U.S.A. and Amer. Assoc. of Univ. Women, $.25. Describes the results of the Stockholm Conference, its declaration, an action plan, and what citizens can do to improve the quality of the earth's environment.

13 – 123 *World Eco-Crisis, International Organization in Response,* David Kay and Eugene Skolnikoff (eds.), 324pp, 1972, U. of Wisconsin Press, $3.45. While some environmental problems, such as the pollution of the oceans or the stratosphere affect all nations, and thus must be dealt with on a global level, others can best be dealt with on the national level.

13 – 124 *Only One Earth, The Care and Maintenance of a Small Planet,* Barbara Ward & Rene Dubos, 225pp, 1972, Norton, $6.00. A report prepared for the U.N. Conference on the Environment which states in more defensible terms than limits to growth, the alarming dangers from environmental deterioration and the need for a global political solution.

13 – 125 *The Global Predicament; Ecological Perspectives on World Order,* David Orr & Marvin Soroos, (eds.) 400pp, 1979, U. of North Carolina, $9.00. Seventeen essays considering the political implications of global ecological problems.

13 – 126 *The New Context for International Relations: Global Ecopolitics,* Dennis Pirages, 283pp, 1978, Duxbury, $7.95. Maintains that three centuries of "rapid growth and expansion are now coming to a close," and examines the five "e's.": energy, economics, environment, ecology, and ethics.

13 – 127 *Global Planning and Resource Management,* Antony Dolman (ed.), 222pp, 1980, Pergamon, $7.95. Proposals for reforming intergovernmental organizations into global institutions for the management of global resources.

13 – 128 *Law and Policy, Petroleum Development, Changing Relations between Transnational Companies and Governments*, Kamal Hossain, 284pp, 1981, Nichols, $32.50. Studies the changing relationship and asks who is exploiting whom.

13 – 129 *Resource Management at the International Level, The Case of the North Pacific*, Oran Young, 260pp, 1977, Nichols, $17.50. Studies the existing regime in Beringia (the North Pacific area) and asks what alternatives are possible and desirable.

13 – 130 *In Defense of Earth, International Protection of the Biosphere*, Lynton Caldwell, 295pp, 1972, Indiana, $8.50. Makes the case for transnational structures to control the human impact on the "biosphere."

N. References

13 – 131 *The Unfinished Agenda: The Citizen's Policy Guide to Environmental Issues*, Gerlad Barney (ed.), 160pp, 1977, Crowell, $3.95. A directory of sources, institutions, and individuals active in environmental and appropriate technology projects.

13 – 132 *International Development and the Human Environment, An Annotated Bibliography*, M. Taghi Farvar, 334pp, 1974, Macmillan, $14.95. A valuable, although dated, resource, which includes short reviews and the key books on a wide range of environment-related subjects. Critics of Mao are disposed of, comments favorable to multinational corporations debunked (agents of imperialism); informative yes, politically neutral, no.

CHAPTER 14

CRISIS AREAS AND CURRENT ISSUES

STEPS toward war, as well as toward peace, often follow from specific decisions by political leaders — the President, the UN Secretary-General, the head of another State, or by decision-making bodies, such as Congress, the UN Security Council, or the Organization of American States. In each global, regional, or local conflict, decisions are made that turn a crisis situation either into a war or into a non-military process for resolving the conflict. Thus, whatever the approach to world affairs, attention must be given to specific choices made within governmental institutions by political leaders.

Crisis areas are those regions of the world where war is being or is likely to be fought. Issues are specific executive and legislative choices. The agenda for most world affairs discussions is made up of these matters. In each specific issue or crisis situation there are two distinct approaches to action: the *ad hoc,* and the value centered. These two approaches differ in that the "ad hoc" approach focuses entirely on a specific crisis or issue and seeks to unite all those for or against a particular outcome, whatever their underlying motivation or reason. The value-centered approach seeks to apply a general set of values and assumptions to various crises and issues and seeks to unite people who share those values and assumptions. The ideas considered in previous chapters are useless abstractions unless they serve as tools which can affect the actions taken.

THE AD HOC APPROACH

Most people develop an interest in world affairs in response to a specific crisis or an immediate issue: "War may break out in the Middle East." "People are being killed." "My son or daughter may be drafted." "I just received an induction notice." "Nuclear war is imminent." "The oceans may die." "People are starving." The invitations to action are many.

People suddenly moved to act are often impatient and reject any suggestion that they step back from the immediate crisis to gain perspective on the larger problem which produced the crisis. What counts, they say, is where one stands on the immediate issue: Are you for or against ratification of a particular treaty? Should the U.S. build a particular weapons system or reject it?

Admittedly, this is an attractive approach to politics: it offers an apparently hardheaded and concrete orientation to a field often dominated by vague and abstract discussion; it is what the media considers newsworthy; it suggests the prospect of collaborative relationships across divisive organizational and political lines; and it promises a larger coalition of people, all agreed on a single issue for whatever reason.

WEAKNESSES OF THE AD HOC APPROACH

Critics of the ad hoc approach maintain that it is self-defeating. Most decisions, they argue, are not made solely on the basis of the facts at hand but result from judgments about the intentions and responses of leaders in other States. World affairs issues are resolved, in part, on the basis of what goals are being sought and what values are to be achieved. Such critics raise these questions: What long-range goals will be advanced by your work on a specific issue? What overall values are you seeking? What is the staying power of your coalition? *Why* are you "for" or "against" a particular issue?

The ad hoc approach rarely leads to a careful analysis of the issue itself. Once a coalition has decided it is against something, it usually finds good reasons to support its judgment.

The ad hoc approach is also weak in that it is based on the lowest common denominator — agreement on opposition to a specific issue. Generally, little thought is given to the goals and measures the coalition *favors*, such as a positive alternative, or how the coalition can respond to opposition in ways that result in a new, perhaps more constructive, position.

THE VALUE-CENTERED APPROACH

The value-centered approach requires permanent structure not dependent on specific issues. This is a weakness in getting organized, and a strength in actual work. The value-centered approach unites in a common task or dialogue those who share an overall political analysis or value orientation, and it welcomes those who may disagree about a specific issue. By seeking to clarify what is at issue and by listening to and responding to opposed views, it offers the possibility of achieving a consensus that will aid in addressing the next specific issue. It is more likely to develop positive and realistic policy alternatives because it gives consideration to conflicting views.

Basic to the value-centered approach is the understanding and statement of the direction in which one wants to move. Once that direction is ascertained it is possible to address questions such as these: What goals are possible (and hence reasonable to pursue) in world politics? What means are legitimate in their pursuit? What countries' policies now pose obstacles to those goals? How could leadership by a country aid in gaining the needed cooperation of others?

An examination of such questions can lead to a clarification of the real issues in the conflict, to the elimination of misperceptions, to the establishment of alternative means to conduct, and to the resolution of violent or potentially violent conflicts. A policy framework adequate to the realities of world politics and relevant to the specific issues can emerge.

WEAKNESSES OF THE VALUE-CENTERED APPROACH

Critics point out that a focus on the general problem of conflict in international affairs may impair the ability to confront a specific crisis or issue. One must specialize in some part of the field and gain expertise in a particular area or issue. Also, the media seldom cover a meeting in which value choices are debated but give prime time and front page coverage to confrontational politics. Consequently, the public is exposed only to the visible manifestations of the larger problem.

Advocates of the value-centered approach concede that their critics are right on both counts, but they are persuaded that their approach is more sound if the aim is to achieve constructive international relations goals.

WHAT IS THE BEST APPROACH TO SPECIFIC ISSUES?

World politics are deeply infused with moral considerations (see Chapter 15). While there are many values involved, our recommendation to those working for a world without war is to concentrate on these:

1. *Nonviolent conflict resolution:* This value, which is now the norm in domestic politics, must permeate world politics.

2. *Realism:* The policies advocated should challenge the military power of every political force, seeking to identify the non-military steps that could make increasingly feasible the resolution of conflicts without violence.

3. *Democratic values:* A commitment to democratic political processes is motivated by a respect for the integrity of the individual, to the open and honest statement of goals, to dialogue and compromise (See Chapter 20).

4. *Political community:* The integrity of the community must be accepted with the majority setting the rules, provided they do not infringe on the rights of the minority.

A commitment to such values, to the development of a more adequate perspective on international conflict, and a need to respond to a specific issue, can lead to actions on crises and issues which: 1) highlight the areas of agreement and disagreement between contending views of how to resolve the issue; 2) clarify the values underlying the debate so that those in disagreement may gain a common sense of direction; 3) introduce into the debate proposals calling for United States leadership toward the goals essential to a world without war; 4) develop proposals for U.S. leadership that maximize the chances of obtaining the needed response of others; 5) build a growing constituency so that successful resolution of a specific issue builds momentum toward a positive resolution of the next issue.

RESOLVING A PARTICULAR CRISIS

There are some guidelines useful in all conflicts. In a world of armed camps, there is always the possibility that local hostilities will escalate into regional or world war. It is therefore important to isolate the military conflict; and international organizations should accept responsibility for intervening when such violence occurs. This does not mean military intervention — which usually compounds the problem — but non-military intervention to resolve the conflict.

Civil wars and regional wars (often fought with external help or influence) are the principal examples of mass, organized violence in world politics today.

Over 150 of these wars have occurred since 1945. Whatever intermediaries seem most effective in a given situation (in some circumstances, regional organizations such as the OAS or the OAU are most appropriate; in others, a single State may be effective; in others, the United Nations), there are six essential requirements for establishing peace in the midst of such conflicts: 1) preventing arms imports into the crisis area or country; 2) achieving and policing a cease-fire; 3) providing relief assistance to the victims of the conflict; 4) establishing a political process, such as an election, to decide who shall rule; 5) protecting the rights of those who lose the first election, through a continued international presence, for a period long enough to gain confidence that withdrawal will not mean loss of those rights; 6) providing economic and other assistance for mutually beneficial projects that foster cooperation among the antagonists.[1]

Much of the material presented in the remainder of this book stresses the usefulness of these guidelines. They parallel the late Adlai Stevenson's argument that the international community has a responsiblity to intervene in violent conflicts by: 1) sealing the borders of the country; 2) calling for a cease-fire; and 3) offering international means of arbitration or other conflict-resolution processes.

Intelligent work on a particular world affairs issue or crisis requires both specialization and a broad background to give perspective to the problem. A focus on a particular crisis issue is not enough. Resource G (page 667) provides a check-list of what one needs to know about a particular conflict in a particular region.

BIBLIOGRAPHY

The bibliography for this chapter introduces a number of regional conflicts in which war is either occurring or is likely to occur. A number of current issues, alternative points of view regarding their resolution, and background information, are also presented. The discussion of current world affairs contexts in Chapter 18 and the outline of how to evaluate the activity of a world affairs organization (Chapter 20) will prove useful in deciding what issues to work on and how to work on them. It may be helpful to keep in mind questions such as these: 1) What is a specific issue? 2) Why is a focus on issue-choices an effective approach to world affairs? How does the impact of the mass media increase its effectiveness? 3) What is the framework of assumptions, beliefs,

[1]*See* "Peace, Security, and the 1980 Elections," World Without War Issues Center – Midwest.

and goals which influences work on issues or on the resolution of a crisis? Which of these contexts does your issues work forward? 4) In building a constituency, is an appeal to agreement around an issue, or to common values underlying disagreement, more effective? 5) How can work on issues help or hinder the effective functioning of a democracy? 6) How can a State, regional, or global organization help resolve a military conflict within or between States? 7) What are the processes available for changing a military conflict into a political conflict? 8) What non-military sanctions can help bring warring parties into an agreement to resolve their conflict without war? 9) What superordinate goals (objectives compelling for the groups involved but unachievable by one group alone) could be sought to help the groups in conflict begin to cooperate? 10) What is the best method for deciding who shall govern a State?

A. Crisis Areas: The World

14 – 1 "A World at War," Center for Defense Information, 16pp, 1980, $1.00. Offers a brief description and world map identifying the cites of over 100 post-World War II wars.

See also, *World Military and Social Expenditures 1980*, page 9 — Lists eighty-three "Wars and Interventions 1960 — 1980."

B. The Middle East

14 – 2 *The Elusive Peace, The Middle East in the Twentieth Century*, William Polk, 201pp, 1979, St. Martin's, $15.95. Provides the background which helps explain why wars are so frequent, peace so precarious, in this region.

14 – 3 *Not By War Alone, Security and Arms Control in the Middle East*, Paul Jabber, 200pp, 1980, California, $12.50. Defines the basic requirements for effective and durable arms control in the region in which armament expenditures are highest.

14 – 4 *Beyond Camp David, Emerging Alignments and Leaders in the Middle East*, Ronald McLourein & Paul Juredini, 170pp, 1980, Syracuse, $8.95. As much an attempt to describe the process as to move beyond it.

14 – 5 *The Camp David Framework for Peace: A Shift toward Shared Rule*, Daniel Elazar, 20pp, 1979, American Enterprise Institute, $1.75. Outlines a plan for federating the West Bank with Jordan and Israel, leaving administration and local government to the Palestinian Arabs and other residents of the territories.

14 – 6 *Middle East Negotiations, A Conversation with Joseph Sicco with Basic Doc-*

uments, 35pp, 1980, American Enterprise Institute, $3.25. Calls for phased steps toward a comprehensive settlement. Includes the texts of the Camp David agreements, UN Security Council Resolutions 242 and 338, and the Palestinian National Covenant of July, 1968. The latter calls it a duty "to repulse the Zionist, imperialist invasion from the great Arab homeland and to pursue the Zionist presence from Palestine."

14 – 7 *A Palestinian Agenda for the West Bank and Gaza,* Emile Nakhleh (ed.), 127pp, 1980, American Enterprise Institute, $5.25. Based on interviews with West Bank and Gaza residents, this collection of articles reflects changing political attitudes since Camp David as well as a variety of economic and social concerns.

14 – 8 *Middle East Panel Report: A Study Document,* National Council of Churches, 34pp, 1980, National Council of Churches, $2.00. A sixteen-page report seeking common ground for a comprehensive settlement with responses by leaders in the American Jewish community and the American Palestinian community.

14 – 9 *The Middle East Today, Questions and Answers for Church Leaders,* Anti-Defamation League, $1.00. Argues that Israel will be flexible and conciliatory toward the Palestinians when they are prepared to accept Israel and to be conciliatory as they were once when Egypt accepted those conditions.

14 – 10 *When Enemies Dare to Talk, An Israeli-Palestinian Debate,* Simha Flapan (ed.), 129pp, 1979, New Outlook, $6.00. A debate between Israeli and Palestinian intellectuals which took place in Jerusalem, September 1978. The basic issues in the conflict are confronted frankly and constructively.

14 – 11 *U.N. Security Council Resolution 242: A Case Study in Diplomatic Ambiguity,* Lord Caradon, Arthur Goldberg, Mohamed El-Zayyat, & Abba Eban, 54pp, 1981, Institute for the Study of Diplomacy, $4.00. Provides the text, background, and assessments of this important U.N. resolution.

14 – 12 *The Implications of Israel-Arab Peace for World Jewry, A Report of the International Economic and Social Commission of the World Jewish Congress,* 119pp, 1981, World Jewish Congress, $3.75. A result of a two-year study in the aftermath of Israel's peace with Egypt that concludes: "the essential next step along the road to peace is an agreement on the autonomy or an alternative formula which will be both consistent with Israel's security needs and acceptable to the Arabs most directly concerned."

14 – 13 *The West Bank and the Rule of Law,* Raja Shehadeh & Jonathan Kuttab, 128pp, 1980, International Commission of Jurists, $7.00. A study by two Palestinian lawyers of the existent laws on the West Bank that concludes the 850 military orders by the Israeli Military Government have effectively eclipsed Jordanian law.

14 – 14 *Arabs in the Jewish State, Israel's Control of a National Minority,* Ian Lustick, 385pp, 1980, Texas, $10.95. A study of the some 500,000 Arabs living within Israel.

14 – 14A *PLO Strategy and Tactics,* Aryeh Yodfat and Yuval Arnon-Ohanna, 225pp, 1981, St. Martin's, $22.50. A thorough study of the origins, ideology, organization, and tactics of the PLO by two Israeli scholars.

14– 15 *Arabs and Israelis, A Dialogue,* Saul Friedlander & Mahmoud Hussein, 223pp, 1975, Holmes & Meier, $12.95. An exploration of common ground intended to gain a sense of direction toward a stable peace.

14– 16 *Jerusalem, Problems and Prospects,* Joel Kraemer (ed.), 256pp, 1980, Praeger, $9.95. An anthology offering diverse views on the current situation in Jerusalem and providing options for the future.

14– 17 *Amnesty International Mission to Israel,* Amnesty International, 71pp, 1979, Amnesty International, $1.50. A report of a fact-finding mission focused primarily on all human rights violations on the West Bank, with an Israeli governmental response and comments by Amnesty.

14– 18 *Amnesty International Report on Syria,* Amnesty, 16pp, 1979, Amnesty International $1.50. A report on human rights violation in Syria. See also *Amnesty International 1980 Report*, 6-135.

14– 19 *Beyond Security, Private Perceptions Among Arabs and Israelis,* John Mroz, 200pp, 1980, International Peace Academy, $8.95. A report on interviews in six Arab countries, Israel and the West Bank seeking suggestions for a comprehensive peace.

14– 20 *The Soviet Union and the Palestine Liberation Organization: Uneasy Alliance,* Galia Golan, 270pp, 1980, Praeger, $25.95. Traces the development of relations between the Soviet Union and the PLO from 1964 to 1979, the support the Soviet Union provides and the price it asks for that support.

14– 21 *American Interests in the Middle East,* Seth Tillman, 57pp, 1980, Middle East Institute, $2.50. Identifies Israel's security, oil, the principle of the peaceful settlement of disputes, and cooperation with the Soviet Union as the essential interests of America and suggests how they can be pursued.

See also Chapter 10, ''Regional Powers and Organization.''

C. Cyprus

14– 22 *Cyprus: The Impact of Diverse Nationalism on a State,* Halil Salih, 224pp, 1978, Alabama, $15.50. A Turkish Cypriot studies the problems of the multi-ethnic State.

14– 23 *Cyprus: Nationalism and International Politics,* Michael Attalides, 1979, St. Martin's $22.50. Places the Greek-Turkish conflict on Cyprus in the context of U.S. – Soviet relationships; superpower rivalry prevents a settlement on the basis preferred by the Greek majority — whatever that decision would be.

14– 24 *The Rise and Fall of the Cyprus Republic,* Kyriacos Markides, 1977, Yale, $14.00. An independent Cyprus composed of two ethnic groups provided a stable basis for government for a period; a movement to unify Cyprus with Greece ended that and brought war, a Turkish invasion, a UN peacekeeping force, and a perilous peace.

D. Lebanese Civil War

14 – 25 *The Lebanese Civil War*, Marius Deeb, 176pp, 1980, Praeger, $24.95. Offers an analysis of the underlying causes, socio-economic makeup of the contestants and the political objectives underlying the conflict.

14 – 26 *Syria and the Lebanese Crisis*, Adeed Dawisha, 208pp, 1980, St. Martin's, $25.00. Studies Syria's peackekeeping role in Lebanon and the role of Soviet military and diplomatic support.

14 – 27 *Lebanon in Crisis, Participants and Issues*, P. Edward Haley & Lewis Snider, 342pp, 1979, Syracuse, $7.95. A balanced collection of essays exploring the religious, political, and economic sources of the war.

14 – 28 *Conflict and Violence in Lebanon: Confrontation in the Middle East*, Walid Khalidi, 217pp, 1980, Harvard Center for International Affairs, $6.95. A valuable analysis of the Lebanese war of 1975 – 76 in both its international and national dimensions.

E. Afghanistan

14 – 29 *Afghanistan: Key to a Continent*, John Griffiths, 200pp, 1981, Westview, $16.00. Provides a history, assessment of Afghanistan's halting modernization efforts, an introduction to its internal divisions and a condemnation of the Soviet invasion. Calls for support for those resisting it.

14 – 30 *Afghanistan*, Louis Dupree, 778, 1980 (rev. ed.), Princeton, $9.95. Offers social and political background on Afghanistan.

F. Iran/Iraq

14 – 31 *The Ideological Revolution in the Middle East*, Leonard Binder, 424pp, 1979, 2nd ed., Krieger, $16.50. An analysis of religious and ideological currents which combine to make the Middle East an explosive region.

14 – 32 *Islam and Revolution*, Hamid Algar (ed. & trans.) 1980, Mizan, $5.95. A translation of Khomeini's 1970 major work and a selection of his speeches designed to build sympathy in America for the Islamic revolution. Khomeini's handbook of Islamic law and chapters on politics and economics are included.

14 – 33 *Iran: From Religious Dispute to Revolution*, Michael Fischer, 303pp, 1980, Harvard, $17.50. A study of the religious underpinnings of the Iranian revolution and of the differing perceptions in Iran of the social/political content of Islam.

14 – 34 *Iran Erupts,* Ali-Reza Nobari, 237pp, 1978, Mizan, $5.95. Offers Iranian voices which are pro-Khomeini, anti-Shah, anti-Soviet Union, anti-U.S. — passionately maintaining that a better future is therefore assured.

G. The Horn of Africa

14 – 35 *Ethiopia: Empire in Revolution,* Marina & David Ottaway, 211pp, 1978 Holmes & Meier, $27.00. An assessment of the effects of the revolution, a critique of the Empire, and an appeal for unity.

14 – 36 *Eritrea, The Unfinished Revolution,* Richard Sherman, 222pp, 1980, Praeger, $19.95. A sympathetic study of the liberation movements in Eritrea and the broader implications of the conflict for Ethiopia, the region, and world politics.

14 – 37 *North Yemen,* Manfred Wenner, 128pp, 1981, Westview, $16.50. Provides background on the civil war and the 1970 compromise, as well as general introductory information.

14 – 38 *South Yemen,* Robert Stookey, 128pp, 1981, Westview, $16.50. A political assessment of the current sect in power, placed there with the aid of Soviet military assistance and East German and Cuban troops.

14 – 39 *Somalia: A Perspective,* Kevin Cahil, 81pp, 1980, State U. of New York, $12.95. A brief assessment of the changing alignment in Somalian politics.

H. Vietnam/Kampuchea

14 – 40 *101 Ways You Could Help End the Famine in Cambodia,* Robert Woito, 4pp 1980, World Without War Issues Center, $.25. Outlines ways to increase the amount of aid, gain publicity and public support for the relief effort, and how to address the problem of getting aid distributed, the war ended, and a political solution found.

14 – 41 *The Third Indochina Conflict,* David Elliot (ed.), 250pp, 1981, Westview, $18.50. Six authors assess the Kampuchean – Vietnamese war, its origins, political signficance, and possible outcome.

14 – 42 *The Boat People,* Bruce Grant, 248pp, 1980, Penguin, $3.50. Describes the origin, risks, and fate of the more than 300,000 people who have left Indochina since 1975.

I. Taiwan

14 – 43 *The Future of Taiwan: A Difference of Opinion,* Victor Li (ed.), 200pp, 1980,

Sharpe, $17.50. A conference report about what fifteen Chinese-Americans believe should be the island's future.

See also Chapter 10, "The Far East."

J. Poland

14 – 44 *Background to Crisis: Policy and Politics in Gierek's Poland,* Maurice Simon & Roger Kanet (eds.), 418pp, 1981, Westview, $27.50. A comprehensive survey of a Communist State in crisis, a description of the nonviolent opposition, and a suggestion that the changes in Poland are irreversible.

K. Northern Ireland

14 – 45 *Northern Ireland: Society Under Siege,* Rona Fields, 1980, Transaction, $5.95. Stresses the impact of the conflict on social life.

14 – 46 *Northern Ireland: A Political Directory 1968 – 79,* W. Flackes, 1980, St. Martin's, $25.00. Provides essential information on leaders.

14 – 47 *Northern Ireland: Between Civil Rights and Civil War,* Liam O'Dowd, et al, 224pp, 1980, Humanities, $8.75. An anthology introducing the participants and issues in the conflict.

L. Angola

14 – 48 *The Angolan Revolution: Exile Politics and Guerrilla Warfare (1962 – 1976),* John Marcum, 473pp, 1978, MIT, $25.00. A richly documented tracing of the bewildering varieties of nationalist organizations and strategies and the emergence of three: Marxist Popular Movement for the Liberation of Angola (MPLA), National Front for the Liberation of Angola (FNLA), and the National Union for the Total Liberation of Angola (UNITA).

14 – 49 *The Angolan War, A Study in Soviet Policy in the Third World,* Arthur Klinghoffer, 231pp, 1980, Westview, $23.75. While arguing that the Soviet Union basically took advantage of a local situation, Soviet military aid, and Cuban military forces are considered decisive; U.S., Chinese, South African, Zairian, and Portugese policies are also assessed.

M. Southern Africa

14 – 50 *Suffer the Future, Policy Choices in Southern Africa,* Robert Rotberg, 311 pp,

1980, Harvard, $15.00. Offers an assessment of the choices once confronted in Rhodesia/Zimbabwe, and now faced in Namibia and South Africa.

14 – 51 *The Apartheid Regime: Political Power and Racial Domination,* Institute of International Studies (Berkeley), $8.95. Eighteen specialists consider the prospects for change including a proposal for a multi-racial parliament.

14 – 52 *Martyrs and Fanatics: South Africa and Human Destinies,* Peter Dreyer, 255pp, 1980, Simon & Schuster, $11.95. Portrays the fear in both the white and black communities but offers little hope of a solution.

14 – 53 *Black Power in South Africa, The Evolution of an Ideology,* Gail Gerhart, 364pp, 1978, California, $5.95. Traces the evolution of the ''Black Consciousness Movement'' and the gathering of forces against apartheid. Also provides an introduction to South African politics.

14 – 54 *Ethnic Power Mobilized: Can South Africa Change?* Herbert Adam and Hermann Gilomee, 307pp, 1979, Yale, $5.95. A study focusing on the Nationalist Afrikaners and what that group loses by maintaining apartheid. Outlines political alternatives including government by a coaliton of leaders from all groups, each with a veto power, each with access to resources and status positions proportionate to their numbers, and each with a significant degree of autonomy.

14 – 55 *Steve Biko, I Write What I Like, A Selection of His Writings,* Adrian Stubbs (ed.), 1979, Harper & Row, $8.95. A Black South African leader of the Black Consciousness Movement explains the aims, objectives, and purposes of the movement.

14 – 56 *U.S. Business in South Africa, The Economic, Political and Moral Issues,* Dezaix Myers and others, 375pp, 1980, Indiana, $17.50. Surveys 20th-century economic and social history, outlines the role of U.S. companies operating there, and presents the positions in the current debate concerning whether they are aids in overcoming or supporting apartheid.

14 – 57 *Decoding Corporate Camouflage: U.S. Business Support for Apartheid,* Elizabeth Schmidt, 140pp, 1980, Institute for Policy Studies, $4.95. A critical assessment of the Sullivan Principles — a fair employment code for corporations operating in South Africa — which concludes the principles are ineffective in improving the black workers' lot and, in any case, leave apartheid unaffected.

14 – 58 *Which Way Is South Africa Going?* Gwendolyn Carter, 176pp, 1980, Indiana, $10.95. A study of separate development, trade unionism, contenders for black leadership, and prospects for change within the white community.

14 – 59 *South Africa into the 1980s,* Richard Bissell & Chester Crocker (eds.), 248pp, 1979, Westview, $22.00. Anthology emphasizing South Africa's strategic importance to the West.

14 – 60 *The Liberal Dilemma in South Africa,* Pierre Van Den Berghe (ed.), 164pp, 1979, St. Martin's, $19.95. Defines a commitment to nonviolence and to change toward democracy without clarity as to how to express those commitments in this setting.

14 – 61 *South Africa's Options: Strategies for Sharing Power,* Frederik Slabbert & David Welsh, 196pp, 1979, St. Martin's, $17.95. Opens an alternative by contrasting South Africa's form of government with democracies; Slabbert leads the opposition in South Africa's Parliament.

N. Central America

14 – 62 *El Salvador Kit,* Robert Woito (ed.), 28pp, 1981, World Without War Publications, $1.00. A loose-leaf collection of articles and analysis focused on how citizens can aid their government foster movement toward democracy without violence.

14 – 63 *El Salvador,* Tommie Sue Montgomery, 128pp, 1981, Westview, $16.00. Provides a history of El Salvador, an assessment of the changes during the 1970s and a forecast of continuing conflict.

14 – 63A *El Salvador: Peace, Revolution or Armed Struggle?,* R. Bruce McColm, 47pp, 1982, Freedom House, $2.00. Argues that democracy's prospects are brighter with the reform-minded military regime than with the guerilla movement, while criticizing the American press for underplaying the land reform program, portraying murders as the result of the government rather than right-wing death squads and left wing terrorists.

14 – 64 *Democracy and Clientelism in Jamaica,* Carl Stone, 270pp, 1980, Transaction, $16.95. Combines social and political data on Jamaica with an interpretation of Jamaica's political evolution.

14 – 65 *The Politics of the Caribbean Community: Regional Integration Among New States, 1961 – 1979,* A.J. Payne, 299pp, 1980, St. Martin's, $25.00. A study of the commonwealth countries, purposes in joining Carifta, Caricom, and functional cooperation outside international organizations, concludes their purposes are nationalistic, not supranational — regional cooperation enhances national objectives and does not lead to political integration.

14 – 66 *Puerto Rico: Commonwealth or Colony?,* Roberta Johnson, 218pp, 1980, Praeger, $8.95. Provides a history of the Island, contemporary political and economic issues, and an analysis of why Puerto Ricans voted overwhelmingly to continue ties with the U.S.

14 – 67 *The End and the Beginning: The Nicaraguan Revolution,* John Booth, 225pp, 1981, Westview, $10.00. Traces the roots of the revolution over a 150-year period, and assesses the first year of the new regime.

14 – 68 *The Dominican Republic,* Ian Bell, 375pp, 1981, Westview, $27.75. Argues that the moderately left-of-center government is making social changes, was elected, and may move the Dominican Republic into the ranks of the newly industrialized.

14 – 69 *Resolution of the Dominican Crisis, 1965, A Study in Mediation,* Audrey Bracey, 64pp, 1981, Institute for the Study of Diplomacy, $3.50. Describes the work of Ellsworth Bunker and the OAS Ad Hoc Committe in mediating the conflict.

See also Chapter 10 for other present or potential crisis areas.

O. Crisis Issues

Most of the subjects in this book contain specific choice points which must be resolved by decision-makers at various levels of nongovernmental and governmental organizational life. Below are listed works on two such issues, with suggestions of others, and references to works cited in other sections of the bibiography. Most issues are best followed in the periodical literature (see "Resources for Action").

THE LAW OF THE SEA

14–69A *Law of the Sea Treaty: Current Choices*, Kurt Carlson (ed.), 64pp, 1982, World Without War Publications, $5.00. Summarizes the Treaty's provisions, the process that led to the 1981 draft, and provides background on the Reagan Administration's review of the treaty.

14–70 *Deepsea Mining*, Judith Kildow (ed.), 251pp, 1980, MIT Press, $17.50. Examines what is at stake in the Law of the Sea negotiations, the proposals as of 1980, and the pros and cons of Treaty ratification.

14–71 *Deep Seabed Resources, Politics and Technology*, Jack Barkenbus, 224pp, 1979, Free Press, $14.95. A study of the economic and political problems in reaching an international agreement for mining the ocean depths, and suggests a solution.

14–72 *The Enclosure of Ocean Resources*, Ross Eckert, 390pp, 1979, Hoover Press, $16.95. An assessment of the UN Law of the Sea Conference which welcomes the new 200-mile coastal economic zone but is critical of many other features of the proposed treaty.

14–73 *Restricting the Concept of Free Seas: Modern Maritime Law Re-Evaluated*, George Smith, II, 260pp, 1980, Krieger, $15.50. Surveys the changes in maritime law concerning coastal waterways, mineral rights, channels and canals, the open ocean, the seabed, and fishing rights.

REFUGEES

14–74 *Refugees, The Humanitarian Dilemma*, William Lewis, 200pp, 1981, Praeger, $19.95. An overview of the growing number of refugees in the world, with a recommended framework for evaluting U.S. policy.

Other Issues: 1) arms control and disarmament (see Chapters 2 and 4): SALT II, MX missile, cruise missile, Trident submarine, B-1 bomber, defensive weapons systems research, conventional armaments, conventional arms transfer, military budgets;

2) international organizations (see Chapter 5): UN Charter review, Security Council reform, weighted voting systems, UN budget, UN peacekeeping, Connelly reservation, International Criminal Court;

3) World Community and Human Rights: UN Human Rights Covenant ratification(s), OAS Human Rights Conventions ratification, UN Human Rights Conventions ratification, UN Commissioner on Human Rights, satellite broadcasting, world press freedom;

4) World Economic Development(see Chapters 7 and 12): foreign aid legislation, World Bank allocations, International Monetary Fund rules, commodity price stabilization, world grain reserve, import restrictions, code of conduct for transnational corporations, debt relief;

5) Environment: pollution control legislation, budget for international Worldwatch System, environmental protection laws.

PART V

DEVELOPING CAPACITIES

Throughout RECORDED human history, individuals have sought to apply ethical insights to the problem of war, to extend the norm of nonviolent conflict resolution from the family to the society and to politics, and to acquire and apply knowledge to achieve peace. Surveying such endeavors is both sobering and instructive: sobering because ethical concepts, nonviolent commitments, or knowledge have rarely had a signficant, continuing impact on the non-military resolution of international conflict. Frequently, moral arguments have led to justifications for war, and knowledge applied to fight, rather than end, wars. The exceptions, however, make the study of ethics and war (Chapter 15), nonviolent theory and practice (Chapter 16), and peace research (Chapter 17) instructive.

In ethics and war, nonviolence, and peace research, significant capacities have already been demonstrated. A conscientious objector to war (aware of and accepting the personal amd social consequences of his or her choice) makes a rare but significant contribution to world politics. Witness to an ideal can help bring that ideal into reality. Martin Luther King, Jr., and Mahatma Gandhi, among others, have demonstrated that nonviolent techniques can build a sense of community between those in conflict and, by doing so, achieve significant change without violence. Peace researchers in a wide range of disciplines have enlarged significantly our knowledge of the origins, frequency, duration, and causes of war and conditions of peace.

In this part of *To End War* contending approaches to problems in each of the three fields are presented. It is essential that we develop our capacities to apply ethical concepts, nonviolence, and knowledge to the world affairs field. When informed by the realities of world politics introduced in Part I, these capacities could increase our chances of gaining the conditions essential to a world without war as presented in Part II.

381

CHAPTER 15

RELIGIOUS AND ETHICAL THOUGHT ON WAR

MANY persons enter the world affairs field with strong moral convictions. They want to change a world in which powerful States threaten death and destruction. They frequently want to end starvation, torture, and exploitation, and other injustices as well.

The meaningful application of moral values to world politics is, however, extremely difficult. Among the problems are disagreement about the source of moral values, about the content or meaning of moral values, and about how values can best be applied.

This chapter presents in summary fashion the contending sources of moral authority, recognizing that disagreement in this area is likely to persist. A number of moral values are then identified, and here disagreement focuses on which is the most important. Finally, answers to this question are considered: "When, if ever, is the organized use of mass violence morally justified in world politics?" A suggestion is offered about how those with differing answers to this question could work together on the problem of war.

WHAT IS THE SOURCE OF ETHICAL PRINCIPLES?

In the past, most people have found the source of their ethical or moral principles in religious faith. There are, to be sure, different views as to whether

382

conscience, reason, or intuition is the faculty through which we learn religious doctrines; conflicting interpretations of God's will have led to countless wars. Nonetheless, it is clear that God's will is the traditional source of moral principles.

The increased secularization of moral and ethical thought has added several non-theistic approaches to moral principles. Two secular theories, utilitarianism and Marxism, suggest an empirical method to determine what is moral. Utilitarianism, as expounded by John Stuart Mill (15-75), maintains that the source of ethical principles lies in reason's ability to measure whether an act "produces the greatest good for the greatest number." Marxists empirically discern in history a pattern, on the fulfillment of which they base their ethical theory (9-28). If historical progress can occur only in the way Marx and Engels said it must, then it is morally right to help fulfill that pattern, morally wrong to oppose it. Neither theory, however, even within its own framework of assumptions and beliefs, has succeeded in combining concepts and facts which would enable ethical disagreements to be resolved on the basis of reason.

A third approach to ethical reasoning traces its roots to Immanuel Kant. In Kantian ethics, the categories through which we perceive the world, not empirical data about the consequences of actions, impose moral imperatives. The morality of an action depends upon the good intentions of the actor. To be moral an act must be selfless and capable of being adopted as a general rule by everyone (Kant, 15-14). A fourth view asserts that the source of moral convictions is a strong feeling that something is right or wrong. But in these latter theories there is disagreement about what is selfless and what selfish, about whether something can be moral if it ignores the consequences of an action, and about how feelings can be distinguished from personal preferences.

In the face of such widespread disagreement about the source of ethical principles, the certainty with which one holds to moral principles should be something less than absolute. One can be wrong about the sources of morality, as about anything else. And irreconcilable disagreement about the application of absolutistic beliefs can cause war when those in disagreement adopt violent means to advance their views. But whether you have a belief, are agnostic or are cynical about the sources of morality, the larger issues of world politics *are* clearly shaped by conceptions of what is right or wrong. Institutions widely perceived as immoral, such as serfdom and slavery, do pass away. When there are contending creeds, one of them, or a new synthesis, may gain wide acceptance. But even then, we will live in a world with chronic disagreement about the source of moral principles.

WHAT PROBLEMS IN INTERNATIONAL RELATIONS RAISE
MORAL QUESTIONS?

If neither religious experience, reason, nor moral intuition provide clear, agreed guidance for justifying ethical principles, how can we meaningfully develop and apply the moral concerns people have about international relations? A first step is to identify the basic moral questions. Among them are these:

1. *Mass Violence:* When, if ever, is the organized use of mass violence justified?

2. *Conduct of War:* If engaged in war, are there limits on how it should be waged?

3. *Nuclear War:* When, if ever, is it morally acceptable to threaten or use nuclear weapons?

4. *Lying:* When may a head of State lie justifiably?

5. *Intervention:* Under what circumstances and with what means can one State or group of States justifiably intervene in the affairs of another State?

6. *Human Rights:* Do individuals have "natural" rights, or other moral rights, that are superior to State-power? If so, what should States do to protect such rights?

7. *Economic systems:* Is capitalism, socialism, decentralized no-growth, or some other economic system morally preferred?

8. *Political systems:* Is a political system that facilitates broad public participation in decision-making processes preferable to a system run by an elite committed to morally desirable ends?

9. *Wealth:* Do wealthy States have a moral obligation to protect their own economic interests or to provide economic aid and guarantee transfers of resources to economically poor States? What constitutes a just distribution of wealth? Can wealth be earned?

10. *Responsibility:* Does an individual's moral responsibility extend beyond the family to the society, the State, and even to humanity? If so, how can that responsibility be expressed?

Such questions present moral issues which heads of State and those active in world politics need to consider, but the answers are far from simple. For example, how can we answer the first question, "when, if ever, is the organized use of mass violence justified?" We cannot possibly calculate the results of conventional or nuclear war today and have to admit that we do not know what the results would be. If we rule out war as a categorical imperative, then we may be leaving the larger issues of world politics to those who *will* use mass violence. Thus, neither the rejection nor the acceptance of war is the obvious moral choice.

WHEN, IF EVER, IS THE ORGANIZED USE OF MASS VIOLENCE JUSTIFIED?

There are at least three different moral traditions that answer this question: 1) *the pacifist,* who answers never; 2) *the just war advocate*, who says in certain circumstances and under certain conditions war is acceptable as the last resort, and 3) *the crusade ethicist*, who maintains that mass violence is a positive moral duty because of the absolute righteousness of the cause or the radical evil of the enemy. These traditions may all agree about what an individual should do if attacked; they diverge when the use of mass violence to promote change or to achieve security is at issue.

PACIFIST THOUGHT

Pacifist thought, like the other traditions, has many sources, applications, and uses *(The Pacifist Conscience,* 15-152). The key element is that it is better to suffer than to inflict suffering on behalf of what you believe to be right. Pacifists thus hold fast to what they believe to be moral, but refuse the use of organized mass violence to further their views. If the consequences are to be killed, a pacifist is prepared to pay that price rather than kill others. Pacifists thus refuse to participate in war, becoming either conscientious objectors, performing alternative service, or, if they deny the authority of the community to make and enforce military conscription, resisting authority in some other nonviolent way.

The strength of the pacifist tradition lies in its combination of moral commitment and the action which expresses that commitment. The pacifist is clear that, whatever else the State may require, it cannot ask him or her to engage in mass violence. The witness for that ideal can be compelling. Pacifist ideals can also be corrupted in their application as when the violence of one side in a conflict is rejected while the violence of another side is condoned or unaddressed. But in its true form, the pacifist tradition condemns all organized mass violence.

Critics of pacifism believe that the withdrawal from the use of organized mass violence will never be politically effective. Refusing to prepare to use mass violence leaves the shaping of the larger questions of world politics to those who are so prepared and willing. The withdrawal of one side from a war allows the other side to win. How will we promote justice or defend ourselves if we reject violence in the face of the clear threat of others to use it?

Pacifists give a number of answers to such questions. Some argue that violence is futile and cannot, itself, promote progress or what is just. Others maintain that the development of nonviolent alternatives can succeed in gaining the agreement of others in the pursuit of conditions essential to a world without war, forcing needed change, or providing for national defense through a civilian-based policy of non-cooperation and nonviolent resistance (see Chapter 16).

A REVITALIZED JUST WAR ARGUMENT?

A second tradition that offers an answer to the question is that based on just war theory. Here careful attention is paid to distinguishing the conditions under which violence is justified. If the circumstances match the criteria which have been developed, war is justified as a necessary or lesser evil. These criteria are stated concisely by Suarez:

> . . .in order that a war may be justly waged, a number of conditions must be observed . . . firstly, the war must be waged by a legitimate power; secondly, the cause itself and the reason must be just; thirdly, the method of its conduct must be proper, and due proportion must be observed at its beginning, during its prosecution, and after victory.[1]

Although offensive war may meet these criteria according to Suarez, it is more likely that a ''just war'' will be defensive in character.

A contemporary application of the criteria runs something like this: the overriding moral evil in world politics today is intervention by one State in the affairs of another; there is no real likelihood of building supranational institutions to prevent such intervention and to resolve conflict; nationalism is the prevailing creed and disarmament is impossible; what is possible and necessary in a world of sovereign States is to distinguish offensive from defensive war — unjust from just wars. Defensive intentions are established by developing defensive weapons systems. Thus, attack tanks are bad, anti-tank weapons are good. Strategic nuclear weapons are bad, strategic defensive weapons are good. Training soldiers to attack is bad but preparing to defend one's country is good.

Those critical of this application of ''just war'' theory point out that it was the strategy designed to prevent World War II, and it failed. Furthermore, it has devastating implications for modern theories of defense, specifically for de-

---

[1]*War and Christian Conscience,* Albert Marrin, (ed.), (Chicago: Regnery 1971), p. 202.

terrence theory. Deterrence depends upon mutual assured destruction. Should one side find a military defense, deterrence would be in jeopardy. One side might then attack, either because it fears attack itself once the other side's defense is in place, or because it has itself acquired a defense. In addition, deterrence is designed to defend not only the powerful States, but their allies as well. Would not allied States seek their own nuclear deterrence forces in such circumstances since they now can be acquired and may be needed? Won't the incentives for nuclear proliferation be increased if one side adopts a "just war" defensive posture and this does not assure that the other will not intimidate non-aligned States? Does not the "just war" argument deny the political bargaining leverage that strategic nuclear weapons provide in the many arenas of political conflict today?

THE CRUSADE ETHIC

The crusade ethic provides a third distinctive answer to the question about the use of mass violence. The Crusades (1096 – 1291) sought to extend Christendom or, more, specifically, recapture the Holy Land from the Moslems. God himself was believed to authorize these expeditions. Their leaders believed in the moral rectitude of their ends and in the evil of the enemy. In modern times, some Americans have seen in "The Hun" or "The Communists" the embodiment of evil requiring war against them. Similarly, wars of liberation or revolution are sometimes interpreted as embodying absolute righteousness either because of the evil of the presumed oppressive power (usually the United States or multinational corporations) or because God is believed to take the side of the oppressed.

In the crusade ethic, initiative lies with the moralist. The violence is a positive good (because a just punishment for iniquity) not an unfortunate last resort. The enemy is to be destroyed, not negotiated with, much less loved (as St. Augustine, a just war theorist, and Gandhi and Martin Luther King, Jr., who were pacifists, required).

Critics doubt that the organized mass violence of conventional, not to mention nuclear, war can ever be the instrument for establishing justice. Modern war, at least, apparently requires the mobilization of mass opinion through propaganda devices, the use of weapons of mass destruction which kill innocent and unintended targets alike, and is nearly as pitiless in what it does to its practitioners as it does to its victims.

LIBERATION THEOLOGY

An influential modern variant of either (or both) the just war or the crusade ethic, depending upon your interpretation, is liberation theory. Some writers in this tradition advocate violence on behalf of justice. Like the other traditions, liberation theology has many versions. The major line of argument proceeds in this vein: the existing circumstances, when viewed from the vantage point of the poor, *are* violent; people in positions of political or economic influence who benefit from such exploitative relationships are the major perpetrators of violence in the world today; the poor who die from starvation or from disease resulting from malnutrition are just as dead as war casualties and there are more of them; violence by the poor is thus, in reality, defensive in character and when successful, a liberating force; movements of the poor and oppressed against people and structures who oppress them are just, whatever the means employed; the means available (terror, guerrilla, or civil war) are proportional to the violent structures which oppress them; peace is possible when the poor and oppressed achieve power and establish new political and economic institutions.

In this survey of writings in the liberation theology tradition, Alfredo Fierro states:

> . . . a distinction between a theology of revolution and a theology of violence is untenable. . . . In Christian analyses of violence . . . violence number one is the institutionalized violence imbedded in and underlying the oppressive power structure. This original violence provokes and unleashes violence number two, which is the violence of the oppressed or the young or revolution in general.[2]

The bridge that makes the initiation of violence defensive in character is the concept of structural violence: "The phase 'opting for violence' is itself ambiguous; one cannot opt for something in which one is already emmeshed" (Domergue).[3] Thus, the violence of liberation movements is understood as a combined form of self-defense and the right of revolution.

Critics attack liberation theology at each point: 1) in its characterization of economic and political institutions as violent; 2) in its analysis which, as liberation theologians themselves widely acknowledge, is heavily dependent upon Marxist categories; 3) in its belief that violence will help eliminate oppression; 4) in its belief that violence will lead to more representative political processes and more equitable economic circumstances; and 5) in its

---

[2]*The Militant Gospel* (15-184).
[3]Quoted in *The Militant Gospel*.

assignment of direct responsibility for hunger in one country to people or institutions often located in other countries.

In a critique of the concept of structural violence, Paskins and Dockrill *(The Ethics of War,* 15-133) argue:

> Structural violence is an inferior substitute for a more precise and articulate concept of just cause . . . it blurs the distinction between a description of events as they are and a proposal for action. It short-circuits the demand for justification . . . . Counter-violence is seen as something that happens, not something that is done.[4]

To label a political or economic institution as violent distorts the meaning of the word, opens the way to violence, and suggests no way to contain it.

ECONOMIC JUSTICE

A related subject is that of "justice" concerning the distribution of wealth. The stress on equality as one of the major values of our time has led to a consensus that political authority must justify itself in part by its ability to produce and distribute equitably economic goods and services. An improved distribution of wealth does not automatically follow from a commitment to a particular economic system. Both capitalist Taiwan and South Korea have done better in distributing wealth than socialist Algeria.[5]

The Soviet Union, in its strenuous efforts to redistribute wealth and achieve what it called justice (little is heard of the goal anymore in Soviet literature), resorted to mass murder and today still has gross inequalities of wealth matching those in the United States. Critics conclude that those versions of liberation theology which recommend violence are adding new obstacles to old — often on behalf of an economic system at least as exploitative and far less democratic than the present one. In short, there is no economic system in existence which guarantees the achievement of economic justice, and it is pointless to call one

---

[4]p. 216.

[5]See Chapters 7 and 12. See, for example, "Capitalist and Socialist Agriculture in Asia," Keith Griffin, World Development, vol. 7, no. 4, 1979, and especially "Growth and Improvement in the Rural Areas of Asia," pp. 361 – 84. In addition, see "Measures of Inequality," Paul D. Allison, American Sociology Review, vol. 13, 1978, pp. 865 – 88 and *The Size Distribution of Income: A Compilation of Data* (Washington: World Bank, 1975).

system structurally violent and another nonviolent, one just and another evil.

Others attack the very concept of justice, arguing that it has as many different definitions as there are political purposes. While equality before the law has gained acceptance, equality of other kinds probably can be achieved only through the coercive instruments of the State and even then, more in theory than in practice.

IS A WORKING CONSENSUS POSSIBLE?

Violence, in its ability to turn a person into a thing, presents itself as the final, unalterable form of injustice that one person can inflict on another. Responsibility for intitiating violence, is, however, hard to locate. Frequently in war, one side blames the other for starting it; each blames the other for its continuance. Those who want to end war because they believe violence itself is unjust, need to present a credible non-military way to resolve a conflict. When they have done so, the side which refuses the solution offered, or offers no other non-military solution, becomes (in most cases) responsible for the violence. A belligerent's willingness to initiate (or reciprocate) a cease-fire is the critical test of peaceful intention.

In revolutionary situations, responsibility for violence is frequently even more difficult to locate. By definition, the State has a monopoly on the legitimate use of violence; it was invented, in part, to prevent the random violence of small groups. A democratic State offers a non-military method for would-be revolutionaries or other dissenters to come to power — the political process. It thus facilitates change and, when fully operating, offers an important alternative to war.

In situations where the political processes are atrophied (as in authoritarian or totalitarian regimes), the appeal of violence (the right of revolution) gains attraction. It is proper that the violence of the oppressed *not* be judged the same as those who use violence to oppress. But even here there are distinct limits. One should not encourage violence from afar; others may die as a result of your advocacy or your refusal to consider and seek the implementation of a non-military alternative. In addition, the instruments of coercion in the hands of the State are usually overwhelming when compared to the ones of those who would challenge it. There is thus little likelihood of success. Those who combine an intention to fulfill some broader conception of humaneness with the level of violence required for success can lose their values in the process. Even when power is won through such instruments of coercion, it then rests on force and is subject to challenge on the same grounds on which it was achieved. Finally, all that violence can do is place a new group in power. Whether this group will use that power for the values you expect, or for quite different ones, always remains an open question. Given such practical considerations in addition to the moral ones, those seeking needed change should first use nonviolent techniques to achieve it. If nonviolent alternatives are not readily available, they should be developed. Who, after all, faces more formidable instruments of State coercion than the Polish workers?

There are many currents of thought and different responses to the question, when, if ever, is the organized use of mass violence justified? The difference between pacifist and just war thought, between focusing on achieving needed change without violence and violent forms of liberation, may never be resolved.

But a common obligation applies to adherents of all positions. The pacifist, who accepts as absolute the norm ''thou shalt not kill,'' must work to establish viable alternatives to mass violence, or become the hapless witness to injustice. The just war advocate, or the liberation theologian who believes that human welfare may require resort to violence, is also obligated to develop alternatives to mass violence. In the values that each seeks to advance, and in the restrictions on means, violence is at best the last resort.

In none of these positions is moral purity possible; in none of them is success guaranteed. But the advocates of each view would improve their current stance by adding a commitment to develop and apply alternatives to war and violent revolution as the means to achieve change, gain security, or prevent conquest. Such a commitment offers the pacifist an answer to the need to meet legitimate security concerns and to force needed change; it offers the just war advocate the means to be certain violence is, in fact, the last resort; it offers the liberation theologian the means to change exploitative situations, but implies that it requires more than merely changing who is in power or the name of the economic system. It asks that in the process of change, means appropriate to the ends should be tested with the resources which would make success possible; it asks how unjust means, oppressive by their very nature, can be the instrument of progress.

CONCLUSION

During the Vietnam war, thousands of young Americans facing the draft (and the families, schools, and religious institutions involved in their lives) hurriedly confronted the problems of ethics and war. Today again the question of conscription brings into focus for many the abstract issues discussed above. The central problem is that we live in a world in which the refusal to be adequately prepared for war can just as surely lead to war as can a commitment to militarism. Thus, neither becoming a conscientious objector nor a conscientious participant in war offers an ideal position. Whichever choice one makes today, the obligation to develop alternatives to war or violent revolution remains. Thinking through the conflicting values of obedience to one's conscience and of responsiblity to one's political community is one valuable step in developing a capacity to apply ethical values to world politics.

BIBLIOGRAPHY

The books listed below trace the history of ethics, offer broad introductions to the subject, and present the pacifist, just war, and liberation theological views concerning violence. They also trace the roots of secular ethical traditions and introduce the discussion of current ethical issues, providing answers to question such as those listed on page 384.

A. The Religious Bases of Ethics

15 – 1 *Holy Bible,* King James Version, 1,024pp, 1980, New American Library, $4.95.

15 – 1A *Good News Bible,* Translated and Published by the United Bible Societies, 1452pp, 1976, $8.95.

15 – 2 *Holy Bible,* Revised Standard Version, 1,120pp, 1980, New American Library, $4.95.

15 – 2A *The New American Bible,* Translated by the Catholic Biblical Association of America, 1,489pp, 1979, Collins Publishers, $13.95.

15 – 3 *The Living Talmud: The Wisdom of the Fathers,* Judah Goldin, trans., 247pp, 1980, New American Library, $1.75. Selections from the teachings of Jewish sages.

15 – 4 *The Teachings of the Compassionate Buddha,* Edwin Burtt (ed.), 247pp, 1955, New American Library, $1.75. A selection of the basic texts of Buddhism.

15 – 5 *The Meaning of the Glorious Koran,* Mohammed Marmaduke Pickthall, trans., NAL, $2.75. English translation of the sacred book of Islam.

15 – 6 *The Way of Life: Tao Te Ching,* Lao Tzu, R.B. Blakney, trans., 134pp, 1955, Mentor, $1.50. The basic teachings of Taoism.

15 – 7 *How to Know God: The Yoga Aphorisms of Patanjali,* 128pp, 1980, Verdanta, $5.95. The classic works on Yoga.

15 – 8 *The Song of God: Bhagavad-Gita,* 143pp, 1980, NAL, $1.50. The gospel of Hinduism.

15 – 9 *The Upanishads: Breath of the Eternal,* trans, Swami Prabhavanada and Frederick Manchester, trans., 128pp, 1980, NAL, $1.50. Forms the core of sacred scriptures and the highest authority for Hinduism.

15 – 10 *The Sayings of Confucius,* James Ware, trans., 128pp, 1980, Mentor, $1.25. The basic philosophy of Confucius.

15 – 11 *Patterns in Comparative Religion,* Mircea Eliade, 484pp, 1980, NAL $4.95. Seeks to establish core religious values.

15 – 12 *What the Great Religions Believe,* Joseph Gaer, 192pp, 1975, Signet, $1.75. An account of the basic beliefs of the world's historic religions . . . adds Zoroastrianism and Jainism to those above.

15 – 13 *All Things Made New: A Comprehensive Outline of the Baha'i Faith,* John Ferraby, 319pp, 1975, Baha'i, $7.95. A new religious faith seeking to unify all others through a change in the spirit of humanity.

B. Non-Theistic Basis of Ethics

Classic
15 – 14 *Foundations of the Metaphysics of Morals,* Immanuel Kant, Lewis Beck, trans., 92pp, 1959, Liberal Arts Press, $3.45. Kant's attempt to construct a moral philosophy free of evidence about how people live. The resultant moral laws are universal, must be devoid of self-interested intention, and dependent on experience only in determining their application.

Classic
15 – 15 *Utilitarianism,* John Stuart Mill, 350pp, 1979, Bobbs-Merrill, $2.95. Mill's defense of the greatest happiness for the great number as the norm on which a rational ethics can be based.

15 – 16 *Ethics Since 1900,* Mary Warnock, 150pp, 1978 (1960) (3rd. ed.), Oxford, $3.50. Introduces 20th century secular thought on ethics including a study of the works of G.E. Moore, Ayer, Rawls, Sartre, and Wittgenstein. Concludes there has been a general shift from Freudian to Marxian assumptions and calls naive the belief that a "pure moral conviction or argument" can stand on its own without reference to the social setting in which it arises.

Intro
15 – 17 *Theories of Ethics,* Philippa Foot (ed.), 187pp, 1967, Oxford, $4.95. An

anthology focusing on the "naturalistic fallacy" (the attempt to derive obligatory rules from descriptive statements) and utilitarianism through current disputes. Especially useful is John Searle's "How to Derive the Ought from the Is."

15–18 *Ethical Judgment: The Use of Science in Ethics,* Abraham Edel, 348pp, 1964, Free Press, $3.00. Edel analyzes seven strands which contribute to ethical relativism: morality is man-made; everything changes; doing your own thing; struggle for power; mechanistic psychology, education, and linguistic theory. He then examines these strands within modern social science disciplines, and concludes that democratic values are well-supported and should be considered the basis for moral criticism.

15–19 *The First Book of Ethics,* Algernon Black, 66pp, 1965, Franklin Watts, $4.90. Explores questions like the meaning of truth, honesty, duty, sacrifice, and obligations.

15–20 *Humanist Manifestos I and II,* Paul Kurtz, 31pp, 1973, Prometheus Books, $1.95. An articulation of liberal humanist values as they apply to a variety of ethical, social and political problems. Urges the abolition of war and the creation of a world community based on law.

15–21 *Janus, A Summing Up,* Arthur Koestler, 354pp, 1978, Random House, $3.95. An assessment of the cultural condition of humanity some thirty years after Hiroshima; Koestler draws heavily on biological evolution to sustain his pessimism: we can and will destroy our species.

15–22 *Morale,* John Gardner, 158pp, 1980, Norton, $3.45. Despite alienation of individuals and disintegration of institutions, Gardner finds cause for optimism in the ability of Western civilization to renew its values and to reform its institutions.

15–23 *The Arrogance of Humanism,* David Ehrenfeld, 286pp, 1978, Oxford, $11.95. An attack on the autonomy of reason, faith in progress and in technology, and an appeal for a sense of limits: all problems are not solvable.

15–24 *Herbert Marcuse: An Exposition and a Polemic,* Alasdair MacIntyre, 114pp, 1970, Viking, $4.95. Concludes "the philosophy of the young Hegelians, fragments of Marxism, and revised chunks of Freud's metapsychology — out of these materials Marcuse has produced a theory that . . . evokes the great names of freedom and reason while betraying their substance at every important point" (p. 106).

15–25 *Duties Beyond Borders, On the Limits and Possibilities of Ethical International Politics,* Stanley Hoffmann, 288pp, 1981, Syracuse, $9.95. A student of international relations examines here three crucial moral issues — the use of violence, the promotion of human rights, and distributive justice — and suggests that force remains "the essence of the international milieu despite all of the efforts of lawyers and statesmen to do away with it."

15–26 *The Theory of Morality,* Alan Donagan, 278pp, 1979, Chicago, $4.95. Examines contemporary secular theories of morality and offers his own theory based on "practical reason."

15 – 27 *Reason and Morality,* Alan Gewirth, 393pp, 1978, Chicago, $20.00. An important contribution to the discussion.

15 – 28 *Evaluation Thesaurus,* Michael Scriven, 149pp, 1980, Edgepress, $6.95. A careful exploration of the language of moral and non-moral evaluation.

15 – 29 *The Social Construction of Reality, A Treatise in the Sociology of Knowledge,* Peter Berger & Thomas Luckmann, 219pp, 1966, Doubleday, $3.50. Seeks to account for why societies take different things for granted.

Classic
15 – 30 *The Treason of the Intellectuals,* Julien Benda, 244pp, 1928, 1969, Norton, $3.95. The primary function of intellectuals is to clarify rational and moral concepts, thus restraining and acting as judges on the powerful. When they enter politics themselves, they betray their station and leave only power to decide what is right.

15 – 31 *The Good Want Power, An Essay in the Psychological Possibilities of Liberalism,* Kathleen Nott, 319pp, 1977, Basic Books, $13.50. A somewhat personal consideration of why liberalism can be neither fully materialistic nor idealistic; the relationship of progress to the achievement of an end; and the hope, not very optimistic, that liberalism will revive.

15 – 32 *Right and Wrong,* Charles Fried, 225pp, 1979, Harvard, $5.95. Maintains that we are constrained but not smothered by morality; lying, participation in the economic life of market economies, and the intrusion of one individual into the life of another are considered.

15 – 33 *Primary Philosophy,* Michael Scriven, 303pp, 1966, McGraw-Hill, $15.95. Argues that reason can decide answers to humanity's primary problems, or when evidence and reason are inconclusive, at least achieve the best interim solution. Concludes that democracy is probably a prerequisite of a moral society but no guarantee of one.

15 – 34 *Doing Good: The Limits of Benevolence,* Willard Gaylin, Ira Glasser, Steven Marcus & David Rothman, 170pp, 1978, Pantheon, $3.95. Four separate essays, studying different times, places, and policies and concluding it is difficult to do good because, for example, you may become dependent upon your benefactor.

C. Applications of Ethics to Social Concerns

15 – 35 *Ethics,* Dietrich Bonhoeffer, 382pp, 1979 (1949), Macmillan, $1.95. A contemporary theological definition of the basis of ethics is: "God as revealed in Jesus Christ." Bonhoeffer maintains that God's creation bestows on humankind, moral obligations for this world's institutions.

15 – 36 *Christian Realism and Liberation Theology,* Dennis McCann, 1981, Orbis, $8.95. Compares Niebhurian theology with the contemporary.

D. Selected Works in the History of Ideas

15 – 37 *The Iliad, or the Poem of Force,* Simone Weil, 39pp, 1956, Pendle Hill, $1.20. A profoundly impressive interpretation of the Homeric epic as teaching the effects of violence on those who use it, as well as those who suffer under it.

Classic
15 – 38 *The Peloponnesian War,* Thucydides, 516pp, 1954, (c. 508 B.C.) Penguin, $3.95. Athenian democracy was degraded by the terrible requirements of war — a classic of history with many ethical and political analogies to the present.

15 – 39 *Complete Plays of Aristophanes,* Moses Hades (ed.), 501pp, 1962, Bantam, $1.45. A Greek pacifist and playwright argues against the Peloponnesian war.

15 – 40 *The Last Days of Socrates,* Plato, 199pp, 1977 (399 B.C.), Penguin, $1.95. An affirmation of truth, of conscience, and of the law; when in conflict, Socrates accepts the verdict of an unjust law.

Intro
15 – 41 *Christian Attitudes toward War and Peace,* Roland Bainton, 299pp, 1980, Abingdon, $5.95. A historical survey and critical appraisal by a well-known historian. Covers the range of ethical perspectives found in the Christian heritage, and explores the historical context in which each emerged. An excellent introduction.

15 – 42 *Ideology, Reason, and the Limitation of War: Religious and Secular Concepts 1200 – 1740,* James Johnson, 291pp, 1975, Princeton, $18.50. Traces the origins of just war, holy war, and natural law concepts; maintains that in the present, relativism restrains holy war advocates, and a "rudimentary international community" offers hope to limit war through a "new and just war doctrine."

15 – 43 *On World Government,* Dante Alighieri, 80pp, 1957, Bobbs-Merrill, $2.90. Dante's plan for a world government of Christian powers, written in 1317.

15 – 44 *On God and Political Duty,* John Calvin, 102pp, 1956, Bobbs-Merrill, $3.25. Calvin argues that obedience to earthly rulers, who are ordained by God, takes precedence over the freedom which Christianity grants to the individual conscience.

15 – 45 *The Essential Erasmus,* John Dolan (ed.), 397pp, 1964, NAL, $1.95. Erasmus of Rotterdam (1466 – 1536) found it "incredible to see the tremendous expenditures of work and effort which intelligent beings put forth in an effort to exchange (peace) for a heap of ruinous evils (war)" *(The Complaint of Peace).*

15 – 46 *Prolegomena to the Law of War and Peace,* Hugo Grotius, 43pp, 1957, Bobbs-Merrill, $2.80. Grotius sets forth the rules for warfare in order that it might be conducted in a more humane manner (1625).

15 – 47 *Rights of Man,* Thomas Paine, 309pp, 1976 (1791 – 2), Penguin, $2.50. Paine's response to Edmund Burke's attack on the French Revolution, in which Paine

justifies revolutionary violence if it brings representative government and promotes human rights. He did not foresee the reign of terror or the Napoleonic dictatorship.

15 – 48 *On History,* Immanuel Kant, Lewis Beck (ed.), 154pp, 1963, Bobbs-Merrill, $3.70. Immanual Kant's (1724 – 1804) "Idea for a Universal History from a Cosmopolitan Point of View" and "Perpetual Peace," plus several essays on beginnings, progress, and goals in history. Perpetual peace is possible between republican States for they make possible juridical legislation.

E. Ethics Within a Society: The Nature of the Enterprise

15 – 49 *Justice, Human Nature and Political Obligation,* Morton Kaplan, 279pp, 1976, Free Press, $14.95. A critique of Toulmin *(Reason in Ethics)* and Rawls *(A Theory of Justice)* maintaining that values can be objectively defined within a system in which political motivation, political obligation, identification, and goals are specified.

15 – 50 *Ethics and Public Policy,* Tom Beauchamp (ed.), 464 pp, 1975, Prentice-Hall, $11.95. Contending views of key issues; Chapter 5 is titled "War."

15 – 51 *Where Do You Draw the Line? An Exploration into Media Violence, Pornography and Censorship,* Victor Cline (ed.), 365ppm 1974, Brigham Young, $7.95. Presents contending views of current issues in the balancing of rights.

15 – 52 *Lying, Moral Choices in Public and Private Life,* Sissela Bok, 326pp, 1979, Vintage, $2.95. Clarifies the nature of the enterprise of applying ethical values to social concerns by carefully considering the various circumstances in which lying might be morally preferred to telling the truth.

F. Ethics Within a Society: Law and Democracy

15 – 53 *The Children of Light and the Children of Darkness: A Vindication of Democracy and a Critique of Its Traditional Defense,* Reinhold Niebuhr, 190pp, 1944, Scribners, $5.95. Argues that democratic ideals often fail to account for the evil which people may do, and that an adequate defense of democracy requires a Christian interpretation of human nature which recognizes human capacities for both good and evil. Defends the idea that democracy is relevant to the emergent world community.

15 – 54 *The Religion of Ethical Nationhood: Judaism's Contribution to World Peace,* Mordecai Kaplan, 205pp, 1970, Macmillan, $5.95. Maintains that secular States threaten us with overpopulation, depletion of resources, and nuclear warfare; the alternative is ethical nationhood of which Israel is considered the first example — a State based on a religion.

15 – 55 *Government and the Mind,* Joseph Tussman, 175pp, 1977, Oxford, $9.95.

Argues that government does influence the mind — through education, regulation of the forums for public discourse (radio, TV, newspapers), and in other ways. It should help create a forum that "can become the sustainer of a mode of communication that is more than a form of conflict."

15 – 56 *The Decline of Democracy, Essays on an Endangered Species,* Ralph Buultjens, 1981, Orbis, $4.95. Argues that democracy represents a recent and temporary aberration within human history.

15 – 56A *Christianity and Democracy,* Richard John Neuhaus, 14pp, 1982, The Institute on Religion and Democracy, $1.50. Makes the case for democracy as the best embodiment of Christian values in its respect for conscience, in its leaving the future open, and in its sustaining of human rights.

15 – 57 *The Philosophy of Law in Historical Perspective,* Carl Friedrich, 297pp, (1963), Chicago, $5.50. Introduces eighteen different interpretations of the basis of law, and concludes with a chapter on "Peace and the World Community of Law."

15 – 58 *The Morality of Consent,* Alexander Bickel, 160pp, 1975, Yale, $3.95. A thoughtful analysis of the limits of civil disobedience, first-amendment-protected behavior, and the moral basis of democratic government.

Classic

15 – 59 *The Origins of Totalitarianism,* Hannah Arendt, 527pp, 1951, 1973, Harcourt, Brace, Jovanovich, $5.95. Maintains that totalitarian governments in Germany and Russia so altered the concept of politics, society, and the State, that our traditional concepts are of little help. The pre-eminence of ideology and terror are the new key elements.

15 – 60 *Political and Legal Obligation,* J. Roland Pennock & John Chapman (eds.), 455pp, 1970. Atherton, $15.00. Studies the moral, legal and political basis of loyalty to a political community, and the conditions for obedience and for civil disobedience. The complexity of these problems is explored here by philosophers and political scientists.

Intro

15 – 61 *The Morality of Law,* Lon Fuller, 202pp, 1965, Yale, $3.95. Usefully distinguishes between the moralities of duty and of aspiration; goes on to the relationship between law and morality; and examines the moral pre-conditions of law.

15 – 62 *The Concept of Law,* Herbert Hart, 263pp, 1976, Oxford, $6.50. An introduction to the philosophy of law, the bases of law and its role in adjudicating disputes.

15 – 63 *The Policy Predicament: Making and Implementing Public Policy,* George Edwards III & Ira Sharkansky, 336pp, 1978, Freeman, $14.00. Identifies the pattern of rational decision-making — outline options, decide on goals, pick most feasible option. Policy is made in a democracy by public opinion, contending interests and values, scarce resources, and much else influencing the policy outcome.

G. Ethics Within a Society: Conscience and War

TEW

15 – 64 *Conscience and War Kit,* World Without War Council of Northern California, 100pp, 1981, World Without War Publications, $5.00. A balanced portrayal of the ethical choices involved in reconciling conflicting obligations to one's conscience, to the community, and to justice, together with statements of those who have made up their mind.

15 – 65 *Handbook for Conscientious Objectors,* 137pp, 1981 (13th ed.), CCCO, $1.75. The basic handbook containing much of the information used by individuals considering becoming conscientious objectors to war.

15 – 66 *Conscription: A World View,* War Resisters International, 166pp, 1968, Housmans, $2.50. Examines the status of conscription, and particularly conscientious objection, in nearly every country in the world.

15 – 67 *The New Exiles: American War Resisters in Canada,* Roger N. Williams, 401pp, 1971, Liveright, $3.45. Captures the many moods and justifications of the exile-community during the Vietnam war.

15 – 68 *Words of Conscience, Religious Statements on Conscientious Objection,* National Interreligious Service Board for Conscientious Objectors, 134pp, 1980, NISBCO, $2.00. Statements supporting conscientious objection to war by over fifty religious bodies.

15 – 69 *Of Holy Disobedience,* A.J. Muste, 18pp, 1968, Greenleaf, $.75. An argument for non-cooperation (a refusal to register for the draft) as morally superior to the C.O. position.

15 – 70 *Conscientious Objection in the Civil War,* E. Wright, 274pp, 1966, Barnes, $5.50. A study of individuals in America who tried to resolve their conflicting obligations to conscience, the State, and social justice.

15 – 71 *Diary of a Self-Made Convict,* Alfred Hassler, 182pp, 1958, Fellowship, O.P. A moving account of the author's experience in prison as a non-cooperating C.O. in World War II.

15 – 72 *The Right to Refuse to Kill, A New Guide to Conscientious and Service Refusal,* International Peace Bureau, 35pp, 1971, $.60. A selection of writings seeking to establish the universal right to declare oneself a conscientious objector to war.

15 – 73 *Conscription of Conscience: The American State and the Conscientious Objector, 1940 – 49.* Mulford Sibley & Philip Jacob, 580pp, 1952, Johnson, $31.00. The most complete account of C.O.'s in the World War II period.

15 – 74 *Conscience in America: A Documentary History of Conscientious Objection in America, 1757 – 1967,* Lillian Schlissel (ed.), 444pp, 1968, Dutton, O.P. An anthology of writings which traces the conflict of individual conscience with the demands of the State concerning warfare. Introduces a wide range of views, too many of which fail to present viable alternatives to violence as a means for achieving security or justice.

15 – 75 *Guidelines for the East Bay Draft Counseling Center,* Robert Pickus and Steve Bischoff, 8pp, 1969, World Without War Council, free. An almost singular example of draft counseling based on the formal cooperation of community organizations; intended to provide unbiased information and a searching examination of the religious, ethical and political dimensions of the draft decision.

15 – 76 *Conscience, War and the Selective Objector,* Richard Niebanck, 62pp, 1969, Board of Social Ministry, Lutheran Church in America, $.60. A careful argument which attempts to establish the real but limited autonomy of conscience. Examines the conflict between civil authority and selective objection to war based on just war arguments.

15 – 77 *Handbook on Non-Payment of War Taxes,* Ernest Bromley (ed.), 50pp, 1980, Peacemakers, $1.00. A manual which describes the procedures to go through if you wish to protest the use of tax revenue for military programs.

H. Ethics Within a Society: The Extent and Limits of Political Obligation

15 – 78 *Obligation and the Body Politic,* Joseph Tussman, 144pp, 1968 Oxford, $3.50. Argues that individuals do belong to organizations they did not join by virtue of the benefits they receive from them. Offers a difficult intellectual challenge to individuals considering conscientious objection, civil disobedience, or other forms of appeal to a higher obligation than that of obeying the law.

15 – 79 *What Belongs to Caesar,* Donald Kaufman, 128pp, 1970. Herald, $2.95. Theories of political obligation examined by a Mennonite theologian, who makes the case against paying taxes which the political community through its representatives appropriated for war.

15 – 80 *Obligations: Essays on Disobedience, War and Citizenship,* Michael Walzer, 242pp, 1971, Simon & Schuster, $2.95. A collection of thoughtful essays showing how the author's commitment to the "consent of the governed" is applied to current political and social issues.

15 – 81 *The New Meaning of Treason,* Rebecca West, 374pp, 1968, Viking, $1.85. Compares the meaning of treason during World War II and in the 1950s and laments the laxer standards of what constitutes treason of the 1950s.

15 – 82 *Obligation and Dissent: An Introduction to Politics,* Donald Hansen & Robert Fowler (eds.), 389pp, 1971, Little, Brown, O.P. An excellent collection of essays which juxtapose contrasting views of such problems as civil disobedience, selective conscientious objection, and the right to revolution. A useful introduction to a number of central questions.

I. Ethics Within a Society: Production and Distribution of Wealth

15 – 83 *The Great Economic Debate: An Ethical Analysis,* J. Philip Wogaman, 182pp,

1977, Westminster, $5.95. A remarkably judicious introduction to five economic systems: authoritarian socialism (Marxism), laissez-faire capitalism, mixed economies, democratic socialism, and the "economic conservatism of the "steady-State" economist — Schumacher, Daly and Stivers. The importance of moral issues is asserted throughout.

15 – 84 *Social Justice in the Liberal State,* Bruce Ackerman, 416pp, 1980, Yale, $17.50. The case for liberalism, based on neither market mechanisms nor State bureaucracies but on a broad definition of individual freedom, and what the State can legitimately do to enhance it.

15 – 85 *The Ethic of Democratic Capitalism, A Moral Reassessment,* Robert Benne, 288pp, 1981, Fortress, $10.95. A response to critics of democratic capitalism arguing that liberty, equality, productivity, and the quality of social and cultural life are best approached in societies permitting market mechanisms to decide price, wages, what gets produced, and how it is distributed.

INF

15 – 86 *A Theory of Justice,* John Rawls, 607pp, 1971 Harvard, $7.50. Rawls seeks to defend the following conception of justice: "All social values — liberty and opportunity, income and wealth, and the bases of self-respect — are to be distributed equally unless an unequal distribution of any, or all, of these values is to everyone's advantage." Rawls indicates that an equitable but not equal distribution of income is to everyone's advantage.

15 – 87 *Justice or Tyranny? A Critique of John Rawls's "Theory of Justice,"* David Schaefer, 137pp, 1979, Kennikat, $12.50. Argues that Rawls's view of political philosophies is a disguised ideology, and that classical problems of political philosophy remain unresolved.

15 – 88 *The New Egalitarianism: Questions and Challenges,* David Schaefer (ed.), 248pp, 1979, Kennikat, $15.00. An anthology responding to the attacks on Western democratic capitalism.

15 – 89 *Liberal Equality,* Amy Autmann, 318pp, 1980, Cambridge, $10.95. Traces the shift from equality of opportunity to equality of outcome, and attempts a synthesis.

15 – 90 *Christian Political Theology: A Marxian Guide,* Joseph Petulla, 256pp, 1972, Orbis, $4.95. The author writes "a primary purpose of this book is the presentation of a Marxian conceptual devise as a contribution to an understanding of economic, political, and social processes from within a Christian theological perspective."

15 – 91 *Religious Life and the Poor, Liberation Theology Perspectives,* Alejandro Cussianovich, 168pp, 1979, Orbis, $6.95. A Peruvian theologian maintains that solidarity with the poor is the religious imperative of the present, which can best be carried out through the acceptance of a life of poverty for oneself.

15 – 92 *Christian-Marxist Dialogue,* Paul Oestreicher (ed.), 156pp, 1969, Macmillan,

$1.95. A discussion between East European Marxists and radical Christians and the similarities and differences between modern radical theology and Marxism.

15 – 93 *Marxism and Religion in Eastern Europe*, Richard DeGeorge and J.P. Scanlon (eds.), 180pp, 1976, Reidel, $27.00. Describes the conflict between the two.

15 – 93A *Must Walls Divide*, James Will, 115pp, 1981, National Council of Churches/Friendship Press, $3.75. An attempt to find uniformity underlying sharp ideological and political differences through an affirmation of Eastern European governments and governmentally recognized religious leaders as the only legitimate spokespersons.

15 – 93B *Must Walls Confuse?*, George Weigel, 16pp, 1981, Institute on Religion and Democracy, $1.50. A critical review of *Must Walls Divide* citing repression of civil and political rights, the crushing of religious dissent, and the subservence of society to the State and the State to the Soviet Union as providing good reason for current divisions.

15 – 93C *Discretion and Valour*, Trevor Beeson, 416pp, 1982, Fortress Books, $15.95. Examines the tension between religious life and State authority and concludes that the "persecution goes on and the suffering remains acute."

15 – 94 *On Synthesizing Marxism and Christianity*, Dale Vree, 206pp, 1976, Wiley, $16.95. Vree believes a synthesis has been sought in Marxist Christian dialogue to the loss of both viewpoints; he warns against illusions, such as denying political liberty to Christians who disagree with the conclusion of dialogue, and of the tendency to turn Marxist claims into articles of Christian faith.

15 – 95 *The Road to Serfdom*, Friedrick Hayek, 250pp, 1956, University of Chicago, $4.95. Argues that the increased expectation of benefits from State action feeds the Leviathan.

15 – 96 *Mind and Politics: An Approach to the Meaning of Liberal and Socialist Individualism*, Ellen Wood, 224pp, 1972, California. $15.75. Clarifies the similar and different conceptions of the individual in the two creeds.

J. Ethics Within a Society: Revolution and Violence

15 – 97 *The Moral Meaning of Revolution*, Jon Gunnemann, 277pp, 1979, Yale, $15.00. Maintains that a revolution shifts a society's view of the nature and origins of evil but does not abolish evil: thus, revolutionary movements, ends, and means are accountable to moral evaluation.

15 – 98 *Philosophy for a New Generation*, Arthur Bierman & James Gould (eds.), 678pp, 3rd ed., 1977, Macmillan, $10.95. Chapters on liberation, political flux, freedom, violence, and revolution.

15 – 99 *Philosophy and Political Action*, Kai Nielsen & Charles Parsons (eds.), 282pp,

1972, Oxford, $4.50. Part I discusses reform, revolution, and violence; Part V, "Defiance of the State."

15 – 100 *Religion and Violence: A Primer for White Americans,* Robert McAfee Brown, 128pp, 1973, Westminster, $4.95. A former pacifist argues that violence is justified in opposition to unjust social systems.

15 – 101 *Violence and the Sacred,* René Girard, 333pp, 1972 (1977), Johns Hopkins, $5.95. Explores concepts of violence linking sacrifice to the sacred, and to the restoration of order to society.

15 – 102 *The Betrayal of the West,* Jacques Ellul, 207pp, 1978, Seabury, $9.95. Calls the assault on Western values lamentable.

K. Ethics Within Society: Utopia

15 – 103 *Utopia,* Thomas More, 154pp, 1965 (1516), Penguin, $2.50. More's ideal society in which criminals are not killed but do penal service, and in which war is loathed but fought in "self-defense, to repel invaders from friendly territory, or to liberate the victims of dictatorships."

15 – 104 *Paths in Utopia,* Martin Buber, 152pp, 1949 (1958), Beacon, $3.95. Critical appraisal of utopian thought.

15 – 105 *Utopian Thought in the Western World,* Frank Manuel and Fritizie Manuel, 896pp, 1979, Harvard, $25.00. Describes many utopias.

15 – 106 *A Pagan Prophet, William Morris,* Charlotte Oberg, 189pp, 1978, Virginia, $13.95. A critique of industrial England on aesthetic grounds by a late 19th-century poet.

15 – 107 *The Peace Revolution: Ethos and Social Process,* John Somerville, 236pp, 1975, Greenwood, $14.95. Argues that the process essential to achieve a world without war must penetrate into all aspects of social life. Argues that contesting social forces must be reconciled to achieve peace, not that they must contest their differences without war.

L. Ethics and World Politics: the Nature of the Enterprise

15 – 108 *Moral Claims in World Affairs,* Ralph Pettman (ed.), 280pp, 1979, St. Martins, $18.95. A study of the nature and force of moral claims when applied to relationships between States.

15 – 109 *Morality and Foreign Policy,* Kenneth Thompson, 240pp, 1980, Louisiana State U. Press, $16.95. A Niebuhrian moralist introduces here a way in which moral categories can realistically be applied to foreign affairs.

15 – 110 *Political Theory and International Relations,* Charles Beitz, 212pp, 1979, Princeton, $3.95. Searches for a normative theory of international relations that rejects the prevailing views that international relations is either a state of nature or like a domestic society. His theory emphasizes the autonomy of States, and distributive justice in economic relationships.

15 – 111 *Philosophy, Morality, and International Affairs,* Virginia Held, Sidney Morgenbesser & Thomas Nagel (eds.), 338pp, 1974, Oxford, $5.95. Secular ethicists use a variety of legal, moral and empirical instruments to criticize U.S. foreign policy as evaluated by opponents of U.S. participation in the Vietnam war.

15 – 112 *The Structure of Nations and Empires: A Study of the Recurring Patterns and Problems of the Political Order in Relation to the Unique Problems of the Nuclear Age,* Reinhold Niebuhr, 306pp, 1959, Kelly, $15.00. An influential Protestant theologian applies the standards of "Christian realist" ethics to international politics in the nuclear age. While the nature and scope of war and weapons have changed drastically, the basic moral problems remain the same.

15 – 113 *Evil and World Order,* William Thompson, 116pp, 1977, Harper, $3.95. Doubts that people know enough to create a desirable world order; thus, the effort is likely to produce chaos in this order.

15 – 114 *The Moral Issue in Statecraft: Twentieth Century Approaches and Problems,* Kenneth Thompson, 127pp, 1966, Louisiana State, $8.95. Identifies and assesses problems of the changing international order from the standpoint of moral and ethical issues. Surveys Anglo-American approaches to moral and political principles. Examines the inevitable tension between morality and political necessity, and looks for alternatives to moral absolutism in politics.

15 – 115 *Global Living Here and Now,* James Scherer, 128pp, 1974, Friendship, $2.25. Maintains that North Americans can live more responsibly by consuming less; believes a global community is coming into existence without addressing how ideological and cultural differences will be overcome.

15 – 116 *U.S. Foreign Policy and Christian Ethics,* John Bennett & Harvey Seifert, 235pp, 1977, Westminister, $7.95. Explores the morality of deterrence, war, economic systems, and change; dismisses the crusade ethics as "anachronistic" and explores areas of cooperation between just war and pacifist ethicists.

15 – 117 *American Foreign Policy and Moral Rhetoric: The Example of Vietnam,* David Little, 117pp, 1969, Council on Religion and International Affairs (hereafter CRIA), $2.00. Little argues that the liberal critics of American policy in Vietnam paradoxically reject moral issues in international relations as irrelevant, while using language which is loaded with unconsidered moral connotations.

15 – 118 *The Great Ideas: A Synopticon of Great Books,* Mortimer Adler and others (eds.), Vol II, pp. 1010 – 1037, 1952, *Encyclopedia Britannica.* "War and Peace" offers a helpful division of the subject matter and an introduction to the basic ideas.

15 – 119 *Ends and Means: An Inquiry into the Nature of Ideals and into the Methods Employed for their Realization,* Aldous Huxley, 386pp, 1937, Greenwood, $18.50. Huxley argues that Western civilization is peculiarly violent and war-prone but that such a limitation can be overcome. See especially Chapter 9, "War."

15 – 120 *The Human Imperative, A Challenge for the Year 2000,* Theodore Hesburgh, 115pp, 1974, Yale, $8.95. Emphasizes the ethical imperatives in overcoming hunger, distributing political power, and in improving education.

15 – 121 *The Philosopher's World Model,* Archie Bahm, 328pp, 1979, Greenwood, $22.95. Maintains that futuristic works are usually linear while we need "multi-dimensionality" in thought to resolve problems in "a rapidly changing, increasingly complex, more intricately interdependent megalopolitan and global society."

M. Ethics and World Politics: Religions and War

Intro
15 – 122 *War and Peace in the World's Religions,* John Ferguson, 166pp, 1978, Oxford, $3.95. Surveys the attitudes of the world's major religions.

15 – 123 *Judaism and War,* Robert Pickus, 40pp, 1968, World Without War Council, $.50. An anthology of materials covering five different perspectives on war which are encountered in the Jewish tradition. Prepared for high school discussion, useful for adults.

15 – 124 *The Peace Bishops and the Arms Race: An Invitation to the Needed Discussion,* George Weigel, 64pp, 1982, World Without War Publications, $2.00. Reprints four statements on nuclear war and weapons by Catholic Bishops and a four-part reply by George Weigel with responses and commentary. Weigel maintains that America "in or out" of world politics, and "build or don't build" weapons are not the critical question. A peace movement must develop an alternative to war as the legitimate means for conducting international conflict.

15 – 125 *War: Four Christian Views,* Robert Clouse (ed.), 210pp, 1981, Inter-Varsity, $5.95. Advocates of "biblical non-resistance" to war, pacifism, just war, and preventive war (to unseat Pol Pot and prevent massacres, for example) here make their case, with responses by advocates of the other three views.

15 – 126 *I and Thou,* Martin Buber, 137pp, 1970, Scribner's, $2.95. Buber believes that the I-Thou (as opposed to the I-It) relationships are the only ethical ones. He draws from this insight, a commitment to nonviolence. A difficult exposition of relationships.

15 – 127 *Tao Te Ching,* Lao Tzu, 192pp, 1964, Penguin, $1.95. A classic expression of a Taoist view of war: the acceptance of a non-just situation is preferable to war. Fighting should be avoided at all costs; one must never be the aggressor. The goal is peaceful co-existence; non-contention will eventually yield justice.

15 – 128 *Islam and Development, Religion and Socio-political Change,* John Esposito

(ed.), 292pp, 1981, Syracuse, $9.95. Assesses Islamic teachings concerning development, and the application of those teachings in many Moslem countries.

15 – 129 *The Law of War and Peace in Islam: A Study of Moslem Internatonal Law,* Majid Khadduri, 145pp, 1955, Garland, $38.00. Traces the development of Moslem law relating to war, peace, and international relations.

15 – 130 *Modern War and the Christian,* Ralph Moellering, 96pp, 1969, Augsburg, $2.50. Argues that the Christian must choose between war and peace. Examines three traditional justifications of war in the Christian heritage, and concludes that none of them will do today.

N. Ethics and World Politics: The Problem of War

15 – 131 *The Ethics of War,* Barrie Paskins & Michael Dockrill, 332pp, 1979, Univ. of Minnesota Press, $28.50. An essay in practical philosophy which considers whether the bombing of cities, terror, and nuclear deterrence can be ethically justified. While clear that nuclear deterrence requires intent to retaliate, deterrence "in addition to violating the principles of proportion and noncombatant immunity, . . . introduces an unacceptable quality of giving hostages to fate" (p. 244).

15 – 132 *War and Moral Responsibility,* R.B. Brandt, et al. 144pp, 1974, Princeton, $3.95. An anthology which surveys the moral and ethical issues involved in war — is it ever just? can it be conducted justly? who decides? Contributors include Richard Wasserstrom, Thomas Nagel and Michael Walzer.

15 – 133 *War and the Liberal Conscience,* Michael Howard, 143pp, 1978, Rutgers, $8.50. Four centuries of effort have not led to the abolition of war. Liberals are "profoundly dissatisfied with their world and confident of the power of reason to change it." But if liberals want to abolish war, their love of justice (variously defined) also entails the call to arms.

15 – 134 *The Critique of War: Contemporary Philosophical Explorations,* Robert Ginsberg (ed.), 360pp, 1969, Regnery, O.P. An anthology which explores the causes of war, its nature in the modern world, and the problem of justifying war today. Examines alternatives to war, including law and nonviolent resistance.

N. Ethics and World Politics: Peace

15 – 135 *The Idea of Peace in Antiquity,* Gerardo Zampaglione, 344pp, 1973, Irvington, $20.00. Discusses different conceptions of peace in the Old Testament, classical Greek and Roman sources, and in early Christian writings. Despite the

prevalence of war, much thought has been given throughout the period to the conditions of peace.

15–136 *Locke on War and Peace,* Richard Cox, 220pp, 1960, Clarendon Press, O.P. Studies Locke's conviction that the central purpose of the State is the defense of property.

15–137 *Religion in the Struggle for World Community,* Homer Jack (ed.), 418pp, 1980, World Conference on Religion and Peace, $7.95. The unabridged proceedings of the Third World Conference on Religion and Peace, with speeches by Jesse Jackson, Robert Muller, Kurt Waldheim, George McGovern, A.K. Brohi, Andrew Young, and others.

15–138 *A Just Peace,* Peter Matheson, 156pp,1981, Friendship Press, $5.95. The results of a two-year study by the Church of Scotland to revise pacifist and just war teachings. Attempts to redefine violence, just war, and just revolution, and ends by condoning violence in a just revolution.

15–139 *War or Peace? The Search for New Answers,* Thomas Shannon (ed.), 255pp, 1980, Orbis, $9.95. Features articles by James Finn, Tom Cornell, Gordon Zahn, and David O'Brien.

15–140 *Philosophers of Peace and War, Kant, Clausewitz, Marx, Engels and Tolstoy,* W.B. Gallie, 147pp, 1979, Cambridge, $5.95. An exposition of the ideas of each philosopher designed to illustrate conflicting views of the subjects. The conclusion attempts to draw them together.

15–141 *Peace and Nonviolence: Basic Writings by Prophetic Voices in the World Religions,* Edward Guinan (ed.), 174pp, 1973, Paulist, $4.95. A selection from 19th and 20th century sources demonstrating the variety of justifications and aims of nonviolent movements.

P. Ethics and World Society: International Law and the Conduct of War

15–142 *War and Morality,* Richard Wasserstrom, 136pp, 1970, Wadsworth, $6.95. An anthology with selections dealing with the moral considerations involved in whether to participate in a war; with the limits imposed on the conduct of war; and with the applicability of the Nuremberg principles to subsequent wars.

15–143 *The Law of War,* Leon Friedman (ed.), 1,800pp, 2 volumes, 1972, Random, $65.00. A collection of materials tracing the laws which govern the conduct of warfare from the Middle Ages to the present. Included are treaties, conventions, and agreements, plus transcriptions of war crime trials and court martials to which those laws were applied. Introduction by Telford Taylor.

15–144 *The Nuremberg Fallacy: War and Crimes Since World War II,* Eugene

Davidson, 1973, Macmillan, $9.95. Examines just and unjust warfare since Nuremberg, through case studies of U.S. and North Vietnamese military action in Indochina, the Russian invasion of Czechoslovakia, the Arab-Israel wars, and others.

15 – 145 *Prohibitions and Restraints in War,* Sydney Bailey, 180pp, 1972, Oxford, $5.95. Describes the just war doctrine in Christain ethics, and international law and current restraints.

15 – 146 *Nuremberg and Vietnam: An American Tragedy,* Telford Taylor, 224pp, 1970, Quadrangle, $1.95. The former war chief counsel for the prosecution at Nuremberg draws disturbing historical parallels between American actions in Vietnam and those the U.S. condemned at Nuremberg. Concludes that ''somehow we failed ourselves to learn the lessons we undertook to teach at Nuremberg, and that failure is today's American tragedy.''

15 – 147 *Home from the War, Vietnam: Neither Victims Nor Executioners,* Robert Jay Lifton, 478pp, 1974, Simon & Schuster, $3.95. A psychiatrist's exploration of the impact of the Vietnam war on U.S. soldiers.

15 – 148 *War Crimes and the American Conscience,* Edwin Knoll & Judith McFadden (eds.), 208pp, 1970, Holt, Rinehart & Winston, $2.95. A partial transcript of a conference called by ten liberal Congressional representatives to apply the major principles of Nuremberg to American conduct of the Vietnam war. Participants included Richard Falk, Jerome Frank, Hannah Arendt, Telford Taylor, and Gabriel Kolko. The Nuremberg principles are reprinted and selectively applied to fit the politics of the participants.

15 – 149 *The Catholic Conception of International Law: Vitoria and Suarez,* James Scott, 1934, Georgetown, O.P. A basic introduction.

Q. Ethics and World Politics: Why Mass Violence Is Never Justified— Pacifism

15 – 150 *The Pacifist Conscience,* Peter Mayer (ed.), 447pp, 1966, Regnery, $3.95. An anthology of writings from Lao-Tzu to Camus with an extensive bibliography. Illustrates the wide variety of thought which has been called pacifist.

15 – 151 *The New Testament Basis of Pacifism,* G.H.C. MacGregor, 160pp, 1968, Fellowship, O.P. A classic statement based on a careful analysis of the New Testament. Sees the obligation to accept suffering as the basis of Christian nonviolence.

15 – 152 *The Dagger and the Cross,* Culbert Rutenber, 138pp, 1965, Fellowship, O.P. A careful survey of the Biblical foundations of pacifism written in the context of contemporary Christian thought.

15 – 153 *The Early Christian Attitude Toward War,* C. John Cadoux, Gordon Press, $69.95. Identifies the currents in Christian pacifism.

15—154 *War, Peace and Nonresistance,* Guy Hershberger, 382pp, 1944, 1969, Herald, $9.95. Traces the biblical roots of the Mennonite pacifism, and the attempts to apply those values in different settings.

15—155 *In Solitary Witness, The Life and Death of Franz Jagerstatter,* Gordon Zahn, 277pp, 1968, Irvington, $18.95. Biography of a conscientious objector in Nazi Germany.

15—156 *Twentieth Century Pacifism,* Peter Brock, 274pp, 1970, Van Nostrand Reinhold, O.P. A history of the principal themes in pacifist thought and activity in this century — conscientious objection in World Wars I and II, Gandhian nonviolence, and nuclear pacifism.

15—157 *Conscience in Crisis,* Richard MacMaster, Samuel Horst & Robert Ulle, 528pp, 1979, Herald, $17.95. History, interpretation and documents of the Mennonites and other peace churches in America and their relationships to the military during the years 1739—1789. Includes documents, statistical charters, and a bibliography.

15—158 *Mennonite Statements on Peace 1915—1966, A Historical and Theological Review of Anabaptist-Mennonite Concepts of Peace Witness and Church-State Relations,* Richard Detweiler, 71pp, 1968, Herald, $1.50. A summary of the content and a sympathetic theological exposition.

15—159 *New Call to Peacemaking, A Challenge to All Friends,* Norval Hadley (ed.), 80pp, 1976, Faith and Life, $1.00. Seven authors seek to re-establish and clarify the Friends commitment to nonviolence, and to then go about building the conditions of peace in world politics.

15—160 *New Call to Peacemakers,* Maynard Shelly, 96pp, 1979, Faith & Life, $2.00. A wide-ranging work calling Christians to simpler lifestyles, to recognition of their "violence" in sustaining U.S. corporations who are accused of exploiting others. The definition of "violence" employed is so broad that it is doubtful if anyone can be nonviolent.

15—161 *Nevertheless: The Varieties of Religious Pacifism,* John Yoder, 144pp, 1972, Herald, $2.50. A typology of over fifteen distinctive yet overlapping varieties of religious pacifism (at least one of which might better be described as a just war position) by the noted Mennonite scholar.

15—162 *On Earth Peace, Discussions on War/Peace Issues Between Friends, Mennonites, Brethren, and European Churches, 1935—1975,* Donald Durnbaugh, 412pp, 1978, Brethren, $9.95. Texts from forty troubled years of affirming a rejection of all violence, asserting the need to witness for that belief and confront the horrors of Nazism, and the argument that violence is needed to achieve change.

15—163 *Pacifism in Britain 1914—1945, The Defining of a Faith,* Martin Ceadel, 300pp, 1980, Oxford, $31.00. The author believes World War I encouraged pacifists to believe pacifism was politically practical; World War II did not.

R. Ethics and World Politics: When Is Mass Violence Justified? — Sometimes: Just War

15—164 *The Original Revolution, Essays on Christian Pacifism,* John Yoder, 208pp, 1972, Herald, $4.95. An attempt to reassert the political significance of Christ's rejection of violence as more fundamental than contemporary justifications for achieving justice through violent revolution.

15—165 *Christian Pacifism in History,* Geoffrey Nuttall, 96pp, 1971, World Without War Publications, $1.25. Traces five Christian avenues of thought justifying a refusal to participate in war.

15—166 *Pacifism in the United States from the Colonial Era to the First World War,* Peter Brock, 1005pp, 1968, Princeton, $30.00. A detailed history of the "peace" churches — Quaker, Mennonite, and Brethren — with a summary of nonsectarian pacifist groups.

15—167 *Pacifism in Europe to 1914,* Peter Brock, 556pp, 1972, Princeton, $8.75. A history of its many variations.

S. Ethics and World Politics: Just War Doctrine

15—168 *The Half-Way Pacifist: Thomas Jefferson's View of War,* Reginald Stuart, 93pp, 1978, Toronto, $10.00. Jefferson knew the economic costs of war, thought reasonable action by us would "provide justice and friendship from others" and yet, found his domestic program overshadowed by the Napoleonic wars. "I hope it is practicable, by improving the mind and morals of society, to lessen the disposition to war, but of its abolition I despair."

INF

15—169 *Just and Unjust Wars: A Moral Argument with Historical Illustrations,* Michael Walzer, 381pp, 1977, Basic, $15.00. Maintains that moral judgment is rightly applied to war and that the just war doctrine still holds true.

15—170 *The Just War in the Middle Ages,* Frederick Russell, 360pp, 1975, Cambridge, $11.95. The development of the doctrine by Aquinas.

15—171 *Modern War and the Pursuit of Peace,* Theodore Weber, 36pp, 1968, CRIA, $.50. A thorough examination of the just war doctrine.

15—172 *Hungry for Peace,* Victor Lamont, 63pp, 1976, Friendship, $2.95. Prose, pictures, graphics designed to point up the absurdity of all war except revolutionary war by the oppressed. More evocative than clear.

15—173 *Faith and Violence: Christian Teaching and Christian Practice,* Thomas Merton, 290pp, 1968, U. of Notre Dame, $3.45. Centered around developing an adequate conception of nonviolence, this volume nonetheless contains reflections on many other subjects.

15 – 174 *Just War and Vatican Council II: A Critique,* Robert W. Tucker, 101pp, 1966, CRIA, $.50. Tucker believes that the diplomat is entrusted with the care of the State and must use whatever means are appropriate to that end. A careful examination of just war doctrine applied to nuclear deterrence.

T. Ethics and World Politics: Mass Violence — the Crusade

15 – 175 *The Origin of the Idea of Crusade,* Carl Erdmann, 446pp, 1977 (1935), Princeton, $32.50. A detailed intellectual history of the idea that offensive warfare is an appropriate instrument of the "Prince of Peace" — the sources of this conclusion vary from the view of sacrificial death in battle as analogous to Christ's death to the "aggressiveness of the Christianized Germanic knights."

U. Ethics and World Politics: Liberation Theology

15 – 176 *Theology in the Americas,* Sergio Torres & John Eagleson (ed.), 438pp, 1976, Orbis, $5.95. Applies liberation theology to the United States. Robert McAfee Brown sets the tone: "Christians cannot be asked to disavow or be suspicious of a position of their own simply because close to two millennia later Karl Marx happened to offer his own version of the same truth."

15 – 177 *Cry of the People, United States Involvement in the Rise of Fascism, Torture, and Murder, & the Persecution of the Catholic Church in Latin America,* Penny Lernoux, 555pp, 1980, Doubleday, $12.95. An impassioned appeal for the Church to lead the revolution — but who will care for the souls of the revolutionaries?

15 – 178 *My Life for My Friends, The Guerrilla Journal of Nestor Paz, Christian,* Nestor Paz, 103pp, 1975, Orbis, $2.95. Tales of combat and love in the service of Che, the revolution and humanity, compressed into eighty days when the guerrilla hero dies of starvation in Bolivia.

15 – 179 *A Theology of Liberation, History, Politics and Salvation,* Gustavo Gutierrez, 288pp, 1973, Orbis, $4.95. Concludes that the Church should be "on the side of the oppressed classes and dominated peoples, clearly and without qualifications" and that "only when the oppressed themselves raise their voice" and "become the protagonists of their own liberation" will we "have an authentic theology of liberation" (p. 307).

INF
15 – 180 *The Gospel of Peace and Justice: Catholic Social Teaching Since Pope John,* Joseph Gremillion, 550pp, 1976, Orbis, $8.95. Contains over 400 pages of documents and about 130 pages of commentary.

15— 181 *A New Moral Order: Studies in Development Ethics and Liberation Theology,* Denis Goulet, 126pp, 1974, Orbis, $3.95. A collection of essays dealing with the need for new moral and ethical perspectives on the development process.

15— 182 *The Militant Gospel, A Critical Introduction to Political Theologies,* Alfredo Fierro, 459pp, 1977, Orbis, $6.95. A Spanish theologian proposes a political theology based on ''an equal mixture of two ingredients: (1) of statements made by Christians who have noted and accepted the obvious correctness of Marxism; (2) of acknowledgments by Marxists who have made a serious effort to understand and appreciate what the Christian faith purports to mean'' (p. 369). Fierro confuses ''historical materialism'' with ''dialectical materialism.''

15— 183 *Camilo Torres, A Biography of the Priest-Guerrillero,* Walter Broderick, 370pp, 1975, Doubleday, $10.00. A detailed account of a priest who joins a guerrilla movement rather than encourage participation in Colombia's political system. Camilo ''did not object to their [the Communist Party's] presence; for after forty years of political activity, the Communist party has its cells operating in every corner of the country and was the most valuable group of all when it came to organizing meetings . . .'' but the party and Camilo disagreed about the tactical values of participating in electoral politics. Torres died in a skirmish with the Colombian Army.

15— 184 *The Church and Third World Revolution,* Pierre Bigo, S.J. 316pp, 1974, 1977, Orbis, $4.95. A liberation theologian with a difference: ''nothing gives evidence that a system which makes revolution the ultimate criterion for conscience will offer protection of any kind to human liberties'' (p. 163). Bigo considers violence a problem and democracy a feature of a liberated society — he aims at some form of democratic socialism.

15— 185 *Camilo Torres: His Life and His Message,* Camilo Torres, 1968, Templegate, $5.95. Writings of a Colombian priest who preached — and waged — revolutionary war, and was killed by government troops whom he was trying to kill.

15— 186 *Evangelicals and Liberation,* Carl Armerding (ed.), 136pp, 1977, Presbyterian & Reformed Publishing, $4.50. Given that liberation theology has become the ''in'' subject, this work explores its biblical roots and contemporary application. Revolutionary socialism is defined as the outcome with one dissent: How does this theology apply to ''the most consistently subservient [church body] to the ruling power . . . where the status quo is Marxist?''

V. Ethics and World Politics: Nuclear War

15— 187 *Peace or Atomic War?,* Albert Schweitzer, 47pp, 1958, 1972, Kennikat, $6.00. An impassioned plea for the renunciation of nuclear weapons after which outstanding differences can be negotiated.

15— 188 *The Limits of Nuclear War, Thinking about the Do-able and the Un-Do-able,*

Paul Ramsey, 56pp, 1963, CRIA, $.50. Maintains that counterforce nuclear war is "the upper limit of rational, politically purposive military action" (p. 10).

15 – 189 *Force, Order, and Justice,* Robert Osgood & Robert Tucker, 374pp, 1971, Johns Hopkins, $4.95. Argues against the viability of nonviolent alternatives to war, but recognizes that nuclear weapons have sharpened the dilemma involved in preparation for war and the use of violence to achieve order or justice.

15 – 190 *The New Nuclear Debate,* Robert Gessest and J. Bryan Hehir, 95pp, 1976, CRIA, $2.00. The authors take different positions concerning nuclear strategy while asking: can it be moral?

15 – 191 *Ethics and Nuclear Strategy,* Harold Ford & Francis Winters, SJ, (eds.), 246pp, 1977, Orbis, $12.95. Fifteen essays focused largely on nuclear weapons and particularly around counterforce doctrines which posit the possibility of fighting a limited nuclear war. Includes an eleven-page bibliography on "ethical issues."

Intro
15 – 192 *The Moral Dilemma of Nuclear Weapons,* William Clancy (ed.), 78pp, 1961, CRIA, $1.50. An anthology of works bringing together political scientists, military strategists, journalists, and theologians. Still the best introduction to the subject.

W. Ethics and World Politics: Economic Relations Between States

15 – 193 *New Hope for the Hungry? The Challenge of the World Food Crisis,* Larry Minear, 140pp, 1975, Friendship, $1.95. Places the food shortage in global perspective and calls for a key role to be played by international organizations and NGOs, especially Churches, in ending persistent hunger.

15 – 194 *On the Development of Peoples (Populorum Progressio),* Pope Paul VI, 53pp, 1967, St. Paul Editions, $.25. A Papal encyclical letter calling for more than economic development although that too is needed. Places the institutions of the Catholic Church on the side of economic development without the imposition of totalitarian governments. Calls for a spirit of world community.

15 – 195 *Cry Justice, The Bible on Hunger and Poverty,* Ronald Sider (ed.), 220pp, 1980, Paulist, $2.45. Selections from the Bible on hunger, poverty, and justice aimed at motivating the rich to help overcome the poverty of the some 750,000,000 people who live on $75 or less per year.

15 – 196 *Religion, Politics, and Social Change in the Third World: A Sourcebook,* Donald Smith (ed.), 286pp, 1971, Free Press, $4.50. Sources, documents, and interpretative essays explore the role of religion in the development process.

15 – 197 *The Emerging Order, God in the Age of Scarcity,* Jeremy Rifkin, & Ted Howard, 1979, Putnam, $10.00. Calls for a New Protestant Reformation to lead the way toward a steady-state economy.

15 – 198 *Enough is Enough: A Biblical Call for Moderation in a Consumer-Oriented Society,* John Taylor, 124pp, 1977, Augsburg, $3.50. Calls for life style changes in response to the limits of growth argument and biblical teachings.

15 – 199 *Foreign Aid as Moral Obligation?* Theodore Sumberg 72pp, 1973, Sage, $3.50. Examines the arguments for considering foreign aid to poor nations a moral duty — and finds them unpersuasive.

15 – 200 *How the Other Third Lives . . . Third World Stories, Poems, Songs, Prayers, and Essays from Asia, Africa, and Latin America,* Margaret White and Robert Quigley, 425pp, 1977, Orbis, $4.95. A mixture of cultural and political messages, the latter featuring Fidel Castro and Ho Chi Minh.

15 – 201 *Bread and Justice, Toward a New International Economic Order,* James McGinnis, 358pp, 1979, Paulist, $8.95. A teacher's book making the case for the NIEO with instructural materials defining the NIEO's goals as just.

X. Ethics and World Politics: International Human Rights

15 – 202 *Human Rights and American Foreign Policy,* Donald Kommers & Gilbert Loescher, (ed.), 345pp, 1979, Notre Dame, $14.95. Weighty contributors suggest how human rights can be advanced along with other foreign policy objectives; includes a section on the advance of human rights in the USSR.

15 – 203 *Claims in Conflict: Retrieving and Renewing the Catholic Human Rights Tradition,* David Hollenback, 224pp, 1979, Paulist, $5.95. Part of a series on topics such as "Human Rights, Needs and Power in an Interdependent World." This work is based on three moral priorities: "1) The needs of the poor take priority over the wants of the rich; 2) the freedom of the dominated takes priority over the liberty of the powerful; and 3) the participation of marginalized groups takes priority over the preservation of an order which excludes."

15 – 204 *Christian Declaration on Human Rights,* Allen Miller (ed.), 190pp, 1977, Eerdmans, $4.95. A series of papers prepared under the auspices of the World Alliance of Reformed Churches, asks if the Christian faith offers a distinctive approach to human rights questions. Various answers are offered: some point out that revolutions of the 20th century have brought totalitarian forms of political organization; others advocate violence as a liberating force.

See Chapter 6, human rights portions.

15 – 205 *Women, Resistance and Revolution, A History of Women and Revolution in the Modern World,* Shiela Rowbotham, 288pp, 1972, Random House, $2.45. An attempt to connect the achievement of women's liberation with the success of world socialist revolution, by adding sexual oppression to economic oppression. Women are considered liberated in China and Cuba.

15 – 206 *New Woman/New Earth: Sexist Ideologies and Human Liberation,* Rosemary Ruether, 221pp, 1975, Seabury, $8.95. Argues that sexism, racism, and capitalism are integrally related.

15 – 207 *Who Really Starves? Women and World Hunger,* Lisa Leghorn & Mary Roodkosky, 40pp, 1977, Friendship, $1.25. An overview touching on women's accomplishments in history, sex discrimination in the United States, and the disproportionate share of hunger experienced by women when compared to men.

CHAPTER 16

SOCIAL CHANGE: NONVIOLENT APPROACHES

THE reality of conflict has been stressed repeatedly in this book. Conflict between States has been the focus, because States are the most powerful actors in world politics, and the threat or fact of war remains for them an acceptable means to resolve basic differences. Conflicts have been considered between ethnic groups, social classes, races, rich and poor, and between groups holding different religious, ideological, or other views. Some of these conflicts, no doubt, arise from misperceptions; but others involve real, incompatible differences. Calling for love or trust in the midst of such conflicts does not provide a sufficient, or even a very helpful, answer.

International conflicts are likely to continue to be resolved by war until the achievement of the conditions introduced in Chapters 4 to 7 as essential to a world without war. A strategy is presented in Chapter 19 through which one country could lead toward their attainment. This peace-initiatives strategy is basically an adaptation of the Gandhian theory of nonviolent conflict, applied to international politics.

At the center of Gandhi's conception of nonviolence was a commitment to certain ideas that made possible the creation of a sense of community between antagonists. War is the denial of community, for it breaks the unity essential to establish non-tyrannical law. In other forms of conflict — interpersonal, small-group, within a society — violence also breaks the sense of community because it seeks to end or limit participation in the decision-making process. That sense of community is also disrupted by discrimination, exploitation, or the unequal administration of the law — but violence breaks it. Any approach that seeks in the midst of conflict to build a sense of community is worthy of careful study.

THE CONTEMPORARY EXPERIENCE

In the post-World War II era nonviolent conflict theory became the subject of careful study. Among those developing the idea were peace researchers among political scientists (see Chapter 17), psychologists, communication specialists, and others focusing on the problem of conflict. Others were inspired by religious traditions and the examples of Mahatma Gandhi and Martin Luther King, Jr. Many joined in the study for practical rather than moral reasons, being fully aware of the terrors of nuclear and conventional warfare and of the tendency of conflicts to escalate.

In the 1970s, however, the cutting edge of nonviolent conflict theory had been blunted and even turned against its developers. Within the peace research field "peace through change" became a prominent slogan; change, as conceived by particular groups, was to be promoted with little regard to the means to be employed; "liberation" in personal or political terms, not reconciliation, became the goal. The moral imperative to find nonviolent means to conduct and resolve conflict became an obstacle to many who knew exactly what the just society looked like and how it could be achieved.

The transition in the civil rights and peace movements from a commitment to principled nonviolence to mass movements in which violence was tolerated and sometimes encouraged, served to discredit and obscure the value of nonviolent theory. But, despite its low credibility in the minds of many today, nonviolent theory, rightly understood and practiced, remains an important body of thought in work for a world without war. Our capacity to end war will be increased if we can clarify the valuable parts of the theory, point out its mistaken applications, and enter into dialogue with those who feel that something went wrong.

TRADITIONAL NONVIOLENT THEORY AND PRACTICE

A wide variety of religious and political traditions teach the rejection of violence. Within the Christian tradition, Brethren, Mennonite, and Friends

(Quaker) churches, among others, a commitment to nonviolence is a matter of doctrine. Other denominations have sometimes supported pacifist beliefs, but official church doctrine has more frequently supported some version of the just war theory (see Chapter 15). Religious texts as old as the Chhandogya Upanishad of ancient Hinduism and the Chinese Tao Te Ching express the central reasons for rejecting violence, as do various sources within the syndicalist, liberal democratic, anarchist, and classical Greco-Roman political traditions.

The refusal to use or condone violence has led to many different practices. Some individuals have withdrawn from society to pursue a life of contemplation or non-involvement or to seek personal fulfillment in isolation from the larger society. Others have devoted their lives to service and the alleviation of suffering.

When the State insists upon its due, pacifists may adopt tactics of passive resistance or civil disobedience. Some, having declared themselves conscientious objectors to war, do public service to the community. Other pacifists, however, feel that public service entails a compromise with the State and refuse to register for the draft, reject the payment of ''war taxes,'' or in other ways limit or reject commitments to ''organizations we never joined.''

Because of the emphasis on the individual, on conscience, or to service, this view is referred to as ''personalist.'' Political institutions, threats from other societies, or mass political movements are reduced to personal terms, and are given little credence or accepted as the evils moral people must suffer. Whether expressed as political anarchism, as a refusal to pay ''war taxes,'' or as an affirmation of a simpler, more self-sufficient lifestyle, this perspective is attractive for many who recognize the dehumanizing effects of war, contemporary ideological conflict, and mass politics. The truth expressed in this personalist tradition is profound; if we lose our humanity by failing to see that other human beings oppose us, if we surrender our responsibility to others for a commitment to the larger terms of politics and history, we have lost an essential insight.

There is a quality of innocence and simplicity in this tradition. Those who embody it are often compelling personalities. How can one deny the harmlessness and appeal of one who asserts that he or she wants only to live a good life of love, and to care for other human beings? But it is misleading to assert that a personal ethic of nonviolence offers an answer to the problems of hunger, war, or injustice. This tradition may lead to a rejection of attempts to deal with the difficult problems of social and political life. Nothing is solved by the simple assertion that the problems would disappear if there were a universal commitment to nonviolence.

THE APPLICATION OF NONVIOLENCE TO SOCIAL PROBLEMS

A second distinct tradition applies the following central principle to achieve social and political change: it is moral to accept suffering for oneself but one cannot inflict it on others, whatever the consequences. The belief that nonviolence could provide a dynamic basis for social change was given modern expression by Mahatma Gandhi and Martin Luther King, Jr. Both brought into the political arena the long tradition of religious and personal witness. They argued that, despite the great coercive powers of States or groups, these cannot compel the individual to act. The withdrawal of consent by refusing to act unleashes a powerful force that will be of great value if properly used in promoting change without violence. This offers a practical alternative, which can build a sense of community between antagonists. In one of the seminal works extrapolating a theory of conflict from Gandhi's experience and fragmentary writings, Joan Bondurant *(Conquest of Violence,* 16-33) identifies ''truth, nonviolence and self-suffering'' as the key values in Satyagraha (holding fast to truth) — Gandhi's approach to conflict. These values were applied in Gandhi's nonviolent campaigns through: 1. a commitment to dialogue concerning the change desired in the opponent and a willingness to re-formulate one's own position in the dialogue; 2. the use of nonviolent techniques (e.g. fasting, personal witness, vigils, pickets, marches, or civil disobedience) as a last resort to open communication; 3. a commitment by both leaders and followers to refrain from violence, not out of fear, but out of the courage born of a willingness to accept suffering, even death if necessary, to demonstrate commitment to the objective; 4. a rejection of the rhetoric and symbolism of violence; 5. a commitment to persist in the objective while seeking to express love and support for the opposition while rejecting the evil they may do. Gandhi believed that these techniques could govern his ''experiments with truth,'' through which he sought to resolve the tension between the truth one's opponent knows and that which one knows oneself.

In the early days of the civil rights movement, Martin Luther King, Jr., sought to apply similar ideas to achieve needed change in race relations in the United States. Gandhi's picture adorned the King family home and his influence can be seen in the following rules excerpted from a ''commitment card'' which every volunteer at the Southern Christian Leadership Conference (SCLC) office signed:

I hereby pledge myself — my person and body — to the nonviolent movement.
Therefore I will keep the following ten commandments:
1. Meditate daily on the teachings and life of Jesus.

2. Remember always that the nonviolent movement in Birmingham seeks justice and reconciliation — not victory.

3. Walk and talk in the manner of love, for God is love.

4. Pray daily to be used by God in order that all men might be free.

5. Sacrifice personal wishes in order that all men might be free.

6. Observe with both friend and foe the ordinary rules of courtesy.

7. Seek to perform regular service for others and for the world.

8. Refrain from the violence of fist, tongue, or heart.

9. Strive to be in good spiritual and bodily health.

10. Follow the directions of the movement and of the captain on a demonstration.[1]

The key elements — truth, nonviolence, a willingness to accept rather than inflict suffering — are evident, as is the commitment to support those whom you are trying to change and to seek reconciliation with them.

PRINCIPLED NONVIOLENCE

These teachings led to the adoption of a number of practical standards which were implemented in SCLC demonstration activity from 1955 to 1964. Among the standard procedures were:

1. Asking permission to hold a demonstration, indicating that it would be nonviolent, and seeking the cooperation of police.

2. Announcing in the call to the demonstration that nonviolence would be strictly adhered to — those who found they could not maintain that discipline were asked not to come, or to leave.

3. Discussing and planning in preliminary meetings to develop precautions against violence:

> a. Designating monitors wearing armbands who would be responsible for their portion of the line of march.
>
> b. Sitting-down, if the provocation of others tempts the resolve of members of the march.
>
> c. Checking rumors and planning how best to call off the demonstration if discipline should break down.
>
> d. Expressing a willingness to end the demonstration, or other pressure, should negotiations become possible.

When followed, such procedures help assure that a nonviolent demonstration remains nonviolent.

---

[1] Martin Luther King, Jr., *Why We Can't Wait* (16-56).

The initial successes of the application of nonviolence to social and political life were astonishing. The power of love — expressed in a willingness to accept rather than inflict suffering — let loose currents of feeling which touched people far removed from those directly involved. In India, M.K. Gandhi emerged as the national leader. His arrests, which were not uncommon, could bring 500,000 others to the jails seeking to join him. British authorities became divided, but only over the form of transition to self-rule.

In the United States, groups long silent about civil rights suddenly considered that silence to be shameful. Religious leaders, at first only a few, but later the great majority, supported the movement. Civic organizations, political parties, labor, business, and community organizations all adopted civil rights resolutions — and more. A new consensus formed. This coalition gathered August 18, 1963, to sing "We Shall Overcome," and meant reconciliation, not victory. Martin Luther King, Jr., spoke eloquently at that march on Washington of the day racial discrimination would come to an end — and it was widely believed that nonviolence would speed that day.

BLURRING THE LINE BETWEEN NONVIOLENCE AND VIOLENCE

This brief summary (and the works in the bibliography on which it is based) identifies a body of thought that is clear, both in theory and practice, in its commitment to nonviolence. It was, however, understood and appreciated only by a minority. That minority is divided today and has become isolated and is largely without influence as a political force. The transition from nonviolence to violence, in both the civil rights and peace movements, as interpreted by the media, was easy, quick, and devastating. Insiders in these movements know that, in many cases, there was a change of leadership by the late '60s, but this is little understood by the public. Profound changes occurred — from principled to tactical nonviolence; from civil disobedience to insurrectionary violence; and from nonviolence which affirms the humanity of those in opposition to that which seeks to drive them out of public life. These changes were frequently resisted by older nonviolent leaders, but were accepted by many once committed in principle to nonviolence.

A full assessment of the violence during the late 1960s would have to weigh the role of the assassinations (John F. Kennedy, Robert Kennedy, and Martin Luther King, Jr.), the escalation of the Vietnam war, and many other factors. But it is also a fact that a significant split occurred within the ranks of those still committed to nonviolence. At the center of the split is disagreement over the relation of nonviolence to democracy.

NONVIOLENCE AND CIVIL DISOBEDIENCE AS EXTENSIONS OF DEMOCRACY

One side argues that representative democracy is "institutionalized nonviolence"; it incorporates the best insights of the nonviolent tradition, i.e. a commitment to rationality, to supportive action for one's opponent, and agreement about how a minority can gain power without violence (by persuading others and becoming a majority). According to this view, civil disobedience, arising out of profound respect for law, allows people nonviolently to challenge laws considered unjust. It can open dialogues once closed and can serve as witness to a commitment to both change and law, for it accepts the penalty of the law.

A contrary view holds that representative democracy has very little to do with nonviolence. Arguing from a variety of perspectives, such advocates of nonviolence reject present democratic institutions as corrupt and turn instead to revolution or disassociation from contemporary American society and government. In this context, "civil disobedience" becomes "resistance" and is applied to almost any act of an illegal but not violent nature. "Resistance" advocates seek to evade the law's penalty and rarely give heed to the climate that results — a climate of disrespect for law.

Those holding such views blur the line between violence and nonviolence in several ways. First, by adopting a stance of "tactical" nonviolence it became possible to build a coalition of people opposed to American involvement in Vietnam which was not agreed that opposition should be expressed through nonviolence. Leaders of that coalition organized the demonstrations at the Democratic Convention in 1968. Some (for example, Tom Hayden and Rennie Davis) thought the "movement would have to move to violent resistance and armed struggle." (Dellinger, *More Power Than We Know*, 16-50). The line between violence and nonviolence was blurred as demonstrators held up bull's-eye placards with the Presidential candidates as targets, hurled projectiles at police, and claimed the right to "shut the convention down."

The Movement for a New Society at one time rejected principled nonviolence in another more subtle way: they posited what they considered to be socially desirable ends and then sought to open dialogue with those who shared those ends and to expose those who did not. While they did not rule out the use of democratic political processes as a tactic, they felt that the purpose of electing candidates was to "expose the facade of democracy" existing in the United States. As for the correct attitude toward "violent liberation movements" in the United States, they argued "it is important that we express our basic solidarity with all those who share our goals, even where we differ on means." *(Moving Toward a New Society* 16-47). Thus, the emphasis was on ends, and on dialogue only with those who shared those ends; the question of nonviolent means was subordinated. This view rejects the Gandhian idea that counsels support for the opponent and the primacy of means since the means tend to become embodied in the ends actually arrived at. More recent statements by the Movement for a New Society suggest a re-commitment to the primacy of nonviolent means.[2]

There was further blurring of the line between violence and nonviolence in the attempt to make a distinction between the destruction of property and the destruction of people. *(More Power Than We Know* 16-50) In fact, blowing up buildings in the late 1960s and early 1970s did cause deaths. Symbolic and actual destruction of property expressed hatred and sought to intimidate the opposition — a most unlikely means for opening dialogue. Also it was argued that the gross violence by the United States in Vietnam made lesser acts of violence by individuals seem insignificant. Why, for example, should we condemn the "Weatherpeople" who were, after all, only "destroying the buildings of American imperialism." (Dellinger, 16-50).

These arguments — for tactical nonviolence, for closing the dialogue about ends, for distinguishing between destruction of property and people, and for remaining silent about the lesser acts of violence — prepared the way for violence in America, in the view of those still committed to democracy and nonviolence. Principled civil disobedience and nonviolence were not what led to the violence in the late 1960s and early 1970s, since they had been rejected by supporters of tactical nonviolence. The insurrectionary violence of that period came out of the climate created by those who advocated alienation and hatred for this society, its institutions, and its leaders.

Genuine nonviolent civil disobedience can be an instrument essential to the proper functioning of democracy although most who appreciate it agree that its use should be limited to special, appropriate circumstances. Those who seek to justify mass civil disobedience must meet the argument that it can destroy respect for law and thereby open the way for violence. In sum, a minority should usually obey laws with which they disagree, while working to change them. Mass civil disobedience should be seen as a last resort.

NONVIOLENCE AND REVOLUTION

Another division among contemporary nonviolent theorists becomes evident when questions of international relations and revolution are discussed. The division is usually along the same lines as the controversy over the relation of

[2]Newsletter of the *Movement for a New Society*, Summer 1979.

nonviolence to democracy. Those who see nonviolent civil disobedience as an extension of democracy frequently support nonviolent means of resolving international conflict. They seek the development of an international peace brigade (or army) — a group, trained in nonviolence, willing to interpose themselves between hostile armies — or of a strategy of specific peace initiatives — acts which enable a State to take a leadership role in building the conditions essential to nonviolent conflict resolution, while putting significant incentives and pressures on other States to reciprocate.

Supporters of nonviolence who identify with revolutionary movements undertaken in the name of oppressed people seek to "humanize" a revolution by making it as nonviolent as possible. They view international conflict as another form of class conflict, and sometimes they put their loyalty to a side in that conflict ahead of their commitment to nonviolence.

What is at first seen as a single, coherent body of thought is now recognized as involving a variety of contradictions. It becomes necessary to ask those committed to nonviolence, as one asks those committed to "peace," to explain precisely what they mean.

PRINCIPLED NONVIOLENCE

The part of the nonviolent tradition affirmed here is that which seeks to maintain comity among people.

> It relies upon love rather than hate, and though it involves a willingness to accept rather than inflict suffering, it is neither passive nor cowardly. It offers a way of meeting evil without relying on the ability to cause pain to the human being through whom evil is expressed. It seeks to change the attitude of the opponent rather than to force his submission through violence. It is, in short, the practical effort to overcome evil with good.[3]

The essence of this kind of nonviolence lies in its ability to resolve conflict without destroying community between those on opposite sides of the battle lines. From this base one can build a distinctive approach to politics. The central problem for advocates of political nonviolence is how to counter the violence others are using or may use; how can one force needed change without becoming an executioner or the accomplice of an executioner? Advocates of nonviolence must face the facts of evil and of aggression and must oppose aggression and exploitation even when proclaimed to be on behalf of the poor

[3]*Speak Truth to Power*, (Philadelphia: American Friends Service Committee 1954)

and oppressed. The nonviolent must be prepared to defend their values by changing their opponents, not destroying them. They must develop ways to resolve conflict while maintaining community. The problem of world peace, stated most simply and most fundamentally, is how to achieve community in the midst of conflict.

The body of thought called "nonviolence" — currently somewhat exotic, divided, and frequently rejected — has much to contribute to the ending of war. Nonviolent resistance to aggression is far from being unrealistic. In some situations (Poland in 1981 is surely one) nonviolence is the only realistic option available. Nonviolence has been demonstrated as practicable even against totalitarian forces, for example, in limiting Nazi rule in Norway (16-37) and in protesting the Soviet invasion of Czechoslovakia (16-53).

BIBLIOGRAPHY

The bibliography surveys thought about violence and social change and about the problem of conflict. It introduces works on violence and nonviolence with the focus on the latter. Nonviolent theory and practice are presented, as are the relationship of nonviolence to problems of democracy, revolution, and as an alternative to military defense. These books will be helpful in answering questions such as: 1) What are the forms of protest that help make insurrectionary or other forms of violence a likely outcome? 2) Why do many advocates of nonviolence believe violence is an inappropriate means to achieve good ends? 3) What desirable goals in history have been claimed to have been achieved through violence? Could they have been achieved without violence? Did the use of violence speed or slow their realization? 4) How can the principled use of nonviolence create a sense of community between antagonists? 5) Why did Gandhi consider his nonviolent campaigns "experiments with truth"? 6) What are the essential characteristics of Satyagraha? 7) What precautions against violence arising from demonstrators did Martin Luther King, Jr. insist upon? 8) Can civil disobedience in a democratic society be justified? 9) Did nonviolent protests in the civil rights and peace movements in the 1950s and early 1960s create a climate in which the violence of the late 1960s became more likely? What portion of the responsibility for violence lies with the slowness of institutions to respond (or even live up to) their own commitments? What portion with the escalation of the Vietnam war? 10) How can nonviolence be applied in world politics?

A. Roots

Classic

16 – 1 *On the Duty of Civil Disobedience*, Henry Thoreau, 16pp, 1975 (1853), Fellowship, $.25. An introduction by Gene Sharp clarifies how the withdrawal of consent from lawful authority can release a powerful force — for both good and evil.

16 – 2 *Tolstoy, On Civil Disobedience and Non-Violence*, Alymer Maude (trans.), 302pp, 1967, Mentor, O.P. Tolstoy's advocacy of cultivating your own and doing no evil even if that requires disobedience to lawful authority.

INF

16 – 3 *Autobiography: The Story of My Experiments with Truth*, M.K. Gandhi, 390pp, 1957, Beacon, $6.95. Gandhi describes his early life, his commitment to nonviolence, and his techniques for transforming an enemy through love. He accepts suffering while making clear his own commitment to certain values. Gandhi coined the word ''satyagrapha'' (holding fast to truth) substituting the more active concept for ''passive resistance.''

INF

16 – 4 *Stride Toward Freedom; The Montgomery Story*, Martin Luther King, Jr., 203pp, 1958, Harper, $10.95. King describes the Montgomery bus boycott and the moral basis of his commitment to nonviolence. He explains why he believes that when nonviolence failed, it was because too little nonviolence was tried.

B. Conflict

16 – 5 *Images of Conflict*, Albert Eldridge, 275pp, 1979, St. Martin's, $5.95. Emphasizes misperception of antagonists and of their conflict as causes of race riots, revolutionary terrorism, and war.

Intro

16 – 6 *Resistance, Rebellion and Death*, Albert Camus, 209pp, 1963, Modern Library, $2.95. An anthology of nineteen essays on nonviolence, rebellions and social obligation. One of the best introductions to Camus' thought.

16 – 7 *The Resolution of Conflict: Constructive and Destructive Processes*, Morton Deutsch, 420pp, 1973, Yale, $5.95. A study of the psychological processes involved in resolving conflict and includes inducing cooperation, adherence to rules and mediation. Also aims to promote peace by encouraging constructive conflict.

16 – 8 *Conflict: Violence and Non-Violence*, Joan Bondurant, and Margaret Fisher (eds.), 206pp, 1971, Atherton, $9.95. An anthology tracing the origins of violent and nonviolent conflict.

C. The Claims of Revolutionary Violence

INF

16– 9 *On Revolution,* Hannah Arendt, 349pp, 1970 (1963), Penguin, $4.95. Maintains that war and revolution have lost their ideological justifications but remain the dominant reality of 20th-century politics.

16– 10 *On Violence,* Hannah Arendt, 106pp, 1970, Harcourt, Brace, Jovanovich, $2.45. Argues that violence is at the center of this century's politics. Rejects all views of violence as an organic, biological, inevitable, or behavorial necessity; it is chosen for political reasons.

16– 11 *Their Morals and Ours,* Leon Trotsky, 96pp, 1974, Pathfinder, $2.95. Trotsky denies there is a valid nonviolent position in a world in revolutionary ferment. He argues that the only choice is between revolutionary violence and the violence of the status quo (the latter is now called structural violence).

16– 12 *Political Violence,* Ted Henderich, 118pp, 1977, Cornell, $7.50. Defends the political utility of violence.

16– 13 *Injustice: The Social Bases of Obedience and Revolt,* Barrington Moore, Jr., 540pp, 1978, Sharpe, $17.50. Recognizes that 20th-century revolutions as often as not have led to more not less oppressive governments. Asks then why the poor are so placid, revolutions so unliberating.

16– 14 *Repression and Repressive Violence,* Marjo Hoefnagels, 194pp, 1977, Transaction, $11.95. An anthology about the use of violence to consolidate positions of power and influence; the political, legal, and psychological effects of "violence from above" are considered.

INF

16– 15 *Reflections on Violence,* George Sorel, 286pp, 1950 (1906), Macmillan, $1.95. Calls for violence to create the class consciousness essential for a proletariat revolution; when material forces fail, social myths can be created to propel history.

16– 16 *The Cult of Violence, Sorel and the Sorelians,* Jack Roth, 384pp, 1981, California, $25.00. Identifies a current of thought which seeks in violence the possibility of a totally renovated society and suggests that the desertion of democracy involved can have tragic consequences.

16– 17 *A Structural Theory of Revolution,* Johan Galtung, 78pp, 1974, Transaction, $5.95. Argues that violent revolutions may be less costly than slow changes of exploitative social structures.

16– 18 *Urban Guerrilla: Studies on the Theory, Strategy, and Practices of Political Violence in Modern Societies,* Johan Niezing (ed.), 149pp, 1975, Transaction, $9.95. A contribution to both theory and contemporary history.

16 – 19 *The Riddle of Violence,* Kenneth Kaunda, 184pp, 1981, Harper, $9.95. Zambia's President seeks to reconcile an appreciation of nonviolence with a defense of forcible struggle for the liberation of Southern Africa.

16 – 20 *Perspectives on Violence: Essays on Concepts of Aggression and Related Behavior,* Gene Usdin, 161pp, 1976. Citadel Press, $3.95. Essays by a historian, a social psychologist, an anthropologist, and a psychiatrist on the origins and alternatives to violence in both inter-personal and inter-group relations.

16 – 21 *Revolution, Reform and Social Justice: Studies in the Theory and Practice of Marxism,* Sidney Hook, 307pp, 1975, N.Y.U. Press, $6.95. A collection of essays by a democratic socialist.

16 – 22 *Black Violence, Political Impact of the 1960s Riots,* James Button, 248pp, 1978, Princeton, $17.00. A study of over ninety riots in the U.S. between 1963 and 1968, most of them in 1967, and their political implications measured in Federal funds spent and white backlash.

16 – 23 *Terror or Love? Bommi Baumann's Own Story of His Life as a West German Urban Guerrilla,* 127pp, 1979, Grove, $6.95. A working-class youth describes how he achieved class consciousness through rock music, found violence "a perfectly adequate means" to express his political views; and later, concludes that "it was only the fear of love, from which one flees into absolute violence" that motivated him; this then becomes a personal rather than a social statement.

16 – 24 *Insurgent Era, New Patterns of Political, Economic and Social Revolution,* Richard Sanger, 235pp, 1977, Potomac, $7.50. A restatement of the old thesis that either democratic changes occur or revolutionary violence will follow; what is new are the examples including the Soviet Union, China, and Cuba; argues for democratic change, but offers few practical proposals.

16 – 25 *Violence, Internal War and Revolution,* Michael Kelly and Thomas Mitchell, 1976, Carleton University (Ottawa), Norman Paterson, School of International Relations. $5.00. A bibliography with 496 items, and a special section on Canadian violence.

16 – 26 *Leaders of Revolution,* Mostafa Rejai with Kay Phillips, 248pp, 1979, Sage, $8.95. Offers a "situational theory of revolutionary leadership" and provides "comparative evidence on the life experiences and ideological orientations of revolutionary leaders."

16 – 27 *Violence in America: Historical and Comparative Perspectives,* Hugh Graham and Ted Gurr, 528pp, 1979, Sage, $8.95. Compares violence here to violence in other industrialized societies.

16 – 28 *Modern Revolutions and Revolutionists. A Bibliography,* Robert Blackey, 257pp, 1976, ABC-Clio, $21.25. Offers references on concepts, theories, findings, and particular revolutions in Europe and throughout the modern world.

16 – 29 *Political Violence in the United States, 1875 – 1974: A Bibliography,* Jarol Manheim and Melanie Wallace, 116pp, 1974, Garland, $21.00.

See also Chapter 3, "The Causes of War" and Chapters 1 and 2 on "War in World Politics."

D. Nonviolent Conflict — Theory

INF

16–30 *The Power of Nonviolence,* Richard Gregg, 192pp, 1960, Attic, $2.75. An important interpretation of the dynamics underlying Gandhi's and others in the use of nonviolence.

16–31 *Nonviolence: A Christian Interpretation,* William Miller, 380pp, 1966, Schocken, $2.95. A comprehensive, carefully written analysis which explores the root values underlying nonviolence in the Christian ethical tradition.

TEW

16–32 *The Politics of Nonviolent Action,* Gene Sharp, Vol. I, *Power and Struggle,* 105pp, $3.95; Vol. II. *The Methods of Nonviolent Action,* 271pp, $5.95; Vol. III. *The Dynamics of Nonviolent Action,* 445pp, $6.95, 1973, Porter Sargent. A massive work introducing the basic ideas, stressing the enormously varied situations, places and times when nonviolence has been tried, and a contribution to the development of a more effective, nonviolent, strategy of change.

TEW

16–33 *Conquest of Violence, The Gandhian Philosophy of Conflict,* Joan Bondurant, 294pp, 1971, California, $4.95. An important contribution to conflict theory and the best single exposition of Gandhi's ideas using concrete examples. Bondurant criticizes the frequent identification of power with military force, given Gandhi's success in transforming his "enemies" through nonviolence.

16–34 *Gandhi's Truth; On the Origins of Military Nonviolence,* Erik Erikson, 510pp, 1969, Norton, $4.95. A leading psychoanalyst's study of the inevitability of conflict and Gandhi's contribution to making conflict creative.

16–35 *Gandhi as a Political Strategist: With Essays on Ethics and Politics,* Gene Sharp, 344pp, 1979, Porter Sargent, $7.95. A collection cf essays examining both the principled and the practical parts of Gandhi's theory of conflict.

16–36 *Gandhi, His Relevance for Our Times,* T. K. Mahadevan, and G. Ramachandran, 290pp, 1972, World Without War Publications, $2.95. An anthology of writings applying Gandhian concepts to a wide variety of situations.

16–37 *Social Power and Political Freedom,* Gene Sharp, 400pp, 1980, Porter Sargent, $8.95. A collection of essays by one of America's leading theoreticians of nonviolence. Addresses the use of nonviolence in limiting oppressive governments and in conducting international conflict without violence. Includes appendices on nonviolent sanctions.

16 – 38 *The Essays of A. J. Muste,* Nat Hentoff (ed.)., 513pp, 1970, Simon & Schuster, $3.45. A valuable collection of essays by a radical pacifist; these essays were written between 1928 and 1966, and reflect Muste's pilgrimage to and from and back to nonviolence; to and from and back to a primary focus on opposing the economic and political structures of America (as opposed to universal standards for action). A towering figure for all who learned from him, even for those who opposed him in his later years when "revolution" again became more important to him than "nonviolence."

E. Gandhi

Classic

16 – 39 *All Men are Brothers,* M.K. Gandhi, 256pp, 1972, World Without War Council, $4.95. Compiled and edited by UNESCO, this anthology includes a brief autobiographical sketch, plus selections on nonviolence, truth, women, democracy, and economic development.

16 – 40 *Collected Works,* Mahatma Gandhi, Government of India, 70 volumes now available, $6.00 each.

16 – 41 *Mahatma: Life of Mohandas Karamchand Gandhi,* Dinanath Tendulkar, 8 volumes, 1960 – 1963, Government of India. The definitive companion, tracing Gandhi's steps day-by-day and providing many illustrations of his life.

16 – 42 *Selections from Gandhi,* N.K. Bose (ed.), 320pp, 1948, Greenleaf Books, $2.00. One of the best anthologies of Gandhi's writings for those interested in problems of nonviolence in politics.

Intro

16 – 43 *Gandhi, His Life and Message for the World,* Louis Fisher, 192pp, 1954, $1.25. A popular introduction to Gandhi's life and to his philosophy.

16 – 44 *The Challenge of the Mahatmas,* Martin Green 256pp, 1978, Basic Books, $11.95. A comparison of Tolstoy and Gandhi, their lives and conversions, and the implications of their thoughts for ending war, imperialism, and materialism.

16 – 45 *The Moral and Political Thought of Mahatma Gandhi,* Ragavan Iyer, 449pp, 1973, Oxford, $5.95. A thoughtful study of the enduring elements of Gandhi's thought and achievement. A chapter on the "Scope and Significance of Satyagrapha" clarifies Gandhi's central concept.

16 – 46 *The Meanings of Gandhi,* Paul Power (ed.), 199pp, 1971, Hawaii, $10.00. Articles describe Gandhi's personality, the transmission of his ideas, and compare his techniques with advocates of violence as well as others who advocate nonviolence.

F. Tactical Nonviolence

16 – 47 *Moving Toward a New Society,* Susan Gowan, George Lakey, William Mover

& Richard Taylor, 296pp, 1976, Movement of New Society Press, $5.00. Maintains that violence "slows the pace of social change," describes U.S. as a "sick society," and states a number of values characteristic of a "healthy society." Expects to make the transition to a decentralized, artisan or small-group cooperative society.

16–48 *The Struggle for Humanity: Agents of Nonviolent Change in a Violent World,* Marjorie Hope and James Young, 305pp, 1977, Orbis, $6.95. A sometimes appealing call for nonviolence to push for a decentralized more equitable society, a sometimes bland endorsement of alternative lifestyles, and a useful introduction to several individuals and organizations working for radical change without violence in the 1970s.

16–49 *Blockade! A Guide to Nonviolent Intervention,* Richard Taylor, 175pp, 1977, Orbis, $2.95. Describes a nonviolent campaign to block the shipment of arms to Pakistan in 1971. Also discusses the tactics of nonviolent campaigns with the emphasis on protesting not building a sense of community. Offers no constructive alternative policies.

16–50 *More Power than We Know: The People's Movement Toward Democracy,* Dave Dellinger, 326pp, 1975, Doubleday, $3.95. A description of Dellinger's commitment to nonviolence, his adoption of coalitional activities with those committed to violent revolution, and his assessment of who is responsible for the violence in the peace movement of the late 1960s.

16–51 *The Nonviolent Cross, A Theology of Revolution and Peace,* James Douglass, 301pp, 1964, Macmillan, $1.95. Attempts to blend themes of nonviolence and revolution.

G. The Practice of Nonviolence

16–52 *The Power of the People: Active Nonviolence in the U.S.,* Robert Cooney & Helen Michalowski (eds.), 240pp, 1977, Peace Press, $9.95. Portrays in pictures and prose the use of nonviolent techniques in American history with a focus on 20th-century labor, women, civil rights, anti-war, and opposition to America movements in the 20th century.

16–53 *Support Czechoslovakia,* Michael Randle & April Carter, 64pp, 1968, Housmans, $1.00. The War Resisters League International protested the Soviet invasion of Czechoslovakia in Moscow and Prague. NATO did not.

16–54 *Report from Palermo,* Danilo Dolci, 310pp, 1959, Viking, $2.45. Nonviolence applied in Sicily to promote social change and to oppose corruption in governemnt.

16–55 *Martin Luther King, Jr., A Documentary . . . Montgomery to Memphis,* Flip Schulke (ed.), 224pp, 1976, Norton, $8.95. Portrays in pictures and text the nonviolent civil rights movement led by King.

16 – 56 *Why We Can't Wait,* Martin Luther King, Jr., 159pp, 1963, NAL, $1.25. King at the peak of his influence as he organized the march on Washington.

16 – 57 *Marching to Freedom, The Life of Martin Luther King, Jr.,* Robert Bleiweiss (ed.), 152pp, 1971, NAL, $1.25. A sympathetic account of King's accomplishments, attributing his achievements to his commitment to nonviolence.

16 – 58 *King, A Biography,* David Lewis, 472pp, 1978, 2nd ed., Illinois, $5.95. A critical evaluation of King's strategy of change.

TEW
16 – 59 *Down the Line, The Collected Writings of Bayard Rustin,* Introduced by C. Vann Woodward, 355pp, 1971, Quadrangle, O.P. From 1942 — when Rustin sat in the front of a Nashville bus and suffered beatings rather than inflict violence — until today, Rustin has combined a commitment to nonviolence with an astute understanding of coalition politics. This volume collects his writings and honors his life.

16 – 60 *The Quiet Battle,* Mulford Sibley (ed.), 386pp, 1969, Beacon, O.P. An anthology of essays presenting instances when nonviolent means have been used to achieve social or political ends.

H. Civilian-Based Defense

16 – 61 *Making the Abolition of War a Realistic Goal,* Gene Sharp, 16pp, 1980, Insitute for World Order, $1.50. Makes the case for a civilian-based defense and argues that such a defense system could be created alongside existing military systems, or used now in circumstances where military defense is impractical, such as in Poland.

16 – 62 *Possibilities of Civilian Defense in Western Europe,* Gustaaf Geeraerts, 172pp, 1977, Transaction, $9.95. An anthology exploring whether a combination of prepared nonviolent activities could provide a more effective defense than weapons. Symbolic activities, activities denying utilization of institutions, and overtly confrontational tactics are distinguished and discussed.

16 – 63 *In Place of War, An Inquiry into Nonviolent National Defense,* Working Party, American Friends Service Committee, 115pp, 1967, Grossman, O.P. Offers a scenario on how a nonviolent defense strategy might work.

I. Civil Disobedience

16 – 64 *Civil Disobedience; Conscience, Tactics and the Law,* Carl Cohen, 222pp, 1971, Columbia, $3.50. Distinguishes civil disobedience from either secret law violations or lawful public demonstrations, and maintains that when the law and conscience conflict, it may be possible to justify public, nonviolent, civil disobedience.

16 – 65 *Democracy and Disobedience,* Peter Singer, 150pp, 1974, Oxford, $7.50. Argues that obedience to laws is more easily justified in a country which is a democracy.

16 – 66 *Theory and Practice of Civil Disobedience,* Art Harvey, 29pp, 1961, Greenleaf, $.30. A statement of the assumptions underlying and the very practical methods for conducting civil disobedience.

16 – 67 *Disobedience and Democracy: Nine Fallacies on Law and Order,* Howard Zinn, 124pp, 1978, Vintage, $1.65. Denies that the rule of law has any intrinsic worth; civil disobedience and disobedience to the law, even willful violation of law, are justified.

16 – 68 *Civil Disobedience and Political Obligation: A Study in Christian Social Ethics,* James Childress, 250pp, 1971, Yale, $16.00. Offers a careful definition of civil disobedience, and then outlines the objections a defense must overcome.

16 – 69 *Civil Disobedience: Theory and Practice,* Hugo Bedau (ed.), 288pp, 1969, Pegasus, $6.30. An anthology of essays which seek to answer the question: ''when is civil disobedience justified in a democracy?'' Includes an extremely valuable article by Richard Wasserstrom, ''The Obligation to Obey the Law.''

16 – 70 *Civil Disobedience, Revolution and Violence,* Mulford Sibley and Robert Pickus, 16pp, 1970, World Without War, $.25. Sibley argues that revolutionary violence is an impediment to achieving democratic and humane goals; Pickus argues that civil disobedience is justifiable, but revolutionary violence is not.

CHAPTER 17

PEACE RESEARCH

THE aim of peace research is to discover the processes that lead to war and those that lead to peace. For years, many scholars in a variety of disciplines, have sought to enlarge our validated knowledge of war and peace, and there is probably no discipline irrelevant to that study. The institutional settings within which this research is done range from the United Nations University (Tokyo), to government, and private, often university-related, institutes. The full range of this activity can only be suggested; our focus is on the peace research movement which came into existence after World War II.

THE PEACE RESEARCH MOVEMENT

The attempt to define war and peace as legitimate objects of scholarly, perhaps even social scientific, inquiry owes much to Quincy Wright. His *A Study of War* (3-1) defined war as a problem, separate from other social problems, which could be studied for the purpose of eliminating it. A second pioneer in the field was an English meteorologist, Lewis F. Richardson, who spent the last twenty years of his life developing mathematical and statistical theories of war and peace. These were published as *Arms and Insecurity* (17-3)

434

and *Statistics of Deadly Quarrels* (17-2). Richardson suggested several equations for predicting when arms races will end in war. But it was Theodore Lenz's *Toward a Science of Peace* (17-1), which Kenneth Boulding credits with "the first clear statement of the problem" (Boulding, *Collected Papers,* 17-11, p. 293).

These scholarly works had their greatest impact on political scientists. A self-defined group of "peace researchers" (*In Search of Global Patterns,* 17-5) developed an interdisciplinary "science of international relations"(p. 91). Among the methods used to increase and validate our knowledge of international relations were simulations (Guetzkow), statistical studies correlating the outbreak of war with other factors (Choucri, Singer), and "cognitive maps" assessing what makes negotiated agreement likely and unlikely (Coplin and Rochester).

By 1965 UNESCO reported the existence of eighty-one "institutions for peace and conflict research," sixty-two of them established since 1945, thirty from 1960 – 62 (*Peace Research, Trend Report and World Directory,* 17-9). In the United States serious and moderately well-financed programs to promote investigation and improve methodology in the field of international conflict were under way at several universities, (Michigan, Northwestern, Stanford) and at other academic centers. Peace research centers also developed outside the academic world, sometimes sponsored by government, occasionally by religious institutions and private groups. Government-sponsored research was inaugurated by the U.S. Arms Control and Disarmament Agency, which developed a plan for general and complete disarmament. *The Journal of Conflict Resolution,* the *Journal of Peace Research, Peace Research Reviews,* and the *Journal of Peace Science* took their places among the journals of the more traditional disciplines. National associations of peace researchers were formed in the United States, Great Britain, Japan, and the Federal Republic of Germany. International communication among scholars developed through the International Peace Research Association, founded in 1964. UNESCO increased awareness of the multinational effort through publication of a directory (*World Directory of Peace Research Institutes,* 21-72).

THE INITIAL CONTRIBUTIONS OF PEACE RESEARCH

A useful categorization of the field and a summary of the major peace research results (1945 – 1969) is provided by Hanna and Alan Newcombe (*Peace Research Around the World,* 17-6). Their categories, each listed with an example, clarify the early focus in peace research:

I. *Fundamental Studies and Theories*
  A. International Systems
    1. Historical-descriptive (Bullough, "The Roman Empire vs Persia: A Study of Successful Deterrence")
    2. Quantitative-historical (Dimension of Nations [DON])
    3. Simulation (Inter-Nation Simulation (INS))
    4. Theories of International Systems (Morton Kaplan)
    5. Data Collection (Bruce Russett, *Peace, War and Numbers*)

  B. Crisis Research
    1. Crisis Decisions (Robert North, et al, Stanford Studies in International Conflict and Integration)
    2. Tension Measurement (Ole Holsti, Kenneth Boulding)

  C. Conflict Studies
    1. History of Conflicts (Michelson Project, Richardson, Beer)
    2. Conflict Theory (Paul Smoker, Morton Deutsch, Thomas Schelling, Anatol Rapoport and Lewis Coser)
    3. Small Group Experiments (Anatol Rapoport)
    4. Causes of War (Quincy Wright, Karl Deutsch, J. David Singer)

  D. Attitudes
    1. Attitude Surveys and Scales (Jerome Laulicht)
    2. Images and Perceptions (Harold Lasswell, Daniel Lerner)
    3. Attitude Change (Herbert Kelman, Leon Festinger)

  E. Research on the Future
    1. Transition to and Nature of Stabilized World (Kenneth Boulding, Robert Jungk)
    2. Disarmed but Revolutionary World (Walter Millis, Arthur Waskow)

  F. Integration Studies
    1. Political Integration (Ernst Haas, Amitai Etzioni)
    2. International Nongovernmental Organization (Robert Angell)
    3. Impact of Student Exchange (Lotte Bailyn)

  G. Economic Studies
    1. Conversion to a Peace Economy (Emile Benoit)
    2. Economic and Technical Assistance (Wassily Leontieff)

  H. International Law
    1. General (Saul Mendlovitz, Richard Falk, Arthur Larson)
    2. Definition of Aggression (Quincy Wright)
    3. Codification of Co-existence (Jan Tinbergen, G.P. Zadoroczn)

I. Disarmament Studies
   1. The Armament-Disarmament Spectrum (J. David Singer, Robert Levine)
   2. Deterrence (Thomas Milbane)
   3. Disarmament Inspection (Lawrence Finkelstein)
   4. U.N. Police Force (Inis Claude)
   5. World Government Plans (Hanna Newcombe, Grenville Clark and Louis Sohn)
II. *Action Research*

  A. Protest Actions
    1. Efficacy of Protest (Kenneth Boulding)
    2. Study of Participants (Paul Ekman)

  B. Nonviolence (Gene Sharp)

III. *Conclusions*

  A. Theoretical Conclusions

  B. Policy Recommendations

  C. Research Recommendations

This research typology reflects the overriding concern with conflict between States and with ways to end or limit the use of military force in the conduct of those conflicts. Other contributions to the field were made by area specialists focusing on a particular region of the world, such as the Middle East; by studies of politics, for example, of political parties; and the role of opinion leaders and internal governmental decision-making.

SELECTED PEACE RESEARCH STUDIES, 1962–1975

Azar, et al. (1974) analyzed (regression and statistical analysis) 11,664 cooperative and conflictful events for twelve pairs of states over 276 months (1950–1971).

Barringer (1972) assessed the dynamics of 20th-century escalation for eighteen conflicts by applying agreement analysis to 300 variables.

Beer (1974) determined the probable number of wars and casualties, 3600 B. C. – 1974 A. D.

Brock and Galtung (1966) delineated for 652 societies the character and correlates of their wars.

Coplin and Rochester (1972) statistically analyzed the resolution of 118 disputes, 1920–1968.

Denton and Phillips (1968) factor analyzed the patterns in 375 wars, 1480–1900.

Dewey (1962, 1964, 1969, 1970) did a cyclic analysis of the number of war battles, 600 B. C. – 1957 A. D.

East (1972) determined the dependence of violence on international status for about 120 states and 381 conflicts, 1948–1961.

Ferris (1973) analyzed the relationship of forty-two wars, 1850–1966, to the power of states.

Gameson and Modigliani (1965, 1968, 1971) tested different foreign policy models of Soviet behavior, 1946–1963.

M. Hass (1970) factor analyzed diverse variables and data on war for twenty-one international systems, 1648–1963.

Jarvad (1968) statistically analyzed the nature of cases before the International Court of Justice, 1946–1966.

Holsti, et al. (1969) statistically analyzed twenty-five U.S.-Soviet documents regarding the 1962 Cuban missile crisis to determine the dependence of the potential for violence on perception.

Mahoney (1976) assessed the predictors of American politico-military operations in 215 actions, 1946–1975.

Melko (1973) determined the characteristics and bases of fifty-two peace societies in recorded history.

Naroll, et al. (1974) determined the war correlates of twenty historical periods.

Onate (1974) analyzed the relationship between internal and external conflict for all states, 1950–1970.

Peterson (1972) statistically determined the dependence of Soviet-American conflict on attitudes, 1955–1964.

Randle (1972) statistically assessed the nature and causes of the outcome of 500 wars, 1500–1971.

Singer and Small (1972) statistically defined all wars, 1816–1965.

Tung (1975) analyzed the conflict and polarization in the East–West system, 1948–1967.

Bendix (1975) factor analyzed over 150 attributes of ninety States in 351 conflicts, 1945–1966, to determine the patterns of East–West conflict and American operations.

Van Atta and Robinson (1975) analyzed (regression) twelve Soviet behavior variables for 1955 and 1963.

Voevodsky (1969) determined the mathematical functions fitting the process and ending of selected 19th and 20th Century wars.

Wallace (1972) assessed the dependence of war, 1882 – 1964 on capabilities and change.

Wright (1965) tested a model of escalation against forty-five international conflicts since 1918.

Zinnes (1971) studied the dependence of wars, 1815 – 1945, on cross pressures.

This list was selected by R.J. Rummel from some 682 studies, out of which he has developed and tested a "field theory of international relations." The field theory draws on all 682 studies and in Rummel's "The New Danger of a Soviet – American War" (1978) it is applied to the question of war between the superpowers in the 1980s. He concludes: "This assessment suggests . . . a new generation is entering a renewed period of dangerous Soviet – American conflict in which war is not only possible, but towards which many forces are pushing."

THREE DEFINITIONS OF PEACE RESEARCH

The initial objectives of peace research came under attack in the 1960s as being too narrow. Johan Galtung characterized the efforts of nearly twenty years as focused only on negative peace — the absence of war. He suggested that to complement the study of what he called "direct violence" — the use of military force in warfare — peace research should develop a conception of "positive peace" in which "structural violence" was eliminated through the realization of "human self-fulfillment." This attack met with significant success and by the early 1970s UNESCO's *Peace Research, Trend Report and World Directory* stated:

> Originally, peace was seen mainly as the absence of war — and still is by many peace researchers. To others, the absence of war and other "direct violence" (sometimes called "negative peace") is now regarded as too narrow. The concept of "positive peace" was used as a description of a situation marked by equity, integration, solidarity — perhaps even harmony. Later, the concept of structural violence was introduced for the kind of violence which does not have a direct "sender" — as when starvation results not from ill-will of any person or group but from distributional inequalities. From a strong orientation in the early and mid-1960s, research on structural violence became more important around 1970. . . .by 1978 the trend seems to have been modified or even reversed. . . .

In American peace studies programs the aim frequently became that of achieving "equity" with racism, sexism, inner peace, and a variety of other subjects competing with, if not crowding out, the earlier focus.

WAR PREVENTION OR NEGATIVE PEACE

Kenneth Boulding points out that the aims of peace research as defined by Quincy Wright and others were not just to describe the international system as it is. The main object always was to clarify "the dynamics of the international system with a view to understanding what kinds of policies, decisions, and strategies can move it in the direction of stable peace and away from the direction of war" (*Collected Papers,* 17-11). Nonetheless, Galtung accurately describes the focus of the research as the transformation of relationships between States and the reduction or elimination of "direct violence" in such relationships.

HUMAN SELF-FULFILLMENT OR POSITIVE PEACE

In the late 1960s and 1970s the concept of "positive peace" arose within the self-styled peace research/peace studies programs. The search for "positive peace" broadened the definition of violence:

> Violence is deprival of life, as in a battle; it is intended and is a quick process. But what if it is not intended, and/or takes place slowly, as in a slum? Is that not violence? It might even be argued that it is usually more violent, for if the victim dies at thirty-two years of age in a battle, he is usually in good health the moment before, whereas a slow death is usually preceded by a process of increasing near-death. . .[1]

Galtung calls this "structural, victim-oriented . . . violence." Structural violence exists wherever there is a denial of "everybody's right and empirical possibility (given some variation) to realize a healthy life for a number of years. If anybody is deprived of that, and it is avoidable, then there is violence at work."

Galtung then broadens the definition of violence still further to include "non-material violence" *(The True Worlds,* 17-17), which is "anything that interferes with mental self-realization." Galtung would thus add to the focus of

---

[1]John Galtung in *Peace Research* (17-9).

peace research on the prevention of war, research on how "human self-fulfillment" can be achieved.

Galtung assigns responsibility for structural violence in third-world countries to Western "capitalist-imperialism." The Marxists in the peace research field naturally welcomed Galtung as providing new reasons for wars of liberation. Galtung, however, disassociates himself from this reading of his contribution to peace research:

> The glibbest escape is to use structural violence as an excuse for the application of direct violence, and even for the failure to do research on how to reduce direct violence. Research on nonviolent revolution and non-military defense is therefore a basic constituent of any peace research program.[2]

Still, the concepts of "structural" and "non-material violence" imply that wars of liberation are a form of self-defense and often attribute suffering in world politics to one source. This implicitly justifies violence.

The question of whether some internal reorganization of a State increases or decreases the likelihood of war remains unanswered. Would an egalitarian society be more or less war-like? Are socialist or capitalist States more likely to engage in war? Some peace researchers (e.g. Rummel) argue that the view that Socialism is a sufficient condition of peace flies in the face of the facts: the Sino-Soviet border is the most heavily armed in the world; Socialist economic performance is dismal; the idea that centralized state authority, in the authoritarian and totalitarian States, solves problem is false; such governments hide their problems. Who today expects war between the industrialized market economies?

A THIRD DEFINITION OF PEACE RESEARCH

If one looks back at the first twenty years of peace research, one is now struck by the absence of studies on international human rights and on the wider range of world economic issues. The focus on conflict between States, underlined and made urgent by the threat of the cold war becoming a nuclear war, obscured part of the positive ingredients needed to achieve peace. One can reject the statement that anything that "interferes with mental self-realization" is violence and yet recognize that an adequate strategy of peace must address more than the armaments problem. That, however, has never really been in question. At issue

---

[2] In *Peace Research*, 17-9, p. 15.

is whether the peace research movement should adopt a "minimalist" or a "maximalist" approach to defining the conditions essential to a world without war. *To End War* maintains such conditions include the achievement of basic human rights, of economic development, and of a global problem-solving capability. This is still a minimalist approach because it focuses on the elimination of war, while asking what institutions are needed to conduct conflicts between those with contending conceptions of justice. The maximalist approach, as advocated by Galtung, focuses on utopian objectives like "mental self-realization" or other desirable objectives, without establishing their relationship to the organized use of mass violence in world politics.

A 1976 survey of Peace Research (*Recent Advances in Peace and Conflict Research,* 17-7) discusses the conceptions of "positive peace" and "structural violence," and concludes that a focus on war prevention and on achieving peaceful change within the world community are recommended. In a preface to *Recent Advances,* Elise Boulding maintains that "peace research is now an established interdisciplinary field," a statement with which one can readily agree and still doubt that a "critical science offering a variety of tools for the analysis of the structures and processes of conflict and peace at global and domestic levels" has resulted. While UNESCO now counts over 2,000 researchers at work, the conclusion of many within and outside the peace research field is that of Richardson: "Our major results have been minor." To help coordinate the efforts to achieve major results, UNESCO has adopted a "Medium Term Plan" in the field which runs from 1977 – 1982. The objective is the

> Promotion of peace research, in particular research on manifestations of violations of peace, causes preventing its realization, ways and means to eliminate them and proper measures to be taken in order to maintain and reinforce a just, lasting and constructive peace at the level of groups, societies and the world. The Medium Term Plan stresses the importance of disarmament and, at the same time, the interrelations between peace, human rights and development.

One can reasonably doubt the current claim to scientific validation but still appreciate the potential importance of work that attempts to measure variables in the patterns of conflict, variables that lead either to war or to peace. Groups at the Duke University Rule of Law Center and Ohio State University's Mershon Center have consistently sought to bring their research to bear on the real problems of those now at work in peace education and action projects. The functional approach to problems of world order (as developed at the Institute for International Studies at the University of California, Berkeley), has yielded many studies on growth toward world community. The Berkeley institute has recently begun to correct the bias in peace research, that has had easy access only to Western sources of information, by publishing assessments by Soviet dissidents of internal Soviet politics, Soviet decision-making processes, and even the Soviet military-industrial complex. While ideologically motivated attacks on the West are sometimes presented as peace research, one now more frequently encounters thoughtful attempts to understand how domestic institutions and patterns in the West, in the Soviet Union, in China, in regional powers, and in the third world affect the chances for war or for peace.

In sum, as in so many areas of the world affairs field, it is essential that there be a highly cultivated ability to distinguish between thoughtful and confused attempts to work for peace. The standards by which such distinctions can be made are being gradually validated.

In an embarrassingly simplified (but, we believe, defensible) fashion, *To End War* has attempted to identify causes of war and to explore alternatives that could either eliminate the cause in question or channel its propensity for producing violent conflict into nonviolent processes of conflict resolution. We have set alongside a cause of war, a condition that would help bring peace. We have, however, offered only a general perspective on these problems, not a systematic and scientifically validated body of knowledge. That is the endeavor of peace research. If our emphasis here has been on a line of argument sustaining a certain approach to foreign policy problems, it is not because of any assurance that all the evidence is in, but rather because of the requirement to act now on the best evidence and thought available, while continuing to search for better answers.

BIBLIOGRAPHY

The bibliography for this chapter traces the development of the peace research movement, presents its major studies, and assesses the results. In addition, the contribution of many other academic disciplines are suggested. The reader will find these works useful in answering questions such as these: 1) What are the appropriate objectives of peace research? 2) What are the major results of the peace research movement? 3) What results would be helpful to government officials in making decisions? 4) Do human origins, the formation of social groups, and the pattern of interaction between groups, suggest that human beings have an aggressive instinct? a malleable nature? 5) Under what circumstances does the incidence of violence increase among groups? decrease? 6) How have cooperative activities aided in breaking down tension and conflict? 7) Are there ascertainable patterns of conflict? Is war an inevitable part of those patterns? 8) How has war been treated in literature — as a patriotic duty? an inevitable part of social life? a curse of the powerful on the weak? a necessary duty in a state-system? 9) Does war have socially beneficial, if unintended, consequences that prevent significant efforts to eliminate it from developing? 10) What are the conditions essential to a world without war?

A. Overviews of Peace Research

17 – 1 *Toward a Science of Peace,* Theodore Lenz, 193pp, 1971 (5th ed.), Halycon, $3.00. A pioneer in the field states the case for peace research.

17 – 2 *Statistics of Deadly Quarrels,* Lewis Richardson, edited by Quincy Wright & C.C. Lienau, 373pp, 1960, Boxwood, $24.00. An influential statistical analysis of the incidence of war.

Classic

17 – 3 *Arms and Insecurity: A Mathematical Study of the Causes and Origins of War,* Lewis Richardson, Nicholas Rashevski & Ernest Trucco (eds.), 307pp, 1960, Boxwood, $15.00. Develops mathematical formulas correlating armaments with the outbreak of war.

17 – 4 *Deadly Quarrels, Lewis F. Richardson and the Statistical Study of War,* David Wilkinson, 249pp, 1981, California, $14.50. A presentation of Richardson's collection of data, with comments, comparison to the data of others, and bibliographic information.

Intro

17 – 5 *In Search of Global Patterns,* James Rosenau (ed.), 389pp, 1976, Macmillan, $17.00. Autobiographical essays, plus research and conceptual articles, make this an excellent introduction to the attempt to approach international relations with a "quantitative, scientific" approach.

17 – 6 *Peace Research Around the World,* Hanna Newcombe and Alan Newcombe, 275pp, 1969, Canadian Peace Research Institute, $5.00. A useful categorization and survey of results to 1968.

17 – 7 *Recent Advances in Peace and Conflict Research: A Critical Survey,* Juergen Dedring, 256pp, 1976, Sage, $8.95. A thorough and perceptive review of recent research, and changes in definitions of what constitutes peace research.

17 – 8 *Review of Research Trends and an Annotated Bibliography: Social and Economic Consequences of the Arms Race and of Disarmament,* International Peace Research Association, 44pp, 1978, UNESCO, $3.25. Offers a short overview, notes the increasing "militarization of the third world" and provides 178 annotated references primarily of U.S. and Western European authors.

17 – 9 *Peace Research, Trend Report and World Directory,* International Peace Re-

search Institute, Oslo, 250pp, 1979, UNESCO, $5.00. Includes an essay by Galtung "Towards a Definition of Peace Research" and another by the Institute on recent trends, then lists 310 institutions with detailed information about each.

17 – 10 *Stable Peace,* Kenneth Boulding, 143pp, 1978, Texas, $3.95. Maintaining that war and peace exist along a continuum, Boulding seeks to identify the forces which increase the carrying capacity of the peace system and those which increase the strain.

INF
17 – 11 *Kenneth Boulding, Collected Papers,* Larry Singell (ed.), 497pp, 1975, Colorado, $12.50. Boulding's essays on "international systems" written between 1953 and 1972 offer assessments of peace research at different times.

17 – 12 *The Changing International Community: Some Problems of Its Laws, Structures, and Peace Research and the Middle East Conflict,* Charles Boasson & Max Nurock (eds.), 414pp, 1973, Mouton, $40.00. An overview with a case study of the Middle East.

17 – 13 *Usable Knowledge, Social Science, and Social Problem Solving,* Charles Lindbloom & David Cohen, 129pp, 1979, Yale, $3.95. Maintains that social science research is rarely applicable to social problem solving, and suggests how that might change.

17 – 14 *Conflicting Concepts of Peace in Contemporary Peace Studies,* L. Gunnar Johnson, 1976, Sage, O.P. Distinguishes between peace studies which seek to end war, to achieve world justice, or to aid in the creation of a new world order.

17 – 15 *Bibliography of Quincy Wright, 1890 – 1970,* Louise Wright, 1974, C.E. Barbour, $7.00.

B. Peace Research

INF
17 – 16 *The Correlates of War: I, Research Origins and Rationale,* 384pp, 1979, Macmillan, $19.95. II, *Testing Some Balance-of-Power Models,* J. David Singer (ed.) 384pp, 1980, Macmillan, $25.00. A detailed attempt to codify and test our knowledge about the causes of war and to suggest paths for future research.

17 – 17 *The True Worlds, A Transnational Perspective,* Johan Galtung, 544pp, 1979, Macmillan, $9.95. Argues that poverty, violence, and oppression are characteristics of an obsolete system of States, and calls for transnational institutions. Galtung focuses, however, on the internal structure of States as the cause of "structural violence" which can be eliminated through nonviolent revolution.

17 – 18 *Studies in Crisis Behavior,* Michael Brecher (ed.), 384pp, 1979, Transaction, $12.95. Theory and case studies, identifying patterns of crises occurring in the last forty years.

17 – 19 *Macro-Quantitative Analysis: Conflict, Development, and Democratization,* John Gillespie & Betty Nesvold (eds.), 576pp, 1971, Sage, $8.95. Offers the results of cross-national, statistical research on such problems as conflict within and between States, the causes of civil strife, the role of democracy in development, and the comparison of political systems.

17 – 20 *Understanding Conflict and War,* Vol. I, *The Dynamic Psychological Field,* Rudolph Rummel, 342pp, 1975, Sage, $20.00. Develops a "field theory" in which war is explained as the result of diverse forces operating in a field of States. Conflict or war between States results when those forces causing war outweigh those forces causing peace. All previous peace research is brought to bear on identifying and weighing each type of force. This volume establishes the psychological foundations of the field theory: perceptions, the self, determinism vs. free will, the role of intentions — each are considered significant, contrary to behaviorialist assumptions.

17 – 21 *Understanding Conflict and War,* Vol. II, *The Conflict Helix,* Rudolph Rummel, 400pp, 1976, Sage, $20.00. Explores how a society of diverse people resolve conflict within a political system, and concludes that libertarian societies do not war; war requires that one State be authoritarian.

17 – 22 *Understanding Conflict and War,* Vol. III, *Conflict in Perspective,* Rudolph Rummel, 197pp, 1977, Sage, $17.50. Draws the causes of conflict into the patterns which produce war and other forms of conflict.

17 – 23 *Understanding Conflict and War,* Vol. IV, *War, Power, Peace,* Rudolph Rummel, 447pp, 1979, Sage, $27.50. Brings together the parts of "field theory" in understanding international relations and the conflict helix within that society of States. Attempts to meld all the variables of past peace research into one field.

17 – 24 *The Just Peace,* Rudolph Rummel, 320pp, 1981, Sage, $22.50. Argues that a social contract model provides the basis for a just society; freedom is the central value that minimizes violence and maximizes economic well-being and happiness.

17 – 25 *The Tensionmeter Prediction of Nations Likely to be Involved in War in the Years 1977 – 1980,* Alan Newcombe & Frank Klassen, 43pp, 1979, Korean Institute of International Studies, $1.00. Maintains that a "Tension-Ratio" predicting the likelihood of war with 96.5% accuracy can be obtained by determining the relationship between GNP per capita and military expenditures per capita.

17 – 26 *Strategies Against Violence, Design for Nonviolent Change,* Israel Charny (ed.), 417pp, 1978, Westview, $24.50. An inter-disciplinary approach to behaviorial patterns considered helpful in producing international peace and nonviolent change.

17 – 27 *Structure of Decision: The Cognitive Maps of Political Elites,* Robert Axelrod (ed.), 375pp, 1976, Princeton, $10.95. A cognitive map represents a decision-maker's concepts and the consequences of action on them graphically to better evaluate decision-making.

17 – 28 *Sociology, War and Disarmament: Studies in Peace Research,* Johan Niezing,

131pp, 1973, Transaction, $8.95. Seeks to combine sociology, social psychology, and political science concepts in an attempt to clarify problems and prospects in substituting law for armaments.

17 – 29 *Strategy and Structure: Studies in Peace Research,* II, Johan Niezing, 68pp, 1978, Transaction, $5.95. Maintains that armament possession affects both international policy and domestic social structures; critical of official and unofficial security concepts.

17 – 30 *National Attributes and Behavior: Data, Dimensions, Linkages, and Groups, 1950 – 1965,* Rudolph Rummel, 472pp, 1979, Sage, $27.50. A research report on the Dimensionality of Nations project, presenting the major data and empirical results, plus Rummel's field theory applied to the period.

17 – 31 *Content Analysis: A Handbook with Applications for the Study of International Crisis,* Robert North, et al., 1963, Northwestern, $3.20. Applies quanitative techniques to language use to assess energy devoted to various pursuits.

17 – 32 *Peace, War, and Numbers,* Bruce Russett (ed.), 312pp, 1972, Sage, $32.50. Offers eleven essays summarizing largely quantitative results, focused on conflict resolution.

17 – 33 *Race, Science and Society,* Leo Kuper (ed.), 370pp, 1975, (1956), UNESCO, $6.00. Papers written during the first ten years of UNESCO's existence which helped to bring submerged racial prejudices into the open; racism is found in many societies and social settings.

17 – 34 *Catastrophe and Crisis,* Jeremy Kingston and David Lambert, 336pp, 1978, Facts on File, $17.50. A catalog of "sudden events" like earthquakes, floods, volcanoes, famines, plagues, accidents, wars and assassinations with a chapter on international relief. An odd mixing of natural and human events.

17 – 35 *The War Disease,* Norman Alcock, 238pp, 1972, Canadian Peace Research Institute, $4.00. An attempt to determine the sufficient conditions for war which identifies thirty factors, highlights territorial disputes between adjacent ideological rivals, and concludes with an attempt to reconcile the views that "the onset of war is the automatic end product of an action-and-reaction 'Richardson process' and that it is also the deliberate choice of national leaders."

17 – 36 *Fifty-Two Peaceful Societies,* Matthew Melko, 223pp, 1973, Canadian Peace Research Institute, $4.00. A study of the conditions which lead to periods of sustained peace within certain geographical areas and of the apparently inevitable breakdown of those conditions.

17 – 37 *War and Rank Among Nations,* Michael Wallace, 160pp, 1973, Lexington, O.P. A study which utilizes data covering the last 140 years. Do rapid changes in status among states lead to war?

C. International Relations

17 – 38 *Main Trends of Research in the Social Sciences*, Part I, 819pp, 1979, UN-ESCO, Part II, *Main Trends of Research in the Social and Human Sciences*, 1591pp, 1979, UNIPUB, $125.00. Part of a massive effort to summarize a wide range of research activity through analytical essays by world renowned scholars.

17 – 39 *The Information Sources of Political Science, International Relations and Organizations: Comparative and Area Studies*, Frederick Holler, 122pp, 1975, ABC-Clio, $4.35. Valuable but not as extensive as the title implies.

17 – 40 *Contemporary Research in International Relations: A Perspective and a Critical Appraisal*, Dina Zinnes, 477pp, 1976, Free Press, $19.95. A sweeping review of methodological issues and an assessment of the validity of results achieved.

17 – 41 *Analyzing International Relations: A Multimethod Introduction*, William Coplin & Charles Kegley, Jr., 381pp, 1975, Praeger, O.P. Designed as a substantive and a methodological overview of academic approaches to the study of international relations. It focuses on U.S. foreign policy, national interactions, and the international system. Includes essays by twenty-two scholars.

17 – 42 *Essays on the Analysis of World Politics, A Three Volume Collection of Essays*, James Rosenau, Vol. I *The Scientific Study of Foreign Policy*, 577pp, 1980, Nichols, $15.00; Vol. II *The Study of Global Interdependence, Essays on the Transnationalization of World Affairs*, 350pp, 1980, Nichols, $15.00; Vol. III *The Study of Political Adaptation*, 300pp, 1980, Nichols, $12.50. The latter argues that all actors in world politics must balance internal and external tensions if they are to move toward their goals.

17 – 43 *Diplomacy: New Approaches in History, Theory, and Policy*, Paul Lauren (ed.), 286pp, 1979, Free Press, $25.00. Essays by prominent historians and international relations professors exploring ways in which each discipline can aid the other.

17 – 44 *Conflict among Nations: Bargaining, Decision-Making, and System Structure in International Crisis*, Glenn Snyder & Paul Diesing, 578pp, 1977, Princeton, $9.50. A theoretical study of crises management and bargaining, alliance formation processing and decision-making.

17 – 45 *International Organization, A Conceptual Approach*, Paul Taylor & A.J.R. Groom (eds.), 466pp, 1978, Nichols, $25.00. Outlines the background to international institutions, the major functional approaches (thirteen in all), emphasizes the importance of nongovernmental organizations, and lists international organizations today.

17 – 46 *Quantitative International Politics: Insights and Evidence*, J. David Singer (ed.), 394pp, 1968, Macmillan, $14.95. Both methodology and results are considered.

17 – 47 *Quantitative International Politics, An Appraisal*, Francis Hoole and Dina Zinnes, 519pp, 1976, Praeger, O.P. A summary of four important peace research

projects; the Correlates of War, the Dimensionality of Nations, Inter-Nation Simulation, and Stanford Studies in International Conflict and Integration Projects, with critical assessments of each.

17 – 48 *International Politics and Foreign Policy, A Reader in Research and Theory*, James Rosenau (ed.), 740pp, 1969, (2nd ed.), Free Press, $19.95. An anthology introducing the field through selections from leading political scientists. The ideas included are a definition of the field, the international system, theory and approaches to the action and interaction of States, and research techniques.

17 – 49 *Quantitative Techniques in Foreign Policy Analysis and Forecasting*, Michael O'Leary & William Coplin, 291pp, 1975, Praeger, $37.50. A study of the potential and limits of quantitative techniques in the gathering and analysis of information and in forecasting events, done with the cooperation of the Department of State.

17 – 50 *Forecasting in International Relations: Theory, Methods, Problems, Pro-spects*, Nazli Choucri & Thomas Robinson, 468pp, 1978, Freeman, $33.00. Suggests what can, and cannot, be forecast.

17 – 51 *Statistical Concepts for Students of International Relations*, Jack Vincent, 70pp, 1978, University Press of America, $3.50. An alphabetical approach to method-ological concepts such as canonical correlations, path analysis and z-scores.

17 – 52 *Dependence and Dependency in the Global System*, James Caparaso (ed.), 300pp, 1978, U. of Wisconsin, $5.00. A special edition on international organization devoted to substantive and methodological issues in evaluating the effect of one State's dependence upon another.

17 – 53 *Theories and Approaches to International Politics*, Patrick Morgan, 302pp, 1981, (3rd ed.), Transaction, $9.95. An attempt to establish the empirical basis for different contexts or perspectives.

17 – 54 *Project Theory, Interpretations and Policy Relevance*, Jack Vincent, 340pp, 1970, University Press of America, $10.75. Presents "hundreds of new statistically significant empirical findings on conflict flows in the international system."

D. Crisis, Diplomacy and Intervention

17 – 55 *Between Peace and War, The Nature of International Crisis*, Richard Lebow, 400pp, 1981, Johns Hopkins, $24.50. A study of twenty-seven specific crises to determine whether deliberate decision or miscalculation is more likely to lead to war.

17 – 56 *From Rhodesia to Zimbabwe: The Politics of Transition*, Henry Wiseman & Alastair Taylor, 170pp, 1981, Pergamon, $9.95. Describes the role of the British mediators in evolving a political process to decide an issue being contested by war.

17 – 57 *Dynamics of Third Party Intervention, Mediation in International Conflicts*, Jeffrey Rubin (ed.), 300pp, 1980, Praeger, $23.95. Kissinger's step-by-step diplomacy

(1973 – 75) in the Middle East is the focus of each essay in this anthology; each essay contains an explicit statement of the assumptions made about third party intervention made by the author.

17 – 58 *International Crisis: Insights from Behavioral Research,* Charles Herman, 1973, Macmillan, $14.95. Seeks to apply the results of peace research to specific situations.

17 – 59 *Bargaining in International Conflicts,* Charles Lockhart, 205pp, 1979, Columbia, $12.50. Explores the applicability of modeling and experimentation in administrative, psychological and economic theory to international conflict, using as case studies the Agadir crisis of 1911, the Cuban missile crisis, and the Vietnam war.

17 – 60 *Conference Diplomacy – A Case Study: The UN World Food Conference, Rome, 1974,* Edwin Martin, 58pp, 1981, Institute for the Study of Diplomacy, $3.00. Provides an overview of the conference, from preparatory committees to the aftermath.

17 – 61 *Resolution of the Yemen Crisis, 1963: A Case Study in Mediation,* Chrisopher McMullen, 56pp, 1980, Institute for the Study of Diplomacy, $3.00. A practical, diplomatic guide.

E. Politics

17 – 62 *Global Public Political Culture,* Norman Walbek, 128pp, 1973, Peace Research Review, $4.00. A study of themes expressed in UN and other intergovernmental organization (IGOs), debates, and of the linkages between "public verbal behavior" and actions inside and outside the IGO setting.

17 – 63 *The Divided Academy; Professors and Politics,* Everett Ladd, Jr. & Seymour Martin Lipset, 351pp, 1976, Norton, $4.95. A study of the political beliefs of academics in the 1960s and early 1970s which concludes that "the intellectual stratum will provide in a continuing fashion . . . pressures for social change."

17 – 64 *The Pathology of Politics: Violence, Betrayal, Corruption, Secrecy, and Propaganda,* Carl Friedrich, 287pp, 1972, Irvington, $24.50. In the absence of law, chaos.

See also Chapter 20.

F. Conflict

17 – 65 *New Ways of Managing Conflict,* Rensis Likert & Jane Likert, 375pp, 1976, McGraw-Hill, $19.95. A contribution to resolving "any kind of conflict except that within a single individual"; it helps to use third parties and initiative acts by the strongest.

17 – 66 *Conflict Regulation,* Paul Wehr, 200pp, 1979, Westview, $9.95. Examines theory and practice in the conduct of conflict from Gandhi to the present.

17 – 67 *Fights, Games, and Debates*, Anatol Rapoport, 416pp, 1974, Michigan, $4.95. An explanation of how games like "prisoner's dilemma" can help map out patterns of conflict.

17 – 68 *Prisoner's Dilemma: A Study in Conflict and Cooperation*, Anatol Rapoport & Albert Chammah, 258pp, 1970, Michigan, $2.95. A detailed discussion of the choices one makes when cooperation is desired but may not be reciprocated.

17 – 69 *Every War Must End*, Fred Ikle, 160pp, 1971, Columbia, $3.50. They do not go on forever. The exits are marked here and the urgency, in the nuclear era, of ending war before it starts is underlined. "It is a tragic paradox of our age that the highly humane objective of preventing nuclear war is served by a military doctrine and engines of destruction whose very purpose is to inflict genocide" (p. 130).

17 – 70 *Managing Interstate Conflict, 1945 – 1974; Data with Synopses*, Robert Butterworth & Margaret Scranton, 544pp, 1976, Pittsburgh, $6.95. A chronicle of 255 interstate security disputes, providing both coded data (forty-eight variables) and a description of each conflict.

17 – 71 *Propaganda and Communication in World History*, Harold Lasswell, Daniel Lerner, and Hans Spier, Vol. I: *The Symbolic Instrument in Early Times*, 645pp, 1978, U. of Hawaii Press, $25.00; Vol. II: *Emergence of Public Opinion in the West*, 700pp, 1979, $25.00; Vol. III: *A Pluralizing World in Formation*, 700pp, 1980, $25.00. Each volume has more than ten contributors addressing how communication processes alter perceptions, influence attitudes, and change behavior.

G. Simulation

17 – 72 *Modelling and Managing International Conflicts: The Berlin Crisis*, Raymond Tanter, 272pp, 1974, Sage, $8.95. A quantitative investigation and a case study.

INF
17 – 73 *Simulations in International Relations: Development for Research Teaching*, Harold Guetzkow, et al., 248pp, 1963, Prentice-Hall, O.P. A pioneering work in the development of simulations.

17 – 74 *Global Simulation Models: A Comparative Study*, John Clark & Sam Cole, 135pp, 1975, Wiley, $10.95. Attempts to clarify the potential and limits of models in forecasting.

17 – 75 *Simulated Worlds: A Computer Model of National Decision-Making*, Stuart Bremer, 249pp, 1976, Princeton, $21.00. States a "macro-level theory of international politics," embodies the theory in an operating computer simulation model and then tests it by determining how well the computer predicts future political events."

17 – 76 *Dynamics of the Vietnam War: A Quantitative Analysis and Predictive Com-*

puter Simulation, Jeffrey Milstein, 254pp, 1974, Ohio State, $12.50. Applies simulation techniques to "hawk" and "dove" policy options during the Vietnam war era.

17 – 77 *Catastrophe or New Society, A Latin American World Model* A. Herrera, H. Scolnik, et al., 108pp, 1976, International Development Resource Center, O.P. A world model, like *The Limits of Growth* and its successor, *Mankind at the Turning Point*.

17 – 78 *Problems of World Modeling: Political and Social Implications,* Karl Deutsch, and others (eds.), 420pp, 1977, Ballinger, $18.50. A technical introduction to the problems and prospects of computer models.

H. Economics

17 – 79 *The History of Economic Thought,* William Barber, 266pp, 1977, 1967, Penguin, $2.95. An introductory overview.

17 – 80 *The Political Economy of War and Peace,* Richard Ashley, 320pp, 1980, Nichols, 320pp, 1980, Nichols, $26.50. Offers a systematic analysis of Sino-Soviet-American relations since 1950. It concludes that peace will require "persistent efforts to resolve a web of reproducing dilemmas in which the dynamics of growth have critical results."

17 – 81 *Ecodynamics, A New Theory of Societal Evolution,* Kenneth Boulding, 367pp, 1978, Sage, $16.95. A broad survey of human history which concludes: "It is the processes of growth and production rather than of conflict that are really significant . . . the Washingtons, the Lenins, and the Maos . . . create eddies in the stream, but contribute very little to human progress." p. 255

See also Chapters 13 and 15.

I. Comparative Politics

17 – 82 *International Events and the Comparative Analysis of Foreign Policy,* Charles Kegley, Jr., Gregory Raymond, Robert Rood and Richard Skinner (eds.), 317pp, 1975, South Carolina Press, $7.95. Presents and assesses the comparative approach to politics.

17 – 83 *The Comparative Study of Foreign Policy, A Survey of Scientific Findings,* Patrick McGowan & Howard Shapiro, 256pp, 1973, Sage, $8.95. States 118 different propositions concerning thirteen subjects and summarizes the results of over 200 research projects.

17 – 84 *Why Nations Act, Theoretical Perspectives for Comparative Foreign Policy Studies,* Maurice East, Stephen Salmore & Charles Hermann (eds.), 234pp, 1978, Sage $9.95. A product of the Comparative Research on the Events of Nations (CREON) Project seeking explanations of leadership decisions in international relations settings.

17 – 85 *Comparing Foreign Policies: Theories, Findings, and Methods,* James Rosenau (ed.), 442pp, 1974, Halsted, $21.50. Attempts to evaluate different approaches.

J. Sociology

17 – 86 *The Last Half-Century, Societal Change and Politics in America,* Morris Janowitz, 582pp, 1979, Chicago, $7.95. An analysis of America's changing social structure.

17 – 87 *Political Socialization, An Analytic Study,* Richard Dawson, Kenneth Prewitt & Karen Dawson, 220pp, 1977, (1969), 2nd ed., Little Brown, $7.95. A study of the personal and social origins of political views which concludes that such views rarely change rapidly.

17 – 88 *Living Systems,* James Miller, 1102pp, 1977, McGraw Hill, $49.50. A study of many types of systems including the system of world politics, which indicates that "only in the twentieth century has a world without war been widely regarded as a valid goal." p. 959

17 – 89 *International Law and the Social Sciences,* Wesley Gould & Michael Barkun, 1970, Princeton, O.P. An attempt to show that international law and social science methodology arise from similar assumptions concerning changing social systems; both general implications for social scientists and specific applications of law result.

17 – 90 *International Behavior, A Social-Psychological Analysis,* Herbert Kelman (ed.), 626pp, 1965, Irvington, $18.50. A valuable survey of research on negotiations, perceptions, images, and the influence of contact on perceptions in international relations.

17 – 91 *States and Social Revolutions, A Comparative Analysis of France, Russia and China,* Theda Skocpol, 407pp, 1979, Cambridge, $8.95. A study of the class conflict, chaos, and dictatorship.

K. History

17 – 92 *The Past Before Us; Contemporary Historical Writing in the United States,* Michael Kammen (ed.), 552pp, 1980, Cornell, $19.95. A summary of the "state of the discipline" with an essay on the historiography of international relations by Charles Maier titled "Marking Time."

17 – 93 *Bibliography on Peace Research in History,* Blanche Cook (ed.), 72pp, 1969, ABC-Clio, O.P. A research guide for historians which includes archival holdings, current and out-of-print books, and peace organization record depositories. Emphasizes international relations, disarmament, nonviolence, and world law.

17 – 94 *The Garland Library of War and Peace: A Collection of 327 Titles,* Blanche Cook, Charles Chatfield & Sandi Cooper (eds.), 136pp, 1971, Garland, Free. An attractive catalogue of reprinted landmarks in thought about war and peace. An introduction to neglected writings in Europe and the U.S during the last 400 years. Included in the 328 volume collection are works by Dante, Erasmus, Cruce, Grotius, Bentham, Kant, Tolstoy, and Norman Thomas. Some of these titles might have been left to mold but overall, this is a most useful collection for a library.

17 – 95 *An Introduction to Contemporary History,* Geoffrey Barroclough, 284pp, 1968, Penguin, $2.95. Argues that there is a great division between the 19th century and today; today a world civilization is taking shape in which a mood of "affirmation and the exploration of the new potentialities which science has opened up" is the characteristic attitude.

17 – 96 *A Distant Mirror: The Calamitous Fourteenth Century,* Barbara Tuchman, 704pp, 1980, Ballantine $7.95. A time of disorder, social dislocation, plague — a time when political communities disintegrated into small groups. Small can be calamitous.

17 – 97 *Inevitable Peace,* Carl Friedrich, 294pp, 1969, (1948), Greenwood Press, $12.50.

17 – 98 *Peacemaking from Vergennes to Napoleon,* Thomas Iiams, 240pp, 1979, Krieger, $12.50. A history of diplomacy.

17 – 99 *Universal Evolution and the Road to Peace,* Bernard Wilson, 104pp, 1980, Dorrance, $5.95. Maintains peace is the outcome of history.

17 – 100 *War and Rural Life in the Early Modern Low Countries,* Myron Guttman, 311pp, 1980, Princeton, $22.50. A study of the role of warfare.

17 – 101 *Against the Current, Essays in the History of Ideas,* Isaiah Berlin, 394pp, 1980, Viking, $16.95. A collection of essays, written over a period of thirty years, addressed to common problems such as liberty, human nature, knowledge, and power as developed in intellectual history.

17 – 102 *New Directions in American Intellectual History,* John Higham & Paul Conkin (eds.), 245pp, 1979, Johns Hopkins, $16.00. Identifies the broadening of intellectual history to include popular ideas, cultural fads, and art as new, as well as an emphasis on the social setting within which ideas are generated.

17 – 103 *The Declassified Eisenhower, A Divided Legacy of Peace and Political Warfare,* Blanche Wiesen Cook, 1981, Doubleday, $15.00. A re-appraisal of the Eisenhower era emphasizing covert operations, anti-communism, and the development of military threat as an instrument of political coercion.

17 – 104 *The Library of World Peace Studies,* Warren Kuehl, editor, Reprints on microfiche periodicals of peace societies in the 19th and 20th centuries. For example, currently available is the journal of the American Peace Society (1837 to 1932), variously titled the "Advocate of Peace," "Advocate of Peace and Universal Bro-

therhood," and "The Advocate of Peace through Justice." Write Clearwater Publishing, 1995 Broadway, New York, N.Y. 10023.

17 – 105 *Violence and Aggression in the History of Ideas*, Philip Wiener & John Fisher (eds.), 288pp, 1974, Rutgers, $4.95. Eighteen scholarly essays on justifications and uses of violence in many different historical settings.

17 – 106 *Fin-De-Siècle Vienna, Politics and Culture*, Carl Schorske, 378pp, 1980, Knopf, $15.95. Combines social class, cultural, and psychoanalytic concepts in an analysis of (and to an extent forerunner of) the ahistorical tendency in modern thought.

17 – 107 *Utopian Thought in the Western World*, Frank Manuel & Fritzie Manuel, 896pp, 1979, Harvard, $25.00. Traces an idea over a 3,000-year career including its Judeo-Christian enlightenment and Marxist forms, and concludes "utopian fantasies have yielded both good and evil in ample measure" (p. 814).

17 – 108 *The Philosophy of International Relations, A Study in the History of Thought*, F. Parkinson, 248pp, 1977, Sage, $8.95. Covers the field from classical antiquity to the present. Includes an extensive bibliography.

L. Philosophy

17 – 109 *War and Peace in Contemporary Social and Philosophical Theory*, Irving Horowitz, 218pp, 1957, 1973, Humanities, $9.00. A study of major 20th-century philosophers and their attitudes toward war and peace: metaphysical harmony (Whitehead), pacifism (Tolstoy), humanism (Einstein), universal individualism (Perry), man against man (Russell), historical vision (Lenin), and others. Concludes with an attempt to develop an "integrated philosophy of peace."

M. Futures/Science/Technology

17 – 110 *The Third Wave*, Alvin Toffler, 576pp, 1981, Bantam, $3.95. The continuing impact of science on society.

17 – 111 *The World That Could Be*, Robert North, 161pp, 1976, Norton, $8.95. A cautiously optimistic look at the future. To be sure, problems of population increase; unprecedented technological change and rapid, though unevenly distributed economic growth, promise revolutionary changes; but, at least, the possibility of political action makes the transition possible.

17 – 112 *Alternative Futures, Designing Social Change*, William Boyer, 132pp, 1975, Kendall/Hunt, $4.95. Less futuristic than present problem-solving; population, pollution, energy, war, and poverty are all mentioned with a summary chapter on "Some Alternative Futures."

17 – 113 *Person/Planet: The Creative Disintegration of Industrial Society*, Theodore

Roszak, 347pp, 1979, Doubleday, $5.95. Sees new values emerging from face-to-face relationships.

17 – 114 *Einstein and Peace,* Bulletin of Atomic Scientists (eds.), 120pp, 1979, $3.00. A special issue commemorating the 100th anniversary of Einstein's birth.

17 – 115 *Planning Alternative World Futures, Values, Methods, and Models,* Louis Beres & Harry Targ (eds.), 340pp, 1975, Praeger, $8.95. Outlines courses of study.

17 – 116 *Political Science and the Study of the Future,* Albert Somit (ed.), 336pp, 1974, Dryden, O.P. Includes careful thought about the twelve different kinds of predictions and an essay by Paul Seabury on "Practical International Futures and Science Fiction model world orders."

17 – 117 *Forecasting: An Appraisal for Policy-Makers and Planners,* William Ascher, 239pp, 1978, Johns Hopkins, $4.95. A study of the success in forecasting population growth, economic development, energy utilization, transportation use, and technological breakthroughs, concludes that short term forecasts only are valuable.

17 – 118 *Handbook of Futures Research,* Jib Fowles (ed.), 822pp, 1978, Greenwood, $39.95. Offers forty-one articles on anticipating the future; more practical than speculative.

17 – 119 *Colonies in Space,* T.A. Heppenheimer, 1978, Warner, $2.50. Explores the idea of space colonies.

17 – 120 *The Future, A Guide to Information Sources,* World Future Society, 722pp, 1979, 2nd ed., World Future Society, $25.00. A directory of 560 individuals, 270 organizations, 120 research projects, 587 books and reports, 105 periodicals, ninety-three films, 109 audiotapes and tape series, forty-five games and simulations, seventeen mixed media presentations, and more than 280 courses and programs offered by educational institutions.

N. Psychology

17 – 121 *War: Studies from Psychology, Sociology, Anthropology,* Leon Bramson & George Goethals (eds.), 434pp, 1968 (rev. ed.), Basic Books, $6.95. Examines the failure of any single cause approach to the study of war, and argues the need for a comprehensive list of causes of war for those interested in its prevention.

17 – 122 *Civilization and Its Discontents,* Sigmund Freud, 99pp, 1963 (1909), Norton, $1.95. One of Freud's attempts to apply psychoanalytic categories to society.

17 – 123 *The Anatomy of Human Destructiveness,* Erich Fromm, 576pp, 1978, Fawcett, $2.95. Aggression is considered an acquired trait which can be rejected.

17 – 124 *Violence and the Struggle for Existence,* David Daniels, Marshall Gilula & Frank Ochberg (eds.), 451pp, 1970, Little, Brown, O.P. The Stanford University

Department of Psychiatry examines the roots of violence and identifies guidelines for developing alternatives to violence.

17 – 125 *The Nature of Prejudice,* Gordon Allport, 456pp, 1958 (abrd. ed.), 1979, (1958), Addison-Wesley, $4.95. One of the basic studies of the nature of prejudice, its origins, manifestations, and consequences.

17 – 126 *Power and Innocence: A Search for the Sources of Violence,* Rollo May, 283pp, 1976, Dell, $3.95. A psychological analysis of the various sources of violence in the human personality: focuses on powerlessness as the primal root.

17 – 127 *Childhood and Society,* Erik Erikson, 445pp, 1964, Norton, $2.95. A noted psychologist studies individual identity crises and their relationship to political identification with nation-States. This is but one strand in a book full of insights.

17 – 128 *Marx's Fate: The Shape of a Life,* Jerrold Seigel, 460pp, 1978, Princeton, $22.00. A biography stressing early childhood and Marx's alternation between political commitment and withdrawal.

17 – 129 *Power and Personality,* Harold Lasswell, 262pp, 1948, 1976, Norton $3.95. Maintains that political power is often sought as a means of overcoming a sense of personal deficiency.

17 – 130 *Decision-Making: A Psychological Analysis of Conflict, Choice & Commitment,* Irving Janis & Leon Mann, 488pp, 1979, Macmillan, $8.95. Includes a section on decision-making and paralysis in foreign policy decisions.

17 – 131 *Negotiations, Social-Psychological Perspectives,* Daniel Druckman (ed.), 416pp, 1977, Sage, $29.95. A theoretical and empirical approach to depicting the interplay among goals, background factors, motives, settings, personality traits, and time in deciding outcomes.

17 – 132 *The Social Psychology of Bargaining and Negotiation,* Jeffrey Rubin & Bert Brown, 360pp, 1975, Academic Press, O.P. Devoted to a tough problem made even more critical by "growing demands and diminishing resources."

17 – 133 *Jung and the Story of Our Time,* Laurens Van Der Post, 276pp, 1977, Vintage, $3.95. An appreciation by a friend of the mind that gave us terms like "extrovert, introvert, and archetype."

17 – 134 *The Authoritarian Personality,* T. Adorno, Else Frenkel-Brunswick, Daniel Levinson & R. Nevitt Sanford, 990pp, 1969 (1950), Norton, $9.95. A pioneer study seeking to delineate the characteristics of an authoritarian personality. The focus is on anti-Semitism and Nazi Germany, but the chapters on "antidemocratic trends" and much else have wider application.

17 – 135 *The Scientific Credibility of Freud's Theories and Therapy,* Seymour Fisher & Roger Greenberg, 502pp, 1977, Basic Books, $22.50. A survey of research assessing the evidence confirming, limiting, and refuting Freudian ideas. The death instinct or other subjects related to war are *not* assessed.

17 – 136 *Life History and the Historical Moment, Diverse Presentations,* Erik Erikson, 283pp, 1975, Norton, $3.95. Speeches illustrating Erickson's work on "identity crises," Gandhi, and revolt.

17 – 137 *Death in Life: Survivors of Hiroshima,* Robert Jay Lifton, 594pp, 1976, Simon & Schuster, $5.95. A psychological study of the world of the survivors.

17 – 138 *Future Science: Life Energies and the Physics of Paranormal Phenomena,* John White & Stanley Krippner, 600pp, 1977, Doubleday, $4.50. An introduction to the scientific study of parapsychology.

O. Literature

17 – 139 *International Relations Through Science Fiction,* Martin Greenberg & Joseph Olander, 236pp, 1978, Franklin Watts, $6.95. Short introductions to conflict, international organization, power politics; and other war/peace themes are illustrated through fifteen short science fiction stories.

17 – 140 *Political Science Fiction, An Introductory Reader,* Martin Greenberg & Patricia Warrick, 415pp, 1975, Prentice-Hall, O.P. Includes five selections on international relations and four on conflict resolutions.

TEW
17 – 141 *War and Peace in Literature, A Select, Annotated Bibliography of Works that Illuminate the Problem of War,* Lucy Dougall, 154pp, 1982, World Without War Publications, $5.00. Approximately 300 works of prose, drama, and poetry from the Western tradition, either annotated or keyed to a list of themes. Also included are references, essays and anthologies.

17 – 142 *The Liberal Imagination, Essays on Literature and Society,* Lionel Trilling, 303pp, 1965 (1940), Scribners, $3.95. Essays affirming "the value of individual existence in all its variousness, complexity, and difficulty" written in part against the Stalinism of a previous era but still telling today.

17 – 143 *War: An Anthology,* Edward and Elizabeth Huberman (eds.), 304pp, 1969, Washington Square, $1.50. Brings together descriptions and condemnations of the human suffering in war written by poets and authors.

17 – 144 *Man and Warfare: Thematic Readings for Composition,* William Irscher, 340pp, 1964, Little, Brown, O.P. A study of the treatment of warfare in works of fiction.

P. Anthropology

17 – 145 *The Human Connection,* Ashley & Floyd Matson, 228pp, 1979, McGraw-Hill, $4.95. An exploration of non-verbal communication, including how the same gestures mean the opposite in different cultures.

17 – 146 *Biological Pacifism, Selected Works,* Hisatoki Komaki, 3 Volumes, 276pp, $12.00. II 286pp, $15.00. III 121pp, $7.00. Histaki Komaki Foundation. Maintains that killing of all mammals is unhealthy, that disarmament and world law are urgently needed, and that all spiritual beings must be immortal and must evolve to be completely happy.

17 – 147 *Sociobiology: The Abridged Edition,* Edward Wilson, 366pp, 1980, Harvard, $9.95. Wilson argues that specific (as yet, unknown) genes dispose humans toward certain types of behavior.

17 – 148 *Cannibals and Kings, The Origins of Cultures,* Marvin Harris, 239pp, 1977, Random House, $10.00. Argues that "it is part of human nature to be able to become aggressive and to wage war." But how and when we become aggressive is controlled by our cultures rather than our genes.

17 – 149 *Learning Non-Aggression, The Experience of Non-Literate Societies,* Ashley Montagu (ed.), 235pp, 1978, Oxford, $3.95. Eight anthropologists ask why are some people aggressive and others gentle?

17 – 150 *The Evolution of Political Society, An Essay in Political Anthropology,* Morton Fried (ed.), 270pp, 1968, Random House, $5.95. Explores the relationship between rank, status, and aggression.

17 – 151 *Life Chances: Approaches to Social and Political Theory,* Ralf Dahrendorf, 191pp, 1980, Chicago, $15.00. The expansion of opportunities for individual choice is offered as a measure of social change; Western democracies are assessed and criticized for the crisis of legitimate authority and the erosion of a public consensus concerning social institutions; concludes that disintegrating societies offer few choices.

Q. Reference Works

17 – 152 *Card Catalog of the Peace Palace Library,* The Hague, J. Van Hall, 1979, Clearwater Publishing. Part of The Library of World Peace Studies, Warren Kuehl, General Editor. Provides on microfiche the outstanding collection of the Library of the Peace Palace, The Hague (Netherlands). Begun in 1913, the library has collected over 140,000 titles, plus more than 2,300 journals. The complete set is $2,200; the Periodical Reference Guide portion, Chronological section (70,000 cards), $350; Author index, 75,000 cards, $380; the Universal Bibliographical Catalogue, 170,000 cards, $875; the Author index, 180,000 cards, $900. Write for a complete description to: Clearwater Publishing Company, 1995 Broadway, New York, N.Y. 10023.

17 – 153 *UNESCO Yearbook on Peace and Conflict Studies,* Division of Human Rights and Peace, forthcoming.

17 – 154 *British Writing on Disarmament 1914 – 1978, A Bibliography,* Lorna Lloyd & Nicholas Sims, 250pp, 1979, Nichols, $27.50. A comprehensive listing of books, articles, papers, essays, and pamphlets.

17 – 155 *Warfare in Primitive Societies, A Bibliography,* William Divale, 123pp, 1973, (rev. ed.), ABC-Clio, $2.00. Lists many references written from the 19th century to the present with emphasis on the post-World War II literature.

17 – 156 *Threat of Modern Warfare to Man and His Environment, An Annotated Bibliography,* International Peace Research Association (IPRA), 25pp, 1978, UN-ESCO, $3.25. Provides a brief introduction to basic ecological concepts and the likely impact of war on the environment, plus a 117-entry bibliography.

17 – 157 *International Relations Theory, A Bibliography,* A.J.R. Groom & C.R. Mitchell (eds.), 222pp, 1980, Nichols, $12.50. Focuses on current theoretical and conceptual approaches to international relations. Includes evaluative essays.

17 – 158 *Peace and War: A Guide to Bibliographies,* Bernice Carroll, Clinton Fink, & Jane Mohraz, 1981, ABC-Clio, forthcoming. An annotated guide to bibiliographies published since 1785. Includes nearly 1400 entries and a subject index.

17 – 159 *Bibliography on World Conflict and Peace,* Elise Boulding, J. Robert Passmore and Robert Grassler, 150pp, 1979, Westview, $18.50. Presents over 1,000 entries in twenty-six subjects on conflict and peace studies. Includes books, annuals, periodicals, abstracts, relevant bibliographies, and special collections.

17 – 160 Public Affairs Information Service, *Bulletin,* New York, 1915.

17 – 161 Social Science and Humanities Index.

SECTION B

CONTEXTS

THIS SURVEY OF the major ideas in the world affairs field is now complete. Such ideas are advocated in American politics within frames of reference that are called "contexts" here. The dictionary defines a context as "that which leads up to and follows and often specifies the meaning of a particular expression."[1] In political discourse, coherent sets of assumptions and judgments come before and after a statement of position on a particular issue and determine that statement's meaning. Other words can also be used to describe a context, such as "ideology," "perspective," or "worldview." With the exception of ideology, which suggests something more systematic than what is intended here, the alternatives could do as well. "Context" suggests the relevance of values and is preferred for that reason.

Every context within which world affairs is viewed coherently is made up of a number of assumptions and judgments that give that context a distinctive thrust. Every context must respond to a number of basic questions which we identify in Chapter 18. The answers provided by eight contexts found in American politics are then sketched out. On the basis of these answers, these contexts are considered inadequate to resolving the problem of war. Chapter 19 presents a context that is considered adequate.

[1] The American Heritage Dictionary of the English Language.

CHAPTER 18

CONTENDING WORLD AFFAIRS CONTEXTS IN AMERICAN POLITICS

MOST discussions of world affairs focus on specific issues or a current crisis. Despite the urgency within which such discussions take place, indeed because of it, it is essential to consider the basic assumptions and goals of those participants. The problem that gives rise to an issue may be endemic to the situation. Saying "yes" or "no" to a particular weapons system only makes sense when what happens next is clear. Will another weapons system be built? Will some other power center continue to build new weapons systems and gain military superiority? Will the rejection of a weapons system by one power lead others also to reject new systems?

NINE BASIC CHOICE POINTS

Any approach to world politics that is sustained over time implicitly or explicitly develops answers around at least nine choice points. "Gut feelings" are a poor substitute for the discipline of making judgments after asking the right questions. The nine choice points are:

1. Systems: will world politics be dominated by powerful States for the foreseeable future *or* could one State, without unacceptable danger to itself, lead in creating a world order in which State power is legally restrained?

462

2. Goals: What goals are achievable within the system chosen above:
   A. Within the State System:
      a. a stable balance of power between the superpowers?
      b. a plurality of power centers?
      c. world hegemony by one State? or group of States?
   B. Within a World Order:
      a. over 150 sovereign States capable of self-defense with international organizations facilitating voluntary cooperation?
      b. autonomous regions of the world?
      c. a limited, supranational disarmament authority?
      d. a supranational world government?

3. Actors: Is the United States basically a force for good or evil in world politics? Is the Soviet Union basically a force for good or evil in world politics? What is the appropriate role today for regional powers and other States? What role is desirable and possible for non-State actors such as individuals, non-governmental organizations (Foreign Policy Association), international non-governmental organizations (Amnesty International), and regional and global international organizations (Organization of American States and the United Nations)?

4. Economic Development: How does participation in world politics influence the production and distribution of wealth, goods, and services within and between States? How should it?

5. Resource Limits: Does environmental deterioration and ways in which scarce resources are utilized require significant changes in world politics? Are world political institutions required?

6. Justice: Is one economic system just? The goals of one State? Class? Ethnic group? Is liberty (civil and political rights) the primary good which politics should aim to secure? Or is some other value the purpose of politics?

7. Means: Are power and ethical considerations both relevant to decisions? What means are legitimate to employ in world politics? Should the organized use of mass violence be accepted or rejected? However the above question is answered, what non-military alternatives are advocated to promote security, resolve conflict, and promote change? With what resources are non-military alternatives developed and tried?

8. Change: How will change come about? Through wiser administration of existing laws? Changes in the laws? Through new social groups coming to power? Through the replacement of economic and political systems?

Is the preferred process of change that of working through existing institutions, reforming the institutions or replacing them?

9. Knowledge: Are new ideas, new information, or changes in world politics considered? Are the basic assumptions and judgments of the context open to challenge and reformulation? Are contending contexts considered?

There are, of course, more questions. But every approach to world politics must answer such questions in some way.

CAUTIONS IN IDENTIFYING CONTEXTS

Several qualifications need to be kept in mind when considering the contexts described below. Thought about world affairs is fragmented. Events occur that are hard to assimilate into any context. Some people adopt ideas across contextual lines. Others join in activities because they are the most dramatic vehicle for expressing outrage, not because they agree with the ideas. People change their minds and move from one context to another. Labels, which are but useful simplifications, sometimes obscure more than they illuminate. Ideas may, at times, be rationalizations for other unstated purposes. A very specific self-interested objective may, for example, be presented as the national interest, and patriotic or class rhetoric used to urge a commitment to that objective. For all of these reasons, one needs to be cautious in labeling the opinions of others and needs to be aware of the diversity within contexts. Nonetheless, an attempt to understand these contexts is essential. The current contexts dominant in U.S. thought are inadequate to resolving the problem of war and peace. Their inadequacy is a primary obstacle to American leadership toward a world without war.

EIGHT CURRENT CONTEXTS IN AMERICAN POLITICS

The eight contexts summarized below do not exhaust the possibilities. They are today's operative contexts, either guiding or offering significant challenges to governmental decision-makers, or expressing currents of thought influential among the public that studies world affairs. Although there are varying emphases within each, each has a clearly identifiable central thrust. They are:

1. Win
2. The Present Danger

3. Realpolitik
4. Liberal Internationalism
5. Environmentalism
6. Change America
7. Marxist-Leninism
8. Traditional Pacifism

The following summaries offer a brief précis of these world affairs contexts. Each statement is based on a judgment about how the main currents within the context respond to the nine basic choice points.* All differ fundamentally from the approach presented in Chapter 19 as a context adequate to the problem of war.

1. WIN: A policy direction that seeks to achieve peace through the American use of military power to defeat Communism.

At the center of this view is the perception that Communism is both evil and expansionist. Communism is a threat to American values and interests; it has spread because the U.S. is unwilling to oppose it resolutely with military force. If the U.S. had used its full military power in Korea or Vietnam, it would have defeated the Communists and ended each war in a short time.

Advocates reason in this manner: the international Communist movement, centered in Moscow, is out to destroy us. Our ways of life are incompatible and we are actually engaged in a life-and-death struggle. We should accept the inevitability of war and use, or threaten to use, military power to advance our way of life. [7] Negotiations, trade, or cooperation with Communist countries in international organizations are pernicious because they strengthen our foes. Communists do not uphold their agreements, they try to make the rest of the world believe that our society is monstrously evil, and they try to lull us into a false sense of security.

Advocates once considered a U.S. pre-emptive nuclear strike as feasible. They now argue for a rapid build-up of our armaments so that the Soviet Union will not be tempted to make such a strike. They believe that the Soviet Union will treat as ''acceptable'' the loss of millions of people in a nuclear war, and believe we must have strategic superiority to inflict very heavy, ''unacceptable'' losses.

The State system is viewed as a permanent feature of world politics. [1] The U.S. must seek hegemony to prevent the Soviet Union from gaining it. [2]

---

*The numbers bracketed in the text in this chapter refer the reader back to the nine basic choices identified on pages 462 to 464. The context's answer to the question is summarized at that point. No answer, however, is offered for question# 9 ''knowledge'' in the belief that while it is an important choice point within a context, all contexts have their advocates who are open and closed to new information, knowledge, and alternatives.

Allies really cannot be relied upon. The U.S. is morally superior, with its commitments to liberty, free enterprise, and Christianity. [6] Economic development is achieved through hard work and is not brought about by foreign aid or other external economic programs. [4] Resource scarcity can be surmounted if we have the will to develop our own or the courage to use our power to break the oil cartel. [5] The case for our society is so clear that there is no need to debate contending conceptions of what is just. [6] Only military means will dissuade our adversaries from their goals. [7] All that we need to know about our adversaries is contained in the works of Marx and Lenin and in the statements of current Soviet leaders. Change in American foreign policy will come when people with a strong commitment to this society are once again in power.[8]

While the ''win'' position is clearly in the minority today, it could permeate other positions and become compelling for many Americans who find it a satisfactory resolution to a protracted conflict they see America eventually losing. It also appeals to fears of Communism and feelings of self-righteousness.

2. PRESENT DANGER: A policy which maintains that a shift in the balance of power, from the United States to the Soviet Union, has taken place that is jeopardizing democratic societies which are already accommodating themselves to the new power realities.

Central to this context is a perception that the Soviet Union now holds the balance of power over the U.S. Its military expenditure has risen steadily while ours is inadequate and, until 1980, rarely kept pace with inflation. We lack the will to confront the projection of Soviet power and to defend America's allies and interests. Ultimately, the Soviets will advance their interests within Western Europe and America, if trends are not altered. As an example of the ''Finlandization'' of America, advocates point to the refusal of detente proponents, and even supporters of human rights, to criticize Soviet human rights violations.

Power is measured largely in military terms; political bargaining between States is influenced greatly by the military force each State possesses. [1] The steady erosion of American military power and political will has jeopardized Western Civilization. We have not yet responded to the threat to energy sources. As a result, our allies, as well as non-aligned countries, find themselves adrift, and out of self-interest are looking about for ways to accommodate to Soviet power.[2]

Some once felt that international organizations would be able to enforce international law for resolving disputes. Now they feel that such organizations undermine, rather than uphold, international law as well as the common norms of diplomacy. Such organizations should be resorted to only as forums in which to conduct an ideological defense of the West against the authoritarian States of the South and the totalitarian States of the East.[3]

In this context, economic assistance to the South is considered either a form of charity or a political lever rightly used to advance Western interests.[4] It is not the economic order itself which is responsible for persistent, abject poverty. The miracle is that one corner of the world overcame economic destitution. Environmental pollution restrictions and the assault on nuclear power make the U.S. more dependent on oil imports. There are no effective political institutions other than national institutions; only they can correct environmental problems. In America, the 1970s witnessed a remarkable reversal of pollution trends. [5]

Some advocates are liberal on domestic issues; they are referred to as "neo-conservatives" because of their staunch defense of political, administrative, and economic institutions in this country. [6] Other advocates are conservative on domestic issues and view world politics with a sense of alarm.

Most view the Soviet leadership as monolithic, all consider it expansionist, and totalitarian; they think we should reassess the Vietnam war in the light of its aftermath and perhaps revise the view that Vietnam was "a mistake." Many valuable objectives were sought and lost — consequently, our will to use military force in world politics has been undermined and we have lost credibility and influence.[7] The cold war never ended in the "East"; it should be waged vigorously by the "West." Change will come as the intellectual leadership in America reaffirms this country's basic values, as human rights policy becomes a rallying cry for a new foreign policy consensus, and as Americans once again understand the role force now plays in world politics.

3. REALPOLITIK: A policy direction which emphasizes the importance of military power to defend the United States and recommends the national interest as the best guide to good policy.

Here attention is paid to the wise management of power between States and not the defense of democracy *per se*. Nationalism is the prevailing ideology and States are the only viable actors on the world scene. [1] Rivalry between the Soviet Union and the United States is the most important relationship in world politics.[2]

Some advocates maintain that revolutionary socialist ideas are nearly irrelevant in determining Soviet foreign policy objectives. Ideology may be modestly useful by projecting the Soviet national interest, but few decisions are made on the basis of ideology.

Such peace as can be achieved will be won, and kept, by the wise manipula-

tion of military threat and by coalitions tied by bonds of self-interest. We must
carefully define the national interest and limit our objectives to whatever clearly
threatens that interest.

Containing the Soviet Union, not Communism, is one goal. Realpolitik
advocates share, with those who hold the ''win'' and ''present danger'' contexts, the position that totalitarianism and the imposition of Marxist-Leninist
controls over a society are repugnant. But here the attempt by one State to
promote human rights in others is given a very low priority. Advocates of
realpolitik would thus play the ''China card,'' if they are alarmed by the Soviet
Union; would not, if they are not. The decision as to whether to help China to
arm itself as an effective counter to Soviet influence would turn on degrees of
alarm at Soviet expansionism.

Among those who hold this context there are disagreements about where the
national interest requires military commitments. Some would limit the United
States' military alliances to Western Europe, Japan, and Israel (perhaps making
aid available to others); others argue that we must project our power in many
other places to limit Soviet expansion.

International organizations are viewed as conclaves furnishing the opportunity to exercise influence but not power. They will never be more nor less than
this. [3] Economic development can best be achieved through the pursuit of
self-interest in international economic relations through trade and the free flow
of investments. However, consideration should be given to mutually beneficial
reforms in the world economic order. [4] The scarcity of resources suggests
new strategic vulnerabilities, but the problem is not serious enough to warrant
limits on growth. Environmental pollution can be controlled through new
technologies. [5]

Peace can be maintained by alliances or coalitions and by the wise manipulation of military threat. Change comes through alterations in power relationships
traceable to technological innovations, resource discoveries, and political continuity. We must carefully measure our resources and our interests and avoid
pursuing objectives we cannot achieve. [7]

In this context there is great skepticism about applying moral values to world
politics — they dangerously confuse individual morality with group morality
and, although they may provide ultimate standards, their application to the
decision-making process is at best uncertain. [6]

4. LIBERAL INTERNATIONALISM: A policy direction focused on the United
States' engagement in world politics to achieve strengthened international
organizations, world economic development, human rights, and arms control
and disarmament while seeking peace now through military deterrence.

These ideas were the lesson American policy makers learned from World

War II and from the first use of atomic weapons. With the onset of the Cold War, the achievement of liberal internationalist goals was thwarted. It became evident that the United Nations could not keep the peace, and the U.S. resorted to the doctrine of containment through military deterrence. [3] & [7] Meanwhile, liberal internationalists, with varying degress of commitment, worked for enlightened trade and foreign aid policies and for strengthened international institutions. [4] They continued to believe that a vigorous, constructive American policy should try to lay the foundation for a stable peace. They had some success in exploring the possibility of disarmament agreements. They distinguish among various States and policies in the Communist world.

In practice, the commitment to containment and deterrence involved the careful manipulation of military threat, bolstering anti-Communist regimes (regardless of their human rights record), and helping anti-Communist leaders come to power in other countries.

During the Vietnam war this approach was termed globalist, if not imperialist. Those advocating the containment of Soviet expansionism were characterized as racists serving the ends of corporate capitalism, or as the best and the brightest committed to erroneous policies. Critics on the right argued that the full use of power more squarely confronts today's realities.

Liberal internationalists remain in disarray today. Many are still committed to the United Nations, believing it to be the repository of our last best hope for keeping and maintaining peace. They argue in defense of the UN that it mirrors reality and that its overall record is much better than a few sensational votes in the General Assembly would indicate. They call for positive participation in world organizations and they champion human rights throughout the world. [6] They affirm world trade, investment by transnational corporations, and market mechanisms for deciding what gets produced at what prices, but advocate also that these mechanisms be offset, to aid in overcoming hunger, if need be. [4] They have tried to do so with devices such as a grain reserve and by commodity stabilization arrangements. They accept a plurality of economic systems and have a more or less pragmatic view of investment. (Host countries must offer benefits or the investor will not invest; corporations must offer benefits to the host country or they will be expelled or nationalized. Nationalization is a cause for compensation, not intervention or war.) Conceptions of power and of morality have an impact on liberal internationalist thinking. [6]

The threat or use of mass violence is seen only as a last resort. Economic self-interest must be given significant freedom of operation, but may be limited if the consequences of self-interest are harmful to too many. [5]

Although the liberal internationalist view in its original conception underestimated the dynamics moving in many third world countries, and overestimated the effectiveness of international organizations, it still retains credi-

bility. It expresses the way many thoughtful Americans would apply democratic and religious values to world politics. It expects that change will come
when the Soviet Union alters its conception of a world order. [8] It thus believes
that the existing State-system must be retained until the day when common
values emerge to permit international institutions to have enough legitimacy
and authority to keep peace. In one version of this context, a global society is
being built daily, piece by piece. Interdependence is celebrated as bringing a
global perspective to all of the earth's inhabitants. In a more pessimistic version
of this context, interdependence is seen as threatening; world institutions may
be possible but whether they will reflect the values of the liberal internationalist
context remains an open question. Why build commitment to political
structures when the values those structures will further are unknown?

THE DIVIDING LINE

Advocates of these first four contexts shade off into each other. Some
advocates of *realpolitik* believe only the possession of a war-winning capability
will deter Soviet adventurism. Some who are now focused on the present
danger would support liberal internationalist goals if it could be shown that the
Soviet Union could be brought to pursue similar goals by non-military means.
Advocates of *realpolitik* may speak of a world community coming into existence in some future time. "Win" advocates may change their central thesis
when a clear commitment to this country is evident among governmental and
societal leaders.

All four contexts are alike in advocating primary reliance on American
military power to achieve what security is possible in today's world. Although
they disagree about how much military spending is necessary, and for what
purposes, they are forthright in their advocacy of some level of American
military might as an aid to the advancement of whatever other goals they
advocate. In contrast, the contexts about to be discussed either actually oppose
American military power or avoid military issues altogether.

5. ENVIRONMENTALISM: A policy direction that sees damage to the environment as the primary problem, and advocates dramatic change, such as setting
limits to economic and population growth, and the adoption of new
technologies, lifestyles, and global institutions.

Although different from the above contexts in the degree of coherence,
newness, and in the absence of a tradition or partial application to world
conflict, nonetheless, environmentalism does offer an important approach to

world politics. More new organizations, magazines, and activities have been launched in this context than any other in the 1970s, but frequently the application of environmentalist ideas to world politics is implied, rather than explicit.

By the 1970s the accumulated environmental results of the post-World War II industrial boom were plainly evident. A more or less coherent new context developed. Its central judgment is that strains on the environment endanger life on earth and require us to recast our conceptions of world politics and re-think our attitudes concerning the right relationship between humankind and the environment.[1] [2]

In this context, deterioration of the environment is a global problem; all countries [3] are involved, even though the industrialized societies have caused the major damage; [2] scarce resources must be allocated by institutions based on "mutual coercion, mutually agreed on"; [6] consumption must be limited. [5]

There is disagreement over whether scarce resources should be allocated by governmental fiat or by market principles, price being one form of coercion.

Attitudes toward economic growth must be changed. There should be a "steady state" (no growth) economy and appropriate technology must be developed to make it achievable and sustainable with limited environmental damage. Population growth must be curtailed. [4]

Beyond their inherent dangers to people, armaments are harmful to the environment. They are the products of growth economies and are used in fighting over industrially created wealth.

Little sustained thought has been given to the way in which a transition can be made from a world of industrialized, armed States to an environmentally safe new world order with disarmed States and globally-conscious citizens. [7] A change in personal life-style to reduce consumption is frequently considered one step. The overwhelming obstacles to such a transition on earth have led some to speculate and plan for creating space colonies. Others prefer the earth as their "spaceship." [8]

This context is viewed by its advocates as the precursor of the world politics of the 21st century, by which time the crisis will be acute. Others believe it is an exaggerated response to a real problem, more likely to break people away from other contexts than offer a significant alternative.

6. CHANGE AMERICA: A policy direction that seeks to achieve peace by structural change in the United States, and until such change occurs, argues for a reduced role by the United States in world politics.

---

[2]See Chapter 13.

Although the belief that American economic and social institutions are the root of the problem is the unifying theme in this context, its adherents come to this conclusion for different reasons. Some are persuaded by a version of the Marxist critique of capitalism. Others notice the wide gap between American ideals and social realities and, holding governmental leadership responsible for the latter, become deeply alienated from the former. Still others see themselves as the carriers of American ideals and take responsibility now only for the evils their country does. Yet others reject all large-scale authority, either on principle (anarchists) or intuitively, and thus count any reduction of American influence as a step in the right direction.

The underlying assumption of this context is that American economic and social institutions are the root of the problem. [3] Some domestic problem (racism, poverty, crime, treatment of native Americans, sexism) or past abuse of power (Vietnam) or economic institutions (corporations) is frequently given as the reason for disengagement of the U.S. from world politics. For example, those holding this context argue variously that the U.S. should not respond to the Soviet invasion of Afghanistan because (1) the invasion was a consequence of our refusal to ratify SALT promptly, (2) it is less alarming than our own involvement in Vietnam, or (3) the Soviet action provides a new excuse for defense spending — planned long before by our military-industrial complex. [2]

Specific foreign policy choices are interpreted as reflecting the malign intent of a foreign policy elite, itself a product of American economic and social structures. Their motives are further demonstrated when our allies violate human rights and we do little to prevent it; indeed, we supply the means through which the violations take place. The United Nations is either seen as a creature of U.S. diplomacy or, at most, as a forum in which the U.S. can be attacked. The United Nations is in any case irrelevant to changing the internal structures of American economic and political life. The reorganization of America is the best hope for peace. [3]

Foreign aid is designed merely to prop up corrupt oligarchies who would otherwise be overthrown by popular movements — movements able to establish viable, self-sufficient economies. The U.S. is responsible for poverty in the poor countries, and their economic development is seen as a matter of justice. [6] Our energy consumption and pollution are an indication of the disordered priorities of our society. [5] Economic progress and redistribution of wealth that does take place in non-communist countries either goes unnoticed or is flatly denied. Sometimes China and Cuba, sometimes Tanzania, are pointed to as model economies; in the democratic socialist version, Sweden is a model. Among holders of this context, such support does not necessarily imply approval of the form of government of those States: as often as not it illustrates "the enemy of my enemy is my friend" type of thinking.

As for armaments and military expenditures, we already have an overkill capacity and our military budget is fixed by the military-industrial complex for its own benefit. [7] The use of military force by the Soviets or their allies or their increased military expenditures are either denied, ignored, or held to be a response to our own military posture. Discussion of the Soviet Union as an adversary, and of expansionist States is rejected because it will revive the "cold war." And besides, the U.S. is just as bad, if not worse.

In this context, morality is often expressed as political identification with the poor in non-Western, non-socialist countries. [6] This identification expresses a sense of guilt because of past Western relations with the formerly colonized world and a desire to compensate for and change exploitative relationships. One strand of thought in this context denies that the Soviet Union is based on Marxist principles and is not reluctant to criticize it. They find in Marx's writings an openness to political democracy; others maintain that Marx's central concepts need to be revised in the light of technological and other changes. Both conclude that a commitment to representative democracy is compatible with a Marxist analysis of American foreign policy. That analysis emphasizes the economic interests of a corporate elite as the animating force behind America's engagement in world politics. [1] & [3] (But despite this unifying theme, American democratic Marxists may be found in all the other contexts.)

In addition, one encounters here a curious admixture of Marxism and anarchism. Marxism renders coherent the analysis of America as the enemy, but the anarchist prescription is frequently offered to change to decentralized institutions, face to face relationships, and small scale production.

In sum, the central thrust of these somewhat different approaches is agreement on challenging American use or abuse of its power. Domestic institutions and political forces are considered responsible for war.

7. **MARXIST-LENINIST:** A policy direction that seeks to transform American economic, political, and social institutions on the basis that war and exploitation are necessary to existing economic institutions. Change can come through domestic and world revolution.

It is difficult to present a short summary of the Marxist – Leninist perspective, there being many varieties of Marxist thought. Traditionally, Marxists believed in a tightly woven theory describing all of history as a product of class conflict, with the proletariat inevitably triumphing through an historical process labeled "dialectical materialism." A careful reading of the early texts also permits the interpretation that both modern classes (bourgeoisie and proletariat) could destroy each other. The concepts of Marxism have broadened to encompass new ideas, and the term "Marxist" has become quite flexible. Some proclaim themselves Marxists because they believe that economic interests are a motivating force in politics (surely a truism); some Marxists consider themselves democrats, while others proclaim the necessity of dictatorship; some argue for mixed economies; some believe that Communism is the fulfillment of Western history, while others are intent upon destroying all vestiges of Western civilization.

Within this mélange of ideas there are two opposed contexts in American politics, both claiming to be the legitimate expression of Marxism. One of these, democratic socialism, is part of the "Change America" context. The second is Marxist-Leninism which argues that all of history is a history of class conflict. Societies necessarily have governments which reflect the interests of the dominant class. Control of the means of production is the central issue in the conflict. Intellectual and social life reflects the stage of development of the productive forces at any given time in history.

Representative government is the political system of the bourgeoisie, and is, in fact, a form of class dictatorship. Religious thought merely reflects material circumstances and class structures and has no independent validity. [6] In the modern era the conflict is between the bourgeoisie and the proletariat; the only possible outcomes are the destruction of the bourgeoisie and the triumph of the proletariat, or the destruction of both social classes. [3]

Some Marxist-Leninists in American politics believe their goals have been more or less achieved in the Soviet Union. New questions, however, must be faced: Can socialism be built in one country or must socialists seize power in all industrialized countries? Is peaceful coexistence, even disarmament, possible with capitalist States? How can conflicts of interests be resolved in supposedly classless societies? Between Communist States?

Many American Marxist — Leninists accept the Soviet Union's claim of the right to intervene in other Socialist States to safeguard the interests of the Socialist bloc as a whole. [1] Opposition to Soviet leadership, whether it comes from China or from contending groups within the Soviet Union, is considered an expression of class antagonism. Environmental problems are seen as endemic to capitalist societies and as a problem that can be resolved only within socialist societies. [5]

Marxist-Leninist groups in American politics focus on the evils of American society and foreign policy. They seek to advance to power in other countries those groups sharing their views; when opposition to American military power is helpful to this end, they form or join such coalitions.

8. TRADITIONAL PACIFISM: A policy direction that seeks to convert people to nonviolence, and holds that war is categorically the worst evil.

The traditional pacifist position is oriented toward individual religious or ethical beliefs rather than toward political institutions. *First* comes the rejection of reliance on violence. [7]

Pacifists emphasize the possibility of agreement across ideological barriers and the importance of economic development [4] and growth toward a sense of world community. [1] Their focus is on what the individual can and should do, and their faith is most easily conveyed in personal terms — meetings between diplomats, student exchanges, work camp experiences, personal opposition to military conscription. [3] Sometimes they advocate support for international institutions and a nonviolent international peace force to aid in eliminating war. [2]

There are many currents of thought in this context. While some argue that the focus should be on the individual and not on institutions, others enter the political arena seeking nonviolent forms of social action and organization. [6] Despite a general agreement that Marxist-Leninist teachings violate pacifist ethical concerns, some view these as responses to the materialism and bellicose foreign policies of the Western world. Some pacifists are apolitical and choose simply to bear witness to their rejection of violence, whereas others emphasize a commitment to forcing change and defending values through nonviolent means. Many now advocate a simplified lifestyle to meet environmental problems. [5] In response to U.S. militarism and American anti-Communism, some pacifists find the "change America" context appealing. Others have seen America as the exploiter of the third world and responsible for its poverty; they argue that "structural violence" is the existing reality and condone the violence of oppressed people as liberating. To many, this latter stance makes them "former pacifists." Still others move on to the context described in Chapter 19 as more adequate to ending war.

Pacifist thought perhaps had its greatest influence at the time of the civil rights movement and in the very early days of the movement against American involvement in Vietnam. A very different situation prevails now, with few pacifists working for the nonviolent resolution of international conflict; more emphasis is given today to the pursuit of a vision of egalitarian justice.

THE IMPORTANCE OF CONTEXTS

Today, major policy decisions, and challenges to them, are made within these contexts. Since opinion leaders' beliefs about foreign affairs are badly fragmented, it is important to consider ways to regain a sense of cohesion and direction. Out of the weaknesses of these contexts, and a study of the questions which any context must resolve, can come a new sense of direction for American politics, one that is adequate to the problem of war.

The consensus underlying U.S. foreign policy in the 1950s was shattered by the Vietnam war.[3] As a result, the beliefs of Americans concerning the U.S. role in world politics in the late 1970s and early 1980s were derived from very different interpretations of the Vietnam experience. More recently, while the post-Vietnam fragmentation has decreased, and agreement has seemed to gather around new projections of American interests largely through military power, the consensus sustaining this approach is a thin consensus, one that is likely to collapse when confronted with obstacles. It is based, in part, on a recognition of the United States as weak in the post-Vietnam era, and a rejection of the consequence: the projection of Soviet power and influence. But the costs of the new policy are yet to be weighed. What results can be expected? What values are neglected if there is a renewed American military engagement in world affairs? To rebuild a consensus that can sustain a continuing American engagement in pursuit of constructive goals in world politics requires a careful consideration of alternative assumptions and goals: What response to the Soviet military build-up and use of force is warranted? What American policy offers the best hope for gaining constructive change in Soviet policy?

Contextual choices are what citizens do best. Few are expert on particular world affairs issues but clarifying the goals, identifying the values, and suggesting what are the appropriate means to use are required of citizens in a democracy.

SUMMARY OF THE EIGHT CONTEXTS

The first four contexts — win, present danger, *realpolitik* and liberal internationalism — place primary reliance on national military power for security, and thus depend upon the institution of war. Only in the liberal internationalist approach is there any attempt to move beyond a State-centered approach. But it is difficult to combine a commitment to deterrence and make credible an intention to move toward disarmament, law, community, and development. The next four contexts — environmentalist, change America, Marxist-Leninist, and traditional pacifism — challenge American military

---

[3]Ole Holsti and James Rosenau, *Vietnam, Consensus, and The Belief Systems of American Leaders* (Los Angeles: Institute for Transnational Studies, U. of Southern California 1977)

power, but rarely go beyond that. And that challenge is sometimes made in the interest of another power-center. Many of the contexts retreat from constructive world political engagement, in effect making no attempt to move world politics toward questions of how to pursue the conditions essential to a world without war. While there is much to learn from each of these contexts, none is regarded as adequate to the problem of war. A more comprehensive approach is required, one which learns from each of the above, yet offers a new approach to international conflict that is capable of building community between adversaries.

CHAPTER 19

A CONTEXT FOR WORK
TO END WAR

IF none of the previously described contexts is adequate to guide work on the problem of war[1] a new context is needed. Such a context must address the realities of power as presented in the State-centered approach, must take as goals the conditions essential to a world without war, and must show how the various actors in world politics can agree to pursue those goals as they resolve specific issues and crises. Such a context must be based on an understanding of the causes of war, but it need not eliminate them all. It must, instead, show how the legitimate functions of war can be replaced by non-military processes for maintaining security, resolving conflict and achieving change. It must, in short, address the reasons why those working in most other contexts consider war a "necessary evil." The "to end war" context is offered as such a context. It maintains that the basic changes needed in the international system can be made. Many of the changes have already been anticipated by the other contexts.

The win position has forcefully stated a portion of the truth when it focuses on the reality of conflict, the facts of the Soviet Union's power, and the hostility of Marxist-Leninist ideology to democracy. But the to end war context points out that, even without the Soviet Union or the United States, this would still be a world characterized by war.

[1]See Chapter 18

478

The to end war view agrees with the traditional pacifist context in rejecting reliance on mass violence for security and accepts the moral responsibility of individuals to work to end war. It shares with many pacifists the commitment to develop alternative, non-military ways to defend values and prosecute conflicts.

The to end war context concurs with the "Change America" and Marxist-Leninist viewpoints that America is part of the problem of war rather than part of the solution, but it emphasizes that this perception applies to the Soviet Union and other power-centers as well. It believes that America can lead toward ending war.

The to end war context agrees that strains on the environment need international monitoring and response, require cooperation across national lines, and offer an opportunity for "regime building." But it argues that a world order must be built out of a process for resolving conflicts between contending solutions to problems such as environmental strain, not out of an analysis of a problem.

The to end war context accepts the goals of the liberal internationalist context — law, community, development, and disarmament — as the essential goals and the perception of the reality of power central to the "present danger" and "Realpolitik" contexts. It demonstrates, however, that the liberal internationalist goals can be sought *now* through a peace initiatives strategy capable of bringing the self-interest of all into political reality while contending without violence the conflicts that persist.

Although the to end war context draws on ideas from each of the others, it stands or falls on its own merits. Those seeking to develop the to end war context must address the same eight choice points as the other contexts.[2]

I. THE EIGHT CHOICE POINTS

1. Systems

The to end war context begins with a recognition that the State system is today's pre-eminent reality. Any State acting outside of its own self-interest, or withdrawing its power and influence from a region, can expect that other powers will take advantage of the vacuum created to advance their interests and power. Yet there are a variety of situations in which the self-interest of each State and the self-interest of all are the same, e.g. mutual arms reduction and avoiding nuclear war.

[2]See Chapter 18, pp. 462-477.

So also, specific problems, like eradicating communicable diseases, limiting environmental damage, and creating a political process through which to conduct conflict, have many features attractive to those who claim self-interest is the only legitimate motivating force in world politics. Work for a world without war, which takes intelligent account of the threats to our security and to democratic values and institutions posed by other power-centers, is in the best interest of our country and expresses the best in our traditions.

Although the State system retains great resiliency, the 20th century has also witnessed an unprecedented change in world politics: the invention of international organizations with significant resources and powers. However one judges the present moment, movement toward economic and political integration has taken place in Western Europe in direct response to the problem of war and the fact of interdependence. In an interdependent world, overshadowed by the ominous presence of war, and confronted by many common enemies, it makes sense to explore institution building at the global level. As we confront specific issues and crises it is possible to adopt a new approach to international conflict which seeks to create a sense of community out of conflict and which seeks to create international institutions and processes for resolving such conflicts by law.

2. Goals

In the past, many of the conditions essential to a world without war were sought in isolation from each other. World law has been the goal of one movement. Disarmament of another. Others have advocated human rights, economic development, or creating a sense of world community. When combined, a commitment to these goals has rarely been tied to gaining the agreement on their pursuit with other powers. The to end war approach maintains that these are interrelated goals; progress toward one will increase the possibility of progress toward others.

What Are the Essential Goals?

A. A world without war is a world in which agreement on universal, complete and enforceable disarmament has been achieved and put into effect.

The U.S. and the USSR agreed to seek this goal in the McCloy-Zorin Accords (1961), and the goal was reaffirmed by over 100 States by signing the Nuclear Non-Proliferation Treaty (1971) and more recently at the (first) Special Session of the U.N. General Assembly on Disarmament (1978). National leaders and the public, however, have turned to the more limited goal of arms control or else have abandoned altogether the idea of limits on armaments. There is a renewed interest in nuclear disarmament, but it has yet to develop a comprehensive strategy capable of pursuing that end. The proposal by a senior Reagan Administration official for START talks (Strategic Arms Reduction Talks), not SALT (Strategic Arms Limitation Talks) could renew interest in moving out of what most now concede is a very dangerous situation.

In 1981 world military budgets totalled in excess of $500 billion. The Soviet Union's military budget has risen rapidly in the 1970s and is, by some calculations, larger now than that of the United States. Many third-world countries spend a higher proportion of their GNP on armaments than either superpower. Efforts to gain disarmament through negotiations have had little success, although a number of treaties are in force limiting areas in which weapons can be deployed, and restricting types of weapons. The U.N. General Assembly's Special Session (1978) initially produced a draft statement in which every clause was disagreed to by someone. Nonetheless, the final document gave a sense of direction toward disarmament, created several new institutions to aid in the process, and offered a series of concrete proposals to begin the process. But no progress has since been made.

Arms control and disarmament measures are both needed. Arms control measures can break the momentum of the arms race and open negotiations on arms reductions. Arms control measures could change the perceptions of adversaries and help create the setting in which negotiations on arms reductions could succeed. In the long run, only disarmament remains capable of being both achieved and sustained. Technological change, different evaluations of military force equivalences, and the political benefits of threat manipulation, limit the likelihood that arms control agreements, if achieved, will last. For example, technological innovations in a field not covered by arms control agreements can quickly offset the progress gained through arms control in one area.[3]

Disarmament alone, however, is not a sufficient objective. Disarmament cannot be maintained without alternative governmental institutions capable of resolving disputes, processing change, and pursuing justice in world affairs. Disarmament cannot be maintained without *law*.

B. A world without war is a world in which conflicts are resolved and change achieved through legal rather than military processes.

---

[3]See Chapters 2 and 4.

World law was once the rallying cry of those seeking an alternative to war. It is still an essential objective. The original emphasis on the United States Constitution as a model has wisely been broadened to include many possible alternative models.

The first steps in this century toward world organization were made by the Hague Conferences and the League of Nations. The United Nations is the current embodiment of this objective. It is, in some ways, a different organization than it was in 1945 when it was chartered, due to the entrance of many new States. Proclaiming the "sovereign equality of States," the majority of the General Assembly is no longer responsible to the political influence or persuasion of the United States. If that change means that the body has become more pluralistic and thus better equipped to keep the peace and promote constructive change, it should be welcomed. But it has meant, instead, that the General Assembly is, at times, as inclined to encourage wars as to prevent them. The U.N. in the 1970s did more to isolate Israel than to promote alternatives to war in the Middle East; it aided violent liberation movements in Southern Africa. The General Assembly has passed resolutions on behalf of terrorist groups seeking independence for Puerto Rico, despite the availability of a democratic political process for deciding Puerto Rico's political future.

The principle of the sovereign equality of States has a place in some global institutions. But it cannot be the only principle. If it is, the more powerful States will either yield little authority or not participate at all. An alternative to the one-State, one-vote formula is a weighted voting system (taking into account financial contribution, population size, and GNP, for example) which allows influence within international institutions to be more nearly proportional to responsibility for implementation than is now the case.

While the institutions of world law that are needed and capable of gaining consent are less obvious than they seemed twenty-five years ago, the objective of law remains essential. Today world law includes a variety of governmental organizations and other institutions — functional agencies, regimes, international conferences, international institutions, and supranational institutions. Yet for all the change in focus, the new complexities, and the many sources of law, the essential objective remains clear: in the final analysis, law is the only alternative to war as the way to resolve conflicts between States.

C. Law cannot be made and enforced without a sense of world community (see Chapter 6).

If a disarmed world under law is to be based on consent instead of imposed by violence, a developed sense of unity and mutual responsibility among people is needed. One indication of the strength of this sense of community is the drafting and ratifying of a wide range of international human rights declarations, covenants, and conventions. In the human rights area, the relationship between the individual and the State is a critical one defined by each political community. The wide range of agreements reached would be truly impressive, if the sense of community were strong enough to go beyond definition to enforcement. As it is, agreement about what human rights the international community is willing to enforce is a task for the 1980s.

The emergence of a world communication system, travel patterns, as well as symbolic events like World Cup Soccer and the Olympic games, can also help strengthen a sense of world community. World community is also aided by the increasing realization that we live on one planet whose common care may, in several important ways, eclipse the importance of national boundaries.

D. A world without war is a world in which world economic and political development take place without the use of organized mass violence.

Most people reject attitudes toward community and institutions of law which thwart changes to better economic and social conditions for themselves. While some Asian, African, and Latin American States have achieved impressive economic growth, most people in the third world continue to live in conditions of deprivation. They want economic, political, and social change. The question is how best to facilitate change so that economic objectives are stated publicly and governments held accountable for helping in their achievement.

One way to hold governments accountable for their stated goals is through the institution of democracy — a free press and the free circulation of ideas, the right to assemble, and to contest for political power. Many in power, who seek a shortcut to an industrialized society, have rejected democratic values as irrelevant or a hindrance to the development process. There is, however, no other way than through democratic processes to get an honest government or to challenge effectively governmental abuse of its power or misuse of societal resources. Only a press capable of resisting a government can discover, publicize, and perhaps limit human rights violations, such as torture, or worse, in prisons. Only an adversary political party or parties are likely to point up the limitations of the government's policies.

These four objectives are the conditions essential to a world without war: 1) general, complete, and enforceable disarmament, 2) world law, 3) a sense of world community, 4) world economic and political development. These conditions constitute the essential goals which those working within the to end war context believe this country should seek in world politics. But another goal is essential to substantial progress toward these goals.

E. Gaining the *agreement* of other powers is essential to a world without war.

Those seeking a world without war want their country to commit itself to the four goals above. They seek to define the specific next steps that the United States could take toward each goal. But, in addition, they recognize that little progress toward any of the goals can be made without change in and agreement with the Soviet Union (see Chapter 9). Regional powers and other States must also be brought into agreement.

Gaining the agreement of allies and of the non-aligned on the need to pursue these goals is both necessary and difficult. The requisites for leadership by this country in this effort include a public which authorizes its elected officials to pursue them, the coordination of policies with allies, and a willingness to share the burdens of their pursuit.

Does the Soviet Union want to pursue such goals? Success clearly requires change in the present policies of the Soviet Union. Without such change, the objectives outlined above will be abandoned when the hard facts of current Soviet capability and policy are encountered. The strategy outlined below recognizes this and proposes non-military ways to induce the needed changes.

Is change possible within the Soviet Union? That change will come is a certainty. The question is the nature and direction of that change. American passivity has its effects. American military programs have theirs. In the Soviet Union as elsewhere, contending groups seek influence in the struggle for power. What persistent, long-term American strategy is most likely to enhance the influence of those who accept the need for peaceful competition? How can outside powers and influences best encourage the kind of changes needed in Soviet policy that would make possible progress toward the goals essential to a world without war? What steps by the United States would best demonstrate our own commitment to such goals and induce the Soviet Union to reciprocate?

Rapid change is possible in world affairs. War is *not* expected between France and Germany now although for over 100 years before World War II ended that fear was rarely absent. Who in the 1950s expected that China would, in the 1980s, be the most vociferous advocate of containing "hegemonism," i.e. Soviet expansionism? In great measure, whether change comes to the USSR or not will depend on what we do, or do not do.

F. A world without war is a world in which social change is achieved without organized mass violence.

In democratic societies, change without violence is achieved through political processes. The philosophies and practices of Mahatma Gandhi and Martin Luther King, Jr. are guides to developing nonviolent strategies of forcing change. Civil disobedience, carried out in a manner which helps fulfill democratic values, can be a valuable adjunct to a democratic political process. We have learned a good deal about non-violent conflict and conflict resolution and can apply it to social change.

G. A world without war is a world in which religious and ethical teachings about the organized use of mass violence are clarified and applied to the conduct of world politics.

Progress toward the achievement of the other goals is unlikely unless people and States are impelled to work for them. While most people accept the values of nonviolence, law, and peaceful change as applied to the family and to the community, those values are rarely applied to world politics. Developing the ability to identify and apply such values in the more difficult arena of world politics constitutes a seventh objective.

Seven goals, then, guide those working within the to end war context: 1) General, complete and enforceable disarmament; 2) World law, 3) A sense of world community, 4) World economic and political development, 5) Agreement, 6) Nonviolent conflict resolution and change, 7) Applying fundamental values.[4]

---

[4]The peace researchers have made us very self-conscious about whether a policy promotes "negative" peace, that is, the absence of war, or "positive" peace, a world of societies with self-fulfilled individuals. We believe our approach is best categorized as neither of these. It has elements of both. Arms control and disarmament are essentially negative goals. They must be sought within the existing system of military threat. Steps through arms control toward disarmament offer opportunities to test the intentions of others to pursue the other goals. Only disarmament is considered an adequate condition of peace. This can be defined as disarmament down to police levels. The next two objectives — law and community — are the prime conditions for keeping peace, and thus are peacekeeping objectives. World economic and political development, and nonviolent change, in conjunction with the promotion of human rights, are the "positive" peace or peacemaking objectives. Progress toward them increases the stake in accepting law and building community. The seventh objective is the motivating reason for pursuing the others, in addition to the practical reasons given earlier.

3. Actors

The ideas underlying the to end war context are those Judaic-Christian values and democratic traditions that pervade political and social life in this country. These traditions, as well as the power of the United States, make this the country most likely to initiate effective action toward the conditions essential to a world without war. There are initiatives our country could take that are more likely to lead the world toward a stable peace than either our present predominantly military approach or the previously stated alternative contexts.

Government provides the processes by which a world without war may be achieved and sustained. Representative, democratic government is considered the best form of government, capable of resolving domestic conflict and promoting change, while advancing human dignity and individuality. This political system is a significant resource in work for a world without war. This is particularly true when the full range of non-governmental and educational organizational activity is considered. Individuals working for a world without war should defend democracy against unwarranted attacks, and work to close the gap between what the American political system is and what it ought to be. Responsibility for such work rests with individual citizens, the attentive public, and organizational as well as political leaders.

The Soviet Union is neither a State controlled by a conspiratorial sect nor just another great power which will reciprocate our own good behavior, if forthcoming. The Soviet Union is, instead, an admixture of a State dominated by a party with a revolutionary, universal ideology, and a superpower pursuing its national interest. It has a totalitarian form of political organization in which there is no legal standing for societal organizations that might challenge, and thereby limit, the power of government. It is, nonetheless, a society influenced by internal changes and external attitudes and events. Intellectual currents, once thought impossible in the Soviet Union, now move in *Samizdat* (underground) literature. The Polish workers have severely tested the myth of the invulnerability of Communist States to internally induced change. The Soviet Union's interpretation of both Marxist and Russian traditions is susceptible to re-interpretation. In addition, the Soviet Union is influenced by demographic, technological, and other influences.[5]

The to end war context recognizes that America, in its participation in world affairs, must meet the threats to its security and to its

---

[5]See Chapter 9

democratic values as posed by power organized in other national and ideological camps. This context must, therefore, seek changes in world political understandings and policies in those power-centers as well as in the United States.

The power and influence of Japan, West Germany, Canada, China, Mexico, Brazil, Saudi Arabia, and Nigeria, to name only a few, are also significant new resources or challenges to those working for a world without war. Initiative action by such powers toward the conditions essential to a world without war is needed; the U.S., however, is not in a good position to ask for that unless it is leading also. There are many regional, as well as global, issues where the action of these powers is crucial to resolution.[6]

Regional and global international organizations, like the Organization of American States (OAS) and the United Nations, are potentially effective agents to constrain States and to limit their war-making capability. This can be done both by decreasing the need for that capability and by increasing the ability of international organizations to resolve conflict. These forces need to be surveyed soberly. There is no assurance that transferring power and authority from national to international decision-makers will result in the wiser use of that power. They, like domestic institutions, are arenas in which good policies must be sought but by no means are they guaranteed.

No set formula is offered by which to reform and strengthen international institutions. As reform attempts are initiated, the variety of proposals already offered plus new ones will need to be critically evaluated.[7]

International non-governmental organizations (INGOs), such as Amnesty International, and non-governmental organizations (NGOs), such as the World Affairs Councils, and certainly individuals, have a critical role to play. They do not face the constraints of governmental responsibility. They need to act and advocate change with the constraints in mind, but they also should explore ideas, channels of communications, and changes which those in power find difficult to pursue. These organizations, and the individuals who work through them or on their own, can help form the basis of a world society.[8]

4. Economic Development:

How does participation in world politics influence the production

[6]See Chapter 10
[7]See Chapter 5
[8]See Chapter 11

and distribution of wealth, goods, and services within and between States? How should it?

There must be meaningful progress on eliminating mass poverty. A world divided between the few who are rich and millions living in desperate poverty will not long remain disarmed. Starvation of part of the human family disgraces the rest. Hunger and development questions provide opportunities to demonstrate the way joint problem-solving can work to overcome obstacles. Eliminating hunger is a "superordinate" goal — one no group can reach alone. Accepting the goal, many groups (INGOs, NGOs, governments, international organizations, and government leaders), should seek the resources required for success. Many countries have different insights and resources that might be helpful. Agricultural research from the United States and China, fertilizers from OPEC countries, information on land reform from Taiwan and Cuba, the assessment tools available through satellite technology, and the adaptation of standard indexes (such as the Physical Quality of Life Index) to measure success, might be combined along with other ingredients, into a successful world poverty elimination effort.[9]

While the North, and much of the South, have good reason to reject the New International Economic Order (NIEO) package as a whole, those proposals include some that are mutually beneficial. Those that are mutually beneficial should be adopted while negotiations on others continue. Proposals unacceptable to the North should be responded to with specific counterproposals, so that substantive negotiations can take place. A sense of meaningful participation in the reshaping of the world economic order is a needed step toward building a sense of world community.

5. Resource Limits

Scientists differ about the extent to which industrialization, the use of fossil fuels, and population growth lead to ecological disaster. The question is not whether there are ecological stresses which require changes: there are. The appropriate role of non-State actors to hold conferences and to press for environmental protection measures is also not in question. International organizations have established their role in monitoring environmental stresses and collecting and making available information on how to limit environmental damage. The basic question is: do these ecological stresses require a global authority to decide access to the "global commons" of today; are imposed limits of

[9]See Chapter 13

resource utilization, pollution, or population the moral imperatives of today?[10]

For the range of problems lumped under the category of the environment, there is not a single answer. The evidence is, at best, inconclusive. There are, however, many opportunities for monitoring the environment, for regime building, and for experimentation with various mechanisms for allocating scarce resources. Here also, building effective regimes requires broad participation in negotiating forums and in the implementation of the results.

6. Justice

The to end war context incorporates a range of positions in the argument between socialists and capitalists, between advocates of various economic theories. People sharing this context have very different views of which economic system is just, and disagree about whether equality of opportunity or some degree of equality in income distribution is the appropriate goal. The area of agreement is to seek the eradication of poverty, which, in itself, would partially close the gap between the rich and the poor States. Beyond that, States committed to both radical and conventional economic theories have built the basis of an industrial order in this century; both approaches have also failed to eliminate poverty.

Those working within this context reject the use of violence to promote justice. They maintain that the organized use of mass violence imposes on those who use it, as well as those who suffer from its use, a discipline that alters them and the ends they pursue. They accept the requirement to develop non-military means to promote change. The to end war context thus offers a "minimalist" approach to justice in that it rejects the argument that peace is the fruition of justice or is a world of harmony. It accepts, instead, the inevitability of conflict between contending conceptions of justice and seeks to develop institutions and understandings capable of conducting that conflict without violence. It accepts that there must be a portion of truth in every honest statement of intention, and that justice must encompass different perceptions.

There is now general agreement within this context on the need to promote universal civil and political rights. There is disagreement on what emphasis to give this commitment when it conflicts with security, tension reduction, or culturally conditioned values. Civil and political rights are not considered an obstacle to economic growth. An elite group accountable to an electorate can make significant mistakes, as

[10]See Chapter 13

can one that is not accountable. The advantage which democratic
societies have is that when mistakes are made, there can be new
approaches by new leaders.

7. Means

In today's world politics, a democracy ought to develop, and to
allocate the necessary resources for testing, all available non-military
means for resolving conflict. War is an inappropriate instrument on
which to base a democracy's participation in world politics. The moral
reasoning supporting this conclusion has been presented previously.[11]
Among the practical reasons are:

A) War, in its most ominous embodiment, nuclear war, threatens
human survival. We do not fully know the damage nuclear war
would bring, but the consequences would be catastrophic to any
vision of human progress or common humanity. Assuming there
were survivors, very different moral values, political conceptions,
and aesthetic values would emerge from such a conflict.

B) Conventional war is not, in its basic moral conception or in its
consequences, different, in kind, from nuclear war. Both threaten
population centers, the morale of the enemy, the public, and the
economic and social life of the opponent. Some conventional
weapons rival nuclear weapons in their destructive capacity. Both
nuclear and conventional war, including guerrilla war, tend to be
total.

C) There have been over 115 conventional wars since the advent
of the nuclear era. While none have escalated into nuclear war,
every conventional war poses the threat of superpower involvement
and escalation. In the absence of arms control between the superpowers, as time passes, the proliferation of nuclear weapons, the
possible access to nuclear technology by terrorists — all of these
increase the dangers of escalation.

Those who agree with these judgments may disagree about how
effective war is in today's world politics and they may disagree about
whether war is needed to promote or defend democratic values today;
they do agree to work within the existing system of military threat to
build a strategy capable of moving from that system to a non-military
security system based on a sense of world community. Those working
on creating a sense of world community know the costs of war, its

[11]See Chapter 15

tendency to turn an enemy from a human being into a thing; they know that the dehumanizing effect of war violates religious and democratic values that sanctify the individual and teach us to love our enemy and to support his or her rights. So they unite in developing a non-military strategy for achieving security and forcing change.

An essential task for those seeking to develop a strategy of peace is to assess accurately the role that war plays in world politics. Much has been written about the futility of war. War is futile for achieving some purposes, but not others. You cannot impose democracy on other people. You cannot fight a nuclear war and call the result national security. You cannot liberate a country by creating a climate of terror. But war does shape political outcomes, in the Middle East, in Indochina, and in world politics generally. Most of the world's national boundaries reflect the outcome of wars. War, and the preparation for war, does influence behavior — many refuse to discuss human rights violations in the Soviet Union because it will antagonize the leaders of the USSR, increase tension, and perhaps increase the likelihood of war. Preparation for war, i.e. military threat, does provide bargaining leverage in many world political arenas, although no precise relationship exists between the threat to use force and political influence.

Much has also been written about the horrors and costs of war. Few who have experienced it believe the written word captures the reality; the silence of those who died in war is also eloquent. The resources consumed by war and preparation for war exceed $500 billion per year. But each of these arguments misses an essential point: if a vital issue is in dispute, Americans (and most, if not all, others) would prefer to face the danger war poses, accept its horrors, and pay its costs. If our own or our allies' security, or some other significant interest is in jeopardy, then all the arguments about the futility of war, its costs and horrors, are likely to fail unless a non-military strategy for avoiding that jeopardy is available. Indeed, assessments of the horrors and costs of war are frequently used to reduce the political will to resist an armed adversary. Part of the political influence the possession of military forces provides comes from manipulating the horrors of their use. Oddly enough, the horrors of war are usually ascribed only to the enemy's army.

Work to end war is in part motivated by the horrors, costs, and futility of war. But it rests on the credibility of a non-military means through which States can resolve their conflicts, defend their values, and achieve security as they act on their presently divergent purposes. It requires nonviolent ways to achieve change. At the end of World

War I and again in the shadow of Hiroshima, the will to end war was manifest. It is no longer. Contemporary politics abounds with justifications for war, whether presented in the guise of achieving national security, promoting change, or overthrowing tyrannical governments. This ninth context is centered on the reaffirmation of the goal of ending war.

8. Change

Change will come about when citizens in this country, through the network of nongovernmental organizations, insist that their country lead in the creatign of the conditions essential to a world without war.[12]

When the agreements needed to end war seem beyond reach, action not dependent on prior agreement can change the situation and make agreement possible. Governmental leaders come to power, however, claiming to provide peace through the manipulation of military threat. Only a consensus formed outside of government can turn this country toward the development of a strategy for gaining the agreement of other States. The development of such a peace initiative strategy is essential for progress toward a world without war.

II. APPLYING THE TO END WAR CONTEXT TO ISSUES

How can the perspective outlined above provide guidance when a specific world affairs issue is encountered? How can the to end war goals be sought in the midst of an immediate crisis?

The goals of the to end war context may appear far off and vague and thus incapable of guiding governmental decision-makers or citizens. This context, however, can be made concrete when specific choices are made in the light of how they advance us toward each goal. Today civil wars and regional wars (often fought with external help or influence) are the principal examples of mass, organized violence in the world. At this writing, wars are being fought in Afghanistan, Kampuchea, Ethiopia, Namibia, Chad, between Iran and Iraq, in El Salvador, and elsewhere. The Middle East remains a tinderbox, even as its political and economic importance increases. Disintegrating States in Southwest Asia or the Middle East may soon erupt into military struggles with global implications and dangers. What strategies can be useful in such conflicts?

In a conflict situation, arms control and disarmament involve stopping the

[12]See the Introduction and Section C, "Action."

flow of armaments into a battle arena and achieving a cease-fire. To accomplish these goals, law must authorize some form of police force to guarantee that the flow of arms has stopped and to police the cease-fire. Political processes are likewise needed to help in resolving the issues in dispute. Support for intermediaries or mediators requires a sense of community. A sense of community must be built between the antagonists to the extent that agreement is possible on a political process to conduct and resolve the conflict. Such mediation must protect the human rights of those participating in the political process, or else the process will degenerate into renewed violence. Relief assistance to the victims of the conflict is needed, and may well be the opportunity to define a superordinate goal — a goal that requires the cooperation of the conflicting parties. In addition, economic development projects could be similarly designed. If successful, the self-interest of the contending factions would be to sustain the peace process to obtain the benefits of the projects. Thus, the long term objectives can apply to specific civil and regional conflicts, although they must be creatively interpreted in any given situation.

A New Form of Conflict

Whether the focus is on settling civil, regional, or international conflicts, or on resolving specific issues, the essential objective is gaining enforceable agreements between adversaries. Faced with the problem of agreement, many thoughtful people lose interest in pursuing the essential goals presented above. They know that more than thirty years of negotiations on specific steps toward such objectives have provided only marginal success, while the pace of events has moved the goals even further away. The fifth goal, agreement, encompasses the others and is a prerequisite to significant progress toward them.

Is there a strategy that begins with today's reality, that can, in the absence of negotiated agreements, bring to bear new incentives and pressures that make agreements more likely?

There is such a strategy. It is a strategy of American peace initiative acts.

III. TOWARD AN INITIATIVES STRATEGY

The word "initiatives" has been badly abused in recent political discourse; it has become almost synonymous with any action taken outside of negotiations. It is meant here in a specific and limited sense: a "peace initiative" is a non-military step, taken outside of negotiations, which is designed to induce reciprocation from other States, and is designed to advance the objectives outlined above.

A policy of U.S. initiatives is based on the belief that a predominantly military foreign policy will not lead to a world without war or develop successful opposition to the spread of totalitarian or authoritarian political systems.[13] A favorable judgment on the feasibility of an initiatives policy does not require an optimistic assessment of the intentions of the Soviet Union, China, or others. One can, for example, be profoundly pessimistic about present policy in the Soviet Union and yet conclude that initiative proposals involve less risk and greater promise for improvement than does military confrontation. The heart of the initiative approach lies in the question it seeks to answer. Instead of asking "how can our military power best influence their political and military policy?" a peace initiative strategy asks, "what non-military acts can we take that give promise of producing the change in their attitude and policies that must come if we are to reach agreement on disarmament and world law?"

The initiatives approach rejects yielding to an opponent's will, but does grant some validity to an opponent's claim. It does not seek the opponent's destruction. It seeks instead to change the opponent and to open a non-military, conflict resolution or decision-making process. A policy of peace initiatives is distinguished by its goals — disarmament, law, community, development, nonviolent change — from the more familiar military initiatives that constitute an arms race. But its dynamic is similar. A policy of peace initiatives does not wait for agreement. It pursues its purposes by independent actions. It recognizes that any final settlement must be based on widespread consent, but that there are situations in which only independent, non-military action, taken without prior agreement, can create a situation in which agreement becomes possible. A peace initiative policy seeks to influence an adversary State move toward agreement on disarmament and world law.

Four Types of Initiatives

There are at least four types of peace initiatives: intention-clarifying, reciprocal, punitive, and coercive initiatives. Some initiatives may simply

---

[13]Totalitarian and authoritarian regimes differ in what they consider a political activity but are alike in controlling all things they consider political. Totalitarian regimes consider everything from theological training to water safety courses a political act; authoritarian regimes consider only activity directly relevant to policy concerns or struggles for power as political acts.

indicate one's intent to pursue new goals. These are frequently symbolic in nature, such as the admittance of the U.S. Ping-Pong team into China. In addition, the assigning of some new task to a government bureau, such as preparing plans for conversion of U.S. military and industrial facilities to peace-time production, may help clarify the sincerity of one's intention.

Peace initiatives may also be examples, that you expect to be reciprocated. For example, if one side reduces its armaments by 5%, and indicates that if the other side does so as well, another 5% reduction will follow, that would be a force reduction initiative. In some cases, it may be desirable to state explicitly that if the initial initiative is reciprocated, a second reduction will follow. In this way, an action-response-new-action process can be established.

Initiatives can be punitive in nature, designed to punish an adversary who does not reciprocate intention-clarifying or reciprocal initiatives. Such punitive measures may be mild or severe, ranging from a loss of prestige to the loss of tangible resources. In addition, coercive initiatives could be tried in an effort to compel an adversary to reciprocate. Such coercive initiatives could include the boycott of a country's exports, or an embargo on its imports; they could include a refusal of the country's passports or currency in international transactions. In a full strategy of peace initiatives, a wide variety of intention-clarifying, reciprocal, punitive, and coercive peace initiatives would be considered, usually in that order. Punitive and coercive initiatives may be counter-productive, closing opportunities opened by intention-clarifying and reciprocal initiatives. Punitive and coercive acts may also be necessary from time to time and, if properly coordinated, limited in duration, and tied to specific objectives, just what is required.

A peace initiative strategy has many uses. It can break negotiating dead-locks, e.g. when John F. Kennedy unilaterally halted U.S. nuclear testing in the atmosphere to help gain a limited Test Ban Treaty (1963) with the Soviet Union. It can signal a change in policy, by jamming or stopping the jamming of a country's broadcasts. It can bring significant pressure to bear on an adversary leadership for a change of policy, such as the Carter Adminstration's freezing of Iranian assets and of military replacement parts.

The peace initiatives approach does not depend upon the existence of an effective peacekeeping/peacemaking system at the outset. It is designed to aid in the creation of such a system. It is important to select those initiatives that offer the best prospect for inducing others to reciprocate. The inducement may be that of good example: "since they have changed their policy, so can we." Anwar Sadat symbolically recognized Israel by his visit to Jerusalem. It may be that the new course offers mutual advantages, opening possibilities closed before. For example, an electoral process was created in Zimbabwe which permitted rival guerrilla factions to contest with the government and with other factions for power. The initiatives may also be punitive or coercive in that failure to reciprocate involves losses of some kind.

Conditions for a Successful Initiatives Policy

How can initiative acts create the conditions that change behavior?

a. *Initiatives can change the world political climate within which the leaders of opposing political systems act.*

When leaders of an adversary state like the Soviet Union do a cost/benefit analysis to help decide their course of action, they must consider world opinion. They must consider the attitudes of heads of other States, and those of leaders of movements external to their country with whom they are seeking influence. An initiative policy seeks to use these pressure points in inducing Soviet leaders to reciprocate; if the Soviets do not, they will be perceived as largely responsible for the costs of the continuing arms race in a variety of world political arenas (such as the U.N. with Communist parties in Western Europe, with the nonaligned, or with movements supported by the Soviet Union in other countries.

b. *Initiatives can change the balance of forces within the opposing system's leadership.*

Leaders within every country debate how public funds should be spent for military and social purposes. Rival factions within the governmental hierarchy, bureaucracy, and regions of a country make different judgments about how funds should be allocated. What acts by an external power would help the factions that seek funds for social or economic development rather than for military purposes? Would such acts add to the constituency already preferring agreement to confrontation?

c. *Initiatives can bring pressure for reciprocal action to bear on and within the opposing society.*

The way others view our society influences what we think of ourselves and how we behave in world politics. Actions by one State can communicate to members of another society what is thought of their leaders' actions. The U.S.-initiated Olympic boycott was felt deeply within Soviet society. Another source of pride for a society is the perception that its leaders are seeking peace — a perception skillfully manipulated by many heads of State. The effect of one country initiating action toward agreed goals for a world without war, if properly presented and communicated, could generate significant pressures for reciprocation. The irony of a workers' strike initiated by a workers' union in Poland, a supposedly workers' State, raises profound symbolic implications for all Communist States. Action by American workers, on behalf of the Free Trade Union movement within the Soviet Union, could bring similar pressures for reciprocation.

d. *Initiatives can open alternative, nonviolent courses of action through which opponents may pursue their goals.*

The pressures set in motion by the initiative actions described above are all negative. They seek to exert leverage through forces external to a society, within the State's leadership, or through the State's allies. This fourth approach is positive. It seeks to open an alternative to violence through which an adversary can pursue goals now sought by military means. This could entail the creation of a new political process or the establishment of a special international conference to hear grievances not previously heard in international forums. Peace initiatives policy would reject violence, even as it accepted the need for new channels for political conflict and conflict resolution.

e. *Peace initiatives offer the prospect of a world without war.*

War and the threat of war is a major obstacle to functional problem-solving, ending world hunger, and the creation of a sense of world community. A country which indicates by its behavior that it is willing to take risks for a different future may change many people's minds about the merits of its system of political and economic organization. An attractive goal, meaningfully pursued, can persuade others to participate.

Initiative acts may not be immediately reciprocated in a given situation but may still be useful and important steps. Properly undertaken, they can aid in establishing the understanding and precedents necessary to preclude new stages in the arms race or new threats of war. Since confusion over who is initiating a new stage and who is merely responding to the other side is the usual justification for each new stage, there is enormous value in acts that can help identify and isolate those political forces committed to imposing their will through violence when an alternative political process is available.

IV. BUILDING AN INITIATIVES STRATEGY.

There is nothing new in the idea of independent initiatives. For years States have indicated changes in policies simply by altering their visa and passport regulations. Inviting a head of State to one's country may in some cases be an intention-clarifying act. Former President Nixon's announcement regarding American cessation of research and stockpiling of bacteriological weapons was an example of an initiative which sought reciprocation. The Carter Administration's curtailment of trade arrangements with the Soviet

Union, in response to their invasion of Afghanistan, was an example of punitive initiatives.

What would be new would be a coherent strategy of peace initiatives underaken in pursuit of the interrelated goals essential to a world without war.[14]

The overall goal of a peace initiative strategy would be a world in which conflict is resolved through political and legal processes. The first steps toward that goal would, of necessity, be modest. They might only clarify our intention to move toward the stated goals. As these initiatives are taken and reciprocated, more dramatic initiatives become feasible. Initiatives can seek reciprocation by being part of sequence which continues if reciprocation takes place, by being for a fixed period of time, so that they end if reciprocation does not occur, and by reducing the forces threatening a society, or increasing the resources or institutions available to resolve a problem. A fully developed strategy of peace initiative acts can produce the maximum amount of positive inducements and negative pressures for reciprocation.

There was a period in the early 1960s when attention was focused on the initiative idea. Premier Khrushchev called for a policy of ''mutual example.'' The fiftieth anniversary project in 1961 of the Carnegie Endowment for International Peace sought suggestions for unilateral steps which the United States could take to improve the prospects for peace. The Stanley Foundation focused its annual ''Strategy of Peace'' conference on the idea in 1962. Other research agencies worked on lists of American initiative acts they considered desirable and feasible. Turn Toward Peace, from which the World Without War Council developed, publicly advocated a peace initiatives strategy. President Kennedy announced in 1963 a unilateral American cessation of nuclear testing in the atmosphere as a step to induce Soviet reciprocation and to clear the way for agreement on the limited nuclear test ban treaty.[15]

Yet no comprehensive peace initiatives strategy has ever been developed by the United States or any other country.

The United States should do so now.

A peace initiatives strategy for the U.S. entails a clear and comprehensive statement of the goals sought in world politics — the conditions essential to a world without war. It requires a planned series of specific initiative acts on

---

[14]Charles Osgood has worked out in great detail some of the steps involved in inducing reciprocation. His articles and books (especially *An Alternative to War or Surrender*) are pioneer works in developing what he called GRIT (Graduated Reductions in Tension-Initiatives). The approach outlined here differs in the goals sought and in including coercive, tension increasing acts but owes much to Osgood's work. Amatai Etzioni's *Hard Way to Peace* and Roger Fisher's *International Conflict for Beginners* are also basic texts.

[15]See Amitai Etzioni, ''The Kennedy Experiment,'' *Western Political Science Quarterly* (Spring 1965)

behalf of those goals. These acts cannot be isolated gestures, but a deliberate, graduated set of initiatives designed to move us toward each goal. Such a policy should include careful thought as to what must be done to create or exploit the conditions (outlined above) that would make reciprocation most likely.

Concerning arms control and disarmament, for example, there are many specific acts which could clarify our intention to pursue the goal of general and complete disarmament. The U.S. could independently adopt and utilize the standardized accounting system developed by United Nations teams to report and measure military budgets. A similar standardized system should also be developed to report current force and weapons levels. After the system is used by the U.S. for a short period, results should be published and international inspection teams invited to verify the accuracy of the report. The U.S. should then indicate that the system will be utilized a second year if the Soviet Union permits similar reporting and inspection.

Such an initiative combines intention-clarification initiative with action designed to gain reciprocation. A standardized accounting system for military forces would be particularly helpful to make significant force reduction initiatives possible. Once in place, for example, a 5% force reduction initiative would be of specified items, could be measured, and could be verified. The expected reciprocation and new initiative, if reciprocation takes place, could be similarly concrete, measurable, and verifiable.

The key to a peace initiative strategy (as opposed to isolated gestures or acts) is the linkage between acts toward one goal and acts toward the other interrelated goals. In the previous example, the initiation of a standardized accounting system could be linked toward strengthening international organizations by reporting the results and asking for verification by the appropriate U.N. agency. A promise to use the reduction in military budgets for economic development objectives might follow, if others adopted the accounting system. The 5% military spending reduction could be deposited in development banks and made available to developing countries also willing to reduce military spending by 5% of their total military spending. These initiatives could be linked to an onsite inspection agency, created as part of the process and augmented by satellite surveillance data. International scientific nongovernmental organization leaders could aid in making these steps credible by participating in the inspection process and by encouraging their members to report to the international, nongovernmental governing board any violations of the accounting and force reduction initiatives. Thus, initiatives in the disarmament field could be linked to strengthening international organizations initiatives and to world economic development and human rights goals. The action-response-new action process toward a superordinate (disarmament) goal, would help build a sense of world community. Encouragement by non-

governmental organization, reward for new initiatives, demands for reciprocation by other powers, and calls for new initiatives, would be critical. Surely
these are the appropriate tasks of the network of citizen peace organizations,
world affairs organizations, and international, nongovernmental organizations.

To develop a full peace initiatives strategy, many questions must be
answered. Since inspection is one key to disarmament, how can satellite
surveillance data be used? Could on-site inspection and the ''inspection by the
people (scientists)'' suggested above, supplement ''national technical means''
of verification now accepted in arms control treaties? At what stage should other
nuclear powers be brought into the process? What are the relationships between
conventional and nuclear force levels and how should nuclear force level
reductions be phased into conventional force level reductions? How can allies
best be brought into the process so they do not believe they are being abandoned? What are the situations in which the United States should lead? When
should it follow the lead of others? What groups within the Soviet Union might
be appealed to (scientists? youths? dissidents? trade unionists?) What Russian
or Marxist traditions might be appealed to? What realities of domestic Soviet
politics and what possibilities of pressure from external forces give promise, if
properly exploited, of a favorable response to an initiative? How does one
overcome the facts of extensive controls within Soviet society and the ideological barriers to a meaningful sense of world community? How can initiatives
toward one goal best be linked with initiatives toward others to maximize the
likelihood of reciprocation? What are the best inducements to reciprocation?
What types of coercive initiatives have the best chance of gaining wide support?
When should they be brought into play? What mixture of benefits and losses is
most likely to induce the desired reciprocation? How can momentum best be
maintained once achieved?

It is this kind of detailed questioning, extended to each of the major goals
considered above, that is necessary to construct an initiative strategy.

An initiative approach requires a carefully thought-out policy involving
prior public announcements of the intention to act, toward what goal it is
designed to advance us, and what form of reciprocation is expected. It may be
an important gesture, but it is not part of an initiative strategy when one country
stops building a weapon-system and expects the other side to guess that it must
stop as well. Political pressure is derived from being clear about your goals;
about how the goals are related to ending war, and by acting explicitly on behalf
of those goals. As such actions are taken, pressure for reciprocation increases as
many external and internal incentives and disincentives are brought to bear.

The degree of risk involved in each step has to be carefully calculated.
What, for example, would we risk or gain if we took seriously the proposals to
turn some satellite surveillance facilities over to the U.N.? How could such

international verification of force levels aid in making more secure not only the U.S. but other countries as well? What would we risk or gain if we tied reduction in our arms budget to problems of financial need in the non-oil exporting developing States?

An initiatives policy could relate disarmament moves to acts transforming international institutions into instruments of world law. One example would be to seek an International Oversight Commission to monitor implementation of the Panama Canal Treaties. What powers should such a commission have over military ships passing through the canal? How could such a commission become an instrument for the peaceful utilization of all the world's narrow waterways? Another example would be what authority should a World Ocean Authority have in relation to implementing a Law of the Sea? Should the International Atomic Energy Agency have authority to monitor all nuclear reactors designed to produce energy? Should its authority be increased so it can prevent the diversion of spent fuel rods for weapons manufacture rather than just report that diversion has happened? Should an International Criminal Court be created to try those suspected of engaging in terrorism? U.N. chartering of transnational corporations, training U.N. functional agency representatives stationed in crucial areas in conflict-resolution skills, creating a world broad-casting system open to diverse, nongovernmental opinion . . . there is no shortage of specific ideas of how initiatives by one country could have a beneficial impact on economic and political relations. No attempt is made here to list all the initiatives in each area, or to evaluate their feasibility. Our purpose is to introduce the idea of a strategy of American peace initiative acts that could open the possibility of achieving a world without war.[16]

Tension-reduction, or Coercive Pressures, or Both?

There have been two very different approaches to a policy of U.S. initiatives. One emphasizes the reduction of international tension and sees as the central problem, creating an atmosphere of mutual trust in which agreements, previously thought impossible to achieve, may be reached. Just as an arms race is a form of unilateral but reciprocal tension-increasing activity, one approach to an initiative policy advocates an independent but reciprocated tension-decreasing activity. Another initiatives approach examines the conflict

[16]A statement outlining twenty-six peace initiatives toward the goals outlined here is available from the World Without War Issues Center – Midwest, 67 E. Madison, Suite 1417, Chicago, IL 60603. Ask for "Peace, Security, and the 1980 Elections" and for a prospectus on a project developing the peace initiative idea.

producing the tension, and focuses on the problem of producing sufficient pressure to move reluctant heads of State to make the desired reciprocal response. To induce reciprocation, this approach recommends a combination of reduction of threat, positive incentives, and punitive measures.

Every plan for peace comes up against the fact that it requires agreement, and agreement cannot be negotiated. A peace initiatives strategy can change the situation so that agreement becomes possible. A policy of U.S. initiatives engages us in the right endeavor: progress on our part toward the right goal and toward an understanding of what must change in Soviet, regional powers, and other States' attitudes and policies to make possible a world without war.

Needed change will not come easily. It will not come in response to calls for trust in international affairs (as if countries were individuals). It will not come at all, except in response to pressures for change and processes to facilitate that change. Some of the pressures are now apparent in our society and in others. The to end war context is offered to guide efforts genuinely intended to open the possibility of peace.

Such an initiatives policy could immediately provide the dynamics to achieve at least these goals: a halt to expansion of the arms race; a serious attempt to narrow the gap between the very rich and very poor States by eradicating desperate poverty; temporary political settlements to defuse crisis areas like those in Central America and Central Asia. Such a policy, however, can go far beyond initial steps and temporary settlements. It can recognize that the awesome threats of nuclear war, refugees, hunger, terrorism, and the widespread violation of human rights, are problems of such a magnitude that only international cooperation by currently adversarial powers and global institutions can resolve them.

Can the Will be Formed?

There is, in the contemporary American political culture, little sustained effort on behalf of the goals essential to a world without war. Few in or out of peace circles encounter coherent ideas that give rational or emotional sustenance to the interrelated goals. Very different currents would move in American politics, were there widely shared ideas of how to pursue the goal of ending war.

Such a context has been offered here. There are understandings that are not now governmental policy which, if developed and acted upon, could make a positive contribution to work for a world without war.

Belief that it is possible to end war — as at one time believing it possible to end slavery — requires what is not now available: experience. Our experiences and our expectations are those of war. What is needed is a willingness to challenge that outlook with a new approach to international conflict. That approach — the peace initiatives approach — opens the possibility, although only the possibility, of a world without war. The resources provided in the concluding section of this book are intended for those who, whatever the odds, want to do something specific and thoughtful to make that possibility the reality.

SECTION C

ACTION

THE SURVEY OF the primary requisites of a world without war is now complete. Disarmament under law sustained by a sense of world community becomes possible as human rights are advanced, economic development achieved, and change takes place through political processes or by non-violent, direct action. Progress toward these objectives can be initiated by the United States, without unacceptable risk to itself. A peace initiative strategy is a significantly changed U.S. policy that offers the best chance of gaining the needed response, agreement, and change from the Soviet Union and others. The demonstration by one country that there is an alternative approach to international conflict that rejects both war and surrender can be of great value in resolving regional crises or specific issues.

In Section B a context for work to end war was offered. In this Section C, resources are provided to help make these ideas public policy. Although selected and designed primarily for those in agreement with the context presented in Chapter 19, the resources in Section C will be useful whatever the point of view.

Chapter 20, ''Democracy and World Affairs Organizations,'' is an extension of the to end war context into domestic politics. It develops the implica-

505

tions for action by United States citizens who want to see democratic values expressed in America's engagement in world politics. It examines how American world affairs organizations can help to achieve a world without war using the democratic political process. Participation by non-governmental organizations in that process is one form of action. This includes working in the society to alter conceptions of what goals should be sought, lobbying and consulting with public officials.

Protest against the policies and actions of governments can also be an important and legitimate form of action. When conducted under the discipline which constitutes a principles non-violent movement,* protest may even include civil disobedience and enhance the democratic process. It is when protest takes on disrespect for the law or encourages violence that it poses a problem. What is considered most effective here, is a combination of steady-long term work to build support for a new policy direction *and* the application of that direction to specific issues and crises. Most of the resources gathered in this section are for people who know that a steady and persistent effort is needed, and that that effort should be conducted within the framework of rights and responsibilities, of governmental prerogatives and non-governmental engagement, that make-up a functioning democracy.

In preparing to act, a person should first examine the democratic political process in this country and consider how to defend and improve it. Chapter 20 provides resources that will help in this.

The world of nongovernmental organizations is bewilderingly complex. There are thousands of such organizations; their goals, programs, skills, and strategies of change differ. Categorizing organizations provides a useful overview of the field and reveals that specialization is at least part of the reason for the number of organizations. Resource A provides such a categorization or typology. After looking at the entire field it is easier to decide where to put your effort. Resource B provides an extensive but nonetheless select list of world affairs organizations, and Resource C is an organization assessment questionnaire.

Chapter 21 turns from organizational activity to the individual. In the world affairs field, one must select an audience with which to work. It can be teachers, children, labor or business leaders, religious organizations, or any of many others. Resource D is designed to help assess one's own strengths and weaknesses, to aid in deciding where particular talents can best be applied. Resource E offers twenty-five answers to the question "But What Can I Do?" Resource F indicates how an individual acting within an organization can work on human rights. The "International Human Rights Quotient: An Organ-

*See Chapter 16.

izational Assessment Tool'' suggests what needs to be considered in developing an organization's policy.

The last two resources are designed to help individuals gain expertise on specific subject. Resource G indicates what is needed to become an expert in a particular area, and keep current in it. Resource H introduces periodicals in the world affairs field.

Taken together, the resources for action are intended to enable concerned individuals make a significant, continuing, and effective contribution to work to end war.

CHAPTER 20

DEMOCRACY AND THE WORLD AFFAIRS FIELD

As one prepares to influence governmental decision-making processes, and assuming one wants to both use and improve the democratic political processes in this country, one needs to consider three basic questions about democracy:

1. *Democratic Theory* : What are the ideas and values underlying democratic and anti-democratic theory? What form of government do you favor?

2. *Democratic Practice*: What activity on behalf of ending war will help achieve a consensus concerning this country's appropriate engagement in world politics? What activity will disrupt democratic decision-making processes and make constructive action unlikely?

3. *Democracy in Other Countries*: How does the fact that most of the countries in the world are not democracies affect your work?

THE IMPORTANCE OF DEMOCRACY

To many, the answers to such questions are obvious. Of course, citizens in this country favor representative democracy and want their work to help that political process work effectively. It is through the democratic process that change in governmental policy can be achieved.

Some who combine a concern for democracy with a commitment to work to end war maintain that democracy has special relevance to world politics. They believe that democratic institutions can achieve community across ideological, racial, ethnic and class barriers and thus make possible change without violence. Moreover, striving for the same conditions in world politics flows naturally from an appreciation of the American experience in uniting, over a very wide segment of the earth's surface, diverse people, interests, and experiences. The United States is the world's first urban, industrialized, multi-racial, multi-ethnic society. Because a world society with similar features is in the making, the ability of democratic institutions in this country to process change without the violence of war remains an experiment of vital significance.

DEMOCRACY AND WAR

The view that democracy is a significant resource in work against war is not universally shared. Many engaged in the search for peace see democracy as a problem. They point to the role of democratic ideas over the past two centuries in initiating wars and revolutions, and to the role nationalistic feelings, derived from democratic ideas, played in the two world wars. They lament the difficulties a commitment to democracy places in the way of peaceful relations with authoritarian and totalitarian States. Peace, they say, requires acceptance of other ideologies and forms of government. Besides, they sometimes ask, is there any fundamental difference?

Several other arguments against the relevance of democratic values to peace concerns have found support within the world affairs field. Some peace activitists hold anarchist views which conclude that all large-scale government is evil. They reject democracy as merely another way of organizing and legitimating the State's use of violence. The key to peace, in this approach, lies in personal witness against all institutions and structures that make demands on the individual against his or her will or conscience.

Other people who argue against the relevance of democracy to work for a world without war maintain that the size of modern institutions is the problem, not their underlying values; others argue from ideological or social scientific standpoints that American democracy disproportionately favors the white middle class (or a more narrow oligarchic elite). Work for peace that fails to challenge American social structures, and the political system which perpetuates them, is regarded with scorn in such circles.

In peace movement organizations, hostility to democracy is widespread. Present institutions and practices are regarded with extreme skepticism. Today's problems are vividly dramatized — war, poverty, pollution, deprivation. Those holding positions of authority are deemed responsible and often viewed with contempt. Civil rights violations, the Vietnam war, the "credibility gap" between Presidential statements and perceived facts, assassinations (and conspiracy theories concerning their perpetrators), Watergate and the media's treatment of it, revelations of CIA and FBI wrongdoings, all have distanced social activists from American institutions.

In world politics, democracy has also suffered reverses. In third world countries, an earlier generation of leaders sought to emulate the more open societies of America, Britain, and France. They argued it was self-evident that new States would be strong human rights advocates for they knew the sting of arbitrary authority, But today many in the new States take the USSR, China, or Cuba as their model. In doing so, they are agreeing with the advice offered by an American economist, Robert Heilbroner:

> Communism may well be the quickest possible way out of underdevelopment and the desperate fact is that in many areas of the world the present non-Communist effort looks like the slowest possible way.[1]

Others maintain that the right wing, authoritarian regimes are more likely to achieve economic development and evolve into democracies. The abandonment of human rights and democratic institutions, however, is not without its critics:

> The boundaries between the state of nature and civil society have blurred in so many Third World countries. Yesterday's victims have beome today's executioners. . . . That the whip is cracked by yesterday's liberators and heroes of national independence, that it should have all come to this, explains much of the anomie, alienation and disillusionment one sees in many Third World societies.[2]

Nonetheless, a deep-seated hostility to democracy remains influential among educated elites in the Third World. For them, the idea of sharing power with the majority is a prescription for their own powerlessness and for continuing political and economic dependence upon outside powers; authoritarian ideas, particularly when systematized by Marxist categories transposed to world politics, provide comforting explanation of their own dictatorial powers, the failure of economic development plans, and of how such problems can best be overcome.

These and other currents of thought have placed on the defensive supporters of democratic ideas and institutions. Among the questions that need to be considered are these:

[1] *The Great Ascent*, p. 138.
[2] Fouad Ajami, "The Fate of Nonalignment," *Foreign Affairs*, Winter 1980/81, p. 370.

1. *Origins:* Did democratic values and institutions originate with the emergence of the middle class or have they existed in varying times and places for over twenty-four centuries? Why has continuous democratic government succeeded only recently? (*The Liberal Interpretation of History, 6-117).*

2. *Setting:* Can democratic institutions exist only in urban, literate, middle class, Western societies; or did democratic values and institutions emerge in settings with few of these features and with per capita GNPs below any country in the world today? Can a government be held accountable without a free press, independent judiciary, periodic elections and other features of democracy?

3. *Justice:* What specific ends are so self-evidently desirable, that when denied, many turn to violence to achieve them? What are the political perspectives that provide for the pursuit of those ends in ways that move toward a sense of community, rather than away from such a sense by the use of violence?

4. *Peace:* Does the search for peace require abandoning a commitment to democratic values? Or conversely, can we achieve peace in a world in which democratic government is not universal?

5. *Development:* Are authoritarian and totalitarian forms of government essential in Asia, Africa, and Latin America to achieve economic goals and to maintain national cohesion, or can political freedom aid in achieving economic and political development?

A DEFENSE OF DEMOCRACY

There are three general responses to the claims against democracy: those based on political theory, on the performance of democratic government, and upon ethical values. A defense of democracy based on political theory begins with an examination of alternative political systems. On what values are they based? What are their goals? How have they worked in the past and what are their future prospects? A defense then examines the values of democracy, such as political equality, the extent and limits of majority rule, and human rights. It considers the theory that governments derive their just powers from the consent of the governed, and that government's essential purpose is to defend the rights of its citizens. In such justifications for democracy, government is frequently held to rest on a "contract" between the governed and the governors; individuals living within a society and accepting the benefits of it give an "implied consent" to the contract, thus legitimating governmental authority. But legitimate authority also requires consent; democracy provides the means by which it can be expressed, changed or withdrawn (*An Introduction to Democratic Theory*, 20-2).

Characteristics of Democratic Government

In a Democracy . . .

1. each individual has a right to be represented in governmental decision-making bodies.
2. the majority has the right to make and carry out policy provided it does not violate the inherent rights of the citizens or the constitution.
3. the minority has the right to contest for power and, if successful, to form a new government as the majority.
4. there are periodic elections in which the consent of the governed is ascertained. To make this meaningful there must be:

    a. the right to form political parties.
    b. the free conflict of ideas throughout the electorate.
    c. the right to publish and disseminate ideas, to peacefully assemble, to petition, etc.
    d. a safeguarded election process which accurately records and reports election results.

5. there is a distinction between the society and the State — the society includes non-governmental organizations (religious, commercial, labor, education, cultural, civil and other organizations) and individuals.
6. there is a set of inalienable human rights enforced by an independent judiciary.

Some critics of democracy argue against it in principle. It is unwise, they say, to base a government on a political system which facilitates broad public participation in decision-making. It is wiser, more just, or fairer to place governmental responsibility with those better qualified to do the specialized tasks of government than the public. At the root of this criticism of democracy is the belief that someone, or some group, knows the public's own best interest better than they do. Claims are made on behalf of particular social classes, races, or ethnic groups, as well as on behalf of particular professions (Spitz, *Patterns of Anti-Democratic Thought*, 20-13).

Another form of anti-democratic argument agrees with democratic theory but argues it is unworkable in practice. Some elite having the knowledge, the wealth, the will, or the position necessarily decides the vital questions. Those who believe democracy is wrong in theory raise the question of the public competence, a question even democrats raise when referring to foreign policy. The view that democracy does not work in practice questions whether the public can become deeply engaged in world affairs discussions.

A defense of the performance of democratic government must resolve the possible contradiction between effective conduct of foreign policy and broad public participation in a democracy's decision-making. The contradiction can be resolved when the appropriate role of citizens and of experts is distinguished. Citizens are best qualified to set the goals a country should seek in world politics and to set limits to the means appropriate for use in their pursuit. Indeed, a recent study has concluded: "the general public is especially competent, probably more competent than any other group — elitist, expert or otherwise — to determine the basic ends of public policy."[3] Experts are needed to decide how to pursue those ends in particular circumstances in consultation with a foreign policy attentive public. The latter, the minority who reads about and studies foreign policy issues, can best be approached through non-governmental, world affairs organizations. When the citizen, the foreign policy attentive public, and the expert decision-makers each intelligently fulfill their task, there need be no contradiction between an informed, realistic and democratic foreign policy.

Such approaches to the defense of democracy are developed in books annotated in the bibliography. Books defending democracy on ethical grounds are also provided.[4]

Defenders of democracy on ethical grounds argue that democracy is based on the belief that the individual is a morally responsible being. Democracy provides the means for exercising that responsibility in public life while, at the same time, limiting the legitimate areas of government authority. The area in which the individual, not the State, is sovereign is large but not unlimited. Clearly the individual can legally form associations, practice his or her religious beliefs, and engage in political advocacy. But none of these rights can threaten the rights of others through malicious slander, threats or use of violence, or by exposing State secrets. Resolving the conflicts between the primacy of conscience and the prerogatives of the State is a difficult task for a democracy: other modern forms of government do not pose the question.

Advocates of a world without war may disagree about the virtues of capitalism or socialism as forms of economic organization. The discussion continues about which economic system is more conducive to peace: Do free trade, the free flow of investment capital, the relationship between economic freedom and political freedom, mean capitalism is more conducive to peace than socialism? (*The Just Peace*, 17-24). Or do the cooperative, humanitarian values that underlie socialist theory make socialism more likely to lead to peace? In a century in which wars between capitalist powers (World War I and II), and between Socialist powers (China vs. Vietnam, Vietnam vs. Kam-

[3] Charles Roll, Jr., and Albert Contril, Jr., *Polls: Their Use and Misuse in Politics* (New York: Seven Locks Press 1980).
[4] See also Chapter 15.

puchea, USSR vs. China, or in different definitions of socialism, Israel vs. Syria, Iraq vs. Iran) have occurred, it is apparent that neither economic system is a sufficient condition for peace. But if democratic institutions are weakened, the most effective political process for the nonviolent conduct and resolution of conflict is damaged. Democratic governments provide arenas in which programs can be developed and implemented. In addition to the formal governmental structures, the complex of independent organizations and communications provides a remarkably flexible process to circulate ideas, test new policies, and initiate constructive change.

THE POLITICS OF PEACE

Too often Americans working in the world affairs field swing from active support for democratic values and processes to practices which erode them. If the aim of a peace movement is to help fulfill the promise of democratic government, to utilize the political processes of this country to gain a consensus for a new approach to international conflict, its leaders should consider carefully these choices:

1. *Distinction Between Society and the State:* Is it important that nongovernmental organizations (business, labor, religious, civic, professional, public interest, educational, and world affairs) have a legitimate standing within the State?

2. *Change of Government:* How can changes of governmental leaders be best facilitated so that those in power express the wishes of the majority while those out of power are free to contest to become the new majority and thus form a government?

3. *Human Rights:* If the press is dependent upon the government, how will governmental abuses of power be known? How, for example, could prohibitions against torture or the murder of nonviolent political opponents be prevented, if government has become all powerful?

4. *Accountability of the Governors to the Governed:* How can those in power be made to account for their expenditures of public funds, their use of power, and their programs? By adversarial parties. If not, how else?

For many involved in American peace and world affairs organizations, the question is not so much the problem of democratic theory, as how to implement that theory in their everyday activity. But choices between practices which help fulfill and those which can undermine democratic institutions are encountered daily. These choices are encountered by organizations. Their response can help fulfill democratic political processes or, perhaps, unintentionally, lend support to anti-democratic tendencies:

1. *Quality of Information:* Do your organization's publications rely on a variety of sources of information and reflect facts which permit a balanced assessment of the issue?

2. *Realistic Assessment:* Does your organization's approach to world affairs recognize the obstacles to its goals posed by power and conflicting purposes of other States as well as in our own?

3. *Contending Ideas:* Are the ideas carried by your organization subject to debate and analysis from many points of view or has the discussion of most issues fallen into a familiar pattern?

4. *Constructive Alternative:* Does your organization present constructive policy alternatives to those you reject? Has it a thought-out context with developed answers to the basic questions?

5. *Contribution to the Public Debate:* Does your organization seek to contribute to the public debate about: a) the goals this country should seek in world politics? b) the obstacles to those goals? c) the values underlying contending policy analysis which might provide common ground? d) the means appropriate to the ends sought?

6. *Attitude toward the Public:* Is the style of your organization one of participation in a society whose leaders and political process you affirm or are your policy differences with leaders treated as occasions for distancing yourself from the society and its political processes?

7. *Coalitions:* Are the coalitions your organization enters composed of groups committed to democratic values or are they made up of whomever happens to agree about opposition to a specific policy? What are the principles of inclusion and exclusion?

IMPROVING AMERICA'S COMPETENCE IN WORLD AFFAIRS

It is against this background of concern for the theory and practice of democracy that we turn to a consideration of organizations that seek to influence this country's foreign policy decision-making process. A large majority of organizations in the world affairs field have a common commitment to democratic values and seek to aid this country resolve conflict in world politics without violence and to promote constructive change. But the leaders of these organizations do few joint projects, and rarely plan common strategies to improve America's competence in world affairs.

One segment of the world affairs field of non-governmental organizations is the peace movement. Its primary focus is on the problem of war or some part of it: disarmament, world economic development, international human rights, world community, international organizations — or, more familiarly, with a protest response to U.S. military policy. Those in peace cause organizations direct their talents and resources to work for world peace. They reject primary reliance on national military power. They rarely offer a constructive alternative. While peace cause groups have, for the most part, attracted only a small minority of the population and seem to have little lasting political influence, they play a role far more important than their numbers or budgets would suggest.

Often it is the members of a small peace cause organization who launch a new peace research center or play crucial roles in establishing international organizations or who persuade major religious or other organizations to put "peace work," variously defined, on their agenda. A planning group for a nation-wide protest has, on occasion, been composed of a very small sect with goals far different from those in the protest (*The Citizen Peace Effort: An Overview* 20-152).

MAINSTREAM VOLUNTARY ORGANIZATIONS

The peace cause world is only part of the world affairs field. Mainstream voluntary organizations, research institutes, and a variety of professional and vocational associations (see Resource A) are also involved. Their focus is usually not on war or peace yet it is these groups which, if seriously and responsibly engaged, could have the needed impact on our society.

Peace cause groups and the mainstream organizations play distinctly different roles in the world affairs field. There are among them and the other groups of organizations no stated goals that are shared, no common strategy for change, no agreed-upon set of priorities. The intellectual, organizational, and programmatic fragmentation is one of the reasons for the sporadic nature of activity, the inadequate funding in the field, the duplication of effort, the inability to attract knowledgeable leadership, and the consequent general ineffectiveness. There are, to be sure, notable exceptions to any generalizations about a field as diverse as that made up of world affairs organizations. But, in general, the quality of discussion, the prescription of new policy, and the assessment of world politics is rarely adequate to the standards necessary to have a cumulative impact on this country's engagement in world affairs.

OVERCOMING FRAGMENTATION

The first thing that occurs to a thoughtful person surveying the world affairs field is that something should be done about uniting the fragments. But this would be last on the list of any experienced person, who knows only too well the reasons for this situation — the conflicting goals, analyses, and strategies. Each organization tries to survive and do useful work and this can lead to rivalry rather than cooperation. Judging from past attempts it is hopeless to coordinate all the groups or to put them together in one overarching structure. But if the goal is more limited — if it aims at some, not all, of the groups, if its mode is functional, not structural, if it offers a continuing process, not a single event or issue, if it increases funding for the field, if it tries to clear up the intellectual and ideological confusions as well as confront the organizational chaos — then, perhaps, something can be accomplished.

This book is an attempt to provide one of the requisites of a more effective world affairs field. It provides a systematic overview, outlines an analysis, and proposes common goals growing out of that analysis (see Chapter 19). The typology of organizations is a step toward establishing the functional specialization of various organizations. What has not been presented, but what is needed, is an approach to programming that is functional in the subjects it treats (like common concerns with the media, funding, leadership, training, relationships to government, and resources) and thoughtful in the substantive programs it offers. An example of the latter are programs that map out the range of views on a subject, clarify the underlying values and goals, and seek to chart a common sense of direction within the world affairs field. This type of substantive program is more likely to give non-governmental organizations a voice in setting policy direction than are programs which gather those already in agreement.

We have a long way to go before a non-governmental, world affairs field exists which has clear standards of professional competence, a demonstrable understanding of world affairs, and a well-conceived sense of direction capable of uniting currently divided poles in the public debate. Among the institutional and programmatic activities required are:

1). A recruiting and training program for professionals considering entry into the world affairs field.

2). A constructive dialogue between the State Department and leaders in world affairs organizations enabled by governmental publications identifying choices *not made* and the reasons for their being rejected as well as the choices made (this would help organizations advance the discussion of ideas) and a willingness to appear in forums in which governmental voices are one of several voices heard.

3). Mainstream organizations which are willing to define their appropriate engagement in the world affairs field, to assign staff and budget resources for such work, and to engage their full instrumentalities.

4). A group in Congress and the Senate committed to clarifying how this country could pursue end war goals (now partially achieved through the work of Members of Congress for Peace through Law).

5). A program to facilitate peace education and global education curriculum in public schools.

6). A series of flexible organizational structures capable of focusing maximum strength on specific issues (e.g. on treaty ratification issues).

7). A strong and morally clear radical wing of people committed to active opposition to American military programs who are capable of resisting the use of mass violence by other States as well.

8). A significant peace research effort.

9). An international, morally authoritative voice offering continuing guidance on the need to pursue non-military conflict resolution and constructive change.

10). National and regional funds which have thought-out standards for the allocation of funds to organizations and projects.

11). National and regional planning, linking, and communication structures which look at the field as a whole, address functional needs common to most organizations within it and who are charged with the responsibility for connecting the above.

There is a considerable difference between building a strong movement opposed to American military programs and building a competent world affairs public in America. The aim of the efforts outlined above would be the latter. Here also there is a difference between competent world affairs organizations and an effective world affairs field. Lasting change requires more than a numerical majority; it requires fundamentally changed understandings of America's role in the world — understandings that permeate the fabric of

American life. One part of that definition of competence would be the development and implementation (with the resources that made success possible) of the many available alternatives to war as a means of resolving international conflict and promoting constructive change. A world affairs field focused on that task and capable of fulfilling it has yet to be formed.

BIBLIOGRAPHY

The books on democracy and the world affairs field listed here introduce democratic and anti-democratic theorists. They trace the history of international and American nongovernmental activity on world affairs. These publications will help answer questions such as those presented on pages 508, 511, 514, and 515.

A. Democratic Theory and Its Critics

20 – 1 *Development of the Democratic Idea: Readings from Pericles to the Present*, Charles Sherover (ed.), 604pp, 1974, NAL, $2.50. An anthology which surveys the foundations of democratic theory. Includes selections by Cicero, Montesquieu, Madison, Mill, Dewey, Hook, and others, with a thoughtful introductory essay before each selection.

20 – 2 *An Introduction to Democratic Theory*, Henry Mayo, 316pp, 1960, Oxford, $5.00. A presentation of the theoretical support for democratic government and a defense.

20 – 3 *Social and Political Philosophy, Readings from Plato to Gandhi*, John Somerville & Ronald Santoni (eds.), 545pp, 1963, Doubleday, $3.50. Includes classic texts and selections from Lenin, Mussolini, Hitler, Dewey and Gandhi.

20 – 4 *The Reason for Democracy*, Kalman Silvert, 136pp, 1977, Viking, O.P. Seeks to secure democratic institutions in a sense of community not in a mechanistic calculus of benefit and loss.

20 – 5 *Democracy*, Jack Lively, 160pp, 1975, St. Martin's, $16.95. Considers different definitions and theories of democracy which focus on political equality as the distinguishing criterion.

20 – 6 *Three Essays: On Liberty, Representative Government, The Subjection of Women*, John Stuart Mill, edited by Richard Wollheim, 550pp, 1975 (1859, 1861, 1860), Oxford, $5.95. Mill's classic essays on liberty and his belief that the "legal subordination of one sex to the other is wrong in itself, and now one of the chief hindrances to human improvement."

Classic

20 – 7 *On Liberty,* John Stuart Mill, David Spitz (ed.), 260pp, 1975, (1859), Norton, $2.95. The classic justification of individual liberty as a requirement for discovering truths and thus the need to limit the demands of the State and society. Reprinted here with critical essays.

20 – 8 *A Preface to Democratic Theory,* Robert Dahl, 154pp, 1956, Chicago, $2.75. An abstruse mathematical argument attempting to demonstrate why traditional theoretical justifications of popular sovereignty fail and to develop an alternative justification.

20 – 9 *Democracy,* Carl Cohen, 302pp, 1971, Free Press, $3.50. Examines the nature, presuppositions, instruments and conditions of democracy. Offers a defense of the prospect for democracy in a thorough and comprehensive way.

20 – 9A *The State,* Stephen Graubard, 183pp, 1981, Norton, $14.95. Reassesses the nation-State as a human invention with political, ethical, and social implications and questions anew whether the State can be replaced as the primary actor in world politics.

20 – 10 *The Democratic Experience: Past & Prospects,* Reinhold Niebuhr & Paul Sigmund, 192pp, 1969, Praeger, O.P. Niebuhr analyzes the history of democracy in the West; Sigmund discusses the relevance of democracy for the developing States. A hopeful view of the prospects.

20 – 11 *Democratic Theory: Essays in Retrieval,* C.B. Macpherson, 250pp, 1973, Oxford, $5.75. A critique of "post-liberal-democratic theory" on behalf of Rousseau or Marx or both.

20 – 12 *The Theory of Democratic Elitism, A Critique,* Peter Bachrach, 125pp, 1980, U. Press of America, $7.25. Argues that democracy and elitist principles can be reconciled; that the theory of democratic elitism is both theoretically sound and practicable.

TEW

20 – 13 *Patterns of Anti-Democratic Thought: An Analysis and Criticism with Special Reference to the American Political Mind in Recent Times,* David Spitz, 347pp, 1981 (1965), Greenwood, $27.50. Distinguishes the forces and attitudes that reinforce democracy from those that undermine it.

20 – 14 *Crisis of the Republic,* Hannah Arendt, 240pp, 1972, Harcourt, Brace, $3.75. A collection of essays on various problems of democracy: civil disobedience, violence, revolution and lying in politics.

20 – 15 *One Dimensional Man,* Herbert Marcuse, 260pp, 1964, Beacon, $2.95. Argues that all industrial society leads to some form of authoritarianism or totalitarianism. Assumes that society is a single entity, which cannot be changed piecemeal but must be wholly replaced.

20 – 16 *Anarchy, State, & Utopia,* Robert Nozick, 367pp, 1974, Basic, $5.95. Concludes that "a minimal State, limited to the narrow functions of protection against force,

theft, fraud, enforcement of contracts, and so on, is justified; that any more extensive State will violate persons, rights . . ."

20—17 *The Modern State,* R.M. MacIver, 504pp, 1966 (1926), Oxford, $5.95. Discusses the origins, nature and evolution of today's most powerful political institution.

INF
20—18 *Political Man, The Bases of Politics,* Seymour Lipset, 584pp, 1981, Johns Hopkins, $7.50. An influential study of the social preconditions for democracy: urbanization, high rate of literacy, large middle class — none of which existed prior to the 20th century.

20—19 *Critique of Pure Tolerance,* Herbert Marcuse, Barrington Moore, & Robert Wolff, 123pp, 1969, Beacon, $3.95. The authors argue against Mill's *On Liberty* on the grounds that certain views, not their own, are too loathsome to be heard.

20—20 *On Pure Tolerance: A Critique of Criticisms,* David Spitz, 16pp, 1971, World Without War Publications, $.50. Advocates of freedom of speech and tolerance of all views, so long as they do not deprive others of basic rights. A response to the above selection.

B. Democracy in Practice

20—21 *Law, Legislation and Liberty,* I. *Rules and Order,* II. *The Mirage of Social Justice,* III. *The Political Order of a Free Society,* F.A. Hayek, 1977, Chicago, $10.00. A defense of classical liberalism — of liberty of the individual, of property rights, of capitalism and of law as the best economic/political system even for the poor.

20—22 *The Crisis of Democracy: Report on the Governability of Democracies to the Trilateral Commission,* Michael Crozier, Samuel Huntington and Jeji Watanuki, 320pp, 1975, NYU Press, $4.95. An assessment of the declining ability of democratic institutions to resolve problems.

20—23 *Democracy, Ancient and Modern,* M.I. Finley, 112pp, 1973, Rutgers, $8.00. An examination of democratic theory in ancient Athens and in the 20th century which responds to intellectual critics from Plato to Michels; concludes that public education, not apathy or heroic leadership, is the safest guardian of democracy.

20—24 *The Democratic Civilization,* Leslie Lipson, 614pp, 1964, Oxford, O.P. A believer in democracy assesses the criteria for democracy, the conditions for its growth, the values sustaining it and the varied political forms of its 2400-year history. He finds it, despite critics from Plato to Hitler, from Aristophanes to Stalin, a civilizing force of value to third world countries and to international organizations.

20—25 *The Breakdown of Democratic Regimes,* Juan Linz & Alfred Stepan (ed.), 4 volumes, 1970, Johns Hopkins, I, *Crisis Breakdown and Reequilibration,* $2.95; II. *Europe,* $3.95; III. *Latin America,* $3.95; IV. *Chile,* $3.95. A comparative study of political change and what makes democracy viable.

20–26 *Community Power & Political Theory: A Further Look at the Problem of Evidence and Interference,* Nelson Polsby, 144pp, 1980(1970), Yale, $5.95. Tests "elitist" and "pluralist" models of who governs and concludes that a new pluralist theory is needed.

20–27 *The Law and Political Protest,* Tom Dove, Senior Editor, 115pp, 1970, World Without War Publications, $1.25. A description of democratically protected political activity with an invitation to defend the institutions that make it possible.

20–28 *The Power Structure: Political Process in American Society,* Arnold Rose, 506pp, 1967, Oxford, $3.50. A study of American political processes, the influence of pressure groups, the power of voluntary organizations and the military-industrial complex. Maintains that the U.S. power structure retains the essential features of a democratic polity: openness to new talent and ideas, and accountable to the electorate.

20–29 *Technological Decisions and Democracy: European Experiments in Public Participation,* Dorothy Nelkin, 104pp, 1977, Sage, $9.95. A study of attempts to balance public participation in technical issues with the need for expertise.

20–30 *Political Oppositions in Western Democracies,* Robert Dahl (ed.), 458pp, 1968, Yale, $5.95. A study of the functions of political opposition in eleven democratic countries.

20–31 *The History of Parliamentary Behavior,* William Aydelotte (ed.) 321pp, 1977, Princeton, $9.95. Nine essays on the functioning of parliaments, using mathematical models to test different hypotheses.

20–32 *Political Parties in Western Democracies,* Leon Epstein, 386pp, 1979, Transaction, $7.95. Studies the styles, organization, and roles of European and American political parties and the expanding effect of mass media on both — particularly the ability of the media to enlarge a constituency for a single issue into a mass movement.

20–33 *Western European Party Systems: Trends and Prospects,* Peter Merkl (ed.), 676pp, 1980, Free Press, $39.95. A major study of parties in democratic states, trends in party membership and the shifting constituencies within and among European States.

C. Democracy in America

Classic

20–34 *Democracy in America,* Alexis de Tocqueville, 317pp, 1956 (1831), (abrd. ed.), NAL, $1.95. A classic study of democratic government and society in America which highlights the role of non-governmental organizations and suggests that democracies are ill-suited for world politics.

20–35 *Clear and Present Dangers: A Conservative View of America's Government,* M. Stanton Evans, 433pp, 1975, Harcourt, Brace, Jovanovich, $9.95. A critique of liberal analysis and causes which turns most of them around; one chapter is titled "Friends of the Earth, Enemies of Man."

20– 36 *American Constitutional Law, Introductory Essays & Selected Cases,* Alpheus Mason, William Beary, 787pp, 1978, (6th ed.) Prentice-Hall, $19.95. Examines the constitutional basis, the legal structure and the case-by-case building up of American constitutional law.

20– 37 *The Constitution and What it Means Today,* Edward Corwin, revised and edited by Harold Chase & Craig Ducat, 394pp, 1979, Princeton, $8.95 plus 1978 supplement, $3.50. A guide to decisions, actions and events of the 1977-78 Supreme Court, describing what applications of constitutional law are currently upheld.

20– 38 *American Government,* Judy Glaske and Walter Vokomer, 1979, Prentice Hall, $11.95. Adds a chapter on world order to a textbook designed for use in a high school civic class.

20– 39 *Political Parties in a New Nation, The American Experience, 1776-1809,* William Chambers, 231pp, 1963, Oxford $4.95. An amazing discovery of the need for political parties to contest differences in a society with a per capita GNP below all but the most destitute today.

20– 40 *Radical Principles, Reflections of an Unreconstructed Democrat,* Michael Waltzer, 192pp, 1980, Basic, $12.95. The case for democratic socialism as an extension of political democracy.

20– 41 *What Does America Mean?* Alexander Meiklejohn, 271pp, 1972, (1935), Norton, $2.50. Answers the title question — "a passion for liberty."

20– 42 *On The Democratic Idea in America,* Irving Kristol, 149pp, 1972, Harper & Row, O.P. A collection of essays which contend that liberal values can now best be defended by conservative principles: the primacy of the community's interests over the individual's in a time of social dissolution.

20– 43 *Toward a Democracy: A Brief Introduction to American Government,* Louis Koenig, 520pp, 1973, Harcourt, Brace, & Jovanovich, $12.95. Examines the theory, institutions and practices of American life and finds them helpful in confronting and working to overcome many problems.

20– 44 *American Democracy in World Perspective,* William Ebenstein, et al, 1980 (1967) (5th ed.) Harper & Row, $17.50. An unusual civics text in its attention to democracy as a conflict resolution mechansim and in its section on "democratic control" of foreign policy.

D. How Democratic Is America?

Inf
20– 45 *The Power Elite,* C. Wright Mills, 423pp, 1977 (1959) Oxford, $4.95. A now classic statement of the view that a largely closed, self-perpetuating elite rules America.

20– 46 *Who Rules America?,* G. William Domhoff, 184pp, 1967, Prentice-Hall,

$3.45. Argues that ''less than 1% of the population comprises the American upper class, if it is a government class it does not rule alone.'' But the others are ''co-opted.''

20 – 47 *Elites in American History: The New Deal to the Carter Adminstration,* Philip Burch, Jr., 545pp, 1980, Holmes & Meier, $14.50. A collective biography of federal officials from 1930 to 1980 which finds a disproportionally high number of businessmen in power.

20 – 48 *The Whole World is Watching: Mass Media in the Making and Unmaking of the New Left,* Todd Gitlin, 350pp, 1980, California, $12.50. A former President of the Students for a Democratic Society argues that the media destroyed the New Left.

20 – 49 *Changing of the Guard: Power and Leadership in America,* David Broder, 512pp, 1980, Simon & Schuster, $14.95. Argues there is a generational division between those for whom the depression, Munich and the Nazi-Stalin Pact were the politically shaping experiences and those for whom it was Vietnam, Watergate and the civil rights movements.

20 – 50 *Welfare, Justice and Freedom,* Scott Gordon, 256pp, 1980, Columbia, $15.00. Maintains that democratic societies have rightly placed significant constraints on property rights to promote welfare.

20 – 51 *The Pursuit of Equality in American History,* J.R. Pole, 395pp, 1980, California, $5.95. Presents the impact of egalitarian ideas on social structure and political institutions.

20 – 52 *Viable Democracy,* Michael Margolis, 211pp, 1979, Penguin, $3.95. Calls for a reform of democratic institutions, using new technologies to permit better information for citizens, greater in-put from them.

20 – 53 *The Moral Foundations of the American Republic,* Robert Horwitz (ed.), 245pp, 1977, Virginia, $2.95. An assessment of the circumstances and the values which influence the constitutional process. Includes essays by Ben Barber, Richard Hofstadter and Wilson Carey McWilliams, among others.

20 – 54 *The American Establishment,* Leonard & Mark Silk, 320pp, 1980, Basic Books, $13.95. Describes the centers of influence within the Eastern Establishment: Harvard, *The New York Times*, The Brookings Institution, The Ford Foundation and the Council on Foreign Relations.

20 – 55 *Power and Politics in the United States: A Political Economy Approach*, G. David Garson, 352pp, 1977, Heath, $6.95. A detailed presentation of the ''elitist'' vs. ''pluralist'' debate about American decision-making and society; an attempt to transcend the debate by concluding that the U.S. has sought elitist ends through pluralist means.

20 – 56 *American Bureaucracy,* Peter Woll, 260pp, 1977 (1963), Norton, $5.95. A study of the fourth branch of government which examines problems of control, the

acquisition of judicial-like power and yet concludes that the Federal bureaucracy "occupies a responsible position within our political system."

20 – 57 *Political Organization,* James Wilson, 374pp, 1973, Basic Books, $11.95. An examination of the functions of groups in seeking to influence public decision-making processes. Considered are political parties, trade union, business organizations, civic associations, protest groups, the bureaucracy and civil rights organizations.

E. Contemporary American Politics

20 – 58 *The Almanac of American Politics,* Michael Barone & Grant Ujifusa, 1981, Almanac of American Politics, $16.95. Includes information on the 1980 elections, the composition of the House and Senate, Governors and big city mayors, plus an assessment of the political implications of the 1980 census information.

20 – 59 *A Tide of Discontent, The 1980 Elections and Their Meaning,* Ellis Sandoz & Cecil V. Crabb, Jr., 225pp, 1981, Congressional Quarterly, $7.50. Asks how an election "too close to call" in late October became a Republican landside with a Republican majority in the U.S. Senate. Considers also the implications for the country's political future.

20 – 60 *Congress Reconsidered, Second Edition,* Lawrence Dodd & Bruce Oppenheimer, 440pp, 1981, Congressional Quarterly, $7.95. Considers the institutional and operational practices of Congress and how one can influence the decision-making process.

20 – 61 *Emerging Coalitions in American Politics,* Seymour Martin Lipset (ed.), 524pp, 1978, Institute for Contemporary Studies, $6.95. Speculations on the role of religion, occupation, regional differences, education and race on voting patterns and the future prospects of the two major parties.

20 – 62 *The Almanac of American Politics 1980,* Michael Barone, Grant Ujifusa & Douglas Matthews, 1,055pp, 1980, Dutton, $10.95. Profiles each Senator, member of the House of Representatives and Governor, their records, States and District.

20 – 63 *The Hammond Almanac of a Million Facts, Records, Forecasts,* 502pp, 1980, Signet, $4.50. The 1980 U.S. election results, as well as census figures, information on government, politics, history and other data.

20 – 64 *American National Election Studies Data Sourcebook, 1952 – 1978,* Warren Miller, Arthur Miller & Edward Schneider, 456pp, 1980, Harvard, $25.00. Data on national elections.

20 – 65 *The American Party System; Stages of Political Development,* William Chambers and Walter Burnham (ed.), 374pp, 1975 (1967), Oxford, $5.95. A history and analysis of the two-party system from 1790 to the 1970s which tests different hypotheses about its durability.

20 – 66 *Transformations of the American Party System: Political Coalitions from the New Deal to the 1970s,* Everett Ladd, Jr., with Charles Hadley, 371pp, 1975, Norton, $4.95. Assesses the future of the two-party system in a time when the majority considers itself independent.

20 – 67 *The Silent Revolution, Changing Values and Political Styles Among Western Publics,* Ronald Ingelhart, 482pp, 1977, Princeton, $9.95. In societies in which more than half the population have college degrees, value change occurs relatively easily. Politics, however, gets congested since everyone has an opinion.

20 – 68 *The Pulse of Politics: The Rhythm of Presidential Politics in the 20th Century,* James Barber, 342pp, 1980, Norton, $14.95. A history of the major 20th-century presidential campaigns, concludes that conciliation, no less than conflict, is a legitimate aim of a presidential campaigner.

F. Decision-Making

20 – 69 *Knowledge and Decisions,* Thomas Sowell, 422pp, 1980, Basic Books, $18.50. A political economist looks at the range of ''free choices'' in American economic and political life and regrets their restriction. The free market and choices over a wide range of social issues have less harsh consequences and more benefits than government decisions.

20 – 70 *Controversies and Decisions, The Social Sciences and Public Policy,* Charles Frankel (ed.), 299pp, 1976, Russell Sage, $10.00. Essays analyzing the relationships between the social sciences and governmental decision-making, morality, and the policy impact of social scientists.

20 – 71 *The American Presidency,* Richard Pious, 491pp, 1979, Basic Books, $6.95. Once again a plea for strong leaders to make decisions.

20 – 72 *Presidential Power & Accountability: Toward a New Constitution,* Charles Hardin, 257pp, 1972, Chicago, $7.95. Offers nine specific proposals for checking the power of the Executive Branch and making all branches more accountable.

20 – 73 *Decision-Making in the White House, The Olive Branch or the Arrows,* Theodore Sorensen, 94pp, 1963, Columbia, $7.50. Examines the extent and limits of Presidential decision-making; the public's values, expectations and goals all limit what the President can do.

20 – 74 *A Primer for Policy Analysis,* Edith Stokey and Richard Zeckhauser, 356pp, 1978, Norton, $7.95. Policy makers in the public sector must allocate scarce resources. Selecting the best policy can be aided by ''establishing the context, laying out the alternatives, predicting the consequences and valuing the outcomes.'' Models, simulations, cost-benefit analysis, decision trees and other techniques are introduced.

G. How Foreign Policy Is Made

20 – 75 *Public Opinion and American Democracy,* V.O. Key, Jr., 566pp, 1961, Knopf, $9.50. A study of public opinion which finds both political activists (broadly defined) and the masses play a significant role in shaping policy-making in American democracy. Key argues that the political activists play a crucial role in developing new ideas but that broad public opinion sets the boundaries within which policy-makers must act.

20 – 76 *The Public's Impact on Foreign Policy,* Bernard Cohen, 222pp, 1973, Little, Brown, O.P. Maintains the government is responsible to informed public opinion but not controlled by it.

20 – 77 *Political Process and Foreign Policy: The Making of the Japanese Peace Settlement,* Richard Cohen, 293pp, 1980, (1957), Princeton, $37.50. A classic study of the domestic processes in the U.S. involved in the formulation and approval of the peace settlement. Examines major elements in the American political system that have foreign policy-making roles and the interrelationships among them.

20 – 78 *Prejudice, War and the Constitution,* Jacobus Ten Broek, Edward Barnhart & Floyd Matson, 464pp, 1954, Calif., $5.95. A study of the ''causes and consequences'' of the evacuation of Japanese-Americans from their homes to internment camps in World War II.

20 – 79 *The American People and Foreign Policy,* Gabriel Almond, 269pp, 1960, Greenwood, $19.75. An assessment of American public attitudes and their impact on foreign policy decision-making.

20 – 80 *Invitation to Struggle: Congress, The President and Foreign Policy,* Cecil Crabb, Jr., & Pat Holt, 234pp, 1980, Congressional Quarterly, $7.75. Through case studies of the Panama Canal treaty ratification debate, the Middle East conflict, and human rights policy, the authority of each branch is clarified and the points of conflict identified.

20 – 81 *Interest Groups, Lobbying and Policymaking,* Norman Ornstein & Shirley Elder, 245pp, 1978, Congressional Quarterly, $6.95. Offers a case study of the B-1 Bomber's initial rejection and other issues to define the extent and limits of public impact on decisions.

See also Chapter 8, U.S. Foreign Policy, and Section K below.

H. Analyses of the Contemporary Age

20 – 82 *The Age of Discontinuity: Guidelines to Our Changing Society,* Peter Drucker, 402pp, 1978 (1968), Harper, $4.95. An impressionistic survey highlighting the

emergence of large organizations, the change from an international to a world economy and the political significance of knowledge.

20 – 83 *The Millennium Postponed: Socialism from Sir Thomas More to Mao Tse-Tung,* Edward Hyams, ed., 277pp, 1975, NAL, $3.95. Introduces the variety of socialist ideas and theories but concludes all have been rendered obsolete by the physical comfort of the masses and the power of the bureaucratic state.

20 – 84 *Essential Works of Socialism,* Irving Howe (ed.), 864pp, 1976, Bantam Books, $1.95. An anthology of socialist thought edited out of the conviction "that no compromise is possible between democratic socialists and the various defenders of authoritarian and totalitarian despotism who have appropriated the name of socialism."

20 – 85 *The American Commonwealth*, 1976, Nathan Glazer and Irving Kristol (eds.), 224pp, 1976, Basic, $3.95. An affectionate assessment of the American experience with Daniel P. Moynihan, Robert Nisbet, Martin Lipset and others participating.

20 – 86 *Inequality in the Age of Decline,* Paul Blumberg, 250pp, 1980, Oxford, $12.95. Assesses the impact scarcity may have on equality.

20 – 87 *Life Chances: Approaches to Social and Political Theory,* Ralf Dahrendorf, 181pp, 1980, Chicago, $15.00. Offers "life chances" — the opportunity for individual choice — as a measure of success in social change, and discusses the question of "legitimacy" of government and the waning consensus underlying Western democracies.

20 – 88 *The Last Half-Century, Societal Change and Politics in America,* Morris Janowitz, 583pp, 1978, Chicago, $7.95. Asserts that the period from 1920 to 1970 witnessed "the transformation of the United States from an industrialized nation to an advanced industrialized nation" and maintains a crucial problem in the new era is the establishment of legitimate authority.

20 – 89 *The Twilight of Capitalism,* Michael Harrington, 431pp, 1977, Simon & Schuster, $4.95. Dedicated to "the foe of every dogma, champion of human freedom and democratic socialist — Karl Marx," and claims modern capitalism is the source of most of problems of the 1970s. Harrington concludes we have three choices: totalitarianism, authoritarianism or democratic socialism. Capitalism is "self-destructive." Marx gave it fifty years in 1850; Harrington says the patient has been restored to life "by a miracle drug (the State) whose side effects will eventually kill him."

20 – 90 *Radical Political Economy: Capitalism & Socialism from a Marxist Humanist Perpective,* Howard Sherman, 431pp, 1972, Basic, $13.50. " . . . only a socialist revolution can lay the foundations for a society where there is equal opportunity for all people, continuing economic prosperity, freedom of expression in culture, politics and science and peace." Offers a "non-dogmatic," "democratic" approach to achieving a radical political economy: "socialism is a necessary condition of democracy, but not a sufficient one" (p. 312).

20–91 *The New Conservatives, A Critique from the Left*, Lewis Coser & Irving Howe, 323pp, 1977, Meridian, $9.95. A critique of neo-conservative intellectuals, "former liberals who got cold feet in the late 1960s; these essays defend equality, affirmative action and government planning against neo-conservative arguments.

20–92 *Breaking Ranks: A Political Memoir*, Norman Podhoretz, 448pp, 1980, Harper, $4.95. A "neo-conservative" explains why he believes liberalism needs to rethink its basic approach to social problems.

20–93 *Legitimacy in the Modern State*, John Schaar, 341pp, 1981, Transaction, $15.95. Maintains that legitimate authority is the basic political question of today because bureaucratized power, manipulated mass opinion, and the decline of public discourse have undermined it.

20–94 *The New American Political System*, Anthony King (ed.), 407pp, 1978, American Enterprise Institute, $9.25. Ten political scientists describe the changes since 1960 which, they conclude, add up to a new system.

20–95 *The New Industrial State*, John Galbraith, 404pp, (1979), 1972, NAL, $3.50. Argues that the large corporations "fix prices and go on extensively to accommodate the consumer to their needs" and advocates "a system of wage and price controls . . . neither inflation nor unemployment is an acceptable alternative."

20–96 *The Cultural Contradictions of Capitalism*, Daniel Bell, 304pp, 1970, Basic, $4.95. A "socialist in economics, a liberal in politics, and a conservative in culture" here examines the cultural manifestations of a society whose central feature is economic activity, not military or religious concerns. Asks whether "liberty and equality" are complementary or contradictory values and suggests the latter.

20–97 *Dialogues on American Politics*, Irving Horowitz & Seymour Lipset, 199pp, 1978, Oxford, $3.95. A discussion of the impact of material scarcity and other contemporary issues in American politics.

I. Problems: Do Democratic Institutions Help Or Hurt in their Solution?

20–98 *Violence in America, Historical & Comparative Perspectives*, Hugh Graham & Ted Gurr (eds.), 528pp, 1979, Sage, $9.95. Updates a 1969 governmentally commissioned study which found "a nation [whose] past was often marred by violence" but that was "neither unique nor beyond explanation and remedy" p. 10.

20–99 *The Meaning of McCarthyism*, Earl Latham (ed.), 198pp, 1973, Heath, $4.95. Traces the roots of McCarthyism to the 1930s and offers conflicting assessments of its meaning.

20–100 *The Ultimate Tyranny, The Majority over the Majority*, Eugene McCarthy, 256pp, 1980, Harcourt, Brace, Jovanovich, $12.95. McCarthy's 1976 Presidential campaign found the procedures of the Federal Election Campaign Law too cumbersome.

Other dangerous bureaucracies cited include the FCC, FBI, CIA, IRS and the Department of Education.

20 – 101 *Protest, Politics and Prosperity: Black Americans and White Institutions, 1940 – 75,* Dorothy Newman, et al, 345pp, 1978, Pantheon, $4.95. A critical survey of Black Americans' changing economic and social circumstances with a call for full employment.

20 – 102 *Assassination on Embassy Row,* John Dinges & Saul Landau, 411pp, 1980, Pantheon, $14.95. A detailed account of the killing in Washington of Orlando Letelier, Chilean diplomat under Allende.

20 – 103 *The American Police State: The Government Against the People,* David Wise, 437pp, 1978, Vintage, $4.95. Although presented as "how the CIA, FBI, IRS, NSA and other agencies have spied on Americans during seven administrations," it covers only the Nixon White House.

20 – 104 *Generating Inequality,* Lester Thurow, 258pp, 1975, Basic, $5.95. Outlines different rules for equity and suggests that by personally analyzing the rules through which one's own wealth was acquired one may gain some appreciation of the complexity of the problem.

20 – 105 *A Minority of Members, Women in the U.S. Congress,* Hope Chamberlin, 391pp, 1974, NAL, $2.25. Brief descriptions of the lives and politics of the seventy-three women who served in Congress from 1917-1973.

20 – 106 *From Brown to Bakke, The Supreme Court and School Integration 1954 – 1978,* J. Harvie Wilkinson, 368pp, 1979, Oxford, $17.95. Assesses both the victories and the losses in the efforts to achieve school integration; concludes that there is no single formula for successful integration but good reason to persist in the effort.

20 – 107 *The American Occupational Structure,* Peter Blau & Otis Uncan, 520pp, 1978, Free Press, $6.95. Concludes "a large amount of upward mobility is found in the American occupation structure. Upward movement far exceeds downward movement . . . Sons from all occupational origins participate in this upward movement."

20 – 108 *Who Gets Ahead? The Determinants of Economic Success in America,* Christopher Jencks, et al. 397pp, 1979, Basic, $17.50. An assessment of the Horatio Alger legend and the closed society analysis.

20 – 109 *The Permanent War Economy, American Capitalism in Decline,* Seymour Melman, 384pp, 1976, Simon & Schuster, $4.95. Maintains that American capitalism is hurt by, not in need of, large military budgets.

20 – 110 *Policing a Free Society,* Herman Goldstein, 371pp, 1977, Ballinger, $8.95. A useful assessment of policy/citizen/public authority issues and the legal and practical problems of police.

20 – 111 *Essays and Data on American Ethnic Groups,* Thomas Sowell, (ed.), 415pp, 1978, Urban Institute, $15.00. A study of different racial and ethnic groups, various

routes toward integration, and an assessment of current policies aimed at reducing inequalities.

J. The Citizen Peace Effort

Classic

20 – 112 *Peace or War: The American Struggle, 1636 – 1936,* Merle Curti, 374pp, 1959, Canner, $7.50. An important study of the various strands in the struggle for peace: religious pacifism, internationalism, and democratic liberalism.

20 – 113 *Twentieth Century Pacifism,* Peter Brock, 274pp, 1979, Van Nostrand Reinhold, $3.50. A history of the principal themes in pacifist thought and activity in this century — conscientious objection in World Wars I and II, Gandhian nonviolence and nuclear pacifism.

20 – 114 *American Thinking about Peace and War: New Essays on American Thought and Attitudes,* Ken Booth & Moorhead Wright (eds.), 1979, Barnes & Noble, $18.50. British and U.S. scholars examine 200 years of thought about peace and war.

20 – 115 *Peace Movements in America,* Charles Chatfield (ed.), 191pp, 1973, Schocken, $3.95. An anthology surveying American peace organizations of the past 100 years; focuses on pacifist, internationalist and peace research efforts.

20 – 116 *The Peace Reform in American History,* Charles DeBenedetti, 245pp, 1980, Indiana, $18.50. An overview of efforts for peace throughout American history.

20 – 117 *Pacifism in the United States: From the Colonial Era to the First World War,* Peter Brock, 1,005pp, 1968, Princeton, $25.00. A detailed history of religious and secular pacifism in America. The author argues that the failure to relate the quest for international peace to the attainment of justice and freedom within the national community was fatal to the peace efforts of the time.

20 – 118 *Response to Imperialism, The United States and the Philippine-American War, 1899 – 1902,* Richard Welch, Jr., 215pp, 1979, U. of North Carolina, $11.50. Describes America fighting in the Philippines and the opposition in America.

20 – 119 *Toward a Warless World, The Travail of the American Peace Movement, 1887 – 1914,* David Patterson, 352pp, 1976, Indiana, $15.00. Describes the various currents of thought and organizational structures during the period.

20 – 120 *The American Peace Movement and Social Reform, 1898 – 1918,* C. Roland Marchand, 441pp, 1972, Princeton, $17.50. Identifies many currents of thought — legalistic, arbitration, arms race opponents, socialist, pacifist — in the peace movement and concludes that domestic concerns shaped their attitudes more than international affairs.

20 – 121 *Eleven Against War: Studies in American Internationalist Thought, 1898 –*

1921, Sondra Herman, 264pp, 1969, Hoover, $2.95. A study of two strands of internationalist thought: one represented by Woodrow Wilson, Elihu Root and others, sought to abolish war through international political organization; the other sought the same end through economic progress.

20 – 122 *Opponents of War, 1917 – 1918,* H. Peterson & Gilbert Fite, 213pp, 1957, U. of Washington, $2.95. Summarizes the various types of opposition to American involvement in World War I and the public response to the opponents which included intolerance, even violence.

20 – 123 *Rebel Passion,* Vera Brittain, 240pp, 1964, Fellowship, $5.00. A study of the various leaders of the international pacifist movement including Norman Thomas, Martin Niemoller, J. Nevin Sayre, and others.

20 – 124 *For More Than Bread: An Autobiographical Account of Twenty-Two Years' Work with the American Friends Service Committee,* Clarence Pickett, 433pp, 1953, Little, Brown, $5.00. A detailed account of the AFSC's peace and related activities during the 1930s and 1940s.

20 – 125 *Women's International League for Peace and Freedom, 1915 – 1965,* Gertrude Bussey & Margaret Time, 255pp, 1965, George Allen & Unwin, $6.75. A detailed record of the origins and development of the WILPF including officers, policy stands, and organizational activity.

20 – 126 *For Peace and Justice: Pacifism in America, 1914 – 1941,* Charles Chatfield, 447pp, 1973, Beacon, $4.45. A study of pacifist attempts to develop a political coalition capable of translating their ideal into reality.

20 – 127 *To End War: The Study of the National Council for the Prevention of War,* Frederick Libby, 188pp, 1969, Fellowship, O.P. The Executive Secretary describes the efforts of his organization to mobilize American voluntary organizations for peace from 1921 to 1954. Portrays the shift in emphasis within the peace movement from supporting world organization in 1921 to neutrality in foreign wars in the 1930s without apparent recognition of the difference. An important document on the peace movement.

20 – 128 *Origins of the Modern American Peace Movement, 1915 – 1929,* Charles DeBenedetti, 281pp, 1978, KTO Press, $15.00. A history of the emergence of secular, democratic ideas in what had been a primarily religious based movement, now concerned about total war between industrialized States. The faith that independence and the right of self-determination would bring peace gives way before social revolution.

20 – 129 *Peace Prophet: American Pacifist Thought, 1919 – 1941,* John Nelson, 192pp, 1968, North Carolina, O.P. Demonstrates that the divergent types of pacifist thought originate in a common religious perspective. Sharply critical of the political alliances and mistaken political judgments made by some pacifists between the World Wars.

20 – 130 *Doves and Diplomats: Foreign Offices and Peace Movements in Europe and America in the Twentieth Century,* Soloman Wank (ed.), 303pp, 1978, Greenwood,

$18.50. A generally critical assessment of the citizen peace efforts that laments, among other things, the focus on single issues, the narrow base of public support, and the absence of strategy for influencing government.

20 – 131 *Rebels Against War: The American Peace Movement, 1941 – 1960,* Lawrence Wittner, 339pp, 1969, Columbia, $2.95. A study of the backbone of the American peace movement in the post-World War II period. A sympathetic treatment of many diverse groups.

20 – 132 *More Power than We Know: The People's Movement Toward Democracy,* Dave Dellinger, 326pp, 1975, Doubleday, $3.95. Traces the evolution of a nonviolent protest movement into a movement committed to insurrectionary violence in the 1960s. One chapter is titled "Losing Our Way."

20 – 133 *Protest: Pacifism and Politics,* James Finn (ed.), 511pp, 1968, Random House, O.P. Interviews with a wide variety of pacifist and radical opponents of American military power.

TEW

20 – 134 *Neither Victims Nor Executioners,* Albert Camus, 62pp, 1972, World Without War Publications, $4.95. Camus' classic essay delineating the line between those who justify the use of mass violence in politics and those who refuse to do so. The introductory essay by Robert Pickus discusses some actions of the peace movement of the 1960s that blurred that distinction.

20 – 135 *Uphill for Peace: Quaker Impact on Congress,* E. Raymond Wilson, 432pp, 1975, Friends United Press, $7.95. An autobiographical account of Quaker work in Washington largely through the Friends Committee on National Legislation (FCNL).

K. Left and Right

20 – 136 *The Politics of Unreason: Right Wing Extremism in America, 1790 – 1977,* Seymour M. Lipset & Earl Rabb, 605pp, 1978 (2nd ed.), Chicago, $7.95. An historical overview of conspiracy theorists, fear-mongers, and demogogues of the right; concludes American political institutions withstood the tests of the 1960s and 1970s.

20 – 137 *The Odyssey of the American Right,* Michael Miles, 371pp, 1980, Oxford, $19.95. A brief history from the New Deal to the Nixon Presidency.

20 – 138 *The Divided Left: American Radicalism 1900 – 1975,* Milton Canton, 248pp, 1978, Hill & Wang, $11.95. An overview of the American Left addressed, in part, to the question of why socialist movements have failed to achieve a mass base in America.

20 – 139 *The Radical Left: The Abuse of Discontent,* William Gerberding & Duane Smith (eds.), 366pp, 1970, Houghton Mifflin, $4.00. A collection of essays, generally critical, on the New Left of the 1960s.

20 – 140 *Anti-Politics in America: Reflections on the Anti-Political Temper and Its Distortions of the Democratic Process,* John Bunzel, 291pp, 1970, Random, $1.95. A searching analysis of why so many on the left and right and in religious sects fail to understand democratic politics.

20 – 141 *Intellectuals and Other Traitors,* Bernard Brown, 196pp, 1980, Ark, $12.95. A critique of New Left and Western intellectuals' rejection of representative democracy.

20 – 142 *Highlights of a Fighting History: 60 Years of the Communist Party USA,* Philip Bart, Theodore Bassett, William Neinstone & Arthur Zipser (eds.), 526pp, 1979, International Publishers, $5.25. An anthology of party statements and social analysis by editors whose "aggregate Party membership is 200 years."

20 – 143 *Something to Guard, The Stormy Life of the National Guardian, 1948 – 1967,* Cedric Belfrage & James Aronson, 362pp, 1979, Columbia, $19.95. Described as the first "non-communist, radical newspaper" in the post-World War II era by the authors.

L. Coalitions?

20 – 144 *The Lesser Evil? The Left Debates the Democratic Party and Social Change,* Michael Harrington & Peter Camejo, 128pp, 1977, Pathfinder, $1.75. A debate between socialists about tactics, third party movements, and how to transform America.

20 – 145 *Homage to Catalonia*, George Orwell, 232pp, 1952, Harvest, O.P. The failure of a united front examined — underlines the difficulties in cooperating with groups with antithetical political objectives and only one common denominator — an enemy.

20 – 146 *Democracy and the Student Left,* George F. Kennan, 208pp, 1968, Bantam, $1.50. An exchange between Kennan and student activitists on the values of democratic decisions-making, rationality in debate and constructive opposition, i.e. opposition which combines a denunciation of current policies with a prescription of thoughtful alternatives.

20 – 147 *An Infantile Disorder? The Crisis and Decline of the New Left,* Nigel Young, 490pp, 1980, Westview, $25.00. A sharp critique of the New Left by a former participant.

20 – 148 *After the Revolution? Authority in a Good Society,* Robert Dahl, 171pp, 1970, Yale, $3.95. An analysis of principles, problems and solutions in any society that seeks both to have and to limit governmental authority.

M. Assessments

20 – 149 *Polls, The Use and Misuse in Politics,* Charles Roll, Jr., & Albert Cantril,

224pp, 1980, Seven Locks Press, $5.95. Assesses the uses of public opinion polls in mainstream politics and how they can be abused; makes the case for the citizens' appropriate role in setting foreign policy goals.

20 – 150 *Public Interest Lobbies: Decision Making on Energy,* Andrew McFarland, 141pp, 1976, American Enterprise Institute, $3.00. Assesses the rise of public interest groups (1965-1975) and outlines how six organizations sought to influence energy policy and their success.

20 – 151 *Lobbying for the People, The Political Behavior of Public Interest Groups,* Jeffrey Berry, 331pp, 1977, Princeton, $5.95. An interesting well-researched study of what leads to the formation of voluntary organizations, how they survive and what is effective and ineffective in influencing Congress. Includes a case study of the WILPF (Women's International League for Peace and Freedom).

20 – 152 *Polling on the Issues, Twenty-One Perspectives on the Role of Opinion Polls in the Making of Public Policy.,* Albert Cantril (ed.), 210pp, 1980, Seven Locks Press, $7.95. Articles by Gallup, Roper, and Field make this a state of the art work; the article ''with a Grain of Salt (II)'' provides insight into the mixed public view of the Treaty and of the groups trying to influence the ratification debate.

TEW

20 – 153 *The Citizen Peace Effort, 1930 to 1980,* George Weigel, 60pp, 1981, World Without War Council, $1.00. Offers an assessment of the primary teachings of the peace movements in different periods, and suggests how the basic questions every peace organization addresses could best be answered in the 1980s.

RESOURCE A: A TYPOLOGY OF WORLD AFFAIRS ORGANIZATIONS

Many non-governmental organizations in the United States influence Americans' understanding of and competence in world affairs. This typology distinguishes nine distinctive purposes of such organizations and provides examples of each. Many organizations fit in more than one category and other categories could be added. Not included, for example, is the world of private philanthropy. Organizations which work directly abroad or which are established and funded by governments are also not included. The typology is designed to provide an overview of the world affairs field and to help you decide where within it you want to help.

Categories	Definitions and Examples
I. ''Mainstream'' Organizations	mass organizations, present in most American communities; formed for other purposes, maintain as one of their activities

	regular and usually staffed programs on foreign policy and world affairs problems.
A. Religious	e.g. U.S. Catholic Conference, Commission on Justice and Peace
B. Business	U.S. Chamber of Commerce; Rotary International
C. Professional	American Bar Association
D. Labor	AFL-CIO Department of International Affairs
E. Youth	U.S. National Student Association
F. Women	American Association of University Women
G. Scientific	American Association for the Advancement of Science
H. Civic	League of Women Voters; YMCA
I. Ethnic	American Jewish Committee, NAACP
II. Arena Organizations	offer a platform for foreign policy, world affairs education and policy discussion from a variety of perspectives.
A. General Audience	City World Affairs Councils, Foreign Policy Association
B. Specialized Constituency	Farmers and World Affairs
C. Problem-Focused	Council on Religion and International Affairs
III. Advocacy Organizations	offer a distinctive ethical, analytical or policy perspective described as contributing to progress toward peace or security.
A. Ideologically Based	embodying a developed ideological perspective, e.g. Socialist Workers Party; American Nazi Party
B. Perspective Setting	concerned with a range of issues and problems but all set in a distinctive context, e.g. Institute for World Order, United Nations Association, Fellowship of Reconciliation, Young Americans for Freedom
C. Problem-Area Focused	focused on education/action in a specific

substantive area, e.g. Arms Control Association, Committee on the Present Danger, Amnesty International

D. Constituency-Focused — organizing or addressing a specific constituency, e.g. Federation of American Scientists, Members of Congress for Peace through Law

E. Single Issue — e.g. Americans for SALT

F. Lobbying — seek to influence national legislation, e.g. Friends Committee on National Legislation, Ripon Society, New Directions

G. Ad Hoc Protest — usually formed around the immediate, publically visible issue or crisis, e.g. Stop the Draft Now!

IV Functional Organizations — provide a specific service.

A. Exchange of People — e.g. American Field Service; Citizen Exchange Corps

B. Development & Aid Programs — e.g. Asia Foundation; CARE, Oxfam

C. Foreign Visitors — e.g. National Council for Community Services to International Visitors

V. Special Purpose — undertake a very specific task.

A. Distinctive Task — Sister Cities International

B. Distinctive Audience — Council on International Programs for Youth Leaders

C. Special Area/Country Focus — e.g. African-American Institute; Japan Society

D. Specific Goal — U.S. Committee for the U.N. University

E. Training — e.g. International Peace Academy

F. Institutionally Focused — World Peace through Law Center

G. Advisory to Government — U.S. National Comm. for UNESCO

VI. Research and Study Center — provide an institutional setting for study and research.

A. University-based Area Studies — e.g. Middle East Studies Institute

B. University-based Problem Centered

e.g. Center for the Study of Armaments and Disarmament

C. Nationalities

e.g. Joint Committee on Eastern Europe

D. Conflict

e.g. Institute for Psychiatry & Foreign Affairs

E. Policy Studies

e.g. Center for Strategic & International Studies, Brookings Institution, Institute for Policy Studies

F. Professional

e.g. American Society for International Law

G. Problem Focused

e.g. Overseas Development Council

VII. Formal Education

accredited public and private educational institutions.

A. Pre-Collegiate

e.g. National Council for the Social Studies

B. Junior College

e.g. Amer. Assoc. of Community & Jr. Colleges

C. College

e.g. Amer. Assoc. of State Colleges & Universities

D. University

e.g. Council of Graduate Schools in the U.S.

E. Adult

e.g. National Advisory Council on Extension and Education

VIII. Related Educational Organizations

offer program services and act as a catalyst to formal educational structures.

A. Exchange of Students

e.g. Institute of International Education

B. Pre-Collegiate

e.g. Global Perspectives in Education

C. Research

e.g. Conference on Peace Research, Education and Development

D. Foreign Students

e.g. National Assoc. for Foreign Student Affairs

E. Advocacy

e.g. Amer. Professors for a Middle East Peace

F. Professional

e.g. Conf. on Peace Research in History

IX. Overview Organizations

seek to influence the development of the field as a whole or subsections thereof.

A. Non-partisan   e.g. International Studies Association,
                                         World Without War Council

B. Partisan   e.g. Coalition for a New Foreign & Military
                                         Policy

RESOURCE B: A SELECT LIST OF WORLD AFFAIRS ORGANIZATIONS[5]

The organizations listed here illustrate every type of organization in the typology (Resource A). The focus is on American organizations active in the non-governmental, world affairs field, but a few international non-governmental organizations are included also. The list is presented in alphabetical order with the exception of U.S. Peace Studies programs, International Peace and Related Institutes, and U.S. International Studies Centers, which are listed separately at the end. The roman numeral next to the name of the organization indicates where we believe it best fits in the typology.

A few types of organizations are not included. For example, ad hoc groups are not listed despite the fact that for a season they may dominate the news. Unaffiliated community-based groups are also not listed, although they undertake the enormously difficult, and occasionally rewarding, task of sustained work at the local level. In any given year just in the United States, one can find between fifteen hundred and two thousand such ad hoc and community-based groups. The number changes rapidly depending on the public mood and international events. Most follow a predictable and short-lived curve of enthusiasm, frustration, discouragement, and dissolution. The organizations named here are, for the most part, a continuing component of the American voluntary organization world. They have staff, well-articulated statements of purpose and policy, clear channels for decision-making, and continuing program goals. But even so, many lack genuine, sizable constituency, and have inadequate staff and modest funding.

The list includes most of the stable organizations working toward the constructive engagement of this country in world affairs, particularly those which seek constructive change and the non-military resolution of international conflict, but it also includes others with different goals.

A person considering work with one or more world affairs organizations should request their descriptive brochures and information about current programs, policies, and possible work opportunities. Such brochures were re-

[5]The information in this resource was prepared by Janet Mackey, a graduate of the University of Chicago and a Peace Interne with the World Without War Council – Midwest during the 1980/81 program year.

quested for the compilation of this list. If the annotation below is enclosed in quotation marks, it was taken from the organization's brochure. Most brochures do not, however, tell you how the organizations are distinct from others in the field, what judgments shape the intellectual focus of their programs, or how, specifically, they work to advance their purpose. It is best to evaluate carefully a variety of organizations before committing time or money. Resource C is designed to help in this evaluation.

Academy for Educational Development VIII C
680 Fifth Ave., New York, NY 10019
212-397-0040

The Academy is an education research and planning organization which has done work in areas of international relations, international negotiation, and global education. It also provides some technical assistance to developing countries.

Ad Hoc Committee on the Human Rights and Genocide Treaties V D
25 E. 78th St., New York, NY 10021
212-535-3700

"A national coalition of civic, labor, religious and ethnic organizations established in 1964 to promote and encourage the advancement of human rights and fundamental freedoms for all, through legally binding conventions and strengthening of world law in this field."

Africa Studies Association VI C
218 Shiffman Center, Waltham, MA 02154
617-899-3079

This independent, non-profit organization is currently located at Brandeis University. It collects, stores, inventories, and promotes research on Africa. Publications include *Issue, African Studies Review,* and *African Studies Newsletter.*

African-American Institute IV A
833 UN Plaza, New York, NY 10017
212-949-5666

"Helps African students get a secondary education in the United States."

African Development Bank IV B
P.O. Box 1387, Abidjan, Republic of the Ivory Coast, West Africa
"Technical assistance/concessional loans, half of them agricultural."

Africare IV B
1601 Connecticut Ave., NW, Washington, D.C. 20009
202-462-3614

"Operates and helps fund rural development programs."

Agricultural Cooperative Development International V E
1012 14th St., NW, Suite 201, Washington, D.C. 20005
202-638-4661
"Consulting and management assistance organization created by the leading agriculture cooperatives and farmer organizations in the United States."

Agricultural Missions IV B
475 Riverside Dr., Room 624, New York, NY 10027
212-870-2553
"Interdenominational agency serving Christian rural work overseas; clearinghouse for information and services for church bodies and mission boards working abroad; recruits and trains for service in agricultural, home life and community development projects; provides technical supplies and assistance in program planning and field studies; publishes *Rural Missions, Christian Rural Fellowship Bulletin.*

The Alan Guttmacher Institute VIII E
360 Park Ave., S., New York, NY 10010
212-685-5858
"Conducts research, public policy analysis and public education in the field of family planning and population. An affiliate of the Planned Parenthood Federation of America, the national family planning agency."

Alternatives, Inc.
1924 E. Third, Bloomington, IN 47401
A public, non-profit organization providing publications dealing with disarmament, transnational corporations, security, hunger, justice and conflict resolution.

American Academy of Political and Social Science II B
3937 Chestnut St., Philadelphia, PA 19104
215-386-4594
"Since 1889 the Academy has served as a common meeting ground for those who have our social and political responsibilities at heart. Its 16,000 members include leading educators, business persons, and professional people." Publishes *The Annals* (bimonthly), holds an annual spring meeting and occasional conferences, and publishes monographs.

American Assembly II B
Columbia University, New York, NY 10027
212-280-3455
"Conducts international, national, regional, state and local Assemblies for community leaders on public affairs issues. Services: Background publi-

cations on Assembly topics, Assemblies' findings and policy recommendations.''

American Association for the Advancement of Science I G
1515 Massachusetts Ave., NW, Washington, D.C. 20005
202-467-4400

"Over 130,000 members in all 50 states and more than 140 other countries, who despite varied backgrounds, nationalities and specialities, . . . have many things in common, including a desire to improve themselves through the publications, meetings, and other activities of the Association and to promote increased public understanding of science and technology.''

American Association for the International Commission of Jurists III C
777 UN Plaza, New York, NY 10017
212-972-0883

"Judges, law professors, attorneys and other members of the legal community in the U.S. dedicated to the promotion of the rule of law through the preservation and dissemination of material on human rights.''

American Association of University Women I F
2401 Virginia Ave., NW Washington, D.C. 20037
202-785-7700

"Conducts study, discussion and action programs; cultural exchange; awards exchange fellowships; takes legislative action; issues study and program materials.''

American Baptist Churches, USA I A
Peace Concerns Program
Valley Forge, PA 19481
215-768-2412

"Our purpose . . . is to make people in the denomination aware of the dangers and moral implications of nuclear weapons and military spending. We seek to accomplish this by giving talks, leading workshops, distributing information, and establishing a network of people in the denomination interested in dealing with the issue of world peace.''

American Baptist Convention, Division of Christian Social Concern I A
Valley Forge, PA 19481
215-768-2000

"Conducts education and action programs on national and international matters; issues study guides on world affairs topics; conducts seminars with special program emphasis on national priorities, military problems, international development.'' Publishes *Concerns for Christian Citizens* (8 times/yr.), Mission (monthly), and *Crusader*(monthly).

American Bar Association, World Order Under Law Committee I C
1800 M ST., NW, Washington, D.C. 20036
202-331-2000
Assesses international treaties and other developments in international law.

American Civil Liberties Union III C
132 W. 43rd St., New York, NY 10036
212-944-9800
"The ACLU is the guardian of the Bill of Rights which guarantees fundamental civil liberties to all of us. . . . When the ACLU was founded in 1920, it consisted of a hundred men and women who were concerned primarily with the rights of conscientious objectors. Though its membership has swelled, and its programs are the broadest of any public interest group in the country, its fundamental ideals remain unchanged: to protect and extend those liberties that inhere to each of us, and by so doing, to create a just humane society for all of us." Affiliates in most states.

American Committee on Africa V C
198 Broadway, New York, NY 10038
212-962-1210
Although founded in order to provide support for African decolonization, the American Committee now acts as lobbyist, political action group, and information base on U.S. foreign policy towards Africa.

American Committee on East-West Accord III B
227 Massachusetts Ave., NE, Suite 300, Washington, D.C. 20002
202-546-1700
Seeks "to reduce tensions between East and West, particularly between the U.S. and the USSR by promoting arms control, non-strategic trade, and exchange programs."

American Council for the United Nations University V D
1211 Kenbar Court, McLean, VA 22101
703-241-1815
"Promote(s) American support of the University as an autonomous body within the framework of the United Nations devoted to the advancement of knowledge about urgent global problems under conditions of academic freedom and objectivity."

American Council on Education VIII C
1 Dupont Circle, Washington, D.C. 20036
202-833-4700

An independent higher education association working as a coordinating body for post-secondary institutions. Serves as the voice of American higher education in Washington and abroad. Serves as an umbrella organization for many international projects (Council for International Exchange of Scholars, International Education Project).

American Council of Voluntary Agencies for Foreign Service IX A
200 Park Ave. S., New York, NY 10003
212-777-8210

"Provides a forum for cooperation, joint planning and the exchange of ideas and information, to avoid duplication of effort and assure the maximum effectiveness of the relief, rehabilitation and development programs of American voluntary agencies following WWII. Operates the Technical Assistance Information Clearinghouse (TAICH), an information center specializing in the socio-economic development programs abroad of U.S. voluntary agencies, missions, foundations and other non-profit organizations." Publishes country reports and directories of organizations.

American Enterprise Institute for Public Policy Research VI E
1150 17th St., NW, Washington, D.C. 20036
202-862-5800

"Conducts research, publication, and TV programs on a range of public policy issues." Its materials are invariably substantial and present an intelligent conservative perspective.

American Ethical Union III B
2 West 64th St., New York, NY 10023
212-873-6500

This private, non-profit organization does research and puts on conferences dealing with human rights, peace, women, the environment, and ethics.

American Federation of Labor-Congress of Industrial Organizations (AFL-CIO)
Department of International Affairs
815 16th St., NW, Washington, D.C. 20006
202-637-5000

"Focuses on issues of political and human rights central to free trade unionism and maintains contact with labor organizations around the world. Through its three auxiliary institutes it conducts training programs and provides aid for labor unions in developing countries. A major force in foreign policy debate, committed to internationalist goals and to peaceful settlement, skeptical of detente if it does not aid liberalizing currents in the Soviet Union or permits USSR military superiority. Critical of all totalitarian and authoritarian rule, both from the right and left, that denies workers their basic human rights and freedoms. Strong advocates of 'fair' trade policies.''

AFS: International/Intercultural Programs Inc. IV A
313 E. 43rd St., New York, NY 10017
212-661-4550
''AFS is students, families, and volunteers in approximately 60 countries who share in the learning and excitement of a high school exchange experience.''

American Freedom from Hunger Foundation III F
1625 I St., NW, Washington, D.C. 20006
202-254-3487
''Citizen support lobby for UN/FAO through fund-raising, testimony before Congress, conferences.''

American Friends Service Committee III B
1501 Cherry St., Philadelphia, PA 19102
215-241-7000
''As a Quaker organization, the AFSC carries on its programs as an expression of a belief in the dignity and worth of each person, and in a faith in the power of love and nonviolence to bring about change.'' Has 10 regional offices.

American Immigration and Citizenship Conference III C
20 W. 40th St., New York, NY 10018
212-221-6750
A 50-year old organization concerned with immigration and refugee policy for the U.S. It seeks to bring together non-profit, non-political groups working for a humanitarian policy.

American Institute of Nutrition I C
9650 Rockville Pike, Bethesda, MD 20014
301-530-7050
''Professional society of experimental nutrition scientists.''

American Jewish Committee 1 I
165 E. 56th St., New York, NY 10022
212-751-4000

"To enlighten and clarify public opinion on problems of Jewish concern, to fight bigotry and protect human rights, and to promote Jewish cultural interests and creative achievement in America."

American Jewish Joint Distribution Committee, Inc. IV B
60 E. 42nd St., New York, NY 10017
212-687-6200

"The major American agency serving Jewish communities abroad. The JDC receives its funds mainly from the campaigns of the United Jewish Appeal."

American Legion III D
700 N. Pennsylvania St., Indianapolis, IN 46204
317-637-6649

Seeks to be second to none in its advocacy of achieving national security through military preparedness.

American Library Association IC
50 E. Huron St., Chicago, IL 60611
312-944-6780

A professional association of librarians; publishes a list of recommended books; concerned about freedom of speech in the U.S. and elsewhere.

American Near East Refugee Aid IV B
1522 K St., NW, #202, Washington, D.C. 20005
202-347-2558

ANERA works "to increase total assistance in cash and kind from Americans to Palestinian refugees and other needy individuals in the Arab world. ANERA also responds to civilian emergencies, usually the result of conflict in the area, and seeks to increase American understanding of the plight of the Palestinians."

American Peace Society III B
4000 Albemarle St., NW, Washington, D.C. 20016
202-362-6195

"Seeks to illuminate through its publication, *World Affairs,* the issues involved in international conflict. Articles are published on international relations, law and organization, foreign policy, comparative politics, theory, and diplomatic history."

American Political Science Association I C
1527 New Hampshire, NW, Washington, D.C. 20036
202-483-2512

"The major professional organization in the U.S. whose members are engaged in the study of politics. Founded in 1903, the Association provides members with services to facilitate research, teaching, and professional development."

American Professors for Peace in the Middle East VIII E
9 E. 40th St., New York, NY 10016
212-532-5005

A group of professors working in support of Israel. Publishes *Bulletin* (five times per year).

American Red Cross IV B
17th and D Sts., NW, Washington, D.C. 20006
202-737-8300

"Emergency relief and extensive social/health services."

American Universities Field Staff VIII C
4 W. Wheelock St., Hanover, NH 03755
603-643-2110

A private, non-profit organization doing research, training, conferences, and publications dealing with international relations, politics, and peaceful coexistence.

Americans for Constitutional Action V A
955 L'Enfant Plaza N., SW, Washington, D.C. 20024
202-484-5525

A political action organization "convinced that if a significant number of dedicated and determined constitutional conservatives are elected to the Congress of the U.S. they will retard and, eventually, reverse the current massive movement of our Nation into Socialism and a regimented society";compiles voting records, does fundraising.

Americans For Democratic Action (ADA) IIIF
1411 K St., NW #850, Washington, D.C. 20005
202-638-6447

"Has consistantly given leadership in the efforts to bring about reductions in U.S. aid to governments guilty of consistent and gross violations of human rights." Once the major liberal presence in Washington, still an important voice.

Americans for Middle East Understanding V C
475 Riverside Dr., Room 771, New York, NY 10027
212-870-2053
   Founded in 1967 to foster understanding in America of the Middle East
and of forces which are shaping American policy in the Middle East, and to
strengthen friendships between all the people of the Middle East and people
of the U.S.

Americans Veterans Committee V B
1346 Connecticut Ave., NW, Suite 930, Washington, D.C. 20036
202-293-4890
   "To achieve a more democratic and prosperous America and a more stable
world."

Amnesty International III C
304 W. 58th St., New York, NY 10019
212-582-4440
Headquarters:
10 Southhampton St., London WC2E 7HF, England
   "A worldwide, independent, non-profit human rights movement working
for the release of prisoners of conscience, people imprisoned anywhere for
their political or religious beliefs, color, ethnic origin, language or sex
provided they have neither used nor advocated violence."

Another Mother for Peace III B
407 North Maple Dr., Beverly Hills, CA 90210
   "A non-profit, non-partisan association whose goal is to eliminate war as a
means of settling disputes between nations, peoples and ideologies."

The Arms Control Association III C
11 Dupont Circle, NW, Washington, D.C. 20036
202-797-6450
   "A non-partisan, membership organization formed in 1971 by a group of
concerned individuals with extensive experience in the field of arms control
and national security policy. Its purpose is to promote understanding of arms
control and its contribution to national security. It acts as a clearinghouse for
information and a catalyst for innovative thinking and fresh initiatives."

The Asia Society V C
725 Park Ave., New York, NY 10021
212-288-6400
   "To increase American understanding and appreciation of current Asian

realities — both problems and achievements — and to educate Americans about the traditional cultures and civilizations of Asia.''

Asia Monitor Resource Center
464 19th St., Oakland, CA 94612
415-835-4691

"Provides all who are concerned about the impact of U.S economic and military power on the nations and working people of Asia with systematically compiled information on topics such as: transnational corporations, the export of hazardous products to Asia, and the U.S. military's role in Asia.''

Asian Development Bank V A
P.O. Box 789, Manila, Philippines
"Development loans.''

Aspen Institute for Humanistic Studies II B
717 Fifth Ave., New York, NY 10022
212-759-1053

"An international, non-profit organization that for more than thirty years has brought together leading citizens from the public and private sectors in the U.S. and abroad to consider interrelated issues of the human mind and spirit in contemporary society . . . . All Institute activities are designed to develop approaches to current issues, identify the implications of alternative approaches and propose possible policies and actions for resolving issues.''

Assembly of Captive European Nations III D
150 Fifth Ave., #832, New York, NY 10011
212-255-9549

Association of East European-Americans and immigrants seeking to free their countries from Soviet domination and communist rule.

Association for Childhood Education International VIII B
3615 Wisconsin Ave., NW, Washington, D.C. 20016
202-363-6963

Concerned with children, their education and their needs around the world. "Members in more than 70 countries . . . look to ACEI for support as they work to improve the quality of life for children everywhere.'' Publishes *Childhood Education.*

Association for Supervision and Curriculum Development (ASCD) VII A
225 N. Washington St., Alexandria, VA 22314
703-549-9110

"Members have joined together for the improvement of curriculum, instruction, and supervision.''

Association for World Education V B
P.O. Box 589, Huntington, NY 11743
516-549-4143

"Studies world issues through problem-oriented and experimental approaches; promotes intercommunication among colleges, universities, and post-secondary institutions for research centers which are working toward a global view in education." Publishes *Journal of World Education*.

Association of Catholic Colleges and Universities VII C
1 Dupont Circle, Suite 770, Washington, D.C. 20036
202-293-5954

Promotes "education for justice" and believes "that it is crucial for our Catholic colleges and universities to discover their unique way of contributing to the effort to mediate justice and peace to a world of war and injustices."

Association of Teachers of Latin American Studies (ATLAS) I C
P.O. Box 73, Lefferts Station, Brooklyn, NY 11225
212-756-0890

"An organization of educators and other persons interested in promoting the study of Latin America in our educational institutions. Inherent in this objective is the desire to increase the understanding of our hemispheric neighbors through a realistic and accurate portrayal of its peoples, languages, customs and heritage."

Atlantic Council of the United States III F
1616 H St., NW, Washington, D.C. 20006
202-347-9353

A non-profit educational organization working with similar organizations in NATO and OECD countries formulating recommendations for action on problems of international significance and presenting these to elected officials in the U.S. and abroad. "The end goal of the Atlantic Council is to encourage and assist the development of free, representative, and democratic political institutions in which consultation is continuous, in order to enable the Atlantic Community to deal adequately with problems with which no existing nation-state can cope successfully alone."

Baptist World Aid, Baptist World Alliance IV B
1628 16th St., NW, Washington, D.C. 20009
202-265-5127

"Relief, development and fellowship assistance programs."

Boy Scouts of America I E
International Relationships Service
U.S. Highway 1, North Brunswick, NJ 08902
201-249-6000
    Administers international scouting programs.

Bread for the World III C,D,F,
32 Union Square East, New York, NY 10009
212-260-7000
    "Christian education/direct action on hunger and poverty . . . .Our
membership is grouped according to state and congressional district so that
selected Congresspersons can be reached."

Brethren Service Committee
1451 Dundee Ave., Elgin, IL 60120
312-742-5100
    The service committee of one of the three historic peace churches; the staff
has been active in Middle East relief work with Palestinians on the West
Bank and through the National Council of Churches on mutual recognition of
Palestine and Israel. Is active on other projects as well.

Broadcasting Foundation of America V A
52 Vanderbilt Ave., Ste. 1810, New York, NY 10017
212-986-6448
    A cultural and educational institution which distributes "selected radio
programs from over 100 foreign countries to commerical and non-
commercial radio stations in the United States."

Brookings Institution VI E
1775 Massachusetts Ave., NW, Washington, D.C. 20036
202-797-6000
    "A private, non-profit organization devoted to research, education, and
publication in economics, government, foreign policy, and the social sciences generally. Its principal purpose is to bring knowledge to bear on the
current and emerging public policy problems facing the American people."

Bureau of Social Science Research VI G
1990 M St., NW, Washington, D.C. 20036
202-223-4300
    Doing research and documentation on social problems including interna-
tional comparisons of social indicators, health services, poverty, communication, and urban problems.

Business Executives Move for New National Priorities III D
901 N. Howard St., Baltimore, MD 21201
301-837-5600

"A nationwide organization of business owners and executives opposed to excessive military spending and favoring meeting more adequately urgent domestic needs. BEM believes the present emphasis on military power decreases our nation's true security and undermines its political, economic and social progress."

California Institute of International Studies VIII D
766 Santa Ynez, Stanford, CA 94305
415-322-2026

Research organization studying international affairs, especially Soviet foreign policy and Latin America. Publishes *World Affairs Report*.

Campaign for UN Reform III F
600 Valley Rd., Wayne, NJ 07470
703-524-2078, 201-694-6333

"Seeks to implement 14-point program to improve the United Nations by lobbying and working to elect Congresspeople who support the Campaign's program. Also evaluates Congressional voting records."

Campaign for World Parliament V D
National Press Bldg., Ste. 440, Washington, D.C. 20045
202-638-2662

Seeks to create a world parliament by direct election of delegates who would then gather to make laws.

CARE (Cooperative for American Relief Everywhere) IV B
660 First Ave., New York, NY 10016
212-686-3110

CARE is a non-profit international development agency focusing on assistance to developing countries through food, medical aid, and self-help partnership programs. In addition, CARE provides disaster relief when requested by a CARE country.

Carnegie Endowment for International Peace II A
11 Dupont Circle, NW, Washington, D.C. 20036
202-797-6400
and
30 Rockefeller Plaza, New York, NY 10112
212-572-8200

"As an operating (not a grant-making) foundation, the Carnegie Endowment conducts its own programs of research, discussion, publication, and education in international affairs and American foreign policy. Program areas change periodically. The Endowment also engages in several co-located joint ventures with other tax-exempt organizations to reinvigorate and extend the domestic and foreign dialogue on world affairs issues. The Endowment publishes the quarterly, *Foreign Policy.*"

Catholic Peace Fellowship III B D
339 Lafayette St., New York, NY 10012
212-673-8990

"The purpose of the Catholic Peace Fellowship is to educate and initiate action programs toward peace and in the spirit of Christian nonviolence. Our focus at present is on disarmament, the impending draft and Central America."

Catholic Relief Services IV B
1011 First Ave., New York, NY 10022
212-838-4700

"Crisis relief, also technical assistance for pilot agricultural projects/training programs/improved food storage facilities."

Catholic Worker Movement III B, D
36 E. First St., New York, NY 10003
212-254-1640

Founded by Dorothy Day, this organization expresses pacifist and anarchist values in its work with the poor in this society.

Center for California Public Affairs VI E
226 W. Foothill Blvd., P.O. Box 10, Claremont, CA 91711
714-624-5212

Non-profit research organization interested in California public affairs, but emphasizing environmental and energy policy in the U.S. and abroad. Includes the Public Affairs Clearinghouse of reference works and directories on world and national affairs.

Center for Defense Information III C
122 Maryland Ave., NE, Washington, D.C. 20002
202-543-0400

"A non-profit, non-partisan, public interest organization dedicated to making available continuing, objective information and analyses of our national defense — information which is free of the special interest of any government, military, political, or industrial organization . . . Supports a strong defense but opposes excessive expenditures or forces. It believes that strong social, economic and political structures contribute equally to national security and are essential to the strength and welfare of our country."

Center for International Policy VI E
120 Maryland Ave., NE, Washington, D.C. 20002
202-544-4666
"Non-profit research group concerned with studying the impact of U.S. foreign policy on developing nations, with particular emphasis on those countries with the most serious record of human rights violations."

Center for Multinational Studies VI E
1625 I St., NW, Ste. 908, Washington, D.C. 20006
202-331-1987
An economic research organization studying the effects of multinational corporations on production, employment, trade, finance and development. Publishes findings and recommendations.

Center for National Security Studies III C
122 Maryland Ave., NE, Washington, D.C. 20002
202-544-5380
"Conducts research and produces information on issues of national security, provides information and expertise to concerned groups, individuals, the press and Congress."

Center for the Study of Democratic Institutions III C
P.O. Box 4068, Santa Barbara, CA 93103
805-961-2611
Taking "Democracy" as the major topic, the Center is "as interested in analyzing its nature and function as we are intent upon cultivating and devising perspectives that might enable us to see it afresh. We believe that this is the most effective way to exercise vigilance over individual liberties, human rights, and personal freedoms."

Center for UN Reform Education VIII E
600 Valley Rd., Wayne, NJ 07470
201-694-6333
"Initiates conferences on United Nations reform proposals; circulates information to its affiliated organizations; undertakes related research."

Center for War/Peace Studies III B
218 E. 18th St., New York, NY 10003
212-475-0850
Publishes *Global Report* which seeks to apply a global perspective to issue

choices such as are involved in the UN Law of the Sea Conference and UN activity on disarmament.

Center of Concern III B
3700 13th St., NE, Washington, D.C. 20017
202-635-2757
   "Opened in 1971 in response to an invitation of the U.S. Catholic Bishops to the international Jesuit Order . . . .Powerlessness, destitution, and structures of socio-economic injustice compel the Center of Concern, through social analysis, advocacy, and education, to work toward a world that is human."

Central Committee for Conscientious Objectors (CCCO) III C
2208 South St., Philadelphia, PA 19146
215-545-4626
Western Region:
1251 Second Ave., San Francisco, CA 94122
415-566-0501
   "Founded in 1948 to aid and work with people taking a stand against war. CCCO's main efforts are with individuals . . . . CCCO believes it is vitally important to reach young people with information on the realities of military life, and on conscientious objection and alternatives to militarism." Opposes the draft, does draft counseling, and publishes materials related to conscientious objection and other draft or military-service related issues.

Chicago Council on Foreign Relations II A
116 S. Michigan Ave., Chicago, IL 60603
312-726-3860
   "Our purpose is to promote — by all appropriate educational means — public understanding of the foreign policy of the U.S. and world affairs to the end that our citizens of all ages may more effectively perform their duties of citizenship."

Chile Legislative Center V C
120 Maryland Ave., NE, Washington, D.C. 20002
202-544-3067
   "Concerned with the restoration of fundamental human rights and democracy in Chile. The CLC is an action-oriented, non-profit educational resource center for both the Congress and the public."

The China Council of the Asia Society VC
1785 Massachusetts Ave., NW, Washington, D.C. 20036
202-387-6500

"Established in 1975 to seek fresh insights to American public education about China. The Council provides outreach through twelve regional councils and collaborative projects, a variety of media-related activities, and a series of studies on modern Chinese history and China's role in the contemporary world."

Christian Aid V A
P.O. Box 1, London SW9 8BH, England
01-733-5500

"Christian Aid is a division of the British Council of Churches. It provides a link between the British churches and their overseas partners, and a channel for their aid programs. It supports long-term projects among poor communities in more than 100 countries, as well as relief programmes after natural disasters."

Christian Life Commission, Southern Baptists I A
460 James Robertson Pkwy, Nashville, TN 37219
615-244-2495

"The Christian Life Commission is the social and moral concerns agency for the 13.5-million member Southern Baptist Convention. It assists Southern Baptists in the propagation of the gospel by helping them to become more aware of the ethical implications of the Christian gospel."

Christian Reformed Church, World Relief Committee IV B
2850 Kalamazoo Ave., SE, Grand Rapids, MI 49508
616-241-1691

"Some agricultural food programs."

Church Center for the UN VB
777 UN Plaza, New York, NY 10017
212-870-2347

"To help Christians and the churches respond to the urgent and fateful problems of the international scene in light of the ethical implications of the Christian faith."

Church Women United I F
475 Riverside Dr., Rm. 812, New York, NY 10027
212-870-2347

"To combat the rising tide of hatred caused by war; to minister to those suffering from the ravages of war; and to dedicate ourselves to the task of demanding of our country that it assume its full responsibility in the days to come in helping to build a world order based on love and justice without which there can be no durable peace."

Church World Service
475 Riverside Dr., New York, NY 10027
212-870-2061
    "CWS is the relief and development arm of the Division of Overseas
Ministries of the National Council of Churches of Christ in the U.S.A."

Church World Service/CROP IV B
28606 Phillips St., Elkhart, IN 46514
219-264-3102
    "Free loan of films on hunger and related issues, world relief and de-
velopment programs and education on global issues."

Citizen Exchange Council IV A
18 E. 41st St., New York 10017
212-889-7960
    "Dedicated to promoting mutual learning and understanding between
American and Soviet Citizens . . .[We] work to provide opportunities for
direct, face-to-face communication between Americans and their Soviet
counterparts." Offers travel and hospitality programs.

The Citizens Committee on Interdependence Education VIII B
1011 Arlington Blvd., Ste. W-219, Arlington, VA 22209
703-525-4400
    "Supports community partnerships between lay citizens and school per-
sonnel so that our students may learn more through the basics about the world
in which they live."

Citizens Committee on the Media V F
407 S. Dearborn, Rm. 1000, Chicago, IL 60605
312-427-4064
    "A broad-based citizens' organization working for reforms in the media.
[It is] dedicated to the belief that open communications are the key to a free
society."

Citizens Energy Project III C
1110 Sixth St., NW, Washington, D.C. 20001
202-289-4999
    Works on a variety of energy-related projects, funded through private
foundations and government contracts, in order to stimulate thought and
research on solar energy and financing renewable energy sources, fossil
fuels, and new energy technologies.

The Clamshell Alliance
Layayette Rd., Route 1, Seabrook, NH 03874
"A coalition of anti-nuclear and safe energy groups in New England. Our goal is to stop nuclear power and encourage the use of decentralized, safe, renewable sources of energy under public control (for people, not profit). We work toward these ends by organizing and participating in non-violent direct actions, which often include civil disobedience."

Clergy and Laity Concerned III D
198 Broadway, New York, NY 10038
212-964-6730
"CALC was founded in 1965 to mobilize opposition to American intervention in Southeast Asia. Responding to worsening domestic and international problems, CALC works for: a freeze on nuclear weapons, compensation for nuclear radiation victims, reduction of the military budget, just food and land policies which promote human rights."

Clergy and Laity Concerned, Human Rights Coordinating Center III C
1114 G St., SE, Washington, D.C. 20003
202-546-8985
"Concentrates its human rights activities on supporting U.S. policies to: ratify international human rights convenants, promote diplomatic concerns for human rights world-wide, recognize and correct domestic human rights violations and end aid and sales to gross violators of human rights unless it directly benefits the needy people."

Cleveland Council on World Affairs II A
601 Rockwell Ave., Cleveland, OH 44114
216-781-3730
"Educates the public in foreign affairs and provides services to foreign students and visitors in the Cleveland area. The Council takes no position on any issues."

Coalition for a New Foreign and Military Policy IX B
120 Maryland Ave., NE, Washington, D.C. 20002
202-546-8400
A "coalition of over 40 peace, religious, labor, and public interest organizations working to create a peaceful, non-interventionist foreign policy. We have a network of several thousand activists doing educational outreach work in their communities. The national staff produces resource material and coordinates grass-roots campaigns and legislative work in Washington."

Commission on the Churches' Participation in Development III C
World Council of Churches
P.O. Box 66, 150, rue de Ferney, 1211 Geneva 20, Switzerland
"Currently the emphasis is on: nuclear disarmament; militarization and underdevelopment; peaceful resolution of conflicts. It provides information on disarmament, promotes actions by churches on disarmament and collaborates with other non-governmental organizations working in this field."

Commission to Study the Organization of Peace VIII C
866 UN Plaza
New York, NY 10017
212-688-4665
"Founded in 1939, a permanent research body to consider the reorganization or replacement of the League of Nations. Since late 1939, the Commission has published 25 reports, 20 Special Recommendations, and several Occasional Statements. The Commission seeks always to anticipate problems . . . the Commission's analysis and recommendations about such new issues as the seabed, outer space, and the environment anticipated by several years the current concern of the UN and its member states."

Committee for Economic Development VIII F
477 Madison Ave., New York, NY 10022
212-688-2063
A non-partisan, non-profit business education research organization whose 200 trustees formulate specific recommendations on domestic and international business issues.

The Committee for National Security III C
1742 N St., NW, Washington, D.C. 20036
202-833-3140
Seeks to broaden the definition of national security believing it cannot be defined in "exclusively military terms . . . .Other factors are equally important — a stable and equitable economy, our ability to meet basic human needs, prospects and opportunities for our citizens to lead productive lives, and the preservation of human rights and of democratic values throughout our society."

Committee for the Free World
211 E. 51st Street
New York, NY 10022
212-759-7737
An international constituency of trade unionists, writers, artists, scien-

tists, and business people who recognize that "free societies are now, more than ever, under attack and who wish to prevent this trend."

Committee on the Present Danger III C
1800 Massachusetts Ave., Suite 601
Washington, D.C. 20036
202-466-7444

"A non-profit, non-partisan organization of citizens devoted to the peace, security and liberty of the nation, [which finds] the principal threat to our nation, to world peace, and to the cause of human freedom [to be] the Soviet drive for dominance."

Committee to Aid Democratic Dissidents in Yugoslavia (CADDY) III C
Willkie Memorial Bldg., 20 W. 40th St., New York, NY 10018
212-730-7744

"CADDY was founded in 1980 under the aegis of Democracy International to extend moral support to those persecuted in Yugoslavia for their views and opinions. The Committee regularly issues bulletins and news releases on violations of human rights in Yugoslavia."

Committee for a Community of Democracies
13306 Fieldstone Lane, Reston, VA 22090
703-620-3467

"Promotes strengthening ties between the democracies, with special attention to the capacity to formulate common policies and take concerted action on vital matters." Linked with similar committees in other parts of the world.

Common Cause I H
2030 M St., NW, Washington, D.C. 20036
202-833-1200

Common Cause is a non-partisan "citizens' action lobby, working at all levels of government to turn the system around, to make it work for us — the people."

Commonwealth Agricultural Bureau III C
Farnham House, Farnham Royal, Slough SL2 3BN, Bucks, England
(02814) 2281

"Exchange of information for researchers"

Community for Creative Nonviolence
1345 Euclid St., NW, Washington, D.C. 20009
202-234-9175

"Poverty and peace community that has a high political profile in Washington, D.C." in disestablishmentarian circles.

Community for Non-Violent Action III B
RFD 1, Box 197, Voluntown, CN 06384
203-376-9970

A pacifist organization active in demonstration activity against U.S. military installations and power plants.

CONCERN
P.O. Box 1790, Santa Ana, CA 92702 IV B
714-953-8575

"CONCERN is an international non-profit organization that seeks to promote education and socio-economic progress in developing countries as well as devoting itself to the relief of hunger and suffering. CONCERN is non-denominational and non-governmental."

Concern, Inc. III B
1794 Columbia Rd., N.W., Washington, D.C. 20009
202-965-0066

"Consumer-oriented environmental protection; education. Provides pamphlets presenting precise summaries on such issues as energy, land use, air and water pollution, and encouraging individuals and groups to act in their communities."

Conference on Peace Research in History VIII C
Department of History, University of Toledo, Toledo, OH 43606
419-537-2845

"Formed to encourage, support, and coordinate peace research among historians and social scientists. Viewing war and its causes as among the most serious problems confronting humanity, members of CPRH seek to apply intellectual resources to the quest for a peaceful world."

Conscience and Military Tax Campaign-U.S. III E
44 Bellhaven Rd., Bellport, NY 11713
516-286-8824

Seeks to "help build the military tax refusal movement to a politically significant level. The goal [is] to gain passage of the World Peace Tax Fund Bill or similar legislation which would provide a legal alternative for tax-payers morally opposed to war."

Consortium on Peace Research, Education, and Development (COPRED) VIII C
Center for Peaceful Change, Kent State University, Kent, OH 44242
216-672-3143

"Links persons and institutions interested in scientific study, action-oriented research, and education on problems of peace and social justice."

Cooperative League of the U.S.A. I H
1828 L St., NW, Ste. 1100, Washington, D.C. 20036
202-872-0550

The national office of the cooperative movement in the U.S. which operates many consumer-owned enterprises.

Coordinating Council for Hunger Concerns IV B
National Council of Churches
475 Riverside Dr., Rm. 868, New York, NY 10027
212-870-2331

"Educational/research/action on domestic and international problems of hunger and poverty."

Coordination in Development (CODEL)
79 Madison Ave., New York, NY 10016
212-685-2030

"A consortium of over 40 Protestant and Catholic mission-sending agencies committed to working collaboratively with the peoples of the developing countries in their aspirations to improve their quality of life."

Council for a Livable World
11 Beacon St., Boston, MA 02108 III E & F
617-742-9395
and
100 Maryland Ave., NE, Washington, D.C. 20002
202-543-4100

"Avert nuclear war and strengthen national security through rational arms control . . . seeks to elect and inform members of U.S. Senate which has unique advise and consent powers in foreign affairs."

Council for Intercultural Studies and Programs III C
60 E. 42nd St., New York, NY 10017
212-972-9877

"A cooperative association of some 500 colleges and universities which believe in the future need for understanding more than one culture."

Council of the Americas III C
684 Park Ave., New York, NY 10021
212-628-3200

"A non-profit business association by member corporations, all of which have major commitments in Latin America. To further the understanding and acceptance of the role of private enterprise as a positive force for the development of the Americas."

Council on Economic Priorities, Conversion Information Center III E
84 Fifth Ave., New York, NY 10011
212-691-8550
An organization devoted to the collection of defense data and conversion data for use in research.

Council on Foreign Relations II A
58 E. 68th St., New York, NY 10021
212-734-0400
"Breaks new ground in the consideration of international issues; to help shape American foreign policy in a constructive, non-partisan manner; to provide continuing leadership for the conduct of our foreign relations."

Council on International and Public Affairs VIII C
60 E. 42nd St., Ste. 1231, New York, NY 10017
212-972-9877
"A non-profit research and educational organization founded in 1954 to promote the study of the U.S. and other nations of the world through conferences, research, publications, and other means . . . . The major part of its work is conducted through independent operating programs such as the Policy Studies Associates and Learning Resources in International Studies which seek to improve college and university instruction."

Council on International Educational Exchange IV A
777 UN Plaza, New York, NY 10017
212-661-0310
"A membership organization whose purpose is to aid the international activities of its institutional members, other exchange organizations and the student, teacher and young adult engaged in educational exchange and travel."

Council on Religion and International Affairs II C
170 E. 64th St., New York, NY 10017
212-838-4120
"Founded in 1914 by religious and civic leaders . . . it was mandated to work toward ending the barbarity of war, to encourage international cooperation, and to promote justice." Publishes *Worldview* (monthly).

Darien Book Aid Plan V A
1926 Post Rd., Darien Ct 06820
203-655-2777
"A women's volunteer organization founded in 1949 to build a foundation of peace, understanding and friendship by the free distribution of books. To

date over 1120 tons of free good quality reading materials have been sent upon request to over 120 countries and 36 states of the United States.''

Democratic National Committee I
1625 Massachusetts Ave., NW, Washington, D.C. 20036
202-797-5900
    National headquarters.

Department of Social Responsibility IA
Unitarian/Universalist Church
25 Beacon St., Boston, MA 02108
617-742-2100
    The catalytic and coordinating center for Unitarian social action work.

Disciples Peace Fellowship III B
P.O. Box 1986, Indianapolis, IN 46219
317-353-1491
    ''A community of Disciple women and men who believe that war is 'pagan, futile and destructive of the values for which the Christian faith stands.' DPF members support a positive, non-violent approach to human conflicts and are determined to work actively for peace. With Martin Luther King, Jr., they believe that 'peace is not merely the absence of tension but it is the presence of justice and brotherhood.' ''

8th Day Center for Justice III A
22 E. Van Buren, Chicago, IL 60605
312-427-4351
    ''8th Day Center's goal is to bring about a more just society by working to change the structures and systems that oppress. Any effort to build a more human world, that reflects the Gospel value of Solidarity, must address the systematic roots of injustice.''

Environmental Action, Inc. II C
1346 Connecticut Ave., NW, Washington, D.C. 20036
202-833-1845
    ''Lobbies Congress on issues such as air, water quality, pesticides.'' Publishes *Environmental Action,* a magazine devoted to a variety of current environmental issues.

Environmental Defense Fund II C
1525 18th St., NW, Washington, D.C. 20036
202-833-1484
    ''Litigation/education.''

Environmental Policy Center II C
317 Pennsylvania Ave., SE, Washington, D.C. 20003
202-547-6500
    "EPC lobbies Congress to reduce our nation's dependence on foreign oil
and nuclear power. It promotes the safe, clean use of coal, oil and gas, energy
and water conservation and protection of prime farmlands."

Episcopal Church, Public Affairs Office I A
815 Second Ave., New York, NY 10017
212-867-8400
    Central office for expressing Episcopal Church concerns on public issues.

Episcopal Peace Fellowship III B
Wisconsin Ave. & Woodley Rd., NW, Washington, D.C. 20016
202-363-5532
    "It endeavors to create, within the Church, an effective body of Christians
pledged to renounce participation in war so far as is conscientious for the
individual, and to espouse non-violence in the works of reconciliation and
peace in one's own milieu as well as in the larger world community."

European Confederation of Agriculture V A
C.P. 87, 5200 Brugg, Aargau, Switzerland
    "Technical, economic, and social problems of European agriculture."

The Experiment in International Living IV A
80 Kipling Rd., Brattleboro, VT 05301
802-257-7751
    One of the largest organizations engaging in international student ex-
change programs with over 80,000 "alumni."

Federal Union, Inc. II B
1875 Connecticut Ave., NW, Washington, D.C. 20009
202-234-2211
    "Seeks . . . a democracy of democracies which can come to grips with
today's problems through a free, open, representative political structure . . .
a federal union of democracies."

Federation of American Scientists I G
307 Massachusetts Ave., NE, Washington D.C. 20002
202-546-3300
    "Professional association of American Scientists that expresses views of
the arms race and other public issues." Publishes *Public Interest Report*.

Fellowship of Reconciliation III B
Box 271, Nyack, NY 10960
914-358-4601

"A world-wide ecumenical organization devoted to the peaceful resolution of international conflict, advancement of human rights, solutions for world hunger and disarmament." A major voice of Christian pacifism.

Food for the Hungry International IV B
International Coordination Center
7729 E. Greenway Rd., Scottsdale, AZ 85260
602-998-3100

Food for the Hungry was organized in 1971 "to offer both disaster relief and long-range self-help assistance." It currently is organizing a new volunteer program called "Hunger Corps."

Ford Foundation IB
320 E. 43rd St., New York, NY 10017
212-573-5000

A large grant-giving Foundation whose founder tried to prevent World War I. Current projects include human rights efforts, arms control studies, and economic development work.

Foreign Policy Association IIA
205 Lexington Ave., New York, NY 10016
212-481-8450

"Founded in 1918, the FPA is a private, nonprofit, nonpartisan, educational organization. Its objective is to help stimulate an informed, thoughtful, and articulate public opinion on foreign policy issues facing the nation. To this end it works closely with many public and private organizations and with colleges and schools. The Association strives to air diverse viewpoints impartially; it advocates none."

Foreign Policy Research Institute IC
3508 Market St., Ste. 350, Philadelphia, PA 19104
215-382-0685

"Research, conferences, and publications intended to provide the attentive public, scholars, and policy makers with analyses to American foreign policy, arms control and disarmament, international relations, and Soviet strategy and power." Publishes *Orbis*.

Foresta Institute for Ocean and Mountain Studies VI G
6205 Franktown Rd., Carson City, NV 89701
702-882-6361

"Research, training, consultation on fauna/flora protection."

Freedom House III C
20 W. 40th St., New York, NY 10018
212-730-7744

"Operates a center for Appeals for Freedom, distributing *samizdat* from oppressive countries to the right and left. Runs the Afghanistan Information Center to provide data on that country and enable its residents to get a better hearing in the U.S. Its Caribbean Basin Project provides similar services for that area." Promotes civil and political rights throughout the world.

Friends Commitee on National Legislation III F
245 Second St., NE, Washington D.C. 20002
202-547-4343

"FCNL, founded in 1943, is registered to lobby the U.S. Congress. It publishes a newsletter and other materials and its program is determined by participating members of the Religious Society of Friends."

Friends of the Earth III C
124 Spear St., San Francisco, CA 94105
415-495-4770

An organization committed to the restoration, preservation, and rational use of the earth. Conducts research and develops educational materials in support of a sound use of the environment.

Friends of the Filipino People VC
110 Maryland Ave., NE, Washington, D.C. 20002
202-543-1517

"Concerned with U.S. military and economic aid, multilateral funding, political prisoners, 'runaway shops' and their effect on U.S. labor, and U.S. bases in the Philippines."

Friends Peace Committee III B
1515 Cherry St., Philadelphia, Pa 19102
215-241-7230

"Work(s) within Philadelphia Yearly Meeting (Quakers) for understanding of the Friends peace testimony . . . and work(s) with Friends and non-Friends for peace in our families, our Meetings, our communities, our country, and our world. We help translate Friends' beliefs into action on issues such as disarmament, non-violent action for justice and peace, education and parenting, U.S. foreign and military policy, peace conversion, military recruiting, and support for an effective United Nations."

The Fund for Peace III B
345 E. 46th St., New York, NY 10017
212-661-5900

"The Fund for Peace, a private non-profit institution, was established in 1967 by a group of concerned citizens, to promote knowledge and understanding of global problems that threaten human survival. It is composed of the following projects: Center for Defense Information, Center for International Policy, Center for National Security Studies, 'In the Public Interest' Radio Programs, and the Institute for the Study of World Politics."

Girl Scouts of the U.S.A. IH
830 Third Ave., New York, NY 10017
212-940-7500

"Fosters international friendship and understanding for girls and women through scouting experiences."

Global Community Network V C
10415 McCormick St. N., Hollywood, CA 91601
213-766-6867

"A non-partisan, non-profit corporation founded to facilitate communication and dialogue among — and services to — non-governmental organizations, corporations, labor and business organizations, government agencies and representatives, and individuals that are concerned with international matters relating to human rights, human needs, economic and social development, world peace, global education, and protection of the environment."

Global Education Associates VIII B
552 Park Ave., East Orange, NJ 07017
201-675-1409

"Facilitates the efforts of concerned people of diverse cultures, talents, and experience, in contributing to a more human and just world order . . . has a network of Associates in 40 countries who collaborate in research, writing and education programs related to this goal."

Global Learning Inc. VIII B
40 S. Fullerton Ave., Montclair, NJ 07042
201-783-7616

"Dedicated to furthering a global perspective in education — primarily elementary and secondary. Professional staff and extensive network of consultants to conduct workshops, inservice courses and institutes on global perspectives, peace, social injustice and ecological concerns."

Global Perspectives in Education, Inc. VIII B
218 E. 18th St., New York, NY 10003
212-475-0850
"A nonpartisan education effort building upon American democratic traditions, to prepare our youth for the challenges of national citizenship in a global age."

Heifer Project, Inc. IV B
P.O. Box 808, Worthen Bldg., Little Rock, AR 72203
501-376-6836
"Livestock improvement assistance for Indian reservations, rural Blacks, also international projects."

Help and Action Coordination Committee III C
Box 6, 77850, Hericy, France
Monitors closely human rights violations in the Soviet Union with daily and weekly lists of those known to have been arrested. Estimates there are some 10,000 political prisioners and prisoners of conscience in the Soviet Union today.

Hudson Institute VI E
Quaker Ridge Rd., Croton-on-Hudson, NY 10520
914-762-0700
Founded in 1961 by Herman Kahn, the Hudson Institute "seeks always to provide immediately useful analyses which can be applied to current issues, policies and programs. . .Hudson tries to perform the research that a decision-maker should do, if he had the time and resources. First known for innovative work in national security policy, in the mid-1960's Hudson branched out into the study of domestic policy and economic development, and in the early 1970's into international business issues."

Humanitas International, Human Rights Committee III C
P.O. Box 818, Menlo Park, CA 94025
415-324-9077
"Established in 1979 by Joan Baez as a non-profit, non-partisan, non-ideological organization working to assist the victims of human rights violations around the world. Humanitas believes that respect for human rights is essential for the preservation of human dignity, works actively to educate the public to the importance of human rights, and acts wherever possible to relieve the suffering that results from the violation of these rights."

Human Rights Internet III C
1502 Ogden St., NW, Washington, D.C. 20010
202-462-4320

Acts as a clearing house of information on human rights for academics, advocates, and the interested public. Publisher *Human Rights Internet Reporter*.

The Hunger Project III C
1735 Franklin, San Francisco, CA 94101
415-775-8100
    "Global education to end hunger."

IMPACT III F
110 Maryland Ave., NE, Washington, D.C. 20002
202-544-8636
    IMPACT is an interreligious network, sponsored by 23 national Protestant, Roman Catholic and Jewish Agencies. It monitors and recommends positions on legislative issues in the following areas: U.S. foreign policy and military spending, U.S. food policy, civil rights and civil liberties, criminal justice, energy and ecology, health care, human services, and public policy affecting women.

Institute for Defense and Disarmament Studies VI E
251 Harvard St., Brookline, MA 02146
617-734-4216
    Studies the factors which deter serious consideration of a world without nuclear weapons and advocates a freeze on strategic delivery systems and nuclear warhead production.

Institute for Ecological Policies III C
9208 Christopher St., Fairfax, VA 22031
703-691-1271
    "National oriented, non-profit organization working to educate and activate individual and community-based organizations to become more involved in constructive grass-roots based solutions to the many problems facing us. Our primary focus is publishing 'how to' books and conducting workshops and seminars in the fields of energy conservation, renewable energy, and political education."

Institute for Education in Peace and Justice VIII E
2747 Rutger St., St. Louis, MO 63108
314-773-8884
    "The Institute is committed to the ideal of peace through justice as stated by Pope Paul VI, 'If you want peace, work for justice.' It is assisting individuals, schools, and religious institutions in finding alternatives for living that incorporate justice into an active quest for peace."

Institute for Food and Development Policy VIII E
2588 Mission Street, San Francisco, CA 94110
415-648-6090

"Founded in 1975 by Francis Moore Lappé and Joseph Collins, the Institute is a not-for-profit research, documentation and education center. It focuses on food and agriculture, always asking: Why hunger in a world of plenty?"

Institute for Mediterranean Affairs VC
428 E. 83 St., #1R, New York, NY 10028
212-988-1726

Has research projects, training programs, and publications about social-economic development and peace.

Institute for Policy Studies VI E
1901 Q St., NW Washington, DC 20009
202-234-9382

"Founded in 1963, the Institute is a transnational center for research, education, and social invention. IPS sponsors critical examination of the assumption and policies which define American posture on domestic and international issues, and offers alternative strategies and visions. Areas of focus include domestic policy, national security, international economics and human rights."

Institute for Psychiatry and Foreign Affairs VI D
2600 Virginia Ave., NW, Washinton, DC 20037
202-338-1851

". . . studies psychological and cultural factors which help determine the course of international relations."

Institute for the Future VI E
2750 Sand Hill Rd., Menlo Park, CA 94025
415-854-6322

A research and consulting group doing studies of the long-term future (defined as five to fifteen years) for both private and public clients.

Institute for World Order III B
777 UN Plaza, New York, NY 10017
212-490-0010

". . .works to formulate practical alternatives to war, social and economic injustice and ecological breakdown. Produces material for college and university level courses and for public education." Sponsor of the World Order Models Project, and of *Alternatives: A Journal of World Policy*.

Institute of International Education IVA
809 UN Plaza, New York, NY 10017
212-883-8224

  "Build (s) understanding . . . and advance(s) a more peaceful and productive international order through the interchange of students and scholars, knowledge and skills."

Institute for Religion and Democracy
1000 16th St., N.W., Washington, D.C. 20036
202-822-8627

  " . . . an interdenominational association of clergy and laity, representing a diversity of theological and political viewpoints, working to revitalize our religious institutions by reaffirming the link between Christianity and democratic values."

Inter-American Association for Democracy and Freedom VC
20 West 40th St., New York, NY 10018
212-221-6790. ext. 1

  "Aims to awaken greater interest in the U.S. in Latin America and its problems; and to further cooperation with the Latin American people in their struggle for political, economic and social democracy . . . Aims to stave off the inroads of communism and neo-fascism with a vital counter-force of democracy."

Intercommunity Center for Justice and Peace VB
20 Washington Sq. North, New York, NY 10011
212-475-6677

  Calls for Christians to "develop educative processes that will inform persons of the moral imperatives to denounce the sinfulness of the arms race and to relate the arms race to the U.S./Global economy . . . ." Also has programs on sexual preference, women's ordination and criminal justice.

Interfaith Center on Corporate Responsibility III C
475 Riverside Dr., Rm 566, New York, NY 10027
212-876-2293

  "Shareholder resolutions on economic conversion, foreign military sales and nuclear weapons." Sponsored by the National Council of Churches.

Interfuture VIII B
150 Nassau St., Ste. 1204, New York, NY 10038
212-964-8861

  "IF is a non-profit educational organization which helps undergraduates design and carry out cross-cultural study projects in the U.S., Europe, and the Third World on issues related to internationalism."

Intermediate Technology Development Group IVB
777 UN Plaza, New York, NY 10017
212-972-9877
"Spreads the word in the U.S. and Canada about small and intermediate scale technologies developed by ITDG in London, the Group established by E.F. Schumacher in the mid-1960s to give practical expression to the ideas and concepts which he set forth in *Small is Beautiful.*"

International Center for Advanced Mediterranean Agronomic Studies VC
11 rue Newton, 75116, Paris, France
"Post-graduate studies and research on Mediterranean and international problems of rural development and world food."

International Commission of Agricultural and Food Industries VC
35, rue du General Fiy, 75008 Paris, France
"Coordinates activities that involve the food industry"

International Commission of Jurists III C
109 Route de Chene, 1224 Geneva, Switzerland
American Section: 777 U.N. Plaza, New York, NY 10017
"Dedicated to the promotion of the rule of law and the independence of the judiciary to uphold and strengthen the observance of human rights . . . sends missions to different parts of the world to observe important political trials."

International Committee of the Red Cross VA
815 Second Ave., Rm. 510, New York, NY 10017
212-972-0704
Organized to enforce the various conventions on wartime practices and to care for the victims of war.

International Council of Voluntary Agencies III A
13, rue Gautier, 1201 Geneva, Switzerland
Works with voluntary agencies and governments on refugee problems.

International Council of Women VB
777 UN Plaza, New York, NY 10017
212-697-2278
"Founded in 1888, the ICW is the oldest international organization working on behalf of the education, advancement, and participation of women throughout the world. Headquartered in Paris, the organization has seventy-three member nations, half of which are in underdeveloped countries. The group has consultative status with the UN."

International Dairy Federation IC
Square Vergote 41, 1040 Brussels, Belgium
"To promote through international cooperation and consultation, the solution of scientific, technical and economic problems in the international dairy field."

International Development Institute IV B
Indiana University, 400 E. Seventh Street, Bloomington, IN 47405
812-337-8596
Studies agricultural development problems in the Third World.

International Food Policy Research Institute VI E
1776 Massachusetts Ave. NW, Washington, DC 20036
202-862-5600
"Policy issues of food production, consumption, availability, distribution."

International Friendship League VA
22 Batterymarch, Boston, MA 02109
617-523-4273
"Headquarters for individuals who wish pen friends in other countries. We carefully match each correspondent individually as to age and interests. Mail from overseas swamps us with letters from sincere persons who wish to know more about the United States."

International Human Assistance Programs, Inc. IVB
360 Park Ave,. S., 14th Fl., New York, NY 10010
212-684-6804
"A non-profit assistance agency that designs and supports self-help programs in the developing world."

International Human Rights Law Group III C
1700 K St., NW Washington, D.C. 20006
202-659-5023
A group of dedicated lawyers fighting for the advancement of human rights in the world. Conducts educational programs and provides legal services.

International League for Human Rights IIIC
777 UN Plaza, New York, NY 10017
212-972-9554
"Successful in calling attention to human rights violations through the publication of special reports, the preparation and submission of documented

complaints to governments and inter-governmental bodies; violations are reported, the dispatch of international judicial observers to trials, direct negotiation with governments, the publicizing of consistent abuses and the support of civil liberties groups throughout the world . . . also works to develop standards of conduct in human rights areas and to improve procedures at the regional and international level."

International Metalworkers' Federation ID
54 bis, route des Acacias, Ch-1227 Geneva, Switzerland
    An international labor union rejecting "violence, extremism and military aggression" and working for "peace, democracy and the right of men and women everywhere to have work and social fulfillment."

International Organization for the Study of Group Tensions VIII F
7 West 96th St., Rm. 17C, New York, NY 10025
    Research and publications dealing with discrimination, violence, and intergroup relations, aiming to promote peace and mutual understanding.

International Peace Academy, Inc. VE
777 UN Plaza, New York, NY 10017
212-986-3540
    "The Academy conducts international training seminars, and produces practitioner — oriented publications and reports of its off-the-record consultations for diplomats and military officers from 115 nations."

International Relations Council IIA
210 Westport Rd., Kansas City, MO 64111
816-531-0089
    "Seeks to promote understanding of international affairs. The Council has monthly programs September-May, films, speakers and educational materials provided free of charge to schools and community organizations, and a small international affairs library open to the public."

International Rescue Committee III C
386 Park Ave. S., New York, NY 10016
212-679-1011
    Founded in the 1930s to aid victims of Nazi Germany, the Committee is active in aiding individuals escape oppressive governments, in caring for refugees, and in emigration law reform.

International Voluntary Services VE
1717 Massachusetts Ave., NW, Washington, D.C. 20036
202-387-5533

"UNESCO-affiliated self-help work camps and projects." Trains young people from the U.S. to work on community service projects in other countries.

Interns for Peace IIB
150 Fifth Ave., Rm. 710, New York, NY 10011
212-242-0532

"An independent, non-political program that seeks to strengthen the social fabric of Israel by increasing interaction between its Jewish and Arab citizens."

Interreligious Taskforce on US Food Policy IVB
110 Maryland Ave., NE, Washington, D.C. 20002
202-543-2800

"A team of 44 Washington-based staff of national religious agencies who work together to influence and help the American community influence US policy for the sake of justice for the hungry at home and abroad."

Jane Addams Peace Association VB
777 UN Plaza, New York, NY 10017
212-682-8830

"A tax-exempt organization sponsoring and financing certain educational programs of the Women's International League for Peace and Freedom. Among these programs are International Disarmament Fund, International Seminars and Nuclear Information Committee."

The Japan Institute for Social and Economic Affairs VC
1333 Gough St., Ste. 6F, San Francisco, CA 94109
415-922-5600

"Offers, among other projects, 20 all-expenses-paid Travel Study Fellowships for social studies educators who are desirous of becoming better acquainted with contemporary Japanese society to enhance teaching of global perspectives in American schools."

Japan Society VC
333 E. 47th St., New York, NY 10017
212-832-1155

Seeks to build good will between Japan and the U.S. through mutual understanding.

Jewish Peace Fellowship IIIb
Box 271, Nyack, NY 10960
914-358-4601

"Unites those who believe that Jewish ideals and experience provide inspiration for a non-violent philosophy of life." Publishes material on Jewish sources of nonviolence and opposition to war. Has counselled conscientious objectors since 1941."

Johnson Foundation VA
P.O. Box 547, Racine, WI 53401
414-639-3211
"Convenes conferences on international understanding, educational excellence, improvement of the human environment, intellectual and arms control issues. Program interests include peace, security and arms control issues. Guidelines for proposals available upon request."

Charles F. Kettering Foundation IXA
5335 Far Hills Ave., Dayton, OH 45429
513-434-7300
A grant-giving foundation which also conducts projects of its own; active in building bridges within the fragmented world affairs field in America and through the Dartmouth Conferences, in promoting Soviet-American dialogue. Publishes *New Ways* (free).

Kiwanis International IH
101 E. Erie St., Chicago, IL 60611
312-943-2300
An international service club active in many community betterment programs and seeking to build international understanding.

League of Women Voters I F
1730 M St., NW, Washington, D.C. 20036
202-659-2685
"Dedicated to strengthening citizen knowledge of and involvement in representative governments. International Relations department deals with international development, international organization, and international trade as well as other issues."

Learning Resources in International Studies VIIIC
60 E. 42nd St., Ste. 1231, New York, NY 10017
212-972-9877
"A cooperative dissemination program of the Consortium for International Studies education, Council on International and Public Affairs, Council for Intercultural Studies and Programs, and Maxwell School of Syracuse University."

Letters Abroad VA
209 E. 56th St., New York, NY 10022
212-752-4290
"A volunteer, non-profit clearinghouse for correspondence between adult Americans and their counterparts in more than 130 countries overseas as a means of promoting global good will."

Lions International IH
400 22nd St., Oak Brook, IL 60521
312-986-1700
"The Lions Clubs, which are non-political and non-sectarian, constitute a tremendous force for international friendship and good will. The Lions official magazine which is published in 12 languages serves as an instrument of truth and information designed to create and foster a more generous consideration among the peoples of the world."

Lutheran Church in America IA
231 Madison Ave., New York, NY 10016
212-481-9600
Advocates the elimination of hunger in the world, support for human rights, economic and social justice for all the world's people."

Lutheran Peace Fellowship IIIB
168 W. 100th St., New York, NY 10025
212-222-7045
"An independent Lutheran organization, striving to maintain a witness for peace and justice within the church."

Lutheran World Relief IVB
360 Park Ave. S., New York, NY 10010
212-532-6350
An economic, refugee, and immigrant assistance program of the Lutheran Church in the USA.

Maryknoll Fathers IIIB
121 E. 39th St., New York, NY 10016
212-697-4470
A Catholic order active in promoting liberation in most of its many varieties.

Members of Congress for Peace through Law (MCPL) VB
501 House Annex 2, Washinton, D.C. 20515
202-225-8550
"A bi-partisan caucus of members of the House and Senate who work

together on foreign and military policy issues. Its prime goals are to control the spread of arms and to strengthen international institutions."

Mennonite Central Committee-Peace Section IIIB
100 Maryland Ave., NE, Washington, D.C. 20002
202-544-6564
Interested in peace and justice concerns as well as their relation to national legislation and policy.

Methodist Federation for Social Action IIID
76 Clinton Ave., Staten Island, NY 10301
212-273-4941
Founded in 1907, "the Federation unites activist United Methodists to promote action on the liberation issues confronting the church and society and to witness the transformation of the social order that is intrinsic to the church's entire life, including its evangelism, preaching, and counseling." Publishes *Social Questions Bulletin,* bimonthly.

Middle East Institute IIC
1761 N St., NW, Washington, D.C. 20036
202-785-1141
Formed in 1946 to develop interest in the Middle East among Americans. It does scholarly research, puts on seminars and conferences, runs a library, and publishes the quarterly, *Middle East Journal.*

Middle East Peace Project VC
339 Lafayette St., New York, NY 10012
212-475-4300
"MEP has been working for ten years as a national, interreligious clearinghouse for those committed to a Middle East peace for both Israelis and Palestinians. MEP is a source of literature, speakers, and advice."

Minority Rights Group
36 Craven St., London, WC2N 5NG England
930-6659
"Educational work on human rights. Has consultative status as a NGO with the UN."

Mobilization for Survival IIIB
3610 Locust Walk, Philadelphia, PA 19104
215-386-4875
"MFS is a nationwide coalition of 140 national and local groups united under the four goals: zero nuclear weapons, ban nuclear power, stop the arms

race, and meet human needs. It is working to build a non-violent survival movement that will awaken people everywhere to the growing threats to their survival, and to channel that awareness into massive public action. A world in which human needs and rights come first is the ultimate goal.''

Movement for a New Society IIIB
4722 Baltimore Ave., Philadelphia, PA 19143
215-724-1464

''A decentralized, nationwide network of small groups working for fundamental social change by nonviolent means. The small groups work collectively in direct action, training/organizing, and the building of alternative institutions.''

National Action/Research on the Military Industrial Complex (NARMIC) IIIC
1501 Cherry St., Philadelphia, PA 19102
215-241-7175

''A project of the American Friends Service Committee, produces well-researched factual yet popular printed & audio-visual materials on nuclear arms and power, U.S. arms sales, new economic order, and military contracts.''

National Association for Foreign Student Affairs (NAFSA) IVA
1860 19th St., NW, Washington, D.C. 20009
202-462-4811

''Serves as a source of professional training, as a guide to standards of performance, and as a spokesman for international educational exchange programs in governmental and educational circles.''

National Association of Arab Americans IIIF
1825 Connecticut Ave., NW # 211, Washington, D.C. 10009
202-979-7757

Established in 1972, the NAAA is officially registered to lobby Congress on Middle East policy. In addition to representing the interest of Arab states, it also produces publications.

National Association of Evangelicals IA
450 E. Gundersen Dr., Wheaton, IL 60187
312-665-0500

''A voluntary fellowship of evangelical denominations, churches, schools, organizations and individuals . . . .Encourages the application of biblical principles to the social needs of the day.''

National Association of World Affairs Councils IIA
L.A. World Affairs Council
900 Wilshire Blvd., Los Angeles, CA 90017
213-638-2333
Acts as a clearinghouse for information and projects of local councils.

National Audobon Society IIIC
950 Third Ave., New York, NY 10022
212-832-3200
"Promotes wildlife conservation through research/education."

National Catholic Education Association VIIA
1 Dupont Circle, Ste. 350, Washington, D.C. 20036
202-293-5954
Curriculum development center and administrative headquarters for the Catholic School systems in the U.S.

National Child Nutrition Project
46 Bayard, New Brunswick, NJ 08901 VI G
201-846-1161
"Technical advice on federal food programs."

National Committee on U.S.-China Relations VC
777 UN Plaza, 9B, New York, NY 10017
212-682-6848
"A private, non-profit, educational organization which encourages public interest in, and public understanding of, China and United States-China relations."

National Conference on Soviet Jewry IIIE
2025 I St., NW, Washington, D.C. 20006
202-293-2262
"The major nation-wide coordinating agency for American activity and policy on behalf of Soviet Jews."

National Congress of Parents and Teachers VIIIB
700 N. Rush St., Chicago, IL 60611
312-787-0977
Headquarters of the PTAs throughout the country; has directed public attention to the impact of TV violence on children's lives.

National Council for a World Peace Tax Fund
2111 Florida Ave., NW, Washington, D.C. 20008
202-483-3751

"Works for the passage of legislation, the World Peace Tax Fund bill (HR 4897/S 880), which will enable taxpayers who are morally opposed to war to pay the military portion of their federal taxes into a special fund for non-military purposes."

National Council for the Social Studies VIIA
3615 Wisconsin Ave., NW, Washington, D.C. 20016
202-966-7840
"A leadership association of social studies educators, representing all levels of education, who share a commitment to improve the quality of teaching, curriculum, research, and service in the world affairs field."

National Council of Catholic Women IA
1012 14th St., NW, Washington, D.C. 20005
202-638-6050
"The nationwide federation in the U.S. of Catholic women and their organizations.. . .It is the representative voice of some 10 million women . . . working together through national program commissions which reflect current issues in the Church and society."

National Council of the Churches of Christ in the U.S.A. IA
475 Riverside Dr., New York, NY 10027
212-870-2227
Through a wide variety of programs, seeks to encourage fellowship among churches, and promotes understanding of global problems in an ethical/spiritual context. A major Protestant ecumenical agency.

National Council on Foreign Language and International Studies IXA
605 Third Ave., 17th Floor, New York, NY 10158
212-490-3520
Formed in 1980 to continue and build upon the work of the President's Commission on Foreign Language and International Studies. It is "A non-profit organization focusing public attention on the crucial importance to the U.S. of effective communication with and comprehensive understanding of the world beyond our borders. [It makes the case] that high quality foreign language and international studies are vital to America's future."

National Farmers' Organization IIB
485 L'Enfant Plaza, SW, Washington, D.C. 20024
202-484-7075
"Marketing problems of owner-operator farmers' products."

National Federation of Priests' Councils IIID
1307 S. Wabash Ave., Chicago IL 60605
312-427-0115

An association of priests throughout the U.S. active in peace and justice issues.

National Federation of Temple Sisterhoods
838 Fifth Ave., New York, NY 10021
212-249-0100

"Members serve the Synagogue, the family and the community. They intensify Jewish knowledge through study and action programs; their projects translate the ideals of Judaism into practical service to Jewish and humanitarian causes."

National Interreligious Service Board for Conscientious Objectors (NISBCO) IV E
550 Washington Bldg. 15th St. & New York Ave., NW, Washington, D.C. 20005
202-393-4868

"Provides professional counseling for those who are working through problems with military service and convictions of conscientious objection, while providing training for religious CO counselors." Formed in 1940.

National Peace Academy Campaign (N-PAC) IIIE
1625 I St., NW, Ste. 726, Washington, D.C. 20006
202-466-7670

"Set up to promote the establishment of a United States Academy of Peace and Conflict Resolution — an institution for training professionals in non-violent conflict resolution and mediation skills at the domestic and international levels. N-PAC lobbied successfully for creation of a Congressional Commission to study the Peace Academy concept."

National Planning Association VIE
1606 New Hampshire Ave., NW, Washington, D.C. 20009
202-265-7685

"A private research organization which has specialized in policy-oriented research on domestic and international issues for almost 50 years. Favors American parity with the Soviet Union in arms, the draft, and a strengthened NATO alliance."

National Urban League IL
500 E. 62nd St., New York, NY 10021
212-644-6500

A major association of Americans promoting the civil rights and economic welfare of blacks.

Network IIIF
806 Rhode Island Ave., NE, Washington, D.C. 20018
202-526-4070

A group representing religious orders and seeking to advance the concerns of the underprivileged in the world by lobbying and seeking to influence national legislation.

North American Coalition for Human Rights in Korea VC
100 Maryland Ave., NE, Washington, D.C. 20002
202-488-5600
National office:
475 Riverside Dr., Rm. 1538, New York, NY 10027
212-678-6260

''Mobilizes the concerns of people in North America for human rights in Korea, facilitates their concerned action in advocacy of these rights, enables the sharing of information and analysis about the immediate situation and its causes, and seeks to support those whose human rights have been violated in Korea.''

North American Congress on Latin America VC
151 W. 19th St., 9th Fl., New York, NY 10011
212-989-8890

Engages in research on the impact of U.S. domestic and foreign policies on Latin America.

Ocean Education Project IIIE
100 Maryland Ave., NE, Washington, D.C. 20002
202-544-2312

''Educates the U.S. public as to the Law of the Sea Treaty implications in preparation for ratification by the U.S. Senate.''

Office for Church in Society IA
United Church of Christ
110 Maryland Ave., NE, Washington, D.C. 20002
202-543-1517

''To assume a leadership function for the social concerns of the United Church of Christ. To provide resources to the national conference and local churches and to strengthen coordination of social action activities within the denomination.''

Office of International Justice and Peace IA
United States Catholic Conference
1313 Massachusetts Ave., NW, Washington, D.C. 20005
202-659-6812

Emphasizes education "of the type that leads to action for peace: action to eliminate the arms race and take steps toward disarmament, as well as action to eliminate the underlying causes of the social unrest that can threaten and lead to war."

Operation Push II
930 E. 50th St., Chicago, IL 60615
312-373-7900

Headed by Jesse Jackson, PUSH's focus is primarily domestic issues with occasional projects on the Middle East, African relief and human rights issues.

Operations and Policy Research, Inc. VI E
4000 Albermarle St., NW, Washington, D. C. 20016
202-362-3329

Non-profit research organization surveys and studies on elections in Latin America and the U.S., ethnic groups, and comparative political institutions.

Organization for Economic Co-operation and Development (OECD) Intergovernmental
2, rue Andre Pascal, 75775 Paris Cedex 16, France

"To promote economic and social welfare throughout the OECD area by assisting member governments in the formulation of policies designed to this end and by co-ordinating these policies; and to stimulate and harmonize members' efforts in favour of developing countries." 24 member countries in Western Europe, North America and the Pacific.

Overseas Development Council VIG
1717 Massachusetts Ave., NW, Washington, D.C. 20036
202-234-8701

"Seeks to increase American understanding of the economic and social problems confronting the developing countries and of the importance of these countries to the United States in an increasingly interdependent world."

Overseas Education Fund VIE
2101 L St., NW, Ste. 916, Washington, D.C. 20037
202-466-3430

"Is the only U.S. private, non-governmental organization which focuses its overseas programs on the integration of the Third World women into the socioeconomic development of their societies."

Oxfam – America IVB
302 Columbus Ave., P.O. Box 288, Back Bay Station, Boston, MA 02116
617-247-3304

Provides relief services to those struck by natural disasters. Conducts educational programs on Third World economic development and seeks to establish self-reliant development projects in rural areas. Its motto: "Helping people around the world to help themselves."

Pacem in Terris IIID
1106 Adams St., Wilmington, DE 19801
302-656-2721

"To facilitate the active participation of Delmarva Peninsula citizens and organizations, especially within the religious community, in the pursuit of world peace and global justice."

Pan American Development Foundation IVB
1625 I St., NW, Ste. 622, Washington, D.C. 20006
202-789-3000

Works with private sector development efforts in Latin America and the Caribbean. Through its Inter-American Forum, it has "developed a solid collaborating network of respected organizations and universities concerned about the hemisphere, who are working toward encouraging a more expansive understanding of the Americas."

Pan American Women's Association IF
20 W. 40th St., New York, NY 10018
212-221-6790

Founded in 1930 to effect the relationships among the Americas through women through cultural means. The organization has a wide range of programs basically in support of human rights and democratic causes.

Path Institute of Research on International Problems VIE
46-393 Holopu Place, Kaneohe, Hawaii 96744

Uses scientific methods and interdisciplinary studies to analyze alternatives to social problems, international relations, conflict, economic growth, and economic development.

Pax Christi USA IIID
3000 N. Mango Ave., Chicago, IL 60634
312-637-2555

"Pax Christi, the international Catholic movement for peace, has as its primary objective to work with all people for peace for all humankind, always witnessing to the peace of Christ. Pax Christi USA has as its priorities disarmament, a just world order, the primacy of conscience, education for peace, and alternatives to violence."

Pax World Fund VA
224 State St., Portsmouth, NH 03801
603-431-8022

"Seeks investment in companies that are not to any degree engaged in manufacturing defense or weapons-related systems."

The Peace Lab VID
438 N. Skinner St., St. Louis, MO 63130

Founded by Theodore Lentz, the Peace Lab seeks to develop a "Science of Peace."

Peace Research Organization Fund VID
First National Bank Bldg, Denver, CO 80202

A private, non-profit organization dealing with peace and education through research and conferences.

Peacemakers for Christ IIID
3355 Briggs Rd., Columbus, OH 43204
614-279-1018

"'The Missing Peace' — A revelation given in Mexico to Pope John Paul — to ban Christians from nuclear war. 'Peacemakers — Voices in the Wilderness' — A news bulletin that hails the actions and witnesses of all Peacemakers."

Peaceworkers
3565 Mt. Diablo Blvd.
Lafayette, CA 94549
415-283-6500

" . . . is building a roster of untrained and trained persons who are willing to volunteer for nonviolent duty as members of a UN Peace Brigade." Peaceworkers pledge to "serve in an unarmed UN Peaceworkers service . . . to prepare for the peaceful settlement of conflicts."

P.E.N. American Center VA
47 Fifth Ave., New York, NY 10003
212-255-1977

"An international association of writers. Its basic goal is to promote cooperation among men and women of letters in all countries in the interest of freedom of expression, exchange of ideas relevant to literature and international good will.''

People-to-People International IVA
2440 Pershing Rd., Ste. G-30, Kansas City, MO 64108
816-421-6343
    An international exchange organization.

Philadelphia Namibia Action Group IIIE
5201 Cedar Ave., Philadelphia. PA 19143
215-474-9592
    ''We are a small collective of the Movement for a New Society using education and direct action to support the struggle of the Namibian people against South African control and multinational corporate exploitation. We distribute a slide show on Namibia, publish irregular updates on Namibian news, and organize demonstrations and workshops.''

Physicians for Social Responsibility
23 Main Street, P.O. Box 144, Watertown, MA 02172
617-924-3468
    A non-profit, non-governmental organization composed of concerned physicians and citizens who wish to halt the nuclear arms race. It educates through films, seminars, and public presentations that dramatically describe the horrors of nuclear war.

Planetary Citizens VA
777 UN Plaza
New York, NY 10017
212-490-2766
    ''Conducts programs designed to stimulate awareness of the capacity individuals have to identify as a species and overcome the threat of war and ecocide and the pestilence of injustice and hunger.''

Planned Parenthood-World Population IIIE
810 Seventh Ave., New York, NY 10019
212-541-7800
    ''Research/education/training on family planning.''

Population Council IIIC
1 Dag Hammarskjöld Plaza, New York, NY 10017
212-644-1300
    ''Research and research funding.''

The Population Crisis Committee IIIC
1120 19th St., NW, Ste. 550, Washington, D.C. 20036
202-659-1833
"Develops worldwide support for international population and family planning programs through public education, policy analysis, and liaison with international leaders and organizations, as well as through direct funding of private family planning projects overseas."

The Population Institute IIIC
110 Maryland Ave., NE, Washington, D.C. 20002
202-544-3300
"Education on population trends and related problems."

Population Reference Bureau, Inc. IIIC
1337 Connecticut Ave., NW, Washington, D.C. 20036
202-785-4664
"Research/education."

Project for Global Education VIIIF
1011 Arlington Blvd., Ste. W-219, Arlington, VA 22209
202-524-2141
"An effort by four organizations to promote global values and world order education. It is intended to stimulate thought and discussion among students, faculty and campus clergy about world problems and model futures."

Project HOPE IG
The Project HOPE Health Sciences Education Center, Millwood, VA 22646
703-837-2100
"Provides educational programs for medical, nursing, dental, and allied health personnel in developing countries. Sponsors policy studies on U.S. and international health care issues."

Promoting Enduring Peace IIIA
P.O. Box 5103, Woodmont, CT 06460
203-878-4769
"Seeks to improve international understanding and good will. It distributes educational materials free and annually gives the Gandhi Peace Award to a person who has made significant contributions to peace."

Public Resource Center VIC
1747 Connecticut Ave., NW, Washington, D.C. 20036
202-483-3321
Does public interest research on the environment, employment, and health internationally.

Radio Free Europe/Radio Liberty IIIC
1775 Broadway, New York, NY 10019
212-397-5300

"Operates radio stations beaming news and entertainment to people behind the Iron Curtain."

The Rand Corporation VIIIC
1700 Main St., Santa Monica, CA 90406
213-393-0411

A private research institute working largely on government defense contracts; studies military strategies and military systems as well as social science questions.

A. Philip Randolph Institute IL
260 Park Ave., S., New York, NY 10010
212-533-8000

National organization promoting the civil rights of blacks; active in forming "black caucuses" in major trade unions in the U.S.

Religious Action Center of the Union of American Hebrew Congregations IA
2027 Massachusetts Ave., NW, Washington, D.C. 20006
202-387-2800

Serves as a resource center and the Washington voice of the reformed Jewish movement in the U.S. on social action issues pertinent to the Jewish community.

Republican National Committee IIIB
310 First St., SE, Washington, D.C. 20003
202-484-6500

National headquarters.

Research Center for Religion and Human Rights in Closed Societies IIIC
475 Riverside Dr., New York, NY 10027
212-870-2440

Documents violations of human rights in totalitarian societies, presents materials for translation — both official documents and underground literature, issues press releases and information updates, and publishes a newsletter.

Resource Center for Nonviolence VIG
P.O. Box 2324, Santa Cruz, CA 95063
408-423-1626

"Offers a wide-ranging public education program in the history and theory, methodology and current practice of nonviolence as a force for personal and social change." Publishes occasional newsletter; internship program.

Resources for the Future VIII C
1755 Massachusetts Ave., NW, Washington, D.C. 20036
202-328-5000
"A private non-profit research organization concerned with the development, conservation, and use of natural resources and with the quality of the environment. To safeguard freedom of inquiry for its staff, RFF does not advocate particular policies nor otherwise adopt institutional positions."

Right Sharing of World Resources Program IVB
Friends World Committee for Consultation, 1506 Race St., Philadelphia, PA
  19102
215-563-0757
"Quaker education and outreach regarding development issues, with support for projects."

The Ripon Society IIIF
419 New Jersey Ave., S.E., Washington, D.C. 20003
202-546-1292
"The Ripon Society believes that innovative public policy proposals can help rejuvenate the Republican Party."

Riverside Church Disarmament Program IIIB
490 Riverside Dr., New York, NY 10027
212-749-7000
Educates the public about the horrors of nuclear war through its publications, seminars, and conferences. Acts as a speaker's referral agency and supports church disarmament programs throughout the country.

The Rockefeller Foundation IB
1133 Avenue of the Americas, New York, NY 10036
212-869-8500
"Both a granting and operational foundation. Its field staffs have contributed to improved public health, to agricultural progress, and to strengthened university centers throughout the world."

Rotary International IB
Service Division, 1600 Ridge Ave., Evanston, IL 60201
312-328-0100
World headquarters of an international service club composed largely of business people. Conducts programs designed to encourage international understanding and cooperation.

Salvation Army I H
120 W. 14th St., New York, NY 10011
212-620-4900
"Social religious welfare projects, clinics, emergency feeding and shelter."

SANE: A Citizen's Organization for a Sane World IIIB
514 C St., NE, Washington, D.C. 20002
202-546-7100

"Established in 1957 for the purpose of achieving a nuclear test ban treaty, which was signed in 1963. Currently our issues revolve around efforts to halt the escalating international arms race, examining the military budget, and supporting economic conversion. We are a membership organization with twelve established chapters and more currently starting up."

Save the Children VA
54 Wilton Rd., Westport, CT 06880
203-226-7241

"Family-oriented self-help and disaster relief."

Shalom Education VIIIE
67 E. Madison, Ste. 1417, Chicago, IL 60603
312-236-7459

"A Chicago-based group of pastors, seminary professors, Christian educators and local church-school teachers, and a national network of concerned groups and individuals working to find and create resource materials so that Christian education programs might be infused with the best methods, basic values and perspectives that will teach the way of peace (a world without war, hunger or systemic injustice)."

The Sierra Club VA
530 Bush St., San Francisco, CA 94108
415-981-8634

Active in defense of the natural environment against encroachment by technological society.

Sister Cities International VA
1625 I St., NW, Ste. 424-26, Washington, D.C. 20006
202-293-5504

Seeks to get cities in different countries to exchange information, visitors, and friendship.

Social Science Education Consortium, Inc. VIIA
855 Broadway, Boulder, CO 80302
303-492-8154

Seeks to "improve social science/social studies education at all levels by providing educators with publications, information services, workshops, consultation, and research."

Society for Citizen Education in World Affairs VII E
c/o Richard Heggie, World Affairs Council of Northern California
312 Sutter St., Ste. 200, San Francisco, CA 94108
415-982-2541

A professional association of individuals making their living in citizen education in world affairs. Meets with National Council of Community World Affairs Organizations.

Society for Cultural Relations USA-USSR IIIB
1154 North Western Ave., Los Angeles, CA 90029
213-469-7525

"Deeply committed to working for understanding and friendly relations between our country and the USSR [from a] commitment shaped by our love for our country and its people. Convinced that our country will benefit more profoundly from friendly relations, trade, and cultural exchanges than from building military bases armed with nuclear missiles pointed at all major cities of the Soviet Union."

The Society for International Development IVB
Palazzo Civilta del Lavoro, EUR, 00144 Rome, Italy
59.55.06 or 59.17.897

"An independent, non-governmental organization whose purposes are to provide a forum for collective reflection and to encourage a mutually educating dialogue on development at all levels."

Society for Social Responsibility in Science VB
221 Rock Hill Rd., Bala Cynwyd, PA 19004

"A body of scientific workers organized to foster throughout the world a tradition of personal moral responsibility for the consequences to humanity of professional activity, with emphasis on constructive alternatives to militarism." Publishes a monthly newsletter.

Sojourners Fellowship IIIB
1343 Euclid St., NW, Washington, D.C. 20009
202-232-2657

A Christian community ministering to the inner-city community in Washington. Interested in peace and justice issues. Publishes *Sojourners* (monthly).

Solar Lobby VA
1001 Connecticut Ave., NW, Washington, D.C. 20036
202-466-6350

Works to influence the formation of energy policy, prods Congress to give solar energy a chance, and serves as a watchdog.

Southeast Asia Resource Center VC
P.O. Box 4000D, Berkeley, CA 94704
415-548-2546

   "Primary function at this time is to coordinate and disseminate information about the countries and issues of Southeast Asia, and on U.S. involvements there."

Southern Christian Leadership Conference IL
334 Auburn Ave., N.E., Atlanta, GA 30303
404-522-1420

   Founded by Martin Luther King, Jr., the SCLC remains an active civic rights organization; the emphasis has shifted from political to economic issues.

The Stanley Foundation IIB
420 E. Third Ave., Muscatine, IA 52761
319-264-1500

   "Encourages study, research, and education in the field of foreign relations, contributing to secure peace with freedom and justice. Emphasis is given to activities related to world organization."

Swarthmore College Peace Collection VIB
McCabe Library, Swarthmore, PA 19081
215-447-7000

   A major depository of peace organizations' records.

Tolstoy Foundation Inc. IIIC
250 W. 57th St., New York, NY 10107
212-247-2922

   "To assist victims of oppression by rehabilitation within the Free World, immigration to countries willing to offer asylum, integration and assimilation in local communities without loss of the distinctive values inherent in their ethnic traditions."

TRANET: Transnational Network for Appropriate Alternative Technologies IVB
P.O. Box 567, Rangley, ME 04970

   "Established to serve appropriate/alternative technology centers in all parts of the world. Its goals are: to help these groups develop bilateral links with one another and to promote the dialogue on A.T. concepts."

Transnational Institute VIIIC
1901 Q St., NW, Washington, D.C. 20004
202-234-9382

and:

Paulus Patterstraat 20, 1017 DA Amsterdam, The Netherlands

A research organization, using researchers from many countries, studying disarmament, human rights, international law, development, militarism, and the new international economic order.

The Trilateral Commission IIIB
345 E. 46th St., New York, NY 10017
212-661-1180

"A non-governmental organization of business, labor, governmental and civic leaders in North America, Western Europe, and Japan that publishes a quarterly magazine *(Trilague)* and issues task force reports including policy recommendations suggesting how the industrial democracies can best cope with a changing, interdependent world."

Twentieth Century Fund VIE
41 E. 70th St., New York, NY 10021
212-535-4441

"A research foundation engaged in policy-oriented studies of economic, political and social issues and institutions" including, in recent years, non-proliferation, energy, secrecy, veterans, and presidential politics.

Union of American Hebrew Congregations IA
838 Fifth Ave., New York, NY 10021
212-249-0100

"The central organization of 750 reform synagogues. Its Commission on Social Action deals with issues of social justice including arms control and world peace."

Union of Concerned Scientists IIIB
1384 Massachusetts Ave., Cambridge, MA 02238
617-547-5552

A non-profit organization of scientists, engineers, and other professionals concerned about the impact of advanced technology on society. UCS has conducted independent technical studies on a range of questions relating to nuclear power plant safety, nuclear arms limitation and liquefied natural gas transport and storage hazards.

Unitarian Universalist Service Committee IA
78 Beacon St., Boston, MA 02108
617-742-2120

"Non-sectarian service with nutrition, education, rural health care programs."

United Automobile, Aerospace, Agricultural, Implement Workers of America (UAW) ID
1757 N St., NW, Washington, D.C. 20036
202-828-8500

> The second largest trade union in the U.S. and Canada works ''to help raise money, enlist candidates, educate members on current issues, register voters, and get members to the polls. [It considers that] the fate of the UAW is tied to the struggle for social justice and world peace.''

United Methodist Church, Board of Church and Society IC
100 Maryland Ave., NE, Washington, D.C. 20002
202-488-5600

> ''The staff, in general, carries on a program of research, education, and action, with a focus on national social policy. It interprets and advocates positions set forth in the Social Principles of the church.''

United Nations Agencies
> Listed at the end of Chapter 5, International Organization and World Law

United Nations Association of the USA IIA
300 E. 42nd St., 8th Fl., New York, NY 10017
212-697-3232

> ''Heightens US public awareness and increases public knowledge of global issues and their relation to the United Nations system; encourages, where appropriate, multilateral approaches in dealing with these issues; builds public support for constructive US policies on matters of global concern; and enhances the effectiveness of the United Nations and other international institutions.''

The U.N. University VIA
Toho Seimei Bldg., 15-1 Shibuya 2-chrome, Shibuya-ku, Tokyo 150, Japan
(03) 499-2811

> ''Provides a network of communication for all scholars at the university level, conducts research on global problems, concentrates currently on three areas: world hunger, human and social development, management and use of natural resources. UNU does not grant degrees or operate within the confines of a central campus.''

U.N. We Believe IIIB
33 E. 43rd St., New York, NY 10017
212-661-1772

> ''The liaison between the business/labor community and the U.N.; seeks to persuade corporations and unions to stimulate greater public confidence in the U.N.''

U.S. Association for the Club of Rome IIIB
1735 DeSales St., NW, Washington, D.C. 20036
202-638-1029
  Circulates and attempts to gain public visibility for Club of Rome studies, such as *The Limits to Growth*.

U.S. Chamber of Commerce, International Division IB
1615 H St. NW, Washington, D.C. 20006
202-659-6000
  "A federation of businessmen and women, firms and organizations, with a membership of over 170,000. . . . The International Division . . . develops and implements policies on international economic issues, conducts the international business relations of the Chamber, and produces studies, publications and programs on a broad range of concerns to the international business community."

U.S. Committee for Refugees IIIC
20 W. 40th St., New York, NY 10018
212-398-9142
  "Seeking to communicate the plight of the world's millions of refugees to the American people through its many public education programs."

U.S. Committee for UNICEF VA
331 E. 38th St., New York, NY 10016
212-686-5522
  Seeks to gain public visibility and raise funds for UNICEF projects.

U.S. Peace Council IIIA
7 E. 15th St., Ste. 408, New York, NY 10003
212-989-1194
  "Seeks to be an organizational vehicle in the U.S. which will work alongside all the peace forces of our United States. We seek also to work in concert with the peace forces of the world who find their most comprehensive expression in the World Peace Council"; an organization closely associated with the Soviet Union's foreign policy objectives.

U.S. Servas IVC
11 John St., Rm. 406, New York, NY 10038
212-267-0252
  "An international cooperative system of hosts and travelers established to help build world peace, good will and understanding by providing opportunities for deeper, more personal contacts among people of diverse cultures and backgrounds."

Veterans of Foreign Wars of the U.S. IC
34th and Broadway, Kansas City, MO 64111
816-756-3390

"A 1.9 million member organization of men and women veterans of foreign engagements around the world. A fraternal, patriotic group whose motto is, 'To honor the dead by helping the living.' The V.F.W. is the oldest major veterans organization and was established in 1899.''

Vietnam Veterans of America
212 Fifth Ave., New York, NY 10010
212-685-3152

An organization of and for Vietnam veterans that seeks better treatment of veterans as a result of better understanding of the war.

Volunteers in Technical Assistance (VITA) IVB
3706 Rhode Island Ave., Mount Rainier, MD 20822
301-277-7000

"A private, non-profit association of concerned engineers, scientists, educators, technicians, and other experts working to promote economic and social development in Africa, Asia, and Latin America. Our focus is on small-scale, low-cost technologies which are appropriate to local human, cultural, and economic conditions, which rely on renewable sources of energy and which do not harm the environment. VITA's services include a technical inquiry service, publications, on-site technical assistance, and (in the field of renewable energy technologies) small project grants.''

War Control Planners, Inc. VA
Box 19127, Washington, D.C. 20036
202-785-0708

Chartered in 1963, War Control Planners "is a citizen effort seeking to foster continuing exploration and discussion of scientific, technical and other achievements which make possible the protection of all nations against future war, and the re-direction of Earth's energies and resources to pro-human purposes instead. In the interest of mutual survival it is time to project a new type of global organization to assure protection and safety for all nations.''

War Resisters League IIIC
339 Lafayette St., New York, NY 10012
212-228-0450

"Secularist, pacifist organization; opposes war and violence through nonviolent action and education; seeks removal of causes of war (e.g. sexism, racism, militarism); programs on disarmament, feminism, opposition to nuclear weapons and power; draft and war tax resistance; publishes yearly Peace Calendar and bimonthly *WRL News*; maintains network of 20 locals.''

Washington Office on Africa IIIE
110 Maryland Ave., NE, Washington, D.C. 20002
202-546-7961
"Established in September 1972 to advocate and work for a United States policy toward southern Africa which would support majority rule."

Washington Office on Latin America III E
110 Maryland Ave., NE, Washington, D.C. 20002
202-544-8045
"Focuses on human rights in Latin America and U.S. policy toward that region and serves as a liaison between Latin America and U.S. institutions affecting foreign policy."

Wilmington College Peace Resource Center VIB
Pyle Center Box 1183, Wilmington, OH 45177
513-382-5338
The Center makes available films, slide shows and books on the Hiroshima/Nagasaki experience, arms race, non-violence, and has research files on H/N, nuclear testing and fallout, nuclear power, nuclear weapons, disarmament, and the peace movement.

Women Strike for Peace IIIB
145 S. 13th St., Philadelphia, PA 19107
215-923-0861
"Dedicated to 'End the arms race — not the human race,' organizer of Proposition #1 which calls on the President to call emergency session of nuclear nations to plan dismantling of nuclear weapons."

Women's International League for Peace and Freedom IIIC
1213 Race St., Philadelphia, PA 19107
215-563-7110
"An international organization working since 1915 by nonviolent means to secure peace, freedom, and justice for all. Universal disarmament, an effective U.N., an end to racism and sexism, education for peace, and putting people before profits are among its goals."

World Affairs Council of Boston IIA
22 Batterymarch St., Boston, MA 02109
617-482-1740
"Pursues its primary goal of creating an informed, articulate and influential public opinion on important foreign policy issues."

World Affairs Council of Northern California IIA
312 Sutter St., Ste. 200, San Francisco, CA 94108
415-982-2541

"Founded in 1947 to promote public study and education about international issues and foreign countries. While the Council's 7000 members are committed to the idea that world affairs are important to all in this ever-shrinking world, they are not necessarily agreed on specific policies, approaches, or solutions. The Council seeks to provide authoritative information and opportunities to explore diverse views through a wide range of activities held in congenial surroundings."

World Affairs Council of Philadelphia IIA
1300 Market St., Philadelphia, PA 19107
215-563-5363

"A year-round service of intellectual stimulation in global and national affairs."

World Affairs Council of Wilmington, Delaware IIA
1 Rodney Square, Wilmington, DE 19899
302-658-6541

Seeks to "promote education in the field of world affairs . . . presents speeches and lectures by recognized experts, sponsors debates, study groups and conferences, distributes literature and other materials bearing on world affairs, to carry out the Council maxim, 'In a democracy agreement is not essential; participation is.' "

World Association of World Federalists IIIB
777 UN Plaza, New York, NY 10017
212-490-2766

Believes that world problems require world organizations, and seeks to assure peace through disarmament, a just world, and the equitable distribution of resources.

World Conference on Religion and Peace VB
777 UN Plaza, New York, NY 10017
212-687-2163

"An international, inter-religious organization working for world peace and justice through greater religious understanding and more effective cooperative effort in reducing the causes of international conflict. It represents all of the major world religions in approximately 60 nations, including the U.S."

World Constitution and Parliament Association IIIB
1480 Hoyt St., Ste. 31, Lakewood, CO 80215
303-233-3548

"Seeks ratification of the Constitution for the Federation of Earth . . . ratification is invited by national parliaments, communities and universities, and, in due course, by popular referendum. When 25 countries have given provisional ratification, the first operative stage of world government will be organized."

World Council of Churches — U.S. Conference IA
475 Riverside Dr., Rm. 439, New York, NY 10027
212-870-2533

An organization of 293 churches in 100 countries which promotes missionary work, aids common activity among churches, and maintains contact with other religious groups.

World Federalists Association IIIB
1011 Arlington Blvd., Suite W-219, Arlington, VA 22209
703-524-2141

Conducts educational programs aimed at the development of global institutions to deal with global problems such as war, hunger, population expansion, environmental pollution, denial of human rights and economic inequities. Publishes *World Federalist Newsletter*.

World Future Society VIIIC
4916 St. Elmo Ave., Washington, D.C. 20014
301-656-8274

Works toward a rational understanding of the future and a recognition of the importance of such studies through workshops and publications; does not engage in political activities or endorse particular ideologies.

World Hunger Education Service IVB
2000 P St., NW, Washington, D.C. 20036
202-223-2995

"Seminars on 'The Politics of Hunger,' monthly journal *Hunger Notes*, and information clearinghouse are the primary services offered. Sees solutions to hunger in terms of policy decisions rather than technology. Works closely with hunger and justice programs of many religious and secular organizations and networks."

World Hunger Year, Inc. IVB
350 Broadway, Ste. 209, New York, NY 10013
212-226-2714

"A nonprofit educational and resource organization dedicated to developing people's awareness of the root cause of hunger to bring about change."

World Leisure and Recreation Association VIIIC
345 E. 46th St., New York, NY 10017
212-697-8783
    "A nonprofit, non-governmental international service agency dedicated to improving individual and community life through recreation and the positive use of leisure."

World Neighbors IVA
5116 N. Portland Ave., Oklahoma City, OK 73112
405-946-3333
    Encourages communication across national boundaries by high school students and others.

World Peace Army VA
Friends Meeting House, 15 Rutherford Place, New York, NY 10003
212-879-5976
    Recognizes the adversarial relationship between the US and the USSR is leading to potential nuclear destruction, and thinks that a third force to bridge the gap between the two superpowers is needed. "The first action we are planning is a march across Western Europe, to be met by our equivalent from the Soviet Union and Eastern Europe."

World Peace Foundation VIIE
22 Batterymarch St., Boston, MA 02109
617-482-3875
    "Sets in motion educational forces . . . advancing the cause of peace through research and education in international relations." Specific research in international organizations, U.S.-Canada Relations, public opinion and world affairs, and public involvement in international relations. Publishes *International Organization*.

World Peace Council (see U.S. Peace Council).

World Peacemakers VB
2852 Ontario Rd., NW, Washington, D.C. 20009
202-265-7582
    "Works within the religious community to raise the great danger, both physical and spiritual, of the nuclear arms race; and to find/communicate real security derived from God's peace. We encourage small groups to form around both the inward and outward journeys of peacemaking."

World Pen Pals VA
1690 Como Ave., St. Paul, MN 55108
612-647-0191
"Links approximately 40,000 young people, ages 12-20 from 175 countries and territories each year in friendly correspondence."

World Service Authority VA
Atlantic Bldg., 930 F St., NW, Ste. 318, Washington, D.C. 20004
202-638-2662
Seeks to build a political identification of world citizens through use of a world passport, issuance of World Government postage stamps, and other actions.

World University Service IVA
Lehman College, Bedford Park Blvd., Bronx, NY 10468
212-960-8000
"Student to student self-help activities and education."

World Vision International IVB
919 W. Huntington Dr., Monrovia, CA 91016
213--357-7979
"Christian childcare, relief agency."

World Without War Council, Inc. IVA
175 Fifth Ave., New York, NY 10010
212-674-2085; 415-845-1992 (Office of the President)
"A consulting agency to an enterprise that does not yet exist — a serious and sustained effort to end war. The Council affirms the possibility of bringing into existence conditions essential to a world without war; it considers the work of American nongovernmental organizations crucial and focuses on alternatives to violence capable of advancing the ideas of a free society in a world persistently hostile to those ideas." Research, publications, conferences, interne training, and a quarterly newsletter (free).

World Without War Issues Center-Midwest III
421 S. Wabash, Chicago, IL 60605
312-236-7459
"Exists to apply the moral and political perspective of the World Without War Council to specific legislative and executive choices."

Worldwatch Institute IVB
1776 Massachusetts Ave., NW, Washington, D.C. 20036
202-452-1999

"Seeks to anticipate global problems and social trends. Through its research and publications, Worldwatch focuses attention on emerging global issues."

YMCA (Young Men's Christian Association) IH
100 E. Wacker, Chicago, IL 60601
312-977-0031

National headquarters of the YMCA which has largely autonomous branches in many countries, and an active international program in this country.

YWCA (Young Women's Christian Association) IH
600 Lexington Ave., New York, NY 10022
212-753-4700

National headquarters of a major national women's service organization with programs designed to meet members' interests.

Youth for Understanding IVA
3501 Newark St., NW, Washington, D.C. 20016
202-966-6808

An international exchange program for students.

Zero Population Growth, Inc. IIIC
1346 Connecticut Ave., NW, Washington, D.C. 20036
202-785-0100

"A non-profit, activist organization dedicated to population stabilization, nationally and internationally. Single copies of *A Basic Case for ZPG in the U.S.* are available free with a first class stamp and a mailing label."

Zonta International IF
59 E. Van Buren St., Chicago, IL 60605
312-939-3850

"A service organization of executive women in business and the professions who, as leaders in their communities, devote themselves to civic and social welfare. Zonta International has been granted consultative status with the United Nations by ECOSOC, UNESCO, UNICEF, and ILO."

UNITED STATES PEACE STUDIES PROGRAMS

This list includes formal programs in peace studies or conflict resolution at American colleges and universities. A few of the entries are annotated to give the reader a flavor of what peace studies involves. Since a program can easily change, it is advisable to contact the school for a current description of its program. In addition to the schools mentioned, many others offer appropriate courses in several fields or allow individual research which can be combined to create an individualized major, minor, or concentration in peace studies.

Akron, University of
Center for Peace Studies
Akron, OH 44325
216-375-7008
    ''Offers an academic program with a Certificate in Peace Studies. Publishes the International Peace Studies Newsletter, has special materials on teaching human rights and reproduces peace and international journals, library card catalogues, and other research aids on microfilm.''

Antioch College
Antioch International Individualized M.A. in Peace Studies
Yellow Springs, OH 45387
513-767-1031

Associated Mennonite Biblical Seminaries
3003 Benham Ave., Elkhart, IN 46514

Avila College Peace Institute
11901 Wornall Road, Kansas City, MO 64145

Bethel College
Peace Studies Program
North Newton, KA 67117
316-283-2500

Boston College
Program for the Study of Peace and War
Gasson Hall, Chestnut Hill, MA 02167
617-969-0100, Ext. 3514

California State University
Peace/War Studies
6000 J St., Sacramento, CA 95819
916-454-6618
    ''An interdisciplinary major concentrated in the Social Sciences concerned with conflict and social change. The program, which can lead to a BA degree in Social Science, is designed to introduce students to the processes of understanding and changing conditions to lead to a more peaceful world and a more just society.''

Catholic University
Peace Studies Program
Marist Hall, Washington, DC 20064

Chapman College
Peace Studies Progam
Orange, CA 92666
714-997-6621

Colgate University
Peace and World Order Studies Program
Hamilton, NY 13346
315-824-1000
    "The Peace and World Order Studies Program (originally Peace Studies)
was established at Colgate in 1970 as a multidisciplinary approach to
peacemaking in international affairs. It is . . . primarily directed to policy-
making and problem-solving. Our purpose is to engage students, faculty, and
others in an active vocational quest for a world community free from mass
organized violence and ordered by a just and viable system of peace."

College of Mount Saint Vincent
Peace Studies Program
Riverdale, NY 10471
212-549-8000

College of William and Mary
Honors and Experimental Programs
Williamsburg, VA 23185

Colorado, University of
Conflict and Peace Studies Program
Muenzinger E 229, Boulder, CO 80302

Cornell University
Peace Studies Program
180 Uris Hall, Ithaca, NY 14850
607-256-6484
    "Interdisciplinary effort concerned with problems of peace and war, arms
control and disarmament, and foreign policy aspects of these issues. Supports graduate and postdoctoral study, research and cross-campus interactions. Sponsors an active seminar series, conferences and workshops, and
teaching related courses."

Dayton, University of
Peace Studies Institute
Dayton, OH 54509

Duke University Law School
Rule of Law Research Center
Durham, NC 27706

Earlham College
Peace Studies Program
Richmond, IN 47374
317-962-6561

The Peace Studies Program at Earlham offers courses that can be combined with a major in another field, a major in Peace Studies, and, in conjunction with the Earlham School of Religion, a Master of Ministry degree in social ministry with a peace emphasis.

Friends World College
Peace Studies Program
Huntington, NY 11743
516-549-1102

Garrett-Evangelical Theological Seminary
The Peace Institute
2121 Sheridan Road, Evanston, IL 60201
312-866-3963

"In February 1975 the Garrett-Evangelical faculty founded the Peace Institute as an expression of its commitment to help prepare the church for its essential ministries of peace and justice in a thermonuclear and neo-colonial era . . . Seeks to provide ministerial students a sound biblical, theological, and ethical basis for the understanding of, and for efforts supporting peace, justice, and liberation."

Georgetown University
Center for Peace Studies
Washington, DC 20057
202-625-4240

Goddard College
Peace Studies Program
Plainfield, VT 05667

Goshen College
PAXCOM
Goshen, IN 46526
219-533-3161

Gustavus Adolphus College
Peace Studies Program
St. Peter, MN 56082
507-931-4300

Harvard University
Conflict and Peace Studies Program
Cambridge, MA 02138

Haverford College
Center for Non-violent Conflict Resolution
Haverford, PA 19041

International College
Peace Studies Program
Los Angeles, CA 90024

Iowa, University of
Center for World Order Studies
College of Law, R. 280, Iowa City, IA 52242

Juniata College
Peace Studies Program
Huntington, PA 16652
814-643-4310

Keene State University
International Studies Program
Keene, NH 03431

Kent State University
Center for Peaceful Change
Kent, OH 44242
216-672-3143
    "The Center is an academic unit at Kent State University offering a
program of study, research, and service activities focusing on the dynamics
of change in human systems. The Center offers a major in Integrative Change
leading to a BS degree under the Arts and Sciences College."

Manchester College
Peace Studies Institute and Program in Conflict Resolution
North Manchester, IN 46962
219-982-2141
"For over 30 years this program has reflected Manchester's tradition of concern for peace and human need through interdisciplinary studies in the understanding of war and peace, social change, and conflict resolution."

Manhattan College
Peace Studies Institute
Bronx, NY 10471
212-548-1400

Mankato State College
Peace Studies Program
Mankato, MN 56001

Maryland, University of
World Order Studies
College Park, MD 20742

Missouri, University of
Peace Studies Program
22 Middlebush Hall
Columbia, MO 65211

New York, State University of
Society for the Study of Social Problems
208 Rockwell Hall, 1300 Elmwood Ave., Buffalo, NY 14222
716-878-5511

North Carolina, University of
Peace Studies Program
Chapel Hill, NC 27514
919-933-2304

Notre Dame, University of
Program in Non-violence
Notre Dame, IN 46556

Oregon State University
Peace Education Resource Group
Corvallis, OR 97331

Pennsylvania, University of
Peace Studies Program
Philadelphia, PA 19104
215-243-7502

Pittsburgh, University of
Peace and Conflict Studies
Pittsburgh, PA 15260

Saint Joseph's College
Faith-Justice Institute
5600 City Ave., Philadelphia, PA 19131
215-879-7906

Southern Illinois University
Peace Studies Program
Edwardsville, IL 62025

Syracuse University
Program in Nonviolent Conflict and Change
Maxwell School
Syracuse, NY 13210
315-423-3870
   "An interdisciplinary program to study, research, and train in creative, peaceful ways of managing conflict and bringing about or resisting change."

Villanova University
Program in Peace and Justice
Villanova, PA 19085

Washington, University of
Committee on Conflict Studies
School of Law
Seattle, WA 98105

Wayne State University
Center for Peace and Conflict Studies
5229 Cass Ave., Detroit, MI 48202
313-577-3453
   "The Center for Peace and Conflict Studies was established in 1966 at Wayne State University. Confronted by the awesome destructiveness of modern warfare, those who founded the Center continue to be aware of the responsibility of both scholars and citizens to search for ways to lessen global conflict."

William Patterson College of New Jersey
Peace Studies Program
500 Pompton Road
Wayne, NJ 07470

Wilmington College
Peace Studies Program
Wilmington, OH 45177
513-382-6661, Ext. 219
    ''Has, as its primary goal, the active involvement of students, faculty and
others in the quest for a way of life (individually, socially and politically)
which is characterized by peace — not merely the absence of war and violence, but also the presence of social and economic justice and a spirit of
mutual helpfulness.''

World University in Ojai
College of World Peace
107 N. Ventura St.
Ojai, CA 93023
805-646-1444
    Advocates a ''world without walls'' and sponsors a weekly ''Peace
Meditation'' Fridays at 5:30 PM. The College of World Peace offers a BA
degree in Irenology, the study of peace.

INTERNATIONAL PEACE AND RELATED INSTITUTES

    This list provides a sample of institutions around the world currently doing
peace research or research in world affairs. Some of these are private, others are
affiliated with universities. In addition, *World Directory of Peace Research
Institutions*(UNESCO, 1981), offers an extensive list of international organizations with information on their research, affiliation, staffing, and publications.

Australia

Strategic and Defense Studies Centre
Research School of Pacific Studies
The Australian National University
Canberra, A.C.T. 2600 Australia
    ''The only academic institution in this field in Australia. The SDCA is

concerned with research and graduate teaching in the areas of global, regional and national security, embracing studies of force structures, postures and arms control.''

Austria

Austrian Society of Foreign Affairs and International Relations
Palais Palffy, Josefplatz 6, Vienna 1, Austria
   ''Non-profit organization; 600 members; lectures; round-tables; library; publication of a journal and editor of books.''

International Institute for Peace
Mollwaldplatz 5, A-1040 Vienna, Austria
   Engaged in research and educational work on topics of disarmament, peaceful resolution of international conflict, and U.S./Soviet relations.

Belgium

Institute of International Law
82 Avenue du Castel, 1200 Brussels, Belgium
Concerned with the application of international law in the furtherance of peace.

University of Peace
Blvd. du Nord, 4, 5000 Namur, Belgium
   ''Seeks the establishment and maintenance of peace through education, training and providing resources for young people. Focuses on disarmament and economic development.''

Canada

Canadian Institute of International Affairs
15 Kings College Circle, Toronto M5S 2V9 Canada
   Studies ''Canada's position and policies in the international community and the policies and attitudes of others toward us. The Institute is thus able to place before government and the public a continuing body of factual knowledge and informed opinion.''

Canadian Peace Research Institute
119 Thomas St., Oakville, Ontario L6J 3A7 Canada
   ''Started in 1961 by a nuclear physicist, Dr. Norman Alcock, it is a privately funded organization. It publishes a quarterly journal and books dealing with peace, mainly on attitudes and government decision-making.''

Centre D'Etudes et de Documentation Européennes, University of Montreal
3150, rue Jean-Brillant, Casa Postale 6128, Montreal, Quebec H3C 3J7
Canada
    Studies integration, especially European integration, European political
systems, and Canada's relationship with integration organizations in Europe.
Publishes *Journal of European Integration*.

Centre for Foreign Policy Studies, Dalhousie University
Halifax, Nova Scotia, B3H 4H6 Canada
    Studies foreign policy and decision-making processes of Canada, USA,
USSR, the United Kingdom, China, and Africa.

Institute of Intergovernmental Relations, Queen's University
Kingston, Ontario K7L 3N6, Canada
    Studies fiscal, political, and administrative implications of intergov-
ernmental relations in federal systems, Canada's in particular.

Peace Research Institute
25 Dundana Ave., Dundas, Ontario L9H 4E5, Canada
    "A non-profit research and publishing organization which focuses on the
causes and prevention of war."

Colombia

CODECAL (Corporation for Cultural and Social Development)
Carrera 21 no. 56-33, Apartado aereo 20439, Bogota, Colombia
    "CODECAL carries activities in the field of social education for adults,
making emphasis in education for peace, justice and respect for human
rights. To achieve this, develops a methodology of group work which
elaborates materials and promotes animators."

Institute of Investigations, Gran Colombia University
Cra. 6a. no. 13-40, Oficina 207, Bogota, D.E., Colombia
    Promotes research on conflict theory, alliance politics, cultural conflicts,
imperialism, agricultural problems, disarmament, and transnational corporations.

Denmark

Institute of Political Studies, University of Copenhagen
Rosenborggade 15, 1130 Copenhagen K, Denmark
    A public, non-profit research institution which concentrates on a variety of
international relations topics. Current research is concerned with strategic
weapons systems, cultural pluralism and world politics, and religion and
politics in Africa.

Finland

Tampere Peace Research Institute
Hameekatu 13b A., P.O. Box 447, SF-33101 Tampere 10, Finland
"Established by the Finnish Parliament in 1970, The Institute is a scientific research base studying the problems of war and peace in the widest sense."

World Peace Council
Lonnrotinkatu 25 A 6 krs.,
00180 Helsinki 18, Finland
Works to gain cooperation among peace research institutes around the world. Publishes *New Perspectives* and the *Peace Courier*.

See also, U.S Peace Council.

France

Atlantic Institute for International Affairs
120 Rue de Longchamp, Paris 75116, France
" . . .a non-governmental and multinational institute which addresses itself to the broad economic and poltical issues which confront our nations."

Germany, Federal Republic of

Institute for Peace Research and Security Policy, University of Hamburg
Falkenstein 1 D-000, Hamburg 55, Federal Republic of Germany
Interested in questions of peace and security, arms control and disarmament, and international economics. Organizes workshops and conferences.

Max Planck Institute for the Study of the Conditions of Life in the Modern World
8130 Stamberg, Riemerschmiedstrasse 7, Federal Republic of Germany
A private, non-profit organization doing research and conferences on problems of underdevelopment, strategic studies, and socialization.

Hungary

Institute for World Economics of the Hungarian Academy of Sciences
Kálló Esperes U. 15, H-1124 Budapest, Hungary
Engaged in research on world economic problems including international economic relations between Western and Eastern countries.

India

Gandhi Peace Foundation
221/223 Deen Dayal Upadhaya Marg, New Delhi 110-001, India
Attempts to construct present day alternatives to violence through the advocacy of Gandhian techniques. Publishes *Gandhi Marg*.

Israel

The Israeli Institute for the Study of International Affairs
P.O. Box 17027, Tel-Aviv 61170, Israel
   A private, non-profit organization conducting research, organizing conferences, and producing publications on international affairs, international law, peace, and the developing countries.

Middle East Peace Institute
ZP. O. Box 1777, Tel-Aviv, Israel
   Primarily a research organization concerned with the potential for detente in the Middle East and the peaceful settlement of disputes.

Italy

Club of Rome
Via Giorgione 163, 00147 Rome, Italy
   A non-profit organization which provides studies, conferences, and publications on world problems such as technology, the new international economic order, development, population, the environment, and peace.

Japan

International Peace Research Association, University of Tokyo
Hongo, Bunkyo-ku, Tokyo 113, Japan
   An interdisciplinary research organization which discusses the causes of war and the strategies for peace through seminars, publications, and primary research.

World Friendship Center
5-8-20 Midori Machi, Minami-ku Hiroshima-shi 734, Japan
   Based on the proposition that a lasting peace should be built, the Center promotes the peaceful resolution of international conflict, and supports the survivors of the atomic bomb.

Mexico

Center for International Studies, Colegio de Mexico
Guanajuato 125, Mexico 7, D.F., Mexico
   A research and documentation organization dealing with international relations, international law, and political integration.

Latin American Peace Research Council
Apartado Postal 20-105, Mexico D.F., Mexico
   A regional organization of peace research institutions throughout Latin America.

The Netherlands

Foundation for Reshaping the International Economic Order
P.O. Box 299, 300A6 Rotterdam, The Netherlands
Conducts research in and promotes education on the changing international economic order and presents strategies for economic development in the Third World.

Netherlands Institute for Studies on Peace and Security
Alexanderstraat 7, 's-Gravenhage, P.O. Box 85581, 2508 CG 's-Gravenhage, The Netherlands
". . .endeavors, in the light of academic knowledge and current world events, to indicate phenomena which could lead to war, and to investigate measures which could curb or thwart the use of force."

Peace Research Center, University of Nijmegen
Van Schaek Mathonsingel 4, Nijmegen, The Netherlands
Besides conducting research on current problems in international relations, the Center is investigating the role of ideology and perception in shaping a country's foreign policy.

New Zealand

New Zealand Institute of International Affairs
P.O. Box 19-102, Aro St., Wellington 2, New Zealand
Studies international affairs, law and economics especially as they affect New Zealand, Oceania, and Southeast Asia.

Nigeria

Nigerian Institute of International Affairs
Kofo Abayomi Road, Victoria Islands, G. P. O Box 1727, Lagos, Nigeria
A public, non-profit organization which conducts research, holds conferences and workshops, and produces publications on international relations.

Peace Research Institute of Nigeria, University of Nigeria
Nsukka, Nigeria
The Institute's primary focus is on the relationship between economic development and peace, and promotes peace education and communication studies.

Norway

International Peace Research Institute
Radhusgata 4, Oslo 1, Norway
Attempts to realize the goal of peace research — the non-military resolu-

tion of international conflict — through intensive research on world militarism, human rights, arms control and disarmament. Publishes the *Journal of Peace Research* and the *Bulletin of Peace Proposals*.

Pakistan

Department of International Relations, University of Karachi
Karachi 32, Pakistan
   A public, non-profit organization dealing with international relations, international organization and law, and peace. Organizes conferences and produces publications.

Poland

Polish Institute of International Affairs
UL. Warecka 1A, POB 1000, 00-950 Warsaw, Poland
   "The main scope of interest: security and cooperation in Europe, problems of armament and disarmament, foreign policy of socialist, capitalist, and developing countries, some aspects of international economic relations, international law and organization, training of research staff, and publishing activity."

Sweden

Department of Peace and Conflict Research, Lund University
Paradisgaten 5, S-223 50 Lund, Sweden
   An interdisciplinary approach to the problem of international conflict, the Department investigates sociological, political, historical, economic, and psychological causes of mass violence.

The Dag Hammarskjold Foundation
Ovre Slottsgatan 2, S-752 20 Uppsala, Sweden
   " . . . was established in 1962 in memory of the late Secretary General of the United Nations. The purpose of the Foundation is to organize seminars, conferences, and courses on the social and economic problems of the developing countries."

Department of Peace and Conflict Research, Uppsala University
P.O. Box 278, S-751 05 Uppsala 1, Sweden
   "Current research at the Department is concentrated on conflict theory, militarization, security problems and disarmament.

Stockholm International Peace Research Institute
Sveavagen 166, S-133 46, Stockholm, Sweden
   "SIPRI is an independent institute for research into problems of peace and

conflict, with particular attention to the problems of disarmament and arms regulation. It was established in 1966 to commemorate Sweden's 150 years of unbroken peace.''

Switzerland

Commission of the Churches on International Affairs
World Council of Churches
150 Route de Ferney, 1211 Geneva 20, Switzerland
    ''The churches' commitment to world peace and justice is continued through the Commission, seeking to articulate the moral and spirtual implications of relations between the nations.''

Geneva International Peace Research Institute
41, rue de Zurich, CH-1201 Geneva, Switzerland
    Conducts research in the area of peace and security, militarism, and arms control.

The Graduate Institute of International Studies
P.O. Box 53, 132 rue de Lausanne, CH-1211, Geneva 21, Switzerland
    ''The Institute is devoted to the advanced study of international relations in a multi-disciplinary approach, which relies upon the methods of history and political science, of law and of economics. English and French are the working languages.''

International Peace Bureau
41 rue de Zurich, 1201 Geneva, Switzerland
    A membership of international peace organizations devoted to developing proposals for disarmament and critiquing existing proposals for their contribution to the nuclear disarmament discussion.

United Kingdom

Pugwash Conferences on Science and World Affairs
9 Great Russell Mansions, 60 Great Russell St., London WC1B 3BE, United Kingdom
    Presents conferences on nuclear arms and disarmament, gathering together scientists from all countries. Publishes the Pugwash Newsletter and other publications.

Richardson Institute for Conflict and Peace Research, University of Lancaster
Department of Politics, Fylde College, Bailrigg, Lancaster LA1 4YF, United Kingdom
    Does research, publications, and conferences on nationalism in the United

Kingdom, imperialism by the British and Americans, and defense in Europe and the Middle East.

Royal Institute of International Affairs
Chatham House, 10 St. James's Square, London SW1Y 4LE, United Kingdom
"An independent, self-governing body whose aim is to advance the objective study and understanding of all aspects on international affairs."

Science Policy Research Unit, University of Sussex
Mantell Bldg., Falmer, Brighton BN1 9RF, United Kingdom
Is specifically interested in the role of science and technology in international politics. Current research is concerned with science and technology in the Third World, energy exploration, and technology as an issue in the North/South debate.

USSR

Institute of General History, Academy of Sciences of the USSR
Akademia Nauk USSR, UL. Dimitria Uljanova 19, Moscow B-36, USSR
Studies Western Europe and the United States from the perspective of class conflict, wars, and political processes.

Institute of World Economics and International Relations of the Academy of Sciences
Jaroslavskaja ul. 13, Moscow, USSR
A research organization studying the politics and economics involved in international relations, peace, and disarmament.

Yugoslavia

Institute of International Politics and Economics
Makedonska 25, P.O. Box 750, 11000 Belgrade, Yugoslavia
A private, non-profit organization which researches security problems, international economy, regional studies, international labor movements, and contemporary international law in relationship to international disputes, conflict, and nuclear energy.

UNITED STATES INTERNATIONAL STUDIES CENTERS

This section contains a select list of centers connected to American universities which do research related to world affairs. Some of them may have government or public policy as their main focus, but they all do some research in international affairs. Research centers focusing on area or regional studies are not included. A list of more than 200 of these can be found in *Research Centers Directory: A Guide to University-Related and Other Nonprofit Research Organizations* (Archie M. Palmer, ed., Gale, 1979). Although some of these centers do adminster undergraduate or graduate courses in international relations, this list is not one of degree-granting programs. Several guides to college and graduate programs are available which provide that information. Private research organizations are included in the list of world affairs organizations, and they are not repeated here.

Arizona, University of
Institute of Government Research
Tucson, AZ 85721
     Studies political theory, comparative governments, Latin American politics, and U.S.-Mexican relations.

Beloit College
Cullister Center for International Studies
Beloit, WI 53511
     Promotes a variety of interdisciplinary research projects, conducts conferences and workshops, works to increase understanding of international events through an extensive collection of world affairs books and periodicals.

Brigham Young University
Language and Intercultural Research Center
240 B-34, Provo, UT 84602
801-378-2651
     Helps meet the intercultural communications needs of professionals and organizations through research and publications on other cultures and countries.

California Institute of Technology
California Seminar on Arms Control and Foreign Policy
P.O. Box 925, Santa Monica, CA 90406
     Studies arms control, national security, international relations, economics, foreign policy, and European security.

California State University
Center for the Study of Armament and Disarmament
151 State College Dr., Los Angeles, CA 90032
213-224-3152
     Seeks "knowledge of the historical, political, economic, philosophical,

technological, and psychological nature of war and the means of controlling it.''

California, University of
Institute of International Studies
2538 Channing Way, Berkeley, CA 94720
   Recent studies have focused on contending elites in internal Soviet politics.

Colorado, University of
Graduate Concentration in the Sociology of Conflict
Boulder, CO 80309
   Studies sociology of conflict, conflict resolution, and the roots of violence.

Colorado, University of
Institute of Behavioral Science
Boulder, CO 80309
   Studies behavioral sciences, population, technology.

Colorado, University of
International Research Center for Energy and Economic Development
216 Economics Bldg., Boulder, CO 80309
   Regularly holds conferences on energy issues, publishes the proceedings as well as the *Journal of Energy and Development.*

Columbia University
Research Institute on International Change
New York, NY 10027
212-280-4638
   Formerly the Research Institute on Communist Affairs, the Institute still is primarily interested in that subject.

Columbia University
Institute of War and Peace Studies
420 W. 118th St., New York, NY 10027
212-280-4616
   The Institute was organized in 1951. Its programs include sponsorship of seminars, publications, and research. The research program has two main parts — one dealing with peace and security and the other involving theoretical and empirical investigations in international and comparative politics and international institutions.

Connecticut, University of
The Thut World Education Center
Box U-32, School of Education, Storrs, CT 06268
203-486-3321

"Begun in 1971 as the World Education Project, TWEC is a statewide program serving educators, schools and colleges, libraries and cultural organizations through graduate courses, in-service workshops and conferences, publications, and consulting on topics related to bilingual, multicultural, international and global education."

Cornell University
Program on International Studies in Regional Planning
200 W. Sibley Hall, Ithaca, NY 14853
607-256-2333

Studies urban/rural development problems, particularly in Latin America, Africa, and Western Europe.

Denver, University of
Center for Teaching International Relations
Denver, CO 80208
303-753-3106

Seeks "the improvement of international/intercultural studies at elementary and secondary school levels."

Georgetown University
Center for Strategic and International Studies
1800 K St., NW, Suite 520, Washington, D.C. 20006
202-833-8595

Studies international policy issues and encourages research to fill information gaps. Uses publications and conferences to aid in information and idea exchange.

Georgetown University Law Center
Centro de Immigracion
600 New Jersey Ave., NW, Washington, D.C. 20001
202-624-8374

"Provides backup services for people doing direct work with migrant workers, monitors legislation on the state and federal level and judicial cases in the Supreme Court and federal courts. The Center also monitors pending regulations pertaining to immigration and conducts research on policy issues."

Georgetown University
Institute for the Study of Diplomacy
School of Foreign Service, Washington, D.C. 20057
202-625-4218
Offers detailed instruction in the art of diplomacy and case studies in pamphlet form of various crises and other practical "how to" information.

Harvard University
Center for International Affairs
6 Divinity Ave., Cambridge, MA 02138
617-495-4420
Studies international affairs and world problems, especially those of advanced industrial societies, force management, and international order.

Hawaii, University of
Dimensionality of Nations Project
2500 Campus Rd., Honolulu, HI 96822
Studies international relations and international law.

Hawaii, University of
East-West Center
1777 East-West Rd., Honolulu, HI 96848
Studies communications, environment and public policy, resources and populations.

Illinois, University of
Committee for Public Service in International Affairs
205 Arcade Bldg., 725 S. Wright St., Champaign, IL 61820
217-333-1465
Offers a wide range of world affairs programming, information and services to citizens of Illinois.

Illinois, University of
Institute of Communications Research
1207 W. Oregon, Urbana, IL 61801
Studies communication, mass communication, culture and language.

Indiana University
Bureau of Public Discussion
302 Owen Hall, Bloomington, IN 47401
812-337-1684
Studies public opinion and public policy information; holds programs of the Midwest University Seminar Committee on U.S. Foreign policy.

Indiana University
Mid-America Program for Global Perspectives in Education
513 N. Park Ave., Bloomington, IN 47401
812-332-0211

"Works with a variety of civic and educational groups to improve and expand global perspectives in education." It helps develop programs which enable "young people to acquire the knowledge, skills and attitudes necessary for responsible participation in an interdependent world."

Iowa, University of
Comparative Legislative Research Center
Iowa City, IA 52242
319-353-5040

Studies comparative legislatures and their role in political development and conflict management, especially in Belgium, Italy, Kenya, Korea, Switzerland, and Turkey.

Johns Hopkins University
Johns Hopkins Foreign Policy Institute
School of Advanced International Studies
1740 Massachusetts Ave., NW, Washington, D.C. 20036

Studies international relations and security and their relation to American foreign policy problems.

Massachusetts Institute of Technology
Center for International Studies
30 Wadsworth St., Cambridge, MA 02139

Studies international relations, arms control, economic development, migration, nutrition, energy, communications, and environmental problems.

Miami, University of
Center for Advanced International Studies
P.O. Box 8123, Coral Gables, FL 33124

Studies the impact of technology, international affairs, and the Middle East, China, Latin America, and the USSR.

Michigan State University
Global Studies Center
513 Erickson Hall, East Lansing, MI 48824
517-355-5522

"Provides inservice assistance, resources/referrals, and instructional materials to Michigan teachers, school personnel, and interested groups wishing to infuse global perspectives/global issues into their curricula."

Michigan, University of
Center for Political Studies
426 Thompson St., Ann Arbor, MI 48109
   A section of the Institute for Social Research which studies cross-national politics, especially the relationship between political elites and the public.

Michigan, University of
Correlates of War Project
Mental Health Research Institute, Ann Arbor, MI 48109
   Deals with the causes and consequences of war.

Minnesota, University of
Minnesota World Affairs Center
306 Wesbrook Hall, 77 Pleasant St., SE, Minneapolis, MN 55455
612-373-3799
   Studies foreign policy and public opinion with an emphasis on encouraging continuing education in world affairs. ''Members share the belief that a sound influence on American foreign policy can best be made by an informed citizenry.''

Minnesota, University of
Quigley Center of International Studies
1246 Social Science Bldg., 267 19th Ave., S., Minneapolis, MN 55455
612-373-2691
   Studies world order, international organization, economics, communications, arms control and disarmament, and foreign policy.

New York University School of Law
Center for International Studies
Room 440C, 40 Washington Square South, New York, NY 10003
212-598-7644
   Studies international relations, foreign policy, politics, international law, the political process, economic growth, and international dispute settlement.

Notre Dame, University of
Institute for International Studies
1201 Memorial Library, Notre Dame, IN 46556
219-283-6587
   Studies diplomacy and international organization; houses the International Documentation Center.

Ohio State University
Mershon Center — Programs of Research and Education in National Security,
  Leadership, and Public Policy
199 W. 10th Ave., Columbus, OH 43201
  Studies international relations, foreign policy, political sociology, and
international organization.

Ohio State University
Service Center for Teachers of Asian Studies
College of Education, 29 W. Woodruff Ave., Columbus, OH 43210
614-422-4872
  "Established by the Association of Asian Studies in 1971, it serves
primarily as a clearinghouse, identifying the existing and continually emerging print and non-print materials on Asia for the pre-collegiate level, and
giving guidance to teachers about the best available materials for the needs of
a given teacher or school situation. Publishes *Focus on Asian Studies* and
'Service Center Papers on Asian Studies.'"

Pennsylvania State University
Institute of Public Administration
205 Burrowes Bldg., University Park, PA 16802
  Studies mainly public administration in Pennsylvania, but has done research on agrarian administration in Latin America as well.

University of Pittsburg
Center for International Security Studies
160 Mervis Hall, Pittsburg, PA 15260
412-624-5572
  Studies international security, arms control and disarmament, regional
instability, and perceptions of threat and security.

Princeton University
Center of International Studies
Princeton, NJ 08540
  A part of the Woodrow Wilson School studying many aspects of world
politics and international relations, including defense and military strategy,
diplomacy, international organization, world order, and modernization.

Rice University
Program of Development Studies
121 Sewall Hall, Houston, TX 77001
713-527-4849
  Interdisciplinary research on social, political, and economic problems of
developing countries, especially Malaysia, Taiwan, Columbia, and Brazil.

South Carolina, University of
International Studies Association
James F. Byrnes International Center, Columbia, SC 29208
803-777-2933
   Studies comparative foreign policy, international organization, the environment, international law, political economy, Soviet-American relations, the military, and peace.

Teachers College
World Council for Curriculum and Instruction
Box 171, Teacher's College, New York, NY 10027
212-678-3000
   Develops curriculum for peace and global community studies and encourages transnational cooperation among educators.

Stanford University
Arms Control and Disarmament Program
Dept. of Political Science, Stanford, CA 94305
   Studies problems of arms control and disarmament.

Stanford University
Hoover Institution on War, Revolution, and Peace
Stanford, CA 94305
415-497-1754
   Studies international relations, foreign policy, social change, and peace.

Texas, University of
Institute of Latin American Studies
Educational Outreach, Austin, TX 78712
512-471-5551
   "Programs focus on the development of cultural understanding through the teaching of intercultural projects, teaching units, films, demonstrations in the public schools. We believe in the positiveness of cultural pluralism, its relevance to American education, and the necessity of all students to learn appreciation and tolerance of different cultural groups, their customs, values, and lifestyles."

Utah, University of
Institute of International Relations
252 Orson Spenser Hall, Salt Lake City, UT 84112
801-581-7031
   Studies foreign policy and international affairs; holds lectures and conferences.

Wisconsin, University of
Institute of World Affairs
P.O. Box 413, Milwaukee, WI 53201
414-963-4251

"To stimulate the interest and broaden the knowledge and understanding of students, faculty, and the community in the field of world affairs. It engages in a wide range of programs of specialized instruction, publication, and public service."

Yale University
World Data Analysis Program
New Haven, CT 06520

Gathers and analyzes data on conflict, military spending, public attitudes and the link between military spending and war.

RESOURCE C: A QUESTIONNAIRE TO EVALUATE A PARTICULAR ORGANIZATION

It is not always easy to get an accurate understanding of the ideas, programs, and goals of a world affairs organization. Getting answers to the questions which follow will help. But explicit answers may not be forthcoming because the organization itself is unclear. Every world affairs organization's outlook is, at least implicitly, in the literature it promotes, in the speakers it sponsors or does not sponsor, and in the priorities it assigns to different activities. Being able to find these answers, and then to choose one's organization intelligently, is an essential requisite for serious and effective work.

As an exercise to test your own understanding, select an organization you know something about and try to determine what answers it would give to the following questions; then ask for an interview with a key staff person to find out if you are right.

I. *Understandings*

The response to the questions below help clarify the basic understandings the organization wants to forward. From the sum total of the organization's behavior, you can learn:

a. *Goals:* How the organization defines its goals (i.e. the changes in the world it seeks to bring about) and purposes (i.e., its own organizational and programmatic objective). Is it focused on the problem of war as a whole, or on some part of the problem (e.g., disarmament, world law, development)? or on a different problem? By what standards does it judge the success of its work?

b. *Causes:* What is the organization's view of the cause of war: a particular ideological, economic, or political system; the absence of world government or law; human nature or the interests of a social class; injustice or oppression; a particular conception of justice; military organization; the distribution of wealth?

c. *Roots:* What motivates the organization's work in the world affairs field? Does it believe new ideas, or increased understanding of old ones, are needed?

d. *Issues:* Does the organization take stands on specific world affairs issues facing the President, Congress, the U.N., or the American public? Every year hundreds of world affairs issues are dealt with in legislation, Presidential directives, treaties or U.N. resolutions. On which of these issues has the organization acted? What position has it taken?

e. *Change:* What does the organization see as the prime levers of social change — the development of new ideas, their widespread distribution, mass political protest, the influence of specific elites? Does it see change as coming primarily when economic or political power is reorganized? On what theoretical assumptions is the group acting when it defines the relationship between grass-roots sentiment and leadership decision-making? What specific sectors of the society are seen as being of special importance in producing changed attitudes and governmental policies?

II. *Politics*

You will frequently encounter world affairs organizations which present themselves as "above politics." However earnest their intention, there is no way to say anything meaningful about world affairs problems without making political judgments. It is, therefore, useful to try to understand the political stance an organization takes.

Action on world affairs problems is action on the central problem of politics: who governs and to what ends? It is, therefore, important to understand the political currents which move within an organization and shape its work. Careful discussion of the questions below is essential if you are to judge whether the enormous energy poured into world affairs and peace cause organizations is guided by a political perspective that you wish to promote.

a. *Stance:* Where does the organization stand concerning the contending power centers? What is its view of American society and of Soviet society? Of regional powers? Of the newly industrialized States? Of the

"Group of 77"? Does the organization clarify its political values and commitments, or does it refuse, claiming that emphasizing political distinction only heightens international tensions or produces dissention among those engaged? Does it argue that it can hope to influence only our own government, and therefore never criticizes other governments (thus building a bias into its work)? Or does it refuse to criticize our own government, assuming others are to blame for war? Does its work reflect a single-villain focus on either America or on the Soviet Union? Does it present itself as opposing the arms race, but in fact only challenge the participation of one side? Does it portray wars of liberation as progressive and deserving of support, as none of our business, as bad solutions to real problems, or as threats to be crushed? Are third-world movements defined as nationalist or as Soviet-inspired?

b. *Strategy*: What policy and strategy emphasis in current conflict does it advocate for this country? Does it argue for American withdrawal from world politics? Does it call for intervention by international organizations or by America in other countries and if so for what purposes and to what ends? Does the organization call for American peace initiatives designed to bring other States into agreement, military deterrence coupled with negotiations and other efforts to remove the causes of conflict, increased use of American military power? Is its primary concern to build a strengthened sense of world community through the U.N. or other intergovernmental organizations? Is it in favor of aid for needed change in the developing States?

c. *Program:* What is its program to achieve its purposes? Does it seek to build a political movement or party, to disrupt, or to build discontent so that present processes can no longer function? Does it plan programs to develop new understandings and values in society so that decisions by political leaders will reflect those understandings no matter what position the prevailing government takes? Does it view protest *per se* as a virtue or does it believe that protest actions can encourage alienation and thus undermine the sense of community on which progress depends?

d. *Justice:* Politics involves more than power; it also defines a common vision of how people should live together. What is the organization's view of the good society? Does it seek to end all conflict or to regulate it? How does it value freedom, law, conscience, equality, peace, community, achievement? What seems most important to the organization?

e. *Coalitions:* How does it relate to other groups acting on world affairs problems? How does it decide whether or not to cooperate with a particular organization in a particular activity?

III. *Profile: Facts about the Organization*

a. *Structure:*

1. *Range:* Does it operate locally, regionally, nationally, internationally? What is the relationship between the branches?

2. *Membership:* Sources, character, requirements? Size — of core group, active participants, supporters, mailing lists?

3. *Control:* Who makes the key decisions? To whom are they accountable? How?

4. *Staff:* How many? For what are they responsible? How paid? Do they initiate activities, or carry out the directives of a policy-making board? Are they trained? What is their level of knowledge of the world affairs field? Of the work of other organizations in the field? In what other public affairs activities do they play leadership roles?

5. *Legal and Financial Status:* Is the organization incorporated? Tax-exempt? How large is its budget? Does it depend on a few large contributions or on many small ones?

b. *History:*

1. Origin: How old is the group? Who organized it and under what circumstances? What was the primary stimulus — a charismatic leader, a new body of thought, a political issue, an outgrowth of an existing tradition?

2. *Development:* What were the shaping events in its history? What ideas or policy changes were important milestones? Who were the key personalities? How does it see itself developing in the future?

IV. *Activity*

Assessing the actual work of an organization is the best way of discerning its primary purposes.

a. *Audience:* What audience is the organization trying to reach — women, business executives, national decision-makers, mass audiences, the labor unions, the unorganized, students, political leaders, religious leaders, the media? The answer to this question will provide evidence on how the organization sees social change taking place.

b. *Materials and Channels:* What tools does the organization use — literature, films, newsletters, demonstrations, study groups, membership mailings, telephone "tree," discussion groups, meetings with opinion leaders, lobbying? Does it work through established institutions such as unions, schools, or political parties? Does it organize groups sharing its view to do its work?

c. *Programs:* What continuing activities does it conduct? Is it focused primarily on engaging its own members in its work? Does it service other organizations? In what ways? Does it have programs for children, aimed at legislators, or designed to increase knowledge?

d. *Criteria for Judging Success:* How does it measure the success of its work — by membership, budget, quality of ideas and materials, size of participating groups at public events, legislation passed or blocked, number of people engaged in work, public visibility, response from decision-makers?

V. *Character*

How is the organization viewed by the community? How does it see itself? A group's character and style are what determines whether a person will support it. Which of the following best describe the kinds of people associated with the organization: achievement-oriented or witness-oriented? radical or conventional? religious or secular? old or young? Who is attracted to it: women, political activists, community leaders, the wealthy, youth, an ethnic or racial group, the upwardly mobile, middle-class youth between school and career? Does the group aim at strengthening a small committed nucleus or does it seek to broaden participation? Is it focused on crisis issues or on a long-range perspective? Is it well financed or does it operate on a shoestring? Do its offices look clean, ordered, expensive, intense, chaotic, sacrificial . . .?

ANALYZING A WORLD AFFAIRS ORGANIZATION: AN OVERVIEW

Many organizations seek to influence the foreign policy decision-making process of this country. Other organizations seek to influence world politics directly. A survey of such activities reveals a bewilderingly complex range of organizations and programmatic activity. Asking these questions will help decide which deserve your support.

Understandings
  Goals: How defined?
    Issues: What specific stands?
      Roots: What is it in the field?
        Causes of War: What leads to war?
          Peace: What will bring about peace?
            Change: How will the goals be achieved?
              Politics: What view towards contending power centers?

Profile
  Structure: Board, leader, staff, constituency managed?
    Range: In what geographical areas does it work?
      Staff: How large? Who trained?
        Control: Who runs it?
          Membership: Size, character, source, requirements?
            Legal and financial status: Tax-exempt, endowed, struggling?

History
  Origins: When? Why? Who?
    Development: What events, ideas, personalities shaped it?
      Patterns: Is there continuity in its activities?

Work
  Audiences: Whom does it try to reach?
    Programs: What activities does it conduct?
      Criteria: How does it judge success?
        Materials/Channels: What tools does it use?
          Quality: To what level of intelligence, fairness, objectivity,
            accuracy, comprehensiveness, and honesty does it aspire?

Character or Style
  Community: Alienated from society, or affirming its basic values?
    Wealth: Poor and proud? Middle income? Affluent?
      Audience: Ethnic group, social strata, opinion leaders, the
        people, or other audience?
      Size: Small, committed, or wide participation?
        Success: Influences policy, enlarges constituency, or witnesses
          for a view?

CHAPTER 21

THE INDIVIDUAL: CHOOSING AN AUDIENCE

IN previous chapters, the ideas, actors, problems, contexts and organizations in the world affairs field were presented. The importance of contexts, the relevance of thought and choice, and the need for steady, sustained work were emphasized. The previous chapter highlights the critical importance of citizen organizations as a vital part of American democracy and as a potential source of direction and initiative toward a world without war. This chapter recognizes that every action or decision is made by individuals. You, the individual, are the ultimate agent in the task of ending war. The resources gathered here are designed to help you fulfill your potential.

BUT WHAT CAN I DO?

To be effective you must reach others. Even if you act alone, you will probably be doing so to communicate with others. Therefore, some of the resources offered here are designed to help you identify the audiences that match your skills and interests. In this field, as in others, it will take time to understand the possibilities, and to pick the places where your abilities are best correlated with challenging and rewarding responsibilities.

634

Some actions can be undertaken by individuals "on their own," or by small groups of like-minded individuals who express their personal commitments together. Some individual acts are dramatic, such as war tax resistance, silent vigils, or civil disobedience. Some acts are more commonplace such as writing letters to the editor, persuading neighbors to act on a particular issue, or changing one's eating habits. The effectiveness and impact of individual acts are often hard to assess, and are sometimes undertaken not so much for their direct effect as for their valid expression of deeply-held values.

To avoid these pitfalls, to find the best place for your own talents, and to help contribute steady and sustained work, a "Self-survey" is recommended (Resource D). Also, the "Twenty-Five Responses to the Question — 'But What Can I Do?' " should be considered to discover what has constituted success for others. Then the basic choices can be made: Where do you want to work? What subject matter most interests you? What skills do you have? What audience is the best target? How much time do you have and how much is required to make a positive contribution? What results are required to make this a successful endeavor?

Some people will find it possible to work for peace in the institutions they already work in. This is most likely for people who are engaged in some form of communication or education, for example, teachers, ministers, or journalists. Most of these professions recognize that peace — if it can be achieved with security and without loss of fundamental values — is part of what is meant by the public good. It is therefore appropriate that people in those professions self-consciously build the discussion of peace into their work. Several resources that follow are specifically designed for those who wish to work to end war within their own professions. Other people will work in one of the many world affairs organizations. In deciding where to work, it is recommended that an individual look over the typology of organizations (Resource A) and the guide to evaluating organizations (Resource C).

RELIGIOUS INSTITUTIONS

In a religious institution, for example, world affairs subjects arise in many places. Is there, in your religious institution, a set of guidelines that recommend the moral and educational context within which world affairs questions are presented? Is there a thought-out policy such as that suggested by the International Human Rights Quotient (Resource F)? Which of the following programs have been deliberately studied and the best values and traditions of your religious institution applied?

a. Youth education program
b. Adult education program
c. Sermons
d. special offerings
e. Response to specific crisis
f. Conscience and war counseling
g. Participation by the local institution in regional, national or world religious institutions
h. Stewardship of contributions
i. Use of bulletin boards
j. Publications
k. People-to-people projects
l. World service
m. Value clarification concerning controversial issues
n. World hunger
o. Human rights
p. Refugees — sponsorship? assistance? policy?
q. Armament or disarmament policy
r. Special committees: peace committee
s. Film programs
t. Relation to governmental decision-makers
u. Men and women's association work
v. Retreats
w. Dialogue with other religions
x. Religious liberty
y. Special holidays
z. Use of media

After an individual is clear what is being done, the next questions are: Is the action appropriate? Does it embody the best in our country's or our religious tradition's or our organization's values? Are the ideas underlying the activity adequate to the challenges we face in world politics? Is action taken within explicit, agreed-to guidelines, or does the staff engage in whatever activities it regards as worthwhile?

The development of guidelines is extremely important: they can anticipate many of the questions which must be faced and develop a response which would then guide the staff. It then becomes possible for an institution, as opposed to concerned individuals, to act responsibly. Among the questions the guidelines need to address are these:

1. What are the central values of our organization which compel us to enter the world affairs field?

2. What are the political and ethical beliefs underlying our work?

    a. Should our work seek to fulfill democratic values and enable a democratic political process to work effectively?

b. Should our work affirm the primacy of conscience? or of law? or seek some resolution of the tension between the two?

c. Should we reject all violence? Should we affirm violence when authorized by competent authority on behalf of security concerns or in promoting change? Or should we focus on the development and use of non-military means for achieving security and promoting change?

d. Should our work address the legitimate security concerns of our country? Of others?

3. What are the obstacles to effective work?
4. By what standards will our work be evaluated?
5. What are the programmatic goals of our undertaking?
6. What administrative procedures are followed?

An organization, whose members have thought through and developed answers to such questions, may then be prepared for a thoughtful and continuing engagement in the world affairs field.

Answering such questions will set the context and the institutional support for the activity. The program areas may include any or all of those listed above, plus the following:

1. Opinion leaders
2. Decision-makers: national
3. Decision-makers: international
4. Policy proposals
5. Public meetings
6. Leadership training
7. Art and cultural events
8. Special observances: human rights day
9. Public demonstrations
10. Seminars and study groups
11. Speakers program
12. Fund-raising
13. Communications
14. Newsletter editor
15. Office work
16. Specific issues in these subjects:
    a. Hunger and economic development
    b. International organization and world law, for example, The Law of the Sea Treaty
    c. Disarmament: arms reductions and negotiations
    d. Conscience and war: conscription
    e. Nonviolence
    f. Human rights

     g. Environment

     h. Other

17. Specific issues or crisis conflict resolution:
     a. The Middle East
     b. Central America
     c. Southern Africa
     d. Southeast Asia
     e. Central Asia
     f. Northern Ireland
     g. USSR/Chinese Border
     h. Other

18. Voluntary organizations
     a. Religious
     b. Professional
     c. Labor
     d. Business
     e. Educational
     f. Peace Cause
     g. Environmental

19. School programs
20. Forecasting new issues
21. Futures
22. Transnational education
23. Intercultural understanding
24. Foreign language skills
25. Peace research
26. People-to-people programs
27. Developing peace initiatives

This approach to work in the world affairs field emphasizes the need for an institution to formulate explicit ideas and programs. It is designed to provide arenas in which different perspectives can join to develop realistic and thoughtful ways to conduct international conflict without violence and how constructive change can be promoted. It is not easy to develop such arenas, but once achieved, they provide many of the safeguards needed so that the best values in our democratic and religious traditions can be applied to choices in the world affairs field.

BIBLIOGRAPHY

The bibliography in this chapter introduces work in a variety of organizational settings, but focuses on business, labor, religious, peace, exchange and education. It offers programmatic resources found to be helpful to many of them, and these illustrate what kinds of resources might be of value in other types of organizations. In addition, directories of organizations are included here, to help the individual pick where he or she wants to work.

A. Overview: Specific Tasks an Individual Could Undertake

TEW
21 – 1 "101 Ways You Could Help End the Famine in Cambodia," World Without War Issues Center, 4pp, 1979, World Without War Publications, $.25. Offers specific suggestions for obtaining adequate supplies of food, for getting it distributed, and for addressing the problem of achieving a political solution to the conflict over who shall rule.

Intro
21 – 2 *Try This, Activities to Learn the Ways of Peace,* Shalom Education, 69pp, 1979, Discipleship Resources, $3.50. A wealth of practical information on activities designed to build confidence that family members can conduct conflict creatively, can learn about other cultures and global interdependence, and can apply the lessons learned to the nonviolent resolution of international conflict.

21 – 3 *International Jobs, Where They Are, How to Get Them,* Eric Kocher, 318pp, 1979, Addison-Wesley, $6.95. A comprehensive guide to over 500 careers in government, business, international organizations and private associations.

21 – 4 *Resignation in Protest,* Edward Weisband & Thomas Franck, 236pp, 1976, Penguin, $2.95. A study of the occasions when conscience was in conflict with a governmental policy and led to the individual's resignation.

21 – 5 *Citizen Participation in America, Essays on the State of the Art,* Stuart Langton, 144pp, 1979, Lexington, $12.95. Examines various ways citizens influence the political process and the society.

21 – 6 *Volunteers and the Making of Presidents,* Jane Dick, 268pp, 1980, Dodd, Mead, $6.95. A study of presidential campaigns from Wendel Willkie's to Adlai Stevenson's which makes the case for the crucial role of volunteers.

B. Forming and Successfully Operating an Organization

21 – 7 *Volunteer Agencies in the International Arena,* Kettering Foundation, 28pp, 1981, Free from the Foundation. A report on a conference designed to increase

the participants' involvement in world affairs in the 1980s and to break down the fragmentation between organizations.

INF

21 – 8 *Marketing the Nonprofit Organization,* Philip Kotler, 436pp, 1975, Prentice-Hall, $17.95. Of the thousands of nonprofit organizations formed each year, only a handful reach their fifth birthday. This will help those that did, reach their tenth.

21 – 9 *Breaking Even, Financial Management in Human Service Organizations,* Roger Lohmann, 316pp, 1980, Temple, $19.50. Offers a clear description of how nongovernmental organizations can plan to break even using cost-benefit analysis, zero-base budgeting, cost analysis, and ratio analysis techniques.

21 – 10 *Fund Raising for the Small Organization,* Philip Sheridan, 240pp, 1968, Evans, $5.95. Helpful advice.

21 – 11 *Fund Raising: A Professional Guide,* William Cumerford, 1978, Peters, $29.95. Pick your targets selectively, plan your campaign thoroughly, describe your need or goals clearly, outline measurable objectives, include evaluation, and you may succeed.

21 – 12 *Grant Writer's Handbook: 1979-1980,* Public Management Institute Staff, 400pp, 1980, Public Management Institute, $37.50. Suggestions for gaining corporate, foundation and government grants.

21 – 13 *Grants in the Humanities: A Scholar's Guide to Funding Sources,* William Coleman, 1980, Neal-Schuman, $12.95. More for academic or research, than organization fund-raisers.

C. An Audience: Students in Exchange Programs

21 – 14 *Open Doors 1979 – 80; Report on International Education Exchange,* Institute for International Education, 200pp, 1981, Institute for International Education, $20.00. A statistical report on foreign and U.S. college students involved in education exchange programs.

21 – 15 *Handbook on International Study for U. S. Nationals,* Mary Taylor (ed.), 293pp, 1970, Institute for International Education, $7.00. Describes higher education in 120 countries. Special editions are available from IIE on study in Europe and in Latin America.

21 – 16 *Study Abroad,* UNESCO, 1011pp, 1980, UNESCO, $9.95. This is the twenty-third edition of a bi-annual publication offering information on international schools, scholarships, financial assistance, and study programs. The list of International Non-Governmental Organizations (INGO's) offering scholarships is impressive.

21 – 17 *Vacation Study Abroad: The Learning Traveler,* Gail Cohen (ed.), 182pp, 1981 (32nd ed.), Institute of International Education, $8.00. Describes college-level study opportunities sponsored by U.S. colleges and universities, foreign institutions, private and governmental agencies. Published annually.

21 – 17A *Directory of Financial Aid for American Undergraduates Interested in Overseas Study and Travel*, Office of International Education, Adelphi University, 1981, $9.00. Lists 108 financial aid offerings good for nine countries.

D. Educators

21 – 18 *Global Studies: Problems and Promises for Elementary Teachers,* Norman Overly & Richard Kimpston, 1976, Association for Supervision and Curriculum Development, request from publisher. Describes how elementary teachers can introduce global studies.

21 – 19 *No Limits to Learning, Bridging the Human Gap,* James Botkin, Mahdi Elmandra & Mircea Malitza, 159pp, 1979, Pergamon, $7.00. Maintains that the current system of world politics is now capable of great leaps forward or backward. The authors and their consultants at the Club of Rome outline innovative educational strategies to improve understanding and prepare for innovation.

21 – 20 *Peace Education in Catholic Schools,* National Catholic Education Association, 133pp, 1976, NCEA, $3.50. A survey of Catholic school course offerings on peace.

21 – 21 *Schooling and Citizenship in a Global Age: An Exploration of the Meaning and Significance of Global Education,* Lee Anderson, 486pp, 1979, Social Studies Development Center, Indiana, $10.00. Offers a definition of global education addressed to a time when exponential growth is forecast in the "globalization of the human condition."

21 – 22 *Education for a World in Change, A Working Handbook for Global Perspectives,* David King, Margaret Branson, & Larry Condon, 100pp, 1976, Center for Global Perspectives, $3.50. Offers a rationale for and examples of Global Perspective education at grades K through 12.

21 – 23 *Education for a World in Change: A Report,* David King, 62pp, 1980, Global Perspectives in Education, $5.00. An assessment of global education and a question and answer response to frequently received queries.

21 – 24 *World Problems in the Classroom, A Teacher's Guide to Some United Nations Tasks*, Herbert Abraham, 223pp, 1972, UNESCO, $5.30. Provides background on the U.N. and describes its role in resolving contemporary problems and suggests how these things can best be taught.

21 – 25 *The Friendly Classroom for a Small Planet, A Handbook on Creative Ap-*

proaches to Living and Problem Solving for Children, Priscilla Prutzman, et al, 105pp, 1978, Avery, $6.95. A handbook for teaching about nonviolent conflict resolution.

21 – 26 *International Education Programs of the U.S. Government: An Inventory,* Helen Wiprud, 1980, U.S. Gov. Printing Office, $8.50. Describes 181 programs in 28 federal departments and agencies with detailed information on each.

21 – 27 *Localizing International Issues: A Community Guide,* Laureen Andrews, 4pp, 1980, League of Women Voters, $.35. Describes links between local and international activitiy.

21 – 28 *Education for a Global Century: A Handbook of Exemplary International Programs,* Council on Learning, 1980, 271 North Ave., New Rochelle, NY 10801. Describes exceptional programs plus documents the need in two other studies: *What College Students Know and Believe about their World* ($5.95) and *College Students' Knowledge and Beliefs: A Survey of Global Understanding,* $10.95.

21 – 29 *Teaching about the United Nations,* UNA-USA (write for current edition).

21 – 30 *Functions of Folk and Fairy Tales,* Donald Baker, 24pp, 1981, Association for Childhood Education International, $2.00. Describes the uses of folk stories from different cultures in education settings; includes a bibliography of books for children ages 2 – 5; books for children, 5 – 15 and background books for teachers and parents.

21 – 31 *Bibliography of Books for Children,* Books for Children Committee, 112pp, 1980, Association for Childhood Education International, $5.95. Published every three years, this guide reviews both fiction and non-fiction works, and offers ordering information.

21 – 32 *How the Children Stopped the Wars,* Jan Wahl, Avon, $1.50. A child sees a vision and sets out to stop the wars. On his way he collects children whose fathers and brothers are dying far from home.

E. College and University Teachers

21 – 33 *The Study and Teaching of International Relations,* R.C. Kent & G.P. Nielsson, 358pp, 1981, Nichols, $26.50. A practical "how to" book on the presentation of key concepts, teaching strategy, and the likely new shape of the discipline.

21 – 33A *The Global Yellow Pages, A Resource Directory*, 193pp, 1981, Global Perspectives in Education, $7.50. Lists 182 professional and non-governmental organizations and provides a brief description of each organization's focus, services, and publications.

21 – 34 *Peace and World Order Studies,* Transnational Academic Program, 386pp, 1981, Institute for World Order, $8.00. Outlines courses and presents syllabi for seminars which offer "a broad overview of just world order concerns."

F. Business and Labor

21 – 35 *Labor Relations in Advanced Industrial Societies,* Benjamin Martin & Everett Kassalow, 206pp, 1979, Carnegie Endowment for International Peace, $10.00. Examines diverse problems common to democratic, industrialized countries including the impact on labor of multinational corporations, the trend toward labor participation in management and the persistent ways in which industrial conflict is resolved.

21 – 36 *Merchants of Peace: Twenty Years of Business Diplomacy through the International Chamber of Commerce,* George Ridgeway, 1938, Columbia, O.P. Describes the origins and development of the International Chamber of Commerce, 1919 – 1938.

G. Religious Institutions

TEW
21 – 37 *Guidelines in Work for a World Without War,* World Without War Program, 64pp, 1972, Diocese (Episcopal) of California, $.75. Guidelines adopted to guide a peace program after very wide consultation throughout the entire Diocese.

21 – 37A *Rumors of War: A Moral and Theological Perspective on the Arms Race,* Charles Cesaretti and Joseph Vitale (eds.), 1982, Seabury Press, $9.95.

TEW
21 – 38 *Conscience and War, A Kit of Materials,* World Without War Council of Northern California, 62pp, 1981, World Without War Council, $3.50. Clarifies the conflicting values underlying a conscientious response to conscription and indicates what questions a thoughtful person needs to consider.

21 – 38A *Lordship as Servanthood: Thirteen Lessons on the Biblical Basis of Peacemaking,* William Keeney, 112pp, 1975, Faith and Life Press, $2.00. A detailed analysis of the Biblical basis of various teachings on war, written from a pacifist perspective.

21 – 39 "Obstacles to Church Centered Work in the World Affairs Field," Tim Zimmer, 8pp, 1971, World Without War Council, $.10. Examines the most frequently raised objections to peace programs in Churches and responds to them.

21 – 39A *Militarization, Security and Peace Education: A Study Program for Concerned Christians,* Betty Reardon, 1982 (forthcoming), American Baptist Convention. An adult education course package focused on starting a peace education program in a religious institution.

21 – 40 "Churches and a World Without War," Lowell Livezey, 10pp, 1971, World Without War Council, $.25. Suggests how Churches which are willing to be institutionally serious about their work for peace, might approach the subject.

21 – 40A *A Matter of Faith: A Study Guide for Churches on the Nuclear Arms Race,*

108pp, 1981, Sojourners, $3.50 for each of 10 study sessions. Includes articles by those critical of American policies.

21 – 41 *Peace or What?* Barbara Page, 200pp, 1981, World Without War Council – Midwest, $5.00. A six session curriculum introducing approaches to world peace.

21 – 41A *Disarming God's World, Peacemaking Ministry*, 104pp, 1981, United Presbyterian Church in the United States of America, $4.00. (A separate study/action guide is an additional $4.00) Introduces nuclear war, the nuclear arms race, American and Soviet motivations, and "Choices for Our Future."

21 – 42 "Violence and New Forms of Peacemaking," Lowell Livezey, 100pp, 1981, United Church of Christ, $5.00 (est.). A future-oriented curriculum introducing new strategies for resolving international conflict.

21 – 42A *Judaism and War*, Robert Pickus, 40pp, 1968, World Without War Council, $1.00. An anthology of materials covering five different perspectives on war which are encountered in the Jewish tradition. Prepared for high school discussion, useful for adults.

21 – 42B *Judaism and War/Peace Issues*, Jeremy Brochin, 50pp, 1974, World Without War Council/American Jewish Committee, $1.00. A syllabus with well-chosen curriculum materials prepared for Jewish educators.

21 – 42C *National Security: Seeking a New Perspective on an Old Problem*, Commission on Peace and War, 1981, Episcopal Diocese of California, $5.00. A three-session study kit designed for use in parishes and with adult education classes.

21 – 42D *New Call for Peacemakers: A Call to Peacemaking Study Guide*, Maynard Shelly, 109pp, 1981, Faith and Life Press, $2.00. Seeks to establish pacifism as the Christian response to violence and ranges widely into other areas of economic and social life.

21 – 42E *The Riverside Church Disarmament Resources Packet*, Free. A packet of materials including bibliographies, film lists, and a class syllabus for church schools.

21 – 42F *Armament or Disarmament?*, Frank Zeidler, 1970, Lutheran Church in America, $1.00. One of a series of four booklets introducing conditions essential to a world without war.

Many of the organizations listed in Resource B also provide religious institutions with curriculum and offer guidance on what constitutes an appropriate engagement for a religious institution. Write to them for their listings.

H. Peace Work

21 – 43 *Peace Eyes*, Richard McSorley, SJ, 219pp, 1978, Center for Peace Studies,

Georgetown, $2.00. Impressions of world travel to meet "peace people" whose intention it is to work for peace. Most work in isolation from each other and from the major political forces within their country. They operate on very different definitions of peace.

See also Chapter 20, Peace Cause Organizations

I. Programmatic Aids

21 – 44 *Annual Program Manual,* United Nations Association of the U.S.A., 110pp, 1981, UNA-USA, free. Practical information on how to plan and carry out a UN program, to celebrate UN Day or to introduce UN-related topics in the classroom. Includes a list of resources available.

21 – 45 *Hunger: Understanding the Crisis through Games, Drama & Songs,* Patricia Sprinkley, 1980, John Knox, $5.95. A variety of activities and some data on the problem.

21 – 46 *Handbook for World Peacemaker Groups,* 24pp, 1980, World Peacemakers, $1.00. Seeks to form groups of two to twelve Christians to consider the arms race, nonviolence and peacemaking; does not address politics or power in international relations.

21 – 47 *Alternative Celebrations Catalogue,* Staff, Annual, Discipleship Resources, $5.00. Offers non-materialist ways to celebrate holidays.

21 – 48 *The War Peace Film Guide,* John Dowling, 188pp, 1980, World Without War Publications, $5.00. The third edition of what has become the standard reference in the field. Offers an extensive listing of films, describes and evaluates them, and provides resources to use them intelligently.

21 – 49 *Nuclear War Films,* Jack Shaheen, 1978, S. Illinois, $4.95. Describes films on nuclear war.

21 – 50 *Teaching Global Issues Through Simulation: It Can Be Easy,* William Nesbitt, 32pp, 1974, Intercom, $1.50. Introduces a number of simulations and offers an adaptation of the "Road Game."

21 – 51 *World Without War Game,* Anne Stadler, Bev Herbert, Jim Leonard and others, World Without War Publications, $10.25. Includes all the materials you need to organize a weekend retreat that introduces the causes of war and ways to work for a world without war. Also can be adjusted for school use.

J. Contacts

21 – 52 *Names and Numbers, A Journalist's Guide to the Most Needed Information*

Sources and Contacts, Rod Nordland, 560pp, 1978, Wiley, $24.95. An invaluable mine of information, now dated. Hopefully a new edition is forthcoming.

K. Standards of Competence

21 – 53 *Strength through Wisdom, A Critique of U.S. Capability, A Report to the President from the President's Commission on Foreign Language and International Studies,* 39pp, 1979, $1.00. An assessment of American Capabilities far beyond foreign language skills. Problems are identfied in nine areas and recommendations for improvement offered in each. In each area, a committee of non-governmental leaders has assessed needs in the field in the Bay Area. These reports are also available: a). Foreign Language; b). Pre-Collegiate Education; c). Undergraduate Education; d). Graduate Education; e.) Business; f). Adult Education; g). Student Exchange; h). Relief and Development; i). Overview of the Field.

21 – 54 "Assuring the Future: A Diplomat's Concern," Charles Bray, 9pp, 1981, International Communication Agency, $.50. Outlines standards of competence.

L. Directories

21 – 55 *Encyclopedia of Associations,* Nancy Yakes & Dennis Akey, 1,600pp, 1980, Gale, Vol 1. *National Organizations of the U.S.,* $135.00. Lists 14,019 organizations and describes each with seventeen points of information. Vol. 2 provides an 816 page Geographic and Executive Index of the associations listed in Vol. 1 arranged by States and Cities. $120.00. Vol. 3 is a listing of "new associations and projects." $135.00.

21 – 56 *Associations' Publications in Print,* R.R. Bowker, 1,900pp, 1981, Bowker, $75.00. A subject organized bibliography with over 100,000 publications produced and sold by some 20,000 national, state, regional and local associations in North America.

21 – 57 *Research Centers Directory,* Archie Palmer, 1,121pp, 1979, Gale, $110.00. Lists 6,268 centers both university related and non-profit organizations in the United States and Canada. "New Research Centers" is available for $96.00 and updates the volume between editions.

21 – 58 *California and the World, A Directory of California Organizations Concerned with International Affairs,* 68pp, 1979, Center for California Public Affairs, $12.00. Describes 553 California organizations concerned with international politics, global food problems, world trade and business, human rights, student exchange and other topics with a description of their purposes, activities, and publications.

21 – 59 *Foreign Area Programs at North American Universities: A Directory,* 1979, Center for California Public Affairs, $15.00. Gives information on over 750 programs.

21 – 60 *North American Human Rights Directory,* 1980, Laurie Wiseberg & Harry Scoble (eds.), 182pp, 1980, Garrett Park Press, $11.00. Identifies and describes the purposes, programs and structure of nearly 500 U.S. and Canadian based organizations.

21 – 61 *Human Rights: An International Directory of Organizations and Information Sources,* 1979, Center for California Public Affairs, $20.00. An extensive listing.

21 – 62 *International Directory of the Trade Union Movement,* A.P. Goldrick & Philip Jones, 1365pp, 1980, Facts on File, $55.00. A guide to trade unions in many countries compiled with the cooperation of the International Labour Organization (ILO), and International Confederation of Free Trade Unions (ICFTU), the World Conference of Labour (WCL) and the World Federation of Trade Unions (WFTU).

21 – 63 *The Future: A Guide to Information Sources,* 512pp, 1980, World Furture Society, $25.00. A guide to people, ideas, and organizations engaged in "futuring."

21 – 64 *Guide to Ecology Information and Organizations,* John Burke & Jill Reddy, 1976, Wilson, $12.50. Describes the sources and those at work.

21 – 65 *Population: An International Directory of Organizations and Information Sources,* 160pp, 1976, Center for California Public Affairs, $18.75. Describes over 600 organizations.

21 – 66 *The Directory of Directories,* James Ethridge (ed.), 722pp, 1980, Gale, $68.00. An annotated listing of 5,100 current directories of all kinds.

21 – 67 *World Directory of Environmental Organizations,* 288pp, 1976, Center for California Public Affairs, $25.00. Covers more than 3,200 organizations throughout the world.

21 – 68 *World Food Crisis: An International Directory of Organizations and Information Sources,* 166pp, 1977, Center for California Public Affairs, $20.00. Describes over 800 organizations and 275 programs.

21 – 69 *Minority Organizations: A National Directory,* Katherine Cole (ed.), 200pp, 1972, Garrett Park Press, $25.00. A directory of over 5,000 organizations "drawing most of their membership from Black, Hispanic, Asian or Native Americans or which provide special services to these groups."

21 – 70 *American Peace Directoy,* Randall Forsberg, 1981, Westview, (forthcoming). A directory of 2,000 American organizations concerned with "peace, disarmament, and related issues." Includes college and graduate programs, research centers, and membership, activist and lobbying groups.

TEW
21 – 71 *Americans & World Affairs, A Directory of Organizations & Institutions in Northern California,* Laurel Elmer (ed.), 210pp, 1981, World Without War Council of Northern California, $5.00. Offers what is rare: a description of the "Perspective on World Politics and Strategy of Work" of each organization.

21 – 72 *United Nations Development Education Directory*, UN, 74pp, 1981, UN Non-Governmental Liaison Service, Palais des Nations, CH-1211, Geneva 10, Switzerland, free. Describes UN-related agencies, sources of development information, services available to NGOs and sources of statistical information.

21 – 73 *World Directory of Peace Research Institutes*, UNESCO, 213pp, 1981, (4th ed.) Unipub, $10.00. Provides information on 312 institutes in forty-three countries.

RESOURCE FOR ACTION D: BUT WHAT CAN I DO? — A SELF SURVEY

Individuals entering the world affairs field need to assess their strengths to determine where and how their effort can help. The following questions can help you clarify your own situation.

I. Who am I?

Name: _____

Address: _____

City _____ State_____ Zip _____

Educational level: _____ Occupation: _____

Religious, political, professional or other organizations to which you

belong: _____

Major peace activities: _____

Work preferences: (check one or more)

leadership role?	nuts and bolts?
help others?	execution?
conceptualization?	meeting new people?
planning?	research?

Groups I enjoy working with: (check one or more)

children?	conservative?
young adults?	liberal?
adults?	radical?
religious?	secular?
professional?	non-vocational?
avant garde?	consensus building?

II. In what war/peace field am I interested? (check one or more)

_____ the U.N., International Organization and growth toward world law

_____ hunger, world economic development, and social development

_____ building a sense of world community

_____ developing human rights conceptions and enforcement procedures

_____ the arms race, arms control and general and complete disarmament

_____ conscience and war: the moral issues and value choices involved

_____ current crisis problems: the Middle East, energy, hunger, Southeast Asia, the B-1 bomber, the law of the sea. . . .

_____ building understanding across ideological, regional, religious, and ethnic barriers

_____ nonviolent methods of forcing change or conducting conflict others:

_____ I need more information before deciding

III. What do I believe?

In a word, how do I describe myself?

_____ world federalist?   _____ pacifist?

_____ personalist?   _____ internationalist?

_____ deterrence advocate?   _____ next step foreign policy?

_____ concerned but confused?   _____ other

IV. What special skills or talents do I have?

_____ public speaking   _____ persuading others

_____ discussion leader   _____ motivating others

_____ office management   _____ organizing groups

_____ identifying unifying factors   _____ raising money

_____ layout and design   _____ research

V. How much time can I give?

_____ full-time   _____ one or two days a week

_____ an hour a day   _____ a few hours a month

VI. What type of work experience do I need to continue?

_____ Uncritical acceptance of every peace activity

_____ Work based on a thoughtful analysis of the reality of conflict purposes and power centers in world politics

_____ Immediate results

_____ A sense of accomplishment

_____ A recognition that the work is badly needed

VII. Where should I work?
_____ Professional organization (psychiatrists, doctors, lawyers . . .)
_____ Religious organization (church, synagogue, temple, mosque . . .)
_____ Business association
_____ Labor unions
_____ Teacher
_____ Opinion leaders
_____ Idea centers
_____ Peace-cause organizations
_____ Major institutions: schools, libraries, businesses. . . .
_____ News media
_____ University
_____ Coalitions

VIII. What type of activity makes most sense?
_____ Developing a film library
_____ Work with elected officials
_____ Making visible intelligent publications in the field
_____ Protest and demonstration activity
_____ Campaigns, petitioning, letter writing
_____ Public meetings
_____ Research and idea development
_____ Symbolic witness
_____ Engaging new organizations
_____ Improving the work of old organizations
_____ Building a transnational constituency
_____ Reaching the mass media
_____ Gaining opinion leader support
_____ Educating

IX. What will I actually do?

The need for serious and specific community work is clear. The variety of possibilities is almost endless. The trick is to match your skills, time and interest with a task which is both challenging and feasible.

RESOURCE FOR ACTION E: BUT WHAT CAN I DO?: TWENTY-FIVE ANSWERS

Here are twenty-five examples written in the first person because they are summaries of actual individual experiences.

WORK WITH DECISION-MAKERS

1. We live in a time of crises. The best way to work is to go directly to the decision-makers themselves. If you do not have access directly, find out who does and get them to go. During the Cuban missile crisis I called key Soviet scientists and key American scientists. They in turn reached government officials. An informal channel of communication was opened to the very top leaders. I think we averted World War III that way. I am worried about the next crisis and have continued to build contacts across the ideological divides in the world. I'm grateful for others who have gathered scientists, opinion leaders, members of nongovernmental organizations, even if the concrete results are meager.

2. Whatever work is done, in this country or elsewhere, pays off in Washington. Therefore, I have helped work with members of Congress to organize them. We meet periodically to plan strategy in Congress, to work out approaches to specific issues, and to connect work on issues to long-term strategy.

WORK ON A TRANSNATIONAL CONSTITUENCY

3. My emphasis has been on transnational relationships. All the focus on this country and on decision-makers in Washington seems to me to be beside the point. We need to develop a transnational constituency for the goals and ideas needed to build a world order. I have thus aided the Institute for World Order in its World Order Models Projects. Through this a transnational academic constituency has developed. Soon it may be possible to form a transnational political party. It is an oddity of American politics that the connections to political organizations in other countries are almost non-existent. Given an interdependent world, we need political officials willing to run for office on platforms designed to address the new scope of foreign policy.

ENLARGING THE KNOWLEDGE BASE

4. When I was young, I knew how to end war. This world is full of surprises. I have turned to an academic career seeking to increase the amount of validated knowledge available to diplomats. There is a large network of peace researchers working in every corner of the world. During the next decade I plan

to test out a simulation of the international system developed through a team effort in this country. We will test the simulation in other cultural and ideological settings to eliminate bias.

DIRECT INVOLVEMENT

5. Enough now is known to work on the problem of war. What is needed is to apply what we know. I, therefore, gather peace researchers and diplomats in conferences to discuss what is relevant to decision-makers. We have also worked with the non-governmental International Peace Academy which trains people for U.N. peacekeeping roles and other mediation efforts. We are interested in new efforts to form nonviolent ''armies'' of people willing to act as mediators even when the parties at war do not ask for mediation. ''Seeding'' individuals with nonviolent conflict mediation skills in crisis areas may be the best way to build local contacts prior to the time when a crisis erupts. They will then be positioned to mediate.

6. My skills are more administrative than academic. I am working to develop the structure of a government-sponsored Peace Institute designed to teach people conflict-resolution skills. I call it the West Point of the peace movement. I have gone to the U.N. University in Tokyo to study how they have worked out curriculum, relationships between contending perspectives, and the support system needed. Setting up such an institution will be an enormous challenge.

THE WORLD AFFAIRS FIELD

7. I have worked full-time in this field for over thirty years. The field is an imbroglio of organizations. Nearly every new issue that comes along leads to the creation of a new organization. After six months they are usually gone. Those that survive carry an idea, conduct a function, create an arena, or serve a specialized constituency. Almost no one looks at the whole field. My task is to gather and link these organizations, to develop functional relationships among them, to create a mosaic of organizations that can work jointly to make this country a competent actor in world politics.

8. You rarely encounter thoughtful discussions of world affairs. I was curious, at first, why this was so. It now appears that the field is particularly susceptible to conspiracy theories — much of the decision-making *is* done in

secret and by elites. I discovered that there is a special role for elites because only a few people are willing to take the time to become experts on an issue or crisis area. Thus, I try to get organizations to sponsor programs that cut beneath the surface questions of issues to the values or the goals involved; then individuals who are not specialists can become experts on ends and means. In the arenas created as a result, no one point of view carries the day. Many points of view are encountered and each must clarify its values. The point is to map out areas of agreement and disagreement so that possibly, just possibly, we can regain a sense of direction.

EDUCATION

9. I'm a social studies teacher. In my field the problem is to keep up with the outpouring of literature from a variety of curriculum development centers, and then to get teachers to use it. School boards, curriculum development centers, research institutes, social studies organizations. . . all of these are places where critical decisions are being made daily on how to prepare children for the world they will face. I work in each area to improve the resources available to teachers and to focus attention on non-military alternatives to war as the means to resolve international conflict.

10. I work in curriculum development. We have tried to break out of the national focus into a global perspective. The nation-State is still the critical actor but the interaction between States, the problems which no State can solve alone provide the challenge to us. Some of the new curricula are very imaginative. Students at each grade level participate in creating connections between people and places, between change and continuity, between cultural differences and underlying uniformities. Since we are continually meeting people from new cultures, ideologies, religions, and various walks of life, it is essential to prepare students first to appreciate and to understand their own values; then comfortably meet and relate to people with different values. That way we can increase the chances that the inevitable conflicts in world politics will be handled without violence because misperceptions resulting from misunderstandings can be reduced, and perhaps institutions created for resolving real conflicts that remain.

MASS MEDIA

11. I'm a writer and a TV producer. Using the skill and channels now open to me obviously makes the most sense. The media is the major ''shaper''

of ideas and attitudes in this society. I'm always on the lookout for intelligent programming which helps clarify how international conflict can be conducted and resolved without violence and which then increases our understanding of others; all of this aids in promoting constructive change. Sometimes this means connecting a resource person with a talk show host; sometimes it means developing a script into a TV series; sometimes it means writing a script from scratch.

12. I have two small children and spend much of the day at home. I have done editing for world affairs organizations which engage in publishing or preparing news releases and grant proposals. In addition, I keep track of all the radio and TV talk shows, the kind of ideas they focus on, and how people who care about world affairs can be heard.

PEACE EDUCATION WITH CHILDREN

13. I believe it is important to work with children. I have, therefore, done a survey of available curricula for churches and temples and found much of it is of real value. We have set up workshops for religious leaders to sort through the available curricula picking those which are open-ended because they have more than one outcome. We have also used inter-generational and intercultural curricula and projects for families and for religious institutions as a means of preparing children for an interdependent world.

REACH OPINION LEADERS

14. There is in my region of the country a select number of people whose judgment really carries weight. The important thing is to get them to put world affairs high among their priorities and to nurture them so they can offer wise leadership. I have a list of fifteen people whom I regularly inform of key decisions and another ten in my profession with whom I maintain regular correspondence.

WORK THROUGH WORLD AFFAIRS EDUCATION ORGANIZATIONS

15. I have been very skeptical of organizations in the world affairs field. For the most part, they are so one-sided in their portrayal of the virtues and vices

of the various actors in the field, so selective in their presentation of facts, so focused in what they want, that I avoid them. Instead, I've joined the World Affairs Council and the Foreign Policy Association. They offer balanced programs and do a sophisticated job of education on the realities of world politics. Each year we study the *Great Decisions* booklet, and form opinions on a variety of world affairs issues. These opinions are then tabulated and passed on to decision-makers. In that way, an informed public opinion can be achieved and it can have an impact on those now responsible for policy.

16. I've found that world affairs organizations rarely challenge the prevailing views in the Department of State. What they do, an important task to be sure, is to create an informed dialogue within the framework of assumptions and beliefs in government. I think far more of our efforts should go into making the United Nations a viable, effective keeper of the peace. I, therefore, focus my energies on the United Nations Association.

CHOOSE AN ISSUE

17. I like to focus all my energy on one issue. Whether it is a new weapon system or one of a whole series of economic issues or a human rights question, or some crisis, I work on what is current. I try to become an instant expert by reading a number of different periodicals, consulting with specialists, reading the newspapers, and by meeting with organizational leaders. Then, I can write letters to the editor, form or join an ad hoc organization, visit my Representative or write the President.

CONSCIENCE AND WAR

18. My church was deeply divided by the draft in the 1960s. Some people did draft counseling that was little different from a resource for people wanting to avoid military service. A group of us in the church challenged this approach, indicating that it was advocating dishonesty. We then studied questions of conscience and war and formulated guidelines for a counseling center. We insisted that the center honestly present information, that counseling be done which challenged people to think carefully about the contending bodies of thought related to war. Some of those we counseled filed for conscientious objector status. Others joined the army. Still others acted out of their judgment by refusing to register. I think most of the people we counseled were aware of

the shortcomings of any position offered in answer to the question: Are you a conscientious objector to war? A few, whatever they decided at the time, have continued to work to develop non-military ways to conduct and resolve international conflict.

BECOME AN EXPERT IN A SPECIFIC PROGRAM AREA

19. I've become an expert on good war/peace films. I've seen most of them. I developed a rating system to aid people conducting programs in schools, religious institutions, or world affairs organizations. The ratings, plus annotations of what is in the films, together with ordering information makes the film resouce list I developed a hot item. It is hard to turn the feelings and ideas engendered by most war/peace films into constructive programs, so resources to aid in that endeavor have been and are being developed.

RELIGIOUS INSTITUTIONS

20. My institution has been skeptical about its appropriate role in the world affairs field. At first we let the small group that cared passionately about issues use a few of our resources. They did not, however, deeply influence the religious instruction, the sermons, or the adult education classes. Then we thought through what should be the institution's response to these issues. To do so required discussion with people with very different perspectives. Out of that discussion came a framework of belief most agreed upon and which then enabled us to engage the institution in a consideration of how its values ought to be applied to world affairs.

PEOPLE-TO-PEOPLE

21. I've always felt that we miss a great opportunity to influence world affairs when we ignore the visitors in our midst. I was amazed at the number of students, visiting officials, business people, diplomats, newspaper correspondents, and others I have met from other countries. I have worked with exchange students. Some of these relationships have continued over the years.

SYMBOLIC ACTS

22. I'm impatient with those approaches which counsel caution. Education is fine, but the major issues of our time are moral questions. Surely these eternal meetings miss the point — the point is to act. I've helped organize a walk across the United States and Europe — from Seattle to Moscow. We plan to talk to everyone we meet urging concern about the threats to our survival.

23. The most important thing you can do is say no. To say no forcefully requires that you put your body on the line. I've learned the techniques of civil disobedience and have organized a mass protest. We plan to encircle the Pentagon, the Soviet embassy, and the Embassy of any country at war at that time.

SUPPORT A PROFESSIONAL

24. I've been impressed by the quality of people working sacrificially in the world affairs field. I am, therefore, making a regular pledge to a world affairs organization. It was hard to decide which one to support. I requested the organizational leaflets of the twenty-five which interested me most, then went to visit the five which seemed particularly well conceived.

BE A PROFESSIONAL

25. I've decided to work full-time in a world affairs organization. It is a challenging choice. We have yet to secure a funding base, so financial sacrifice is the reality. But the challenge of developing ideas, organizations, and resources makes it worthwhile.

RESOURCE FOR ACTION F: ACTING WITHIN AN ORGANIZATION

AN ORGANIZATIONAL

INTERNATIONAL HUMAN RIGHTS QUOTIENT

. . . AN ASSESSMENT TOOL

We know that the question of peace and the question of human rights are closely related.

Without recognition of human rights, we shall never have peace.

It is only within the framework of peace that human rights can be fully developed.
—*Dag Hammarskjold*

THE ASSESSMENT

First, your own perspective:
A concern for international human rights is now an important element in U.S. foreign policy. What is your reaction?
In answering the following questions, try to assess both your national organization's and your local organization's work in the field of international human rights.

I. INTERNATIONAL HUMAN RIGHTS AND YOUR ORGANIZATION:

FACTS

1. In your judgment, should advancing international human rights have a prominent place on your organization's agenda?
   1a. Does it now?
   1b. If it does, are there formal guidelines or policy statements to direct the organization's international human rights work? How valuable are these?

2. *What kinds* of international human rights *violations* have been the objects of your organization's concerns?

3. *What countries'* human rights practices have received your organization's attention in the past five years?
   3a. How has that attention been expressed?

4. Is there a committee and/or staff person assigned responsibility for international human rights work in your organization?

nationally: _____committee _____staff person

locally: _____committee _____staff person

II. INTERNATIONAL HUMAN RIGHTS AND YOUR ORGANIZATION:

CONCEPTS

These questions are to help you assess your organization's ideas on international human rights (or, if not developed), what they should be.

Standards

5. In developing its human rights concepts, does your organization assert that there are *universal* human rights — fundamental rights of all people, which constitute moral standards to which we can appeal in making judgments about countries with traditions different from our own?

6. The world being as it is, human rights violations are legion. Limitations of time and energy require choosing those cases of human rights violations to which your organization will respond. Is your organization clear on what it considers a "persistent pattern of gross violations of human rights," requiring an expenditure of organizational energy and resources?
   6a. Is there a statement in writing of how your organization makes that judgment?

7. Is your organization's human rights activity vulnerable to charges of being suspiciously selective — directed towards Chile, South Korea, and Iran, but not Cuba, Vietnam, and Mozambique (or vice versa)?
   7a. Since no organization can work on everything, most develop a pattern of response or activity in the human rights field. If your organization has, is that pattern desirable and appropriate to the organization? Is it vulnerable to a charge of "double standard"?

8. Should there be a single standard, or are there other values and goals in our foreign policy that, in some cases, should take priority over our human rights concerns? If so, what are they?

Balance

9. There are societies committed to and working on a broad range of human rights, societies which are open to scrutiny and criticism. There are also societies in which gross violations of human rights are a matter of state policy, and reporting these is difficult because information is rigidly controlled.

   In between these two extremes are a variety of intermediate arrangements. Does your organization understand this situation, and deal with it wisely?

Intervention

10. What is your reaction to this statement: "The U.S. Government should not interfere in the internal affairs of other countries."?

11. If you think there are situations where the U.S. should intervene, what means should be used?

12. Do you think that the human rights situation in the U.S. today is such that this country can legitimately seek to forward human rights internationally?

Scope

13. Here are two statements:

    A. The language and concepts of human rights cannot be restricted to the traditional North Atlantic civil and political liberties, nor to the question of government in its relationship to individuals. Human rights must include those fundamental claims to food, work, medical care, education, and culture that are primary requisites of a human life.

    B. The language and concepts of human rights should be reserved to the arena of political and civil liberties. Other language and concepts will serve us better in seeking to meet other basic human needs.

       This is because there is a difference between the essential goals of any enlightened political community, and identifying those goals as entitlements to be delivered primarily by governments under the rubric of human rights. Government may not be the best way to reach those goals, and the price of giving government this power may be a serious encroachment on the civil and political liberties that define a democratic society.

13a. Which of these statements most accurately reflects *your* approach to human rights?

13b. Which of these statements most accurately reflects *your organization's* approach to human rights?

Rationale

14. Much of the current discussion of international human rights invokes ethical or legal concepts. Are there *practical* reasons which our country should give a high priority for advancing international human rights?

III. INTERNATIONAL HUMAN RIGHTS AND YOUR ORGANIZATION:

ACTION

We're approaching this from the point of view of a member of an American nongovernmental organization (NGO).
You are asked first to outline your organization's international human rights work at various levels, and then to survey your attitude towards the range of human rights programming available to a U.S. NGO.
   A. Check the levels of your organization which presently conduct international human rights activity and, where possible, give an example.

Examples

15.____ for its local members   20.____ with the international NGO

16.____ for the local community   to which your organization

17.____ as a national organization   relates

18.____ in relation to the U.S.   21.____ with other international
       government   NGOs and governments

19.____ in relation to the U.N.
       and its agencies

   B. Elements of a Developed International Human Rights Program for an American NGO. (circle appropriate category)

      A. Would welcome my organization doing this.

      B. We're doing it nationally.

C. We're doing it here locally.

22. *Publications:*
Do you publish materials
that draw on your organization's
tradition, discipline, or
function to set out your role
in the international human
rights field?   A.   B.   C.

23. *Newspaper, newsletter, or
other information services:*
Regular reporting on international
human rights problems?   A.   B.   C.

24. *Statements:*
By your organization's leader (s)
on U.S. international human
rights policy?   A.   B.   C.

25. *Statements:*
By your organization's leader (s)
on international human rights
as a program focus of your
organization?   A.   B.   C.

26. *Leadership training:*
Are there opportunities for those
wanting to take responsibility in
this field to learn the business
— ideas, perspectives, other
organizations, government actors
and agencies, program-funding
strategies, etc.?   A.   B.   C.

27. *Education programs for your membership:*
a. for adults?   A.   B.   C.
b. for young people?   A.   B.   C.
c. for children?   A.   B.   C.

28. *Programs for the local community:*
    a. arena-setting events?   A.   B.   C.
    b. media visibility?   A.   B.   C.

29. *Legislative information:*
    Does your organization keep
    abreast of current Congressional
    action that bears on U.S.
    international human rights policy?   A.   B.   C.

30. *Congressional and executive action:*
    Response to or attempts to
    encourage action (by the
    Congress, the President, the State
    Department, or other federal
    agencies) your organization
    thinks is necessary?   A.   B.   C.

31. *Advocacy:*
    Petitions, boycotts, issue
    campaigns, etc.?   A.   B.   C.

32. *Action in relation to the
    international NGO to which
    you are linked:*
    Joining its international
    human rights activities in
    both substance and program;
    catalyzing needed action?   A.   B.   C.

33. *Action in relation to the
    U.N. and its affiliate
    agencies:*
    Monitoring action and
    resolutions; formulating
    positions in relation to
    theirs; acting through NGO
    channels in New York and Geneva?   A.   B.   C.

34. *Symbolic events/public witness
    activity:*
    Special services or days designed
    to highlight and remind your
    organization and the wider
    community of the fundamental
    commitments from which all
    this activity arises.   A.   B.   C.

35. *Mass media activity:*
    Press releases, press
    conferences, etc.?   A.   B.   C.

36. *Direct action in support of
    victims of human rights
    violations abroad:*
    Aiding in visibility, funding,
    and support before relevant
    governments and/or U.N. agencies?   A.   B.   C.

IV. INTERNATIONAL HUMAN RIGHTS AND YOUR
ORGANIZATION:

PROBLEMS AND COUNTRIES

*A. On which of these problems is your organization currently working (either
in a human rights context, or as a means of meeting basic human needs and
aspirations)?*

	Concern of my organization	Understood and worked on in a ''human rights'' context.
37. adequate medical care (physical and mental health)		

38. adequate standard of
    living (food, clothing,
    housing)
39. arbitrary arrest and
    detention
40. benefits of authorship
    or invention
41. emigration
42. employment
43. equal pay for equal work
44. equal status before
    the law
45. ethnic language and
    culture
46. form and maintain a
    family
47. free assembly
48. free press
49. free speech
50. free and compulsory
    primary education
51. freedom of conscience,
    thought, and religion
52. genocide
53. leisure time
54. participation in cultural
    life
55. racial discrimination
56. safe working conditions
57. self-determination
58. sex discrimination
59. social security
60. torture
61. other:

B. Which of these countries is presently the focus of your organization's international human rights concern and action? (The list is not exhaustive; feel free to add others.)

_____62. Argentina

_____63. Bangladesh

_____79. South Korea

_____80. Libya

_____64. Brazil

_____65. Burma

_____66. Central African Empire

_____67. Chile

_____68. China (PRC)

_____69. China (Taiwan)

_____70. Cuba

_____71. Ethiopia

_____72. India

_____73. Indonesia

_____74. Iran

_____75. Northern Ireland

_____76. Israel

_____77. Kampuchea

_____78. North Korea

_____81. Mexico

_____82. Mozambique

_____83. Namibia

_____84. Pakistan

_____85. Philippines

_____86. Poland

_____87. Romania

_____88. Saudi Arabia

_____89. South Africa

_____90. Syria

_____91. Uganda

_____92. U.S.S.R.

_____93. Vietnam

_____94. Zimbabwe

_____95. Other:

V. INTERNATIONAL HUMAN RIGHTS AND YOUR ORGANIZATION:

THE QUALITY OF THE ENDEAVOR

In short . . .

As you look at the full range of your organization's international human rights thought and activity, not quantitatively but qualitatively, *is it an expression of the best in your tradition and values?*

1   2   3   4   5   6   7   8   9   10

unclear, thoughtless,   lots of problems,   speaks from the
confused, hypocritical   but basically on the   very best of
                                 right track   our roots, and
                                                            addresses these
                                                            issues wisely
                                                            and effectively

Or . . .

_____*It's not really on our present agenda.*

RESOURCE G: SPECIALIZING IN A SUBJECT AREA: AN EXAMPLE

Most of the material in this book is intended to give you a general overview of the world affairs field. As you become familiar with the ideas and problems in the field, you may want to deepen your knowledge of some section of it which is of special interest to you. Whether the subject is disarmament or development, the Middle East or South Africa, ethics and war, or transnational corporations, there is a need for specialized knowledge plus an understanding of how a particular problem area relates to the overall problem of progress toward an end to war. What does the latter require? Using the disarmament area as an example, to develop a specialist's understanding, you should come to know:

1. *The crucial periodicals that deal regularly with issues of arms control and disarmament* (e.g. *Foreign Affairs, Foreign Policy, The Bulletin of Atomic Scientists,* etc.)

You probably already follow arms control and disarmament issues in the general circulation magazines and newspapers. It is important that you also familiarize yourself with the relevant specialist and scholarly journals, and become acquainted with general circulation periodicals which present a range of political perspectives on arms control problems.

2. *The best introductory pamphlets, books and research center reports dealing with disarmament problems.*

Go back to the arms control and disarmament bibliographical portions of Chapters 2 and 4 and select the major books in the field. They will give you a start. From them and from some of the specialized periodicals listed in Resource H you will be able to develop a more exhaustive reading list.

3. *The government agencies, congressional committees and staff in the executive branch who are responsible for arms control and disarmament policy.*

You should know: who on the President's staff are influential on arms control and disarmament questions, who in the National Security Council, the Pentagon, the State Department, and the CIA are responsible for arms control and disarmament matters, who heads the U.S. Arms Control and Disarmament Agency and what staff officers are most helpful, who chairs the relevant Congressional committees and who are the key staff? Are you on their mailing lists?

4. *The staff and members of committees and sections of the United Nations that deal with disarmament questions; the specialized international agencies involved.*

Does the U.N. General Assembly have disarmament questions on its agenda for this year? What issues are being discussed? Is another Special

Session on Disarmament planned? Is the Committee on Disarmament meeting? What is the Secretary-General doing to promote disarmament negotiations and agreements? What is the U.N. Centre for Disarmament doing? Who in the U.S. delegation to the U.N. is especially concerned with disarmament questions?

5. *What specific arms control and disarmament issues will confront the President, Congress, the United Nations, bilateral and multilateral negotiators, and the American public this year?*

What new technological developments are shaping the course of the nuclear and conventional arms races? When will this year's arms control impact statements be issued? What new weapons systems will require Congressional authorization? What disarmament legislation is pending before Congress? What other issues will be discussed in public media — nuclear proliferation, zonal disarmament, nuclear strategy, international supervision and inspection, conventional disarmament, arms embargoes?

6. *The international and national nongovernmental organizations and thought centers which do educational, political and research work on arms control and disarmament issues; the positions they have taken on specific issues. What coalitions or interorganizational policy approaches have been adopted? What policies have been discussed by representatives and people from different ideological camps?*

Look over the listing of organizations in Section C, Resource C, and pick out those that are particularly interested in disarmament questions. Write to them for information on their activities and publications. Many mainstream community organizations have taken positions on disarmament issues. Compile a list of such organizations and the positions they have taken.

7. *The individuals articulating the major distinct approach to arms control and disarmament problems, their arguments and responses to their critics' arguments.*

As the debate over an issue takes shape, it is important to know the contending schools of thought. As you follow the discussion in general circulation and scholarly journals, you will probably notice that within each school of thought most spokespersons defer to the arguments of a particular scholar or expert. You should know who these experts are and be familiar with their perspectives.

8. *Educational resources in the field: bibliographies, films, tapes, reports, article reprints, speakers available locally and nationally, and program materials prepared for work at both levels.*

There is a wealth of educational materials available, but you need to know how to evaluate them, what they are useful for and where they can be obtained.

9. *Your own context, standards, values, goals and conception of what you are doing.*

This is a reminder that although you may acquire much specialized knowledge, you will be working on only one part of the problem of war. How does work on disarmament relate to problems of world law, economic development, and building a sense of world community? How might the goals, which you pursue in the areas of arms control and disarmament, be aided by international agreements in other areas?

10. *What specific peace initiatives by one country could demonstrate a willingness to move beyond arms control toward disarmament?* Is its initiative simply to reduce its own level of threat or does it combine such reduction with efforts to gain reciprocal reductions by others?

This is the essential task and one "pay-off" for a specialist. It is rarely done well. When you take policy proposals which are offered throughout the literature and turn them into specific acts one country (or other international actor) can take which initiate a process toward disarmament goals (and others), then you are working within the context recommended by *To End War*. (See Chapter 19).

All of these may sound too much for one person to handle; but a minimal filing system, a relationship with one of the good world affairs organizations in your subject area, links to a few important centers of thought nationally, and a sustained intention to build your own understanding will soon enable *you* to make a significant contribution to the policy decision-making process.

Passion and ignorance are too frequently combined in the world affairs field. It is essential that you do your homework on your part of the field. You'll be a valuable resource person in your community or organization if you do.

RESOURCE H: KEEPING INFORMED: A SELECTED LIST OF WORLD AFFAIRS PERIODICALS[1]

Periodicals play an important role in the public discussion of world affairs problems. It is a little depressing to realize how often a person's point of view can be identified simply by the magazine he or she reads. Few make a conscious effort to seek out a variety of points of view or to become acquainted with scholarly or other sources of more objective information. It is worth the trouble.

The periodicals listed here each offer a point of view, provide insight into an area of specialization, or reach a level of intelligence that makes them worth seeking out. They are grouped in six categories, although in many cases a particular periodical could readily fit in more than one. In many cases the publisher will provide a sample copy for your own assessment.

---

[1] The information for this resource was compiled by Kurt Carlson, a graduate of Beloit College, and a Peace Interne with the World Without War Council – Midwest during the 1980/81 program year.

The publications listed here range from political opinion weeklies to scholarly journals and include specialized publications that regularly cover foreign policy issues and topics related to world affairs. No newspapers are included. You may want to seek out one of the U.S. newspapers which has its own foreign policy reporters: The Boston Globe, The Chicago Tribune, The Christian Science Monitor, The Los Angeles Times, The New York Times, The St. Louis Post Dispatch, and the Washington Post.

World Without War Council Peace Internes have four or more periodical assignments which they have found helpful in developing capabilities for work in this field. Each Interne is assigned a scholarly journal, a perspective setting magazine, a mass circulation periodical, and an organizational newsletter, in which he or she follows the treatment of a world affairs problem. Internes also construct a spectrum of magazines from those listed in the ''perspective setting'' section.

For more comprehensive but unannotated listings of periodicals consult Ulrich's *International Periodicals Directory* or Ayer's *Directory of Newspapers and Magazines,* both of which list thousands of periodicals in many categories. *Magazines for Libraries,* Bill Katz, editor, is less comprehensive but its lively, intelligent annotations make it useful to the general reader. More specialized are *The Information Sources of Political Science* and *The Annotated Guide to the Social Sciences* (Volume I: ''International Relations and Current History''), both in the ABC – Clio Bibliographic Series. Topically organized indices of specific articles and essays can be found in *The Reader's Guide to Periodical Literature* (general interest magazines and newspapers), in *The Social Science and Humanities Index* (including some more scholarly and specialized periodicals), and in the *Public Affairs Information Service Bulletin,* which includes many government publications.

I. General Interest and World Affairs Arena Periodicals

  A. Scholarly World Affairs Periodicals

   Armed Forces and Society:
   An Interdisciplinary Journal
   Sage Publications
   275 S. Beverly Drive
   Beverly Hills, CA 90212   Quarterly, $18/year

   Current History
   4225 Main Street
   Philadelphia, PA 19127   Monthly, $18.85/year

Foreign Affairs
Council on Foreign Relations
58 E. 68th Street
New York, NY 10021   5 times/year, $22/year

Foreign Policy
Carnegie Endowment for International Peace
11 Dupont Circle
Washington, DC 20036   Quarterly, $15/year

International Studies Quarterly
International Studies Association
University of South Carolina
Columbia, SC 29208   Quarterly, Membership Required

Journal of International Affairs
School of International Affairs
Columbia University
420 W. 118th St.
New York, NY 10027   Semi-annually, $7/year

Orbis:
Journal of World Affairs
Foreign Policy Research Institute
3508 Market St., Suite 350
Philadelphia, PA 19101   Quarterly, $15.00/year

The Washington Quarterly:
A Review of Strategic and International Studies
Transaction Periodicals
Rutgers University
New Brunswick, NJ 08903   Quarterly, $16.00/year

World Affairs:
Quarterly Review
American Peace Society
4000 Albermarle St., NW
Washington, DC 20016   Quarterly, $10.00/year

World Affairs Report
California Institute of International Studies
766 Santa Ynez
Stanford, CA 94305   Quarterly, $9.00/year

World Politics:
A Quarterly Journal of International Relations
Princeton University Press
Princeton University
Princeton, NJ 08544   Quarterly, $12.00/year

The World Today
The Royal Institute of International Affairs
Oxford University Press
Press Road, Neasden
London NW 10, England

B. Scholarly Periodicals Which Include World Affairs

American Bar Association Journal
77 S. Wacker Dr.
Chicago, IL 60606   Monthly, $15.00/year

American Journal of Political Science
University of Texas Press
Box 7819
Austin, TX 78712   Quarterly, $30.00/year

The American Political Science Review
The American Political Science Association
1527 New Hampshire Ave., NW
Washington, DC 20036   Quarterly, $35.00/year

The American Scholar
United Chapters of Phi Beta Kappa
1811 Q. St., NW
Washington, DC 20009   Monthly, $10.00/year

The Annals of the American Academy
of Political and Social Science
3937 Chestnut St.
Philadelphia, PA 19104   Bi-monthly, $18.00/year

Canadian Journal of Political Science
Canadian Political Science Association
Wilfrid Laurier University Press
75 University Ave.
Waterloo, Ontario N2L 3C5
Canada   Quarterly, $35.00/year

Columbia Journalism Review
700 Journalism Bldg.
New York, NY 10027   Bi-monthly, $14.00/year

Daedalus
American Academy of Arts and Sciences
7 Linden St.
Harvard University
Cambridge, MA 02138   Quarterly, $16.00/year

The Economist (London)
515 Abbott Dr.
Broomall, PA 19008   Weekly, $85.00

The Humanist
American Humanist Association
7 Harwood Dr.
Amherst, NY 14226   Bi-monthly, $12.00/year

International Journal of Politics:
A Quarterly Journal of Translation
M.E. Sharpe, Inc.
White Plains, NY 10603   Quarterly, $30.00/year

International Political Science Review
Sage Publications
275 S. Beverly Drive
Beverly Hills, CA 90212   Quarterly, $18.00/year

International Social Science Journal
Unipub
345 Park Ave., S.
New York, NY 10010   Quarterly, $23.00/year

Journal of Social and Political Studies
Council on American Affairs
1716 N. Hampshire Ave., NW
Washington, DC 20009　　Quarterly

Pacific Affairs
University of British Columbia
2075 Westbrook Place
Vancouver, BC
V6T IW5 Canada　　Quarterly, $12.00/year

Partisan Review
128 Bay State Road
Boston, MA 02215　　4 issues/year, $12.50/year

Political Science Quarterly
Academy of Political Science
619 W. 114th St., Suite 500
New York, NY 10025　　Quarterly, $17.50

Political Theory:
An International Journal of Political Philosophy
Sage Publications
275 S. Beverly
Beverly Hills, CA 90212　　Quarterly, $32.00/year

Radical History Review
Radical Historians Organization
445 W. 59th St.
New York, NY 10019　　3 times/year, $12.50/year

Society
Transaction Periodicals
Rutgers University
New Brunswick, NJ 08903　　Bi-monthly, $18.00/year

Western Political Quarterly
University of Utah
258 OSH
Salt Lake City, UT 84112　　Quarterly, $20.00/year

The Wilson Quarterly:
A National Review of Ideas and Information
Woodrow Wilson International Center for Scholars
   Smithsonian Institute
Washington, DC 20560   Quarterly, $14.00/year

C. Mass Market Periodicals Which Include World Affairs

The Atlantic
8 Arlington St.
Boston, MA 02116   Monthly, $18.00/year

Harper's Magazine
2 Park Ave
New York, NY 10016   Monthly, $14.00/year

Newsweek
444 Madison Ave.
New York, NY 10022   Weekly, $32.50/year

Time
Time and Life Bldg.
New York, NY 10020   Weekly, $35.00/year

U.S. News & World Report
2300 N. St., NW
Washington, DC 20037   Weekly, $32.00/year

D. International Business Periodicals

African Business
IC Magazine Ltd.
62 Long Acre
London WC2E 9JH
England   Monthly, $50.00/year

Barron's National Business and Financial Weekly
Dow Jones and Co.
22 Cortlandt St.
New York, NY 10007   Weekly, $49.00/year

Business Week
1221 Ave. of the Americas
New York, NY 10020   Weekly, $34.95/year

Columbia Journal of World Business
Graduate School of Business
Columbia University
408 Uris Hall
New York, NY 10027   Quarterly, $32.00/year

8 Days Magazine:
Middle East Business
Empire House
414 Chiswick High Road
London W4 5TF
England   Weekly, $87.00/year

Forbes Magazine
60 Fifth Ave.
New York, NY 10011   Bi-weekly, $30.00/year

Fortune Magazine
Time and Life Bldg.
New York, NY 10020   Bi-weekly, $33.00/year

Harvard Business Review
P.O. Box 3000
Boston, MA 01888   Bi-monthly, $24.00/year

Multinational Monitor
P.O. Box 19312
Washington, DC 20036   Monthly, $15.00/year

Nation's Business
1615 H St., NW
Washington, DC 20062   Monthly, $22.00/year

World Business Weekly
Financial Times of London
135 W. 50th St.
New York, NY 10020   Weekly, $98.00/year

E. U.S. Government Periodicals

Congressional Record
U.S. Government Printing Office
Washington. DC 20402   Daily, $75.00/year

Department of State Bulletin
Department of State
Washington, DC 20520   Monthly, $19.00/year

Department of State Newsletter
U.S. Government Printing Office
Washington, DC 20402   Monthly, $13.00/year

Government-Sponsored Research on Foreign Affairs
Office of External Research
U.S. Department of State
Washington, DC 20520   Quarterly

NATO Review
Bureau of Public Affairs
Department of State
Washington, DC 20520   Bi-monthly, Free

Problems of Communism
International Communications Agency
U.S. Government Printing Office
Washington, DC 20402   Bi-monthly, $10.00/year

II. Subject Periodicals

A. Military Strategy

Air University Review
Building 1211
Maxwell Air Force Base
Alabama 36112   Bi-monthly, $13.00/year

Army
Association of the U.S. Army
2425 Wilson Blvd.
Arlington, VA 22201   Monthly, $13.00/year

Aviation Week and Space Technology
1221 Ave. of the Americas
New York, NY 10020   Weekly, $35.00/year

Comparative Strategy
3 E. 44th St.
New York, NY 10017   Quarterly, $36.00

Defense and Foreign Affairs
1777 T Street, N.W.
Washington, DC 20009   Fourteen issues/year, $70.00/year

Foreign Policy and Defense Review
American Enterprise Institute
1150 17th St., NW
Washington, DC 20036   Bi-monthly

International Security
MIT Press
28 Carleton St.
Cambridge, MA 02142   Quarterly, $15.00/year

Military Review
U.S. Army Command and General Staff College
Fort Leavenworth, KS 66027   Monthly, $12.00/year

Naval Affairs
Fleet Reserve Association
1303 New Hampshire Ave., NW
Washington, DC 20036   Monthly, $2.00/year

Strategic Review
United States Strategic Institute
1612 K St., NW Suite 1204
Washington, DC 20006   Quarterly, $14.00

Survival
The Institute for Strategic Studies
23 Tavistock St.
London WC2E 7NQ
England   Bi-monthly

Washington Report
American Security Council
Boston, VA 22713   Monthly, $12.00/year

B. Arms Control

Arms Control Today
Arms Control Association
11 Dupont Circle, NW
Washington, DC 20036   Monthly, $20.00/year

Defense Monitor
Center for Defense Information
122 Maryland Ave., NE
Washington, DC 20002   10 issues/year, $15.00/year

C. International Organizations, Regional Organizations, and World Law

American Journal of International Law
American Society of International Law
2223 Massachusetts Ave., NW
Washington, DC 20008   Quarterly, $47.00/year

Americas
Organization of American States
17th and Constitution Ave., NW
Washington, DC 20006   Monthly, $10.00/year

The Atlantic Community Quarterly
Atlantic Council of the United States
1616 H St., NW
Washington, DC 20006   Quarterly, $15.00/year

European Community
European Community Information Service
2100 M St., NW
Washington, DC 20037   Monthly, Free

Harvard International Law Journal
Harvard Law School
Austin Hall
Cambridge, MA 02138   3 times/year, $12.00/year

International Interactions
Gordon and Breach Science Publishers
42 William IV St., London W.C.2
England   2 volumes/year, $36.50 per volume

International Organization
MIT Press
292 Main St.
Cambridge, MA 02142   Quarterly, $15.00/year

Review
International Commission of Jurists
109 Route de Chene
1224 Chene-Bougeries
Geneva, Switzerland   11 times/year

United Nations Monthly Chronicle
UN Publications, Room LX 2300
United Nations
New York, NY 10017   Monthly, $11.00/year

UN Observer and International Report
Room 2020
Pan Am Bldg.
New York, NY 10017   20 times/year, $15.00/year

The UNESCO Courier
Unipub
345 Park Ave., S.
New York, NY 10010   Monthly, $11.00/year

World Health
World Health Organization
Avenue Appia
1211 Geneva 27
Switzerland   Monthly, $12.50

D. World Economic Development

Asian Development Bank Quarterly Review
Asian Development Bank
Information Office
P.O. Box 789
Manila, Philippines 2800   Quarterly

Ceres:
The FAO Review on Agriculture and Development
Food and Agriculture Association of the UN
Unipub
345 Park Ave., S.
New York, NY 10010   Bi-monthly, $12.00/year

Development Dialogue:
A Journal of International Development Cooperation
Dag Hammarskjold Foundation
Oevre Slottsgatan 2
752 20 Uppsala
Sweden   Bi-annually, Free

Development Education Exchange
Action for Development
Food and Agriculture Organization
of the UN
Via della Terme di Caracalla
00100 Rome, Italy   Bi-monthly, Free

Development Forum
United Nations Division for Economic
and Social Information
Palais des Nations, CH-1211
Geneva 10, Switzerland   Monthly, Free

Economic Development and Cultural Change
University of Chicago Press
5801 Ellis Ave.
Chicago, IL 60637   Quarterly, $35.00/year

Finance and Development
International Monetary Fund
700 19th St., NW
Washington, DC 20431   Quarterly, Free

Food Monitor
Institute for Food and Development Policy
P.O. Box 1975
Garden City, New York 11530   Monthly, $15.00/year

Ideas and Action
Food and Agriculture Organization of
the United Nations
I-00100 Rome, Italy   8 times/year, free

New Internationalist
113 Atlantic Ave.
Brooklyn, NY 11201   Monthly, $19.00/year

Population and Development Review
The Population Council, Center for Policy Studies
1 Dag Hammarskjold Plaza
New York, NY 10017   Quarterly, $12.00/year

Survey of International Development
Society for International Development
1346 Connecticut Ave., NW
Washington, DC 20036   Bi-monthly

E. Environment and Resources

Green Revolution:
A Voice for Decentralized and Balanced Living
School of Living
P.O. Box 3233
York, PA 17402   10 times/year, $8.00/year

Mother Earth News
P.O. Box 70
Hendersonville, NC 28791   Bi-monthly, $15.00/year

Environmental Action
1346 Connecticut Ave., NW
Washington, DC 20036   Monthly, $15.00/year

Fusion
Fusion Energy Foundation
888 Seventh Ave.
New York, NY 10019   10 issues/year, $20.00/year

New Ecologist
73 Molesworth St.
Wadebridge, Cornwall
England   Bi-monthly, $9.00/year

Scientific American
P.O. Box 5919
New York, NY 10017   Monthy, $21.00/year

Solar Age
P.O. Box 4934
Manchester, NH 03108   Monthly, $20.00/year

Technology and Culture
University of Chicago Press
5801 Ellis Ave.
Chicago, IL 60637   Quarterly, $27.00/year

Tranet
Appropriate Technology Review
P.O. Box 567
Rangley, ME 04970   Quarterly, $15.00/year

Undercurrents
27 Clerkenwell Close
London EC1R OAT
England $11.00/year

F. Religion and Peace

The American Baptist
Valley Forge, PA 19481   Monthly, $4.75/year

The Brethren Journal
5905 Carleen Drive
Austin, TX 78731   Monthly, $4.00/year

The Christian Century:
An Ecumenical Weekly
407 S. Dearborn St.
Chicago, IL 60605   Weekly, $18.00/year

Christianity and Crisis
537 W. 121 St.
New York, NY 10027   Bi-weekly, $15.00/year

The Churchman
1074 23rd Ave., N.
St. Petersburg, FL 33704   Monthly, $6.50/year

Commonweal
232 Madison Ave.
New York, NY 10016   Bi-weekly, $22.00

The Episcopalian
1930 Chestnut St.
Philadelphia, PA 19130   Monthly, $4.00/year

Friends Journal
152A N. 15th St.
Philadelphia, PA 19102   Semi-monthly, 10.50/year

The Lutheran
2900 Queen Lane
Philadelphia, PA 19129   Semi-monthly, $3.50/year

National Catholic Reporter
P.O. Box 281
Kansas City, MO 64141   Weekly, $18.00/year

Radical Religion
Community for Religious Research and Education
2401 LeConte Ave.
Berkeley, CA 94709   Quarterly, $7.00/year

Unitarian Universalist World
25 Beacon St.
Boston, MA 02108   19 times/year, $2.50/year

G. Institutional/Social Change

Fellowship
Fellowship of Reconciliation
523 N. Broadway
Nyack, NY 10960   8 times/year, $8.00/year

Manas:
A Journal of Independent Inquiry
P.O. Box 32112, El Sereno Station
Los Angeles, CA 90032   Weekly, $10.00/year

Peace News:
For Nonviolent Revolution
8 Elm Ave.
Nottingham 3
England   Bi-weekly, $13.00/year

Socialist Review
4228 Telegraph Ave.
Oakland, CA 94609   Bi-monthly, $15.00/year

Sojourners
1309 L St., NW
Washington, DC 20005   Monthly, $12.00/year

WIN Magazine
326 Livingston St.
Brooklyn, NY 11217   Bi-weekly, $15.00/year

Working Papers for a New Society
Center for the Study of Public Policy
Transaction Periodicals
Rutgers University
New Brunswick, NJ 08903   Bi-monthly, $15.00/year

H. Peace Research and Peace Education

Bulletin of Peace Proposals
Box 258
Irvington-on-Hudson
NY 10533   Quarterly, $20.00/year

Current Research on Peace And Violence
Tampere Peace Research Institute
Tammelanpuistokatu 58 B
Tampere, Finland   Quarterly, $12.50/year

Global Report
Progress Toward a World of Peace with Justice
Center for War-Peace Studies
218 E. 18th St.
New York, NY 10003   4 times/year, $15.00
                         (includes other publications)

The Journal of Conflict Resolution:
Research on War & Peace Between and Within Nations
SAGE Publications
275 S. Beverly Dr.
Beverly Hills, CA 90212   Quarterly, $22.50/year

Journal of Peace Research
International Peace Research Institute, Oslo
Box 258
Irvington-on-Hudson
NY 10533   Quarterly, $24.00/year

Journal of Peace Science:
An International Journal of Scientific
Study of Conflict and Conflict Management
Department of Peace Science
3718 Locust St.
University of Pennsylvania
Philadelphia, PA 19174   2 times/year,

Peace and Change:
A Journal of Peace Research
Center for Peaceful Change
Kent State University
Kent, OH 44242   Quarterly, $12.00/year

Peace and the Sciences
International Institute for Peace
Moellwaldplatz 5
A-1040 Vienna
Austria   Quarterly

Peace Research Abstracts Journal
Peace Research Institute-Dundas
25 Dundana Ave.
Dundas, Ontario
Canada L9H 4E5   Monthly

Peace Research Reviews
25 Dundana Ave.
Dundas, Ontario
Canada L9H 4E5   6 times/year, $20.00/year

Peace Science Society Papers
3718 Locust Walk
Mcneill Bldg.
University of Pennsylvania
Philadelphia, PA 19174   Semi-annually, $6.00/year

The Peacemakers
Box 627
Gaberville, CA 95440   Monthly, $6.00/year

I. Science and World Affairs

American Scientist
345 Whitney Ave.
New Haven, CT 06511   Bi-monthly, $15.00/year

Bulletin of the Atomic Scientists
1020-24 E. 58th St.
Chicago, IL 60637   10 times/year, $19.50/year

New Scientist
Commonwealth House
1-19 New Oxford St.
London WCIA ING
England   Weekly, $74.00/year

Science
American Association for the Advancement of Science
1515 Massachusetts Ave., NW
Washington, DC 20005   Weekly, $43.00/year

Scientific America
415 Madison Ave.
New York, NY 10017   Monthly, $21.00/year

J. Public Opinion and Political Processes

Congressional Digest
3231 P St., NW
Washington, DC 20007   Monthly, $18.00/year

Congressional Quarterly
1414 22rd St., NW
Washington, DC 20037   Quarterly

Current
4000 Albermarle St., NW Suite 504
Washington, DC 20016   10 times/year, $12.00/year

Policy Review
Heritage Foundation
113 C. St., NE
Washington, DC 20002   Quarterly, $15.00/year

The Public Interest
10 E. 53rd St.
New York, NY 10022   Quarterly, $14.00/year

Public Opinion
American Enterprise Institute
1150 17th St., NW
Washington, DC 20036   Bi-monthly, $18.00/year

Social Policy
33 W. 42nd St.
New York, NY 10036   5 times/year, $15.00/year

Vital Speeches of the Day
Box 606
Southhold, NY 11971   Semi-monthly, $18.00/year

K. Education

Facts on File
119 W. 57th St.
New York, NY 10019   Weekly, $329.00/year

Journal of World Education
Association for World Education
Box 589
Huntington, NY 11743   Quarterly, $20.00/year

Social Education
National Council for the Social Studies
3615 Wisconsin Ave., NW
Washington, DC 20015   7 times/year, $25.00/year

L. The Future

Futures:
The Journal of Forecasting and Planning
IPC Business Press
205 E. 42nd St.
New York, NY 10017   Bi-monthly, $104.00/year

The Futurist
World Future Society
4916 St., Elmo Ave.
Washington, DC 20014   Bi-monthly, $20.00/year

Next
Next Publishing Co.
708 Third Ave.
New York, NY 10017   Bi-monthly, $12.00/year

Omni
909 Third Ave.
New York, NY 10022   Monthly, $18.00/year

III. Regional or Area Study Periodicals

  A. General

    Comparative Political Studies
    Sage Publications
    275 S. Beverly Dr.
    Beverly Hills, CA 90212   Quarterly, $20.00/year

    The Courier
    Africa-Caribbean-Pacific-European Community
    200, rue de la Loi
    1049-Brussels
    Belgium   Bi-monthly, Free

    Journal of Developing Areas
    Western Illinois University
    900 W. Adams St.
    Macomb, Il 61455   Quarterly, $12.00/year

    South: The Third World Magazine
    South Publications
    New Zealand House
    80 Haymarket
    London SW1 4TS   Monthly, $28.00/year
    England

    Survey:
    A Journal of East & West Studies
    Oxford University Press
    Press Road, Neasden
    London NW 10
    England   Quarterly, $27.00/year

B.   The Middle East

Arab World
Anglo Arab Association
21 Collingham Road
London SW5 ONU
England   Quarterly, $9.00/year

Journal of Palestine Studies
Institute for Palestine Studies
Washington, DC 20036   Quarterly, $15.00/year

The Middle East
P.O.Box 261
63 Long Acre
London WC2E 9LR   Monthly, $34.00/year

Middle East International:
Devoted to the Middle East and Its
Place in World Affairs
21 Collingham Road
London SW5 ONU
England   Monthly, $60.00/year

The Middle East Journal
Middle East Institute
1761 N. St., NW
Washington, DC 20036 Quarterly, $12.00/year

Mideast Observer
P.O. Box 2397
Washington, DC 20013   Semi-monthly

New Outlook
Jewish-Arab Institute
8 Karl Netter St.
Tel Aviv, Israel   Monthly, $24.00/year

C. Africa

Africa:
An International Business, Economic, and
Political Monthly
African Journal
Kirkman House
54 Tottenham Court Road
London W1P Obt   Monthly, $28.00/year

Africa Now
50 Pall Mall
London SW1 5JQ
England   Monthly, $33.00/year

Africa Today
Graduate School of International Studies
University of Denver
Denver, CO 80208   Quarterly, $15.00/year

African Report
Transaction Periodicals
Rutgers University
New Brunswick, NJ 08903   Bi-monthly, $15.00/year

Frontline
402 Dunwell
35 Jorissen St.
Braamfrontein
South Africa   Monthly, $7.00/year

Journal of Modern African Studies
Cambridge University Press
32 E. 57th St.
New York, NY 10022   Quarterly, $29.50/year

New Africa
63 Long Acre
London WC2 9JH
England   Monthly,$34.00/year

Rural Africana
African Studies Center
Michigan State University
100 International Center
East Lansing, MI 48823   3 times/year, $8.00/year

West Africa
West Africa Publishing Co.
53 Holborn Viaduct
London EC1A 2FD
England   Weekly, $75.00/year

D. Asia

Asia
Asia Society
725 Park Ave
New York, NY 10021   Bi-monthly, $16.00/year

Asian Survey:
Review of Contemporary Asian Affairs
University of California Press
Berkeley, CA 94720   Monthly, $20.00/year

Bulletin of Concerned Asian Scholars
P.O. Box W
Charlement, MA 01339   Quarterly, $14.00/year

China Quarterly:
An International Journal for the Study of China
School of Oriental and African Studies
London University
Malet St.
London WC 1E 7HP
England   Quarterly, $20.00/year

China Reconstructs
Peace Book Co.
Chung Shang Bldg. 7/F, 9-10
Queen Victoria St.
Hong Kong   Monthly, $3.00/year

Far Eastern Economic Review
Datamovers
38 W. 36th St.
New York, NY 10018   Weekly, $62.00/year

Free China Review
Chinese Information Service
159 Lexington Ave.
New York, NY 10016   Monthly, $3.00/year

Harvard Journal of Asiatic Studies
2 Divinity Ave.
Cambridge, MA 02138   Semi-annually. $12.50/year

Journal of Asian Studies
One Lane Hall
University of Michigan
Ann Arbor, MI 48109   Quarterly, $30.00/year

Journal of Japanese Studies
The Society for Japanese Studies
Thomson Hall
University of Washington
Seattle, WA 98185   Semi-annually, $16.80/year

Modern China
SAGE Publications
275 S. Beverly Dr.
Beverly Hills, CA 90212   Quarterly, $32.00/year

Micronesian Report
Public Information Office
Trust Territory of the Pacific Islands
Saipan, Mariana Islands 96950   Quarterly, $4.00/year

Peking Review:
A Magazine of Chinese News and Views
China Publication Centre
Box 399
Peking, People's Republic of China   Weekly, $4.50/year

E. Latin America

Latin American Digest
Center for Latin American Studies
Arizona State University
Tempe, AZ 85281   Quarterly,$5.00

Latin American Research Review
University of North Carolina
Hamilton Hall
Chapel Hill, NC 27514   3 times/year, $13.00/year

NACLA:
Report on the Americas
North American Congress on Latin America
151 W. 19th St.
New York, NY 10011   Bi-monthly, $13.00/year

Journal of InterAmerican Studies
and World Affairs
Sage Publications
275 S. Beverly Dr.
Beverly Hills, CA 90212   Quarterly, $18.00/year

F. Eastern Europe and the Soviet Union

East Europen Quarterly
University of Colorado
Regent Hall
Boulder, CO 80302   Quarterly, $12.00/year

Reprints from the Soviet Press
Compass Publications
115 E. 87th St., Box 12-F
New York, NY 10028   Semi-monthly, $35.00/year

The Russian Review
Hoover Institution
Stanford, CA 94305   Quarterly, $12.00/year

Soviet Life
Embassy of the Soviet Union in the USA
1706 18th St., NW
Washington, DC 20009   Monthly, $6.00/year

IV. Problem-Focused Periodicals

  A. Human Rights

Amnesty Action
Amnesty International, USA
304 W. 58th St.
New York, NY 10019   11 times/year, membership required

Cultural Survival
11 Divinity Ave.
Cambridge, MA 02138   Quarterly, $15.00/year

Freedom at Issue
Freedom House
20 W. 40th St.
New York, NY 10018   Bi-monthly, $7.50

Human Rights Internet Reporter
1502 Ogden St., NW
Washington, DC 20010   5 times/year, $25.00/year

Human Rights Quarterly:
A Comparative and International
*   Journal of the Social Sciences,*
*   Philosophy, and Law*
The Johns Hopkins University Press
Journals Division
Baltimore, MC 21218   Quarterly, $16.00/year

The Journal of Intergroup Relations
National Association of Human Rights Workers
P.O. Box 60
Louisville, KY 40201   4 times /year, $11.00/year

Universal Human Rights
Conklin Hill Road
Stanfordville, NY 12581   Quarterly, $19.50/year

B. Terrorism

Terrorism
3 East 44th St.
New York, NY 10017   Quarterly, $40.00/year

C. Disarmament

Disarmament Times
777 UN Plaza - 7B
New York, NY 10017   8 times/year, $15.00/year

D. Law of the Sea Treaty

Soundings:
Law of the Sea News & Comment
Ocean Education Project and United Methodist
Law of the Sea Project
100 Maryland Ave., NE
Washington, DC 20002

E. Conscience and War

CCCO Newsletter
Central Committee for Conscientious
    Objectors
2208 South St.
Philadelphia, PA 19146   Quarterly, Free

Reporter for Conscience Sake
National Interreligious Service Board for
Conscientious Objectors
550 Washington, Bldg.
15th and New York Ave., NW
Washington, DC 20005   Monthly, $2.50/year

V.   Perspective-Setting Periodicals

Alternatives:
A Journal of World Policy
777 UN Plaza
New York, NY 10017   Quarterly, $15.00/year

American Opinion
395 Concord Ave.
Belmont, MA 02178   Monthly, $15.00/year

The American Spectator
P.O. Box 1969
Bloomington, IN 47402   Monthly, $15.00/year

The Center Magazine
Box 4068
Santa Barbara, CA 93103   Bi-monthly, $15.00/year

Commentary
165 E. 56th St.
New York, NY 10022   Monthly, $27.00/year

Dissent
505 Fifth Ave
New York, NY 10017   Quarterly, $12.00/year

Encounter
59 St. Martins Lane
London WC2N 4JS
England   Monthly, $19.00/year

The Guardian:
The Independent Radical Newsweekly
33 W. 17th St.
New York, NY 10011   Weekly, $17.00/year

Human Events
422 First St., SE
Washington, DC 20003   Weekly, $25.00/year

Inquiry
1700 Montgomery St.
San Francisco, CA 94111   20 times/year, $16.00/year

The Interdependent
300 E. 42nd St.
New York, NY 10017   8 times/year, $10.00/year

Manchester Guardian
164 Deansgate
Manchester M60 2RR
England   Weekly, $35.00/year

Monthly Review
62 W. 14th St.
New York, NY 10011   Monthly, $15.00/year

Mother Jones
625 Third St.
San Francisco, CA 94107   Monthly, $18.00/year

The Nation
72 Fifth Ave.
New York, NY 10014   Weekly, $30.00/year

National Civic Review
47 E. 68th St.
New York, NY 10021   Monthly, $15.00/year

The National Review
150 E. 35th St.
New York, NY 10016   Bi-weekly, $24.00/year

New America
275 Seventh Ave.
New York, NY 10001   Monthly, $8.00/year

The New Leader
212 Fifth Ave.
New York, NY 10010   Bi-weekly, $20.00/year

The New Republic
1200 19th St., NW
Washington, DC 20036   Weekly, $32.00/year

New Statesman
10 Great Turnstile
London WCiV 7HJ
England   Weekly, $34.00/year

New Times
406 S. Franklin St.
Syracuse, NY 13202   Weekly, $12.95/year

The New York Review of Books
250 W. 57th St.
New York, NY 10019   Bi-weekly, $20.00

The Other Side
Box 12236
Philadelphia, PA 19144   Monthly, $15.00/year

The Progressive
409 E. Main St.
Madison, WI 53703   Monthly, $17.00/year

Ripon Forum
800 18th St., NW
Washington, DC 20006   Monthly, $15.00/year

Saturday Review
1290 Ave. of the Americas
New York, NY 10019   Bi-weekly, $18.00/year

Socialist Forum
Room 617
853 Broadway
New York, NY 10003

Transnational Perspectives:
An International Journal of Federalism
and World Affairs
Case Postale 161
1211 Geneva 16
Switzerland   Quarterly, $7.00/year

Trialogue
The Trilateral Commission
345 E. 46th St.
New York, NY 10017   Quarterly, $12.00/year

The Village Voice
842 Broadway
New York, NY, 10003   Weekly, $26.00/year

The Washington Monthly
2712 Ontario Road, NW
Washington, DC 20009   Monthly $22.00/year

The Washington Spectator
P.O. Box 442
Merrifield, VA 22116   22 times/year, $10.00/year

World Press Review:
News and Views From the Foreign Press
230 Park Ave.
New York, NY 10017   Monthly, $16.00/year

Worldview
170 E. 64th St.
New York, NY 10021   Monthly, $15.00/year

VI. Special Audience Periodicals

Akwesasne Notes
Native American Movement
Mohawk Nation
Via Roosevelton, NY 13683   5 times/year

American Legion Magazine
700 N. Pennsylvania St.
Indianapolis, IN 46206   Monthly, $3.00/year

Ebony
820 S. Michigan Ave.
Chicago, Il 60605   Monthly, $14.00/year

MS. Magazine
119 W. 40th St.
New York, NY 10018   Monthly, $12.00/year

The New Yorker
25 W. 43rd St.
New York, NY 10036   Weekly, $28.00/year

Present Tense:
The Magazine of World Jewish Affairs
American Jewish Committee
165 E. 56th St.
New York, NY 10022   Quarterly, $12.00/year

Psychology Today
One Park Ave.
New York, NY 10016   Monthly, $13.97/year

Rolling Stone
745 Fifth Ave.
New York, NY 10022   Bi-weekly, $15.95/year

Soul Force
Southern Christian Leadership Conference
Atlanta, GA 30303   Monthly, $2.50/year

VFW Magazine
Veterans of Foreign Wars
34th and Broadway
Kansas City, MO 64111   Monthly, $2.00/year

THE WORLD WITHOUT WAR COUNCIL

The conditions essential to a world without war are known. They do not now exist. The World Without War Council affirms the possibility of bringing them into existence and the crucial role of American non-governmental organizations in so doing. In more than two decades of work, the Council has compiled a singular record. It has demonstrated how key independent sector organizations and institutions in this country can contribute effectively and appropriately to progress toward the nonviolent resolution of international conflict.

The Council has not sought to add one more set of initials to the jungle of American peace organizations. It has, instead, acted to bring out of the present sporadic, fragmented, ideologically troubled peace effort a broader, steadier, wiser and more coherent endeavor: one which more adequately confronts the policies of adversary societies and the incapabilities of the present international system because it improves American competence in world affairs. To this end the Council has organized and manages both national and regional planning centers. Through them leaders of research, education, exchange, and citizen-involvement organizations launch joint efforts to build an independent sector that is better-linked, better-funded, more knowledgeable and more effective.

In such work the Council has forged useful bridges between specialist agencies and the mainstream organizations of American life. Council staff have catalyzed and directed programs for groups as diverse as the National Catholic

703

Education Association, Seattle, First National Bank, the American Jewish Committee, the National Council on Philanthropy, and United Ministries in Higher Education.

Ideas offered from various points on the political spectrum must be combined if sound policies and a common sense of direction are to emerge. We have therefore worked to strengthen those currents in the discussion capable of recognizing truths at more than one pole of the argument, and have successfully drawn into our programs an impressive array of spokespeople for a wide range of foreign policy perspectives.

A peace organization which defies all the standard stereotypes, the Council has broken sharply with those currents of thought which oppose only American military programs. It focuses insteas on developing alternatives to violence capable of advancing the ideas of a democratic society in a world persistently hostile to those ideas.

Write for a complete introduction to the ideas, programs, and work opportunities to the office nearest you. Council Offices:

> 421 S. Wabash, Chicago, IL 60605
> 1730 Grove Street, Berkeley, CA 94709
> 1514 N.E. 45th Street, Seattle, WA 98105
> 1838 S.W. Jefferson, Portland, OR 97201
> 175 Fifth Avenue, New York, NY 10010

TITLE INDEX

This index includes all of the titles listed in this book. It is followed by an author index. Organizations are listed in various parts of the book: 1) United Nations Agencies, pp. 135–138; 2) American World Affairs Organizations and a few International Non-Governmental Organizations, pp. 539–604; 3) United States Peace Studies Programs, pp. 604–611; 4) International Peace and Research Institutes, pp. 611–619; 5) United States International Studies Centers, pp. 619–628. Directories of additional organizations are listed on pp. 646–648. If you are looking for a particular type of organization, refer to the typology on pp. 535–538. The list of organizations, pp. 539–604, is keyed to the typology.

AUTHOR INDEX